MATERIALS ON

ACCOUNTING FOR LAWYERS

CONCISE FOURTH EDITION

by

DAVID R. HERWITZ
Austin Wakeman Scott Professor of Law
Harvard University Law School

MATTHEW J. BARRETT
Associate Professor of Law
Notre Dame Law School

FOUNDATION PRESS

2006

© 1978, 1980, 1997, 1998, 1999, 2000, 2001 FOUNDATION PRESS
© 2006 By FOUNDATION PRESS
        395 Hudson Street
        New York, NY 10014
        Phone Toll Free 1–877–888–1330
        Fax (212) 367–6799
        foundation–press.com
Printed in the United States of America

ISBN 978-1-59941-040-1

 TEXT IS PRINTED ON 10% POST CONSUMER RECYCLED PAPER

To Kate, Kevin, Wilson, Luke and Maggie
M.J.B.

To Carla

D.R.H.

*

PREFACE TO THE CONCISE FOURTH EDITION

Is there any such thing as "accounting for lawyers?" No matter how you answer that question, these materials attempt to highlight the importance of issues involving accounting to the practice of law. As a matter of professional responsibility, every lawyer should understand certain fundamental things about accounting. At the same time, clients and employers will likely expect every lawyer to have developed at least some working knowledge of accounting.

In the last five years, we have watched as corporate and accounting fraud led to Enron's collapse in late 2001 after quickly becoming the nation's fifth largest company, Andersen's conviction for obstructing justice the following year, and the Supreme Court's subsequent reversal earlier this year. The additional scandals at WorldCom and other publicly traded companies led to the landmark Sarbanes-Oxley Act of 2002 ("SOx"), the most significant piece of accounting-related legislation since the 1930s. Even now, however, stories about accounting fraud and the resulting criminal trials, administrative proceedings, and civil suits continue to appear in the financial and general press almost daily.

We may all be tired of reading about Enron, but that corporation's collapse painfully illustrates the importance of financial accounting to *all lawyers and law students*. As the third editions note, accounting has long been called "the language of business." Virtually every lawyer represents businesses, their owners, or clients with adverse legal interests, such as creditors and customers. Moreover, accounting issues also arise regularly in the representation of not-for-profit enterprises, including governmental bodies, and even in private individual matters, such as local rent control. Almost all lawyers, therefore, will encounter financial statements at some time in their professional careers or personal lives, and will draft, negotiate or sign an agreement or legal document containing accounting terminology or concepts. Of special importance are potential discovery issues related to contingencies and audit inquiry letters, which affect every lawyer or law firm that represents businesses or legal interests adverse to those businesses. Finally, all competent lawyers should recognize certain "red flags" which suggest that their client or another party has committed financial fraud, such as misstating inventories or other assets, recording revenues before they are earned, allocating expenses to the wrong accounting period, or failing to record or disclose liabilities.

Accounting issues constantly arise in different areas of law practice, such as calculating damages in contract and tort cases, disclosure requirements under the federal securities laws, significant cost allocation and disclosure issues under environmental laws, resolving reimbursement claims, in the health care industry, and determining an appropriate rate for a public utility.

While accounting rules have become increasingly complex, and few law students or lawyers receive formal training in accounting, lawyers can watch financial statements and related disclosures for "red flags." Just as the prefaces to the third editions contain a listing of the top ten things that every lawyer should know about accounting, we begin here with a listing of the top ten accounting lessons for lawyers from the Enron scandal:

1. Where's the beef?

A complete set of financial statements includes an income statement, a balance sheet, a statement of cash flows, a statement of changes in owners' equity, and the accompanying notes. The Enron crisis accelerated when the company's 2001 third quarter earnings press release on October 16, 2001, provided only an income statement, and not a balance sheet, statement of cash flows, or statement of changes in shareholders' equity. (Remarkably, Enron failed to provide the other financial statements in its earnings releases beginning in 1996.) In response to questions from analysts, Enron's management later disclosed that Enron recorded a $1.2 billion reduction in shareholders' equity. Because the income statement does not reflect this item, without a balance sheet or statement of changes in shareholders' equity, investors could not see a complete and accurate picture of Enron's financial condition and operating results. In addition, the cash flow statement, possibly the lawyer's best friend in such situations, also would have alerted a careful reader to problems, including the business's declining profitability. As Enron's collapse demonstrates, a missing financial statement may indicate that the enterprise seeks to hide disappointing results. Enron's eventual issuance of its missing balance sheet, and the large write-down of shareholders' equity in that financial statement, triggered a loss of investor confidence, which caused Enron's share price to fall, accelerated debt repayment obligations, and ultimately led to Enron's bankruptcy. The Enron scandal illustrates that *each* financial statement offers important information necessary to maintain investor and creditor confidence. A lawyer should ask probing questions any time an enterprise does not provide a complete set of financial statements, plus accompanying notes.

2. Old dogs, new tricks.

Generally accepted accounting principles (GAAP) often offer choices in financial accounting treatments. Although the "consistency principle" generally requires enterprises to use the same accounting principles to treat the same transactions similarly from year-to-year, this consistency requirement does not apply to new business

activities. The business community refers to the "rules" governing the compilation of accounting data into financial statements and the accompanying notes as "GAAP." GAAP, however, typically allows choices among permissible alternatives and almost always requires estimates and assumptions that affect the amounts shown in the financial statements, including the reported amounts of assets, liabilities, revenues and expenses. Especially in today's world, business transactions and practices evolve more rapidly than rule-makers can promulgate accounting rules. For several reasons, therefore, GAAP does not provide a set of black-and-white rules that produce a single "bottom-line" number that a lawyer can use natural law to verify. Commonly referred to as "earnings management," corporate managers can often use GAAP's flexibility to show operating results in line with projections and expectations. Especially when an enterprise's business changes (witness Enron's evolution from a regional natural gas company to a global energy and commodities trader), lawyers should pay particular attention to the accounting principles an enterprise uses to account for transactions arising from the new business activities.

3. Looks aren't everything.

Pro forma reporting can distort an enterprise's financial appearance. In its 2001 third quarter earnings release, Enron reported "recurring" net income of $393 million. Such "pro forma" reporting, which provides numbers "as if" certain (often undescribed) assumptions apply, does not follow GAAP. Even a simple analysis of the earnings release reveals that Enron actually suffered a $618 million *net loss* under GAAP. By labeling $1.01 billion as "one-time" or "non-recurring" charges, mostly related to investment and asset write-downs and restructuring charges, the company turned its $618 million net loss, purportedly using GAAP, into $393 million in net income. Such write-downs and charges, however, would seem to represent normal business expenses and losses.

In an effort to focus investors on results from "normal" business operations, an enterprise may, knowingly or innocently, mislead investors. Initially, pro forma reporting can hide troubling financial results. For instance, in its 2000 fourth quarter earnings release, Enron boasted a 25 percent increase in earnings per share ("EPS") for the full year 2000 over 1999 and a 32 percent increase in earnings per share for the 2000 fourth quarter over the 1999 fourth quarter. Buried in the last section of its earnings release, however, the company told a very different story. Enron disclosed that EPS for 2000, including non-recurring charges, increased only from $1.10 per share in 1999 to $1.12 per share in 2000. These amounts translated to an increase of only 1.8 percent, compared to the 25 percent increase Enron reported at the beginning of its earnings release. Next, Enron disclosed that 2000 fourth quarter EPS, after non-recurring charges, totaled $0.05, a *decrease* of 83.8 percent from the 1999 fourth quarter, in contrast to the 32 percent increase it reported at the beginning of the release. Interestingly, earlier in the quarter, Enron predicted that it would post fourth quarter EPS of $0.35.

Excluding what it called non-recurring items allowed Enron to exceed those expectations. If Enron had included the non-recurring items, its results would have fallen below that prediction.

Second, an enterprise can use pro forma reporting to manage earnings. Earnings management typically tries to increase net income (or reduce the size of a loss), relative to what the business would otherwise report under GAAP. Enterprises, however, sometimes exclude non-recurring gains in an effort to report lower net income, which translates to smaller profit-sharing payments to employees (or reduced income tax obligations). Lawyers drafting agreements that rely on earnings to set prices or trigger payments, for example, should distinguish pro forma earnings from net income calculated in compliance with GAAP. Without distinguishing between the two benchmarks, parties to such an agreement can manipulate earnings by labeling some items as one-time or non-recurring.

4. Sometimes, looks are everything.

Auditor independence matters—both in appearance and in fact. During the late 1990s, the largest public accounting firms increasingly provided non-audit services, such as consulting, internal audits, and tax advising, often for the very enterprises they audited. During 2000, Enron paid $52 million to Arthur Andersen—$25 million for auditing services, and an additional $27 million for non-auditing services—and ranked as Andersen's second largest client. In addition, an internal Andersen memo regarding the retention of Enron as an audit client refers to $100 million a year in potential revenues from Enron.

Unlike lawyers who must zealously represent their clients, auditors' real responsibilities flow to the investing public, not the enterprise that hires them. By evaluating an enterprise's financial statements and expressing an opinion as to whether those statements fairly present, in all material respects, the enterprise's financial position and operating results, an auditor seeks to help maintain investor and creditor confidence. To satisfy generally accepted auditing standards, an auditor must remain independent from any enterprises it audits—both in fact and in appearance. When non-audit fees comprise a substantial piece of an auditor's income from the audit client, those fees might tempt an auditor to overlook an enterprise's "aggressive" accounting simply to retain the client's non-audit business. At a minimum, substantial fees paid to auditors for non-audit related services call the appearance of independence into question. Even if the auditor continues, in fact, to exercise objective judgment, such relationships impair the appearance of independence. As the recent malaise that has afflicted the stock markets in the United States ably demonstrates, even the *perception* of a lack of independence can shake investor confidence in the quality of financial statements. Because investors view a lack of independence, whether in appearance or in fact, with a critical eye, lawyers should encourage clients to preserve independence, both in fact and in appearance. Lawyers should also carefully scrutinize financial statements, disclosures, and transactions that involve an auditor who may have compromised independence, whether in fact or in appearance.

5. With friends like these, ...

Related-party transactions, especially those involving a special purpose entity ("SPE"), can distort an enterprise's apparent financial condition and operating results. Although related-party transactions may increase efficiency in transacting business, they may also allow an enterprise to manipulate its earnings by the way the enterprise sets prices or allocates expenses. Similarly, an enterprise may use SPEs for legitimate purposes, such as to limit exposure to risk in certain investments, including credit card receivables or residential mortgages. An enterprise, the "sponsor," generally forms an SPE to transfer risks from such investments to outside investors.

Enron's transactions with its SPEs, including the so-called Chewco and LJM partnerships, highlight the dangers that can arise from related-party transactions. As a small, but relatively simple example, Enron sold an interest in a Polish company to LJM2 for $30 million on December 21, 1999. While Enron intended to sell the interest to an unrelated party, the company could not find a buyer before the end of the year. The sale allowed Enron to record a gain of $16 million on a transaction that Enron could not close with a third party. Remarkably, Enron later bought back LJM2's interest for $31.9 million after it failed to find an outside buyer. Another deal allowed Enron to *report* a $111 million gain on the transfer of an agreement with Blockbuster Video to deliver movies on demand, even after Enron realized that no real profits would ever flow from the underlying agreement.

The related-party transactions with SPEs, often occurring at the end of a fiscal period, allowed Enron to manipulate its reported earnings, to close deals at desired amounts qui ckly, to hide debt, and to conceal poorly performing assets. Such transactions, which frequently closed at the end of a quarter or year, allowed Enron to meet its earnings expectations and to sustain its stock price. In fact, Enron sometimes even backdated such transactions to the previous period, in an effort to "manufacture" income for that period. Because Enron entered into those transactions with "friendly" related parties, the company could quickly and easily negotiate terms that allowed its earnings to appear on target. In addition, Enron used its earliest SPEs to obtain financing, without showing the related liability on its balance sheet. Finally, Enron used SPEs to move poorly performing assets off of its balance sheet. By transferring such assets to SPEs, Enron could hide later declines in the value of those assets.

GAAP requires an enterprise to disclose information about material related-party transactions in the notes to the financial statements. In particular, an enterprise must disclose: the nature of any relationships involved; a description of the transactions for each period for which the financial statements present an income statement, including any information necessary to understand the transactions' effects on the financial statements; the dollar amounts of the transactions and the effects of any changes in the method used to establish terms when compared to those followed in the preceding period; and amounts due from or to related parties on each balance sheet date and the related terms governing those amounts. The disclosures should not imply that the transactions contained terms equivalent to those that would have prevailed in an arm's-length transaction unless management can substantiate that claim. Enron did disclose various related-party transactions in the notes to its financial statements, but not in any detail.

Lawyers who assist in related-party transactions should carefully examine the transactions and their client's securities disclosures in an effort to assure that those disclosures accurately describe the transactions' true nature and effects on the financial statements. Likewise, lawyers negotiating other transactions or pursuing other claims, especially when future or past earnings determine legal rights and obligations, should keep in mind that an enterprise can use related-party transactions to manipulate earnings.

6. Details, details, details.

Corporations should develop and adhere to internal controls (both administrative and accounting). Administrative controls generally refer to an enterprise's plan of organization, procedures, and records that lead up to management's approval of transactions. Accounting controls, by comparison, describe the plans, procedures, and records that an enterprise uses to safeguard assets and produce reliable financial information. Enron's administrative controls included policies designed to minimize conflicts of interest and to ensure that transactions fairly benefitted the company. Not only did recent events prove Enron's administrative controls inadequate, but those events also showed that Enron failed to follow the controls that it had put in place. For example, when Enron's board approved a policy that allowed the company to enter into transactions with certain entities owned by Enron officers, the implementing procedures explicitly required management to use a "Deal Approval Sheet." By requiring certain disclosures and the approval of Enron's chief executive officer, the Deal Approval Sheets sought to ensure that the contractual provisions in such transactions would closely resemble the terms that would have materialized in an arms'-length transaction. In fact, the chief executive officer's signature does not appear on the sheets for several specific transactions. Moreover, the current absence of sheets for other transactions suggests that Enron did not complete any such document in those transactions. As another example, Andrew Fastow, Enron's former chief financial officer and, for a time, the general partner of the several partnerships that entered into transactions with Enron, reportedly earned more than $30 million from his investments in those enterprises. Even though the board seemed to recognize the conflict of interest inherent in such related-party transactions, the board failed to require that Mr. Fastow report his profits from the partnerships to the company. Such disclosures almost certainly would have alerted the board to the possibility that the underlying transactions unfairly benefitted the related parties, to the detriment of Enron and its shareholders. Other items in this list document that Enron failed to implement adequate accounting controls.

Although top management bears the initial responsibility to develop, implement, and, when necessary, revise adequate internal controls, overall oversight falls to the board of directors, who often rely on lawyers for advice. Internal controls work effectively only when those who bear responsibility for developing, implementing, and overseeing those controls stress the need to adhere to all policies and procedures and lead by adhering to those rules themselves. In recent years, the SEC has brought administrative actions and imposed so-called "tone-at-the-top liability" under the Foreign Corrupt Practices Act, which applies to all SEC registrants, including enterprises that engage only in domestic operations. Strong internal controls enhance the likelihood that the enterprise will engage in sound, beneficial transactions and reduce the chances that an enterprise will incur the enormous losses that can result from internal control failures.

7. If it walks like a duck, ...

In recognizing revenue (and accounting generally), substance prevails over form. Under GAAP, an enterprise cannot recognize revenue until the business has substantially completed performance in a bona fide exchange transaction. If a transaction does not unconditionally transfer the risks that typically accompany a "sale," the enterprise may not recognize revenue.

Enron's announcement regarding a $544 million after-tax charge to earnings in October 2001 revealed a serious flaw in its prior financial statements: Enron had improperly recognized revenue from transactions with its SPEs. In short, Enron recorded revenue after transferring certain assets to those SPEs, even though credit guarantees, promises to protect the purchasers from any loss from decline in value, or buyback agreements caused the company to retain the risks of ownership even after the transfers. As a result, Enron had not truly "earned" the revenue it reported.

Enron's "sham" transactions resemble schemes that ultimately led to the demise of Drexel Burnham and the imprisonment of Michael Milken, that appeared so frequently during the savings and loan crisis, and that accompany most financial accounting frauds today. Milken ultimately pled guilty to charges involving "parking," whereby Drexel Burnham purchased securities from third parties with the understanding that the investment banking firm would quickly resell the securities back to the third parties at a fixed price. Similarly, the Federal Home Loan Bank Board (FHLBB) took control of Lincoln Savings & Loan Association in 1989 after discovering, among other things, that Lincoln or its affiliates had recognized income on sales of real estate even though the funds for the down payments had emanated from Lincoln itself. In substance, Lincoln or its affiliates had retained the risks of ownership and could not recognize revenue from the sales.

The issue of substance over form applies not only to managers and accountants, but to attorneys as well. The litigation that follows financial frauds can impose enormous financial costs. In addition, a lawyer who fails to investigate, or perhaps spot, a "red flag," such as a side agreement or guarantee, can face staggering personal liability for malpractice. Whether drafting, negotiating, or interpreting contractual provisions that refer to "net income" or "earnings," performing "due diligence" to determine whether a particular transaction will further a client's best interests, or rendering a "true sale" opinion regarding whether a transferor that retains some involvement with the transferred asset (or the transferee) has surrendered economic control over the asset to justify treating the transaction as a sale for financial accounting purposes, substance over form requires an attorney to look beyond the form of a transaction and to try to identify any arrangements that may affect the transaction's economic realities. In particular, understanding the motivations for a transaction offers an important clue to the transaction's substance. Enron often transferred assets to SPEs to hide losses or to remove liabilities from its balance sheet. Although most clients or adversaries will not expressly state such desires, such effects should also alert attorneys to issues of substance over form.

8. Promises, promises.

Any time an enterprise guarantees the indebtedness of another in material amounts, the enterprise must disclose the nature and amount of the guarantees in the notes to the financial statements. When Enron's SPEs sought credit, the lenders often required that Enron guarantee the debt. On several occasions, Enron guaranteed amounts that various SPEs borrowed by promising to pay cash or to issue additional common shares to repay the debt, if the market price of Enron's common shares dropped under a set amount or if Enron's bond rating fell below investment grade. While the notes to Enron's financial statements disclosed guarantees of the indebtedness of others, Enron did not mention that its potential liability on those guarantees, which shared common debt repayment triggers, totaled $4 billion. When material, GAAP specifically requires an enterprise to disclose the nature and amount of guarantees of the indebtedness of others. Again, inadequate disclosure can subject enterprises to liability and lawyers to malpractice claims.

9. If it sounds too good to be true, ...

An enterprise cannot recognize income from issuing its own shares and generally should not record a net increase in shareholders' equity when it issues stock in exchange for a note receivable. At the risk of oversimplifying, Enron used related-party SPEs to hedge, or to protect itself from declines in the market value of, certain investments that Enron used current market prices to value on its books. In these arrangements, Enron transferred its own stock to an SPE in exchange for a note or cash. In addition, Enron guaranteed, directly or indirectly, the SPE's value. The SPEs in turn hedged the underlying investments, using the transferred Enron stock as the principal source of payment for the hedges. The value of the underlying investments decreased, but the hedges allowed Enron to recognize a corresponding increase, resulting in a wash. The SPEs, however, could reimburse Enron for any decline in value of the investments only as long as the market price of Enron's common shares remained stable or increased. When the value of Enron's common shares fell, Enron had to issue additional shares pursuant to its agreements with the SPEs and the related guarantees. These additional shares reduced Enron's stock value, which triggered additional guarantees. In the interim, Enron recognized about $500 million in revenues from the hedges, which had really arisen from the issuance of the company's own shares. GAAP, however, does not allow an enterprise to record gains from the increase in the value of its capital stock on its income statement.

As previously mentioned in the first item, Enron announced on October 16, 2001, that it had recorded a $1.2 billion reduction in shareholders' equity, arising, in large part, from an accounting error. When Enron issued its common shares to several SPEs in exchange for notes receivable, Enron recorded the notes receivable as assets, thereby overstating shareholders' equity by $1 billion. Although GAAP usually allows an enterprise to record notes receivable as assets, a different rule applies when an enterprise issues stock in exchange for the notes. GAAP states that an enterprise should treat any notes received in payment for the enterprise's stock as an offset to shareholders' equity. Only when the obligor pays the note can the enterprise record an increase in shareholders' equity for the amount actually paid.

Many credit agreements allow the lender to accelerate the repayment of the debt if the borrower's debt-to-shareholders' equity ratio exceeds a certain level or if the borrower fails to maintain a certain credit rating. Although Enron's $1.2 billion reduction in shareholders' equity did not itself trigger any debt repayment obligations, investment ratings companies immediately placed Enron on review for downgrade. Soon after, the ratings companies downgraded Enron's credit rating to below investment grade. Because provisions in many of Enron's credit agreements required the company to maintain an investment grade credit rating, the downgrades triggered debt repayment obligations, which accelerated Enron's bankruptcy.

10. When the going gets tough, ...

Lawyers' duties to their clients include an obligation to object when a client proposes or uses questionable accounting policies or practices. In his well-publicized opinion in the *Lincoln Savings and Loan* case, Judge Sporkin asked where the lawyers were when Lincoln consummated various improper transactions, wondering why they did not attempt to prevent those transactions or disassociate themselves from them. Now, more than ten years later, we hear similar questions directed to Enron's lawyers. While Enron's lawyers, both in-house and outside counsel, did question some practices, Enron officers and employees often either ignored the lawyers' advice, or changed the transactions just enough to get around the lawyers' particular concerns. In some cases, Enron's lawyers apparently helped to complete the very transactions they questioned.

The attorney-client privilege prevents lawyers from disclosing client confidences. That privilege, however, does not prevent lawyers from discussing concerns with their clients, attempting to persuade their clients to choose another course of action, going up the "corporate ladder," or even withdrawing from representing their clients if a client declines to follow the lawyer's advice. When Enron's lawyers questioned Enron's practices, they voiced their concerns to Enron's in-house lawyers and its management, but not to the board of directors or the audit committee. Blind deference to accountants and auditors seems unwise and dangerous. We'll never know, but without hearing the concerns of Enron's lawyers, the board of directors or the audit committee arguably could not see an objective picture of those transactions and Enron's financial accounting practices.

Standing up takes courage. Let's hope that Enron's collapse, the well-publicized scandals at WorldCom, which led to the largest bankruptcy in U.S. history, and the Sarbanes-Oxley Act of 2002 encourage more lawyers to for accounting "red flags" and to respond courageously when they see them.

This book's roots date back to Professor Robert Amory, Jr.'s pioneering first casebook on accounting for law students in 1948. Five years later, Professor Covington Hardee joined Professor Amory on a second edition. In 1959, Professor Donald T. Trautman joined the senior author for an earlier third edition. These materials continue to benefit from our predecessors' contributions and the comments and research assistants, and many colleagues and fellow teachers who are listed in the unabridged fourth edition. However, we should especially acknowledge the valuable contributions of Christopher Lee Wilson, JD Harvard 2006, and Melissa Anderson, Harvard Law School, 2009, whose proof-reading, editing, indexing, and general polishing efforts combined with the devoted and tireless work on the manuscript by Delona Wilkin, with a very welcome helping hand from Minoee Modi, to make it possible to put out this temporary version of the concise fourth edition. Also, very warm thanks to Mr. John Bloomquist, President of Foundation Press, for his gracious and continuing support of this unexpectedly extended venture.

These materials strive to instill confidence in its readers so they can begin to master the principles of accounting and develop command of the basic tools that lawyers need in this field. To accomplish this objective, we have built the materials around explanatory text designed to lead the students through the subject's technical aspects. To keep the focus on the interests of law students, each chapter begins with a section which explains the topic's importance to lawyers, and both the materials and the problems seek to highlight the lawyer's role in dealing with accounting issues.

We gratefully acknowledge the graciousness of Starbucks Corporation for permission to reprint substantial excerpts from its annual report and securities regulation documents for the fiscal year ended October 2, 2005, and Ben & Jerry's Homemade Holdings, Inc. for permission to reprint cartoons that appeared in the company's 1992 annual report.

FASB Statement No. 5, *Accounting for Contingencies*, is copyrighted by the Financial Accounting Standards Board, 401 Merritt 7, P.O. Box 5116, Norwalk, Connecticut 06856-5116, U.S.A. Portions are reprinted with permission.

One final comment: we want our materials to be as accurate, current, and helpful as possible and plan to continue our recent practice of updating them regularly. Apart from isolated "subsequent events," this text uses April 30, 2006 as the cut-off date for developments. If you find any errors or omissions, we hope that you will call them to our attention so that we can incorporate any corrections into future supplements and editions. We also welcome any other comments or suggestions that you might be willing to share. You can reach Matt Barrett at <Matthew.J.Barrett.1@nd.edu>, by calling him at (574) 631-8121, or via fax at (574) 631-4197, and David Herwitz at (617) 495-3121, or fax at (617) 495-1082.

David R. Herwitz
Matthew J. Barrett

November 1, 2006

*

TABLE OF CONTENTS

CHAPTER I Introduction to Financial Statements, Bookkeeping and Accrual Accounting

CHAPTER II The Development of Accounting Principles and Auditing Standards

CHAPTER III The Time Value of Money

CHAPTER IV Introduction to Financial Statement Analysis and Financial Ratios

CHAPTER V Legal Issues Involving Shareholders' Equity and the Balance Sheet

CHAPTER VII Contingencies

CHAPTER VIII Inventory

*

TABLE OF SIGNIFICANT CASES

TABLE OF ACRONYMS

AAER	SEC Accounting and Auditing Enforcement Release
ABA	American Bar Association
AcSEC	Accounting Standards Executive Committee of the AICPA
AICPA	American Institute of Certified Public Accountants
APB	Accounting Principles Board of the AICPA
ARB	Accounting Research Bulletin
ASB	Auditing Standards Board of the AICPA
ASR	Accounting Series Release
AU	Codification of Auditing Standards
AudSEC	Auditing Standards Executive Committee of the AICPA
CEO	Chief executive officer
CFO	Chief financial officer
EBITDA	Earnings Before Interest, Taxes, Depreciation, and Amortization
EBIT	Earnings Before Interest and Taxes
EC	European Commission
EITF	Emerging Issues Task Force
EU	European Union
FASB	Financial Accounting Standards Board
FIN	FASB Interpretation
FRR	SEC Financial Reporting Release
GAAP	Generally Accepted Accounting Principles
GAAS	Generally Accepted Auditing Standards
ISB	Independence Standard Board
IAS	International Accounting Standard
IASB	International Accounting Standards Board
IASC	International Accounting Standards Committee
IFRS	IASB International Financial Reporting Standard
IPR&D	In-process research and development
ISA	International Standards on Auditing
MD&A	Management's Discussion and Analysis
PCAOB	Public Company Accounting Oversight Board
SAB	SEC Staff Accounting Bulletin
SAC	IASB Standards Advisory Council
SAP	Statement of Auditing Procedure
SAS	Statement of Auditing Standards
SFAC	Statement of Financial Accounting Concepts
SFAS	Statement of Financial Accounting Standards
SOP	AICPA Statement of Position
SOx	Sarbanes-Oxley Act of 2002
SPE	Special Purpose Entity
VIE	Variable Interest Entity

CHAPTER I

INTRODUCTION TO FINANCIAL STATEMENTS, BOOKKEEPING AND ACCRUAL ACCOUNTING

A. IMPORTANCE TO LAWYERS

Accounting is often called the language of business. Even if a lawyer does not represent businesses or their owners, almost every lawyer will represent clients with legal interests adverse to businesses or their owners. Lawyers, therefore, must understand certain fundamental concepts about accounting.

Resolving accounting problems that lawyers encounter ordinarily demands much the same kind of analysis and judgment needed to solve other legal problems. A lawyer must unscramble other people's troubles or, even better, help avoid trouble before it develops. Before a lawyer can accept an assignment where accounting issues are involved, however, the lawyer faces a special difficulty. Accountants, and more generally people in business and finance, have their own way of expressing the data with which they are concerned. At first, it may seem akin to an unfamiliar language. But the basic principles on which this language is built are simple enough. This chapter is designed to show you that if you had set out to devise a technique for recording financial data, you might well have come out about the same as the current system, which has certainly stood the test of time: the underlying process had already been in use for a couple of hundred years when it was described and analyzed by a Renaissance monk named Luca Pacioli, in his 1494 text, the first published work on accounting.

You should not assume, however, that every aspect of the current system was inevitable. Certainly the application of the system in particular situations is open to doubt and to analysis, and in later chapters of this book, which deal with the function of accounting statements in business life, we will occasionally question the appropriateness of the "language" as applied in particular contexts.

Before discussing specific accounting issues, we must first understand the system for reporting and recording financial information. Accountants use four different financial statements—the *balance sheet*, the *income statement*, the *statement of changes in owner's equity* (the ownership interest), and the *statement of cash flows*—to describe an enterprise's financial condition and the results of its operations. We will see that accountants may use different names to refer to these financial statements, or different formats to present the data involved, but they provide the same basic information.

The balance sheet presents an enterprise's assets, liabilities and residual equity at a particular moment, typically at the end of a specified period of time. The income statement shows how well (or badly) the enterprise has done, and the resulting change in the owners' equity, during that time period. The statement of changes in owners' equity portrays the ups and downs in the ownership interest from all causes during the period. Finally, the statement of cash flows analyzes the changes in the enterprise's cash during the particular period. We will discuss each financial statement in this chapter.

As discussed in the preface, the Enron crisis illustrates the importance of a complete set of financial statements. Adopting the custom of many other companies, Enron stopped providing a balance sheet in the press releases announcing its quarterly results in 1996. That practice became significant when Enron reported its 2001 third quarter earnings in October 2001. In response to questions from analysts, Enron's management later disclosed that the company recorded a $1.2 billion reduction in shareholders' equity during that third quarter. Because the income statement does not reflect this item without a balance sheet or statement of changes in shareholders' equity, investors could not see a complete and accurate picture of Enron's financial condition and operating results. Enron's eventual issuance of its missing balance sheet, and the large write-down of shareholders' equity in the balance sheet, triggered a loss of investor confidence, which caused Enron's share price to fall, accelerated debt repayment obligations, and ultimately led to Enron's bankruptcy.

Perhaps, even more significantly, the cash flow statement, possibly the lawyer's best friend in such situations, would have alerted a careful reader to the serious problems at Enron, including the business's declining profitability. As early as 1999, Enron's cash flows from operations dropped when compared to the previous year, even though net income for 1999 had increased. During the first six months of 2001, which reflects the period immediately before Enron's collapse, Enron reported negative cash flows from operations exceeding $1.3 billion.

The Enron scandal illustrates that *each* financial statement offers important information about an enterprise's financial health. An incomplete set of financial statements may prevent a reader from seeing the whole picture.

These financial statements, however, represent the "ends" in a process which accountants refer to as *double-entry bookkeeping*. The "means" in the process consists of that special technique which business enterprises use to recognize and record the entity's various transactions. The financial statements are derived from these accounting records, and the special technique will be introduced shortly, when we discuss the bookkeeping process.

At the time when Pacioli published his analysis of the bookkeeping system, most business ventures did not last very long. Today, most businesses expect to continue indefinitely, so what both management and investors need are periodic financial statements, which in turn requires allocation of revenues and expenses among the various accounting periods regardless of when the cash expenditures or receipts occur or when the obligations to pay or the rights to receive cash arise. That is the goal of *accrual accounting*, which consists of a set of principles and rules for classifying and measuring economic events in the real world through the process of bookkeeping.

To begin our study of bookkeeping and accrual accounting, we should understand the first important financial statement, the balance sheet.

B. THE BALANCE SHEET

The object of bookkeeping is to make it as easy as possible for anyone who understands the language to get a clear and accurate summary of how well a business is doing. As one way of determining how well a business is doing, we can compare what the business owns with what it owes. The difference between what a business owns—its *assets*—and what it owes—its *liabilities*—represents the ownership interest, often referred to as *equity, or net worth*. As the first basic financial statement that we will study, the balance sheet shows a business's assets, liabilities, and equity at a particular moment in time.

At this point, take a look at the cartoons in Appendix C, *infra*, which are reprinted, with permission, from the 1992 annual report of Ben & Jerry's Homemade, Inc., particularly those on pages C-2 and C-4, which try to explain simply the balance sheet and its components, namely assets, liabilities and equity. After that introduction, we can proceed to discuss those components in more detail, beginning with assets.

1. ASSETS

Suppose we want a financial picture of E. Tutt, who recently graduated from law school and has opened a law office. Certainly one important facet is how much she owns. Because we really are concerned with her business and not her personal affairs, we forget her car, her clothes, and other personal property, and we look to see what she has in her office:

(a) Office furniture

(b) Office equipment

(c) Stationery and supplies

(d) Library

(e) Cash in the bank

All of these would be understood by a layperson to be what the accountant calls them: assets.

Accountants view *assets* as future economic benefits which a particular accounting entity, whether a natural person, business enterprise or charitable organization, owns or controls as a result of a past transaction or event. Accountants classify economic resources as assets when the entity satisfies three requirements pertaining to the resource. First, the entity must control it Second, the entity must reasonably expect the resource to provide a future benefit. Third, the entity must have obtained the resource in a transaction so that the entity can measure it.

Several examples can illustrate these requirements. Would E. Tutt's friendly personality qualify as an asset which she can list on her balance sheet? No. Although Tutt can control her personality and a friendly personality should help a lawyer, she did not acquire her personality in a transaction. If Tutt purchases a computer for her office, paying $2,000 in cash, and expects the computer to last two years, can she show the computer as an asset on her balance sheet? Yes. Tutt controls the computer, which should provide at least two years of service to her law practice, and she acquired the computer in a transaction. If Tutt spends $300 to send her secretary to a training session on using software for the computer, can she treat the training cost as an asset? No. Unless Tutt and her secretary have signed an employment contract, as an at-will employee the secretary could choose to quit her job at any time, taking along the training. Although Tutt expects to receive future benefits from the training and a transaction has occurred, Tutt does not have control over her secretary.

Before we can show an asset on a balance sheet, we need some measure for the resource. In other words, we need to assign some dollar amount to the asset. Because the price at which property was bought is ordinarily much easier to ascertain and less subjective than the current fair market value of the property, accountants generally record assets at *historical cost*. We should always remember that the balance sheet usually does not show assets at their fair market value.

We should also remember that the balance sheet shows only assets which satisfy the three requirements described above. The balance sheet does not reflect many important things which we might consider as valuable to a business. For example, the value that an outstanding management team brings to a business, good morale among the enterprise's employees, or loyal and satisfied customers do not appear as assets on the balance sheet.

For these reasons, the balance sheet, like the other financial statements which we will discuss, provides little, if any, contemporary or prospective information.

2. SOURCES

If E. Tutt bought all her property out of her own funds and has not yet earned anything, we could simply add up the assets to find out how E. Tutt stands in her business. But if she has borrowed money from a bank to buy some of her assets or, perhaps more likely, has bought some on credit, E. Tutt's personal "stake" in the business would not be as large as if she had bought everything from her own funds. To give a true picture of her financial position, we would want to know where the money came from to buy the assets. Suppose we find that she acquired the assets as follows:

(a) Office furniture: bought on credit from Frank Co. for $400;

(b) Office equipment: bought on credit from Elmer Co. for $300;

(c) Stationery and supplies: bought from Stanley for $100 on a promissory note;

(d) Library: purchased for $200 cash, out of Tutt's original "stake" of $1,000; and

(e) $800 cash: balance of Tutt's original "stake" remaining.

We could then list, in parallel columns, the assets and their sources:

Assets		Sources		
(a) Office furniture	$400	Frank Co.	$400	(a)
(b) Office equipment	300	Elmer Co.	300	(b)
(c) Stationery and supplies	100	Stanley	100	(c)
(d) Library	200			
(e) Cash (balance remaining)	800	E. Tutt	1,000	(d, e)
Total	$1,800	Total	$1,800	

This parallel listing of assets and their sources is what accountants usually call a *balance sheet*. This listing may also be referred to as a *statement of financial position* or a *statement of financial condition*. As preliminary matters about the balance sheet, we should note two things. First, whatever the name, the totals of the two columns must always be equal. For this reason, we will refer to this financial statement as the balance sheet. Second, no matter how complicated a business or how long its history, the balance sheet shows, at one particular point in time, what assets the business owns and where the money came from to acquire those assets. Because the balance sheet reflects one instant in time, we can compare the balance sheet to a snapshot.

To give a somewhat clearer picture of how well off E. Tutt herself is, we can separate the sources of assets into two groups: "outside" sources—money which the business owes to creditors; and "inside" sources—amounts that Tutt herself has invested in the business. We turn our discussion to those "outside" sources.

a. LIABILITIES

The "outside" sources would also be understood by a layperson to be what the accountant calls them: liabilities. Accountants characterize duties or responsibilities to provide economic benefits to some other accounting entity in the future as *liabilities*. Liabilities arise from borrowings of cash, purchases of assets on credit, breaches of contracts or commissions of torts, receipts of services, or passage of time. Accountants treat duties or responsibilities as liabilities when the underlying debt or obligation possesses three characteristics. First, the debt or obligation must involve an existing duty or responsibility. Second, the duty or responsibility must obligate the entity to provide a future benefit. Finally, the debt or obligation must have arisen from a transaction which has already occurred so that the entity can reasonably measure the obligation.

Again, several hypotheticals can illustrate these characteristics. If Tutt accepts delivery of the computer on August 1 and agrees to pay for it in full on October 1, has Tutt incurred a liability? Yes. A transaction that has already occurred has legally bound Tutt to pay $2,000 to the seller. If Tutt orders law books worth $200, but the seller has not yet delivered the books, has she incurred a liability? No. When delivery takes place, Tutt will owe the $200, but until that time Tutt has not incurred a liability. The transaction does not become complete until the delivery takes place; only then must Tutt pay for the supplies or return them. If Tutt accepts a $300 retainer from one of her clients to prepare and file articles of incorporation in advance of rendering legal services, has she incurred a liability? Yes. Tutt has an obligation to deliver legal services worth $300 to the client. If she cannot provide the services, she must refund the client's payment. She has incurred a legal obligation and a transaction has already occurred.

Just as the balance sheet does not show "positives" that do not satisfy the accounting requirements for assets, the balance sheet also may not list "negatives" which could adversely affect the business. For example, poor management, labor problems, unsatisfied customers or poor reputation in the community would not appear as liabilities on a balance sheet. By ignoring these factors, which obviously present difficult measurement issues, the balance sheet can convey a false impression about a business's financial condition.

Unless the business has given a creditor a security interest in a particular asset or a law grants such an interest, liabilities attach to the business's assets generally rather than to the specific assets that the creditor may have helped the business acquire. If the business does not pay its debts, creditors may force the business to liquidate. In that event, creditors rights laws require the entity to satisfy its liabilities before paying any "inside" claims.

b. EQUITY

Because creditors' claims enjoy priority in liquidation over "inside" claims, any liabilities reduce E. Tutt's personal stake or equity in the business. Accountants use the term *equity* to refer to the arithmetic difference between an entity's assets and it's liabilities. In other words, if the entity sold its assets, and satisfied its liabilities, for the amounts shown on the balance sheet, we call the remainder equity because the owners could claim that residual amount.

Equity increases when the owners invest assets into the business. The equity in E. Tutt's law practice increased when she contributed $1,000 to the business. Equity decreases when the owners withdraw assets from the business.

Depending on the type of entity involved, accountants assign different names to the residual ownership interest. Owners can use sole proprietorships, partnerships, corporations, or hybrid organizations such as limited partnerships, limited liability partnerships and limited liability companies, to conduct business. We will now consider the residual ownership claims in these different forms of business organization.

As the name suggests, one person owns a *sole proprietorship*. The owner usually also manages and operates the business. Many small service-type businesses, including E. Tutt's law office, operate as sole proprietorships. Sole proprietorships generally offer simplicity as an advantage. Anyone can start a sole proprietorship, and the owner can keep any profits. The owner, however, must bear any losses and remains personally liable for any debts which the business incurs. Although the law does not recognize any distinction between the business and the owner, we recognize the business as a separate accounting entity. Accountants refer to the residual ownership interest in a sole proprietorship as *proprietorship*.

A *partnership* arises when two or more persons engage in business for profit as co-owners. If E. Tutt and her law school classmate, Jennifer King, decide to practice law together, they could form a partnership, which they might call "King Tutt." In many ways, a partnership resembles a sole proprietorship except that the business involves more than one owner. Again, partnerships generally offer simplicity, but the partners frequently sign partnership agreements which set forth various terms regarding the partnership, such as each partner's initial investment, responsibilities and duties, profit and loss sharing ratio, and vote in management, and the procedures for ending the partnership. As a huge disadvantage, each partner incurs unlimited personal liability for the partnership's debts. Despite this unlimited personal liability, accountants recognize partnerships as separate accounting entities to segregate partnership affairs from the partners' personal activities. Accountants refer to the residual ownership interest in partnership as *partners' equity,* or *capital.* With multiple owners, however, partnerships keep separate equity accounts for each partner.

One or more persons owning a business could also form a *corporation* by complying with certain statutory requirements. Laws in every state treat corporations as legal entities separate from their owners. Corporate laws divide the residual ownership interest in a corporation into *shares.* Generally, each share entitles the owner to: (1) participate in corporate governance by voting on certain matters, such as the election of directors who manage the corporation's business and affairs; (2) share proportionally in any earnings, in the form of dividends, which the directors may declare for the corporation to distribute to shareholders; and (3) share proportionally in residual corporate assets upon liquidation.

The owners of the shares, usually referred to as *shareholders*, enjoy limited liability. The corporation's creditors cannot hold the shareholders personally liable for the corporation's debts. Shareholders can transfer their shares to other investors without dissolving the corporation. On the downside, federal income tax law treats corporations as separate taxpaying entities. This treatment creates double taxation because corporations must pay taxes on their income, and shareholders generally must pay taxes on any amounts that the corporation distributes as dividends.

Accountants refer to the ownership interest in a corporation as *shareholders' equity.* For practical reasons related to the free transferability of shares and the possibility that thousands, or even millions, of shareholders could own a stake in a corporation, corporations do not maintain separate equity accounts for each shareholder.

All states permit business owners to form hybrid entities such as *limited partnerships, limited liability companies,* or *limited liability partnerships.* These hybrid entities possess both partnership and corporate characteristics. The hybrid entities all follow partnership accounting.

Two or more persons can form a limited partnership in any state by complying with the applicable statutory requirements. A limited partnership requires one or more general partners and one or more limited partners. As a general rule, general partners manage the partnership's business while limited partners provide additional capital. Although the limited partners enjoy limited liability, the general partners remain personally liable for the limited partnership's debts. As with partnerships, accountants refer to the residual ownership interest in the limited partnership as partners' equity. Limited partnerships keep separate equity accounts for each partner, whether general or limited.

By following state law requirements, one or more owners can form a limited liability company ("LLC") as a separate legal entity in every state. The LLC's owners, usually referred to as *members*, enjoy limited liability. Accordingly, an LLC's creditors cannot hold the members personally liable for the LLC's debts. LLCs offer significant flexibility because the members can structure their *operating agreement* in almost any way they want. LLCs have become very popular because they can avoid the double tax problem. Accountants refer to the residual ownership interest in an LLC as *members' equity*. Because LLCs possess some partnership characteristics, LLCs keep separate equity accounts for each member.

Almost all states permit two or more owners to organize a limited liability partnership ("LLP"), or an existing partnership to convert to an LLP. Depending on the statute, partner in an LLP enjoy limited liability from either certain tort-type liabilities or from all liabilities. LLPs, therefore, offer partners either partial or full shields against the LLP's obligations. As with any other partnership, accountants refer to the residual ownership interest in an LLP as partners' equity. Similarly, LLPs keep separate equity accounts for each partner.

We will discuss, in more detail, the different accounting treatments that accountants use to account for partners' equity and shareholders' equity later in the chapter.

3.   THE FUNDAMENTAL ACCOUNTING EQUATION

No matter what organizational form the owners choose, we can express the relationship between equity, assets and liabilities in the following mathematical equation:

Equity = Assets — Liabilities

Under this equation, E. Tutt's equity, which we might also call her *net worth*, equals the difference between the law practice's assets and liabilities.

Accountants, however, rearrange the equation in two steps. First, they reverse the equation's two sides so that the equation reads:

Assets — Liabilities = Equity

Second, they add Liabilities to both sides of the equation to produce the restated equation:

Assets = Liabilities + Equity

Accountants refer to this restatement as the *fundamental accounting equation* because the equation serves as the underlying basis for the balance sheet. In fact, the fundamental accounting equation sustains the bookkeeping process and the accrual accounting system.

We might rearrange E. Tutt's assets, listing them in the order in which they are likely to be used up. We might also separate the source of the assets between liabilities and owners' contribution. The result would be a simple balance sheet that might look like this:

E. Tutt, Esquire
Balance Sheet, after transactions (a) - (e)

Assets			Liabilities & Proprietorship		
			Liabilities:		
(e) Cash		$800	Accounts Payable		
(c) Supplies		100	Frank Co.	$400	(a)
			Elmer Co.	300	(b)
(b) Equipment		300	Note Payable: Stanley	100	(c)
(a) Furniture		400	Total Liabilities	$800	
(d) Library		200	Proprietorship	1,000	
	Total	$1,800	Total	$1,800	(d, e)

Note that no change has been made except a change in presentation of the list of assets and sources which appears on page 5, *supra*. The essential meaning remains the same.

Having discussed each component in the balance sheet and the fundamental accounting equation, we should remember four very important points about the balance sheet. First, total assets must equal the sum of liabilities and equity. Second, the balance sheet speaks at, or as of, one particular instant in time. Third, the balance sheet records assets at historical cost. Fourth, the balance sheet shows only assets and liabilities which meet certain accounting requirements. The balance sheet, therefore, may not reflect many important things which we might consider as valuable or detrimental to the business.

4. THE CLASSIFIED BALANCE SHEET

Thus far, we have purposely kept the discussion about the balance sheet simple. The balance sheet becomes more useful to managers, creditors, owners and potential investors, however, when the entity classifies assets and liabilities into various categories.

Accountants generally classify assets into four types: *current assets, long-term investments, fixed assets* and *intangible assets*. They generally treat cash and other assets which the particular accounting entity would normally expect to convert into cash or use within one year as *current assets*. Current assets could include: *marketable securities*, such as stocks and bonds, which the entity holds as short-term investments; *notes receivable*, amounts due to the entity under promissory notes; *accounts receivable*, uncollected amounts owed to the entity for goods or services sold on credit; *inventories*, or goods held for sale or resale; and *prepaid expenses*, such as insurance premiums paid in advance for insurance coverage during the next year. In contrast, accountants generally classify resources which an accounting entity would not normally expect to convert into cash or use within one year as *long-term investments*. Long-term investments include stocks and bonds which the entity intends to hold; notes receivable or accounts receivable which the entity cannot collect for more than a year; and prepaid expenses, such as insurance premiums paid in advance for insurance coverage more than one year into the future. *Fixed assets* include tangible resources such as land, buildings, plant and equipment, machinery, or furniture and fixtures which the entity acquired for extended use in the business. *Intangible assets* lack physical substance and include patents, copyrights and trademarks acquired for extended use in the business.

Accountants usually show assets on the balance sheet in the order listed in the previous paragraph. Typically, a balance sheet lists current assets first and according to declining *liquidity*. Liquidity refers to the relative ease and time necessary to convert an asset into cash. Within current assets, the balance sheet starts with cash and proceeds to marketable securities, notes receivable, accounts receivable, inventory and prepaid expenses in that order. Long-term investments typically follow current assets. The balance sheet then proceeds to list fixed assets, usually according to permanence, and finishes with intangible assets.

Accountants also divide liabilities into two types: current and long-term. They generally classify liabilities which will require payment in one year or less as *current liabilities*. Current liabilities include: money borrowed under promissory notes due within one year, usually called *notes payable*; amounts owed for purchases on credit, or *accounts payable*; money owed for services already performed, usually referred to as *accrued liabilities or wages*; those portions of long-term debt which the business must repay within one year; taxes payable; and *unearned revenues*, amounts which the entity will have to refund if it does not perform the required services.

In contrast to current liabilities, accountants generally consider obligations, or parts of obligations, which would normally not require payment for more than one year as *long-term liabilities*. Long-term liabilities typically include notes payable that do not require repayment for more than one year; *bonds payable*, which usually represent borrowings from numerous investors through the financial markets, rather than a loan from one creditor which gives rise to a note payable; lease and mortgage obligations due in more than one year; and obligations under employee pension plans.

Because liabilities enjoy priority in liquidation over ownership claims, the balance sheet lists liabilities above equity. Again, accountants usually show liabilities on the balance sheet in the order listed in the previous two paragraphs. Current liabilities come first, usually starting with notes payable and, then, accounts payable. Balance sheets frequently list other current liabilities in descending order of magnitude. Long-term liabilities follow, with any *secured claims* or liabilities for which the borrower has pledged one or more assets as collateral, usually listed first. Finally, the balance sheet shows equity.

We might rearrange E. Tutt's balance sheet according to these conventions. We might also show the assets above the liabilities and equity. The result would be a somewhat more refined balance sheet that might look like this:

E. Tutt, Esquire
Balance Sheet, after transactions (a) - (e)

Assets

	Current Assets:		
(e)	Cash		$800
(c)	Supplies		100
	Total Current Assets		$900
	Fixed Assets:		
(b)	Equipment		$300
(a)	Furniture		400
(d)	Library		200
	Total Fixed Assets		$900
	Total Assets		$1,800

Liabilities & Proprietorship

	Liabilities		
	Current Liabilities:		
(c)	Note Payable: Stanley		$100
	Accounts Payable:		
(a)	Frank Co.	$400	
(b)	Elmer Co.	300	700
	Total Liabilities		$800
(d, e)	Proprietorship		1,000
	Total Liabilities and Proprietorship		$1,800

Accountants refer to such a balance sheet as a *classified balance sheet* in *report form*. Again, note that no change has been made except a change in presentation. The essential meaning again remains the same. But because clear disclosure is one of the accountant's main concerns, matters of presentation are important. The classified balance sheet helps the user to determine whether the accounting entity owns enough current assets to pay liabilities as they come due. The classified balance sheet also shows the relative claims between short-term and long-term creditors.

C.   DOUBLE-ENTRY BOOKKEEPING

As Tutt engages in practice, many events will occur to affect her financial position, and the balance sheet figures will change. If, for example, in transaction (f), she pays off the note to Stanley, her cash would decrease by $100, so that the cash balance remaining would be $700, and the liability to Stanley of $100 would disappear. If, in transaction (g), Tutt paid Elmer Co. $200 of the amount owed for equipment, cash would be further decreased, to $500, and the liability of $300 to Elmer Co. would be decreased to $100. After these two transactions, Tutt's balance sheet, in simple form, would read as follows:

E. Tutt, Esquire
Balance Sheet, after transaction (g)

	Assets		Liabilities & Proprietorship		
			Liabilities:		
(e,f,g)	Cash	$500	Accounts Payable		
(c)	Supplies	100	Frank Co.	$400	(a)
(b)	Equipment	300	Elmer Co.	100	(b,g)
(a)	Furniture	400	Total Liabilities	$500	
(d)	Library	200	Proprietorship	1,000	(d, e)
	Total	$1,500	Total	$1,500	

Note that each of these two transactions affected two items on the balance sheet and did so in equal amounts. This is not a coincidence; the fact is that every transaction has two separate aspects of equal importance. If, (h), Tutt bought more books for $100 in cash, it would tell only half the story to record just the decrease in cash of $100; her "holdings" of books—represented by the asset, *Library*—have increased by $100. If, (i), Tutt took a chair costing $50 from her office for use thereafter at home, reducing *Office Furniture* by $50 would not tell the whole story because her stake in the enterprise, *Proprietorship*, has also been reduced by $50.

Tutt's balance sheet, again in simple form, after these two transactions:

E. Tutt, Esquire
Balance Sheet, after transaction (I)

	Assets		Liabilities & Proprietorship		
			Liabilities:		
(e,f,g,h)	Cash	$400	Accounts Payable		
(c)	Supplies	100	Frank Co.	$400	(a)
(b)	Equipment	300	Elmer Co.	100	(b,g)
(a,i)	Furniture	350	Total Liabilities	$500	
(d,h)	Library	300	Proprietorship	950	(d,e,i)
	Total	$1,450	Total	$1,450	

You will note that recognition of the two aspects of each transaction, which are always equal in amount, may change the totals of the balance sheet columns but does not upset their equality. That should not be surprising; we have already seen that the two columns of the balance sheet mirror the two sides of the fundamental accounting equation. The balance sheet reflects the assets and their sources at any given time, and the inherent equality of the fundamental accounting equation cannot be affected by changes in the mix of assets and their sources. To illustrate, an increase in an asset may come about in one of two ways: either another asset has been exchanged for it, or an additional source of funds has been supplied to acquire it (as, for example, if Tutt bought an asset on credit from a new supplier). On the balance sheet, the increase in the asset column would either be offset by a decrease in the asset column or be balanced by an increase in the sources column. Likewise, a decrease in an asset may come about in one of two ways. If assets have been exchanged, we have the transaction already discussed, but stated in reverse order—the decrease in assets will be accompanied by an increase in assets reflecting the acquisition of the new asset. The other possibility is a decrease in the sources column, reflecting use of an asset to pay off a claim, such as the use of cash to discharge the note payable to Stanley. Finally, there can be an exchange of sources, which would be reflected by equal increases and decreases in the sources column, as, for example, if Tutt should give a note to a creditor to whom she owed money on open account.

To simplify the number of possible combinations involved, we might first set out all the possibilities:

One Effect of Transaction		Accompanying Effect
(1) Increase in Asset	(a)	Increase in Source
	(b)	Decrease in Asset
(2) Decrease in Asset	(a)	Decrease in Source
	(b)	Increase in Asset
(3) Increase in Source	(a)	Increase in Asset
	(b)	Decrease in Source
(4) Decrease in Source	(a)	Increase in Source
	(b)	Decrease in Asset

Obviously, a number of these possibilities simply restate others, but in reverse order: e. g., (1)(a) and (3)(a). Indeed, the four types of balance sheet effects involved could be grouped as follows:

Increase in Asset	Increase in Source
Decrease in Source	Decrease in Asset

for all transactions are some combination of an item on one side of this table with one of the two items on the other side of the table.

The balance sheet itself is simply the summary to date of all the individual transactions, and the inherent equality of its columns is confirmed by the fact that each individual transaction has two equal effects on the balance sheet.

A single transaction can have more than two effects. If, in transaction (j), Tutt bought another piece of office equipment from Elmer Co. for $100, paying $50 down, *Office Equipment* would increase $100, *Cash* would decrease $50, and *Accounts Payable: Elmer Co.* would increase $50. This transaction shows that sometimes two combinations may be involved at the same time; the transaction here involves an increase in an asset balanced half by a decrease in an asset and half by an increase in a source.

Tutt's balance sheet, in simple form, after the above transaction becomes:

E. Tutt, Esquire
Balance Sheet, after transaction (j)

	Assets		Liabilities & Proprietorship		
			Liabilities:		
(e,f,g,h,j)	Cash	$350	Accounts Payable		
(c)	Supplies	100	Frank Co.	$400	(a)
(b,j)	Equipment	400	Elmer Co.	150	(b,g)
(a,i)	Furniture	350	Total Liabilities	$550	
(d,h)	Library	300	Proprietorship	950	(d,e,i)
	Total	$1,500	Total	$1,500	

Even with these few transactions, the balance sheet has been changed several times. While we could rewrite the balance sheet every time something happened, it is more efficient for a business to keep a separate record of the ups and downs of each item on the balance sheet, so that the business can determine at any time the net effect on that item of all transactions since the bookkeeper drew up the last balance sheet. Look at cash. Tutt's first balance sheet, shown earlier, showed a cash balance of $800. The bookkeeper would take a separate card, or page in a book, entitle it *Cash*, and enter the $800 from the balance sheet as the opening balance. Since we ultimately want the net result of all the ups and downs in cash, it would be convenient to divide the page into two columns, one for recording the increases in cash, the other for reflecting the decreases; and it would be sensible to use the same column for increases as the one which has the opening balance. This record is called the Cash *account*. Here, transactions (e), (f), (g), (h) and (j) would each produce an *entry* in the Cash account. When the time for drawing up a new balance sheet arrived, it would be simple to add the total of the increases in cash to the opening balance and subtract the total of the decreases to find the balance in the cash account. The process is about the same as entering the balance forward, deposits and withdrawals in the stubs of a checkbook. The Cash account for Tutt, beginning at the date of the balance sheet on page 10, *supra,* would look like this:

Order in which entries were made

Cash		
	(+)	(−)
(e) Opening balance(from last balance sheet)	(e) $800	
(f) To pay off Stanley		$100 (f)
(g) To pay off Elmer Co.		200 (g)
(h) To purchase books		100 (h)
(j) To purchase equipment		50 (j)
Current balance		$350

Because this record is shaped like a "T," it is often called a *T-account*. The total of the plus column of the T-account, showing the opening cash balance plus any increases, less the total of the minus column, showing decreases, gives the current balance of $350, which would appear on the new balance sheet.

The T-accounts for the other assets, with the opening balance in each case coming from the previous balance sheet, would be as follows:

Office Furniture		
	(+)	(−)
(a) Opening balance	(a) $400	
(i) On removal of chair from business		$50 (i)
Current balance		$350

Office Equipment		
	(+)	(−)
(b) Opening balance	(b) $300	
(j) On new purchase from Elmer Co.	(j) $100	
Current balance		$400

Office Supplies		
	(+)	(−)
(c) Opening balance	(c) $100	

(No further entries, as nothing has happened to affect the Office Supplies account)

Library		
	(+)	(−)
(d) Opening balance	(d) $200	
Current balance		$300

In the T-accounts for assets, it is customary to enter the opening balance in the left-hand column. This corresponds to the fact that assets are recorded on the left-hand side of the balance sheet. As noted, the increases are entered in the same column as the opening balance, just as bank deposits are added to the previous balance in a checkbook.

T-accounts similar to those illustrated for the asset accounts are also set up for the liability and the proprietorship accounts. By a convention to be analyzed in the next paragraph, the opening balance in these accounts (which, as with assets, comes from the previous balance sheet) is entered on the right-hand side of the T-account. To keep this important switch in mind, remember that these accounts are the ones on the right-hand side of the balance sheet. As with assets, increases in these accounts are entered on the same side as the opening balance; but for these accounts that means the right-hand side, with decreases on the left. Tutt's liability and proprietorship T-accounts are as follows:

Accounts Payable: Frank Co.

		(−)	(+)	
(a)	Opening balance		$400	(a)

Accounts Payable: Elmer Co.

		(−)	(+)	
(b)	Opening balance		$300	(b)
(g)	To show partial payment of the account	(g) $200		
(j)	On new purchase of equipment		50	(j)
	Current balance		$150	

Note Payable: Stanley

		(−)	(+)	
(c)	Opening balance		$100	(c)
(f)	To show payment of note	(f) $100		
	Current balance		$0	

Proprietorship

		(−)	(+)	
(d,e)	Opening balance		$1000	(d,e)
(i)	On removal of chair from business	(i) $50		
	Current balance		$950	

At first, this switch of the plus and minus columns may seem clumsy. But it has one very practical advantage which makes the bookkeeper's job easier: it results in having every transaction, no matter what accounts are affected, give rise to equal left-hand and right-hand entries in the T-accounts. To see that this is so, you should first recognize that a transaction affecting accounts on only one side of the balance sheet must produce an equal increase and decrease, and never two increases alone, or two decreases alone. Therefore, if a transaction affects only one side of the balance sheet, such as assets only or sources only, one entry will be a left-hand entry and the other a right-hand entry. In these cases there is no necessity for any convention calling for a switch between asset accounts and source accounts as to the side of the T-account on which an increase or decrease is entered.

It is when a transaction affects both sides of the balance sheet that the advantage of this convention appears. Remember that a transaction affecting accounts on both sides produces either an equal increase on both sides or an equal decrease on both sides, but never an increase on one and a decrease on the other. Whether the change on both sides of the balance sheet is an increase or a decrease, by virtue of this convention the change on one side will be a left-hand entry and the change on the other a right-hand entry. For example, an increase in assets is a left-hand entry, whereas the corresponding equal increase in liabilities or proprietorship is a right-hand entry. Again, a decrease in the assets column will be a right-hand entry, and the corresponding decrease in liabilities and proprietorship will be a left-hand entry. The table given earlier, then, actually constitutes a summary of the possible combinations of left-hand and right-hand entries:

Left-hand entries	**Right-hand entries**
Increase in Asset	Increase in Source
Decrease in Source	Decrease in Asset

This convention as to the side of the T-accounts on which increases and decreases are entered, operating in conjunction with the fact that every transaction has two equal aspects which must be recorded, forms the basis of the system which accountants call double-entry bookkeeping.

At this time, we should mention that some small businesses use *single-entry bookkeeping*. A checkbook register illustrates a single-entry bookkeeping system. If Tutt opened a checking account for her law office and deposited all cash receipts in the account and wrote checks for all cash payments, her checkbook register would tell us the balance in her checking account, where she collected cash and where she spent cash. In that example, the register would show a $350 balance in the checking account and that Tutt deposited $1,000 in the account to start the business. The register would also provide information about five cash expenditures: (1) the purchase of the library for $200, (2) the $100 payment to Stanley for stationery and supplies, (3) the $200 partial payment to Elmer Co. for office equipment which Tutt purchased on credit, (4) another $100 to purchase books for the library, and (5) the $50 down payment to Elmer Co. for another piece of office equipment. The checkbook register, however, does not tell us what other assets the business owns or what business obligations Tutt owes. For example, the checkbook register does not tell us: (1) that Tutt also owns office furniture that she bought on credit from Frank Co., (2) whether Tutt still owns the library books, (3) whether the business has used the stationary and supplies, (4) whether E. Tutt still owns the office equipment she purchased from Elmer Co., or (5) whether the business owes any other creditors. In this last regard, the checkbook register does not tell us that Tutt owes Frank Co. $400 for the office furniture that she bought on credit. Finally, the checkbook register does not reveal that Tutt took a chair which cost $50 from her office for use at home. Double-entry bookkeeping permits more comprehensive financial reports.

To see how double-entry bookkeeping is used, take another look at the transactions already considered. When Tutt paid off Stanley's note, there was a decrease in a liability, *Note Payable: Stanley*, a left-hand entry, and a decrease in an asset, *Cash*, a right-hand entry. And when Tutt bought more office equipment from Elmer Co. for $100, paying $50 down, the left-hand entry showed a $100 increase in an asset, *Office Equipment*; the right-hand entries included: (1) a $50 decrease in an asset, *Cash*, and (2) a $50 increase in a liability, *Accounts Payable: Elmer Co.* The left-hand and right-hand entries for each transaction are equal, no matter how many accounts are affected.

The terms "left-hand entry" and "right-hand entry" are cumbersome. Bookkeepers instead use shorthand terms. Left-hand entries are *debits* and right-hand entries are *credits*. When Tutt buys more books, the bookkeeper speaks of a *debit* to *Library*, or *debiting Library*, and a *credit* to *Cash*, or *crediting Cash*. Whatever meaning these terms have in other contexts, here debit and credit, which accountants often abbreviate "Dr." and "Cr." respectively, mean nothing more than left-hand and right-hand entries in the T-accounts. We could restate the T-accounts which appear on pages 16 to 18, *supra,* as follows:

Cash

		Dr.	Cr.	
(e)	Opening balance(from last balance sheet)	(e) $800		
(f)	To pay off Stanley		$100	(f)
(g)	To pay off Elmer Co.		200	(g)
(h)	To purchase books		100	(h)
(j)	To purchase equipment		50	(j)
	Current balance	$350		

Office Furniture

		Dr.	Cr.	
(a)	Opening balance	(a) $400		
(i)	On removal of chair from business		$50	(i)
	Current balance	$350		

Office Equipment

		Dr.	Cr.	
(b)	Opening balance	(b) $300		
(j)	On new purchase from Elmer Co.	(j) 100		
	Current balance	$400		

Office Supplies

		Dr.	Cr.	
(c)	Opening balance	(c) $100		

Library

		Dr.	Cr.	
(d)	Opening balance	(d) $200		
(h)	On purchase of new books	(h) 100		
	Current balance	$300		

Accounts Payable: Frank Co.

		Dr.	Cr.	
(a)	Opening balance		$400	(a)

Accounts Payable: Elmer Co.

		Dr.	Cr.	
(b)	Opening balance		$300	(b)
(g)	To show partial payment of the account	(g) $200		
(j)	On new purchase of equipment		$50	(j)
	Current balance		$150	

Note Payable: Stanley

		Dr.	Cr.	
(c)	Opening balance		$100	(c)
(f)	To show payment of note	(f) $100		
	Current balance		$0	

	Proprietorship	
	Dr.	Cr.
(d,e) Opening balance		$1000 (d,e)
(i) On removal of chair from business	(i) $50	
Current balance		$950

For convenience, the bookkeeper first records transactions chronologically in a separate book, usually referred to as the *journal*. For each transaction, the journal shows the debit and credit effects on specific accounts. Businesses may use various kinds of journals, but every business will use a *general journal*. A business may also create a journal to record transactions in various functions, such as a sales journal, a purchases journal, a cash receipts journal, or a cash disbursements journal. Today, many businesses use computers to keep their journals, but the fundamental concepts remain the same.

The general journal usually contains five columns for the date, the accounts involved and any explanation of the transaction, a cross-reference for the account number to which the bookkeeper transferred the amount in the journal entry, and separate columns for debits and credits. The general journal for a business typically looks something like this:

General Journal

Date	Account	Ref.	Debit	Credit

For each transaction, the bookkeeper first enters the date. Then, the bookkeeper writes the account to be debited as a result of the transaction and the amount of the debit. Next on the following line, but indented, is written the account to be credited and the amount. Indentation separates the credits from the debits. These items are often followed by a brief description of the transaction which makes it possible to check later to see whether the transaction was recorded properly. Representative *journal entries*, in simplified form without the reference column or the linear grids, for some of Tutt's transactions would be:

(f) Note Payable: Stanley $100
      Cash $100
   (To record payment of the note to Stanley)

(h) Library   100
      Cash   100
   (To record the purchase of additional books)

(j)	Office equipment	100	
	Cash		50
	Accounts Payable: Elmer Co.		50

(To record purchase of additional business
equipment from Elmer Co.)

These entries are then recorded in the appropriate accounts, a process known as *posting* from the journal to the *ledger*. Accountants refer to the ledger as the collection of all the accounts that a business maintains. The ledger, therefore, stores in one place all the information about changes in specific account balances. Again, businesses often keep various kinds of ledgers, but every business will use a *general ledger*. The general ledger contains all the asset, liability and equity accounts for the business. A business may also keep *sub-ledgers* when it needs to keep very detailed records. For example, an accounting entity may use an accounts receivable sub-ledger to record the individual amounts that each customer owes to the business. The accounts receivable account in the general ledger would keep track of the total amount owed to the firm by all its customers. The sum of the subsidiary accounts in the sub-ledger must equal the balance in the accounts receivable account in the general ledger.

For each ledger, businesses often use a looseleaf binder or card file with each account kept on a separate sheet or card. Businesses usually number each account for identification purposes and usually place the accounts in the general ledger in balance sheet order, starting with assets. Liabilities and equity accounts usually follow. As with journals, many businesses today use computerized ledgers, but the underlying concepts still remain the same.

Most business have developed a *chart of accounts* which lists each account and the account number which identifies the account's location in the ledger. To understand a business's accounting records, you should start with the chart of accounts. For example, E. Tutt's chart of accounts might list the following accounts and account numbers:

E. Tutt, Esquire
Chart of Accounts

Number   Account

Assets

1	Cash
5	Accounts Receivable
9	Supplies
11	Equipment
13	Furniture
15	Library

Liabilities

| 21 | Notes Payable |
| 23 | Accounts Payable |

Owner's Equity

31 Proprietorship
99 Profit and Loss

Revenues

51 Professional Income
55 Miscellaneous Income

Expenses

71 Rent Expense
75 Secretary Expense
79 Telephone Expense
83 Miscellaneous Expense

We will discuss revenues, expenses and profit and loss in the next section. For now, you should notice, however, that the account numbering system in the chart of accounts contains gaps to permit the bookkeeper to insert new accounts as needed.

To summarize the bookkeeping process, the bookkeeper first periodically records transactions in the journal. Next, the bookkeeper posts the information in the journal to the ledger by periodically transferring the information in the journal to accounts in the ledger. If the bookkeeper wants to prepare a balance sheet at any point in time, the bookkeeper determines the balance in each account by netting one side against the other and uses the balances in the asset, liability and equity accounts to prepare the balance sheet.

From this summary, you can already imagine that bookkeeping involves a tedious process. As previously mentioned, computers have become so important in bookkeeping and accounting that all large businesses and many, if not most, smaller businesses use computerized bookkeeping or accounting systems. Computerized systems can save enormous amounts of time because software can automatically record each journal entry in the ledger, concurrently compute the new balance in the account, and simultaneously prepare updated financial statements if desired. Beneath the computer software, however, lies the double-entry bookkeeping system.

PROBLEMS

You have now read about the basic foundations of bookkeeping. What is called for at this point is some practice in applying these techniques yourself.

Problem 1.1A. Immediately following is the balance sheet for E. Tutt on January 1 of her second year of practice, followed by a list of some of Tutt's transactions during the month of January, on the dates indicated.

(1) Set up T-accounts for each of the items on the balance sheet on one sheet of paper, with the opening balance on the appropriate side. Then on a separate piece of paper write the journal entry for each of the transactions listed, and then post them to the appropriate T-accounts, adding new T-accounts as necessary.

(2) Unless your instructor directs otherwise, prepare a simple balance sheet for E. Tutt as of January 12.

E. Tutt, Esquire
Balance sheet, January 1 of Second Year

Assets		Liabilities & Proprietorship	
		Liabilities:	
Cash	$450	Accounts Payable	
Supplies	50	Brown	$200
Equipment	420	Frank Co.	250
Furniture	550	Total Liabilities	$450
Library	630	Proprietorship	1,650
Total	$2,100	Total	$2,100

Transactions in January:

Jan.   1   Bought a new chair for the office for $75 cash.

4   Paid Brown $100 on account.

6   Purchased a new office machine from Jones Co. for $220 on credit.

7   Purchased a new copy of the Ames Code Annotated from the East Publishing Co. for $120, paying $60 down, with the other $60 due in February.

9   Received a birthday gift from her parents of $300 cash to help her stay in business—she deposited the money in her business bank account.

11   Paid Frank Co. the $250 she owed it.

12   Gave some law books she no longer needed, which cost her $100, to her law school's library.

Problem 1.1B. Immediately following is the balance sheet for Joe's Diner on June 30, followed by a list of some of transactions during the month of July, on the dates indicated.

(1) Set up T-accounts for each of the items on the balance sheet on one sheet of paper, with the opening balance on the appropriate side. Then on a separate piece of paper write the journal entry for each of the transactions listed, and then post them to the appropriate T-accounts, adding new T-accounts as necessary.

(2) Unless your instructor directs otherwise, prepare a simple balance sheet for Joe's Diner as of July 31.

Joe's Diner
Balance Sheet, June 30

Assets		Liabilities & Proprietorship	
		Liabilities:	
Cash	$4,000	Accounts Payable	
Inventory	2,200	Larkin	$4,200
Equipment	12,000	Proprietorship	14,000
Total	$18,200	Total	$18,200

Transactions in July:

July 2 Joe invested an additional $1,500 in the business.

5 Joe used $300 worth of inventory at cost for a personal party for which he paid $300 cash to the business.

8 The business acquired additional inventory from Larkin on credit for $1,200.

13 Using funds in his business bank account, Joe purchased a new fax machine for the diner for $600 cash.

17 Joe withdrew $1,000 from the business for his personal use.

20 Larkin accepted a promissory note for the total balance due to him.

Problem 1.1C. Immediately following is the balance sheet for Jaline's Dental Shop on June 30, followed by a list of some of transactions during the month of July, on the dates indicated.

(1) Set up T-accounts for each of the items on the balance sheet on one sheet of paper, with the opening balance on the appropriate side. Then on a separate piece of paper write the journal entry for each of the transactions listed, and then post them to the appropriate T-accounts, adding new T-accounts as necessary.

(2) Unless your instructor directs otherwise, prepare a simple balance sheet for Jaline's Dental Supply as of July 31.

Jaline's Dental Supply
Balance Sheet, June 30

Assets		Liabilities & Proprietorship	
		Liabilities:	
Cash	$7,000	Accounts Payable	
Inventory	5,200	Justice	$5,200
Equipment	19,000	Proprietorship	26,000
Total	$31,200	Total	$31,200

Transactions in July:

July 2   Jaline withdrew $6,500 from the business for her personal use.

     5   Jaline sold equipment which cost the proprietorship $5,500 to Ron Gant for that same amount.

     8   She acquired additional inventory from Terry Pendleton on credit in the amount of $1,200.

    13   Jaline purchased, for the proprietorship, a new drill machine for $3,500 in cash.

    17   Jaline withdrew $1,000 from the proprietorship capital for personal use.

    20   Justice demanded payment on the total balance due to him, and Jaline promised payment to him by the end of the month.

D.   THE INCOME STATEMENT

We have already seen how the balance sheet gives a reader one way to determine how well a business is doing by comparing what the business owns with what it owes. The balance sheet shows the present status of the assets and their sources resulting from all transactions since the business was formed. It is drawn up at regular intervals which will vary with the needs of the business. The balance sheet, however, cannot tell a reader very much about the business's ability to earn a profit.

As another, and probably more important way, to assess how a business is doing, we could also compare the amounts which the business's activities generate—its *revenues*—with the costs incurred to produce those revenues—its *expenses*. The *income statement*, the second basic financial statement, shows the extent to which business activities have caused an accounting entity's equity, or net worth, to increase or decrease over some period of time. Again, you may find helpful those cartoons from the 1992 annual report of Ben & Jerry's Homemade, Inc., set out in Appendix C: the two which try to explain the income statement in simple terms are on pages C-3 and C-5.

As preliminary matters, we should note three things about the income statement, which businesses sometimes call the *statement of earnings* or the *statement of operations*. First, the fundamental distinction between the balance sheet and the income statement is that, while the balance sheet speaks as of a particular date, the income statement covers a period of time between successive balance sheet dates. Just as we compared the balance sheet to a snapshot, we can compare the income statement to a motion picture. Income statements usually cover one year. Business owners or managers, however, may also prepare such statements on a monthly or quarterly basis. Accountants usually refer to these monthly or quarterly statements as *interim reports*.

Second, the income statement only shows the extent to which a business's activities have caused an increase or a decrease in equity, or net worth, over some period of time. If revenues exceed expenses, the resulting net income increases equity. In contrast, if expenses exceed revenues, the net loss decreases equity. You should recall, however, that a business's equity can also increase if an owner invests assets in the business or decrease if an owner withdraws assets from the business. Recall that equity increased when E. Tutt contributed $1,000 as her original stake in her law office and decreased when she removed a chair from her office to use at home. The income statement, therefore, only gives a summary of earnings or losses between balance sheet dates.

Third, the income statement, like the balance sheet and the other financial statements which we will discuss, does not provide prospective information. The income statement shows only the results from a business's operations for a period in the past. Past results, however, may provide some indications about the business's prospects.

In later chapters of this book we will have occasion to consider the relative importance of the balance sheet and the income statement. For this chapter, we must simply understand their relationship. You may need a little time to grasp the relation between the two statements and to get accustomed to the way in which double-entry bookkeeping performs a neat "bridging function" between them. But there is nothing mysterious about the income statement as such.

1.   REVENUES AND EXPENSES

Drawing up a simple income statement for E. Tutt, say for the month of June, may be the easiest way to start explaining that financial statement. Suppose that during the month she receives fees of $600 and $400 for legal services.

(1)	Professional Income	$600
(2)	Professional Income	$400

Accountants define *revenues* as increases in assets, decreases in liabilities, or both, resulting from delivering goods, rendering services, or engaging in ongoing major or central operations. In this example, E. Tutt produces $1,000 in revenues during June from her principal business activity, namely performing legal services. In contrast, accountants classify increases in assets or decreases in liabilities from peripheral or incidental transactions, other than contributions by owners, as *gains*. Because both revenues and gains increase assets or decrease liabilities, with corresponding increases in owner's equity, accountants occasionally describe revenues and gains as "positives" — they result in consequences that a business views as favorable.

To find E. Tutt's net income, we must subtract her expenses for the month from the month's revenues. Accountants define *expenses* as decreases in assets, increases in liabilities, or both, resulting from using goods or services to produce revenue. In contrast, accountants classify decreases in assets or increases in liabilities from peripheral or incidental transactions which do not involve distributions to owners as *losses*. Once again, because both expenses and losses decrease assets or increase liabilities, with a corresponding decrease in owner's equity, accountants may say that expenses and losses produce a "negative" effect on a business.

Suppose that E. Tutt's operating expenses were as follows:

(3) Rent	$200
(4) Secretary	230
(5) Telephone	15
(6) Heat & Light	5
(7) Miscellaneous	5

Suppose further that during the month a thief broke intoTutt's office and stole $20 cash. This loss is treated as any other expense:

(8) Theft Loss	$20

There is no particular form required for an income statement, so long as it is a clear and fair statement of the information. An acceptable one might look like this:

E. Tutt, Esquire
Income Statement for June

(1 & 2)	Professional Income			$1,000
	Less: Expenses			
(3)	Rent	$200		
(4)	Secretary	230		
(5)	Telephone	15		
(6)	Heat & Light	5		
(7)	Miscellaneous	5		
(8)	Theft Loss	20		
	Total Expenses			$475
	Net Income			$525

To see how the income statement fits into the balance sheet we might ask where Tutt's net income shows up on her balance sheet. In lay terms, Tutt's net income is an increase in her stake in the business, which we have been calling Proprietorship. Hence, if no other change in her stake occurs, the balance sheet figure for Proprietorship on June 30 should be $525 larger than on June 1.

How does this work out in the accounts? Upon receipt of the $600 fee for legal work completed in June, Tutt will debit *Cash*, since cash has increased by $600:

Cash	$600	
?		$600

Because the corresponding entry must be a credit of $600, the alternatives are a decrease in assets, an increase in liabilities, or an increase in proprietorship (or some combination thereof). But no asset has decreased, nor has any liability increased. Therefore, the credit must be an increase in proprietorship of $600.

This result makes sense. The assets of Tutt's law practice have increased, and because she is the residual owner of this enterprise, the increase redounds to her benefit; in other words, her stake in the enterprise has gone up. But common sense tells us that Tutt's "stake" has not been augmented by a full $600. Light, heat, rent, supplies, secretarial services and miscellaneous items have all gone to produce this $600 fee (and while the theft loss of $20 has not actually helped to produce any fees, it too is a cost of doing business). These items, then, should appear as decreases in proprietorship; in the same way that income increases the stake of the proprietor, expenses decrease her stake. For example, when rent is paid, the entry could be:

Proprietorship	$200	
Cash		$200

If all revenues and expenses were entered in the Proprietorship account, the account would reflect the net increase or decrease in proprietorship for the period. The T-accounts for Cash and Proprietorship for Tutt would be:

Cash

(Bal.)	$350		
(1)	600	$200	(3)
(2)	400	230	(4)
		15	(5)
		5	(6)
		5	(7)
		20	(8)
(Bal.)	$875		

Proprietorship

		$950	(Bal.)
(3)	$200		
(4)	230		
(5)	15		
(6)	5		
(7)	5	600	(1)
(8)	20	400	(2)
		$1,475	(Bal.)

Just as it is inconvenient to draw up a new balance sheet every time something happens, so it would be inconvenient, and indeed uninformative, to enter all the many operating items directly in Proprietorship. Instead, the Proprietorship account is broken up into separate T-accounts. The left-hand side of the Proprietorship account, the side on which decreases in proprietorship are recorded, is subdivided into separate T-accounts, called *expense accounts*, such as Rent Expense or Utility Expense, or sometimes *loss accounts*, such as Theft Loss, and the decreases in proprietorship other than withdrawals by Tutt are entered in those accounts rather than directly in the Proprietorship account. Similarly, the right-hand side of the Proprietorship account, on which increases are recorded, is subdivided into separate T-accounts called *income accounts*, such as Professional Income or Dividend Income, or sometimes *gain accounts*, such as Gain on Sale of Equipment, and increases other than capital investments by owners are recorded in those accounts. The relationship between the expense and income T-accounts and the Proprietorship T-account might be symbolized in the following manner:

Proprietorship

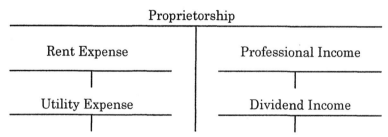

Because an expense constitutes a decrease in proprietorship, which is a debit entry, an expense is of course reflected by a debit or left-hand entry in the appropriate expense T-account. Indeed, because the expense T-accounts are subdivisions of just the left-hand side of the Proprietorship account, you may wonder why the expense accounts themselves have two sides. The answer is simply a practical one: sometimes a portion of an expense previously paid is refunded, perhaps as a rebate, or because it was inadvertently overpaid, and it seems more sensible to record this as a reduction in the expense, by a right-hand entry in the expense T-account, than as an increase in proprietorship, either by a credit directly to that account or to some income account. In addition, right-hand entries in expense T-accounts facilitate the mechanics of double-entry bookkeeping, as we shall see shortly.

In the same vein, since income constitutes an increase in proprietorship, which is a credit, an income item is reflected by a credit or right-hand entry in the appropriate income T-account; and the presence of a left-hand side in the income T-accounts simply makes it convenient to reflect any refund of an income item, such as a return by E. Tutt of an overpayment of a fee, as a reduction in the income by a debit to the income T-account (while again also facilitating double-entry bookkeeping).

The number of different expense and income T-accounts set up depends upon the extent to which we want to identify separately in the books the various items of income and expense. For example, Tutt may want to show rent and secretarial expense as separate items, because they are individually important, but may be satisfied to lump together telephone, heat and light in a single Utility Expense account.

Tutt's journal entries for the income and expense transactions during the month would be as follows:

(1)	Cash	$600	
	Professional Income		$600
(2)	Cash	400	
	Professional Income		400
(3)	Rent Expense	200	
	Cash		200
(4)	Secretarial Expense	230	
	Cash		230
(5)	Utility Expense	15	
	Cash		15
(6)	Utility Expense	5	
	Cash		5
(7)	Miscellaneous Expense	5	
	Cash		5
(8)	Theft Loss	20	
	Cash		20

As these entries show, cash received for professional income has as its corresponding right-hand entry a credit to Professional Income, which is in effect an increase in proprietorship. When cash is paid out for expenses for the period, there are corresponding left-hand entries in the various expense accounts that are in effect decreases in proprietorship. When these entries have been posted to the T-accounts, the T-accounts would appear as follows:

	Cash		Proprietorship	
Bal.$ 350	$200 (3)			$950 Bal.
(1) 600	230 (4)	[Expense Items]	[Income Item]	
(2) 400	15 (5)			
	5 (6)	Rent Expense	Professional Income	
	5 (7)			
	20 (8)	(3) $200	$600 (1)	
Bal. $875			400 (2)	
		Bal. $200	$1,000 Bal.	

Rent Expense

(3) $200	
Bal. $200	

Secretarial Expense

(4) $230	
Bal. $230	

Utilities Expense

| (5) $15 | |
(6) 5	
Bal. $20	

Miscellaneous Expense

(7) $ 5	
Bal. $ 5	

Theft Loss

(8) $20	
Bal. $20	

Professional Income

| | $600 (1) |
	400 (2)
	$1,000 Bal.

2. THE CLOSING PROCESS

Income and expense accounts differ from other accounts in one important respect: as subsidiary accounts of proprietorship, they never appear on the balance sheet. Instead, after the accounts have performed their function of collecting in one place all items of the same kind of income or expense for the period, the net balances in these accounts are brought together in a single account. The net figure in that account, net income or loss, shows the effect of the operations of the period on proprietorship. In other words, whereas at the beginning of the period we broke the Proprietorship account down into several sub-accounts for income and expense items, at the end of the period we bring these sub-accounts back together, and the net figure is the increase or decrease in proprietorship due to operations.

Of course, the income and expense accounts could be brought back together in the Proprietorship account itself, by simply debiting the Proprietorship account with the various expense items, and crediting the Proprietorship account with the income items. That is ordinarily not done, however, since it is desirable to isolate in a single special account all the items relating to operations for the particular period. If the income and expense items were brought back together in the Proprietorship account, that isolation would not be achieved, since the Proprietorship account also reflects other transactions having nothing to do with the operations of the business—for example, a withdrawal from the business during the period, such as Tutt's removal of the chair from the office. A separate account is needed to show just the results of operations; that account called *Profit and Loss*, serves as the consolidating account for all the income and expense items. Accordingly, the income and expense items are transferred, or, in accounting jargon, *closed* to the Profit and Loss account.

The bookkeeper uses journal entries to transfer the balances in these individual accounts to the Profit and Loss account. Since the separate income and expense accounts are to disappear, the bookkeeper makes an entry in each of these accounts equal to and on the opposite side from the net balance found in the account. This entry, by making the two sides of the account equal, closes the account, and the bookkeeper draws a double line across the bottom of the account to show that it is closed. The corresponding opposite-hand entry is then made to the Profit and Loss account, thus putting the balance in each account on the same side of the Profit and Loss account as it was in the account from which it came, i. e., expenses on the left-hand side, income on the right. The bookkeeper would record Tutt's *closing entries* as follows:

(a)	Professional Income	$1,000	
	Profit and Loss		$1,000
(b)	Profit and Loss	200	
	Rent Expense		200
(c)	Profit and Loss	230	
	Secretarial Expense		230
(d)	Profit and Loss	20	
	Utility Expense		20
(e)	Profit and Loss	5	
	Miscellaneous Expense		5
(f)	Profit and Loss	20	
	Theft Loss		20

The T-accounts would become:

Cash		Proprietorship	
Bal.$350			$950 Bal.
(1) 600	$200 (3)		
(2) 400	230 (4)		
	15 (5)		
	5 (6)	[Expense Items]	[Income Item]
	5 (7)		
	20 (8)	Rent Expense	Professional Income
Bal.$875		(3) $200			$600 (1)
			$200 (b)		$400 (2)
				(a) $1,000	$1,000 Bal.
		Secretarial Expense		
		(4) $230		
			$230 (c)	
		Utilities Expense	
		(5) $15		
		(6) 5		
		Bal. $20	$20 (d)	
		Miscellaneous Expense	
		(7) $ 5		
			$ 5 (e)	
		Theft Loss	
		(8) $20		
			$20 (f)	

Profit and Loss

(b) $200	$1,000(a)
(c) 230	
(d) 20	
(e) 5	
(f) 20	
	$525 Bal.

What has been achieved? Compare the Profit and Loss account with the income statement which we made up on page 29, *supra,* at the beginning of this section. They are of course essentially the same, for the income statement is nothing more than a somewhat more detailed presentation of the Profit and Loss account. The creation of separate income and expense accounts in effect sets up slots for recording the transactions as they occur; it permits the immediate classification of the various categories of income and expense and provides a single place for the orderly accumulation and preservation of all items of the same category. The utility of a separate Profit and Loss account, reflecting solely the operations of the business, will become increasingly apparent.

The final step is to close the Profit and Loss account into the Proprietorship account: because at present the net figure in the Profit and Loss account is a credit of $525, we need a debit to Profit and Loss of $525 to close the account, and a credit to Proprietorship in the same amount:

(g) Profit and Loss $525

    Proprietorship $525

Nothing more is happening, of course, than to transfer the credit of $525 to the Proprietorship account, where it would have been in the first place if we had not created the separate income and expense accounts. The T-accounts then appear as follows:

Cash		Proprietorship	
Bal. $875		$ 950	Bal.
		525	(g)
		$1,475	Bal.

Profit and Loss			
(b)	$200	$1,000	(a)
(c)	230		
(d)	20		
(e)	5		
(f)	20		
(g)	525	$ 525	Bal.

The circle is now complete; the resulting balances of $875 in the Cash account and $1,475 in the Proprietorship account are exactly the same as we saw earlier in this section, before we went through the bookkeeping processes for expense and income items. If no change in other assets or liabilities has occurred, so that the balances in those accounts remain as they were on page 15, *supra,* the ending balance sheet, in simple form, would be:

E. Tutt, Esquire
Balance Sheet, End of June

Assets		Liabilities & Proprietorship	
		Liabilities:	
Cash	$875	Accounts Payable	
Supplies	100	Frank Co.	$400
Equipment	400	Elmer Co.	150
Furniture	350	Total Liabilities	$550
Library	300	Proprietorship	1,475
Total	$2,025	Total	$2,025

To summarize our discussion of the bookkeeping process in the context of both the balance sheet and the income statement, the bookkeeper first records transactions in the journal. Second, the bookkeeper posts the information in the journal to the ledger. At the end of an accounting period, the bookkeeper closes the books by transferring the balances in the revenue, gain, expense and loss accounts to owner's equity.

During the *closing process*, the bookkeeper first determines the balance in each account by netting one side against the other. Next, the bookkeeper prepares closing journal entries which transfer the balances in the revenue and expense accounts to the clearinghouse Profit and Loss account and posts those entries to the ledger. Then, the bookkeeper prepares a final closing entry which transfers the balance in the Profit and Loss account to the Proprietorship account and posts this entry to the ledger.

As the final step in the bookkeeping process, the bookkeeper prepares financial statements.

PROBLEMS

You have now read about the basic principles underlying the balance sheet and the income statement. At this point, we should practice the techniques we have read about.

Problem 1.2A. As a continuation of Problem 1.1A, below are the rest of E. Tutt's transactions for the month of January in her second year. Prepare the journal entries for these transactions, and post them to the appropriate T-accounts, setting up any additional T-accounts that may be needed (including, of course, the necessary expense and income accounts). Then close the expense and income accounts to the Profit and Loss account, and close the Profit and Loss account to the Proprietorship account. Prepare an income statement for the month of January and a simple balance sheet as of the end of January, using the forms set out after the list of transactions.

Additional Transactions in January:

Jan 13   Gave Smith some legal advice and received $150.

15   Got a reminder from her landlord that she had not paid te rent of $150 for her office for January, and sent a check immediately.

16   Paid her secretary a salary of $200 for the first half of January.

20   Received $375 for her work during January on Bolton's Estate.

23   Paid an electrician $20 to repair a lighting fixture.

25   Purchased some supplies for $75 cash from Stanley Co.

27   Did some work for Sam's Book Store, and in exchange received a new East's Digest which sells for $220.

29   Prepared a deed for Ingersoll and received a fee of $250.

30   Paid her secretary $200 for the second half of January.

31   Went to Telephone Co. and paid her bill of $50 for the month of January.

E. Tutt, Esquire
Income Statement
For the Month of January

Professional Income		$ _995_
Less: Expenses		
Secretary	$ _400_	
Rent	_150_	
Telephone	_50_	
Miscellaneous	_95_	
Total Expenses		$_____
Net Income		$_375_

E. Tutt, Esquire
Balance Sheet, January 31

Assets		Liabilities & Proprietorship	
		Liabilities:	
Cash	$ _____	Accounts Payable:	$ _____
Supplies	_____	Brown	_____
Equipment	_____	Jones Co.	_____
Furniture	_____	East Publishing	_____
Library	_____	Total Liabilities	$ _____
		Proprietorship	_____
Total	$_____	Total	$_____

Problem 1.2B. The balance sheet on December 31 of James Stief, Attorney at Law, appears below.

James Stief, Attorney at Law
Balance Sheet, December 31

Assets		Liabilities & Proprietorship	
Cash	$4,000	Accounts Payable	$1,400
Office Equipment	3,500		
Library	3,000	Proprietorship	9,100
Total	$10,500	Total	$10,500

During January, Stief's office engaged in the transactions listed below. Prepare journal entries for those transactions and post them to the appropriate T-accounts, setting up any additional T-accounts that may be needed (including, of course, the necessary expense and income accounts). Then close the expense and income accounts to the Profit and Loss account, and close the Profit and Loss account to the Proprietorship account. Unless your instructor directs otherwise, prepare an income statement for the month of January and a classified balance sheet as of the end of January, using the forms set out after the list of transactions.

Transactions in January:

Jan. 1   Paid $500 on his account due to Jackson.

4   Rendered legal services to Lee and received payment in the amount of $700.

5   His secretary, Lulu, purchased for cash $85 worth of office supplies that she used before the end of the month.

8   Received payment in the amount of $1,500 for legal services rendered to Jones.

11 Purchased a set of state reporters from West Group for $1,200 on account.

15 Paid $1,100 rent for the month to the landlord of the office building.

20 Received and paid a bill of $75 for printing services.

31 Paid Lulu $500 as her monthly salary.

James Stief, Attorney at Law
Income Statement
For the Month of January

Professional Income		$_____
Less: Expenses		
Rent	$_____	
Secretary	_____	
Office Supplies	_____	
Printing	_____	
Total Expenses		$_____
Net Income		$_____

James Stief, Attorney at Law
Balance Sheet, January 31

Assets		Liabilities & Proprietorship	
Current		Liabilities (all current):	
Cash	$_____	Accounts Payable:	
Fixed		Jackson	$_____
Office Equipment	_____	West Group	_____
Library	_____	Total Liabilities	$_____
Total Fixed Assets	_____	Proprietorship	_____
Total	$_____	Total	$_____

3. THE TRIAL BALANCE AND SIX-COLUMN WORKSHEET

To assist in the closing process, many bookkeepers will also prepare either a *trial balance* or a *worksheet*. Lawyers and law students can benefit from understanding both of these bookkeeping tools. The trial balance presents another application of the fundamental accounting equation while the worksheet further illustrates the relationship between the income statement and the balance sheet.

You will recall that to begin the closing process, the bookkeeper determines the balance in each account by netting one side against the other. Before proceeding any further, many bookkeepers will then prepare a *trial balance*. The trial balance lists all accounts and their temporary balances. As the final step in completing the trial balance, the bookkeeper totals the debits and credits.

Using the T-accounts on page 32, *supra,* and the balances in the other accounts from the balance sheet on page 35, *supra,* because no change in those accounts has occurred, we could prepare a trial balance for E. Tutt as follows:

E. Tutt, Esquire
Trial Balance for June

Account	Debit	Credit
Cash	$875	
Supplies	100	
Equipment	400	
Furniture	350	
Library	300	
Accounts Payable: Frank Co		$400
Accounts Payable: Elmer Co.		150
Proprietorship		950
Professional Income		1,000
Rent Expense	200	
Secretary Expense	230	
Utility Expense	20	
Miscellaneous Expense	5	
Theft Expense	20	
Totals	$2,500	$2,500

If the debits do not equal the credits, the bookkeeper has made an error. Under the fundamental accounting equation and double-entry bookkeeping, debits must always equal credits. In this way, the trial balance provides a minimal check on the process of recording and posting daily transactions. Preparing a trial balance will detect any addition or subtraction errors that the bookkeeper may have made, any incomplete journal entries or postings to the ledger, and transposition errors in posting amounts to the ledger. The trial balance, however, only detects errors that result in unequal debits and credits. The trial balance will not detect incorrect, but equal amounts, which the bookkeeper may have recorded in the journal entries, entries to the wrong accounts, or omitted or duplicate transactions.

After determining that the debits equal the credits in the trial balance, many bookkeepers will use a *worksheet* to aid in the closing process and the preparation of financial statements. The worksheet allows the bookkeeper to separate the revenue, gain, expense and loss accounts in the trial balance which flow into the income statement and the asset, liability, and equity accounts which will appear on the balance sheet. The worksheet also helps the bookkeeper prepare the closing entries which we have already discussed.

Without going into elaborate detail, a common type of worksheet contains six columns of figures, preceded by a list of all the accounts in the ledger, plus a caption for net income (or loss). The first and second columns display the debit and credit balances, respectively, from the trial balance. The third and fourth columns show the debit and credit balances, respectively, for the revenue, gain, expense and loss accounts which will appear on the income statement, while the fifth and sixth columns, respectively, compile the debit and credit balances for the asset, liability and equity accounts which will appear on the balance sheet. Consequently, a six-column worksheet would look something like this:

E. Tutt, Esquire
Six-Column Worksheet for June

Account	Trial Balance Debit	Trial Balance Credit	Income Statement Debit	Income Statement Credit	Balance Sheet Debit	Balance Sheet Credit
Cash	$875				$875	
Supplies	100				100	
Equipment	400				400	
Furniture	350				350	
Library	300				300	
Accounts Payable: Frank Co.		$400				$400
Accounts Payable: Elmer Co.		150				150
Proprietorship		950				950
Professional Income		1,000		$1,000		
Rent Expense	200		$200			
Secretary Expense	230		230			
Utility Expense	20		20			
Miscellaneous Expense	5		5			
Theft Expense	220		20			
Subtotals	$2,500	$2,500	$475	$1,000	$2,025	$1,500
Net Income			525			525
Totals			$1,000	$1,000	$2,025	$2,025

The debit entry for net income balances the income statement columns and the credit entry balances the balance sheet columns. The credit in the balance sheet column also indicates the increase in equity from net income. Consequently, the worksheet powerfully illustrates the interrelationship between the income statement and the balance sheet. Once again, we see how the income statement shows the change in equity from net income or loss resulting from operations during an accounting period.

PROBLEMS

You have now read about the basic techniques underlying the trial balance and the six column worksheet. At this point, we should practice what we have learned.

Problem 1.3A. Based on the following trial balance for Chamberlain's Romance Book Store, construct a six-column worksheet and prepare August financial statements (balance sheet and income statement only). Ignore depreciation and any other accruals or deferrals.

Chamberlain Romance Book Store
Trial Balance, August 31

Account	Debit	Credit
Accounts Payable ⌐		$3,500
Accounts Receivable A	$1,500	
Advertising Expense ⏐	2,800	
Book Binding Expense ⏐	1,300	
Cash A	8,700	
Equipment A	8,000	
Notes Payable ⌐		2,400
Proprietorship OE		13,700
Rent Expense ⏐	5,000	
Revenue ⏐		16,000
Salary Expense ⏐	6,000	
Supplies Expense ⏐	1,500	
Traveling Expense ⏐	800	
Totals	$35,600	$35,600

Problem 1.3B. Based on the following trial balance for Dave Dutile, Attorney at Law, construct a six-column worksheet and prepare July financial statements (balance sheet and income statement only). Ignore depreciation and any other accruals or deferrals.

Dave Dutile, Attorney at Law
Trial Balance, July 31

Account	Debit	Credit
Accounts Receivable	$9,800	
Accounts Payable		$3,300
Cash	5,700	
Notes Payable		10,000
Office Equipment	8,100	
Proprietorship		10,800
Rent Expense	800	
Revenue		2,200
Salary Expense	1,600	
Supplies Expense	100	
Telephone Expense	200	
Totals	$26,300	$26,300

Problem 1.3C. Based on the following trial balance for Glen's Ice Cream Shop Co., construct a six-column worksheet and prepare June financial statements (balance sheet and income statement only). Ignore depreciation, income taxes and any other accruals or deferrals.

Glen's Ice Cream Shop Co.
Trial Balance, June 30

Account	Debit	Credit
Accounts Receivable	$2,600	
Accounts Payable		$3,500
Cash	15,000	
Food Expense	4,000	
Notes Payable		6,500
Notes Receivable	4,100	
Office Equipment	5,000	
Office Supplies	1,500	
Proprietorship		18,200
Rent Expense	7,500	
Revenue		15,000
Salary Expense	2,300	
Supplies Expense	1,200	
Totals	$43,200	$43,200

E. THE STATEMENT OF CHANGES IN OWNERS' EQUITY

We have now studied both the balance sheet and the income statement. We have seen how the income statement serves as a "bridge" between two balance sheets. The income statement, however, only shows the extent to which a business's activities have caused an increase or a decrease in equity over some period of time. During that same period of time, equity could have also increased if an owner invested assets in the business or decreased if an owner withdrew assets from the business. The *Statement of Changes in Owners' Equity* fully reconciles the changes in net worth between balance sheet dates.

To distinguish between the changes in equity that arise from operations and those from investments and withdrawals by owners, accounting entities often maintain different accounts for *capital*, *drawings*, and *retained earnings*. Accountants use capital accounts to record an owner's investment in the business. Investments obviously increase equity and capital. An owner also may withdraw cash or some other asset for use outside the business, as when Tutt removed a chair from her law office for personal use. Such withdrawals decrease equity and could be credited directly to capital. Accountants, however, normally prefer to use a separate account, referred to as Drawings, to track an owner's total withdrawals for an accounting period. For a corporation, accountants usually net any withdrawals, which we usually refer to as *distributions* or *dividends*, against the corporation's cumulative net income or loss in an account called Retained Earnings. We will examine the accounting treatment for the equity section in the three basic business forms, sole proprietorship, partnership and corporation.

1. SOLE PROPRIETORSHIP

In a sole proprietorship, accountants might describe the account to record capital as either Proprietorship or Capital. When E. Tutt invested $1,000 in her legal practice, the bookkeeper could have recorded the following entry in the general journal:

(d) Cash $1,000
        Proprietorship $1,000
       (To record original investment in business)

Similarly, when Tutt removed the chair from her law office, the bookkeeper could have used the following journal entry for the transaction:

(i) Drawings $50
        Furniture $50
       (To record withdrawal of chair for personal use)

At the end of the accounting period, the bookkeeper would close the Drawings account to the Proprietorship account as follows:

Proprietorship $50
　　Drawings $50
(To close drawings)

To reconcile the equity amounts which appear in the earlier balance sheets, we could prepare the following financial statement:

E. Tutt, Esquire
Statement of Changes in Owner's Equity
For the Month of June

Proprietorship, beginning of period	$1,000
Net income	525
Subtotal	$1,525
Less: Drawings (the chair Tutt removed)	50
Proprietorship, ending of period	$1,475

The statement of changes in owner's equity, therefore, reconciles the amount of the residual ownership interest from the beginning to the end of an accounting period. In other words, the statement summarizes the various changes that have occurred in equity since the last balance sheet. Either net income or additional investments can increase equity, while a net loss or withdrawals decrease equity. Depending on the accounting entity involved, the statement of changes in owner's equity can assume different forms. We turn next to the statement in a partnership context.

2.   PARTNERSHIP

You may recall that accountants assign different names to the residual ownership interest depending on the accounting entity involved. In a partnership, accountants call that interest *partners' equity*. Having multiple owners, however, partnerships maintain separate equity accounts for each partner. Therefore, the King Tutt partnership would keep separate equity accounts for both E. Tutt and Jennifer King. The partnership might call their capital accounts *Partner's Equity, E. Tutt* and *Partner's Equity, J. King*, as respectively. Similarly, the partnership might also call their drawings accounts *Drawings, E. Tutt* and *Drawings, J. King*.

Assume that E. Tutt and Jennifer King both invested $1,000 to start King Tutt on September 1. We could record their contributions as follows in the general journal:

Cash $2,000
　　Partner's Equity, E. Tutt $1,000
　　Partner's Equity, J. King $1,000
(To record original investment in partnership)

If during September, the partnership collects $2,000 for professional services and incurs $800 in expenses, the partnership would show $1,200 net income. Further assume that each partner withdrew $400 for living expenses during the month. When the partners withdrew $400 each, we could record the following journal entry:

Drawings, E. Tutt	$400	
Drawings, J. King	$400	
Cash		$800
(To record draws)		

At the end of the accounting period, we could close the Drawings accounts to the Partner's Equity accounts as follows:

Partner's Equity, E. Tutt	$400	
Partner's Equity, J. King	400	
Drawings, E. Tutt		$400
Drawings, J. King		400
(To close the drawings accounts)		

Because the partnership earned $1,200 in net income, the Profit and Loss account would contain a $1,200 credit balance after transferring the balances in the revenue and expense accounts. To close the Profit and Loss account, we could make the following entry to divide the net income for the month equally between E. Tutt and Jennifer King:

Profit and Loss	$1,200	
Partner's Equity, E. Tutt		$600
Partner's Equity, J. King		600

To reconcile the changes in partners' equity during September, we could prepare the following financial statement:

King Tutt
Statement of Changes in Partners' Equity
For the Month of September

	Tutt	King	Total
Partners' Equity, September 1	$-0-	$-0-	$-0-
Original investment	1,000	1,000	2,000
Net income	600	600	1,200
Subtotals	$1,600	$1,600	$3,200
Less: Drawings	400	400	800
Partners' Equity, September 30	$1,200	$1,200	$2,400

If the partnership included more than two partners, the bookkeeper could add a column for each partner. At some point, however, a partnership may move to a summary approach to the statement as follows:

King Tutt
Statement of Changes in Partners' Equity
For the Month of September

Partner's Equity, September 1	$–0–
Original investment	2,000
Net income	1,200
Subtotals	$3,200
Less: Drawings	800
Partners' Equity, September 30	$2,400

3. CORPORATION

Rather than operate her legal practice as a sole proprietorship, E. Tutt could have formed a corporation to practice law, as is now permitted in all fifty states. If Tutt had incorporated, she would have contributed her $1,000 initial investment to the corporation in exchange for shares in the corporation, and that would have constituted the corporation's initial proprietorship, or capital. The shares issued to E. Tutt would represent the residual ownership interest in the corporation. A corporation may have a great many shareholders, or very few (even only one), and as a general rule shareholders can transfer their shares at any time, so corporations do not create separate equity accounts for each shareholder. Under corporate law a shareholder has no claim to any specified amount of the corporation's assets, but upon liquidation each shareholder has the right to share proportionately with all other holders of the same class, after the corporation has satisfied any prior interests. More important, unlike partners or sole proprietors, shareholders are not personally liable for the debts of their enterprise; that is, the creditors of a corporation can look only to the assets of the corporation for the payment of their claims. Accordingly, the total capital invested in the corporation is a very important figure, since it represents the amount which the owners have placed at risk in the enterprise.

a. CONTRIBUTED CAPITAL

In earlier days, the incorporation documents required to be filed with a state official specified the total amount of capital to be raised from the stockholders, thereby providing notice to prospective creditors as to what the corporation's financial strength would be at the outset. This total capital figure was normally described as divided into a specified number of shares. For example, the Tutt, Inc. documents might have provided that "the capital of this corporation shall be $1,000, divided into 100 shares." Each share then bore the figure designating the fractional portion of the total capital that the share represented, here $10. Eventually, lawyers referred to this figure as the share's *par value*. It is unfortunate that this term included the word "value," because, except perhaps at the very outset, the figure bears no necessary relation to the share's actual worth. But the figure did represent the minimum amount of consideration received for each such share: the corporation statutes uniformly mandated that no share of stock be issued for any less than the par value, in order to be sure that the full amount of the intended capital would be raised (and that each shareholder would pay at least a minimum price for his shares).

It was also very important to know just how much capital had been raised and permanently committed to the enterprise, since in effect that amount served as a substitute for the personal liability of the owners of the enterprise to creditors — it represented a safety margin for creditors, providing a greater likelihood that the corporation would be able to repay its debts. Accordingly, from the beginning corporate statutes provided that the amount of capital contributed by the stockholders should be disclosed: a common way of doing this was to require that shares have a designated par value (which the incorporators were free to fix at any figure they liked), with that very important corollary that shares not be issued for less than the specified par value, in money or money's worth. Accordingly, the total par value of the corporation's outstanding stock in effect represented a statement that at least that amount had in fact been contributed by the shareholders as permanent capital. That figure was usually called *Capital Stock* by accountants, or sometimes *Stated Capital*; lawyers, on the other hand, pretty generally used that term *Stated Capital* for the total par value, although they also often refer to it as the *Legal Capital*, because it was subject to certain legal requirements, starting with that mandate that the corporation receive as invested capital from the shareholders at least as much as the total par value of the outstanding stock. (A corporation may receive more than par value for the shares it issues, but as we will see shortly any excess over par value is likely to be largely if not entirely free of the constraints on legal capital.)

Of course this safety margin represented by the legal capital could be dissipated by operating losses — that is a risk that all corporate creditors take. But creditors should not have to run the risk of a voluntary reduction of the legal capital safety margin by way of a distribution to shareholders. Accordingly, under the legal capital system the corporate statutes commonly prohibited any distribution of corporate assets to shareholders, by way of dividends or otherwise, which would leave the corporation with assets amounting to less than the sum of the corporation's liabilities plus its stated or legal capital. In other words, corporations were forbidden to reduce voluntarily their net assets (assets less liabilities) to an amount less than the legal capital safety margin, thereby giving creditors some assurance that the legal capital would be permanently dedicated to the corporation's activities and obligations (subject of course to losses in the operations of the business).

However, over the years the ingenuity of lawyers has undermined the legal capital system, and it has now been abandoned in about three-quarters of the states (though not including Delaware, where perhaps half of the publicly-traded corporations are incorporated) in favor of merely prohibiting distributions that cause or increase insolvency. One notable weakness in the legal capital system developed when corporations were permitted to issue shares without any specified par value. Known as no-par shares, they obviously avoid the legal restriction against issuing shares for less than the par value; they also complicate the determination of legal capital and hence tend to water down the prohibition against returning any of the legal capital to the shareholders. More important, as to shares which do have a par value it became common to use a very low par figure, as low as $1, or even 1¢. Such shares are typically issued for substantially more than the par value, but since it was generally accepted that only the par figure constituted legal capital subject to the stringent restrictions on distribution to shareholders, that did not provide much protection for the creditors.

The separate account to reflect the amount contributed by shareholders in excess of stated or legal capital was traditionally called *Capital Surplus,* but accountants now prefer the term *Additional Paid-In Capital.* Although not as limited with respect to distributions to shareholders as legal or stated capital, capital surplus may be more restricted than the third component of shareholders' equity, accumulated earnings – that is, earnings retained in the business rather than distributed to the shareholders – traditionally called *Earned Surplus,* but accountants now prefer *Retained Earnings.*

A corporation can also issue more than one class or type of shares, with one class representing the basic residual ownership rights while any other class is likely to have some special rights or preferences, but be subject to some limitations as well. For example, such a class, usually called *Preferred Shares,* might give the holders the right to receive a fixed amount of dividends each year before the corporation can distribute any amount to the common shareholders; but as a consequence the preferred shareholders would normally get nothing more than the specified dividend each year no matter how much the corporation might earn. Preferred shares typically also entitle shareholders to receive a fixed amount upon liquidation before the common shareholders receive anything.

(1) Shares with Par Value

When a corporation issues shares at par value, the company debits the appropriate asset account, whether cash, property, or other consideration, and credits a capital stock account for the par value amount. To illustrate, if Tutt, Inc. issues 100 shares, $10 par value, to E. Tutt for $1,000, the corporation's bookkeeper would record the following journal entry:

```
Cash                              $1,000
   Common Stock, $10 par value              $1,000
(To record the issuance of 100 shares to E. Tutt)
```

If instead, Tutt, Inc. issues five shares of $100 par value preferred stock to Tutt for $500 and fifty shares of $10 par value common stock to her for another $500, the bookkeeper would make the following entry:

Cash	$1,000	
Preferred Stock, $100 par value		$500
Common Stock, $10 par value		500

(To record the issuance of five preferred shares and fifty common shares to E. Tutt)

In the common case when shares are issued for more than their stated par value, as noted above the excess is reflected in a separate account, called *Capital Surplus* by lawyers, but *Additional Paid-In Capital* by accountants. Thus, it is the combination of the common stock account, plus the Preferred Stock account, if there is one, and any Additional Paid-In Capital that makes up the corporation's total contributed capital.

So, if Tutt, Inc. had issued 100 shares of $1 par stock for $1,000, the bookkeeper would have recorded the following entry:

Cash	$1,000	
Common Stock, $1 par		$100
Additional Paid–In Capital		900

Note that the balance sheet discloses certain important information about the corporation's capital structure. First, the shareholders' equity section shows the par value set for the common shares (or that the shares are no-par). It is also common to indicate the number of shares the company is authorized to issue, and the number of shares which the corporation has issued in fact.

(2) No–Par Shares

For no-par shares, the legal capital system presumptively treats the entire amount of consideration paid for the shares as legal or stated capital, but most statutes in this system permit the board of directors to allocate some of the total amount received for shares without par value to the separate capital surplus (or additional paid-in capital) account. Usually, only the amount recorded in stated capital would constitute legal capital which the corporation cannot distribute to the shareholders. The amount per share that ends up in stated capital with respect to no-par shares, whether the entire consideration received for the shares or what is left after some has been allocated to capital surplus, is often referred to as *Stated Value*, a misnomer because, like par value, the stated value figure does not necessarily bear any relation to the share's actual value.

From an accounting standpoint, if the board of directors does not elect to treat some of the consideration received for no-par shares as capital surplus, the company debits the appropriate asset account and credits the full consideration to stated capital; if instead the board decides that less than all of the consideration received for no-par shares should constitute legal capital, that smaller figure will be credited to stated capital, with the excess credited to capital surplus. In either case, the so-called stated value per share is equal to the quotient of stated capital divided by the number of no-par shares.

In summary, both accountants and lawyers recognize the division of contributed capital into two categories, but they refer to them differently. Accountants use an account called stated capital, or sometimes capital stock, for either common stock or preferred stock, to portray the amount which represents the product of the number of issued shares times the par value or stated value per share, whereas lawyers often call this legal capital. Accountants refer to any payment in excess of par or stated value as additional paid-in capital, while lawyers are more likely to use the term capital surplus.

b. EARNED CAPITAL

As already mentioned, the other basic source of shareholders' equity is earnings retained in the business (rather than distributed as dividends), which accountants call *Retained Earnings* but the legal capital system has traditionally referred to as *Earned Surplus*. At the end of each accounting period, a corporation closes the Profit and Loss account to Retained Earnings; that account is debited for any distribution to shareholders, with a corresponding credit to cash or whatever other asset might be used.

To reconcile the equity amounts from the balance sheet which appeared earlier, we could prepare a Statement of Shareholders' Equity:

E. Tutt, Inc.
Statement of Changes in Shareholders' Equity
For the Month of June

Shareholders' Equity, beginning of period	$1,000
Net income	525
Subtotal	$1,525
Less: Distribution (the chair Tut removed)	50
Shareholders' Equity, ending of period	$1,475

F. ACCRUAL ACCOUNTING

Thus far, we have been studying bookkeeping, or the technique for recording a business's transactions. In addition to recording business transactions, accrual accounting seeks to provide quantitative information, primarily financial in nature, about a business's activities, for use in decision-making. When the bookkeeping system was being developed, most ventures did not last very long. Bookkeepers could determine an enterprise's total net profit by calculating the difference between what the owners contributed to the business and what they received at the venture's conclusion. Most businesses today, however, continue indefinitely, so they prepare periodic financial statements to determine income and net worth.

Accrual accounting, or accounting for short, seeks to allocate revenues and expenses to accounting periods, regardless of when the cash receipts or expenditures actually occur. From an accounting standpoint, earning revenue does not require a cash receipt. Similarly, an expense may not require a cash expenditure in the accounting period in which the business incurred the expense. Under accrual accounting, an enterprise recognizes revenues when earned and expenses when incurred, without regard to the actual cash receipts or payments.

We can illustrate these points by returning to our example involving E. Tutt. You will recall that during the month of June, Tutt received $1,000 in fees for legal services that she performed during the month. What if Tutt had sent a bill for $300 to a client on June 29 for services which had been performed earlier in the month, but the client did not pay the bill until July 3? Under the *cash method*, an accounting entity recognizes revenues when the enterprise actually receives cash in payment for goods or services. If Tutt used the cash method, she would not recognize the $300 revenue until the client paid the bill in July, even though she actually performed the services in June. In contrast, under the accrual method, an accounting entity recognizes revenues when the business delivers the goods or performs the services. If Tutt had adopted the accrual method, she would have included the $300 in June's revenues because she performed the services during the month.

These same distinctions apply to expenses. An accrual-method enterprise records expenses when it actually incurs them. Under the cash method, the business would not record the expenses until it paid them. To illustrate, assume that Tutt hired a company supplying janitorial service to clean her office for $50 per month starting June 1. The company performed the requested services during June, but did not bill Tutt until July 1. Tutt paid the bill promptly on July 5. When should she record the expense? If Tutt uses the cash method, she would not record the expense until July, when she paid the bill. Under the accrual method, however, Tutt would have recorded a $50 janitorial expense in June because the company performed the requested services during June, which means that Tutt incurred those expenses during the month.

In both examples, the underlying event preceded payment. Sometimes, however, cash precedes the underlying event. For example, Tutt could collect a retainer, or legal fee prepayment, from a client in July for services that she would not perform until August. Under the cash method, Tutt would include the retainer in July's revenue, even though she has not earned anything yet. The accrual method would require her to wait until she performed the services to recognize the income. Similarly, during July, Tutt might prepay a registration fee for a seminar that she planned to attend in September. If she used the cash method, she would record the prepayment as an expense in July. Under the accrual method, Tutt would treat the prepayment as an asset until she attended the seminar in September, at which point she would eliminate the asset and record an expense.

Accrual accounting seeks to recognize revenues when earned and to match expenses with the revenues that they produce. Accrual accounting includes the processes of accrual and deferral, which we will discuss in detail shortly. Very briefly, *accrual* refers to the process whereby an accountant records a revenue or expense during the current accounting period even though no payment occurred during the current period. In accrual, the accountant "pulls" the future payment into the current period. In our example, during June, the accountant would accrue the income from the billed, yet unpaid, legal services and the expense from the janitorial services. *Deferral*, in contrast, refers to the process whereby the accountant delays an event involving cash or cash's worth in the current period until a subsequent accounting period or periods. In deferral, the accountant "pushes" a payment already received into the future. In our example, at the end of July, the accountant would defer the retainer and the seminar prepayment until August and September, respectively.

In summary, accrual accounting refers to those rules and principles that accountants use to classify and measure "real world" economic events in numbers to fit into the bookkeeping process. Before we begin our detailed study of accrual accounting, as opposed to bookkeeping, we should understand the basic assumptions, principles, and modifying conventions underlying the process.

1. INTRODUCTION

Many accounting practices make sense only if you understand the assumptions, principles and modifying conventions underlying accrual accounting. As we discuss and attempt to resolve various accounting issues, we should ask whether the general assumptions still apply in the specific circumstances and whether the basic principles and modifying conventions suggest a particular accounting treatment.

a. ASSUMPTIONS

Several basic assumptions underlie accrual accounting. These suppositions include the economic entity assumption, the monetary unit assumption, the periodicity assumption, and the going concern assumption. Thus far, we have only implicitly considered these suppositions. We will now explicitly consider each assumption and its implications.

(1) Economic Entity Assumption

Accountants presuppose that they can separate the activities of a business from those of its owners and any other business. Under this assumption, accountants identify economic activity with a particular accounting entity even though the law may not recognize that enterprise as a distinct legal entity. Recall that we kept separate accounting records for E. Tutt's legal practice even though the law recognizes no separation of Tutt from her law practice, and holds a sole proprietor personally liable for a proprietorship business's obligations. We did not want the accounting records for the law office to include Tutt's personal expenses.

(2) Monetary Unit Assumption

Accountants recognize that money serves as the common denominator that enables businesses to conduct economic activity. In the United States, the applicable monetary unit, the dollar, theoretically provides an appropriate basis for accounting measure and analysis. This assumption implies that the monetary unit best communicates economic information regarding exchanges of goods and services as well as changes in owner's equity, and thereby assists in rational, economic decision-making.

As a practical matter, accountants use the monetary unit because that measure offers a simple, universally available, and easy to understand standard. This selection assumes that the unit of measure—again, the dollar in the United States—remains reasonably stable. As a result, accountants add 1960 dollars to 2001 dollars without any adjustment for inflation. Accountants, therefore, assume that we can ignore the difference in purchasing power between 1960 dollars and 2001 dollars. In a period of inflation with continuous and significant rises in prices, users of financial statements should question this assumption. In the inflationary period of the 1970s and early 1980s, accountants required and provided additional information to reflect the effect of inflation on financial statements. With inflation in relative control as we begin the new millennium, accountants usually do not provide that supplemental information.

(3) Periodicity Assumption

As we have already suggested, an accountant could most accurately measure an enterprise's financial results by waiting until the enterprise's liquidation. The accountant could then determine the enterprise's net profit by calculating the difference between what the owners contributed to the business and what they received at liquidation. However, management, investors, lenders, and governments cannot wait indefinitely to assess an enterprise's financial performance (and wouldn't be that interested in a liquidated enterprise anyway). Consequently, periodic evaluation of an enterprise's operations becomes important.

The periodicity assumption presupposes that an accountant can divide an accounting entity's economic activities into artificial time periods. In dividing continuous operations into separate time periods, accountants must determine the relevance of each business transaction or event to distinct accounting periods. The shorter the time period, the more difficult it becomes to determine what belongs in the period.

(4) Going Concern Assumption

Under the going concern assumption, accountants presume that the accounting entity will continue normal operations into the future. If an accountant doubts a business's ability to continue as a going concern, the accountant will want to provide different information to the users of the financial statements, particularly by way of showing assets at net realizable value, rather than using figures based upon historical costs.

b.   BASIC PRINCIPLES

Given the fundamental assumptions underlying accounting, accountants follow certain basic principles and rules in recording transactions. We have already met some of these principles: the basic ones include the historical cost principle, the objectivity or verifiability principle, the revenue recognition principle, the matching principle, the consistency principle and the full disclosure principle. We will discuss various exceptions to these principles in subsequent chapters.

(1) Historical Cost Principle

As we have already seen, accountants initially record assets at original or historical cost. Thereafter, accountants have historically continued to use a figure based on historical cost because that measure offers a definite and determinable standard. Of course a figure based upon historical cost may not provide the most relevant or helpful information for decision-making purposes because that measure will only coincidentally reflect an asset's fair market value: indeed, opponents have criticized the historical cost principle on the ground that users of financial statements increasingly want contemporary or prospective information, whereas particularly during inflationary periods original cost soon becomes out of date. At the same time, we should not forget that using current fair market value would offer less precision and require more estimates.

(2) Objectivity or Verifiability Principle

As an ideal, accountants prefer a system that will reach essentially similar measures and conclusions if two or more qualified persons examine the same data. The objectivity principle seeks to attain that goal and provides additional support for the historical cost principle. If we asked two accountants to record the transaction in which E. Tutt purchased her office equipment from Elmer Co., they would record the office equipment at $300.

If we asked the accountants to determine the equipment's fair market value, they would probably give us two different answers. Under the verifiability principle, which most accountants consider as a corollary to the objectivity principle, accountants prefer accounting treatments which can be supported by available and reliable evidence.

We should not overstate this objectivity principle. As we will see in this section on accrual accounting, financial accounting requires estimates. Consequently, financial statements do not present completely objective information. Nevertheless, as long as the basis for the estimate is disclosed, and others can corroborate the supporting data and methodology, accountants consider an estimate objective and verifiable.

(3) Revenue Recognition Principle

Apart from income tax considerations, most businesses would prefer to recognize income as soon as possible and defer expenses as long as possible. Under the revenue recognition principle, however, accountants usually recognize revenue only when: (1) an exchange transaction has occurred, and (2) the accounting entity has completed or virtually completed the earnings process. We will discuss this principle and its exceptions at length in Chapter VI.

(4) Matching Principle

At periodic intervals, accountants compute the results of operations, seeking as much accuracy as possible. The matching principle dictates that an accounting entity try to match expenses and the revenue they produce in the same accounting period. If the revenue recognition principle precludes an entity from recognizing certain revenue yet, the current income statement should also not show the expenses necessary to produce that revenue. On the other hand, as to any income that *is* being reported in the current period, the income statement should also show those related expenses incurred to generate that income, even though no cash outflow has occurred for those expenses.

(5) Consistency Principle

Under the consistency principle, accounting entities must give economic events the same accounting treatment from accounting period to period. If readers can compare financial statements with similar reports for prior periods, accounting statements and records become much more useful. The consistency principle restricts an accounting entity from changing an accounting method between accounting periods to those situations in which accountants would consider the newly adopted principle as preferable to the old method. If an accounting entity does change an accounting principle, the entity must disclose the change's nature and effect, as well as the justification, for the accounting period in which the entity adopts the change. However, because accounting practices vary from business to business, comparisons between the financial statements of different businesses can prove quite difficult.

(6) Full Disclosure Principle

This basic accounting principle generally requires an accounting entity to report in the financial statements any facts important enough to influence an informed reader's judgment. Common methods for satisfying this disclosure requirement include presenting an account as a line item in the financial statements, adding an accompanying parenthetical disclosure, and including an explanatory footnote. For this reason, it is important to read the footnotes!

(7) An Emerging Fair Value or Relevance Principle

Because financial statements based solely on historical costs often do not provide the most relevant or helpful information for decision-making purposes, in recent years accounting has looked increasingly in the direction of using fair value or market value, at least for financial assets and liabilities, even though that could call into question the objectivity, revenue recognition, consistency and full disclosure principles. In 1999 the Financial Accounting Standards Board, the private-sector body responsible for establishing accounting rules, published a document setting forth its preliminary views on measuring and reporting certain financial assets and liabilities at fair value. While this document could have been seen as the opening shot in a movement toward requiring fair value for all financial assets and liabilities, in fact the rulemakers specifically stated that they had not resolved all the conceptual and practical issues related to determining the fair values of financial assets and liabilities, and therefore they were not prepared to urge that the basic financial statements report such fair values. As possible alternatives, the rulemakers noted that they could require enhanced disclosures about fair value, or a separate set of financial statements based upon fair value. In any event, because for many financial assets there is no readily ascertainable market price, enterprises would need to develop valuation models which would inherently depend upon subjective assumptions. PRELIMINARY VIEWS ON MAJOR ISSUES RELATED TO REPORTING FINANCIAL INSTRUMENTS AND CERTAIN RELATED ASSETS AND LIABILITIES AT FAIR VALUE (FASB 1999). After starting a project in 2001 to require additional disclosures about the use of fair values in financial statements, the rulemakers decided in 2003 to remove that project from their agenda so that they could concentrate first on issues related to fair value measurement. The rulemakers, however, continue to express their commitment to recording financial assets and liabilities at fair value as a long-term goal.

In the meantime, as we shall see later in these materials, fair-value reporting has become required for marketable securities like listed stocks which an enterprise holds for trading purposes.

c.   MODIFYING CONVENTIONS

Accountants realize that they cannot regard the basic accounting principles as infallible rules. Not only do exceptions apply to almost every basic accounting principle, but certain practical considerations lead to *modifying conventions*, including materiality, conservatism and industry practices.

(1) Materiality

Accounting's practical side recognizes that precise attention to theory can impose unreasonable costs and burdens. At times, the added complication and cost involved in attempting to determine the most desirable treatment for an item that is of little size or significance do not justify the benefit that any user of the financial statements would derive: in that event, the concept of materiality permits the accountant to disregard otherwise applicable accounting principles and rules.

Materiality includes quantitative as well as qualitative components, and hence involves questions of both relative size and importance. In other words, materiality depends not only on an item's size, but also on the business's size. To illustrate, an accountant would consider $20,000 in missing inventory material for a small business showing $100,000 in annual sales, while that amount in missing inventory would not qualify as material for Starbucks Coffee Company. From a qualitative standpoint, materiality can vary with an item's nature. For example, an accountant might consider any illegal payment, even a very small payment, material for certain businesses.

(2) Conservatism

As another modifying convention, accountants frequently refer to conservatism. Over the years, accountants have tried to avoid overly optimistic financial statements by anticipating and recording possible losses, while at the same time being reluctant to recognize potential but still uncertain income. In a nutshell, the convention pushes accountants toward the pessimistic side, to offset the natural optimism, if not exuberance, of business owners or managers in reporting the results of their operations. Accountants have summed up this convention's theme in the adage, "Recognize all losses, anticipate no gains." To avoid later unpleasant surprises, accountants try to reflect all losses or expenses as soon as they appear likely, while delaying the recognition of income or gain until it is virtually assured.

Conservatism counsels the accountant to choose the approach least likely to overstate assets and income. As a result, this modifying convention can lead to an accounting entity understating its income, assets and equity. Although conservatism still enjoys considerable influence, accountants increasingly recognize that undue pessimism in reporting financial results can cause almost as many undesirable consequences as over-optimism. For example, unduly discouraging financial statements could lead an investor to sell an investment for too low a price. Accordingly, application of this convention, as with any other accounting doctrine, requires the exercise of sound judgment: remember, too, that the convention only applies when uncertainty or doubt exists.

(3) Industry Practices

As a final modifying convention, peculiarities in some industries and businesses allow departure from basic accounting principles. For example, while accounting entities generally use historical cost to value inventories, businesses engaged in the meat-packing industry sometimes carry inventories at sales price less costs of distribution, because a meat-packer would find it difficult, and expensive, allocate the cost of an animal among the ribs, chucks and shoulders.

Having discussed the assumptions, principles and modifying conventions underlying accrual accounting, we can now turn to discuss the process itself in some detail. The process involves both accrual and deferral. We begin our discussion with deferral.

2.   DEFERRAL OF EXPENSES AND INCOME

As briefly mentioned already, deferral refers to the process whereby an accountant postpones recognition of an expense paid in advance, or revenue received in advance, until the subsequent accounting period or periods where the item belongs. In other words, the accountant delays treating at least some of a cash expenditure as an expense until the later time when the business will enjoy the benefit of the expenditure, or delays recognizing a cash receipt as income until the subsequent period when it was earned.

a.   EXPENSES

You will recall that in the example on page 52 involving the prepayment of a registration fee for a seminar, *supra,* the accountant classified the prepayment as an asset so that E. Tutt would not treat it as an expense until she attended the seminar in September. Until then, the prepayment would appear as a current asset on E. Tutt's classified balance sheet.

(1) In General

As a practical matter, the fact that both assets and expenses   are increased by a debit and decreased by a credit is not coincidental. There is a significant relationship between assets and expenses. To further illustrate, suppose that when Tutt first hangs out her shingle, she pays $60,000 to purchase a small building to use as her office. She would debit the asset Building for $60,000, and credit the Cash account in the same amount, and no income or expense account would be affected. If instead she pays a week's rent for an office, a debit to the Rent Expense account would be appropriate. But what if she pays advance rent for six months? Ten years? Ninety-nine years? Clearly at some point it can no longer be said that Tutt is "out" or "poorer" by the amount of the advance payment, or that her stake in the enterprise has been reduced in that amount. Rather, she has exchanged cash for an asset, just as she did when she purchased a building; here the asset would be the right to occupy the office for the period covered by the payment.

Actually, any expense paid in advance creates an asset, although that asset may be short-lived; even the payment of rent in advance for a week gives rise to an asset—the right to occupy for one week. By the end of the week, however, the asset has been used up, and the payment has become an expense. By the same token, almost all assets are simply prepaid expenses, since ultimately they will be used up and disappear. For the key to deciding how much of an advance payment is an expense and how much is an asset, remember that the income and expense accounts collect the items affecting proprietorship *in a particular period*. The amount of an advance payment which is used up during the period is an expense for that period; any portion of the payment not used up in the current period is something the business still owns, and hence is an asset as of the end of the period. Thus, if Tutt pays $60,000 advance rental for ten years, at the end of the first year $6,000 is an expense, and $54,000 remains as an asset. If, as we have been assuming, Tutt prepares statements each month, then for the first month $500 (1/120 of $60,000) is an expense, and the remaining $59,500 is an asset at the end of the first month.

If for simplicity we assume that the useful life of a building can be estimated with precision and we ignore scrap or other salvage value at the end of the useful life, the purchase of a building with a useful life of, say, 10 years for $60,000 may be thought of in exactly the same way as an advance rental for ten years. Like the advance rental asset, the cost of the building will be completely used up at the end of the tenth year; that cost, therefore, should be apportioned among the periods in which the building helps to produce income under the matching principle.

To see how the bookkeeper uses entries to handle prepaid expenses, suppose that on January 1 of her first year Tutt pays $15,000 for rent for three years in advance. At the end of the first year, no matter how the entries are made during the year, she should end up with an expense of $5,000 and an asset of $10,000. Because at first blush a payment for rent seems like an expense, Tutt's bookkeeper might make this entry on January 1:

Rent Expense	$15,000	
Cash		$15,000

Assuming for the moment that we are only concerned with Tutt's annual statements, the various income and expense accounts will be closed into the Profit and Loss account at the end of the year. But only $5,000 of the $15,000 now in the Rent Expense account "belongs" to the first year; thus if the whole $15,000 is closed to the Profit and Loss account, rent expense for that year will be overstated and net income will be understated. At the same time Tutt's balance sheet for December 31 will not include all of her assets since the asset representing the right to occupy the premises for two more years will be missing. What is needed, then, is a reduction of the expense to the amount actually used up and the creation of an asset to show what Tutt actually still owns. To show the existence of the asset, that is, the right-to-occupy, a debit of $10,000 should be made to that asset account. To decrease the expense from $15,000 to $5,000, a credit to the Rent Expense account of $10,000 is needed. A single entry would accomplish both objectives. The entry could be journalized as follows:

Deferred Rent Cost (asset)	$10,000	
Rent Expense		$10,000

The term deferral describes this process of reducing an expense to the amount actually used up during the accounting period while creating an asset to show something the business still owns at the end of the period. The word appropriately connotes the fact that part of the expenditure is held back from the current period because it has not yet been used. Accordingly, the asset created is often called a *deferred cost* or, perhaps, a deferred expense—here the asset might also be called *Deferred Rent Expense*. Some accountants would hesitate to use the word "Expense" in a balance sheet account, preferring to limit the use of the word to income statement accounts.

Accountants commonly refer to such an asset as a prepaid expense, in this case, *Prepaid Rent*, or *Prepaid Rent Cost*, which, of course, connotes the fact that a future expense has been paid in advance. The fact that a single entry, often referred to as an adjusting entry, accomplishes both the reduction in the expense and the creation of the asset in the proper amount is another example of the neat "bridging function" which double-entry bookkeeping performs between the balance sheet and the income statement. Notice that adjusting entries of this kind utilize the right-hand side of expense T-accounts in facilitating the double-entry bookkeeping process, as was suggested back on pages 30-31.

Look now at the case in which, at the beginning of her first year, Tutt purchases a building with a useful life of ten years to use as her office. This is clearly a purchase of an asset, and the entry would be:

Building	$60,000	
Cash		$60,000

Unless some entry is made at the end of the first year, however, the balance sheet drawn up then will show the asset Building at $60,000. That would be an overstatement of Tutt's assets, because the building would have a remaining useful life of only nine years. In addition, Tutt's net income for the first year would be overstated, since there would be no deduction for the expense of using the building, although one-tenth of the total life of the building has been used up during the year. What is called for, then, is the creation of an expense of $6,000, which we could call *Building Expense*, and a reduction of the asset Building to $54,000. Again, a single entry would do the job:

Building Expense	$6,000	
Building		$6,000

As we will see on pages 62-63, *infra*, the accountant would normally not call the expense Building Expense nor credit the Building account. In any event, the adjusting entry properly puts an expense of $6,000 into the current year and reduces the asset figure to $54,000 to show what is really left for future years.

It might be noted, incidentally, that the advance payment for rent could have been handled in exactly the same way, rather than as we did it above. Upon payment of the $15,000 on January 1 of the first year, the entire payment could have been recorded as a Deferred Rent Expense asset:

Deferred Rent Expense	$15,000	
Cash		$15,000

In that event, on December 31 an adjusting entry creating an expense of $5,000 and decreasing the asset by the same amount would have been necessary to show that one-third of the asset had been used up:

Rent Expense	$5,000	
Deferred Rent Expense		$5,000

The product of these two entries is exactly the same as the one we obtained by first recording the entire advance payment as an expense and then deferring the portion not used up during the period.

As a third alternative, the bookkeeper could have used a single entry to reflect the obvious split between rent expense for the first year and deferred rent:

Rent Expense	$5,000	
Deferred Rent Expense	10,000	
Cash		$15,000

That entry leads to the same end result as the first two approaches, while avoiding the need for any adjusting entry. In the two subsequent years, however, as with the other two approaches, an adjusting entry would be needed to create an expense of $5,000 and reduce the asset by the same amount, to show how much of the asset was used up in each of those years.

Which of these methods the bookkeeper uses depends entirely upon whether the bookkeeper initially records the expenditure as an asset, an expense, or a combination; the end result is the same. Therefore, if you find it easier, handle any advance payment which may not be used up in the current period just as you would an obvious asset like a building—that is, first record the payment as an asset, and then at the end of the period reduce the asset, and create an expense, to the extent that the asset was used up during the period. In practice, however, the initial entry for an expenditure often depends upon whether it looks more like an expense or an asset in the lay sense; hence, a payment of rent to a landlord will normally be debited to an expense account initially, even though it may cover far more than the current period. That is because the bookkeeper's functions are fairly mechanical and do not include, except in obvious cases, deciding how much of a particular expenditure the business will use up during the current period. Resolving that question, which is often quite difficult, and will receive considerable attention in later chapters of this book, is taken care of by the accountant who supervises the closing of the books at the end of the period and makes whatever adjusting entries are necessary.

(2) Depreciation Accounting

We have already seen that a close relationship exists between deferred expenses and fixed assets, such as buildings, which may benefit several, or even many, accounting periods. For example, suppose E. Tutt purchases computer equipment for her law office for $2,000. Because this expenditure will benefit the business in future months and years, Tutt must not treat the entire amount as an expense in the month in which she buys the computer equipment. Rather, most of the expenditure reflects a future benefit or unexpired cost, which she should record as an asset. Computer equipment, however, like most tangible fixed assets other than land, will not last forever. Ultimately, Tutt will retire the computer equipment. At some point, the computer will physically wear out or become inefficient to operate. Alternatively, technological changes may cause Tutt to replace the machine. In any event, the $2,000 that she spent to acquire the computer equipment, less any *salvage value* which Tutt will receive in exchange for the equipment when she decides to retire it, constitutes an expense of producing revenues during the time she uses the computer equipment, which accountants usually refer to as the computer's *useful life*. If we assume that Tutt will retire the computer in three years, and sell it then for $200, she should allocate $1,800, the difference between the $2,000 cost and the $200 salvage value, to expense in some reasonable and systematic manner during the computer's three-year useful life. Accountants refer to this allocation process as *depreciation* for fixed assets and as *amortization* for intangible assets. We should note that the term depreciation in this context does not refer to diminution in the asset's value: although almost all equipment declines in value as time passes, depreciation does not attempt to measure that decrease.

Assuming Tutt decides to use the straight-line method of depreciation, that is, allocates the $1,800 equally among the three years over which she plans to use the computer equipment in her law office, she should treat $600 per year, or $50 per month, as depreciation expense for the computer equipment. We could express this computation as the following formula:

$$\text{Monthly Depreciation Expense} = \frac{(\text{Cost} - \text{Salvage Value})}{\text{Useful life in months}}$$

At the end of the first month, therefore, Tutt might record the following entry:

Depreciation Expense	$50	
Computer Equipment		$50

If Tutt bought the computer in the middle of the month, she might only treat $25, or one-half the normal monthly amount, as depreciation expense.

Using a general term like *Depreciation Expense* enables Tutt to lump together, under one heading, all of the expenses of using up fixed assets during an accounting period. Although Tutt does not own many fixed assets, a large company might own thousands or even millions of individual fixed assets.

As another practical matter, an accountant would normally not credit the Computer Equipment account. Instead, the accountant would credit a separate *contra-asset* account called *Accumulated Depreciation* which would appear as an offset to, or deduction from, the Computer Equipment account on the balance sheet. As the name suggests, a contra-asset account records reductions in a particular asset account separately from the relevant asset account. Basically, the Accumulated Depreciation account at any time simply represents the cumulative amount of the fixed asset's cost that the enterprise has charged to expense. Accountants use this account so that they can preserve the fixed asset's original cost in the accounting records and show it on the balance sheet. Hence, we could restate the previous journal entry as:

Depreciation Expense	$50	
Accumulated Depreciation:		
Computer Equipment		$50

At the end of the first month, the computer equipment would appear as a fixed asset on Tutt's balance sheet, perhaps as follows:

Fixed Assets:	
Computer Equipment	$2,000
Less: Accumulated Depreciation	50
Net Computer Equipment	$1,950

Accountants often refer to the net amount, original cost less accumulated depreciation, as the asset's *book value*. The book value, therefore, represents the amount of the original cost remaining to be allocated to future periods, plus any estimated salvage value. If Tutt purchases additional equipment for her office, such as a copy machine or a fax machine, her bookkeeper will likely lump together all such office equipment so that only a single figure showing the total cost of all office equipment would appear on Tutt's balance sheet, together with an offsetting figure for the total accumulated depreciation on the equipment.

b. REVENUES

A relation similar to that between expenses and assets exists between income items and liabilities, both of which are decreased by a debit and increased by a credit. Consider the bookkeeping for Ohner, the lessor of the building in which E. Tutt rents office space for three years by paying $15,000 in advance. When Ohner receives the $15,000, he might make the following entry in his books:

Cash	$15,000	
Rent Income		$15,000

Without some further entry, this $15,000 item will be closed into the Profit and Loss account along with the other income and expense items at the end of the year. We should remember, however, that the income accounts, like the expense accounts, are supposed to collect items affecting proprietorship *in the current period*. The entire $15,000 of rent income does not belong to the first year; $10,000 of that amount was received for the second and third years. Thus, if the whole $15,000 is closed to the Profit and Loss account for the first year, rent income for that year will be overstated, leading to an overstatement of net income for the year. In addition, net income for each of the next two years would be understated, because there would be no rent income for those years, although there would still be such expenses as insurance, janitor service, property taxes and the like.

At the same time, there would be an item missing from Ohner's balance sheet for the end of the first year. If for some reason Ohner defaulted in his agreement to furnish Tutt with office space for the next two years, presumably Ohner would at least be required to refund to Tutt the $10,000 paid for those two years. To put it another way, as of the end of the first year, Ohner has an obligation to provide office space to Tutt for the next two years, and the most convenient measure of this obligation is the $10,000 Tutt paid for those two years. This obligation should appear on Ohner's balance sheet as a liability at the end of the first year.

What is needed, then, is a reduction of rent income to the amount actually applicable to the current period, here $5,000, and the creation of a liability in the amount of $10,000 to show Ohner's future obligation. To reduce rent income to $5,000, a debit of $10,000 should be made to that account. To create the liability account, which is typically called *Unearned Rent*, or perhaps, *Deferred Income*, or even, *Deferred Rent Income*, because it results from deferring income from the current period, a credit of $10,000 should be made to that account. Again, a purist would prefer not to use the word "Income" in a balance sheet account, but you may encounter such account titles in practice. The entry would be journalized as follows:

Rent Income	$10,000	
Unearned Rent		$10,000

Once again a single adjusting entry has accomplished both objectives—and we see here a nother example of the bridging function of double-entry bookkeeping (and an illustration of the usefulness of a left-hand side for income T-accounts, in facilitating the bookkeeping process).

Just as it is permissible to record an advance payment which may not be used up during the current period initially as an asset rather than as an expense, so an advance receipt can properly be recorded first by a credit to the appropriate liability account rather than as income. Such an entry for Ohner would be:

Cash	$15,000	
Unearned Rent		$15,000

In that event, at the close of the period it would be necessary to make an adjusting entry crediting the Rent Income account in the amount of $5,000 and decreasing the liability by the same amount. Again, a single entry will do the job:

Unearned Rent	$5,000	
Rent Income		$5,000

This entry properly puts income of $5,000 into the current year, and reduces the liability to $10,000 to show a more meaningful measure of Ohner's obligation for future years. The result of these two entries is exactly the same as the one we obtained by first recording the entire advance receipt as income and then deferring the amount not applicable to the current period.

As a third alternative, the bookkeeper for Ohner could have split the $15,000 advance payment between rent income and unearned rent as follows:

Cash	$15,000	
Rental Income		$5,000
Unearned Rent		10,000

Again, the one entry produces exactly the same effect as the first two approaches, while also avoiding the need for an adjusting entry at the end of the first year. In the two subsequent years, however, as in the earlier illustration, the bookkeeper would need to make an adjusting entry to create income of $5,000 and decrease the liability by the same amount, to show how much income was earned in each of those years.

Determination of the period or periods in which to reflect, or as the accountants say, *recognize*, the income represented by a payment received in advance is not always as easy as in the foregoing illustration. Actually, the advance rent example, in which the total income involved is allocated pro rata among the periods affected, is somewhat atypical; in many situations, all of the income from a single transaction is recognized in just one period, and not allocated among several periods. That treatment flows from the general rule governing revenue recognition which has been mentioned before and will be developed in more detail later, in Chapter VI. Under that rule, accountants recognize income only in the period in which it is earned; based in part on conservatism, accountants do not consider any of the income from a particular transaction earned until the recipient has "substantially performed" everything required under the contract. Applying this test, a lawyer who receives a fee from a client for a professional undertaking which will not be completed until a later period would normally not recognize any income from the transaction until the period in which the lawyer in fact substantially completes the assignment, even if the lawyer does some of the work in a prior period; and any portion of the fee received prior to completion would be treated as a liability, such as Unearned Fees. Similarly, a seller of goods who receives payment in advance ordinarily would not recognize any of the income from the transaction until the period in which a transfer of the goods to the customer (or some counterpart indication of substantial completion of performance) occurs. Even if some of the work is done in the period in which the advance receipt was received, or in an intervening period, none of the income would be allocated to either period: all of the advance payment would be deferred until the period in which performance is substantially completed. As you might expect, some close questions arise as to what amounts to "substantial performance" or constitutes a single transaction, whether in the practice of law, the sale of goods, or whatever the activity. We will also examine these issues in Chapter VI.

Returning to our example involving Ohner's receipt of an advance payment of rent for three years, it might seem that Ohner would not have completed his agreed-upon performance until the end of the third year, and therefore would not have earned any of the income involved in the transaction until that time. However, transactions in which the performance by the recipient of income consists primarily of permitting another to enjoy the use of property or money for a period of time, as in the case of rent or interest, are usually treated differently from the standard types of business activity like the practice of law or the sale of goods. These transactions involving leasing property or lending money at interest, which produce income by virtue of the passage of time, are viewed as though they consist of a series of separable agreements covering the consecutive accounting periods over which the entire transaction runs, and the income proportionate to the passage of time during each accounting period is regarded as having been earned in that period. Hence, one-third of the income from Ohner's advance receipt of three years' rent would be treated as earned at the end of the first of the three years. Similarly, for anyone interested in monthly periods, one-twelfth of the one-third earned in the first year would be regarded as earned during each of the twelve months of that first year. This difference in treatment for income arising from the passage of time seems justified because there is so little risk that, say, a lender of money will not substantially complete the required performance, since the lender no longer has control of the borrowed funds (and the situation of the lessor of property is comparable).

3.   ACCRUAL OF EXPENSE AND INCOME

Thus far we have been considering the proper treatment of expense and income items when cash has been paid or received. We have seen that cash receipts or payments do not necessarily determine the amount of income or expense for the current period. As a matter of fact, the time when cash changes hands in a business transaction is often governed by factors which have little to do with the question of when the income or expense represented by the cash should be reflected. That holds true whether the cash moves beforehand, as in the deferral cases we have been considering, or moves afterward, as in accrual: the absence of cash receipts or payment does not negate current income or expense.

a.   IN GENERAL

As noted earlier, accrual refers to the process whereby an accountant records a revenue or expense during the current accounting period even though no payment occurred during that period. In accrual, the accountant "pulls" the future event involving cash or cash's worth into the current period. In the examples on pages 51-52, an accountant would accrue in June both the income from the completed and billed legal services and the expense for the janitorial services enjoyed during the month, even though no cash changed hands during the month with respect to either item.

(1) Expenses

Let us look in more detail at a situation where no cash has moved. Suppose Tutt signed a three-year lease of office space calling for rent of $5,000 per year, payable at the end of each year. Obviously, if Tutt paid the $5,000 due for rent at the end of the first year, an entry debiting Rent Expense in the amount of $5,000 and crediting Cash in the same amount would be routine. But suppose instead that due to inadvertence, or otherwise, Tutt failed to pay the rent due at the end of the first year. If the movement of cash were controlling, then there would not be any entry reflecting rent expense during the first year; hence, when Tutt closed her books at the end of that first year, net income for the year would be overstated because there would be no deduction for the expense of using the office during the year. Moreover, when Tutt pays the $5,000 for the first year's rent shortly into the second year, presumably it would be debited to the current Rent Expense account at that time; but if Tutt also pays the rent for the second year by the end of that year, as she is supposed to, that too would be charged to current rent expense, with the result that the income statement for the second year would be burdened with $10,000 of rent expense, and net income for the year would be seriously understated.

What is needed, then, is the creation of an expense in the first year in the amount properly allocable to that year. That is, the first year should bear its fair share of the total cost of utilizing office space, even though none of that cost was actually paid during the first year. A bookkeeping entry can be used to accomplish this purpose. The debit part is simple enough, for that is dictated by the judgment that rent expense in the amount of $5,000 belongs in the current (first) year. There is only one way to reflect an expense in a particular year, and that is to debit the appropriate expense account in that year, so that it will be closed to the Profit and Loss account at the end of the year and netted with all of the other expense and income items for the period.

Rent Expense	$5,000	
?		$5,000

As to the credit, of course if cash had been paid that would be easy. But since Tutt has not paid, as she was supposed to, is it not clear that she owes the $5,000 at the close of the year, just as clearly as if she had bought more office equipment for $5,000 on account? The credit, therefore, should be to a liability account to reflect her obligation to pay. This process of pulling an expense into the current period even though it has not yet been paid, while creating a liability account reflecting the obligation to pay, constitutes accrual. Taken together with deferral, accrual makes it possible to free the reporting of expense items from the movement of cash. When cash has moved in an amount greater than the expense that belongs in the current period, deferral makes it possible to charge only the proper amount to expense for the current period. When an expense belongs in the current period even though the cash has not moved as yet, accrual makes it possible to reflect the expense in the current period.

Incidentally, with regard to the name given the liability account which is created when an expense is accrued, it would probably not be called an Account Payable, because that term is usually reserved for credit purchases of goods and supplies; moreover, it is often helpful to identify other liabilities as to their source. Hence, the liability would more likely be called something like *Accrued Rent Payable*, which serves as a reminder that the liability results from the accrual of an expense into the current period. Other common terms for such a liability include *Rent Expense Payable* or *Accrued Rent Expense,* which also connote that the liability arises because an expense has been charged to the current period although it has not been paid yet. So the entry here might be:

Rent Expense	$5,000	
Accrued Rent Payable		$5,000

This entry puts $5,000 of rent expense into the current year, and creates a liability account to show that Tutt owes this amount for rent at the end of the first year.

Now suppose that Tutt's lease of office space for three years had not called for payments at the end of either of the first two years, but instead provided that the total of $15,000 should all be paid at the end of the third year. Once again, unless some entry is made when Tutt closes her books at the end of the first year, net income for the first year will be overstated since there will be no deduction for the expense of using an office during the year. Moreover, presumably the entire $15,000 payment in the third year would have to be treated as an expense of that year, with the result that net income for the third year would be greatly understated. Here, too, we need to accrue in the first year the amount of rent expense properly applicable to that year, even though no amount has been paid during that year. Because one-third of the total rent of $15,000 is properly applicable to the first year, an entry exactly the same as before is called for, with a debit of $5,000 to Rent Expense, and a credit of $5,000 to Accrued Rent Payable or some similarly titled account.

To be sure, because Tutt has agreed to pay only at the end of the third year, strictly speaking she is under no legal obligation to pay anything at the end of the first year. Nevertheless, in an accounting sense, Tutt does owe $5,000 at the end of the first year, since she must pay it ultimately, and, what is more significant, $5,000 of the total commitment has been used up in the current period. Hence, it is entirely appropriate to credit some liability account like Accrued Rent Payable. Tutt, however, may want to separate on the balance sheet liabilities of this sort, which do not have to be paid for quite some time, from current liabilities which she must pay within one year. The important point is that an expense which belongs in the period may be accrued, that is, reflected in a current expense account, even though it not only has not been paid but there is not yet even a current obligation to pay it.

Notice that in this case when the rent expense is accrued for the first year, the corresponding liability, whatever the name used, reflects only an amount equal to the expense related to that year, not the entire rent obligation for the three-year period. That is because the very purpose of an accrual is to reflect an expense currently, with the creation of the liability being simply a corollary, to provide a companion credit to go along with the debit to an expense account, and obviously that credit must be in the same amount as the debit. Indeed, unlike the case of an advance payment, when of course some entry must be made to reflect the reduction in cash even though not all of the payment is chargeable to current expense (which is where deferral comes in), in the case of an expected future payment it is usually not necessary to make any entry at all in the current period except if, and then only to the extent that, a charge to current expense is called for. So if Tutt signed a three-year lease for office space during the year before the beginning of the lease, no entry at all relating to the lease commitment would be called for in that year. If material, however, it would be desirable to disclose the existence of the lease commitment somewhere in the financial statements for the current year: at a minimum, the statements must include disclosure of the future minimum rental payments required under leases for each of the next five years. As we shall see, the use of footnotes or other adjuncts to the financial statements may provide suitable mechanisms for such disclosure.

When the rent for the three years is ultimately paid, the debit will be to that liability credited earlier (Accrued Rent Payable, Rent Expense Payable, or whatever else it may be called), just as any debtor who pays money owed on open account debits the account payable:

Accrued Rent Payable	$15,000	
Cash		$15,000

The important fact is that no account on the income statement is affected by the actual payment, which is as it should be since the expense has already been reflected at an earlier time.

We should observe that there may be occasions when the full amount of an obligation should be recorded as a liability on the balance sheet, not just disclosed, say, in a footnote, even though some, or even all, of the obligation will not be properly chargeable to expense until future periods. As a prime example, if an obligation is currently due and payable under an enforceable contract, it should presumably be included among the liabilities on the balance sheet, no matter when it will be charged to expense; and that may also be true even if the obligation is not yet due, if it is relatively very large, i.e., just too significant a liability not to appear on the balance sheet. In either case, the recording of a liability in excess of the amount charged to current expense must be accompanied by a debit to a prepaid or deferred asset account; normally such an entry is only made in conjunction with an advance payment of cash, but here recording the liability serves as a kind of substitute for that.

(2) Revenues

Similar accrual techniques are available when income should be recognized in a period prior to the receipt of cash. Look at the bookkeeping for Ohner when he leases an office to Tutt for three years, for a total rent of $15,000. Ohner's recognition of income from this transaction should not depend upon when he receives the cash; the amount of income reflected in the first year, or any subsequent year for that matter, should be the same, whether Ohner (1) received cash during the year, or (2) was entitled to receive cash but Tutt inadvertently failed to pay, or (3) was not entitled to receive any cash until the end of the three years. As to the amount of income to be reflected in the first year, recall that under the rules for recognizing income noted earlier, the income represnted by rent and interest is regarded as earned uniformly with the passage of time. Accordingly, at the end of the first year Ohner has earned $5,000 of the rent, and therefore he should recognize $5,000 in current income, even though no cash has been received, or is even due as yet.

Once a judgment has been made that $5,000 of rent income belongs in the first year, it follows that a credit in that amount must be made to the Rent Income account for that year. Paralleling the counterpart treatment of an expense, the only way to implement a judgment that an item of income belongs in the current year is to credit a current income account during that year. This is another example of accrual; the rent income is accrued, i. e., pulled into the current period, although the cash has not yet been received. As to the accompanying debit, which would of course have been to cash if the $5,000 had been received, a receivable should be created, to reflect the fact that although the cash has not been received Ohner has a right to receive it in the future. This receivable might be called *Accrued Rent Receivable* or *Accrued Rent Income*, or *Rent Income Receivable*, terms which connote the fact that the receivable reflects the right to receive an amount which has been recognized as income prior to the receipt of cash. So the entry might be:

Accrued Rent Receivable	$5,000	
Rent Income		$5,000

Notice that if the lease provided that none of the rent was due until the end of the third year, then technically Ohner would not have any legal right to $5,000 at the end of the first year. Nevertheless, in the same sense that Tutt owed $5,000 at the end of the first year even though she was not obligated to pay anything until the end of the third year, so Ohner would have a right to $5,000 at the end of the first year since he is entitled to receive it ultimately, and it has been earned during the first year. Therefore, it is entirely appropriate to debit some type of receivable account like Accrued Rent Receivable. On the balance sheet, Ohner may again want to separate long-term receivables like this, on which the cash will not be received for more than one year, from receivables which qualify as current assets because they are expected to be converted into cash within one year. Note that, paralleling the accrual of expenses, the primary purpose of accrual of income is to reflect an item in current income even though cash has not yet been received, and the creation of a receivable account is merely an adjunct needed to show that there is a right to receive the cash in the future. Hence, as with the counterpart payables discussed earlier, these receivables will normally show only that portion of a future receipt which has been earned, rather than the full amount of the expected future payment.

When Ohner ultimately receives the money for the entire three-year period, the credit will be to the receivable account, say Accrued Rent Receivable, just as a creditor who receives money owed to him on open account credits the account receivable:

Cash	$15,000	
Accrued Rent Receivable		$15,000

The important fact is that no account on the income statement is affected by the actual receipt, which is as it should be since the income has already been recognized.

As we noted in connection with advance receipts, transactions involving the rental of property, as here, or lending money at interest, are atypical so far as recognition of income is concerned, because in such cases the income is viewed as earned by the passage of time, and hence is not subject to the general rule that all of the income from a transaction is to be recognized in the one period in which substantial completion occurs. Another, much less substantial, exception to the general rule is that sometimes recognition of income from performance of services is delayed until a bill has been sent, to avoid the need for estimation, and perhaps also to provide greater assurance that performance has indeed been completed. What is important is that it does not matter whether the cash has been received as yet, so long as the income has been earned. Accrual provides the mechanism for recognizing the income in the period in which it is earned, even though no cash has been received.

Notice that, unlike the case of an advance receipt where some entry must be made to reflect the receipt of cash even though the related income has not been earned in the current period, in the case of an expected future receipt no entry is called for in the current period if the income has not yet been earned. An entry will be made only in the period when the income is finally earned, unless, of course, the cash moves sooner, in which event the case becomes simply one of an advance receipt.

One special aspect of the treatment of an expected receipt deserves brief mention here. It arises because accounting, mirroring business in this regard, still attributes considerable importance to the ultimate receipt of cash, even though it does not make such receipt a pre-condition for the recognition of income. Obviously, no question about the ultimate receipt of cash can arise in cases involving advance receipts, because the cash has already been received. In the case of an expected future receipt, however, there can be substantial doubt as to the ultimate collectibility of cash – for example, because of the insolvency of the debtor; if so, no income is recognized from the transaction even though it has been earned in the current period. It should be emphasized that this qualification applies only when there is some special reason for concern about collectibility, not just the general risk of non-payment that is inherent in any business done on credit. For the latter, other tools exist, which will be introduced when this subject is discussed in more detail in Chapter VI.

PROBLEMS

The following problems involve both deferral and accrual techniques.

Problem 1.4A. Andrew Company borrowed $50,000 from Bradford, Inc. at twelve percent annual interest on January 1. Twelve percent annual interest on a $50,000 loan translates to $6,000 in interest per year, or $500 in interest each month. The promissory note requires Andrew Company to pay the $500 monthly interest on, or before, the last day of each month. Andrew Company made three interest payments, $600 on January 15, $250 on February 20, and $350 on March 10.

(a) Prepare appropriate journal entries for Andrew Company for the months of January, February and March, assuming each month is a separate accounting period.

(b) Prepare appropriate journal entries for Bradford, Inc. for the months of January, Febr uary and March, assuming each month is a separate accounting period.

Problem 1.4B. Jones Company leased a machine from Smith, Inc. on January 1. Under the terms of the lease, Jones Company agreed to pay $250 rent per month, due on the first day of each month. Jones Company made two rental payments, one of $300 on January 1 and the other of $350 on February 14.

(a) Prepare appropriate journal entries for Jones Company for the months of January, February, and March, assuming each month is a separate accounting period.

(b) Prepare appropriate journal entries for Smith, Inc. for the months of January, February, and March, assuming each month is a separate accounting period.

Problem 1.4C. Dallas Inc. borrowed $30,000 from Crayne Corporation at eight percent annual interest on January 1. Eight percent annual interest on a $30,000 loan translates to $2,400 in interest per year, or $200 in interest each month. The promissory note requires Dallas Inc. to pay the $200 monthly interest on, or before, the last day of each month. Dallas Inc. made three interest payments, $100 on January 15, $250 on February 25, and $150 on March 5.

(a) Prepare appropriate journal entries for Dallas Inc. for the months of January, February and March, assuming each month is a separate accounting period.

(b) Prepare the appropriate journal entries for Crayne Corporation for the months of January, February and March, assuming each month is a separate accounting period.

b.   INCOME TAX ACCOUNTING

Income taxes present a special application of accrual accounting for corporations, unless they file an S corporation election, which would make the corporation's income taxable to the shareholders rather than to the corporation. Sole proprietorships, partnerships and most S corporations do not pay federal income taxes; instead, the owners must report their allocable share of the business's income on their personal federal income tax returns and pay taxes on that income. On the other hand, regular corporations, being separate legal and taxable entities, generally must file federal income tax returns, and pay taxes on their taxable income. State and local laws may also require corporations and other businesses to pay income taxes. In most cases, a business will not pay all of its income taxes attributable to income from a particular accounting period during that period, and instead must accrue income tax expense during the closing process.

If we assume that Tutt, Inc. earned $525 in taxable income during the month and that the corporation will pay taxes at a forty percent total rate for all federal, state and local income taxes, the corporation will owe $210 in income taxes on the month's income. To properly match expenses against revenues, Tutt, Inc. should accrue $210 as income tax expense for the month as an adjusting journal entry. To reflect this income tax expense, at the end of the month the bookkeeper could record the following entry:

Income Tax Expense	$210	
Accrued Income Taxes Payable		$210

Accountants usually show *Income Tax Expense* as a separate caption on the income statement. Accordingly, assuming the facts from the income statement on page 28, *supra,* we could restate Tutt, Inc.'s income statement for the month as follows:

E. Tutt, Inc.
June Income Statement

Professional Income		$1,000
Operating Expenses		
Rent	$200	
Secretary	230	
Telephone	15	
Heat & Light	5	
Miscellaneous	5	
Theft Loss	20	475
Net Income Before Income Taxes		$525
Income Taxes		210
Net Income		$315

On the company's balance sheet, Accrued Income Taxes Payable would normally appear as a current liability because it will usually require payment within one year.

4. PRACTICE PROBLEM

Deferral and accrual are the most important tools of bookkeeping, and it is therefore essential that you master the mechanics of these two techniques. They are easy enough to summarize: deferral problems arise only after cash has moved, and the objective is to allocate an expenditure or a receipt between the current period and future periods; accrual problems arise only when cash has not yet moved, and the objective is to bring into the current period an item of income or expense which properly belongs there. However, here, as in so many areas, there is no substitute for practice. To gain the necessary confidence in handling these mechanics you must satisfy yourself that you can make them work as they should. Then we will be ready to turn to the matters that make the field of Accounting worth your time and attention as a prospective lawyer, that is, the questions of judgment and discretion involved in determining the period in which particular items of income and expense should be recognized.

The following problem is designed to afford some additional practice in bookkeeping. Set out after the list of transactions are the appropriate journal entries, with explanatory comments, the completed T-accounts, and the final balance sheet and income statement. However, you would do best to work out the problem on your own, before looking at the recommended solution and the comments.

Assume that E. Tutt's balance sheet on June 30 was as follows:

E. Tutt, Esquire
Balance Sheet, June 30

<u>Assets</u>		<u>**Liabilities & Proprietorship**</u>	
Cash	$1,150	Liabilities	
Accounts Receivable:		Accounts Payable:	
Southacre Corp.	300	Ropes Law Book Co.	$40
Georgina Hats, Inc.	100		
Jack Self Clothes	125		
Office Equipment	575		
Library	650	Proprietorship	2,860
Total	$2,900	Total	$2,900

The following transactions occurred during July (ignore depreciation):

July   1   Purchased a piece of land for a contemplated new office building for $1,800. She paid $600 down, and gave a one-year 5% note for the balance, interest payable at maturity.

        2   Paid $75 cash to landlord for rent for July.

3 Paid $100 cash to Douds for painting interior of office.

5 Bought adding machine for $200 from P. M. Ryan on account.

9 Received $150 cash for legal services rendered on July 7 and 8 to Jones.

11 Mailed bill for $225 to Potter for legal services rendered in July.

13 Paid Ryan $100 cash on account.

15 Received check from Southacre for $200 on account.

16 Paid temporary secretarial replacement $180 cash for salary for first three weeks in July.

18 Jack Self settled account with $25 cash and clothes for Ms. Tutt.

20 Paid Ropes Law Book Company $40 cash.

21 The executor of Uncle Zeke Tutt's estate delivered law books worth $100 which had been bequeathed to E. Tutt.

25 In litigation for client Coogan, paid $15 filing fee to Clerk of Court, subject to understanding that Coogan will reimburse any fees advanced.

26 Tutt carelessly dropped a cigarette, starting a fire which destroyed books costing $120, for which she had no insurance.

28 Received $200 advance retainer from Annan.

29 Received telephone bill of $25 for July.

30 Probate court allowed Tutt a $1,000 fee for services to executor of Estate of Smith.

31 Paid temporary secretary $180 salary for last week in July and first two weeks in August.

RECOMMENDED SOLUTION

<u>July</u>

1 Land		$1,800	
	Cash		$600
	Note Payable		1,200

Comment: This entry records Tutt's purchase of land, partly for cash and partly on credit by giving a note. Notes payable are shown separately from accounts payable because not only is there a written instrument, typically with interest, but it may be negotiable, which puts it on a different legal footing. Notice that nothing is done at this time to record the obligation for interest, since no interest expense has been incurred yet.

2 Rent Expense	$75	
Cash		$75

Comment: Tutt debits Rent Expense because it is an important category, for which she wants a separate record. Since this payment is all for July, it is all an expense for July, and no asset will appear on the balance sheet on July 31.

3 Miscellaneous Expense	$100	
Cash		$100

Comment: Tutt might have used a separate account for Maintenance Expense, in which case the debit would have been to that account. Note also that there is a deferral problem: because the paint job will doubtless have utility beyond the month of July, should all this expense be considered a cost of doing business in the month of July? Factors affecting the accounting judgment of whether some of the $100 should be allocated to later periods will be considered in Chapter IX; here, for simplicity, Tutt treats this item as an expense of the current period.

5 Office Equipment	$200	
Accounts Payable: Ryan		$200

Comment: If Tutt distinguished among the various kinds of office equipment that she owned, such as Computers, Printers, and Copying Machines, the debit would then be to the appropriate one of these accounts, which would be in effect subaccounts of Office Equipment. Note that in fact Tutt has moved in the opposite direction, and now includes both Furniture and Equipment in the Office Equipment account.

9 Cash	$150	
Professional Income		$150

Comment: Because Tutt has performed all the services called for by the agreement, the income arising from this receipt has been earned and is therefore income for the current period.

11 Accounts Receivable: Potter	$225	
Professional Income		$225

Comment: Although no cash has yet been received, Tutt has earned the income in July. Therefore, unless Potter is insolvent or for some other reason collection is not reasonably assured, the income should be recognized in the current period. The debit might just as appropriately be to Fees Receivable:

Potter; there is no uniform practice where income from personal services is involved.

If Tutt had not yet sent a bill, she might postpone the recognition of this income; the recognition of income from services is often postponed until the sending of a bill, even though the services have been completed and collection of the income is reasonably assured, because of uncertainty as to the amount to be charged.

| 13 Accounts Payable: Ryan | $100 | |
| Cash | | $100 |

Comment: This is exactly like payment of the amount due Elmer Co., described earlier in this chapter; note that the transaction affects both sides of the balance sheet, resulting in a decrease on both sides of $100.

| 15 Cash | $200 | |
| Accounts Receivable: Southacre | | $200 |

Comment: Note that the income account is not affected. An entry like that of July 11 had already been made in a prior period, and Tutt is now simply converting into cash the asset she then recorded.

| 16 Secretarial Expense | $180 | |
| Cash | | $180 |

Comment: Because this payment will be completely used up in July, it is entirely an expense for the current period, and no deferral problem will arise.

18 Cash	$25	
Proprietorship	100	
Accounts Receivable: Jack Self		$125

Comment: The troublesome element, the debit of $100 to Proprietorship, is exactly the same in theory as the entry upon Tutt's removal of a chair from the office for use at home.

| 20 Accounts Payable: Ropes | $40 | |
| Cash | | $40 |

Comment: This is exactly like payment of the amount due Ryan on July 13. Once again, the transaction affects both sides of the balance sheet, resulting in a decrease on both sides of $40.

| 21 Library | $100 | |
| Proprietorship | | $100 |

Comment: Here, in effect, Tutt has contributed $100 more assets to the business, and there is an increase in Proprietorship.

25 Accounts Receivable: Coogan $15

       Cash $15

Comment: The $15 is chargeable to Coogan, not an expense of Tutt's.

26 Fire Loss $120

       Library $120

Comment: Tutt lost one of her assets other than cash. Nevertheless, this loss, like the theft loss described earlier in the text, is one of the costs of doing business, and is therefore treated like an expense. Fire Loss may be regarded as simply shorthand for Fire Loss Expense. The credit to Library reduces that account by the amount of the books lost.

28 Cash $200

       Client Advances $200

Comment: Since this receipt is identified as an advance retainer, it seems clear that Tutt will not have performed the services by the end of this period, so the income arising from this receipt will not have been earned and should not be recognized currently; therefore, the credit is to Client Advances, or Deferred Income, which will appear as a liability account on the balance sheet at the end of July. If Tutt did happen to substantially complete the agreed-upon performance by July 31, the income would be recognized currently, by a debit to whichever liability account was used and a credit to Professional Income.

29   Telephone Expense $25

       Telephone Expense Payable $25

Comment: This is an example of accrual of expense. Since this expense clearly belongs in the current period it should be reflected currently. That would be true even if no bill had been received: recognition of an expense applicable to the current period is usually not postponed until the receipt of a bill, despite uncertainty as to the amount of the charge; instead a reasonable estimate of the charge is made. This differs somewhat from the treatment often adopted in connection with accrual of income. See the Comment to the entry on July 11.

30 Accounts Receivable: Smith Estate $1,000

       Professional Income $1,000

Comment: The accrual problem here is exactly like that in the transaction of July 11.

31 Prepaid Salary $180

       Cash $180

Comment: Here the payment will not be completely used up by the end of the period. When Tutt initially records the payment as an asset, an adjusting entry must be made to create an expense and reduce the asset in the amount used up during the period. The adjusting entry:

(a) Salary Expense $60
    Prepaid Salary $60

Alternatively, it would be equally proper first to record the payment as an expense. In that event, the initial entry would be:

31 Salary Expense $180
    Cash $180

Then Tutt's adjusting entry, upon closing her books at the end of the period, would defer the amount not used up during the period as follows:

(a) Prepaid Salary $120
    Salary Expense $120

Since the appropriate end result is so obvious at the outset, Tutt could simply allocate the original entry between expense and unexpired asset, thereby eliminating the need for an adjusting entry at the end of July.

31 Salary Expense $60
    Prepaid Salary   120
    Cash $180

The net effect of each alternative is that Tutt treats $60 as salary expense for July and defers $120 to August.

One other adjusting entry is necessary:

(b) Interest Expense $5
    Accrued Interest Payable $5

Comment: Recall that no entry reflecting interest expense was made at the time of the borrowing transaction on July 1, because the note had then just been given. However, the interest which Tutt will ultimately have to pay should not all be treated as an expense in the month when she makes the payment. This is just like the situation in the text above in which we saw that Tutt should not charge the entire payment of three years' rent to the third year simply because it was all paid in that year. Instead, Tutt should attribute a *pro rata* share of the total interest expense to each month during the time that she has the use of the money, just as she charged a *pro rata* share of the rent expense to each of the years in which she had the use of the office premises. Because the interest charge per year is 5% of $1,200, or $60, one-twelfth of $60, or $5, should be treated as an expense in each month. Hence, Tutt should debit an expense account, here Interest Expense, to reflect this expense in the current period; the credit is to a liability account, such as Accrued Interest Payable, to reflect the eventual liability for this current expense. Tutt will make similar entries during the next eleven months, so the liability account will rise to $60. When Tutt ultimately pays the interest at maturity, she will record the following entry:

Accrued Interest Payable	$60	
Cash		$60

Note that no entry is called for to reflect the fact that the due date of the principal amount of the note is one month closer. Just as the borrowing of the funds did not affect Tutt's income statement, neither will the repayment. Therefore, no further entry need be made in connection with the ultimate liability to pay the principal until the note is actually discharged, at which time the entry will be simply:

Note Payable	$1,200	
Cash		$1,200

The T-accounts that follow reflect the journal entries we have been discussing:

Cash

Bal.	$1,150		
7-9	150	$600	7-1
7-15	200	75	7-2
7-18	25	100	7-3
7-28	200	100	7-13
		180	7-16
		40	7-20
		15	7-25
		180	7-31
Bal.	$435		

Accounts Payable: Ropes

		$40	Bal.
7-20	$40		

Proprietorship

		$2,860	Bal.
7-18	$100		
		100	7-21
		810	(j)
		$3,670	Bal.

Note Payable

	$1,200	7-1

Accrued Interest Payable

	$5	(b)

Accounts Receivable: Southacre

Bal.	$300		
		$200	7-15
Bal.	$100		

Accounts Payable: Ryan

		$200	7-5
7-13	$100		
		$100	Bal.

Accounts Receivable: Georgina

Bal.	$100

Accounts Receivable: Jack Self

Bal.	$125		
		$125	7-18
Bal.	$ 0		

Telephone Expense Payable

	$25	7-29

Library

Bal.	$650		
7-21	100	$120	7-26
Bal.	$630		

Office Equipment

Bal.	$575		
7-5	200		
Bal.	$775		

Accounts Receivable: Potter

7-11	$225		

Accounts Receivable: Coogan

7-25	$15		

Accounts Receivable: Smith Estate

7-30	$1,000		

Land

7-1	$1,800		

Prepaid Salary

7-31	$180		
		$60	(a)
Bal.	$120		

Deferred Income

		$200	7-28

Rent Expense

7-2	$75		
		$75	(c)

Miscellaneous Expense

7-3	$100		
		$100	(d)

Salary Expense

7-16	$180		
(a)	60		
Bal.	$240	$240	(e)

Telephone Expense

7-29	$25		
		$25	(f)

Fire Loss Expense

7-26	$120		
		$120	(g)

Interest Expense

(b)	$5		
		$5	(h)

Professional Income

		$150	7-9
		225	7-11
		1,000	7-30
(i)	$1,375	$1,375	Bal.

Profit and Loss

(c)	$75	$1,375	(i)
(d)	100		
(e)	240		
(f)	25		
(g)	120		
(h)	5		
(j)	$810		Bal.

Using the T-accounts, we can prepare the following income statement for the month of July, and balance sheet as of July 31:

E. Tutt, Esquire
Income Statement
For the Month of July

Professional Income		$1,375
Less: Expenses:		
Rent	$75	
Secretarial	240	
Telephone	25	
Miscellaneous	100	
Fire Loss	120	
Interest	5	565
Net Income		$ 810

E. Tutt, Esquire
Balance Sheet, July 31

Assets

Cash		$435
Accounts Receivable:		
Smith Estate	$1,000	
Potter	225	
Southacre Corp.	100	
Georgina Hats, Inc.	100	
Coogan	15	1,440
Prepaid Salary		120
Land		1,800
Office Equipment		775
Library		630
Total Assets		$5,200

Liabilities & Proprietorship

Liabilities:	
Note Payable	$1,200
Accounts Payable: Ryan	100
Accrued Expenses Payable	30
Client Advances	200
Total Liabilities	$1,530
Proprietorship	3,670
Total Liabilities and Proprietorship	$5,200

PROBLEMS

Problem 1.5A. Below is the balance sheet for E. Tutt on March 1, followed by Tutt's transactions during March. Prepare the journal entries and post them to the appropriate T-accounts; then make up the income statement for the month of March and the balance sheet as of March 31. Ignore depreciation and income taxes. Blank forms for these financial statements are set out after the list of transactions.

E. Tutt, Esquire
Balance Sheet, March 1

Assets		Liabilities & Proprietorship	
		Liabilities:	
Cash	$345	Accounts Payable	
Accounts Receivable		Jones Co.	$220
Smith Estate	500	Stanley	100
Potter Corp.	225	Telephone Expense	
Supplies	110	Payable	40
Prepaid Salary	200	Client Advances	300
Office Furniture &		Total Liabilities	$660
Equipment	1,250		
Library	870	Proprietorship	2,840
Total	$3,500	Total	$3,500

Transactions in March:

March 1 Purchased a three-section Super Fireproof Safe for $480 from Jarald Co. on credit.

      2 Paid the landlord $150 rent for her office for March.

      5 Paid $120 for a one-year liability insurance policy ordered the week before and running through next February 28.

      7 Paid $60 for a one-year subscription to the local weekly legal journal, to start on April 1.

      9 Purchased a $100 treatise on bankruptcy from East Publishing Company on credit.

    11 Received $350 from Homer Co. for legal advice given during the week.

    13 A new client, Fashion Corp., sent her $250 as a retainer for an argument on a motion scheduled for April 10.

    14 Completed the work for which Anderson paid her $300 in advance last month.

15 Borrowed $480 from First State Bank on a one-year note, with interest at 10%, payable at maturity, and immediately paid her *— adjusting entry* debt to Jarald Co.

16 Paid $50 to Manpower, Inc. for temporary typing assistance last week.

17 Received bill from landlord for additional rent of $15 due for March under the fuel adjustment clause in her lease.

Accrual

20 Sent $40 to the telephone company to pay her outstanding bill.

21 Gave tax advice to Olson and received $200 for it.

22 Prepared and filed incorporation papers for Nelson, Inc. and sent a bill for $250.

24 Received $300 of the $500 due from Smith's Estate.

26 Rented a section of her new safe to Bilder, a lawyer in the adjacent office, for 90 days, at a rental of $90 payable at the end of the term. *— adjusting entry*

30 Paid her secretary $100 of the $200 owed for the second half of March. *— what happened to the $ 1ST half of march*

31 Checked with telephone company and learned that her bill for March would be $45.

E. Tutt, Esquire
Income Statement
For the Month of March

Professional Income	$_____	
Rent Income	_____	$_____
Less Expenses:		
Rent	$_____	
Insurance	_____	
Secretarial	_____	
Telephone	_____	
Interest	_____	$_____
Net Income		$_____

E. Tutt, Esquire
Balance Sheet, March 31

Assets		Liabilities & Proprietorship	
		Liabilities:	
Cash	$_____	Note Payable	$_____
Accounts Receivable	_____	Accounts Payable	_____
Accrued Rent		Accrued Expenses	
Receivable	_____	Payable	_____
Supplies	_____	Client Advances	_____
Deferred Costs	_____	Total Liabilities	
Office Furniture &			$_____
Equipment	_____		
Library	_____	Proprietorship	_____
Total	$_____	Total	$_____

Problem 1.5B. Tomlin Realty Company began business on January 1 and engaged in the transactions listed below during its first month.

(a) Unless your instructor directs otherwise, prepare journal entries, including any adjusting entries, post them to T-accounts, complete the closing process, and prepare an income statement for January and a classified balance sheet as of January 31. Ignore income taxes and depreciation on all assets except for the building. The company uses straight-line depreciation for the building.

Jan. 1 Issued all 1,000 authorized shares of $1 par value common stock as follows:

> 200 shares to Michael Smith for $20,000.

> 300 shares to Gregory Myers for marketable securities worth $30,000.

> 500 shares to Steven Braggs for land worth $50,000.

  1 Purchased land and building from William Marzano for $25,000, $5,000 down and the balance pursuant to a 9% simple interest per annum note secured by a mortgage. Interest on the unpaid balance of the note is payable annually on December 31. The note is due in ten annual installments of $2,000 each at the end of each calendar year, plus accrued interest. The land is valued at $5,000. The useful life of the building is 25 years and estimated salvage value is $5,000.

  7 Purchased for $365 in cash a one-year liability insurance policy, effective through next January 6, for the building.

12 Mrs. Hayes, a sales agent, sold a parcel of real estate for a client and the company received a $6,000 commission, half of which it paid to Mrs. Hayes.

15 Paid Angie Roberts, a secretary, $500 salary for the first half of January.

17 Made a down payment of $250 for office equipment costing $750 which was ordered but not received.

19 Received a $1,000 dividend check on the marketable securities.

21 Mailed a check for $120 to South Bend News, Inc. for a six month subscription to Realty News, beginning on February 1.

22 Sold marketable securities which were worth $10,000 at the time of their transfer to the company on January 1 for $10,500.

29 Paid Angie Roberts, the secretary, $300 of the $500 the company owed her as salary for the second half of January.

30 The previously ordered office equipment arrived.

31 Received a telephone bill for January for $30.

(b) Use the same facts as above, but assume that the corporation pays income taxes at a forty percent (40%) rate.

Problem 1.5C. Nemo Hand, a great grandchild of a prominent high-court judge, decided to pursue the field of optometry after receiving an F in his first-year torts class.

(a) Unless your instructor directs otherwise, prepare journal entries, including any adjusting entries, post them to T-accounts, complete the closing process, and prepare an income statement for June and a classified balance sheet as of June 30 from the following information for Hand Optometry, Inc. Ignore depreciation on all assets except for the building. The company uses straight-line depreciation for the building.

June 1 Issued 500 of the 1000 authorized shares of $5.00 par value common stock as follows:

    (1) 150 shares to Benjamin Cardizi for $3,000
    (2) 250 shares to Brian White for marketable securities worth $5,000
    (3) 100 shares to Sandy Connors for farmland worth $2,000

1 Paid $730 for a one-year professional liability insurance policy effective through next May 31.

2   Purchased eyeglasses and contact lenses for inventory on account from Rice Optometry for $3,150.

4   Paid an assistant named Charlie his $300 salary for the first two weeks of June in advance because Charlie was strapped for cash.

7   Made a down payment of $500 to Tidmarsh Supply for optometry equipment costing $1,500, which was ordered but not received.

9   Received a $100 dividend check on the marketable securities.

12   Received a check for $450 from a customer, $250 of which was for optometry services rendered and the remainder was for a pair of glasses which Nemo purchased from Rice Optometry on June 2 for $100.

16   Purchased land and a building adjacent to the farmland for $31,000, $1,000 down and the balance pursuant to a 10% simple interest per annum note secured by a mortgage. Interest on the unpaid balance of the note is payable annually on December 31. The note is due in five annual installments of $6,000 each at the end of this year and each of the next four calendar years, plus accrued interest. The land is valued at $3,000. The useful life of the building is thirty years and its estimated salvage value is $10,000.

19   Sold the following investments in marketable securities:

   (1)   Received $2,200 for J.B. Hunt stock worth $2,000 at the time of its transfer to the company on June 1.

   (2)   Received $2,250 for Consolidated Defense, Inc. stock. Nemo expected this stock to decline drastically in the future. These shares were worth $2,500 when transferred to the company on June 1.

22   Mailed a check for $360 to the Journal of Optometry for a one-year subscription beginning on August 1.

25   Tidmarsh Supply received the equipment that was ordered on June 7.

28   Received a telephone bill for June for $40.

29   Paid Charlie's $300 salary for the last two weeks of June.

30   Sent bills totaling $2,250 to various insurance companies for services provided during the month. These bills reflected optometric services of $1,400 and $850 for glasses and contact lenses which Nemo purchased from Rice Optometry on June 2 for $450.

   (b) Use the same facts as above, but assume that the corporation pays income taxes at a forty percent (40%) rate.

G. ACCOUNTING FOR MERCHANDISE INVENTORY

Many businesses earn profits from the sale of goods rather than, like Tutt, from providing services. In such a business, inventory, or goods held for sale or resale in the ordinary course of business, comprises one of the business's basic assets. Inventory differs from the assets which Tutt owns because the goods in inventory are constantly turning over; sales take goods out of inventory, and purchases are made to replace them. As we will see in Chapter VIII, for an enterprise engaged in manufacturing, the process is a bit more complex: the manufactured, or, as they are often termed, "completed," goods are sold and replaced by purchases of raw materials which will be turned into completed goods through the manufacturing operations. This section is designed to introduce you to the special techniques used to deal with the problems that this constant turnover creates.

To take a simple example, suppose Marty Jones operates a retail store which sells inexpensive shoes. Further suppose that during the month of January he sells 1,000 pairs of shoes for $10 a pair. To calculate his net income, Jones must include in his expenses not only the ones like Tutt had, such as rent, utilities, and salaries, but also the cost of the shoes sold. In bookkeeping language, the business sold shoes for $10,000 from which Jones must deduct the cost of the goods sold, as well as his other operating expenses, to determine his net income. If the shoes cost Jones $7 a pair, and his other operating expenses for the month came to $1,000, his net income would be $2,000. A simplified version of his income statement might look something like this:

Jones Shoes
Income Statement
For the Month of January

Sales	$10,000
Less: Cost of Goods Sold	7,000
Gross Profit	$ 3,000
Less: Operating Expenses	1,000
Net Income	$ 2,000

The chief differences between this statement and Tutt's are the different name given to the income account, the introduction of the Cost of Goods Sold account, and the new caption "Gross Profit." We will discuss these differences in sequence.

1. SALES

Sales, or Sales Revenues, are simply another type of income (i. e., increase in proprietorship resulting from operations), and the Sales account reflects the total amount of sales completed during the period. Invariably, however, some customers will bring back goods for various reasons. Customers may return damaged, defective, unwanted or unneeded goods for credit or a cash refund. Accountants call these transactions *sales returns*. Sometimes, the customer may decide to keep the goods if the seller grants an allowance or deduction from the selling price. Accountants refer to these transactions as *sales allowances*, but usually combine sales returns and sales allowances into a single account, *Sales Returns and Allowances*. We can describe this account as a contra-revenue account to the Sales account. The Sales Returns and Allowances account normally contains a debit balance. Accountants use this contra-revenue account, rather than debiting the Sales account directly, to separately identify and disclose sales returns and allowances in both the accounts and in the income statement. Debiting the Sales account directly would hide the comparative size of the returns and allowances relative to sales. Large returns or allowances suggest inferior goods, sloppy sales techniques, or poor handling, shipping or delivery practices. The caption *Net Sales* simply shows the numerical difference between the Sales and Sales Returns and Allowances accounts.

To illustrate, suppose that Jones actually sold 1,020 pairs of shoes during January, but that customers returned twenty pairs for refunds and Jones restored those shoes to inventory. In bookkeeping language, Jones sold shoes for $10,200, from which he must subtract $200 in sales returns, leaving him with $10,000 in net sales. We could restate his income statement as follows:

Jones Shoes
Income Statement
For the Month of January

Sales	$10,200
Less: Sales Returns and Allowances	200
Net Sales	$10,000
Less: Cost of Goods Sold	7,000
Gross Profit	$ 3,000
Less: Operating Expenses	1,000
Net Income	$ 2,000

2. COST OF GOODS SOLD

There are various ways to determine the figure for the cost of goods sold during an accounting period. For example, Jones might keep a record of the cost of each pair of shoes as they are purchased for resale and then sold. Accountants usually refer to such a system as a *perpetual inventory system* because the accounting records continuously show the quantity and cost of the goods which the business holds as inventory at any time. As the business sells goods, the bookkeeper transfers their cost from the Inventory account to the Cost of Goods Sold account. At the end of the period, the balance in the Cost of Goods Sold account would give Jones the cost of all the shoes sold during the period. Ordinarily, however, it might be difficult, and it would certainly be time-consuming, to identify the cost of each pair of shoes sold.

As an alternative, Jones could merely keep a record of the cost of the shoes on hand at the beginning of the period and the cost of the shoes acquired during the period. Then at the end of the period Jones can *take inventory*, that is, count up the number of shoes he has left and determine their total cost. By subtracting the cost of what he has left from the sum of what he had at the beginning of the period and what he acquired during the period, he can compute the cost of what he sold. Accountants call this system the *periodic inventory method* because the accounting entity determines inventory only at the end of an accounting period.

Suppose, for example, that Jones had an inventory at the beginning of January of 300 pairs of shoes which cost $7 per pair, and that during the month he purchased another 1200 pairs of shoes at $7 per pair. Because Jones sold 1,020 pairs of shoes during January, but 20 pairs were returned and placed back in inventory, upon taking inventory at the end of the month, he would find 500 pairs of shoes which cost a total of $3,500. The difference between that figure and the sum of what Jones had on hand and what he acquired, $10,500, gives the cost of goods sold figure of $7,000 which we had previously assumed.

A somewhat more detailed version of his income statement might then look like this:

Jones Shoe
Income Statement
For the Month of January

Net Sales		$10,000
Cost of Goods Sold:		
Opening Inventory	$ 2,100	
Purchases	8,400	
Goods Available for Sale	$10,500	
Less: Closing Inventory	3,500	7,000
Gross Profit		$3,000
Operating Expenses		1,000
Net Income		$2,000

At this point, we can take a closer look at the term *gross profit* and its presentation on the income statement.

3. GROSS PROFIT AND THE MULTI-STEP INCOME STATEMENT

The "Gross Profit" caption in the income statement reflects the difference between net sales and the cost of goods sold. Accountants use the term *multiple-step* to describe an income statement which lists gross profit as an intermediate figure in computing net income or loss. Such an income statement will show two steps: first, the gross profit, calculated by subtracting the cost of goods sold from net sales, and second, the net income, computed by deducting operating expenses from gross profit. Although gross profit does not measure the business's overall profitability, users of financial statements often pay particular attention to that figure, which frequently serves as a better guide to market conditions and the efficiency of the selling operations than the net income figure.

If we assume that Jones has incorporated the business and that the corporation pays income taxes at a forty percent tax rate, a multi-step income statement for Jones Shoe Co. might look something like:

Jones Shoe Co.
Income Statement
For the Month of January

Sales	$10,200	
Less: Sales Returns and Allowances	200	
Net Sales	$10,000	
Cost of Goods Sold:		
Opening Inventory	$2,100	
Purchases	8,400	
Goods Available for Sale	$10,500	
Less: Closing Inventory	$3,500	7,000
Gross Profit		$3,000
Operating Expenses		
Rent Expense	$600	
Selling Commission Expense	$250	
Utility Expense	100	950
Operating Income		$2,050
Non–Operating Items		
Rental Income	50	
Interest Expense	(100)	50
Income Before Taxes		$2,000
Income Taxes		800
Net Income		$1,200

As you see, the multi-step presentation can also provide additional information by separating the business's operating activities and non-operating activities and presenting more detailed information about revenues and expenses. You will recall that businesses derive revenues and incur expenses both from normal operating activities and from peripheral or incidental transactions. Here, Jones Shoe has only interest expense, and rental income from sub-leasing part of the store, in the non-operating section; other items might have included gain or loss from the sale of office equipment, or a major fire loss. Note that the non-operating items are shown immediately after operating income, and they are netted, with the net figure deducted from (or added to) operating income to determine income before taxes.

Compare the so-called *single-step* income statement format, under which all items are classified into just the two categories: revenues, which includes both operating revenues and gains, and expenses, which includes cost of goods sold, operating expenses and losses. To determine net income or loss, the single-step income statement subtracts total expenses from total revenues. The following illustrates a single-step income statement for Jones Shoe Co.:

Jones Shoe Co.
Income Statement
For the Month of January

Revenue		
Net Sales	$10,000	
Rental Income	50	
Total Revenues		$10,050
Expenses		
Cost of Goods	$7,000	
Operating Expenses	950	
Income Taxes	800	
Interest Expenses	100	
Total Expenses		8,850
Net Income		$1,200

4.   PERIODIC INVENTORY SYSTEM

Let us now see how the bookkeeper uses T-accounts and entries to make these computations under the periodic inventory system. On his balance sheet at the beginning of the period, Jones has an asset, Inventory, in the amount of $2,100. This account, which was derived by taking inventory at the close of the period just ended, becomes *Opening Inventory* for the new period. During the period, Jones opens a T-account called *Purchases* to which the amount of purchases made during the period is debited; the corresponding credit is to Cash or an account payable, depending upon whether the purchase is made for cash or on credit. Actually, the purchases during the period could as well be debited directly to the Inventory T-account, thus eliminating the need for a Purchases account; but in practice it appears that a separate T-account for purchases is commonly used.

don't debit inventory directly

If Jones returns any purchases or a seller grants any allowance for defective or damaged goods, the bookkeeper would credit an account called *Purchase Returns and Allowances*, which is a contra account to Purchases, and would normally contain a credit balance. Similar to Sales Returns and Allowances, the purpose of utilizing this contra account, instead of crediting the Purchases account directly, is to separately identify and disclose purchase returns and allowances; on the income statement, the account called *Net Purchases* shows the difference between Purchases and Purchase Returns and Allowances. Crediting the Purchases account directly would hide the comparative size of the returns and allowances relative to purchases. Large returns or allowances suggest sloppy purchasing procedures or unreliable suppliers.

Thus, if Jones purchased the entire $8,400 worth of goods acquired in January in a single cash transaction, the entry would be:

(a)   Purchases $8,400
            Cash $8,400

Whether or not Jones purchased all the goods at the same time, or purchased them all for cash, the T-account for Purchases would show a total debit balance of $8,400 at the end of the month of January.

At the end of the period the bookkeeper sets up a new T-account called *Cost of Goods Sold*. As we have already seen, Cost of Goods Sold is an expense and therefore this account should be increased by a debit and decreased by a credit. The bookkeeper then closes Opening Inventory and Purchases (plus any offsetting Purchase Returns and Allowances) to the Cost of Goods Sold account in much the same way that expense and income accounts are closed to the Profit and Loss account. Because Jones did not return any purchases, the entries would consist of debits to the Cost of Goods Sold account, and credits to the Opening Inventory and Purchases accounts respectively to close them out:

(b)   Cost of Goods Sold $2,100
           Inventory $2,100

(c)   Cost of Goods Sold $8,400
           Purchases $8,400

If there had been any purchase returns or allowances, that account would have contained a credit balance, which the bookkeeper would have closed out by debiting Purchase Returns and Allowances and crediting the Cost of Goods Sold account.

The bookkeeper then learns from the person who took inventory at the end of the month how much inventory remains unsold—here $3,500. This information has two aspects of equal significance to the bookkeeper. It tells the bookkeeper that there remains at the end of the period an asset of $3,500 of closing inventory which should appear on the balance sheet at the end of the period. It also tells the bookkeeper that the cost of goods sold is $3,500 less than would be indicated simply by adding together the opening inventory and the purchases. The bookkeeper can reflect both these facts by a single journal entry:

(d)   Inventory $3,500
           Cost of Goods Sold $3,500

The amount debited to the Inventory account is balanced by a credit to the Cost of Goods Sold account. The Cost of Goods Sold account performs the subtraction of what Jones has left from the sum of what he had at the beginning of the period plus what he bought during the period; the net debit in the Cost of Goods Sold account is the cost of what was sold during the period.

A little thought will show that this entry debiting the amount of the goods still on hand at the close of the period to Closing Inventory, and crediting the same figure to the Cost of Goods Sold account, is just another example of deferral. The sum of what Jones originally had on hand and what he bought during the period constitutes an overstatement of the expense applicable to the current period; the cost of merchandise remaining at the end of the period should not be included as an expense of the current period, but rather should be deferred to later periods. Thus *Closing Inventory* could just as readily be called *Deferred Cost of Goods Sold Expense*. The closing inventory will appear as an asset, usually called simply Inventory, on the balance sheet at the end of the period, like any other deferred item. The Inventory account on the balance sheet will then become Opening Inventory for the new period, and the cycle will start all over again.

It is not necessary to use separate T-accounts for opening inventory and closing inventory. Instead, the bookkeeper usually uses a single T-account called simply Inventory. At the close of each period, this account is temporarily closed out with a credit in the amount of the opening inventory and an equal debit to the Cost of Goods Sold account. The bookkeeper then reopens the Inventory account with a debit in the amount of the closing inventory.

Once the net figure in the Cost of Goods Sold account is arrived at, here $7,000, that cost, like any other expense, is closed to Profit and Loss:

(e)   Profit and Loss $7,000
           Cost of Goods Sold $7,000

Here is a summary of the journal entries described above, along with the related T-accounts.

(a)   Purchases $8,400
           Cash $8,400

(b)   Cost of Goods Sold $2,100
           Inventory $2,100

(c)   Cost of Goods Sold $8,400
           Purchases $8,400

| (d) | Inventory | $3,500 | |
| | Cost of Goods Sold | | $3,500 |

| (e) | Profit and Loss | $7,000 | |
| | Cost of Goods Sold | | $7,000 |

	Inventory		
Bal.	$2,100		
		$2,100	(b)
(d)	$3,500		

	Cost of Goods Sold		
(b)	$2,100		
(c)	8,400	$3,500	(d)
Bal.	$7,000	$7,000	(e)

	Purchases		
(a)	$8,400	$8,400	(c)

The Profit and Loss account would then look like this (after Cost of Goods Sold, together with the Sales Income of $10,000 and the other expenses of $1,000, have been closed to it):

	Profit and Loss		
(e)	$7,000	$10,000	
	1,000		
		$2,000	Bal.

and this balance of $2,000 would be closed to Proprietorship.

The foregoing illustrates the mechanics of handling inventory under the periodic inventory system. Since the system relies upon a physical count of closing inventory at the end of a period to determine the amount of inventory sold during the period, it is not surprising that some difficult problems can arise in particular situations, such as determining the cost of the particular items left in closing inventory if the price Jones had to pay for the items fluctuated during the period. It is not necessary to do more than allude to such problems here; they are considered in detail in Chapter VIII.

5.　SUMMARY OF THE BOOKKEEPING AND ACCRUAL ACCOUNTING PROCESS

At this point, we should summarize our entire discussion of the bookkeeping and accrual accounting process in outline form and provide a format for a classified balance sheet and multi-step income statement:

A.　Prepare original journal entries

B.　Post journal entries to accounts in the ledger after entering beginning balances from previous balance sheet, if applicable

C. Prepare necessary adjusting entries after reviewing the beginning
balance sheet and current period transactions:
   1. Defer paid but unused expenses
   2. Defer received but unearned revenues
   3. Record depreciation
   4. Accrue incurred but unrecorded expenses
   5. Accrue earned but unrecorded revenues
   6. Complete periodic inventory accounting
      a. Transfer beginning balance in Inventory account to Cost of
         Goods Sold
      b. Transfer balances in Purchases and Purchase Returns and
         Allowances accounts to Cost of Goods Sold
      c. Record ending inventory and reduce Cost of Goods Sold,
         after:
         (i) Physically counting inventory at end of period, and
         (ii) Calculating cost of ending inventory
   7. Accrue income taxes
D. Post adjusting entries to the ledger
E. Close revenue and expense accounts
   1. Determine the account balances
   2. Prepare trial balance
   3. Prepare worksheet
   4. Make closing journal entries
      a. Transfer debit balances to Profit and Loss account
      b. Transfer credit balances to Profit and Loss account
      c. Transfer balance in Profit and Loss to Owners' Equity
   5. Post closing journal entries to the ledger
F. Preparing the financial statements
   1. Income Statement
      Sales
      Less: Sales Returns and Allowances
      Net Sales
      Cost of Goods Sold
         Beginning Inventory
         Purchases
         Less: Purchase Returns and Allowances
         Net Purchases
         Cost of Goods Available for Sale
         Less: Ending Inventory
         Cost of Goods Sold
      Gross Profit
      Operating Expenses
      Operating Income
      Non–Operating Items (interest and non-recurring items)
      Income Before Income Taxes
      Income Taxes
      Net Income

2. Balance Sheet
   Assets
      Current Assets
         Cash
         Marketable Securities
         Notes Receivable
         Accounts Receivable
         Inventory
         Prepaid Costs
            Total Current Assets
      Long–Term Investments
      Fixed Assets
         Land
         Buildings
           Less: Accumulated Depreciation
         Equipment
           Less: Accumulated Depreciation
           Total Fixed Assets
      Intangible Assets
           Total Assets
   Liabilities and Owners' Equity
      Liabilities
         Current Liabilities
           Notes Payable
           Accounts Payable
           Accrued Liabilities
           Taxes Payable
           Unearned Items
             Total Current Liabilities
         Other Liabilities
            Total Liabilities
      Owners' Equity
         Proprietorship
         Partners' Equity
          Partners' Capital
          Drawings
         Shareholders' Equity
          Capital Stock
            Preferred Stock
            Common Stock
          Additional Paid–In Capital
          Retained Earnings
            Total Owners' Equity
  Total Liabilities and Owners' Equity

PROBLEMS AND QUESTIONS

The following problems and questions are designed to provide some experience in handling the mechanics of accounting for inventory, as well as some additional practice in bookkeeping generally.

Problem 1.6A.

(a) The Nifty–Novelty Company was organized as a partnership on February 1, to operate a wholesale knick-knack business at rented premises formerly occupied by Samuel Nifty. The following transactions during February are to be recorded on the firm's books. Make the appropriate journal entries and post them to the T-accounts. Draw up a simplified income statement for the month and a balance sheet as of February 28. Ignore depreciation and taxes.

Feb. 1   Samuel Nifty contributed store fixtures valued at $10,000; Hiram Novelty contributed merchandise valued at $2,000 and $8,000 in cash.

1   Paid February rent for store of $200.

2   Paid painter $72 for lettering on store front which will not have to be redone for a year.

3   Purchased costume jewelry on account from Acme, Inc., for $1,000.

4   Purchased counter and trays for displaying merchandise from Blake & Co. for $1,500 on account.

6   Sold merchandise for $550 cash.

8   Received $400 from Ritter for goods to be delivered in March.

9   Sold party decorations and favors to Lincoln Hotel on account for $310.

11   Paid February wages of $260 to salesperson.

12   Paid $500 on account to Acme, Inc.

15   Sold merchandise for $2,150 cash.

17   Purchased merchandise from Klips Corp. giving note for $1,300 due in six months.

20   A display tray which cost $19 was accidentally destroyed.

22   Received $100 on account from Lincoln Hotel.

24   Paid Blake & Co. $1,000 on account.

26   Sold merchandise for $700 cash.

28 Determined that telephone bill for February will amount to $20.

28 Distributed $100 to each of the partners.

Assume further that:

(i) Rent of $105 will be due Smith Corp. on April 30 for storage space leased to Nifty Novelty on Feb. 1 for 3 months.

(ii) A physical inventory on February 28 discloses $1,700 worth of merchandise on hand.

Nifty Novelty Company
Income Statement
For the month of February

Sales		$_____
Cost of Goods Sold		
Opening Inventory	$_____	
Purchases	_____	
Goods Available for Sale	$_____	
Less: Closing Inventory	_____	_____
Gross Profit on Sales		_____
Less: Expenses		_____
Net Income		$_____

Nifty Novelty Company
Balance Sheet, February 28

<u>Assets</u>		<u>Liabilities & Partners' Equity</u>	
		Liabilities:	
Cash	$_____	Note Payable	$_____
Accounts Receivable	_____	Accounts Payable	_____
Inventory	_____	Accrued Exp. Payable	_____
Deferred Costs	_____	Deferred Income	_____
Store Fixtures	_____	Partners' Equity	$_____
Total	$ _____	Total	_____

(b) Could any of the above transactions have been overlooked by the bookkeeper, and hence not recorded, without changing either the balance sheet totals or the net income figure?

(c) Suppose the Nifty–Novelty bookkeeper was not aware of the lease of storage space from Smith Corp. referred to in (i) above, and made no entry reflecting this transaction. What would the effect of this omission be on Nifty–Novelty's financial statements?

Problem 1.6B

(a) The balance sheet of Camera Sales Co. as of March 31, Year 1 shows the following:

Camera Sales Co.
Balance Sheet, March 31, Year 1

<u>Assets</u>

Current Assets:		$14,800
Cash		2,700
Accounts Receivable		2,100
Inventories (21 cameras)		
Prepaid Insurance (unused cost of a one-year		
policy purchased on January 1, Year 1 $300)		225
Total Current Assets		$19,825
Fixed Assets:		
Land		$10,000
Buildings	$40,000	
Less: Accumulated Depreciation	11,700	
Net Buildings		28,300
Furniture and Fixtures	$3,600	
Less: Accumulated Depreciation	480	
Net Furniture and Fixtures		3,120
Total Fixed Assets		$41,420
Total Assets		$61,245

<u>**Liabilities and Stockholders' Equity**</u>

Liabilities:	
Current Liabilities:	
Accounts Payable	$7,900
Accrued Interest Payable	225
Total Current Liabilities	$8,125
Long–Term Liabilities:	
Note Payable, due December 31, Year 5,	
bearing nine percent interest payable	
annually on December 31 of each year	$10,000
Total Liabilities	$18,125
Shareholders' Equity:	
Common Stock (1,000 shares, $10 par value,	
authorized, issued and outstanding)	$10,000
Retained Earnings	33,120
Total Shareholders' Equity	$43,120
	$61,245
Total Liabilities and Shareholders' Equity	

Unless your instructor directs otherwise, prepare journal entries for the following transactions which occurred during April, prepare any necessary adjusting entries, post to T-accounts, construct a six-column worksheet, prepare and post closing entries and prepare April financial statements (multi-step income statement and classified balance sheet only). Assume that Camera Sales Co. pays income taxes at a flat rate of thirty percent (30%) of net income and uses the periodic inventory method and separate accounts for sales returns and allowances and purchase returns and allowances. The building has an estimated useful life of thirty years and a salvage value of $4,000. The furniture and fixtures have an estimated useful life of ten years and no salvage value.

Apr. 1   Purchased ten cameras for $100 each on account from Kodak, Inc.

      2   Returned one camera to Kodak, Inc. for credit because of a slight defect.

      4   Sold eight cameras in various cash sales totaling $1,325.

      7   Sold three cameras to *The Observer* for $675. *The Observer* paid $75 down and issued a promissory note, due in three months, for the $600 balance with interest at the rate of ten percent per annum.

      9   Sold fourteen cameras for $2,300, $1,700 on account and $600 cash.

    11   Sold camera to Thelma Bird for $175 on account.

    14   Thelma Bird returned the camera she purchased for credit.

    15   Paid salaries of $500 for the first half of the month.

    18   Purchased fifteen cameras on account at $100 each from Nikon Inc.

    21   Gave George Land, the President, a $600 advance for May salary.

    23   Paid $100 in wages which had been negligently overlooked to a former employee who was fired in January.

    25   Paid $24 for April telephone bill.

    27   Accepts a $100 down payment from a customer to order a camera costing $200, which the company will sell to the customer for $500.

    30   Physical inventory reveals seventeen cameras in inventory. All cameras were purchased for $100 each. Bookkeeper decides not to pay $500 in salaries for the second half of the month until May.

(b) Could any of the above transactions have been overlooked by the bookkeeper, and hence not recorded, without changing the figures on the balance sheet, the balance sheet totals, or net income?

(c) Suppose the bookkeeper for Camera Sales Co. was not aware of prepaid insurance described in the balance sheet as of March 31, and made no entry during April regarding this insurance. What would the effect of this omission be on the company's financial statements?

H. THE STATEMENT OF CASH FLOWS

Under accrual accounting, as we have seen, the movement of cash does not control the determination of expenses and income for an accounting period. On the other hand, a business's *cash flow*, that is, the net movement of cash into and out of the enterprise, may well determine the business's financial success. To remain in business, an enterprise must either own or have access to the cash needed to meet recurring expenses, such as payroll and rent, to pay its accounts payable to suppliers, and to satisfy its outstanding debt obligations as they come due. In addition, any distributions which the enterprise makes to its owners normally come from cash. Accordingly, judging a business's future prospects calls for some consideration, and comparison, of the business's cash-generating potential and cash needs, over both the short and long terms.

Obviously, an enterprise's revenues from operations provide its primary source of cash, while its expenses serve as the principal cash drain. Estimated future earnings, therefore, provide some indication as to expected cash resources. But operations afford only a starting point, because transactions not reflected in the income statement, such as borrowing money, paying cash dividends, or purchasing long-lived assets like buildings, machinery, and equipment, may significantly increase or decrease a business's cash. We must also keep in mind that, as a corollary of deferral or accrual, some expenses do not involve any current or prospective cash outflow. For example, when an enterprise has prepaid an expense, the periodic charge off, or amortization, of the resulting deferred expense asset, like E. Tutt's deferred insurance expense, is not accompanied by any current outlay of cash. A much more important example is depreciation on tangible fixed assets purchased for cash: here too, the cash expenditure occurs in the earlier accounting period when the enterprise acquired and paid for the asset, while the expense comes in the subsequent accounting periods over which the business depreciates the asset. Similarly, when an expense is accrued it is not accompanied by any outflow of cash at that time, since the actual expenditure comes later.

On the income side, when income is earned in a period after the one in which the cash was received, that later recognition of income is offset by elimination of the deferred income account created back when the cash came in, and there is no related movement of cash in the later period. And again, in the accrual situation, the recognition of income is not accompanied by the receipt of cash, which will come later. However, special note should be taken of the fact that whenever the cash is not expected until quite a while after the income recognition, this delay can significantly affect an enterprise's overall financial picture, a subject that will receive detailed discussion later.

By comparing an enterprise's current balance sheet with the previous one, a reader can glean some useful information relating to cash flow. For example, the relative amounts of cash and accounts receivable, and the change in those figures from the end of the prior year, may indicate significant trends. A number of important transactions, however, such as borrowing, issuing new stock, or buying capital assets, greatly affect cash, but they do not appear in the income statement for the period, and they emerge on the balance sheet at the end of the period only as accomplished facts. While a reader may surmise what happened by comparing the current balance sheet with the prior one, users of financial statements often want more explanatory information.

Accordingly, prudent investors and creditors look for a statement of cash flows which details the effect on cash of both an enterprise's regular operations during the year and those other types of significant transactions. Common cash inflows include sales for cash; collection of accounts receivable; short and long-term borrowings; sale of property, plant and equipment; and issuance of stock for cash. Common cash outflows include current operating costs; acquisition of property, plant, equipment, and other long-term assets; repayment of short and long-term debt; and distributions to owners. As enterprises increasingly rely on debt to finance activities such as expanded operations, buy-outs, and mergers, attorneys as well as accountants, financial analysts, creditors, investors and others must increase their awareness of the mechanics and usefulness of the statement of cash flows. Both the Enron and Tyco scandals illustrate that lawyers should understand not only the statement of cash flows itself, but also the ways that enterprises can manipulate that financial statement.

The W.T. Grant Company illustrates the importance of the statement of cash flows to both investors and creditors. In 1975, the company, then the nation's largest retailer, filed for protection under the federal bankruptcy laws because the company did not have enough cash to pay its debts. For almost ten years before the company filed for bankruptcy, its income statement reported steady profits; but its operations produced a cash deficit, which required W.T. Grant to borrow huge sums of money to continue the business. If investors and creditors had examined a statement of cash flows, they would have noticed that the company's operations did not generate any positive cash flow and that the company had to borrow cash year after year to offset the decline in cash.

1. HISTORY

Accountants have prepared statements that explain flows of cash and other financial resources for many years. The names of these statements have included *Statement of Sources and Uses of Funds, Funds Statement, Statement of Changes in Financial Position,* and most recently, *Statement of Cash Flows,* which became the required title in 1988. Several problems inherent in the previous cash flow reporting practice caused the change to the statement of cash flows. These problems included the ambiguity of terms, such as "funds"; lack of comparability among statements resulting from different definitions and different formats; and the reporting of net changes in amounts of assets and liabilities rather than gross inflows and outflows of cash.

We should note that statutes, regulations and legal documents may use outdated terminology. In particular, a number of state corporation statutes continued to use the term "statement of changes in financial position" instead of "statement of cash flows" well after the adoption of the current accounting standard, and some may still do so.

Today, the statement of cash flows complements the other major financial statements. The statement of cash flows reports the changes in cash and cash equivalents during an accounting period, and, most importantly, *explains* those changes. Whereas the balance sheet summarizes an enterprise's assets, liabilities and owner's equity at a specific point in time, and the income statement summarizes the enterprise's performance on an accrual basis, the statement of cash flows allows its reader to assess an enterprise's cash transactions.

2. THE PURPOSE OF THE STATEMENT OF CASH FLOWS

According to accounting pronouncements, the statement of cash flows should provide relevant information about an enterprise's cash receipts and payments during an accounting period. That information, if used with related disclosures and information in the other financial statements, should help investors, creditors and other users of financial statements to:

(a) assess the enterprise's ability to generate positive future net cash flows;

(b) assess the enterprise's ability to meet its obligations, its ability to pay dividends, and its needs for external financing;

(c) assess the reasons for differences between net income and associated cash receipts and payments; and

(d) assess the effects on an enterprise's financial position of both its cash and noncash investing and financing transactions during the period.

To achieve this purpose, the statement of cash flows should report the effects of an enterprise's operations, its investments in capital assets, and its financing transactions, on its cash during a period. For an example, see Starbucks' Statement of Cash Flows from its financial statements for fiscal 2005, on page 109, *infra*.

3.   CASH AND CASH EQUIVALENTS

The statement of cash flows explains the change during the period in *cash and cash equivalents*. To establish consistency in financial reporting, companies must report the changes in "cash and cash equivalents", thereby getting away from that ambiguous term "funds." Cash includes not only currency, but bank accounts that the enterprise can access "on demand." The applicable accounting pronouncement defines cash equivalents as "short-term, highly liquid investments." To satisfy this definition, cash equivalents must meet two requirements:

1. An enterprise must be able to convert the equivalents to cash readily, and

2. These equivalents' original maturity dates must not exceed three months, so that changes in interest rates do not threaten to affect adversely their value.

Examples of cash equivalents include United States Treasury bills, certificates of deposit, commercial paper and money market funds. The original maturity date means the maturity date when an enterprise acquires the investment. For example, a five-year U.S. Treasury note purchased three months from maturity qualifies as a cash-equivalent because the note will mature in three months. On the other hand, a five-year U.S. Treasury note purchased two years before its maturity date does not become a cash equivalent three months before its maturity because the note's maturity exceeded three months on the acquisition date. According to accounting standards, an enterprise must combine cash and cash equivalents on the balance sheet and on the statement of cash flows. These same standards require an enterprise to include its definition of cash equivalents in a related disclosure to its statement of cash flows. For an example, see Starbucks' definition of cash and cash equivalents in Note 1 to the 2005 financial statements on page 45 in Appendix A.

4.   CLASSIFICATION OF THE STATEMENT OF CASH FLOWS

An enterprise must classify its statement of cash flows into three separate categories: operating, investing and financing activities. These three categories represent an enterprise's three major functions and help the readers of the statement of cash flows recognize important relationships between the three activities. Each activity can produce a cash inflow or outflow to the enterprise. Once again, note Starbucks' Statement of Cash Flows, from its financial statements for fiscal 2005, on page 109, *infra*.

Along with separating these three sections, the statement of cash flows must reconcile the total change in cash and cash equivalents for the period with the beginning and ending balances which appear on the current and prior balance sheets.

The **operating activities** of an enterprise involve acquiring and selling it's products and services. For example, Starbucks' operating section would mainly report cash disbursements and receipts from roasting coffee beans and selling coffee and other beverages. For a service organization, such as a law firm, this section would include inflows from legal fees, and outflows for associate and secretarial salaries, rents, and utilities. Cash inflows from operating activities include interest on loans to, and dividends from ownership investments in, other enterprises, while cash outflows from operating activities include cash interest payments to lenders and other creditors. This category also serves as a "catch all" for any cash flows from transactions which do not qualify as investing or financing activities.

The **investing activities** of an enterprise include acquiring and disposing of long-term investments and long-lived assets. The investing section also shows cash expenditures to acquire other companies through mergers or stock acquisitions. Manufacturing enterprises typically spend the largest amount of cash on such long-lived assets as property, plant and equipment, which accountants sometimes refer to as *capital expenditures*. Note that investing activities do not refer to all investments in the usual sense of the word: the term does not, for example, cover the purchase or sale of U.S. Treasury bills which qualify as cash equivalents, nor does it include interest and dividends from long-term investments.

The **financing activities** of an enterprise include the obtaining of resources from owners and providing them with a return on, and a return of, their investment. Financing activities also include the issuance and retirement of short and long-term debt. Cash outflows from financing activities include cash dividends or other distributions to owners.

5.   THE OPERATING SECTION

An enterprise may use the direct or indirect method to report its cash flows from operations. The direct method requires an enterprise to report major classes of cash receipts and cash payments which relate to the enterprise's operations. Enterprises that use the direct method must report, at a minimum, the following seven classes of cash transactions, if they exist:

1.   Cash collected from customers, including lessees and licensees
2.   Interest and dividends received
3.   Other operating cash receipts
4.   Cash paid to employees and other suppliers of goods or services, including suppliers of insurance and advertising
5.   Interest paid
6.   Income taxes paid

7.   Other operating cash payments

Although the authoritative accounting pronouncement expresses a preference for the direct method, only a very small percentage of large, publicly-traded companies actually use that method. The following is an illustration of the direct method:

Widgets, Inc.

Statement of Cash Flows
For the Year Ended December 31, 2005

Cash Flows From Operating Activities:

Cash receipts from:	
Customers	$1,150,000
Interest	15,000
Other receipts	100,000
Total Cash Receipts	$1,265,000
Cash Payments for:	
Inventory	$ (650,000)
Salaries and wages	(140,000)
Utilities	(40,000)
Interest	(55,000)
Income Taxes	(90,000)
Total Cash Payments	$ (975,000)
Net Cash Provided from Operating Activities	$ 290,000

Under the indirect method of presenting net cash flows from operations, an enterprise must reconcile net income, determined pursuant to accrual accounting, to net cash from operations. This reconciliation involves adjusting net income to remove the effect of any current recognition of income or expense derived from a past deferral of operating cash receipts or payments, and all accruals of future operating cash receipts and payments; also to be eliminated are any gains or losses from the sale of long-term investments and property, plant and equipment, the proceeds from which will be included in the inflows from investing activities. These adjustments require an enterprise to add back (1) depreciation, amortization and other non-cash expenses, (2) so-called "sources" of cash from decreasing accounts receivable, inventories, or prepaid expenses, and from increasing payables, and (3) losses from the sale of long-term investments and property, which reduced net income. The enterprise must also subtract so-called "uses" of cash to increase accounts receivable, inventories or prepaid expenses, or to reduce payables, plus any gains from the sale of long-term investments and property, which increased net income. Because the indirect method starts with net income, any inaccuracies in the income statement directly affect the statement of cash flows. Starbucks' Statement of Cash Flows in its financial statements for fiscal 2005 illustrates the indirect method of reporting cash flows from operations, and is set out on the following page for convenient reference.

STARBUCKS CONSOLIDATED STATEMENTS OF CASH FLOW (*in thousands*)

Fiscal Year Ended	Oct 2, 2005	Oct 3, 2004	Sept 28, 2003
OPERATING ACTIVITIES			
Net earnings	$ 494,467	$ 388,973	$ 265,355
Adjustments to reconcile net earnings to net cash provided by operating activities:			
Depreciation and amortization	367,207	314,047	266,258
Provision for impairments and asset disposals	20,157	13,568	7,784
Deferred income taxes, net	(31,253)	(3,770)	(6,767)
Equity in income of investees	(49,633)	(31,801)	(21,320)
Distributions of income from equity investees	30,919	38,328	28,966
Tax benefit from exercise of nonqualified stock options	109,978	63,405	36,590
Net accretion of discount and amortization of premium on marketable securities	10,097	11,603	5,996
Cash provided/(used) by changes in operating assets and liabilities:			
Accounts receivable	(49,311)	(24,977)	(8,384)
Inventories	(121,618)	(77,662)	(64,768)
Accounts payable	9,717	27,948	24,990
Accrued compensation and related costs	22,711	54,929	42,132
Deferred revenue	53,276	47,590	30,732
Other operating assets and liabilities	56,894	36,356	8,554
Net cash provided by operating activities	923,608	858,537	616,118
INVESTING ACTIVITIES			
Purchase of available-for-sale securities	(643,488)	(887,969)	(481,050)
Maturity of available-for-sale securities	469,554	170,789	218,787
Sale of available-for-sale securities	626,113	452,467	141,009
Acquisitions, net of cash acquired	(21,583)	(7,515)	(69,928)
Net additions to equity investments, other investments and other assets	(7,915)	(64,747)	(47,259)
Net additions to property, plant and equipment	(643,989)	(412,537)	(377,983)
Net cash used by investing activities	(221,308)	(749,512)	(616,424)
FINANCING ACTIVITIES			
Proceeds from issuance of common stock	163,555	137,590	107,183
Borrowings under revolving credit facility	277,000	—	—
Principal payments on long-term debt	(735)	(722)	(710)
Repurchase of common stock	(1,113,647)	(203,413)	(75,710)
Net cash provided/(used) by financing activities	(673,827)	(66,545)	30,763
Effect of exchange rate changes on cash and cash equivalents	283	3,111	3,278
Net increase in cash and cash equivalents	28,756	45,591	33,735
CASH AND CASH EQUIVALENTS			
Beginning of period	145,053	99,462	65,727
End of period	$ 173,809	$ 145,053	$ 99,462
SUPPLEMENTAL DISCLOSURE OF CASH FLOW INFORMATION			
Cash paid during the year for:			
Interest	$ 1,060	$ 370	$ 265
Income taxes	$ 227,812	$ 172,759	$ 140,107

See Notes to Consolidated Financial Statements.

To illustrate the kind of adjustment needed to reconcile net income to net cash flow from operations under the indirect method, we can use the actual figures from a well-known public company a few years ago, when it sold for $310 million in cash a long-term investment with a book value of $181 million, resulting in a $129 million gain. Since the $310 million must appear as a cash inflow from investing activities, and it necessarily includes the $129 million of gain, the gain would be in the investing cash flows, and that is where it belongs because it arose from the sale of an investment rather than from an operating activity. But of course, as an accounting matter the $129 million gain was included in net income, so that amount has to be subtracted in going from net income to net cash flow from operating activities, or else the statement of cash flows would have double-counted the cash inflow from that gain, including it in both the operating section and in the investing section. In addition, the statement would not have reconciled to the ending amount of cash and cash equivalents.

Regardless of whether an enterprise uses the direct or indirect method for reporting cash flows from operations, a user of financial statements should note several important disclosures. First, accounting standards require an enterprise that uses the direct method of reporting net cash flows from operations to include an indirect operating presentation in its financial statements. On the other hand, because the indirect method does not disclose certain details involving operating receipts and disbursements, an enterprise that chooses the indirect method must also disclose the amounts of interest and income taxes paid during the period, either parenthetically or in the footnotes to the financial statements. The indirect operating section must also report separately the changes in inventory, receivables and payables.

Until the recent financial scandals, many readers of financial statements erroneously assumed that dishonest corporate executives could not manipulate the statement of cash flows, especially cash flows from operating activities. Because the indirect method starts with net income, however, any inaccuracies in the income statement directly affect cash flows from operating activities. In addition, numerous public companies that provide vendor financing to customers, either directly or indirectly through subsidiaries, incorrectly classified certain cash flows arising from the sale of inventory as cash flows from investing activities rather than as operating cash flows. Rapoport, *GE Cuts Past Operating Cash Flows*, Wall St. J., Mar. 7, 2005, at C3.

Both the Enron and Tyco scandals illustrate devious techniques that so-called "financial engineers" can use to manufacture fictitious operating cash flows. For example, in a series of complex transactions, usually referred to simply as "prepays", Enron treated more than $6 billion that it in effect obtained from two large banks as cash from operations rather than as loans. In the "Mahonia transactions," Mahonia Ltd. functioned as a front for Chase bank in the following manner: Enron entered into contracts that purported to sell various commodities to Mahonia, which borrowed the necessary funds to pay for the commodities from the bank. At the same time, Enron bought back the identical commodities on credit, on terms mirroring the repayment terms of Mahonia's loan from Chase, so in effect Enron took over that loan. This left Enron as the seller and purchaser of the same amounts of a commodity, at the same price, on the same day. Enron received billions in cash from the transactions, which it later paid back, with interest, to the bank. Nevertheless, Enron treated the transactions as sales that generated operating cash flows, rather than as loans giving rise to financing cash flows. In 2003, the Financial Accounting Standards Board issued a new pronouncement which provides that when such "prepays" really represent borrowing, the borrower must report all cash inflows and outflows from the transactions as financing activities.

Tyco relied upon a different technique to boost its cash flows from operations. Rather than treat as operating cash outflows the approximately $830 million Tyco spent in 2001 to buy about 800,000 individual customer contracts for its security-alarm business from a network of independent dealers, Tyco treated these amounts as investing outflows. At the same time, Tyco treated as operating cash inflows every penny of the monthly fees that those individual customers paid. Reporting those inflows as being from operations, while relegating the closely-related outflows to a non-operating category, gave a misleading picture of the net cash flow from operations. In early 2003, however, Tyco announced its plans to change the accounting treatment for the amounts expended to acquire customer accounts.

6. NONCASH INVESTING AND FINANCING ACTIVITIES

Occasionally, an enterprise will engage in an activity that does not involve a cash transfer and which, therefore, does not fall into any of the three prescribed sections. For example, an enterprise may exchange its own stock for the assets of another company. Although this exchange involves both an investing and financing activity, accounting standards do not require the enterprise to report the transaction on the statement of cash flows since cash did not change hands. Because of the possible significance of these types of events to readers of the financial statements, however, accounting standards do require any enterprise which engages in a material noncash activity to disclose the transaction in the footnotes to the financial statements. Other examples of noncash activities include converting debt to equity, acquiring assets by assuming related liabilities, entering into a lease to obtain a capital asset, exchanging noncash assets for other noncash assets, and converting preferred stock to common stock.

7.   SUMMARY OF REQUIRED DISCLOSURES

An attorney should keep in mind the disclosures described above which are required by accounting standards in connection with a statement of cash flows. First, there is the required disclosure of the enterprise's policy for determining which items it treats as cash equivalents (remember the Starbucks illustration); if an enterprise changes that policy, a change in accounting principle has occurred and the enterprise must restate any statements for earlier years which are currently included for comparative purposes. Second, a business that reports its net cash flow from operations under the direct method must disclose in footnotes what it would look like under the indirect method, while an enterprise using the indirect method must separately report changes in inventory, receivables and payables, and also must disclose in footnotes the amounts of interest and income taxes paid during the period. Third, the notes to the financial statements must disclose any material noncash investing or financing activities. Finally, accounting standards forbid the reporting of the cash flow per share figure in the financial statements.

I.   CONSOLIDATED FINANCIAL STATEMENTS

A corporation which carries on two or more businesses may own all of them directly or hold one or more in the form of a wholly- or substantially-owned subsidiary. Although corporate law treats a corporation and its subsidiaries as separate legal entities, accountants aggregate financial data for a parent company and its subsidiaries as if the parent and the subsidiaries constitute a single economic or accounting entity. Such treatment provides more meaningful information to readers: to take the simplest example, it should not make any difference in the overall evaluation of an enterprise whether one or more of its businesses is owned directly, or is held in the form of a wholly-owned subsidiary; and that is pretty much true even if the subsidiary is not wholly-owned, as long as the parent has as much control over the subsidiary as over directly-owned assets.

Accountants refer to the process of combining the accounts of two or more affiliated corporations to present a unified, composite picture of the overall enterprise as *consolidating*. Today, companies must consolidate all subsidiaries, whether foreign or domestic, which are at least majority-owned, unless control does not rest with the majority owner. Circumstances in which a corporate parent may not control a subsidiary include bankruptcy, legal reorganization, foreign exchange restrictions or other governmentally imposed limitations, or uncertainties so severe that they cast significant doubt on the parent's ability to control the subsidiary.

However, an accountant cannot simply add the assets of the affiliated corporations together because the parent's assets will include the investment in the subsidiary's stock, which reflects the subsidiary's residual ownership interest, or, in other words, the subsidiary's assets less liabilities. Similarly, an entity cannot recognize earnings by entering into revenue-producing transactions with itself: therefore, in the consolidating process the accountant or bookkeeper eliminates reciprocal accounts, that is, those which represent the relationship, or any dealing, between the parent and the subsidiary, and combines only nonreciprocal accounts.

In recent years, the subject of consolidating controlled entries virtually exploded in importance, largely as a result of the Enron scandal. Enron demonstrated that an enterprise may retain control or significant influence over an entity without holding a majority voting interest, through the use of contractual agreements, the entity's organizational instruments, or other governing documents. In its "financial engineering," Enron designed a number of so-called "special purpose entities" ("SPEs"), which appeared to be sufficiently independent but were in fact entirely under the control of Enron or its officers. Enron used these SPEs to generate manipulated profits, to conceal poorly performing assets, and to hide large amounts of debt. Following Enron's collapse, accounting standard-setters in the United States issued new rules adopting an additional test for consolidation, along with the so-called "voting interests model". Under this new "risk and rewards model, the primary beneficiary of an SPE or other such entity must consolidated it when the beneficiary receives a majority of the SPE's expected residual returns,, absorbs a majority of the entity's expected losses, or both. We will pursue this important topic in more detail in Chapter VI; here we need only an introduction to the process of consolidation.

Assume that X Corp. purchases all of Y Corp.'s stock. Before the purchase, simplified balance sheets for X and Y show the following:

X Corp
Balance Sheet, Before Transaction

Assets		Liabilities & Equity	
Cash	$300,000	Liabilities	$250,000
Plant	400,000	Common Stock	300,000
	$700,000	Retained Earnings	150,000
			$700,000

Y Corp
Balance Sheet, Before Transaction

Assets		Liabilities & Equity	
Cash	$50,000		
Plant	150,000	Common Stock	$200,000
	$200,000		$200,000

If X purchases all the Y stock for $200,000 in cash, X's balance sheet might then be:

X Corp
Balance Sheet, After Transaction

Assets		Liabilities & Equity	
Cash	$100,000	Liabilities	$250,000
Investment	200,000	Common Stock	300,000
Plant	400,000	Retained Earnings	150,000
	$700,000		$700,000

Because each share of capital stock in a corporation is a proportionate interest in the equity of the corporation and consequently an indirect interest in its net assets, X's purchase of all of Y's stock amounts to an indirect purchase of Y's net assets. If X and Y engage in related operations, we might want to show, both to the outside world and to X's stockholders, the enterprise's composite picture. Because X's investment indirectly represent's Y's assets, we can achieve this composite or *consolidated* picture by substituting Y's assets for the asset *Investment* which appears on X's balance sheet. X's balance sheet would then appear as follows:

X Corp. and Subsidiary
Consolidated Balance Sheet, after Transaction

Assets		Liabilities & Equity	
Cash	$100,000	Liabilities	$250,000
Cash (Y)	$ 50,000		
Plant (Y)	150,000	Common Stock	300,000
Plant	400,000	Retained Earnings	150,000
	$700,000		$700,000

and, after combining similar items:

X Corp. and Subsidiary
Consolidated Balance Sheet, after Transaction

Assets		Liabilities & Equity	
Cash	$150,000	Liabilities	$250,000
		Common Stock	300,000
Plant	550,000	Retained Earnings	150,000
	$700,000		$ 700,000

This last statement presents the consolidated balance sheet for X and its affiliated subsidiary, Y. Although X and Y must maintain their separate legal entities for most legal purposes, as a practical matter X could dissolve Y at any time and bring all the assets together under one corporate roof. Even without dissolution or merger, consolidating the corporations' accounts may provide a more meaningful picture—both to outsiders interested in the enterprise as a whole and to X's stockholders—about the assets that X actually controls.

We assumed, for the sake of simplicity, that Y did not owe any liabilities. Unless "intra-family" obligations between X and Y exist, the consolidation process remains about the same if Y did have debts to creditors. Assume that Y's balance sheet at the time of acquisition reflected the following financial position:

Y Corp
Balance Sheet, Before Transaction

Assets		Liabilities & Equity	
Cash	$150,000	Liabilities	$100,000
Plant	150,000	Common Stock	200,000
	$300,000		$300,000

When, as here assumed, Y has the same net assets as before, other things being equal the purchase price might also be the same. To consolidate the accounts of the two corporations, we replace the asset Investment on X's balance sheet with the actual assets and liabilities which that investment represents. This presentation provides the most meaningful picture of what the composite enterprise owns and owes as a whole. The consolidated balance sheet would appear as follows:

X Corp and Subsidiary
Consolidated Balance Sheet, After Transaction

Assets		Liabilities & Equity	
Cash	$250,000	Liabilities	$350,000
Plant	550,000	Common Stock	300,000
	$800,000	Retained Earnings	150,000
			$800,000

"Intra-family" obligations between X and Y do not belong in the composite picture. An accountant would eliminate any liabilities between X and Y in the consolidation process by canceling the receivable in one corporation's accounts against the payable on the other corporation's books.

The same consolidation procedure applies when the acquired corporation's balance sheet has retained earnings at the time of acquisition. Suppose that Y's balance sheet appeared as follows:

Y Corp
Balance Sheet, Before Transaction

Assets		Liabilities & Equity	
Cash	$50,000	Common Stock	$100,000
Plant	150,000	Retained Earnings	100,000
	$200,000		$200,000

Here again X's purchase of Y's stock amounts to an indirect acquisition of Y's net assets. The source of the subsidiary's net assets, whether capital stock, additional paid-in capital, or retained earnings, does not matter. Again, when the amount of Y's net assets remains the same as before, the purchase price for the investment might also stay the same. To accomplish the consolidation, we again replace the asset Investment on X's balance sheet with the actual assets and liabilities which that investment represents. The consolidated balance sheet would then appear as follows:

X Corp and Subsidiary
Consolidated Balance Sheet, After Transaction

Assets		Liabilities & Equity	
Cash	$150,000	Liabilities	$250,000
Plant	550,000	Common Stock	300,000
	$700,000	Retained Earnings	150,000
			$700,000

Note that the figure for retained earnings on the consolidated balance sheet does not include any of the retained earnings which appeared on Y's balance sheet at the acquisition date, just as the common stock figure on the consolidated balance sheet does not include any portion of Y's common stock account. As noted above, when X purchased all the stock of Y, X in effect bought Y's net assets by buying Y's assets and assuming its liabilities, and whether the source of Y's net assets is capital contribution or retained earnings has no effect on the consolidated picture. In other words, Y's equity at the time of X's acquisition does not belong in the composite picture

To summarize, when preparing a consolidated balance sheet the accountant or bookkeeper eliminates the parent's investment in the subsidiary, substituting instead the subsidiary's assets and liabilities, while eliminating the subsidiary's equity accounts. In addition, and among other things, the consolidation process eliminates any intercompany transactions, such as intercompany loans or intercompany sales, and reclassifies any transaction involving the sale of inventory when that is necessary to prevent recognition as operating cash inflow until a member of the consolidated group actually receives cash from an outside customer.

Thus far, we have considered only very simple consolidations. When X acquires Y's stock by issuing its own stock instead of paying cash, the accounting becomes much more complex. Additionally, in the real world, unlike our simplistic examples, the price which the acquiring corporation pays would ordinarily differ from the book value of the acquired corporation's net assets. Finally, as noted above, consolidation is not limited to 100 percent owned subsidiaries; as long as a subsidiary is at least majority-owned or controlled, consolidated financial statements may present more meaningful information than separate company statements. In such cases, the interest in the net assets of the subsidiary which the parent corporation does not own is reflected by an account on the consolidated balance sheet called *Minority Interests,* which usually appears with the long-term liabilities. For an illustration, see note 11 to Starbucks' 2005 financial statements, on page 63 in Appendix A, which includes "minority interests liability" among the company's long-term liabilities. Because these minority interests do not represent present obligations of the parent to pay cash or to distribute other assets to minority shareholders, some companies report these amounts in a section between liabilities and equity on the balance sheet. Although the basic consolidation process outlined above generally applies to less than wholly-owned subsidiaries, and also to transactions involving acquisitions for shares rather than cash, or acquisitions for amounts other than book value, these situations may call for some complicated adjustments, which for the present can be ignored.

We should also briefly mention two other presentation formats. First, it can be helpful in illustrating the process involved in consolidating financial statements to use a chart which starts with the financial statements of the two individual companies in separate columns, followed by a third column showing the eliminations, and a fourth column presenting the final consolidated financial statement. Such a chart for X and Y might appear as follows:

X Corp. and Subsidiary
Consolidating Balance Sheet

	X Corp.	Y Corp.	Eliminations	Consolidated
Assets				
Cash	$100,000	$50,000	-0-	$150,000
Investment	200,000	-0-	($200,000)	-0-
Plant	400,000	150,000	-0-	550,000
Totals	$700,000	$200,000	($200,000)	$700,000
Liabilities & Equity				
Liabilities	$250,000	-0-	-0-	$250,000
Common Stock	300,000	$200,000	($200,000)	300,000
Retained Earnings	150,000	-0-	-0-	150,000
Totals	$700,000	$200,000	($200,000)	$700,000

Second, it is often useful to aggregate the accounts of commonly-controlled companies that do not share a corporate parent, for example, so-called *brother-sister* corporations whose stock is owned by the same individual or group. The process involved in producing a combining balance sheet is much the same as for consolidating; if we assume that X has an investment in Y of $50,000, with the other $150,000 of Y's stock owned by the same individual or group that owns all of X's stock, and that X has $150,000 less in liabilities and $50,000 less in retained earnings, a combining balance sheet for X and Y might appear as follows:

X Corp. and Y Corp.
Combined Balance Sheet

	X Corp.	Y Corp.	Eliminations	Consolidated
Assets				
Cash	$100,000	$ 50,000	–0–	$150,000
Investment	50,000	–0–	($50,000)	–0–
Plant	400,000	150,000	–0–	550,000
Totals	$550,000	$200,000	($50,000)	$700,000
Liabilities & Equity				
Liabilities	$150,000	–0–	–0–	$150,000
Common Stock	300,000	$200,000	($50,000)	450,000
Retained Earnings	100,000	–0–	–0–	100,000
Totals	$550,000	$200,000	($50,000)	$700,000

J.   ILLUSTRATIVE FINANCIAL STATEMENTS

A number of references have been made in this chapter to the Starbuck's Coffee Company's consolidated financial statements for fiscal 2005, set out in Appendix A starting at page 40 Although those consolidated financial statements involve numerous complexities not present in E. Tutt's financial statements, the same principles as discussed in this chapter determined their preparation and presentation. The important difference lies in the many difficult judgment questions that large companies, particularly if publicly-owned, have to resolve when preparing their statements. We will refer to these financial statements from time to time throughout the remainder of the book.

CHAPTER II

THE DEVELOPMENT OF ACCOUNTING PRINCIPLES AND AUDITING STANDARDS

A. IMPORTANCE TO LAWYERS

Having been introduced in Chapter I to the mechanics of bookkeeping which underlie the accounting process, we turn to examine the elements of accounting that require judgment and hence make it a professional discipline.

Although we sometimes hear accountants referred to as "bean counters," the term mischaracterizes the profession. Deciding how to reflect a particular transaction, i.e., whether, to take a couple of very simple examples, to defer certain income, or accrue an expense, is subject to "rules" governing the compilation of accounting data into financial statements, plus the form and content of those statements, rules which the business community refers to as *generally accepted accounting principles* (abbreviated as *GAAP)*. Since GAAP often offers a choice among alternatives, or, conversely, does not provide a specific rule for the particular transaction at all, selecting the appropriate treatment calls for the exercise of judgment. As will be reviewed in more detail later in this chapter, historically the GAAP rules have been set by a private sector official standards-setter, which is currently the Financial Accounting Standards Board ("FASB"). We will also see that while the Securities and Exchange Commission ("SEC") can play a very important role in connection with accounting for publicly-traded enterprises, which are almost always subject to its jurisdiction, the SEC has generally deferred to the private sector's official standards-setter. In the Sarbanes-Oxley Act of 2002 ("SOx"), Pub. L. No. 107-204, 116 Stat. 745, to which repeated reference will be made throughout these materials because of the enormously important impact of the legislation on accounting for publicly-traded companies, the SEC was given express authority to recognize accounting principles established by a private standard-setting body as "generally accepted" for purposes of the federal securities laws, and the SEC designated the FASB as that body.

Subject to certain limitations, an enterprise's management makes the choice when there are acceptable accounting treatment alternatives, and decides how the enterprise will report an event when no specific rule exists. To be able to serve a client's interests, a competent lawyer must understand not only GAAP, but also GAAP's shortcomings. In addition, the notes to the financial statements address and explain the choices and judgments that management has made, so lawyers and all other users of financial statements must pay close attention to the notes.

Enterprises supply financial statements to owners, creditors, potential investors and lenders, and governmental bodies. These users want assurances that the financial statements contain reliable representations about the business's financial health. As a result, an outside accounting firm is brought in to examine independently, i.e., to audit, the financial statements that management has presented, and that independent reviewer is referred to as an "auditor". In an audit, the auditor seeks to gather evidence about the various representations made by management in the financial statements about the enterprise's assets and liabilities at a specific date, and the transactions during a particular accounting period. Ultimately, the auditor must express an opinion as to whether the financial statements fairly present the enterprise's financial condition, results of operations, and cash flows in accordance with generally accepted accounting principles.

Lawyers must understand the difference between the role of an auditor and the role of a lawyer. Responsibility to the public and independence from the client are the cornerstones of the auditing profession, whereas a lawyer generally must remain loyal to a client and keep the client's confidences.

During the audit, the auditor must act in certain ways and perform certain procedures, which accountants refer to collectively as *generally accepted auditing standards* ("GAAS"). Historically, GAAS have been set by a private sector organ, most recently the Auditing Standards Board of the American Institute of Certified Public Accountants ("AICPA"), together with custom and practice. However, in the SOx legislation Congress created the Public Company Accounting Oversight Board ("PCAOB") and authorized it to establish or adopt auditing standards for audits of publicly-traded companies (subject to SEC approval).

One of the most important steps in an audit is the auditor's assessment of the enterprise's internal accounting control. Lawyers should understand the important role that *internal control* plays in accounting and the law. Internal control refers to those systems, procedures and policies that an enterprise uses to help assure that an appropriate individual properly authorizes transactions and that, once authorized, the enterprise appropriately executes and records the transaction. If the enterprise has designed and implemented strong internal control, the auditor can better rely on the accounting records and can reduce the necessary testing otherwise applied to the data that the accounting system has produced. Even more significant to lawyers, however, poor accounting may violate the federal securities laws under the Foreign Corrupt Practices Act and its amendments, which incidentally apply to many businesses that do not engage in any operations outside the United States. Here too, SOx adds a new dimension:

an express provision in the statute requires a public corporation's management to assess it's internal controls annually and include the assessment in the enterprise's annual report, to be in turn attested to and reported on by the auditor; however, because of the considerable effort and expense entailed, the smaller public companies have been able to delay their required compliance until at least 2007.

If the examination of an entity's accounting statements satisfies the auditor that the financial statements fairly present the enterprise's financial position, operating results and cash flows in conformity with generally accepted accounting principles, then the auditor will issue an unqualified or "clean" opinion. Lawyers should understand that an auditor does not guarantee the accuracy of financial statements: even an unqualified opinion provides only "reasonable assurance" that the financial statements fairly present, in all material respects, the enterprise's financial condition, results of operations, and cash flows in conformity with generally accepted accounting principles. (The questions of whether "fairly present" and generally accepted accounting principles always coincide, and how to proceed if they don't, are dealt with a little later in this Chapter.)

In addition, lawyers should recognize that many businesses do not need audited financial statements. Nevertheless, these businesses may engage an independent accountant to perform a *review* or a *compilation*. Reviews offer only limited assurance that the financial statements fairly present the enterprise's financial position, operating results and cash flows in conformity with generally accepted accounting principles. Compilations merely report data which management has supplied, with no independent testing or review, so they provide no assurance that the financial statements provide fair representations.

Like lawyers, accountants must examine and interpret various authorities — statutes, regulations, administrative rulings and releases; but they must also look in official pronouncements of accounting bodies for answers to accounting and auditing questions. Lawyers should know where and how to find and apply these authorities, so we will be taking a closer look at them shortly.

A lawsuit involving a failed enterprise's financial statements may illustrate the difference between accounting principles and auditing standards. A plaintiff, perhaps either a shareholder who invested in the business or a creditor who made a loan to the enterprise based on its financial statements, seeks to recover from the auditor, as well as the enterprise and its management, because the financial statements prepared by the management and given an unqualified opinion by the auditor did not properly reflect the enterprise's financial condition or operating results. If the basis for the claim is that the statements included one or more accounting treatments that were misleading or inappropriate, then the complaint would be that the company did not follow GAAP and the auditor failed to object; if the claim was that there was one or more factual errors in the financial statements, then the complaint would be that the mistakes were not detected by the auditors because they failed to comply with generally accepted auditing standards. See the many examples described in section F of this chapter, Accountants' Legal Liability.

In summary, the enterprise's management and accounting staff prepare financial statements, while an independent auditor examines those statements. Whether assisting management in preparing financial statements or auditing those statements, accountants, like lawyers, must exercise judgment. As a result, lawyers should always consider accounting an art, rather than a science.

B. THE NEED FOR ACCOUNTING PRINCIPLES & AUDITING STANDARDS

Take a look at the following data relating to a hypothetical corporation, which J. Evans and C. Lewis formed in 2003 to manufacture and sell souvenir plastic cups for the 2004 Olympic Games in Athens, Greece. At the conclusion of the games, Evans and Lewis decided to liquidate the business rather than design a similar product for the 2008 Olympics. The following summary tabulates the corporation's receipts and expenditures from organization to liquidation:

Receipts		Expenditures	
Original investment	$100,000	Organization expenses	$10,000
		Office rent	60,000
Borrowings	200,000	Purchase of computer	
		equipment	25,000
Payments from		Raw materials	200,000
customers	750,000	Freight charges	10,000
		Salaries and wages	250,000
Damages collected		Utility charges	15,000
on patent		Insurance premiums	30,000
infringement	50,000	Miscellaneous expenses	25,000
		Interest paid	20,000
Interest received on		Income taxes	100,000
bank deposits	15,000	Dividends	100,000
		Repayment of loans	200,000
Proceeds of sale of		Amount left for	
computer equipment	5,000	shareholders upon	
		liquidation	75,000
Total	$1,120,000	Total	$1,120,000

Since the business venture has ended, and the corporation has sold its assets and paid its liabilities, we can easily determine how well the enterprise performed during its existence and how much the owners received on their investment. Obviously, there are no questions as to how assets and liabilities were recorded since everything has been reduced to cash; moreover, since we are in at both the beginning of the venture and its end, there are no periodic issues. If accounting involved only the orderly collection of data, and its presentation as in the simple arithmetic exercise above, no one would consider accounting a profession or devote much time to learning about it. Usually, however, financial statements are prepared by bookkeepers and accountants only for on-going enterprises—indeed, very few people care about the financial statements for a business winding up its affairs. The various parties concerned with an on-going enterprise's welfare and prospects, particularly existing and prospective investors and creditors, need a reasonably current picture of the business's financial position and results of operations, at least annually, amd usually more often. But at any point in time, at the end of any period, whether it be a year, a quarter or a month, a business will be in various stages of many different transactions. It is determining how to reflect, or "account for," these partially completed transactions in the most meaningful fashion that requires professional accounting judgment.

As noted earlier, GAAP includes the needed ground rules and guidelines for presenting various types of financial data in the financial statements. Some rules are virtually self-evident: for example, businesses should treat similar transactions similarly, so that users of financial statements can compare the financial statements with those for different enterprises, or from successive periods for the same business. But with regard to the question on the merits as to what presentation most meaningfully shows any particular type of transaction or item, reasonable minds can disagree. For example, some accountants believe that enterprises should treat costs to develop new products as assets that benefit future accounting periods, while others maintain that businesses should classify these outlays as expenses because any attempt to estimate the amount of their possible benefits beyond the current accounting period involves too much speculation. Or suppose there are two or more acceptable accounting modes: how should an enterprise choose between them? Ground rules and conventions covering these kinds of matters constitute accounting principles, and one may properly inquire as to where these principles come from, and how they become generally accepted and hence included in GAAP.

Before pursuing that topic, however, we must consider the question of who bears the ultimate responsibility for a company's financial statements, and what role the accounting profession plays in that process. Historically, the business community has always assumed that management supplies the representations in the financial statements. After all, the managers of the company are intimately acquainted with its affairs, and they are well-positioned to prepare the financial statements. One of the important functions of the financial statements, however, is to report on how the managers have employed the resources entrusted to them, and how successful they have been—their "stewardship," as it is often termed. But of course the managers are not the most objective reporters of their own performance; accordingly, from the beginning the owners of an enterprise who did not manage it often engaged independent accountants to review the records of the managers and seek to verify the financial statements prepared by these "stewards." As the ownership of business enterprises passed into the hands of disparate groups of public investors, it became all the more important to have independent accountants "audit" the managers' reports, to confirm that they were not manipulated to give an unduly rosy hue to the picture, or, even worse, to conceal improprieties.

Hence, the practice developed of having an independent public accountant—the auditor—report on management's financial statements, or in other words, express an opinion as to whether those statements were consistent with fact and presented in accordance with accounting principles which are generally accepted as sound and appropriate in the circumstances. Notice the two-fold responsibility involved in the auditing process: (1) some check on the underlying facts represented in the financial statements (e.g., physically observing inventory to test whether the company appears to have the amount of inventory recorded, and seeking evidence confirming that the company owes no more than the liabilities indicated); and (2) a review of the principles applied in portraying the information (e.g., whether a particular expenditure should be recorded as an expense of the current year). If the auditor finds that the financial statements suffer from a deficiency in any material respect, the auditor will not give an unqualified report, but instead will qualify the opinion, or perhaps even give an adverse opinion, depending upon the particular circumstances.

From management's point of view, any response other than an unqualified opinion constitutes a most unwelcome development. A qualified opinion can lower an enterprise's credit rating, discourage potential investors and creditors, attract scrutiny from governmental regulators, and generally harm the enterprise's reputation in the business community, any of which can lead to lower market value for the enterprise's securities. That could also significantly affect management's personal wealth, since most managers have a financial interest in their companies, at least in the form of outstanding stock options, if not actual investment pursuant to exercise of options or otherwise; thus, management's own stake in the enterprise, together with the desire to retain the support of the shareholders, provides a powerful incentive to obtain an unqualified opinion. For an illustration of an unqualified opinion on Starbucks Coffee Company's 2005 financial statements, see page 76 in Appendix A.

To instill greater public confidence in the role of the certified public accountants that serve as independent auditors, the various states developed standards of education and experience as minimum qualifications for accountants authorized to perform this function. For example, most states require that a certified public accountant earn an undergraduate degree in accounting, satisfy an experience requirement and pass a two-day, fifteen and one-half hour uniform exam that the AICPA administers in all fifty states. We can compare the AICPA to the American Bar Association ("ABA") in the sense that both organizations represent national, voluntary membership, trade associations. In general, both the ABA and the AICPA enjoy limited authority, but no regulatory power. Similar to the ABA's role in accrediting law schools whose graduates qualify to take the bar exam in numerous states, the AICPA administers a uniform exam.

The Sarbanes-Oxley legislation (SOx) mentioned earlier was a response to "Enronitis", and one of its central goals was to ensure that the auditors of publicly-traded firms will function independently from the subject enterprise and its management. That is because of the constant threat to an auditor's independence stemming from the fact that auditors are anxious to retain their clients' patronage. Even in publicly-traded firms that must establish audit committees to hire and fire the independent auditors, management can influence the auditor's selection and dismissal; in private firms, management may completely control the process. The demise of the once-renowned Andersen accounting firm in the course of the Enron scandal seems to have been due in no small measure to Andersen's desire to please the Enron management, which tends to lead the auditors to compromise their independence by yielding to pressure to go along with management's accounting.

As part of the audit process, the auditor's report must express an opinion as to whether the financial statements conform to generally accepted accounting principles. We turn to a more detailed review of that subject below, but first we should note that the financial reporting process for publicly-traded companies involves not only managements and independent auditors, but also audit committees, securities analysts, regulators and oversight bodies, accounting-standard setters, and the press. Since SOx also imposes new obligations on some of these participants, this is probably a sensible place for a little fuller look at this legislation which generated such great, indeed revolutionary, change in the world of accounting.

Change was certainly called for because the concerns expressed by former SEC Chairman Levitt in his remarks at pages 340- 348, *supra,* proved to be astonishingly prescient, as the years 2001 - 2003 witnessed a dizzying array of restatements of prior published financial statements of public companies, necessitated by improprieties which were either missed by the outside auditors or, occasionally, actually approved. Some of the largest companies in the country were guilty of overstating revenues, understating expenses, concealing liabilities, and the like. With the nation's financial markets badly shaken, and confidence in the whole reporting system for public enterprises at a very low ebb, in 2002 Congress responded with the SOx legislation, which recites as its purpose "[t]o protect investors by improving the accuracy and reliability of corporate disclosures made pursuant to the securities laws, and for other purposes". In its effort to strengthen the corporate governance of public enterprises and the process of auditing their financial statements, as noted above the Act completely overhauls the regulation of auditing of public companies by turning over complete control to the new Public Company Accounting Oversight Board (PCAOB), subject to the watchful eye of the SEC. Pursuant to its statutory mandate to "further the public interest" in the preparation of informative, accurate and independent reports" for investors in public companies, the PCAOB has registered all accounting firms which audit publicly-held companies, and has been carrying out its mandate to inspect them regularly (indeed, annually in the case of firms which regularly audit more than 100 issuers).

In addition, the new board will be in charge of establishing or adopting standards governing auditing, particularly including quality control and independence. Despite the relevance of auditing experience to these tasks, SOx requires that no more than two of the five members of the PCAOB be CPA's, with the further limitation that the chairman of the Board not have been a practicing CPA for at least two years prior to appointment.

The statute also directs some immediate changes in existing auditing practices. Most notable is the substantial enhancement of the role of the audit committee of the Board of Directors, which is given responsibility for hiring and firing the audit firm and generally overseeing the company's entire accounting system. Consistent with these new responsibilities, audit committee members are required to be completely independent, thereby ruling out any paid consultant as well as any affiliate of the company or a subsidiary. Congress was also much concerned with the potential impairment of auditor independence resulting from the existence of lucrative consulting contracts with auditing clients, which often produced much larger fees than the auditing; accordingly, SOx lists some eight types of consulting services which auditors are flatly barred from providing to an audit client, and requires the approval of the audit committee for the auditor to provide any other non-audit services. See Notes 5 and 6 on pages 203 - 204, *infra*.

The new statute does not take over the promulgation of accounting principles; instead, as pointed out above, the SEC was authorized to recognize a private-sector body as the institution to establish accounting principles, and as expected the FASB was designated. However, the requirement that the FASB report to the SEC annually indicates that the latter retains ultimate authority over accounting principles for public companies. In addition, it is the SEC which is directed to study the possibility of a switch to a so-called principles-based accounting system (to be discussed below), instead of the FASB's current emphasis on detailed rules governing the accounting treatment of various types of transactions.

The embrace of this new legislation goes well beyond auditors and the accounting process, dealing extensively with various aspects of corporate governance which are relevant to corporate financial regulation, and imposing a number of obligations on the top executives of public companies. Some of them have special accounting significance, particularly the requirement that the SEC adopt rules requiring each public company's principal executive officer and financial officer to certify, among other things, that as to any financial report filed with the SEC, based on such officer's knowledge the financial statements and other financial information included in the report fairly present in all material respects the financial condition of the company and results of operations. This certification very much parallels the opinion to be rendered by the auditor, but with one very important exception: the executives' certification is not limited by reference to generally accepted accounting principles. According to the SEC's release promulgating the certification requirement, Congress was seeking "assurances that the financial information disclosed in a report, viewed in its entirety, meets a standard of overall material accuracy and completeness that is broader than financial reporting requirements under generally accepted accounting principles". SEC Release No. 34-46427, 2002 WL 31720215. The release repeats the SEC's traditional view that "conformity with generally accepted accounting principles may not necessarily satisfy obligations [of full and fair disclosure under] the federal securities laws", a subject discussed in detail later in this chapter.

The financial scandals involving Enron, WorldCom, Tyco, and other companies during the early 2000s battered investor confidence. The resulting crisis in confidence, in which investors questioned the integrity of corporate financial statements, is said to have erased literally trillions of dollars in value from the stock market and cost the average U.S. household nearly $60,000. Cummings & Schroeder, Lesser-Known Candidates Head List for SEC Chief, Wall St. J. , Nov. 15, 2002, at A3. In response, many corporations, including General Electric Co., then the company with the largest market value in the world, and computer giant International Business Machines Corp., began providing more detailed financial information and disclosures about its various business operations.

C. GENERALLY ACCEPTED ACCOUNTING PRINCIPLES

Accountants define "accounting principles" as those guidelines, rules or procedures which enterprises use to prepare financial statements, and generally accepted accounting principles refer to those practices which enjoy substantial support at a particular time. GAAP reflects a consensus of what the accounting profession and financial community consider desirable, or at least appropriate, accounting practices. Even though GAAP provides rules for many situations, as noted earlier acceptable alternatives are often offered, and some situations may not be covered at all, largely because business transactions evolve more rapidly than accounting principles. For example, *derivatives*, or financial contracts whose value is based on some underlying asset, such as bonds or foreign currency, emerged in the 1980s. Accounting for transactions involving derivatives did not fit neatly into existing accounting principles, with the result that financial statements did not contain adequate disclosures about the financial risks underlying derivatives.

To summarize, management selects the accounting principles to be used in preparing the enterprise's financial statements; the independent auditor then examines the financial statements, seeking reasonable assurance that they fairly present the enterprise's financial condition, results of operations, and cash flows in accordance with GAAP. The power of the management to pressure an auditor to go along with management's accounting has been reduced by the provision in Sarbanes-Oxley which assigns to the audit committee of public companies the power to hire, fire and compensate the auditor. In addition, today public companies must disclose whether the auditor has expressed to the audit committee any concerns about the company's accounting principles, even some that may comply with GAAP. If the auditor believes that management has selected an accounting principle which does not conform with GAAP, the auditor can issue a qualified opinion, with all the adverse consequences that entails for the company.

1. THE ESTABLISHMENT OF ACCOUNTING PRINCIPLES

Since, as indicated above, the SEC has generally deferred to the accounting profession and the private sector in the establishment of accounting principles, and of course there are many privately-held businesses which do not fall within the SEC's jurisdiction but may nevertheless have to provide audited financial statements for banks, other creditors, or investors, it seems sensible to first review the development of accounting principles in the private sector, which historically is where the process began.

a.   THE PRIVATE SECTOR

The accounting profession's first formal efforts to develop accounting principles occurred in 1939, when the AICPA created two committees, the Committee on Accounting Procedure ("CAP") to determine the proper accounting approach or approaches in particular areas of concern, and the Committee on Accounting Terminology ("CAT") to submit recommendations regarding the definition of certain accounting terms and their subsequent use in financial statements. The two committees published their views in the form of Accounting Research Bulletins ("ARBs"), which were widely circulated, but these pronouncements did not bind the profession, much less anyone else. Each ARB bore the concluding comment that "the authority of the bulletins rests upon the general acceptability of opinions so reached." While promulgations from subsequent principle-setting groups have modified many of these early statements, others remain in force today.

Although the ARBs represented a useful start, the absence of any significant amount of supporting research meant that they simply represented a consensus of committee members, reflecting their experiences and viewpoints. The ARBs frequently approved alternative practices or otherwise equivocated, reflecting the compromises on conclusions and wording necessary to obtain the required two-thirds vote of the committee members.

In an effort to give more effective leadership in the determination of accounting principles, the AICPA established the Accounting Principles Board ("APB") in 1959. The APB's membership included AICPA members, mostly in public practice, with representatives from each of the largest accounting firms, at that time the "Big Eight," plus a number from smaller firms and some from academia. Supported by a greatly expanded research capacity, the APB considered, and reached some conclusions on, basic concepts and accounting principles. The Board also tried to resolve the more important problem areas involving accounting practices and financial reporting, in an attempt "to narrow the areas of difference and inconsistency in practice". By the time the AICPA dissolved the APB in 1973, the Board had issued thirty-one "Opinions" and four "Statements," which defined and narrowed the acceptable parameters of accounting methodology. In these materials, we will refer to APB Opinions as "APB Op. No.—" or merely "APB No.—."

Beginning in the late 1960s, the AICPA authorized the Institute's staff to issue "AICPA accounting interpretations" to provide guidance on a timely basis about accounting questions having general interest to the profession without the formal procedures which the APB's rules required.

Despite the added research dimension, the APB suffered from some of the same deficiencies which marked its predecessor. The compromises needed to secure the required two-thirds vote of the members often led to results that failed to satisfy anyone and sometimes produced long delays in reaching any conclusion. There was also continuing disquiet about whether the practicing members could sufficiently divorce themselves from their major clients' desires on various issues.

In an effort to improve the process, in 1971, the AICPA appointed a Committee on the Establishment of Accounting Principles. Pursuant to that committee's recommendations, the accounting profession created the Financial Accounting Standards Board in 1972 as a new body to replace the APB as the organization responsible for determining and promulgating accounting principles.

The FASB differs from its predecessors in that it exists independently from the AICPA. The controlling organization is the Financial Accounting Foundation ("FAF"), an independent charitable corporation, whose sixteen trustees appoint the FASB's seven full-time members to staggered five year terms. The Board's members typically include three public accountants, two corporate executives, one financial analyst and one academic. To assure independence, the FASB's members must terminate all other employment ties in exchange for a generous salary, which amounted to $575,000 for the chairman and $468,000 for the six other members in 2004.

Eleven of the sixteen FAF trustees come from eight sponsoring organizations: three from the AICPA, a total of three from two associations of government accountants, and one each from five other groups, such as accounting educators and financial executives. Those eleven in turn appoint the additional five trustees.

The FAF trustees also appoint, from the sponsoring organization s' various constituencies, approximately thirty members of the Financial Accounting Standards Advisory Council ("FASAC"), which functions as an advisory body to the FASB on pending and proposed projects. In 2002, as a result of the then recent accounting scandals, the FASB established the User Advisory Council ("UAC") to increase the participation in the accounting standards-setting process by securities analysts and other users of financial statements, like mutual funds, banks, and rating agencies. The UAC offers advice on agenda priorities and specific projects, particularly those that could affect the financial information available to users.

The FAF and FASB initially had to rely upon contributions and sales of publications to fund their operations, and increasing pressures to offer free, electronic access to FASB materials had begun to present potentially serious financial problems. That has now changed pursuant to section 109 of SOx, which requires issuers to pay an annual support fee to fund the FASB's operations now that the SEC has designated the FASB as the private standard-setting body that may establish "generally accepted accounting principles" for federal securities law purposes.

The FASB operates under two basic premises in establishing financial accounting standards. First, the Board attempts to respond to the needs and viewpoints of the entire economic community, not just the public accounting profession. Second, the Board strives to operate in full public view through a "due process" system that gives interested persons ample opportunity to share their views. Under the FASB's due process procedures, the Board works from a public agenda that its constituencies help to establish, employs a technical staff to research and analyze various issues and solutions, puts out detailed discussion memoranda which attempt to focus issues under consideration by the Board, publishes exposure drafts of contemplated pronouncements, conducts public hearings, and promulgates formal Statements of Financial Accounting Standards when a majority of the seven FASB members approve the pronouncement. These materials will refer to FASB Statements as "SFAS No.—," "FASB Statement No.—," or "FASB No.—."

The FASB also develops and issues authoritative pronouncements other than the Statements. The FASB's Interpretations seek to clarify the application of its Statements (and of any outstanding APB Opinions and ARBs, which the FASB's rules treat as continuing in force until amended or replaced by an FASB Statement). FASB Interpretations modify or extend existing accounting standards and carry the same authority as FASB statements. There are also Statements of Financial Accounting Concepts ("Concepts"), which set forth fundamental objectives and concepts that the Board plans to use in developing future financial accounting and reporting standards. Accountants use these Concepts to formulate accounting treatments when the FASB has not spoken on an issue.

Over the years, the FASB has adopted a "problem approach" toward setting accounting standards. Areas and issues where disparities already exist in accounting treatments usually comprise the Board's agenda. The FASB has only rarely acted before a dispute arises. In 1984, the FASB created the Emerging Issues Task Force ("EITF") with fourteen members drawn from the profession, to deal with short-term accounting issues so that the FASB can work on more pervasive long-term problems.

If the EITF can reach a consensus, with no more than two members disagreeing with the proposed treatment, the FASB will not take any further action. The SEC's Chief Accountant has stated that the SEC staff will challenge any accounting that differs from a EITF consensus position because that represents the best thinking on issues for which there are no specific authoritative pronouncements.

Rule 203 of the AICPA's Code of Professional Conduct assures the FASB a more authoritative role in setting accounting standards than its predecessors enjoyed: as a matter of professional ethics members cannot express an opinion that financial statements conform with generally accepted accounting principles if the statements contain any departure from an accounting principle which the FASB has sanctioned, including ARBs and APB Opinions which the FASB has not revoked or amended, and if such departure materially affects the statements taken as a whole. An earlier rule had only required accountants to disclose any departure from a principle which the APB had approved. The rule does recognize a single exception: when the auditor believes that conformity with a sanctioned accounting principle would result in a misleading financial statement, in which event the auditor must disclose the departure and its effects. Auditors have almost never asserted the exception.

Although the AICPA can admonish, suspend or expel a member for violating the Code of Professional Conduct, the Institute cannot bar a person from practicing accounting because only state accountancy boards can grant or revoke an accountant's license to practice. Nevertheless, potential liability for misrepresentation, fraud, or other legally recognizable claims deters an auditor from issuing an unqualified opinion if the financial statements contain a material departure from GAAP.

Until late 2002 various committee of the AICPA, particularly the Accounting Standards Executive Committee ("AcSEC"), helped to establish accounting principles by promulgating Industry Guides specific to particular industries, and Statements of Position ("SOP's") to influence the development of new accounting and reporting standards, or to propose revisions or clarifications of existing standards. However, in an effort to streamline the accounting rule-making process, FASB announced that AcSEC would stop issuing statements that create GAAP.

b.   SECURITIES AND EXCHANGE COMMISSION

The enactment of the Securities Act of 1933 and the Securities Exchange Act of 1934 tremendously boosted the significance of accounting within the business community. Congress enacted those laws in response to the 1929 stock market crash and sought to ensure that investors in public companies could rely on financial statements, particularly those of companies whose stocks were traded in the nation's securities markets. The SEC was given the responsibility to oversee the reporting requirements for companies subject to its jurisdiction, which is the basis for the assumption noted earlier that the SEC has the authority to prescribe accounting rules for the financial statements which enterprises must file with the Commission, and perhaps for all financial statements for those businesses.

The federal securities laws generally require any business proposing to issue securities to the public to file financial statements with the SEC. In addition, similar requirements apply to *registrants,* a term which includes most of the country's largest corporations, specifically those companies whose shares are listed on a national securities exchange, such as the New York Stock Exchange or Nasdaq, as well as any entity with at least $10 million in assets *and* 500 or more owners of any class of equity securities. 17 C.F.R. § 240.12g–1 (2003). Registrants generally must file a quarterly report, Form 10-Q, within thirty-five days after the end of a fiscal quarter, and an annual report, Form 10-K, within sixty days after the end of a fiscal year. In addition, registrants must file a current report, Form 8-K, within two business days after certain significant events which could have a substantial impact upon the financial position of the enterprise.

As mentioned earlier, the SEC has usually left the development of accounting principles to the private sector. This historical practice was confirmed in SOx section 108, which expressly allows the SEC to recognize as "generally accepted" for purposes of the federal securities laws any accounting principles established by a private standard setting body that meets certain criteria. It was under this provision that, as noted earlier, in

2003 the SEC, having determined that the FASB and its parent FAF satisfied the criteria, designated the FASB's financial accounting and reporting standards as generally accepted for purposes of federal securities law. The SEC stated that it would continue to monitor FASB's procedures, qualifications, capabilities, activities, and results. Commission Statement of Policy Reaffirming the Status of FASB as a Designated Private-Sector Standard Setter, Financial Reporting Release No. 70 (2003), *available at* http://www.sec.gov/rules/policy/33-8221.htm.

However, the SEC has by no means remained entirely passive in connection with the development of accounting principles, and years ago had specifically noted that there was "always the possibility that the Commission may conclude it cannot accept an FASB standard in a particular area". Notable examples include the SEC's decision in 1978 to reject the FASB's approach to income recognition in the oil and gas industry, and, more recently, issues involving executive compensation and derivatives in the 1990s. In the most recent illustration of the SEC's primacy, in 2005, as described on page 138, *infra*, the Commission overruled the FASB and allowed companies an additional six months to comply with the Board's new requirement that stock options be expensed, after the FASB had already granted one six-month extension, and had rejected the SEC's request for an additional six-month delay.

Immediately after the original revelations that WorldCom had engaged in a staggering $3.8 billion fraud (which later turned out to be as much as $11 billion!), the SEC issued an order requiring the senior officers at the 900 or so largest public companies to file sworn statements regarding the accuracy of their company's financial statements. Congress codified similar requirements in Sarbanes-Oxley: section 302 requires the chief executive and the top financial officers of a registrant to certify in each quarterly and annual report that the report does not contain any material misrepresentations or omissions, and that the financial information included in the report fairly presents in all material respects the entity's financial condition and results of operations. SOx section 906 adds a provision to the criminal laws containing a separate certification requirement that creates new criminal penalties for a knowing or willful false certification. SOx also requires the SEC to review all public companies at least once every three years, and in 2005 the agency reviewed more than 6,000 of the 18,000 that report to the SEC, as the first three-year cycle ended.

More generally, the SEC imposes numerous reporting and disclosure requirements pursuant to its Regulation S-X, which contains lengthy and detailed provisions prescribing the specific items which must be disclosed or addressed in financial statements filed with the Commission by registrants (other than those which qualify as "small business issuers"). In addition, over the years the SEC has issued many types of releases relating to accounting topics, including particularly Accounting Series Releases

("ASRs"), which express the opinions of the Commission and its Chief Accountant (who probably qualifies as the most influential accountant in the world), with respect to various accounting and financial reporting issues. More than three hundred ASRs had been published by 1982, when the SEC promulgated the "Codification of Financial Reporting Policies," to consolidate the accounting positions in the ASRs. The Commission also announced that to update the Codification it would use Financial Reporting Releases ("FRRs"), of which some seventy had been issued by June 30, 2003, mostly addressing problem areas the profession has failed to deal with.

One other type of release is the Staff Accounting Bulletin ("SAB"), which is used to present interpretations and practices followed by the Chief Accountant and the Division of Corporate Finance in reviewing financial statements. Though SABs do not carry the Commission's official approval, they do provide useful guidance. In 1981 SAB No. 4 codified the prior SAB's; subsequent SAB's are integrated into the Codification by using questions and staff interpretations.

The SEC also exerts significant influence over the financial statements which registrants do not file with the Commission, notably the annual report which corporations customarily send to shareholders. Under federal securities laws, registrants that solicit proxies in connection with an annual meeting at which the shareholders will elect directors must send, either previously or concurrently, an annual report satisfying detailed requirements; registrants must send substantially equivalent information to security holders even if proxies are not solicited.

Despite the consistent use of the word "principles" in describing the current accounting regime, *e.g.* GAAP, in fact over the years standard setters in the United States have relied upon rather specific rules in establishing the governing standards. Although the specific, detailed provisions that result from this approach can give helpful guidance, that very detail can allow enterprises to structure transactions to circumvent a rule's intent. In contrast, other countries and, as we shall see, international accounting standards setters have adopted an approach that articulates broad principles and policies, and relies more on professional judgment to decide how any particular transaction should be presented. The latter is generally referred to as "principles-based", while the U.S. system is termed "rules-based". In the aftermath of Enron's financial engineering, Sarbanes-Oxley directed the SEC to conduct a study to determine whether the financial reporting system in the United States should switch to a principles-based standard-setting process, and to submit a report to Congress within one year.

In July, 2003 the SEC's staff issued the mandated report, which concludes that a combination of the two approaches, sometimes referred to as "objectives-oriented", offered the best approach to establishing accounting standards. The SEC staff warns that under a rule-based system, exceptions, bright-line tests, and internal inconsistencies can cause financial reporting to degenerate into "an act of compliance rather than an act of communication." At the other extreme, principles alone typically offer insufficient guidance to financial statement preparers and auditors, leaving room for too much subjective judgment when applying the broad standards to specific transactions and events. As a result, a principles-only approach could reduce comparability among enterprises, and also invite more litigation with both regulators and private plaintiffs.

The SEC staff's idea of an optimal standard is a concise statement of substantive accounting principle, derived from a coherent conceptual framework of financial reporting. The statement should include the accounting objective, provide sufficient detail and structure so that users can apply the standard on a consistent basis, and avoid exceptions and percentage tests that might allow financial engineers to achieve technical compliance while evading the standard's intent. The report acknowledges that neither generally accepted accounting principles in the United States nor current international accounting standards follow the "objectives-oriented" standards as described, but notes that U.S. standard setters have already begun to shift in that direction. STUDY PURSUANT TO SECTION 108(d) OF THE SARBANES-OXLEY ACT, *available at* http://www. sec. gov/news/studies/principlesbasedstand.htm.

c. CONGRESS

It seems implicit that Congress, having enacted the federal securities laws and granted the SEC the power to prescribe accounting principles, also retains the right to legislate on accounting principles and standards. Even though Congress has only rarely, if ever, mandated any specific accounting treatment, Congress has used its legislative power to influence the SEC, the FASB, the AICPA and the financial community.

The continuing controversy over the accounting treatment of stock options perhaps best illustrates how Congress can influence accounting standards. Stock options give corporate executives and employees the right to purchase the corporation's shares at a fixed price in the future. As early as 1993, the FASB proposed rules which would have required corporations to treat the value of these stock options as compensation expense on the income statement. The FASB reasoned that stock options were simply a non-cash form of paying for services. In the past, accounting standards did not require companies to record the grant of a stock option as an expense as long as the option price was not below the market price of the stock at the time of the grant. After legislators introduced bills in both the House of Representatives and the Senate to preclude the FASB from acting, on the grounds that the rule change would negatively affect small companies in the technology industry which rely heavily on stock options to attract and retain personnel, the Board changed its position.   Ultimately, the FASB issued SFAS No. 123, *Accounting for Stock-Based Compensation*, which merely encourages corporations to treat stock options as an expense based on their fair market value on the date the options are granted, leaving companies free not to expense options as long as they supply additional disclosure in the notes to the financial statements.

The issue heated up again when the FASB voted to put accounting for stock options on its agenda after the financial frauds at Enron, WorldCom, Tyco, and other public companies.   Once again lawmakers rushed into action, introducing legislation in both the House of Representatives and the Senate to prevent for three years any new rule on how to account for stock options. At one point, the House actually approved a narrower bill, which would have limited any required expensing of stock options to those awarded to a company's top five executives.   On the opposite side of the stock option debate, several Senators introduced legislation that would have pressured companies to expense stock options by prohibiting any tax deduction for stock options unless the company included the expense on its income statement for financial accounting purposes.

In any event, this time the FASB persisted, and in 2004 adopted Statement 123R, which originally mandated stock option expensing starting in 2005, but was subsequently revised to postpone the starting date to the first interim or annual period beginning after June 15, 2005 (or after December 15, 2005 for small business issuers).   Faced with a number of complex issues in complying with this new requirement, particularly questions of how to value the stock options, while also struggling with the other new demands of Sarbanes-Oxley, especially with respect to internal controls, issuers sought a further delay in the starting date, but the FASB refused, even after the SEC joined in the request.   However, the SEC decided to move on its own, announcing on April 14, 2005 adoption of a new rule giving companies a six-months reprieve.   The new starting date was the first quarter of a company's next fiscal year beginning after June 15, 2005, so a calendar year company did not have to implement the new requirement until the first quarter of 2006, although those with fiscal year ending on or after June 15 had to start sooner.

It now appears that the risk of legislative interference with accounting for stock options has abated, although those difficult questions with respect to valuation of the options, among others, remain to be worked out.   However, the combined efforts of the profession and the regulators should prove equal to the task, and perhaps this episode will make legislative intervention in any accounting matters less likely in the future.

d. INTERNATIONAL ACCOUNTING STANDARDS COMMITTEE

In today's global economy, investors, businesses and their lawyers need to understand local financial accounting and reporting practices. Different taxation systems, economic conditions, political processes and cultural traditions contribute to a diversity in accounting practices between nations in matters such as inventory valuation, depreciation, consolidations, and disclosure requirements. While serving as the chairman of the SEC in the early 1990s, Richard C. Breeden estimated that about eighteen percent of foreign companies would report more income on financial reports under U.S. standards than they did under their own countries' standards. In contrast, about thirty-three percent would report less under U.S. standards. Although these variations often occur on a country-by-country basis, they can differ from company-to-company in a particular country. Kirchheimer, *SEC Chief Accountant Offers New Definition Of 'Asset,'* TAX NOTES, Jan. 18, 1993, at 338-9.

To illustrate further, recall that U.S. accounting standards generally follow the historical cost principle to report assets; but in many foreign countries, particularly nations experiencing high inflationary rates, businesses record their assets at current value. As another example, German and Japanese businesses have traditionally relied upon banks rather than the equity markets for financing: accordingly, the needs of creditors, rather than investors, have disproportionately influenced the financial reporting in those two countries relative to the United States.

The international business community needs and wants globally accepted accounting practices to facilitate the flow of capital between markets. Multinational enterprises around the world, especially in Germany, Switzerland and other European countries, increasingly seek to raise capital across borders and to list their securities on more than one stock market. As of 2003, some 1400 foreign companies had registered here in the United States with the SEC. These enterprises would prefer to use one set of accounting rules worldwide, so that they do not have to bear the burden and expense of reconciling financial statements prepared using their home country's accounting principles to generally accepted accounting principles in the U.S. or other jurisdictions. At the same time, the New York Stock Exchange and exchanges in Canada, Europe, London and Japan have been pressing for international accounting rules.

Serious efforts to harmonize accounting standards world-wide got started in 1973, when an agreement among professional accountancy bodies from most of the developed countries, including the United States, established the International Accounting Standards Committee ("IASC"), and within a few years every country with a professional accountancy body had become a member. As of 1987, most of the standards issued by the IASC's board had been relatively loose, permitting optional treatment, and so they were largely ignored by the founder countries, who by then had developed their own accounting standards, which they viewed as superior. However, in 1988 the IASC, with strong support from the International Organization of

Securities Commissions (IOSCO), started reviewing its earlier standards to eliminate most of the optional treatments, to enhance the required disclosures, and to specify in greater detail how each standard was to be interpreted. As of 1997 the IASC and IOSCO agreed to develop and endorse international accounting standards, and within a year the SEC had decided to provide some guidance, having concluded that the push for global harmonization could ultimately make the IASC standards relevant in the U.S. securities markets. The SEC announced that to be acceptable in the U.S. IASC standards must:

(1) include a core set of accounting pronouncements that constitute a comprehensive, generally accepted basis of accounting;
(2) be of "high quality", in that they provide transparency, compatibility and full disclosure;
(3) be rigorously interpreted and enforced.

In 2000 the IASC's standards resulting from that review of the earlier ones, plus a few new standards, were endorsed by IOSCO, with the understanding that each country's securities regulators could impose additional requirements, including reconciliation of IASC-based financial statements with the country's own GAAP, akin to reconciliation of their statements with U.S. GAAP that the SEC requires of foreign registrants.

In that same year, as urged by the SEC, the IASC restructured itself into a more independent body, along the lines of the FASB, in order to earn legitimacy in the eyes of the world's capital markets. There is an independent foundation run by trustees, paralleling the FAF in the U.S., and they select the members of IASC's board, now formally designated as the International Accounting Standards Board (IASB), which has sole responsibility for setting accounting standards. In an important change from IASC's previous structure, twelve of the fourteen members of the Board must be full-time employees of the Board, severing all employment relationships with their former employers and holding no position with economic incentives that might call into question their independence of judgment in setting accounting standards.

The Board will follow the FASB practice of publishing an exposure draft for public comment and considering any comments before issuing final International Accounting Standards ("IASs"), sometimes referred to as International Financial Reporting Standards.

The Board also has two associated panels, one of which, the Standards Interpretation Committee ("SIC"), can decide "contentious" accounting issues arising in the application of IASs. In essence, SIC will perform the same function for IASC as the Emerging Issues Task Force does for the FASB: that is, interpret IASs, publish draft interpretations for public comment, consider timely comments before finalizing an interpretation, and obtain IASC Board approval for final interpretations. The other panel, the Standards Advisory

Council ("SAC"), will assist the Board on agenda decisions and priorities for the Board's work, and advise on major rulemaking projects.

In its new format the IASB wasted no time in demonstrating that it intends to be a major player on the global accounting scene, tackling before the end of 2002 perhaps the toughest current topic of all, accounting for employee stock options, and by 2004 had decided to require expensing. In the meantime, the European Union approved a regulation requiring all listed companies in the EU to adopt IASB standards in their financial statements by 2005. Under the aegis of the European Commission, a whole new support structure has emerged for screening new IASB standards on both a technical and political level. The former is provided by the European Financial Reporting Advisory Group, set up by private interests and supplied with an expert group from practice and academia to advise on the technical propriety of a proposed standard. The political input comes from an Accounting Regulatory Committee consisting of representatives from the fifteen EU governments. Query if this Committee will be subjected to the same sort of lobbying by multinational corporations and trade associations that, as noted earlier, has befallen Congress on occasion: a particular basis for concern is the provision in the EU's accounting regulation to the effect that the EC "should take into account the importance of avoiding competitive disadvantages for European companies operating in the global marketplace," presumably an effort to preclude any IASB standard that might lead to lower net income figures than some other accounting system, such as U.S. GAAP.

This EU provision was probably provoked in large measure by the prospect of a requirement that stock options be recorded as expenses on a corporation's income statement, which both the IASB and the FASB were considering, but the IASB seemed to be moving more quickly than the FASB. The IASB did indeed adopt the proposed rule first, denominated International Financial Reporting Standard 2 (IFRS 2), but the rule did not become binding until after appropriate confirmation by the EU. That required presentation to the EU member states by the European Commission, which initially held off the vote because of objections from industry. However, after the EU's Accounting Regulatory Committee (ARC), which advises the European Commission on adoption of international accounting standards, gave a favorable opinion on the proposal, it was submitted to, and received the approval of, the member states in December, 2004, and was endorsed by the European Parliament in 2005. In the meantime, in the U.S. the FASB had caught up, having determined in 2004 to require stock option expensing. Though as detailed at page 138, *supra,* the starting date in the U.S. for implementation was postponed a couple of times, it does appear that convergence on this issue has been achieved.

Another potentially serious obstacle to full accounting convergence, especially between the U.S. and Europe, may well have been averted because, as discussed at pages 173-174, *infra,* SOx seems to have confirmed that conformity to GAAP does not necessarily satisfy the accounting objective to "present fairly" the financial picture of an enterprise. That has never been an issue in the United Kingdom, which, though more closely paralleling U.S. accounting standards than any other country does, has long made the requirement of a "true and fair" presentation the ultimate test, and the U.K. approach was adopted by the EU early on.   To be sure, a test as general as "true and fair" is somewhat subject to the "eye of the beholder", and hence it is not surprising that the interpretation of the phrase can vary substantially from country to country. Thus, the use of reserves to "smooth" earnings may be regarded as entirely "fair" in one country, while in another such a practice might be viewed quite critically, as former SEC chairman Levitt did, in his oft-cited remarks quoted in Chapter 6.   But adherents to the "true and fair" test generally agree that when compliance with the applicable accounting principles leads to a statement that does not fully and fairly portray the financial condition and results of operations of an enterprise, an override of the stated principles is called for.

In theory, the literal posture of the two systems was not so different even before SOx: IAS No. 1 ordains full compliance with all accounting standards and applicable interpretations except in the "extremely rare circumstances" when application of a standard would result in misleading financial statements; under Rule 203 of the AICPA Code of Ethics, the "strong presumption" in favor of adherence to officially established accounting principles can be overcome in "unusual circumstances", when literal application of principles would render financial statements misleading. However, in practice British accountants have been more willing than their U.S. counterparts to exercise the override exception. To encourage the practice further, back in 1981 the U.K. amended its Companies Act to *require* affirmative departures from otherwise applicable standards if necessary to achieve a true and fair presentation. On the other hand, there is a problem with easy departure from express rules, since that can just as readily support efforts to escape a rule that actually should be applied, but is very much undesired. Indeed, Australia, which had initially followed the U.K. approach, reversed course and dropped the override technique in favor of a requirement to add any information necessary to give a true and fair view.

The governing EU regulation, formally termed the Fourth Directive, leaves member states with some flexibility as to how best to achieve the required true and fair picture, and the responses have varied from the preference of a few for strict compliance with stated accounting rules, to allowing clarifying additional information, to permitting, if not requiring, an actual override if necessary, or allowing each company a choice between the last two. And in the EU context, it must be recalled, with its inherent language translation aspect, "true and fair" takes on various shades of meaning, occasionally even being reduced in effect to a single word, like "faithful". In addition, in some countries accounting developed largely as a necessary element of taxation, and that continues to influence the interpretation of true and fair.

These multiple variations have led one thoughtful commentator to suggest that the increasingly important cash flow statement may afford an opportunity to bridge the gaps among competing accounting systems in the quest for harmonization. Cunningham, *Semiotics, Hermeneutics, and Cash: An Essay on the True and Fair View*, 28 N.C.J. Int'l L.& Com. Reg. 893 (2003). Professor Cunningham observes that cash flow statements are not affected by most accounting differences, and are far less tied to particular accounting systems. This could reduce the impact of the differences between the U.S. and the U.K. accounting systems, both of which developed largely from practice by the profession and are aimed mostly at the equity capital markets, and also between the U.S. and the accounting systems of the other European countries (and Japan), which were mainly established by law, and were largely influenced by the needs of creditors and tax reporting.

Another barrier to global convergence of accounting systems is the fact that, as discussed on page 136, *supra*, the U.S. approach is based upon specific and elaborate rules, while the rest of the world prefers to rely upon broader, more general principles. Indeed, in 2004 the chairman of the IASB pronounced this difference the biggest obstacle to full convergence. However, as described on pages 136-137, pursuant to a directive in SOx the SEC undertook a study to determine if a switch from rules-based to principles-based accounting standards in the U.S. would be desirable, and concluded that an approach partway between the two, which it called "objectives-oriented", would be the best course. Perhaps this can provide the common ground for overcoming this difference between the IASB and the FASB.

One other hurdle for global convergence of accounting systems lies in the realm of enforcement of the applicable standards. On that score the U.S. has historically been well ahead of other countries, due to the strong role of the SEC, with its broad administrative and regulatory powers; but the U.K. and its close cousins in Canada and Australia have been moving in that direction, with the development of either public or private sector institutions which provide some oversight of company compliance with accounting standards. In the EU, the EC saw that the necessary stronger regulation of financial reporting was likely to be most effectively achieved within the framework of securities regulation. The result was the promulgation in 2002 of a proposed Statement of Principles of Enforcement of Accounting Standards in Europe by a committee of European securities regulators, which was designed to assist member states in the development of their securities law regulation, including the effort to achieve conformity with accounting standards.

In the meantime, the IASB has been busily engaged in developing additional international standards in a number of important areas. Its formal agenda up to 2005 had included consolidation and the treatment of special purpose entities, lease accounting, and a joint project with the U.K.'s Accounting Standards Board on a proposed radical revision of the format in which income and other measures of enterprise performance would be presented in financial statements; at the same time, the IASB is also completing the revision of its first twelve accounting standards. Indeed, so full was the IASB's plate in 2003 that the Board scheduled a "quiet period" between 2004 and 2006, during which no new accounting changes would be required, so that some 7000 European public companies would have a chance to catch up with the international standards adopted to date.

At the same time, the push toward global convergence continues at a steady pace. For example, the FASB is working in tandem with the IASB on (1) the very different format for the portrayal of operating performance referred to in the previous paragraph, (2) revenue recognition, and (3) business combinations. In addition, the IASB and the FASB are carrying on a "short-term project on convergence," seeking to reach agreement on a substantial number of less significant accounting differences between the two systems, such as the computation of earnings per share, or accounting for income taxes, simply by one of the two sides agreeing to adopt the approach of the other.

As indicated above, the SEC has been supportive of these harmonization efforts, while attempting to insure that any final joint product is of sufficiently high quality to meet its standards. The SEC also paid special respect to the development of international accounting standards in its recent release adopting the rules requiring certification of financial statements by corporate officers, described in section B above. The release cites IAS 1 in support of the conclusion that a basic standard for financial disclosure, like "fairly presents", goes beyond compliance with generally accepted accounting principles, and takes account of other elements " in determining whether an issuer's financial information, taken as a whole, provides a fair presentation of its financial condition and results of operations." Securities Act Release 8124, Fed. Sec. L. Rep. (2002 Transfer Binder) ¶ 86,720 at 86, 126, n. 56.

As the movement toward harmonization continues, some have wondered about the FASB's long-term future, but for the time being it seems clear the FASB will continue to assume an important role in standard-setting. One possibility is a two-tier reporting system in the United States, under which multinational firms would use international accounting standards, while domestic companies would continue to apply U.S. GAAP. Critics, however, complain that such a scenario would create an unlevel playing field in accounting. *See generally* Cox, *Regulatory Duopoly in U.S. Securities Markets*, 99 COLUM. L. REV. 1200, 1202, 1214 n.35 (1999) (concluding that the SEC should continue to promote convergence between IASs and U.S. GAAP and describing the biggest political issue as whether to limit IASs to foreign issuers or to permit domestic firms to use IASs to satisfy SEC reporting requirements).

The effort to achieve convergence got a strong boost in October, 2004, with the approval of a joint project of the IASB and the FASB aimed at developing a common conceptual framework. In February, 2005 the staffs of the two boards produced a draft plan to establish project phases and a five-year timetable for the undertaking. Herzfeld, *FASB Sets Five-Year Plan to Complete Conceptual Framework Project with IASB*, 37 Sec. Reg. & L. Rep. 381 (Feb. 28, 2005). Another plus came in April, 2005, when the E.U. internal market commissioner and the SEC Chairman agreed on a "roadmap" for eliminating the requirement that foreign issuers using International Financial Reporting Standards reconcile their statements with U.S. GAAP. The goal agreed to by the SEC is to end the reconciliation requirement as soon as possible, but by 2009 at the latest. 37 Sec. Reg. & L. Rep. 748 (April 25, 2005).

2. HOW DO ACCOUNTING PRINCIPLES BECOME "GENERALLY ACCEPTED?"

You will recall that the term "accounting principles" refers to the rules, procedures and conventions that enterprises use to maintain accounting records and to prepare financial statements. The phrase "generally accepted accounting principles" connotes those conventions, rules and procedures which represent accepted accounting practice at a particular time. Experience, reason, custom, usage and practical necessity develop these principles. As a result, GAAP evolves and changes. Furthermore, to say that an accounting method conforms with GAAP does not imply precision: GAAP often leaves considerable leeway, and sometimes may not provide any definite rules for treating transactions. In addition, various federal and state laws may also require an enterprise to file financial reports with regulatory agencies which require accounting treatments differing from GAAP. Here is what the Supreme Court said on the subject in *Shalala v. Guernsey Memorial Hospital*, 514 U.S. 87, 101, 115 S.Ct. 1232, 1239, 131 L.Ed.2d 106, 119-120 (1995):

> Financial accounting is not a science. It addresses many questions as to which the answers are uncertain, and is a "process [that] involves continuous judgments and estimates." * * *
>
> GAAP is not the lucid or encyclopedic set of pre-existing rules that the dissent might perceive it to be. Far from a single-source accounting rulebook, GAAP "encompasses the conventions, rules, and procedures that define accepted accounting practice at a particular point in time." GAAP changes and, even at any one point, is often indeterminate. "[T]he determination that a particular accounting principle is generally accepted may be difficult because no single source exists for all principles." There are 19 different GAAP sources, any number of which might present conflicting treatments of a particular accounting question. When such conflicts arise, the accountant is directed to consult an elaborate hierarchy of GAAP sources to determine which treatment to follow.

a.   THE HIERARCHY

As we have already stated, an interrelationship exists between accounting principles and auditing standards. Auditing standards require an auditor to opine in the audit report whether the financial statements fairly present the enterprise's financial position and results of operations and cash flows in conformity with GAAP. Accountants generally agree on the basic characteristics that GAAP possess. Unfortunately, no single source supplies or details GAAP. To help the auditor determine whether a particular rule, procedure or treatment enjoys general acceptability and hence whether the financial statements conform to GAAP, auditing standards establish a hierarchy which lists five categories of sources for accounting principles and ranks those categories from highest to lowest levels of authority.

In the United States, the highest level of authority, which accountants refer to as "Category (a)," belongs to those principles officially promulgated by a body that the AICPA Council has designated to establish such principles under Rule 203 of the AICPA Code of Professional Conduct. As a result, this top level includes FASB Statements; FASB Interpretations; APB Opinions and their Interpretations which the FASB has not superseded; and nonsuperseded ARBs. In addition, the SEC's rules and interpretative releases carry a status similar to Category (a) for SEC registrants.

Category (b), the next highest level of authority, includes pronouncements from bodies of expert accountants that deliberate accounting issues in public forums to establish accounting principles or to describe existing accounting practices that qualify as generally accepted. To qualify in this Category (b), however, the relevant body must have exposed the pronouncement for public comment, and a body which qualifies to establish Category (a) principles must have cleared the pronouncement.

The third highest level of authority, "Category (c)," includes (1) those pronouncements from bodies of expert accountants that were formed by a Category (a) organization, and that deliberate accounting issues in public forums to establish or interpret accounting principles or to describe existing accounting practices that qualify as generally accepted, and (2) pronouncements that would otherwise qualify for Category (b) except that the promulgating body did not expose the pronouncement for public comment.

The final two levels include the knowledgeable application of generally accepted pronouncements to specific circumstances plus practices that accountants acknowledge as enjoying general acceptance, and, finally, other accounting literature.

b.   REGULATORY ACCOUNTING PRACTICES

Over the years, various federal and state governmental bodies and agencies that regulate certain industries, such as banks, thrifts, credit unions, utilities, and insurance companies, have issued their own accounting rules and requirements for businesses subject to their jurisdiction. Although the governmental organizations usually based these regulatory accounting practices ("RAP") on GAAP, RAP often modified or supplemented GAAP. As a result, differences between GAAP and RAP often required businesses in regulated industries to prepare separate financial statements, and in some instances to keep separate sets of accounting records, for financial accounting and regulatory purposes. In *Shalala v. Guernsey Memorial Hospital,* page 145, *supra,* the Supreme Court's opinion explicitly recognized that GAAP's underlying goal to inform investors does not always advance regulatory objectives.

3. WHO SELECTS AMONG GENERALLY ACCEPTED ACCOUNTING PRINCIPLES?

As we have heard, GAAP often sanctions alternative treatments for the same transaction. Given the various permissible choices, one academic calculated that in a typical income statement a business enterprise could select from more than a million possible bottom lines. Moreover, the fact that established accounting principles and other accounting literature do not, and indeed could not, address every conceivable situation leaves additional choices. Consequently, the question becomes: Who selects among the permissible alternatives?

We have already heard the answer: Accounting practice has long placed the responsibility for an enterprise's financial statements on management. As a result, management chooses, in the first instance, the accounting principles from among the acceptable alternatives or selects an accounting treatment when established principles do not apply to a transaction or event. However, an independent auditor who examines the financial statements may be able to influence management's selection of accounting principles. As we will be discussing in more detail shortly, if an auditor believes that the accounting principles that management has chosen do not fairly present the enterprise's financial condition, its operating results or its cash flows, the auditor can threaten to issue a qualified opinion, which can significantly and negatively affect an enterprise's financial status.

However, keep in mind that prior to the enactment of SOx in 2002 selection of the independent auditor was usually controlled, at least indirectly, by the enterprise's management, which was therefore in position to exercise pressure by threatening to terminate the auditor's engagement. This ability of management to go looking for an auditor who would acquiesce in a questionable accounting treatment, often referred to as "opinion shopping", was somewhat curtailed when the SEC adopted rules requiring full disclosure of the circumstances by a registrant upon any change in auditors, plus a letter from the former auditor to the SEC commenting on the statements made by the registrant in its report. More recently, the SEC in connection with the stock exchanges had been working both to strengthen the role of audit committees of the board of directors, particularly in connection with hiring and firing auditors, and to enhance the independence of the members of the audit committee. On the other hand, as mentioned earlier, in these later years lucrative consulting contracts had become a more important source of revenue to auditors than auditing, thus restoring, if not increasing, the pressure on auditors to go along with management's desired accounting treatment. In any event, the enactment of SOx in 2002 codified the reform efforts, thereby changing the picture dramatically with those provisions noted above: (1) making the hiring and firing of auditors the exclusive province of the audit committee of the board of directors, which cannot include any member of management or any other interested director, and must have at least one financial expert or explain the reason why not; and (2) drastically limiting the types of consulting services auditors can take on for audit clients and requiring approval by the audit committee for services not absolutely barred.

Pursuant to its authority under SOx, the SEC has adopted rules implementing, among others, the statutory requirement relating to a financial expert on the audit committee. The rule requires companies to disclose whether at least one "audit committee financial expert" serves on the committee, and if so, to state whether the person qualifies as independent of the company's management.

The change from the statutory term "financial expert" to "audit committee financial expert" came after the SEC's first proposed rules as to what type of experience qualified a person as a "financial expert" were criticized as too narrow, and the SEC concluded that the more distinct lab el of "audit committee financial expert" better suggests that the designated person should have experience specifically applicable to his role on the audit committee. Under the rules, an "audit committee financial expert":

- Understands generally accepted accounting principles and financial statements;
- Can assess the general application of such principles in connection with the accounting for estimates, accruals and reserves;
- Has experience preparing, auditing, analyzing or evaluating financial statements that present a breadth and level of complexity of accounting issues that are generally comparable to those that can reasonably be expected to be raised by the registrant's financial statements, or experience actively supervising one or more persons engaged in such activities;
- Can evaluate internal controls and procedures for financial reporting; and
- Possesses an understanding of audit committee functions.

Importantly, the SEC created a safe harbor provision for individuals identified by their companies' boards of directors as audit committee financial experts, by providing that a person so identified incurs no additional duties, obligations or liability in excess of the duties, obligations and liability each member of the board of directors normally assumes. Further, designating an expert does not diminish the responsibilities or liability of the non-expert members of the audit committee and board of directors.

PROBLEMS

2.1A. Suppose that the Nifty–Novelty "management" in Problem 1.6A on pages 99 - 100, *supra*, had decided not to defer the sales income involved in the transaction of February 8, on the ground that "these things even up over time." As the outside auditor, how would you respond?

2.1B. Suppose that the Camera Sales "management" in Problem 1.6B on pages101 - 103, *supra*, had decided not to accrue the salaries for the second half of the month on the ground that "these things even up over time." As the outside auditor, how would you respond?

D.   GENERALLY ACCEPTED AUDITING STANDARDS

We have already noted that an audit involves a process whereby an independent accountant examines an enterprise's financial statements and expresses an opinion regarding whether the financial statements fairly present, in all material respects, the enterprise's financial position, results of operations and cash flows in conformity with GAAP. In that way, auditors provide some assurance to the investing public as to the reliability and credibility of financial statements.

This is particularly important to the shareholders of a corporation, who, through the board of directors, in effect function as principals that hire the corporation's management as agents to operate the business. The interests of the principal and the agent can often diverge: for example, an enterprise's management may want to keep their jobs, even though their continued employment may not further the principals' best interests. Indeed, in some situations the shareholders would likely replace management if the shareholders knew all relevant information about the existing management's past efforts and results. As we saw earlier, however, the ultimate responsibility for an enterprise's financial statements rests with management, which either prepares the financial statements or oversees their preparation.

In most situations, an absent principal does not enjoy the agent's access to information. As a result, the absent principal encounters *information risk*, that is, the chance that the agent has not shared all details relevant to the relationship, leading principals to want an independent monitor's services to reduce information risk. The agent (management) is willing to accept such monitoring arrangements because it can reduce the information risk to the principal, which in turn will lower the cost of capital for the agent because the lower risk means that the principal will accept a lower return. For this reason, the demand for auditing services would exist, and does exist, even absent the regulatory requirement that publicly-traded enterprises file audited financial statements with the SEC.

An equally important reason for audits is the desire of the various users of financial statements, including owners, creditors, potential investors and lenders, and regulatory bodies, for assurances that the financial statements accurately portray the enterprise's financial condition and operating results. In an audit, therefore, the auditor seeks to verify the underlying transactions and events reported in the financial statements, and to test the application of GAAP to those facts. For this reason, the Supreme Court has described auditors as "public watchdogs," in the *Arthur Young & Co.* case described on the next page.

During an audit, the auditor must follow certain standards and perform certain procedures, which accountants refer to collectively as "auditing standards." In some areas Congress has explicitly given the SEC the power to mandate certain auditing standards. More generally, the federal securities laws have probably conveyed, at least implicitly, power to establish standards for auditing registrants. To date, however, the SEC has only occasionally established auditing standards, so it has been mostly the accounting profession, through the AICPA's Auditing Standards Board, which has determined "generally accepted auditing standards" or "GAAS." And of course from now on, establishing auditing standards will be in the domain of the PCAOB, subject to approval by the SEC.

If the examination allows the auditor to develop reasonable assurance that the financial statements fairly present the enterprise's financial position, operating results and cash flows in conformity with GAAP, the auditor will issue an unqualified or "clean" opinion. If the auditor cannot reach this comfort level, then the auditor will issue either a qualified opinion or an adverse opinion, or disclaim an opinion. Lawyers should understand, however, that even an unqualified opinion does not guarantee the financial statements' accuracy. An unqualified opinion provides only reasonable assurance about the financial statements because of course auditors do not purport to check every transaction, and the necessary resort to "sampling" often translates to testing five percent or less of a company's total annual transactions.

1. THE INDEPENDENT AUDITOR'S ROLE

By requiring that a report from an independent auditor accompany financial statements that registrants file with the Commission, the SEC has endorsed the accounting profession's role as the auditor of management's statements. But the role is not available to an accountant who lacks independence or objectivity—for example, if the CPA's firm, or a member of the firm, owns a direct, or material indirect, financial interest in the registrant or any parent entities, subsidiaries or other affiliates, or holds a close connection with the registrant as a director, officer, or employee.

a. INDEPENDENCE

To see why independence is so important for the auditing profession, we must understand the distinct role that auditors play and appreciate the difference between the responsibilities of an auditor and those of an attorney. Basically, lawyers act as advocates, while auditors serve as independent attestators: in essence, an auditor must treat the financial markets, rather than the enterprise undergoing the audit or its management, as the real client.

In *United States v. Arthur Young & Co.*, 465 U.S. 805, 104 S.Ct. 1495, 79 L.Ed.3d 826 (1984), the Supreme Court's description of the role of independent auditors, in holding that an auditor must disclose audit workpapers in response to a subpoena from the Internal Revenue Service, was in sharp contrast to the role of attorneys as confidential advisors and advocates for clients, with a duty of loyalty which requires the lawyer to present the client's case in the most favorable possible light. The Supreme Court wrote:

> By certifying the public reports that collectively depict a corporation's financial status, the independent auditor assumes a public responsibility transcending any employment relationship with the client. The independent public accountant performing this special function owes ultimate allegiance to the corporation's creditors and stockholders, as well as to the investing public. This "public watchdog" function demands that the accountant maintain total independence from the client at all times and requires complete fidelity to the public trust.

465 U.S. at 817-18, 104 S.Ct. at 1503, 79 L.Ed.2d at 835-36.

To maintain the public's confidence in our system, an auditor must remain independent. To do so, and thereby avoid violating SEC rules and professional standards, auditors must not only comply with the strict financial interest limitations already noted, but must also satisfy the requirement of both intellectual honesty and honesty in appearance. To qualify as honest in appearance, an auditor must avoid any circumstance that a reasonable person might consider likely to influence independence adversely. For example, the general public might question an auditor's independence if the auditor's spouse worked for the client even though the auditor exercised intellectual honesty during the audit. Other examples of compromised independence include owning stock in a client, simultaneously representing the client as an attorney, participating in an audit after accepting an employment offer from the client, and accepting business or personal loans from a client.

The independence requirement recently forced many of the 140,000 employees of Price Waterhouse and Coopers Lybrand to sell investments in the audit clients of the other firm prior to the merger which created PricewaterhouseCoopers. These employees faced reduced choices for reinvesting the proceeds from these sales because the merged firm will audit about a quarter of all publicly traded companies and more than half the mutual funds in the United States.

Recall the reference on page 128, *supra*, to the temptation posed by lucrative consulting contracts that can threaten an auditor's independence, and the antidote provided by SOx, described in more detail on pages 203-204, *infra*. For years before SOx came along the accounting profession, with the support of the SEC, had been trying to strengthen independence standards, leading to the creation of a separate panel within the AICPA, the Independence Standards Board (ISB). Consistent with its policy of looking to the private sector for leadership in establishing accounting principles and auditing standards, the SEC agreed to accept the independence standards set by the ISB. Of course, that role will now be played by the new Public Company Accounting Oversight Board (PCAOB), whose responsibility in overseeing firms which audit public companies includes establishing rules regarding independence, along with audit performance, quality control, and ethics.

b. THE AUDIT PROCESS

Financial statements represent assertions that fall into five broad categories: (1) that reported assets and liabilities exist and that recorded transactions occurred during the particular accounting period; (2) that the financial statements present all transactions and accounts; (3) that the listed assets represent the enterprise's rights and the reported liabilities show the business's obligations; (4) that the financial statements record the enterprise's assets, liabilities, revenues and expenses at appropriate amounts; and (5) that the enterprise has properly classified, described and disclosed the financial statements' components. EVIDENTIAL MATTER, Statement on Auditing Standards No. 31 (American Inst. of Certified Pub. Accountants 1980). An audit gathers evidence about these five assertions.

At one time in history, auditors reviewed each transaction during the period which the financial statements covered to ensure that the enterprise properly recorded each transaction. As commerce developed, however, the number of transactions grew and became too numerous to review individually. Today, auditors rely on the enterprise's internal controls over its accounting processes, plus sampling techniques to test selected transactions, to obtain reasonable assurance that the financial statements do not contain any material misstatement. Internal control refers to those systems, procedures and policies which an enterprise uses to ensure that an appropriate individual authorizes all transactions and that the enterprise properly executes and records those transactions.

As the number of transactions actually reviewed decreases, an auditor's professional judgment becomes exceedingly important. In seeking the reasonable assurance that the financial statements do not contain any material misstatements or omissions, auditors strive to design an effective and efficient audit that holds *audit risk* below a reasonable level. Audit risk refers to the possibility that an auditor will unknowingly fail to detect materially misleading financial statements.

Because GAAS does not define "reasonable assurance," the standard depends on the facts and circumstances underlying a particular audit engagement. Although the same auditor may examine a business's financial statements every year, each audit probably will vary in scope and detail. Accepted auditing practices require the auditor to assemble sufficient evidence to form an opinion regarding whether the financial statements fairly present the client's financial condition and operating results. An auditor, however, may encounter various problems during the audit. For example, the client's management or employees may not follow internal control procedures. Mistakes can always be made. In the sample testing by the auditor, observed deviations may indicate larger, more significant problems. Auditors rely on their experience and professional judgment to decide whether such deficiencies likely indicate a material error in the financial statements. Until the auditor issues the audit report, the auditor must constantly exercise professional judgment, and, if necessary, modify the audit strategy to attain the requisite reasonable assurance.

A standard audit includes three phases: planning the audit, implementing the audit program, and reporting the results. We will discuss them in order.

(1) Planning the Audit and Assessing Internal Control

To plan an audit properly, the auditor must gather information about the client and assess the enterprise's internal control before developing an audit program. After accepting an audit engagement, the independent auditor will investigate the client's business and accounting policies. In this process, the auditor will gather information about conditions in the industry, the business's products or services, sales trends, major customers, production and marketing techniques, characteristics of management, personnel, budgeting and accounting systems, affiliations with outside influences, such as foreign governments or political groups, and similar matters. In particular, the auditor will review prior years' audit results.

During this phase, the auditor will also obtain and document an understanding of the client's accounting system. Generally accepted auditing standards require the auditor to assess the enterprise's *internal control*, which, as noted above, means those systems, procedures and policies that an enterprise employs to help assure that the organization properly authorizes, executes and records transactions. Those mechanisms for internal control include both administrative controls, consisting of an enterprise's plan of organization, procedures, and records that lead up to management's authorization of transactions, and accounting controls, including the plans, procedures and records which the enterprise uses to safeguard assets and produce reliable financial records.

An enterprise's internal controls should segregate the responsibilities for authorizing and recording transactions and safeguarding assets between different individuals to detect errors and prevent fraud, thereby insuring greater accuracy and reliability in the accounting records and financial statements. Illustrative internal controls include cash registers that display prices and totals to customers and allow management to total all transactions during a shift to discourage clerks from "pocketing" sales revenues; consecutive numbers on checks, purchase orders and invoices to allow better accountability; rules that require certain employees, especially in banks and other financial institutions, to take continuous, two-week vacations each year to reduce the chance that those employees can hide any irregularities; arrangements that require at least two authorized individuals to sign any check exceeding a certain amount; the division of accounting functions so that different individuals write checks and reconcile bank statements against the cash account; and the separation of purchasing, receiving and accounting functions so that the same individual does not order, accept and pay for goods.

As a practical matter, auditors rely extensively on client internal controls because as we know an audit cannot test every transaction. Accordingly, the auditor performs compliance tests to determine whether the internal controls function properly. The auditor may also examine sample transactions or records to ascertain how accurately the client's financial and accounting systems document transactions. In a process which accountants refer to as *vouching*, an auditor selects a transaction recorded in the business's books to determine whether underlying data supports the recorded entry. Alternatively, an auditor may use a process known as *tracing*, which involves following a particular item of data through the accounting and bookkeeping process to determine whether the business has properly recorded and accounted for the data. Based upon this evaluation, the auditor decides whether to rely on some or all of the internal control systems to reduce the need to test actual transactions and account balances. To the extent that the business does not regularly observe the internal controls or those controls do not adequately prevent errors or frauds, however, the auditor must design auditing procedures which gather additional audit evidence to permit the auditor to render an opinion regarding the financial statements.

Over the years, there has been a constant effort to strengthen internal controls. But clients have often resisted spending the time, effort, and funds that might be necessary to significantly upgrade their internal control systems. At one point a Board created by the AICPA went so far as to recommend that the SEC require registrants to include two reports — the first by management and the second from the registrant's independent accountant — on the effectiveness of the enterprise's internal control system relating to financial reporting. As we shall see shortly, that is in effect just what SOx now requires. However, at the time the ABA Committee on Law and Accounting recommended against an enterprise voluntarily issuing a report on its internal control because "such reports are 'liability documents' of uncertain but potentially broad scope." *Management Reports on Internal Control: A Legal Perspective*, 49 Bus. Law. 889, 929 (1994).

a) INTERNAL CONTROL UNDER THE FEDERAL SECURITIES LAW

In the meantime, federal securities laws came to play a greater role in bringing about improved internal control systems. In particular, inadequate internal accounting controls or poor record-keeping can violate the Foreign Corrupt Practices Act of 1977 (the "1977 FCPA") and the 1988 Amendments (collectively, the "FCPA"). Notwithstanding their titles, these statutory provisions apply to all SEC registrants, including enterprises that engage only in domestic operations.

In the 1977 FCPA, Congress responded to the discovery that U.S. companies had bribed foreign officials and engaged in disreputable conduct to secure business in other countries. That legislation contained two parts: antibribery provisions and accounting requirements. Presumably, Congress enacted the accounting rules to improve corporate accountability on the theory that any failure in record-keeping or internal controls threatened the disclosure requirements under the federal securities laws.

In any event, the FCPA imposes two distinct accounting requirements on all registrants, including those that do not engage in any operations outside the United States. First is the record-keeping obligation, which requires all registrants to "make and keep books, records, and accounts, which, in reasonable detail, accurately and fairly reflect the transactions and dispositions of the assets of the issuer." Under this provision, the SEC promulgated two rules, one prohibiting any person from falsifying any book, record or account which the statute requires, and the other forbidding any officer or director from, directly or indirectly, making a materially false or misleading statement or failing to state a material fact to an accountant in connection with any audit or other required filing.

Second, to establish adequate internal accounting controls all registrants must "devise and maintain a system of internal accounting controls sufficient to provide reasonable assurances" that the enterprise: (1) executes transactions in accordance with management's authorization, (2) records transactions in a way that enables the enterprise to prepare financial statements in conformity with GAAP, and to maintain accountability for assets; (3) permits access to assets only in accordance with management's authorization; and (4) compares recorded assets against actual assets at reasonable intervals and takes appropriate action regarding any differences. These four clauses were taken from an authoritative accounting promulgation offering guidance to auditors as to what they should be looking for in evaluating internal control during an audit; but notice the big difference here, in that the FCPA provisions directly impose a statutory obligation on registrants, and hence their managements, to comply with the requirements.

Congress amended the 1977 FCPA in 1988 to provide that the "reasonable detail" and "reasonable assurances" with which registrants must keep "books, records, and accounts" and maintain the requisite internal controls, respectively, mean "such level of detail and degree of assurance as would satisfy prudent officials in the conduct of their own affairs", while also limiting criminal liability to knowing violations. In one of its Accounting Bulletins the SEC staff has reminded registrants that immaterial but intentional misstatements can indeed violate the FCPA record-keeping and internal controls requirements.

In 1998, a private sector group issued a report highlighting recent regulatory and legal developments that increasingly compel businesses to focus on internal fraud detection. As basic principles in the "battle against fraud and other illegal activity," the report identifies setting the tone at the top through example and communication to create a clear policy against improper conduct, explicitly focusing on fraud risk, and developing an effective communication process between directors, officers, senior managers and employees.

Although a company's top management bears the initial responsibility to develop and implement adequate internal controls, and, when necessary, revise them, overall oversight falls to the board of directors, who often rely on lawyers for advice. Internal controls work effectively only when those who bear responsibility for developing, implementing, and overseeing those controls stress the need to adhere to all policies and procedures and set a good example themselves. Strong internal controls enhance the likelihood that the enterprise will engage in sound, beneficial transactions, and reduce the chances that an enterprise will incur the enormous losses that can result from internal control failures. Some notable examples from the 90's include the $2.6 billion in losses from unauthorized copper transactions suffered by Sumitomo Corp., a Japanese trading concern, Daiwa Bank's $1.1 billion in losses from unauthorized bond trading over an eleven-year period, and numerous instances of unauthorized trading in derivatives, like the $1 billion loss which led to the failure of the British investment bank Barings PLC.

For a more recent example, we need look no further than Enron, where some of the controls were inadequate, but others that were in place were not followed. First, when Enron's board approved a policy that allowed the company to enter into transactions with certain entities owned by Enron officers, the implementing procedures explicitly required management to use a "Deal Approval Sheet." By requiring certain disclosures and the approval of Enron's chief executive officer, the Deal Approval Sheets sought to ensure that the contractual provisions in such transactions would closely resemble the terms that would have materialized in an arm's-length transaction. In fact, the chief executive officer's signature does not appear on the sheets for several specific transactions, and the absence of any sheet for other transactions suggests that Enron did not complete any in those cases. Second, when Fastow, Enron's former chief financial officer, reportedly earned more than $30 million from partnerships that entered into transactions with Enron, the board failed to require that he report those profits from the partnerships to the company; such disclosures almost certainly would have alerted the board to the possibility that the underlying transactions unfairly benefitted Fastow, to the detriment of Enron and its shareholders.

Congress reacted to the revelations about lax internal controls at Enron and other large companies by requiring in SOx section 404 that the SEC create and enforce regulations intended to foster a more stringent internal control environment in public companies. That provision also directed the SEC to adopt rules requiring public companies to include in the annual financial statement a report from management on the company's internal control over its operations, particularly the authorization and recording of transactions, i.e., the data which constitutes the raw material for financial reporting: the required report must (1) state management's responsibility for establishing and maintaining an adequate internal control structure and procedures for financial reporting; and (2) contain an assessment, as of the end of the company's most recent fiscal year, of the effectiveness of the company's internal controls and procedures. In addition, the registered public accounting firm that audits the company must attest to, and report on, management's assessment of the company's internal controls, pursuant to standards that the PCAOB will set. After the SEC had adopted these required new rules, the Director of the Division of Corporation Finance, speaking to an ABA meeting of corporate lawyers, asserted that these rules mark the most important development in SOx, will cause the biggest impact on attorneys, and will require a greater commitment of money and time than any other regulation resulting from SOx.

For purposes of implementing these provisions, the SEC has defined "internal control over financial reporting" as a process designed by, or under the supervision of, a company's principal executive and principal financial officers, which the company's board of directors implements to provide reasonable assurance regarding the reliability of financial reporting and the preparation of financial statements for external purposes in accordance with GAAP. These controls include procedures to ensure that a company maintains records which reasonably reflect the company's transactions and dispositions of assets, and provide assurance that those records will enable the company to prepare financial statements in accordance with GAAP. Further, internal controls should aim to make sure that a company's receipts and expenditures have been appropriately authorized by management or the board of directors, and should provide reasonable assurance that unauthorized acquisition, use or disposition of the company's assets cannot occur without detection.

The requirement noted above that the firm which audits the company's books must also make the attestation report regarding internal controls increases the risk of auditor liability because auditors formerly tested internal controls before the end of each reporting period, but now they must attest to their quality as of the last date of the reporting period. Thus, auditors cannot claim that errors in their reports result from management making changes in internal controls after the auditor's review.

b) IMPACT OF THE NEW SOX RULES REGARDING INTERNAL CONTROL

The starting date for these new rules for the largest public companies, referred to as "accelerated filers" (i.e., companies that have a public float of at least $75 million, have been subject to the SEC's periodic reporting for at least 12 months, and are not eligible to use the SEC's small business reporting forms), was originally fiscal years ending after November 15, 2004 (extended to December 30, 2004 for smaller companies in this category). For the smaller public companies, so-called "non-accelerated filers", the deadline for compliance with the new rules, has already been extended several times, taking it to two years beyond the originally scheduled first fiscal year ending on or after July 15, 2003, and the SEC has announced plans for yet one more short extension. However, the SEC has resisted calls for providing a different, milder requirement for such companies, rejecting the recommendation of its Advisory Committee on Smaller Public Companies made in 2006, and announcing instead that "ultimately, all public companies will be required to comply with the internal control reporting requirements". The SEC anticipates that even non-accelerated filers will be filing reports for fiscal years beginning on or after December 16, 2006.

In any event, the large companies and their auditors were faced with applying these new rules for their 2004 financial statements. It is probably fair to say that these new internal control requirements have occasioned more complaints by companies and their auditors than all the other SOx provisions combined. The core of the objections has been the very large increase in the cost of both internal accounting and outside auditors, plus the considerable drain on the time and energy of senior management. Some surveys have indicated that the accounting costs, both inside and outside, increased fifty percent or more, not counting the high-priced time of top executives. The regulators were not unsympathetic to these complaints, but pointed out that large numbers of deficiencies in internal controls were being detected, and often remedied: although many of the deficiencies discovered were not very significant, SEC officials observed that of the more than 2,500 internal controls reports filed by March 31, 2005, eight percent reported deficiencies which fit the statutory test of "material weakness". Bologna, Official Seeks to Calm Fears over Internal Controls Problems, 37 Sec. Reg. & L. Rep. 749 (April 25, 2005). Nevertheless, critics continued to argue that the additional burdens, financial and otherwise, imposed upon the companies far outweighed the benefits, and sought legislative relief. That seems unlikely to be forthcoming, particularly in view of a survey of financial executives showing that about seventy-five percent of them believed that their companies benefitted, and internal controls were improved, as a result of compliance with these SOx requirements that management assess the company's internal controls, and that the independent auditor report on that assessment; a smaller percentage of those surveyed, but still a majority, felt that despite the substantial increase in cost it was a good use of corporate funds in the interest of shareholders. 2004 Oversight Systems Financial Executive Report on Sarbanes-Oxley Compliance, referred to by SEC Commissioner Glassman, according to McTague, 37 Sec. Reg. & L. Rep. 378 (Feb. 28, 2005).

Needless to say, from the outset the new PCAOB has been actively reviewing this very contentious area, and in March, 2004 the Board issued Auditing Standard No. 2 (AS 2), which in June received the approval of the SEC, as required by SOx section 103. AS 2 was intended to provide guidance for accounting firms in discharging the responsibility they have under SOx section 404 to report on a company's internal controls and management's assessment of their effectiveness. AS 2 was not a great success. Critics claimed that much of the increased costs imposed by this new requirement came from what they saw as a mandate in AS 2 that auditors do substantial testing of a public company's internal control themselves, rather than relying to a considerable extent on the company's internal accountants. In addition, AS 2 was thought by many to take an overly rigid approach to the responsibilities of auditors in implementing this new internal controls obligation, leading to the fear that perhaps auditors would be expected to check virtually every element of internal control in every case, as if pursuant to a checklist. In various forums, PCAOB representatives sought to mollify these concerns, disclaiming any notion that AS 2 contemplated a checklist, or "one size fits all", approach. It was also pointed out that adapting to a new regimen is always more expensive and complicated at the outset. Nevertheless, there did seem to be evidence that, because of the very serious potential consequences for a failure to comply with SOx section 404, auditors were adopting a very conservative, risk-averse approach, interpreting the requirements too strictly, spending too much time on non-critical controls, and failing to communicate with the inside accountants and thereby avoid unnecessary duplication. It was clear that more guidance from the regulators was called for, and both the PCAOB and the SEC responded, with separate releases in mid-May, 2005. The PCAOB took the lead, with a policy statement which focuses on the scope of the internal controls audit, and how much testing is required. These issues were described as the primary drivers of cost, and hence in need of prompt attention in order to be of help in the 2005 audit process. The policy statement primarily tells auditors to:

1. integrate an audit of internal controls with the audit of the company's financial statements;

2. exercise judgment in planning an audit of internal controls so as to focus on the risks faced by the particular client rather than a scatter-shot reliance on checklists, making it possible to minimize the attention given to accounts which have only a remote possibility of material misstatement;

3. use the work of others wherever feasible; and

4. communicate fully with the management and the internal accountants of audit clients.

As to the communication point, the Board wanted to make it clear that extensive interchange with an audit client does not necessarily threaten the auditor's independence, as had been feared by many. In an interview, the PCAOB chairman sought to illuminate the line between proper and inappropriate communication: an auditor should not answer questions for an audit client who acknowledges that it does not know how a particular internal control works, because the auditor would end up inspecting its own work; but if a client describes what it is planning to do with respect to a particular control and asks what the auditor thinks, there is no reason for the auditor not to give a full response.

The SEC release was entirely consistent with the PCAOB's, emphasizing in particular that it is the responsibility of management to determine the appropriate form and level of internal controls. The SEC also suggested that in making the required disclosure of any material weakness that may have been discovered, it would be desirable to indicate the impact that the weakness could have on the company's financial reporting, and, if it has not been remedied, management's plans for doing so. It should be noted that disclosure of any material weaknesses discovered is required even if they have been remedied by the time of the auditor's review of management's assessment, but in such cases disclosure of how they were remedied should be included. In any event, the regulators have urged that investors not overreact to disclosures of material weaknesses, but rather take comfort in the fact that they have been discovered. Most recently, in May, 2006, the

SEC announced new efforts to improve implementation of the new internal control rules, including additional guidance for companies and auditors, and oversight of the 2006 PCAOB inspection program, which is to focus on whether auditors had achieved cost-saving efficiencies.

(2) Implementing the Audit Program

After gathering information about the client and assessing the internal controls, the auditor develops a plan, which accountants refer to as the *audit program*, which sets forth the detailed procedures that the auditor will perform to test transactions and account balances to reach that reasonable assurance that the financial statements present fairly, in all material respects, the business's financial condition and operating results. Based on the information that the auditor has gathered about the client and the internal control, the auditor makes a preliminary materiality judgment and risk assessment which determine the nature, timing, and extent of the procedures which the auditor will perform during the engagement. Most large auditing firms use a standard audit program which they tailor to each engagement according to the reliability of the internal controls and the specific audit risks that the client presents.

Professional standards require an auditor to obtain sufficient competent evidence, either through inspection, observation, inquiries, or confirmations, to reach an opinion about the financial statements. In a typical audit, the auditor verifies that tangible assets exist, observes business activities, confirms account balances, checks mathematical computations, and seeks representations from management and outside counsel. The audit procedures may include substantive testing where the auditor uses statistical sampling to test the financial records. For example, in auditing the accounts receivable ledger, which contains information about all customers that owe money to the client, an auditor might select customers on a random basis to confirm their outstanding balances.

The auditor documents the various procedures and findings in audit *working papers*, which lawyers may hear referred to as "workpapers." In any legal dispute involving a failed audit or other accounting issue, a lawyer will want to examine the working papers, which contain the schedules, memoranda and analyses which the auditor prepared while carrying out the various audit procedures and tests, the corresponding results and information obtained, and the pertinent conclusions reached regarding significant matters.

During an audit, the auditor constantly examines the findings to determine whether they provide a "reasonable basis" to enable the auditor to express an opinion on the financial statements. If the findings have not reached that level, the auditor must conduct additional tests or procedures.

For example, suppose that the auditor selects twenty random customers to confirm their outstanding balances and six customers affirmatively disagree with the balances which appear in the client's accounting records. In those circumstances, the auditor must exercise "professional skepticism" and expand the test sample or seek alternative procedures to gain assurance that the accounting system properly recorded the accounts receivable.

(3) Reporting the Audit Results

As the most important step in the audit process, the auditor prepares an audit report which represents the audit's end product. The standard audit report states that:

(1) the financial statements remain management's responsibility;

(2) based on the audit, the auditor will express an opinion on the financial statements;

(3) the auditor conducted the audit in accordance with generally accepted auditing standards which require the auditor to plan and perform the audit to obtain reasonable assurance that the financial statements do not contain material misstatements; and

(4) the financial statements present fairly, in all material respects, the financial position, the results of operations, and cash flows, in conformity with generally accepted accounting principles.

We will discuss the standard audit report in greater detail later.

2. THE ESTABLISHMENT OF GENERALLY ACCEPTED AUDITING STANDARDS

As in the case of accounting principles, under the federal securities laws the SEC probably has the power to dictate standards for audits involving reporting companies. Even more so than with accounting principles, the SEC has deferred to the accounting profession with respect to auditing standards. Although, as noted above, the accounting profession turned the responsibility to develop and promulgate GAAP over to a body separate from the AICPA (currently the FASB), the corresponding duty to set auditing standards remained with the AICPA through the Auditing Standards Board ("ASB"), until SOx came along in 2002 and delegated complete power over auditing standards to the newly-created PCAOB. However, some of the intervening history is instructive, so we turn to a brief review of the pre-SOx development of auditing standards.

Modern audit procedures trace their development to a famous scandal and failed audit involving McKesson & Robbins Incorporated, a company whose shares were traded on the New York Stock Exchange. Price, Waterhouse & Co. audited the financial statements for McKesson & Robbins and its subsidiaries for the year ended December 31, 1937. The consolidated financial statements reported total assets exceeding $87 million. This total, however, contained approximately $19 million in fictitious assets, including about $10 million in feigned inventories and approximately $9 million in fabricated receivables. For 1937, fictitious sales amounted to more than $18 million on which the consolidated income statement reported fictitious gross profit exceeding $1.8 million.

To accomplish this fraud, Philip M. Musica, a previously convicted swindler who served as the corporation's president under the alias Frank Donald Coster, and his three brothers devised a clever scheme. McKesson & Robbins pretended to purchase merchandise from fictitious vendors that supposedly retained the goods for shipment directly to the corporation's customers. The perpetrators also prepared invoices to document fabricated sales to customers. Musica caused McKesson & Robbins to issue checks to the fictitious vendors, intercepted and cashed the checks, and used the proceeds for partial payments to the corporation on the fabricated sales to customers. Musica and his assistants, however, pocketed about $2.8 million in the scheme. Because the auditors did not observe the inventories or confirm the receivables, the audit did not detect the fraud.

The SEC held administrative hearings to review this failed audit, and issued a report which concluded that

> Auditing procedures relating to the inspection of inventories and confirmation of receivables, which, prior to our hearings, had been considered optional steps, should . . . be accepted as normal auditing procedures in connection with the presentation of comprehensive and dependable financial statements to investors.

The Private Securities Litigation Reform Act of 1995 specifically requires any audit which the securities laws mandate to include, among other things, procedures designed to provide reasonable assurance that the audit will detect any illegal acts that would directly and materially affect the determination of financial statement amounts. In addition, the legislation specifically gives the Commission authority to modify or supplement certain generally accepted auditing standards in at least three areas—illegal acts, related party transactions, and the registrant's ability to continue as a going concern—and a financial reporting release expressed the SEC's desire to alert auditors and issuers to the possibility that, in certain circumstances, the Commission may mandate additional audit procedures, beyond those that GAAS require.

As another way to influence auditing standards, the SEC can impose disciplinary sanctions on accountants and other professionals, including lawyers. Rule 2(e) of the Commission's Rules of Practice allows the SEC to prohibit an accountant from practicing before the Commission for a variety of reasons, including lack of the requisite qualifications, character, or integrity; engaging in violations of the securities laws; or engaging in unethical or improper conduct.

In response to the McKesson–Robbins fraud, the AICPA established the Committee on Auditing Procedures. The Committee's first official promulgation specifically required auditors to observe inventories and to confirm receivables, but at that early date the Committee did not have the power to bind the profession. At the same time, the failure to establish definitive accounting principles hindered significant improvements in auditing.

Since then the Committee's successors, most recently the Auditing Standards Board ("ASB"), has issued many authoritative rulings, called Statements on Auditing Standards ("SASs"), which are comparable to the promulgations on accounting principles by the FASB and its predecessors, except that the FASB is separate from the profession as embodied by the AICPA.

However, that is all past history, since, as noted earlier, in one of its most important reforms SOx provided in section 101 for the creation of the new Public Company Accounting Oversight Board (PCAOB), investing it with responsibility to register, regulate and inspect accounting firms that audit publicly traded companies; to establish or adopt auditing standards for such audits, including quality control, ethics and independence, subject to SEC approval; and to conduct investigations and disciplinary proceedings to enforce compliance with the law and professional standards. The chairman of the Board receives $615,000 per year, and the other members $500,000. SOx section 102 provides that, in registering with the PCAOB as the Act requires, each auditing firm must provide a statement of its quality control policies for its accounting and auditing process.

While it is developing its own standards, the PCAOB has adopted as "Interim Professional Auditing Standards" the auditing standards that the accounting profession, through the AICPA's Auditing Standards Board had promulgated up to April 16, 2003. PCAOB took this action to assure continuity and certainty in the standards that govern audits of public companies. However, in its own first auditing standard, AS 1, PCAOB has required that the reference in audit reports be changed to state explicitly that the audit complied with the PCAOB's auditing standards. As described on pages 159-160, *supra,* in March, 2004 PCAOB issued AS 2, dealing with auditors' responsibility under SOx section 404 to report on management's assessment of internal controls, and followed up with a further policy statement on the matter in May, 2005.

Under SOx section 104(a), PCAOB must conduct a continuing program of inspections to assess each registered public accounting firm's compliance with SOx, SEC and PCAOB rules, and professional standards: all firms must be inspected at least every three years, but those with more than 100 public companies as audit clients must be inspected every year. During 2003, PCAOB conducted limited inspections at the eight largest accounting firms, the "Big Four," plus BDO Seidman, Grant Thornton, Crowe Chizek, and McGladrey & Pullen, all of which audit more than 100 public companies. In fact, collectively these eight firms audit about 15,000 public companies. The examinations covered the internal inspection program at each firm to understand the firm's goals; the approach to compensation below the partner level; the communication between the firm and each client's audit committee chairman; and the hiring and firing processes as related to clients. Early indications were that those inspections were turning up surprisingly apparent violations of GAAP. *So Far, Audit Firm Inspections Turn Up 'Startling' GAAP Violations, Goelze Says*, CORP. L. DAILY (BNA), Feb. 27, 2004.

In August, 2004 the PCAOB released its initial reports on the limited 2003 inspections of the Big Four firms. The reports confirmed that significant audit and accounting issues were found, as well as problems with the firms' quality control systems and documentation process. However, the portions of the inspection reports dealing with quality control issues were not disclosed, because a provision of SOx, which was added after intense lobbying by the Big Four, required those portions to be kept confidential for a year, to give the firms time to address the PCAOB's concerns and correct their processes. A number of commentators expressed not only dismay at the outcome of the inspections, but also concern that the disclosures in the confidential parts might be even more troublesome. Some have urged that the confidentiality provision be dropped from SOx, especially so that audit committees could be fully informed when they are choosing an auditor. They commended KPMG for taking steps to further transparency by voluntarily disclosing some of the confidential information in the KPMG report. Other commentators have been more optimistic, taking the view that the flaws which turned up in the inspections were fairly modest in the total scheme of things. In any event, there was a call for strong enforcement of its standards by the PCAOB, so that accounting firms performing poorly would be held accountable, and hence would have some incentive to improve. Carpenter, Experts Weigh In on Big Four PCAOB's First Inspection Reports, 36 Sec. Reg. & L. Rep. 1694 (Sept. 20, 2004).

During 2004 the PCAOB conducted its first full-blown inspections at approximately 200 auditing firms. These inspections were expected to include an intensive review of audit engagements and financial statements, and to focus on audit firm culture, the free flow of information between predecessor and successor auditors, the detection of fraud, inadequate documentation, and risk assessment.

In the meantime, in February, 2005 the PCAOB released reports on eight small accounting firms, of the ninety-one inspected in 2004. Two of the firms were found to have significant audit deficiencies, while for the other six no deficiencies were discovered. It may be interesting to note that one of the firms that was not up to standard, with four name partners, had only one public company audit client, while the other, a sole practitioner, had seventeen! Among the deficiencies of the latter were failures to note departures from GAAP, or to appropriately test revenues and expenses. As before, any quality control issues were kept confidential.

In May, 2005 the PCAOB took its first-ever disciplinary action, stripping a small New York auditor of its registration, making it no longer able to audit a public company, and barring the managing partner from the industry. He and two partners had concealed information and submitted phony documents in a 2004 inspection, but the other two partners later voluntarily informed the inspectors and cooperated with the probe, so they received less onerous penalties. Later in the year two other firms were stripped of their registrations.

3. COMPONENTS

The audit process incorporates both accepted auditing standards and recognized auditing procedures. Auditing standards differ from auditing procedures in that the former broadly addresses an audit's objectives and seeks to ensure a certain performance level, while the latter refers to the specific acts that an audit entails.

a. AUDITING STANDARDS

Auditing standards involve not only the auditor's professional qualities but also the judgment that the auditor exercises in the audit and the audit report. The AICPA's membership has approved and adopted ten basic statements which the profession refers to as "generally accepted auditing standards." Collectively, these ten basic statements, plus the professional rulings to date that build upon them by providing additional specificity, comprise GAAS, which Rule 202 requires AICPA members to follow.

(1) Basic Standards

The ten basic statements fall into three groups: (1) general standards, (2) standards of fieldwork, and (3) standards of reporting.

The accounting profession recognizes three general standards for audits and auditors. An auditor must, first, possess adequate technical training

and proficiency before undertaking an audit; second, maintain an independent mental attitude in all matters relating to the assignment; and, third, exercise due professional care while performing the examination and preparing the audit report.

Three separate tenets comprise the standards of field work. An auditor must, first, adequately plan the work and properly supervise any assistants; second, properly study and evaluate the existing internal controls to assess the extent to which the auditor can rely on those controls and thereby avoid additional tests and procedures; and third, obtain sufficient competent evidence, whether through inspection, observation, inquiries, or confirmation, to afford a reasonable basis for an opinion regarding the financial statements under examination.

As perhaps the most important step in the audit process, the auditing profession recognizes four basic standards for reporting. First, the audit report must express an opinion as to whether the financial statements comply with generally accepted accounting principles. Second, the report must identify any inconsistency in the application of GAAP between the current period and the preceding period. Third, the profession regards informative disclosure in the financial statements as reasonably adequate unless the audit report specifically states otherwise. Finally, the report should either express an opinion regarding the financial statements, taken as a whole, or explain why the auditor must disclaim an opinion.

b.   AUDITING PROCEDURES

Audit procedures refer to the various acts that an auditor performs during an audit. These acts include tests that the auditor makes to obtain comfort that the financial statements fairly present the enterprise's financial condition and results. Common audit procedures include reconciling the cash amounts reflected in the business's ledger with the balances reflected in statements from the financial institution; observing physical inventories; price-testing inventories; confirming assets and liabilities; transactional testing involving expenses, purchases, sales, and payroll; performing cut-off tests between accounting period s; reading minutes of shareholder and director meetings; and obtaining representation letters from management and attorneys. Official promulgations require very few audit procedures in interpreting the ten basic standards, and do not establish specific requirements to guide auditors' decisions, such as minimums for determining sample size, or rules for selecting sample items for testing, and evaluating results. Although more bright line requirements might help address difficult audit situations, such rules might not keep pace with today's rapidly changing business environment.

4. WHO SELECTS THE AUDITING PROCEDURES?

In definite contrast to accounting principles, the client's management does not choose the auditing procedures that the auditor will perform. Although the financial statements remain management's responsibility, the auditor assumes full responsibility for the audit and the audit opinion. As a result, the auditor selects the auditing procedures that the auditor will use to reach an opinion about whether the financial statements satisfy the basic test, i.e., present fairly, in all material respects, the financial condition, results of operations, and cash flows. In selecting auditing procedures and performing the audit, the auditor must act within the confines of GAAS.

PROBLEMS

Problem 2.2A. If a creditor asked you to audit the financial statements of Nifty–Novelty as of the close of February in the problem on pages 99 - 100, *supra,* what steps would you take? What questions would you ask and to whom would you address them?

Problem 2.2B. If a shareholder asked you to audit the financial statements of Camera Sales Co. as of the close of April in the problem on pages 101 - 103, *supra,* what steps would you take? What questions would you ask and to whom would you address them?

5. THE EXPECTATION GAP

Differing perceptions exist between the assurance auditors provide and that which investors and other users of financial statements expect. A recent survey revealed that almost half of the investors surveyed believed that audited financial statements provide absolute assurance against errors or unintentional misstatements. In that same survey, more than seventy percent expressed a belief that audited financial statements provide absolute assurance against fraud or intentional misstatements. As we have seen, however, an audit provides only reasonable assurance against material misstatements, whether intentional or unintentional, in the financial statements. Moreover, experience shows that frauds, especially forgery and collusion, can more easily avoid detection even in a properly planned and executed audit than unintentional errors. The survey indicates, however, that investors set a higher standard for auditors to uncover fraud than to discover errors and that expectations exceed the assurance actually provided. The accounting profession has labeled these misconceptions as the "expectation gap."

In reality, an audit does not guarantee that error or fraud has not affected the financial statements. And of course, an audit does not offer any assurance about the safety of an investment in the enterprise. However, the auditor is required to assess the risk that errors and fraud may cause the financial statements to contain material misstatement, and hence the auditor must design an audit to provide reasonable assurance that the audit will detect material errors and misstatements, and then must properly perform and evaluate audit procedures to attain the required assurance.

We must keep in mind, however, that the legal standard for materiality may differ from the auditing standard. As a general rule, auditors treat any amount which does not exceed five percent of income before taxes as immaterial, and usually consider any item which does exceed ten percent of income before taxes as material. Both the courts and the Securities and Exchange Commission, however, have rejected these mathematical standards, preferring a facts and circumstances analysis. Under the federal securities laws, the Supreme Court has concluded that an omitted fact qualifies as material if a substantial likelihood exists that a reasonable investor would have considered the omitted fact important because disclosure would have significantly altered the "total mix" of available information. Basic Inc. v. Levinson, 485 U.S. 224 (1988); *see also* 17 C.F.R. §§ 230.405, 240.12b–2 (1999) ("The term 'material,' when used to qualify a requirement for the furnishing of information as to any subject, limits the information required to those matters to which there is a substantial likelihood that a reasonable investor would attach importance in determining whether to purchase [or sell] the securit[ies] registered.").

An example of how a quantitatively immaterial item might nevertheless qualify as material is BankAmerica Corp.'s failure in 1998 to disclose information about its $372 million write-down of a loan to D.E. Shaw & Co., a New York investment firm. Even though bank officials knew about possible losses on the loan as early as August, the bank did not disclose the extent of the losses before shareholders voted in late September to approve a $43 billion merger with NationsBank, which created the nation's second-largest bank. A *Wall Street Journal* article quotes the merged bank's chief financial officer as saying that "'[$372 million is] a big number but it's not material to a company' that is as big as Bank America." When the merged bank announced the write-down in mid-October, the stock price dropped eleven percent in a single day.

In a 1999 Accounting Bulletin, the SEC's staff explicitly rejected the view that any financial statement misstatements or omissions which fall under a five percent threshold were acceptable as long as there were no particularly egregious circumstances, such as misappropriation by senior management. The staff emphasized that registrants and their auditors must consider qualitative factors in materiality determinations. For example, a quantitatively small misstatement or omission could nevertheless qualify as material when it:

• arises from an item capable of precise measurement;

- masks a change in earnings or other trends;

- hides a failure to meet analysts' consensus expectations for the enterprise;

- changes a loss into income or vice versa;

- concerns a segment or other portion of the registrant's business that has been identified as playing a significant role in the registrant's operations or profitability;

- determines the registrant's compliance with regulatory requirements;

- affects the registrant's compliance with loan covenants or other contractual requirements;

- increases management's compensation – for example, by satisfying requirement for the award of bonuses or other forms of incentive compensation; or

- involves concealment of an unlawful transaction.

In assessing multiple misstatements, the bulletin reminds registrants and auditors that they must consider all misstatements or omissions both separately and in the aggregate to determine whether, in relation to the individual line item amounts, subtotals or totals in the financial statements, the misstatements or omissions materially misstate the financial statements taken as a whole.

Finally, the bulletin warns registrants that even immaterial misstatements, if intentional, can violate the federal securities laws, particularly the FCPA record-keeping and internal controls requirements.

a. "PRESENT FAIRLY"

At this point it is appropriate to take a closer look at the precise language which has traditionally been used by auditors in expressing their opinion on the financial statements: *i.e.,* whether the statements "fairly present" the enterprise's financial condition, results of operations, and cash flows "in accordance with generally accepted accounting principles". There is a patent ambiguity here, as to what an auditor should do if despite scrupulous application of GAAP the resulting statements do not fairly present the financial picture, whether because of a misleading representation in some respect, or a failure to disclose some relevant information, or whatever. To put it another way, the traditional language raises the question of whether compliance with GAAP may be presumed in and of itself to satisfy the "fairly present" test. Over the years, the accounting profession has at least leaned toward the position that an auditor's responsibilities end with making sure that the financial statements comply with GAAP, implying that conformity with GAAP confirms that the financials are a "fair" presentation.

Investors and other users, however, have believed, and continue to believe, that accountants accept an additional burden of ensuring that the financial statements present the underlying transactions in a reasonable and fair manner. That view got a significant boost under federal securities law from the very influential decision in *United States v. Simon,* 425 F.2d 796 (2d Cir.1969), *cert. denied,* 397 U.S. 1006 (1970). In that case, Roth, the president of Continental, caused the company to lend substantial sums to an affiliated entity, which Roth also controlled. Roth in turn borrowed the money from the affiliate to use for his personal purposes. Roth's financial situation had deteriorated, leaving him in no position to repay the affiliate, and the collateral he had put up, consisting mostly of stock and securities of Continental, was worth substantially less than the amount of the loan, so the loan receivable from the affiliate on Continental's books was of doubtful collectibility. For failing to insist upon fuller disclosure of these facts, the three accountants from the large firm auditing Continental were charged under various federal statutes with conspiracy to commit fraud. At the trial eight outstanding accounting experts testified that Continental's treatment of the receivable was not inconsistent with GAAP, which did not require disclosure of either the make-up of the collateral or the fact of Roth's borrowings from the affiliate. The trial judge refused to give the defendants' requested instruction that the defendants could be found guilty only if according to GAAP the financial statements did not constitute a fair presentation. Instead, the judge instructed the jury that the critical test was whether the financial statements fairly presented Continental's financial position, and if not, whether the defendants had acted in good faith, as to which compliance with GAAP would be "evidence which may be very persuasive but not necessarily conclusive". The conviction of the defendants was upheld on appeal, in a much cited opinion by Judge Friendly, holding that if literal compliance with GAAP produces a materially misleading impression, the unqualified acceptance by knowing auditors could result in criminal liability.

It should be noted that the Simon case could be construed narrowly, and limited to the special fact that the auditors were aware that the president was running the business for his own benefit rather than in the best interests of the shareholders. As the following excerpt indicates, Judge Friendly's opinion certainly stressed this point:

We join defendants' counsel in assuming that the mere fact that a company has made advances to an affiliate does not ordinarily impose a duty on an accountant to investigate what the affiliate has done with them or even to disclose that the affiliate has made a loan to a common officer if this has come to his attention. But it simply cannot be true that an accountant is under no duty to disclose what he knows when he has reason to believe that, to a material extent, a corporation is being operated not to carry out its business in the interest of all the stockholders but for the private benefit of its president.... Generally accepted accounting principles instruct an accountant what to do in the usual case where he has no reason to doubt that the affairs of the corporation are being honestly conducted. Once he has reason to believe that this basic assumption is false, an entirely different situation confronts him. Then ... he must "extend his procedures to determine whether or not such suspicions are justified." If . . . he finds his suspicions to be confirmed, full disclosure must be the rule, unless he has made sure the wrong has been righted and procedures to avoid a repetition have been established.

However, later cases without such clear-cut impropriety have followed the Simon approach, at least for the purpose of imposing civil rather than criminal liability upon accountants. In Herzfeld v. Laventhol, Kreckstein, Horwath & Horwath, 378 F. Supp. 112 (S.D.N.Y. 1974), rev'd in part on other grounds, 340 F. 2d 27 (2d. Cir. 1976), the District Court put it this way:

The policy underlying the securities laws of providing investors with all the facts needed to make intelligent investment decisions can only be accomplished if financial statements *fully and fairly portray* the actual financial condition of the company. In those cases where application of generally accepted accounting principles fulfills the duty of full and fair disclosure, the accountant need go no further. But if application of accounting principles alone will not adequately inform investors, accountants, as well as insiders, must take pains to lay bare all the facts needed by investors to interpret the financial statements accurately. 378 F. Supp. at 121-2.

Of course these decisions rest upon construction of federal securities laws, such as SEC Rule 10b-5, and do not necessarily fix the test for the responsibility of auditors pursuant to generally accepted auditing standards. But liability, criminal or civil, is just as painful whether imposed under securities laws or professional responsibility, so the Simon approach might have been expected to significantly influence auditor conduct. Nevertheless, the profession continued to display considerable ambivalence about the scope of the auditor's duty. For example, the most recent official promulgation on the subject, by the Auditing Standards Board (ASB) of the AICPA, Statement No. 69, The Meaning of Present Fairly in Conformity with Generally Accepted Accounting Principles in the Independent Auditor's Report (1992), while broadening the responsibility of the auditor somewhat beyond mere literal compliance with GAAP, still stopped short of adopting the standard enunciated in Simon. SAS No.69 requires an auditor to assess whether:

    a) the accounting principles that management has selected and applied enjoy general acceptance;

b) the accounting principles are appropriate in the circumstances;

c) the financial statements, including the related notes, provide information about those matters that may affect their use, understanding and interpretation;

d) the financial statements classify and summarize the information that they present in a reasonable manner that neither provides too much detail nor too few specifics; and

e) the financial statements reflect the underlying transactions and events in a manner that presents the financial position, results of operations, and cash flows stated within a range of acceptable limits that the enterprise can reasonably and practicably attain.

In any event, it would appear that the issue of fair presentation versus GAAP is back on center stage by virtue of the two Sarbanes-Oxley provisions requiring certification of financial statements by the top corporate executives. While there are some differences between SOx sections 302 and 906, such as criminal liability rather than civil, or the breadth of the information covered, the two provisions are identical in casting the obligation in terms of certifying that the information involved "fairly present[s] in all material respects the financial condition and results of operations of the issuer", with no qualifying reference to generally accepted accounting principles. In the light of the long history of the traditional language of the auditor's report, it would be hard to believe that this failure to refer to GAAP was inadvertent, and, not surprisingly, the SEC expressly takes that view in its release adopting the implementing Rule required by section 302. In its Securities Act Release No. 8124, the SEC put it this way (after adding "cash flows" to the financial information specifically required by section 302 to be certified as "fairly presented"):

> The certification statement regarding fair presentation of financial statements and other financial information is not limited to a representation that the financial statements and other financial information have been presented in accordance with "generally accepted accounting principles" and is not otherwise limited by reference to generally accepted accounting principles. We believe that Congress intended this statement to provide assurance that the financial information disclosed in a report, viewed in its entirety, meets a standard of overall material accuracy and completeness that is broader than financial reporting requirements under generally accepted accounting principles. In our view, a "fair presentation" of an issuer's financial condition, results of operations and cash flows encompasses the selection of appropriate accounting policies, disclosure of financial information that is informative and

reasonably reflects the underlying transactions and events and the inclusion of any additional disclosure necessary to provide investors with a materially accurate and completer picture of an issuer's financial condition, results of operations and cash flows."
Fed. Sec. L. Rep. [2002 Transfer Binder] ¶86,720, at 86,126, n. 56.

While this Release relates only to the required certification by corporate officers, its message is likely to be extended to auditors' duties: there is little reason to impose a heavier burden on the corporate officers with respect to fair presentation than on the outside auditor (as long as the auditor knows or has reason to know the facts). That is a welcome development to the proponents of harmonization of U.S. accounting with international accounting standards, as indicated in the discussion of international accounting at pages 141-142, *supra*.

b.   THE AUDITOR'S RESPONSIBILITY TO DETECT AND REPORT ERRORS, FRAUD AND ILLEGAL ACTS

As we have seen, after assessing the risk that errors, fraud or illegal acts may cause the financial statements to contain misrepresentations, the auditor must plan and perform appropriate procedures to enable the audit to attain the required reasonable assurance against material misstatements.

Because of the characteristics of certain frauds and illegal acts, particularly those involving forgery and collusion, a properly designed and executed audit may not detect a material irregularity. For example, GAAS does not require an auditor to authenticate documents. In addition, audit procedures that effectively detect unintentional misstatements may not uncover collusion between the client's employees and third parties or among management and employees.

In the recent past, public perceptions and court decisions imposing liability on auditors have caused the accounting profession to reassess the role which auditors play in society, and public opinion about the level of assurance that an audit should provide. To close the expectation gap, the accounting profession could either educate the public or increase the level of assurance to meet expectations. The profession has chosen to do both. In 1988, the ASB changed the language in the standard audit opinion in an attempt to provide better information about what an unqualified opinion means, and also issued two Statements on the auditor's responsibility to detect errors, fraud and illegal acts: one called for auditors to be more sensitive to the possibility of material fraud in every audit; the other prescribed the consideration that an auditor should give to the possibility that a client's illegal acts or omissions may materially affect the financial statements, and provided guidance when the auditor detects a possible illegal act.

When those efforts did not produce the hoped-for results, the AICPA supported the Private Securities Litigation Reform Act of 1995 which, as noted earlier, requires any audit mandated by the securities laws to include, among other things, procedures designed to provide reasonable assurance that the audit will detect any illegal acts that would directly and materially affect the determination of financial statement amounts. In addition, the legislation requires auditors to take certain actions if they uncover an illegal act or suspect that such an act may have occurred. If an illegal act has likely occurred, unless it qualifies as "clearly inconsequential" the auditor must make sure that the audit committee or the entire board of directors is informed, and may have to notify the SEC if the registrant doesn't.

In 1997 the ASB issued Statement No. 82, Consideration of Fraud in a Financial Statement Audit ("SAS No. 82"), which requires auditors to assess specifically, and document, in every audit the risk that fraud may cause material misstatements. In this context, fraud includes both intentional misrepresentations in financial statements, sometimes referred to as "cooking the books," and misappropriation or theft of assets. SAS No. 82 expands an auditor's responsibilities to plan and perform an audit so as to obtain the required reasonable assurance. The Statement describes various frauds and accompanying characteristics, identifies factors that an auditor should consider in assessing the risk that fraud has caused material misstatements in the financial statements, and provides guidance about how the auditor should respond to the assessment's results. In addition, the standard suggests how an auditor should evaluate test results as they relate to the possibility that fraud may cause material misstatements; requires the auditor to document the risk assessment and response; and reaffirms the requirement that the auditor inform management, the audit committee and perhaps government regulators about any material fraud that an audit detects.

In 2002, SAS No. 99, with the same name as SAS No. 82, reinforced the need to keep the risk of fraud very much in mind, requiring that auditors extend the exercise of professional skepticism to the possibility that fraud may cause a material misstatement. In particular, auditors must evaluate specific fraud risks and document the plan and procedures used to evaluate those risks. Nevertheless, it is still the case that audits provide only reasonable assurance that fraud has not caused a material misstatement in the financial statements, so even scrupulous compliance with the auditing standards may not result in detection of such impropriety.

6. AUDIT REPORTS

The auditor's standard report may express the desired conclusion, i.e., that the financial statements present fairly, in all material respects, an entity's financial position, results of operations, and cash flows in conformity with GAAP, only when an audit, performed in accordance with GAAS, has enabled the auditor to form an opinion about the financial statements. Limitations in the auditor's examination, deficiencies in the client's financial statements, or other unusual conditions, however, may prevent the auditor from rendering the standard report. In those circumstances, the auditor must carefully modify the audit report to highlight those problems or conditions for the users of the financial statements.

a. STANDARD REPORT

The auditor's standard report identifies the financial statements audited in an opening or introductory paragraph, describes the nature of an audit in a scope paragraph, and expresses the auditor's opinion in a separate opinion paragraph. Generally, the financial statements present the enterprise's financial condition and operating results on a comparative basis, showing the numbers from both the present and one or more previous years. The auditor's report for the Starbucks financial statements for fiscal 2005, illustrating the three paragraph types and the reference to comparative figures for the two previous years, appears on page 76 in Appendix A in the casebook.

Notice that the introductory paragraph highlights the fact that the responsibility for the financial statements rests with the enterprise's management, whereas the role of the auditor is to express an opinion on the financial statements based on the audit. The second paragraph describes the scope of the audit, including the need to conform to GAAS and what that entails, and whether the auditor believes the audit provides a reasonable basis for an opinion.

Of course, the most important paragraph in the audit report is the opinion paragraph, which states the auditor's opinion as to whether the financial statements present fairly, in all material respects, the enterprise's financial position as of the balance sheet date, plus the results of its operations and its cash flows for the period then ended, in conformity with generally accepted accounting principles. If the auditor can attain reasonable assurance that the financial statements satisfy this standard, the auditor will render the standard unqualified opinion affirming each of those conclusions.

(1) REPORT ON INTERNAL CONTROL OVER FINANCIAL REPORTING

As noted above, SOx section 404 has added important new elements to the auditor's reporting function, consisting of an opinion on management's assessment of the effectiveness of the company's internal controls, and the auditor's own opinion on the effectiveness of the internal controls. If a registered public accounting firm issues separate audit reports on a public company's financial statements and on the company's internal controls underlying the financial reporting, the audit report on the financial statements must contain a paragraph cross-referencing the audit report on the effectiveness of the company's internal controls.

The auditor's standard report expressing an unqualified opinion on management's assessment of the effectiveness of the company's internal controls, and an unqualified opinion on the effectiveness of the internal controls, also contains the following discrete and essential paragraphs: an opening or introductory paragraph, a scope paragraph, a definition paragraph, an inherent limitations paragraph, an opinion paragraph, and a paragraph that references the audit report on the company's financial statements. The report accompanying the Starbucks 2005 financial statements, set out on pages 77-78 in Appendix A, illustrates these different paragraphs.

b. OPINIONS OTHER THAN UNQUALIFIED

Instead of the standard unqualified opinion, the auditor's report may take one of four other forms:

(1) Explanatory Language Added to an Unqualified Opinion

Certain circumstances, while not affecting the auditor's unqualified opinion on the financial statements, may require the auditor to add explanatory language to the audit report. These situations include (1) use of another auditor's work, (2) a change in accounting principles or in the method of their application materially affecting the comparability of financial statements between accounting periods, or (3) the financial statements depart from a promulgated accounting principle, in order to avoid a misleading presentation.

(2) Qualified Opinion

In a qualified opinion, the auditor in effect states that, *except for* the effects of the matter to which the qualification relates, the financial statements present fairly, in all material respects, the enterprise's financial picture. Among the reasons for a qualified opinion are (1) inadequate accounting records, which prevented the auditor from performing a full audit, (2) the auditor could not observe the counting of physical inventories at year-end, or (3) there is a departure from GAAP, including when the financial statements fail to disclose information that GAAP requires. A qualified opinion will always contain the words "except for" or "with the exception of".

(3) Adverse Opinion

An adverse opinion states that the financial statements do not present fairly the financial position, results of operations, or cash flows of the entity in conformity with generally accepted accounting principles. When an enterprise departs from a GAAP principle, the auditor may issue either an adverse opinion or a qualified opinion, depending upon the materiality of the departure. The SEC does not generally accept filing of financial statements with an adverse opinion from the auditor, presumably to put pressure on the registrant to correct the deviation from GAAP; in effect, then, an adverse opinion is likely to prevent an enterprise from complying with the SEC's filing requirements, which in turn would substantially impair or even eliminate the enterprise's ability to raise capital or borrow money. As a result, the client will do almost anything to avoid such an opinion, and auditors are quite cautious about rendering them. Nevertheless, sometimes there is clear evidence that one is called for, as in the following example of an adverse opinion where the enterprise deviated from the historical cost principle:

> As discussed in [a] Note to the financial statements, the Company carries its property, plant and equipment accounts at appraisal values, and provides depreciation on the basis of such values. . . . Generally accepted accounting principles require that property, plant and equipment be stated at an amount not in excess of cost, reduced by depreciation based on such amount. . . .
>
> In our opinion, because of the effects of the matters discussed in the preceding paragraphs, the financial statements referred to above do not present fairly, in conformity with generally accepted accounting principles, the financial position of the Company as of December 31, 19X2 and 19X1, or the results of its operations or its cash flows for the years then ended.

(4) Disclaimer of Opinion

A disclaimer of opinion states that the auditor does not express an opinion on the financial statements. A typical reason is that the auditor has not performed an examination sufficient in scope to be able to form an opinion on the statements. The following audit report illustrates the necessary disclaimer when the auditor did not observe physical inventories:

> The Company did not make a count of its physical inventory in 19X2 or 19X1 . . . . Further, evidence supporting the cost of property and equipment acquired prior to December 31, 19X1, is no longer available. The Company's records do not permit the application of other auditing procedures to inventories or property and equipment.
>
> Since the Company did not take physical inventories and we were not able to apply other auditing procedures to satisfy ourselves as to inventory quantities and the cost of property and equipment, the scope of our work was not sufficient to enable us to express, and we do not express, an opinion on these financial statements.

E. ALTERNATIVES TO AUDITS

Privately-owned enterprises do not need to file audited financial statements with the SEC. Unless a loan agreement or some other contract requires audited financial statements, these enterprises often prefer to avoid the costs which accompany an audit. Nevertheless, these same firms may want accountants to help prepare their financial statements. As a result, at least two other types of reports may accompany unaudited financial statements. In a *review*, the independent accountant performs certain analytical and other procedures to reach a reasonable basis for expressing limited assurance that the financial statements do not require any material modification to comply with GAAP. The independent accountant will compare financial data to corresponding data for prior periods, to ascertain whether or not the data appears reasonable, while also discussing the enterprise's operations with management to determine whether any changes in the business or operating procedures might explain variations in the financial data or suggest that the financial data from a previous period should change. In a *compilation*, the independent accountant does not express any assurance or opinion on the accompanying financial statements. Instead, the accountant simply prepares financial statements based upon information that management has supplied. The standards for performing reviews are less demanding than the GAAS which govern audits, and are even lower for compilations. Nevertheless, the same accounting principles apply: the review and compilation standards both state that the GAAP hierarchy also applies to those engagements.

F. ACCOUNTANTS' LEGAL LIABILITY

Arthur Andersen's quick and stunning demise illustrates the staggering consequences that can flow from an auditor's malpractice. The audit failure at Enron destroyed the firm's reputation, led to Andersen's conviction for obstructing justice, left thousands looking for new jobs, and spawned lawsuits against the firm seeking more than $25 billion for Enron's investors and former employees. In addition to a $500,000 fine and probation for five years, the conviction barred Andersen from auditing public companies. Although in 2005 the Supreme Court reversed Andersen's conviction on the ground that the trial court's instructions failed to require sufficient evidence of scienter, Arthur Andersen LLP v. U.S., 544 U. S. 696 (2005), it came too late to be of any help to the firm. In 2005 the KPMG firm escaped a similar fate by admitting criminal wrongdoing in connection with its sale of improper tax shelters, paying a fine of $456 million, and accepting a deferred prosecution agreement of the sort described in Chapter VI, on pages 319-320, *infra*.

While what happened to the Andersen firm is the most serious consequence ever visited upon an accounting firm for improper conduct, accountants had much earlier already been incurring all kinds of penalties and liabilities for failure to perform properly. Back in1990 Laventhal & Horwath, at that time the seventh largest accounting firm, went out of business after declaring bankruptcy in the face of liability claims. Between 1991 and 1995, the major accounting firms paid $1.7 billion in cases alleging securities fraud and other wrongdoing. *Big Six Have Paid $1.7 Billion Since 1991 in Securities Fraud Case, Study Finds*, 27 Sec. Reg. & L. Rep. 1723 (1995). During that period, Ernst & Young agreed to a $400 million settlement with federal banking regulators to settle various cases arising from failed audits involving financial institutions; Deloitte & Touche paid $312 million to settle federal regulators' claims involving flawed audits of several banks and savings and loan associations; and KPMG agreed to pay $186.5 million to settle claims that the Federal Deposit Insurance Corp., the Resolution Trust Corp., and the Office of Thrift Supervision brought against the firm.

This sad parade of all kinds of sanctions on accounting firms continued unabated right on into the new century, audit failures related to the recent corporate scandals have left each of the Big Four facing potentially enormous legal liability. Industry sources estimate that the Big Four spend more than ten percent of their auditing and accounting revenues each year to defend and settle lawsuits. For one recent example. Deloitte reportedly paid about $250 million during 2005 to settle litigation related to the collapse of Fortress Re, once the largest aviation reinsurer in the world. Interestingly, Deloitte never received more than $100,00 in any year from that engagement. Maremont and Inada, *Deloitte Pays Insurers More than $200 Million*, WALL ST. J., Sept. 21, 2005, at C3. KPMG agreed in 2003 to pay $125 million to settle shareholder litigation related to former audit client Rite Aid Corp., and another $75 million to resolve an audit failure at Oxford Health Plans Inc. In 2005, a federal judge ordered PricewaterhouseCooper to pay $182.9 million after a jury found the auditing firm jointly and severally liable to an audit failure at Ambassador Insurance Co. Weil, *Pricewaterhouse Is Ordered to Pay $162.9 Million*, WALL ST. J., Oct. 1, 2005.

The SEC has imposed seemingly ever-growing fines against audit firms. In 2005 Deloitte agreed to pay a $25 million civil penalty to the SEC and another $25 million into a fund to compensate victims of the financial fraud at Adelphia Communications Corporation. Even though Deloitte had identified Adelphia as one of its highest risk clients, the accounting firm allegedly failed to implement audit procedures designed to detect illegal acts. To date, the amount stands as the largest fine that the SEC has ever imposed on an auditing firm, surpassing the previous-record $22.5 million that was collected from KPMG after inadequate audits at Xerox Corp. Hughes, *Deloitte Auditors Are Charged by SEC in Adelphia Case*, WALL ST. J., Oct. 1, 2005. Scannell, *KPMG Apologizes for Tax Shelters*, WALL ST. J., June 17, 2005, at A3. The Xerox case also involved the largest civil penalties, $150,000, that the SEC has ever imposed against individual auditors. Reilly,

SEC Obtains Record Penalties From KPMG Auditors of Xerox, WALL ST. J., Feb. 23, 2006, at C3.

Also in 2004, the SEC suspended Ernst & Young from accepting any new public audit clients for six months because of violating the SEC's auditor independence rules. The SEC found that while auditing PeopleSoft, Inc., E & Y had significant business relationships with the client, including partnership arrangements and licensing agreements intended to boost E & Y's consulting revenues. The State of California Board of Accountancy (CBA) served a reminder of the ever-present but rarely-exercised power of state regulators under their licensing authority, pressing the same charges against E & Y under state law. E & Y agreed to a settlement with CBA calling for a three-year probation for the firm; payment for an independent consultant to conduct an investigation to determine that the firm has taken steps reasonably calculated to remedy the violations; reimbursement of up to $100,000 for CBA's expenses incurred pursuing E & Y; and contribution of the funds needed for CBA to host a continuing education program of no less than eight hours, which all the firm's personnel licensed in California must attend. Gilroy, *E & Y Accepts Probation, Fine to Settle Calif. Independence Charges*, 36 Sec. Reg. & L. Rep. 1804 (Oct. 4, 2004).

The following case discusses many issues involving accountants' legal liability.

Bily v. Arthur Young & Company

Supreme Court of California, 1992.
3 Cal.4th 370, 11 Cal.Rptr.2d 51, 834 P.2d 745.

■ LUCAS, CHIEF JUSTICE.

We granted review to consider whether and to what extent an accountant's duty of care in the preparation of an independent audit of a client's financial statements extends to persons other than the client.

Since Chief Judge Cardozo's seminal opinion in Ultramares Corp. v. Touche (1931) 255 N.Y. 170, 174 N.E. 441 (Ultramares), the issue before us has been frequently considered and debated by courts and commentators. Different schools of thought have emerged. At the center of the controversy are difficult questions concerning the role of the accounting profession in performing audits, the conceivably limitless scope of an accountant's liability to nonclients who may come to read and rely on audit reports, and the effect of tort liability rules on the availability, cost, and reliability of those reports.

Following a summary of the facts and proceedings in this case, we will analyze these questions by discussing the purpose and effect of audits and audit reports, the approaches taken by courts and commentators, and the basic principles of tort liability announced in our prior cases. We conclude that an auditor owes no general duty of care regarding the conduct of an audit to persons other than the client. An auditor may, however, be held liable for negligent misrepresentations in an audit report to those persons who act in reliance upon those misrepresentations in a transaction which the auditor intended to influence, in accordance with the rule of section 552 of the Restatement Second of Torts, as adopted and discussed below. Finally, an auditor may also be held liable to reasonably foreseeable third persons for intentional fraud in the preparation and dissemination of an audit report.

I. *Summary of Facts and Proceedings Below*

This litigation emanates from the meteoric rise and equally rapid demise of Osborne Computer Corporation (hereafter the company). Founded in 1980 by entrepreneur Adam Osborne, the company manufactured the first portable personal computer for the mass market. Shipments began in 1981. By fall 1982, sales of the company's sole product, the Osborne I computer, had reached $10 million per month, making the company one of the fastest growing enterprises in the history of American business.

In late 1982, the company began planning for an early 1983 initial public offering of its stock, engaging three investment banking firms as underwriters. At the suggestion of the underwriters, the offering was postponed for several months, in part because of uncertainties caused by the company's employment of a new chief executive officer and its plans to introduce a new computer to replace the Osborne I. In order to obtain "bridge" financing needed to meet the company's capital requirements until the offering, the company issued warrants to investors in exchange for direct loans or letters of credit to secure bank loans to the company (the warrant transaction). The warrants entitled their holders to purchase blocks of the company's stock at favorable prices that were expected to yield a sizable profit if and when the public offering took place.

Plaintiffs in this case were investors in the company. They include individuals as well as pension and venture capital investment funds. Several plaintiffs purchased warrants from the company as part of the warrant transaction. Others purchased the common stock of the company during early 1983. For example, one plaintiff, Robert Bily, who was also a director of the company, purchased 37,500 shares of stock from company founder Adam Osborne for $1.5 million.

The company retained defendant Arthur Young & Company (hereafter Arthur Young), one of the then-"Big Eight" public accounting firms, to perform audits and issue audit reports on its 1981 and 1982 financial statements. (Arthur Young has since merged with Ernst & Whinney to become Ernst & Young, now one of the "Big Five" accounting firms.) In its role as auditor, Arthur Young's responsibility was to review the annual financial statements prepared by the company's in-house accounting department, examine the books and records of the company, and issue an audit opinion on the financial statements.

Arthur Young issued unqualified or "clean" audit opinions on the company's 1981 and 1982 financial statements. Each opinion appeared on Arthur Young's letterhead, was addressed to the company, and stated in essence: (1) Arthur Young had performed an examination of the accompanying financial statements in accordance with the accounting profession's "Generally Accepted Auditing Standards" (GAAS); (2) the statements had been prepared in accordance with "Generally Accepted Accounting Principles" (GAAP); and (3) the statements "present[ed] fairly" the company's financial position. The 1981 financial statement showed a net operating loss of approximately $1 million on sales of $6 million. The 1982 financial statements included a "Consolidated Statement of Operations" which revealed a modest net operating profit of $69,000 on sales of more than $68 million.

Arthur Young's audit opinion on the 1982 financial statements was issued on February 11, 1983. The Arthur Young partner in charge of the audit personally delivered 100 sets of the professionally printed opinion to the company. With one exception, plaintiffs testified that their investments were made in reliance on Arthur Young's unqualified audit opinion on the company's 1982 financial statements.

As the warrant transaction closed on April 8, 1983, the company's financial performance began to falter. Sales declined sharply because of manufacturing problems with the company's new "Executive" model computer. When the Executive appeared on the market, sales of the Osborne I naturally decreased, but were not being replaced because Executive units could not be produced fast enough. In June 1983, the IBM personal computer and IBM-compatible software became major factors in the small computer market, further damaging the company's sales. The public offering never materialized. The company filed for bankruptcy on September[13], 1983. Plaintiffs ultimately lost their investments.

Plaintiffs brought separate lawsuits against Arthur Young * * *. Plaintiffs J.F. Shea & Co., et al. (the "Shea plaintiffs"), brought one lawsuit; plaintiff Robert Bily brought another. The two actions were consolidated for trial. The focus of plaintiffs' claims was Arthur Young's audit and audit opinion of the company's 1982 financial statements.

Plaintiffs' principal expert witness, William J. Baedecker, reviewed the 1982 audit and offered a critique identifying more than 40 deficiencies in Arthur Youn g's performance amounting, in Baedecker's view, to gross professional negligence. In his opinion, Arthur Young did not perform its examination in accordance with GAAS. He found the liabilities on the company's financial statements to have been understated by approximately $3 million. As a result, the company's supposed $69,000 operating profit was, in his view, a loss of more than $3 million. He also determined that Arthur Young had discovered material weaknesses in the company's accounting controls, but failed to report its discovery to management.

Although most of Baedecker's criticisms involved matters of oversight or nonfeasance, e.g., failures to detect weaknesses in the company's accounting procedures and systems, he also charged that Arthur Young had actually discovered deviations from GAAP, but failed to disclose them as qualifications or corrections to its audit report. For example, by January 1983, a senior auditor with Arthur Young identified $1.3 million in unrecorded liabilities including failures to account for customer rebates, returns of products, etc. Although the auditor recommended that a letter be sent to the company's board of directors disclosing material weaknesses in the company's internal accounting controls, his superiors at Arthur Young did not adopt the recommendation; no weaknesses were disclosed. Arthur Young rendered its unqualified opinion on the 1982 statements a month later.

The case was tried to a jury for 13 weeks. At the close of the evidence and arguments, the jury received instructions and special verdict questions including three theories of recovery: fraud, negligent misrepresentation, and professional negligence. * * *

* * *

The jury exonerated Arthur Young with respect to the allegations of intentional fraud and negligent misrepresentation, but returned a verdict in plaintiffs' favor based on professional negligence. No comparative negligence on plaintiffs' part was found. The jury awarded compensatory damages of approximately $4.3 million, representing approximately 75 percent of each investment made by plaintiffs. The Court of Appeal affirmed the resulting judgment in plaintiffs' favor with respect to all matters relevant to the issue now before us.

II. *The Audit Function in Public Accounting*

Although certified public accountants (CPA's) perform a var iety of services for their clients, their primary function, which is the one that most frequently generates lawsuits against them by third persons, is financial auditing. * * *

* * *

Arthur Young correctly observes that audits may be commissioned by clients for different purposes. Nonetheless, audits of financial statements and the resulting audit reports are very frequently (if not almost universally) used by businesses to establish the financial credibility of their enterprises in the perceptions of outside persons, e.g., existing and prospective investors, financial institutions, and others who extend credit to an enterprise or make risk-oriented decisions based on its economic viability. The unqualified audit report of a CPA firm, particularly one of the "Big [Five]," is often an admission ticket to venture capital markets—a necessary condition precedent to attracting the kind and level of outside funds essential to the client's financial growth and survival. As one commentator summarizes: "In the first instance, this unqualified opinion serves as an assurance to the client that its own perception of its financial health is valid and that its accounting systems are reliable. The audit, however, frequently plays a second major role: it assists the client in convincing third parties that it is safe to extend credit or invest in the client."

* * *

The AICPA's professional standards refer to the public responsibility of auditors: "A distinguishing mark of a profession is acceptance of its responsibility to the public. The accounting profession's public consists of clients, credit grantors, governments, employers, investors, the business and financial community, and others who rely on the objectivity and integrity of certified public accountants to maintain the orderly functioning of commerce. This reliance imposes a public interest responsibility on certified public accountants."

III. *Approaches to the Problem of Auditor Liability to Third Persons*

The complex nature of the audit function and its economic implications has resulted in different approaches to the question whether CPA auditors should be subjected to liability to third parties who read and rely on audit reports. Although three schools of thought are commonly recognized, there are some variations within each school and recent case law suggests a possible trend toward merger of two of the three approaches.

A substantial number of jurisdictions follow the lead of Chief Judge Cardozo's 1931 opinion for the New York Court of Appeals in Ultramares, *supra*, 174 N.E. 441, by denying recovery to third parties for auditor negligence in the absence of a third party relationship to the auditor that is "akin to privity." In contrast, a handful of jurisdictions, spurred by law review commentary, have recently allowed recovery based on auditor negligence to third parties whose reliance on the audit report was "foreseeable."

Most jurisdictions, supported by the weight of commentary and the modern English common law decisions cited by the parties, have steered a middle course based in varying degrees on Restatement Second of Torts section 552, which generally imposes liability on suppliers of commercial information to third persons who are intended beneficiaries of the information. Finally, the federal securities laws have also dealt with the problem by imposing auditor liability for negligence-related conduct only in connection with misstatements in publicly filed and distributed offering documents.

In this section we will review and briefly analyze each of the recognized approaches to the problem before us.

A. Privity of Relationship

In Ultramares, *supra,* 174 N.E. 441, plaintiff made three unsecured loans totalling $165,000 to a company that went bankrupt. Plaintiff sued the company's auditors, claiming reliance on their audit opinion that the company's balance sheet "present[ed] a true and correct view of the financial condition of [the company]." Although the balance sheet showed a net worth of $1 million, the company was actually insolvent. The company's management attempted to mask its financial condition; the auditors failed to follow paper trails to "off-the-books" transactions that, if properly analyzed, would have revealed the company's impecunious situation.

The jury, precluded by the trial judge from considering a fraud cause of action, returned a verdict in plaintiff's favor based on the auditor's negligence in conducting the audit. The New York Court of Appeals, speaking through Chief Judge Cardozo, reinstated the fraud cause of action but set aside the negligence verdict.

The auditor in Ultramares knew the company was in need of capital and that its audit opinion would be displayed to third parties "as the basis of financial dealings." In this regard, it supplied to the company 32 copies of the opinion "with serial numbers as counterpart originals." (Ibid.) Plaintiff's name, however, was not mentioned to the auditor nor was the auditor told about any actual or proposed credit or investment transactions in which its audit opinion would be presented to a third party.

With respect to the negligence claim, the court found the auditor owed no duty to the third party creditor for an "erroneous opinion." In an often quoted passage, it observed: "If liability for negligence exists, a thoughtless slip or blunder, the failure to detect a theft or forgery beneath the cover of deceptive entries, may expose accountants to a liability in an indeterminate amount for an indeterminate time to an indeterminate class. The hazards of a business conducted on these terms are so extreme as to enkindle doubt whether a flaw may not exist in the implication of a duty that exposes to these consequences."

* * *

The court emphasized that it was not releasing auditors from liability to third parties for fraud but merely for "honest blunder." It questioned "whether the average business man receiving [an audit report] without paying for it, and receiving it as one of a multitude of possible investors, would look for anything more."

* * *

The New York Court of Appeals restated the law in light of Ultramares . . . and other cases in Credit Alliance v. Arthur Andersen & Co. (1985) 65 N.Y.2d 536, 493 N.Y.S.2d 435, 483 N.E.2d 110. Credit Alliance subsumed two cases with different factual postures: in the first case, plaintiff alleged it loaned funds to the auditor's client in reliance on audited financial statements overstating the client's assets and net worth; in the second, the same scenario occurred, but plaintiff also alleged the auditor knew plaintiff was the client's principal lender and communicated directly and frequently with plaintiff regarding its continuing audit reports. The court dismissed plaintiff's negligence claim in the first case, but sustained the claim in the second.

The New York court promulgated the following rule for determining auditor liability to third parties for negligence: "Before accountants may be held liable in negligence to noncontractual parties who rely to their detriment on inaccurate financial reports, certain prerequisites must be satisfied: (1) the accountant must have been aware that the financial reports were to be used for a particular purpose or purposes; (2) in the furtherance of which a known party or parties was intended to rely; and (3) there must have been some conduct on the part of the accountants linking them to that party or parties, which evinces the accountants' understanding of that party or parties' reliance."

Discussing the application of its rule to the cases at hand, the court observed the primary, if not exclusive, "end and aim" of the audits in the second case was to satisfy the lender. The auditor's "direct communications and personal meetings [with the lender] result[ed] in a nexus between them sufficiently approaching privity." In contrast, in the first case, although the complaint did allege the auditor knew or should have known of the lender's reliance on its reports: "There was no allegation of either a particular purpose for the reports' preparation or the prerequisite conduct on the part of the accountants ... [nor] any allegation [the auditor] had any direct dealings with plaintiffs, had agreed with [the client] to prepare the report for plaintiffs' use or according to plaintiffs' requirements, or had specifically agreed with [the client] to provide plaintiffs with a copy [of the report] or actually did so."

The evolution of the New York rule illustrates a primary difficulty of articulating a standard of auditor liability to third parties: As one moves from privity of contract to privity of relationship, a wide variety of possible circumstances and relationships emerges. From preengagement communications with its client, an auditor may acquire full knowledge of third party recipients of the audit report and a specific investment or credit transaction that constitutes the "end and aim" of the audit. As a consequence, the auditor is placed on notice of a specific risk of liability that accompanies the audit engagement. Yet, under the Credit Alliance test, the auditor appears to have no liability in this situation in the absence of further, distinct conduct "linking" the auditor to the third party in a manner that "evinces [auditor] understanding" of third party reliance.

The New York court offers no rationale for the distinct "linking" element of its rule nor does it specify what conduct is required to satisfy this element, although direct communications between auditor and third party were deemed sufficient on the facts. One might question whether "linking" conduct should be necessary if, as in the example given in the previous paragraph, the auditor knows his engagement is for the express purpose of benefiting an identifiable class of third parties. . .

* * *

From the cases cited by the parties, it appears at least nine states purport to follow privity or near privity rules restricting the liability of auditors to parties with whom they have a contractual or similar relationship. In five states, this result has been reached by decisions of their highest courts. In four other states, the rule has been enacted by statute. Federal court decisions have held that the rule represents the law of three additional states whose highest courts have not expressly considered the question. The more recent of the cited cases generally follow the New York rule as reformulated in Credit Alliance.

B. Foreseeability

Arguing that accountants should be subject to liability to third persons on the same basis as other tortfeasors, Justice Howard Wiener advocated rejection of the rule of Ultramares in a 1983 law review article. (Wiener, Common Law Liability of the Certified Public Accountant for Negligent Misrepresentation (1983) 20 San Diego L.Rev. 233 [hereafter Wiener].) In its place, he proposed a rule based on foreseeability of injury to third persons. Criticizing what he called the "anachronistic protection" given to accountants by the traditional rules limiting third person liability, he concluded: "Accountant liability based on foreseeable injury would serve the dual functions of compensation for injury and deterrence of negligent conduct. Moreover, it is a just and rational judicial policy that the same criteria govern the imposition of negligence liability, regardless of the context in which it arises. The accountant, the investor, and the general public will in the long run benefit when the liability of the certified public accountant for negligent misrepresentation is measured by the foreseeability standard." Under the rule proposed by Justice Wiener, "[f]oreseeability of the risk would be a question of fact for the jury to be disturbed on appeal only where there is insufficient evidence to support the finding."

Following in part Justice Wiener's approach, the New Jersey Supreme Court upheld a claim for negligent misrepresentation asserted by stock purchasers against an auditor who had rendered an unqualified audit report approving fraudulently prepared financial statements. (Rosenblum v. Adler (1983) 93 N.J. 324, 461 A.2d 138.) The court found no reason to distinguish accountants from other suppliers of products or services to the public and no reason to deny to third party users of financial statements recovery for economic loss resulting from negligent misrepresentation. From its review of the purpose and history of the audit function, it concluded: "The auditor's function has expanded from that of a watchdog for management to an independent evaluator of the adequacy and fairness of financial statements issued by management to stockholders, creditors, and others." Noting the apparent ability of accounting firms to obtain insurance against third party claims under the federal securities laws, the court posited the same or similar protection would be available for common law negligent misrepresentation claims.

From a public policy standpoint, the court emphasized the potential deterrent effect of a liability-imposing rule on the conduct and cost of audits: "The imposition of a duty to foreseeable users may cause accounting firms to engage in more thorough reviews. This might entail setting up stricter standards and applying closer supervision, which should tend to reduce the number of instances in which liability would ensue. Much of the additional cost incurred either because of more thorough auditing review or increased insurance premiums would be borne by the business entity and its stockholders or its customers."

Notwithstanding its broad pronouncements about the public role of auditors and the importance of deterring negligence by imposing liability, when the New Jersey court formulated a rule of liability it restricted the auditor's duty to "all those whom that auditor should reasonably foresee as recipients from the company of the statements for its proper business purposes, provided that the recipients rely on the statements pursuant to those business purposes." According to the court, its rule would preclude auditor liability to "an institutional investor or portfolio manager who does not obtain audited statements from the company" or to "stockholders who purchased the stock after a negligent audit" unless they could demonstrate "the necessary conditions precedent."

The New Jersey court offered no principled basis for its "conditions precedent" requirement. Institutional investors, portfolio managers, or prospective stock purchasers who may pick up an audit report from a stockbroker, friend, or acquaintance or otherwise acquire it indirectly are no less "foreseeable" users. In view of the lack of any effective limits on access to audit reports once they reach the client, an auditor can foresee its reports coming into the hands of practically anyone. Thus, the court's approach evinces an Ultramares-like concern about the prospect of unlimited auditor liability, but offers no reasoned explanation of its decision to establish a limit based solely on the company's distribution, a factor over which the auditor has no control.

Two other state high courts—those of Wisconsin and Mississippi—have endorsed foreseeability rules...

* * *

In the nearly 10 years since it was formally proposed, the foreseeability approach has not attracted a substantial following. And at least four state supreme courts have explicitly rejected the foreseeability approach in favor of the Restatement's "intended beneficiary" approach since the New Jersey court's decision in Rosenblum.

* * *

C. The Restatement: Intent to Benefit Third Persons

Section 552 of the Restatement Second of Torts covers "Information Negligently Supplied for the Guidance of Others." It states a general principle that one who negligently supplies false information "for the guidance of others in their business transactions" is liable for economic loss suffered by the recipients in justifiable reliance on the information. But the liability created by the general principle is expressly limited to loss suffered: "(a) [B]y the person or one of a limited group of persons for whose benefit and guidance he intends to supply the information or knows that the recipient intends to supply it; and (b) through reliance upon it in a transaction that he intends the information to influence or knows that the recipient so intends or in a substantially similar transaction." To paraphrase, a supplier of information is liable for negligence to a third party only if he or she intends to supply the information for the benefit of one or more third parties in a specific transaction or type of transaction identified to the supplier.

Comment (h) to subdivision (2) of section 552, Restatement Second of Torts, observes that the liability of a negligent supplier of information is appropriately more narrowly restricted than that of an intentionally fraudulent supplier. It also notes that a commercial supplier of information has a legitimate concern as to the nature and scope of the client's transactions that may expand the supplier's exposure liability. As the comment states: "In many situations the identity of the person for whose guidance the information is supplied is of no moment to the person who supplies it, although the number and character of the persons to be reached and influenced, and the nature and extent of the transaction for which guidance is furnished may be vitally important. This is true because the risk of liability to which the supplier subjects himself by undertaking to give the information, while it may not be affected by the identity of the person for whose guidance the information is given, is vitally affected by the number and character of the persons, and particularly the nature and the extent of the proposed transaction."

To offer a simple illustration * * * , an auditor engaged to perform an audit and render a report to a third person whom the auditor knows is considering a $10 million investment in the client's business is on notice of a specific potential liability. It may then act to encounter, limit or avoid the risk. In contrast, an auditor who is simply asked for a generic audit and report to the client has no comparable notice.

The authors of the Restatement Second of Torts offer several variations on the problem before us as illustrations of section 552. For example, the auditor may be held liable to a third party lender if the auditor is informed by the client that the audit will be used to obtain a $50,000 loan, even if the specific lender remains unnamed or the client names one lender and then borrows from another. However, there is no liability where the auditor agrees to conduct the audit with the express understanding the report will be transmitted only to a specified bank and it is then transmitted to other lenders. Similarly, there is no liability when the client's transaction (as represented to the auditor) changes so as to increase materially the audit risk, e.g., a third person originally considers selling goods to the client on credit and later buys a controlling interest in the client's stock, both in reliance on the auditor's report.

Under the Restatement rule, an auditor retained to conduct an annual audit and to furnish an opinion for no particular purpose generally undertakes no duty to third parties. Such an auditor is not informed "of any intended use of the financial statements; but * * * knows that the financial statements, accompanied by an auditor's opinion, are customarily used in a wide variety of financial transactions by the [client] corporation and that they may be relied upon by lenders, investors, shareholders, creditors, purchasers and the like, in numerous possible kinds of transactions. [The client corporation] uses the financial statements and accompanying auditor's opinion to obtain a loan from [a particular] bank. Because of [the auditor's] negligence, he issues an unqualifiedly favorable opinion upon a balance sheet that materially misstates the financial position of [the corporation] and through reliance upon it [the bank] suffers pecuniary loss." Consistent with the text of section 552, the authors conclude: "[The auditor] is not liable to [the bank]."

Although the parties debate precisely how many states follow the Restatement rule, * * * the Restatement rule has been for many, if not most, courts a satisfactory compromise between their discomfort with the traditional privity approach and the "specter of unlimited liability."

* * *

D. Federal Securities Law

Auditors may also incur liability to third persons under the federal securities laws. Under section 10(b) of the Securities and Exchange Act of 1934 (1934 Act) and rule 10(b)–5 of the Securities Exchange Commission (SEC), accountants may be held liable to actual purchasers or sellers of securities for fraud or gross negligence.

Accountants may incur liability to third parties without a showing of fraud or gross negligence under section 18 of the 1934 Act or section 11 of the Securities Act of 1933 (1933 Act). [The United States Supreme Court has described the basic elements of liability under section 11 as follows: "Section 11 of the 1933 Act allows purchasers of a registered security to sue certain enumerated parties in a registered offering when false or misleading information is included in a registration statement. The section was designed to assure compliance with the disclosure provisions of the Act by imposing a stringent standard of liability on the parties who play a direct role in a registered offering. If a plaintiff purchased a security issued pursuant to a registration statement, he need only show a material misstatement or omission to establish a prima facie case. Liability against the issuer of a security is virtually absolute, even for innocent misstatements".] * * * An accountant or other professional within the scope of section 11 can escape liability for a false or misleading statement by proving due diligence, i.e., that after "reasonable investigation" he or she had "reasonable ground to believe and did believe" that the statement was "true and not misleading."

The liability of accountants and other professionals to third parties under section 11 of the 1933 Act is circumscribed by several factors: (1) the accountant's liability is limited to situations in which he or she prepares or certifies the accuracy of a portion of a registration statement and thus is aware he or she is creating part of a communication to the public; (2) liability is limited to third parties who actually purchase securities; (3) damage exposure is limited to the out-of-pocket loss suffered by the purchaser and can be no greater than the amount of the offering. Thus, under section 11: "[T]he plaintiff class, the proof of violation, and the measure of damages are statutorily defined in a manner that enhances the accountant's ability to gauge, ex ante, its liability exposure."

Section 18 of the 1934 Act imposes liability on accountants for misstatements contained in documents filed with the SEC. Liability is limited to third persons who, in reliance on the accountant's statement, "have purchased or sold a security at a price which was affected by such statement, for damages caused by such reliance." The accountant may successfully defend the action by proving that "he acted in good faith and had no knowledge that such statement was false or misleading."

     * * *

IV. Analysis of Auditor's Liability to Third Persons for Audit Opinions

     * * * Civil liability for injury to others is imposed based on causes of action in tort, which include, insofar as relevant to this case: negligence, negligent misrepresentation, and fraud.

A. Negligence

     * * * [W]e decline to permit all merely foreseeable third party users of audit reports to sue the auditor on a theory of professional negligence. Our holding is premised on three central concerns: (1) Given the secondary "watchdog" role of the auditor, the complexity of the professional opinions rendered in audit reports, and the difficult and potentially tenuous causal relationships between audit reports and economic losses from investment and credit decisions, the auditor exposed to negligence claims from all foreseeable third parties faces potential liability far out of proportion to its fault; (2) the generally more sophisticated class of plaintiffs in auditor liability cases (e.g., business lenders and investors) permits the effective use of contract rather than tort liability to control and adjust the relevant risks through "private

ordering"; and (3) the asserted advantages of more accurate auditing and more efficient loss spreading relied upon by those who advocate a pure foreseeability approach are unlikely to occur; indeed, dislocations of resources, including increased expense and decreased availability of auditing services in some sectors of the economy, are more probable consequences of expanded liability.

In a broad sense, economic injury to lenders, investors, and others who may read and rely on audit reports is certainly "foreseeable." Foreseeability of injury, however, is but one factor to be considered in the imposition of negligence liability. Even when foreseeability was present, we have on several recent occasions declined to allow recovery on a negligence theory when damage awards threatened to impose liability out of proportion to fault or to promote virtually unlimited responsibility for intangible injury.

* * *

In line with our recent decisions, we will not treat the mere presence of a foreseeable risk of injury to third persons as sufficient, standing alone, to impose liability for negligent conduct. We must consider other pertinent factors.

1. Liability Out of Proportion to Fault

An auditor is a watchdog, not a bloodhound. (In re Kingston Cotton Mill Co. (1896) 2 Ch. 279, 288.) As a matter of commercial reality, audits are performed in a client-controlled environment. The client typically prepares its own financial statements; it has direct control over and assumes primary responsibility for their contents. (See In re Interstate Hosiery Mills, Inc. (1939) 4 S.E.C. 721 ["The fundamental and primary responsibility for the accuracy [of financial statements] rests upon management."].) The client engages the auditor, pays for the audit, and communicates with audit personnel throughout the engagement. Because the auditor cannot in the time available become an expert in the client's business and record-keeping systems, the client necessarily furnishes the information base for the audit.

The client, of course, has interests in the audit that may not be consonant with those of the public. "Management seeks to maximize the stockholders' and creditors' confidence in the company, within the bounds of [GAAP and GAAS]; whereas, the public demands a sober and impartial evaluation of fiscal performance."

Client control also predominates in the dissemination of the audit report. Once the report reaches the client, the extent of its distribution and the communications that accompany it are within the exclusive province of client management. Thus, regardless of the efforts of the auditor, the client retains effective primary control of the financial reporting process.

Moreover, an audit report is not a simple statement of verifiable fact that * * * can be easily checked against uniform standards of indisputable accuracy. Rather, an audit report is a professional opinion based on numerous and complex factors. [T]he report is based on the auditor's interpretation and application of hundreds of professional standards, many of which are broadly phrased and readily subject to different constructions. Although ultimately expressed in shorthand form, the report is the final product of a complex process involving discretion and judgment on the part of the auditor at every stage. Using different initial assumptions and approaches, different sampling techniques, and the wisdom of 20–20 hindsight, few CPA audits would be immune from criticism.

Although the auditor's role in the financial reporting process is secondary and the subject of complex professional judgment, the liability it faces in a negligence suit by a third party is primary and personal and can be massive. The client, its promoters, and its managers have generally left the scene, headed in most cases for government-supervised liquidation or the bankruptcy court. The auditor has now assumed center stage as the remaining solvent defendant and is faced with a claim for all sums of money ever loaned to or invested in the client. Yet the auditor may never have been aware of the existence, let alone the nature or scope, of the third party transaction that resulted in the claim.

         * * *

Investment and credit decisions are by their nature complex and multifaceted. Although an audit report might play a role in such decisions, reasonable and prudent investors and lenders will dig far deeper in their "due diligence" investigations than the surface level of an auditor's opinion. And, particularly in financially large transactions, the ultimate decision to lend or invest is often based on numerous business factors that have little to do with the audit report. The auditing CPA has no expertise in or control over the products or services of its clients or their markets; it does not choose the client's executives or make its business decisions; yet, when clients fail financially, the CPA auditor is a prime target in litigation claiming investor and creditor economic losses because it is the only available (and solvent) entity that had any direct contact with the client's business affairs.

The facts of this case provide an apt example. Although plaintiffs now profess reliance on Arthur Young's audit report as the sine qua non of their investments, the record reveals a more complicated decisionmaking process. As a group of corporate insiders and venture capitalists who were closely following the Cinderella-like transformation of the company, plaintiffs perceived an opportunity to make a large sum of money in a very short time by investing in a company they believed would (literally within months) become the dominant force in the new personal computer market.

Although hindsight suggests they misjudged a number of major factors (including, at a minimum, the product, the market, the competition, and the company's manufacturing capacity), plaintiffs' litigation-focused attention is now exclusively on the auditor and its report. Plaintiffs would have us believe that, had the Arthur Young report disclosed deficiencies in accounting controls and the $3 million loss (on income of over $68 million), they would have ignored all the other positive factors that triggered their interest (such as the company's rapid growth in sales, its dynamic management, and the intense interest of underwriters in a public offering) and flatly withheld all their funds. Plaintiffs' revisionist view of the company's history, the audit, and their own investments, suggests something less than a "close connection" between Arthur Young's audit report and the loss of their invested funds.[12]

In view of the factors discussed above, judicial endorsement of third party negligence suits against auditors limited only by the concept of for[e]seeability raises the spectre of multibillion-dollar professional liability that is distinctly out of proportion to: (1) the fault of the auditor (which is necessarily secondary and may be based on complex differences of professional opinion); and (2) the connection between the auditor's conduct and the third party's injury (which will often be attenuated by unrelated business factors that underlie investment and credit decisions).

As other courts and commentators have noted, such disproportionate liability cannot fairly be justified on moral, ethical, or economic grounds. As one commentator has summarized: "The most persuasive basis for maintaining the limited duty [of auditors] is a proportionality argument.... It can be argued as a general proposition in these cases that the wrongdoing of an accountant is slight compared with that of the party who has deceived him (his client) as well as the plaintiff. This rationale for nonliability is similar to the proximate cause grounds on which willful intervening misconduct insulates a 'merely negligent' party from liability."

2. The Prospect of Private Ordering

Courts advocating unlimited auditor liability to all foreseeably injured third parties often analogize the auditor's opinion to a consumer product, arguing that the demise of privity as a barrier to recovery for negligence in product manufacture implies its irrelevance in the area of auditor liability as well. Plaintiffs advance similar arguments. The analogy lacks persuasive force for two reasons. Initially, as noted above, the maker of a consumer

---

[12]With one exception, each of the plaintiffs testified that he had read and relied on Arthur Young's audit report dealing with the company's 1982 financial statements in making his investment in the company. Without deprecating plaintiffs' testimony, we note that third party professions of reliance on audit reports may be easily fabricated. Because there may be no record showing the distribution of the audit report by the client, it may be difficult for the auditor to prove any particular plaintiff did not receive, read, or rely on the report. Although instances of uncorroborated, self-interested testimony are also present in other litigation contexts, the prospect of huge numbers of financially large, complex claims of doubtful merit that cannot be readily sorted out in pretrial litigation is an additional factor to be considered in determining whether negligence liability ought to be imposed. * * *

product has complete control over the design and manufacture of its product; in contrast, the auditor merely expresses an opinion about its client's financial statements—the client is primarily responsible for the content of those statements in the form they reach the third party.

Moreover, the general character of the class of third parties is also different. Investors, creditors, and others who read and rely on audit reports and financial statements are not the equivalent of ordinary consumers. Like plaintiffs here, they often possess considerable sophistication in analyzing financial information and are aware from training and experience of the limits of an audit report "product" that is, at bottom, simply a broadly phrased professional opinion based on a necessarily confined examination.

In contrast to the "presumptively powerless consumer" in product liability cases, the third party in an audit negligence case has other options—he or she can "privately order" the risk of inaccurate financial reporting by contractual arrangements with the client. For example, a third party might expend its own resources to verify the client's financial statements or selected portions of them that were particularly material to its transaction with the client. Or it might commission its own audit or investigation, thus establishing privity between itself and an auditor or investigator to whom it could look for protection. In addition, it might bargain with the client for special security or improved terms in a credit or investment transaction. Finally, the third party could seek to bring itself within [an] exception to Ultramares by insisting that an audit be conducted on its behalf or establishing direct communications with the auditor with respect to its transaction with the client.

As a matter of economic and social policy, third parties should be encouraged to rely on their own prudence, diligence, and contracting power, as well as other informational tools. This kind of self-reliance promotes sound investment and credit practices and discourages the careless use of monetary resources. If, instead, third parties are simply permitted to recover from the auditor for mistakes in the client's financial statements, the auditor becomes, in effect, an insurer of not only the financial statements, but of bad loans and investments in general.[13]

---

[13]The dissent argues that unsophisticated third parties who rely on audit reports are left unprotected by our decision. In our view, the argument itself poses a dilemma. If a third party possesses sufficient financial sophistication to understand and appreciate the contents of audit reports (which often include complex financial data and accounting language as well as technical terms like "Generally Accepted Accounting Principles" and "Generally Accepted Auditing Standards"), he or she should also be aware of their limitations and of the alternative ways of privately ordering the relevant risks. If, on the other hand, a third party lacks the threshold knowledge to understand the audit report and its terms, he or she has no reasonable basis for reliance. In either event, there is no sound basis to extend potentially unlimited liability based on any alleged lack of sophistication.

3. The Effect on Auditors of Negligence Liability to Third Persons

Courts and commentators advocating auditor negligence liability to third parties also predict that such liability might deter auditor mistakes, promote more careful audits, and result in a more efficient spreading of the risk of inaccurate financial statements. For example, the New Jersey Supreme Court reasoned: "The imposition of a duty to foreseeable users may cause accounting firms to engage in more thorough reviews. This might entail setting up stricter standards and applying closer supervision, which would tend to reduce the number of instances in which liability would ensue. Much of the additional cost incurred because of more thorough auditing review or increased insurance premiums would be borne by the business entity and its stockholders or its customers.... Accountants will also be encouraged to exercise greater care leading to greater diligence in audits." (Rosenblum v. Adler, *supra*, 461 A.2d at p. 152.)

We are not directed to any empirical data supporting these prognostications. From our review of the cases and commentary, we doubt that a significant and desirable improvement in audit care would result from an expanded rule of liability. Indeed, deleterious economic effects appear at least as likely to occur.

In view of the inherent dependence of the auditor on the client and the labor-intensive nature of auditing, we doubt whether audits can be done in ways that would yield significantly greater accuracy without disadvantages. Auditors may rationally respond to increased liability by simply reducing audit services in fledgling industries where the business failure rate is high, reasoning that they will inevitably be singled out and sued when their client goes into bankruptcy regardless of the care or detail of their audits. As a legal economist described the problem: "The deterrent effect of liability rules is the difference between the probability of incurring liability when performance meets the required standard and the probability of incurring liability when performance is below the required standard. Thus, the stronger the probability that liability will be incurred when performance is adequate, the weaker is the deterrent effect of liability rules. Why offer a higher quality product if you will be sued regardless whenever there is a precipitous decline in stock prices?" (Fischel, The Regulation of Accounting: Some Economic Issues (1987), 52 Brooklyn L.Rev. 1051, 1055.) Consistent with this reasoning, the economic result of unlimited negligence liability could just as easily be an increase in the cost and decrease in the availability of audits and audit reports with no compensating improvement in overall audit quality.

In light of the relationships between auditor, client, and third party, and the relative sophistication of third parties who lend and invest based on audit reports, it might also be doubted whether auditors are the most efficient absorbers of the losses from inaccuracies in financial information. Investors and creditors can limit the impact of losses by diversifying investments and loan portfolios. * * * In the audit liability context, no reason appears to favor the alleged tortfeasor over the alleged victim as an effective distributor of loss.

* * *

The dissent acknowledges, as we do, the complexity of the problem before us and the necessity of a legislative process of study, debate, experimentation, and careful rulemaking. In view of the nature of the problem, we refrain from endorsing a broad and amorphous rule of potentially unlimited liability that has been endorsed by only a small minority of the decided cases. * * *

For the reasons stated above, we hold that an auditor's liability for general negligence in the conduct of an audit of its client financial statements is confined to the client, i.e., the person who contracts for or engages the audit services. Other persons may not recover on a pure negligence theory.[16]

There is, however, a further narrow class of persons who, although not clients, may reasonably come to receive and rely on an audit report and whose existence constitutes a risk of audit reporting that may fairly be imposed on the auditor. Such persons are specifically intended beneficiaries of the audit report who are known to the auditor and for whose benefit it renders the audit report. While such persons may not recover on a general negligence theory, we hold they may, for the reasons stated in part IV(B) post, recover on a theory of negligent misrepresentation.

The sole client of Arthur Young in the audit engagements involved in this case was the company. None of the plaintiffs qualify as clients. Under the rule we adopt, they are not entitled to recover on a pure negligence theory. Therefore, the verdict and judgment in their favor based on that theory are reversed.

B.   Negligent Misrepresentation

One difficulty in considering the problem before us is that neither the courts (ourselves included), the commentators, nor the authors of the Restatement Second of Torts have made clear or careful distinctions between

---

[16]In theory, there is an additional class of persons who may be the practical and legal equivalent of "clients." It is possible the audit engagement contract might expressly identify a particular third party or parties so as to make them express third party beneficiaries of the contract. Third party beneficiaries may under appropriate circumstances possess the rights of parties to the contract. This case presents no third party beneficiary issue. Arthur Young was engaged by the company to provide audit reporting to the company. No third party is identified in the engagement contract. Therefore, we have no occasion to decide whether and under what circumstances express third party beneficiaries of audit engagement contracts may recover as "clients" under our holding.

the tort of negligence and the separate tort of negligent misrepresentation. The distinction is important not only because of the different statutory bases of the two torts, but also because it has practical implications for the trial of cases in complex areas such as the one before us.

Negligent misrepresentation is a separate and distinct tort, a species of the tort of deceit. * * *

Under certain circumstances, expressions of professional opinion are treated as representations of fact. * * * There is no dispute that Arthur Young's statements in audit opinions fall within these principles.

But the person or "class of persons entitled to rely upon the representations is restricted to those to whom or for whom the misrepresentations were made. Even though the defendant should have anticipated that the misinformation might reach others, he is not liable to them."

Of the approaches we have reviewed, Restatement Second of Torts section 552, subdivision (b) is most consistent with the elements and policy foundations of the tort of negligent misrepresentation. The rule expressed there attempts to define a narrow and circumscribed class of persons to whom or for whom representations are made. In this way, it recognizes commercial realities by avoiding both unlimited and uncertain liability for economic losses in cases of professional mistake and exoneration of the auditor in situations where it clearly intended to undertake the responsibility of influencing particular business transactions involving third persons. * * *

* * * [The Restatement rule requires that the supplier of information receive notice of potential third party claims, thereby allowing it to ascertain the potential scope of its liability and make rational decisions regarding the undertaking. T]he identification of a limited class of plaintiffs to whom the supplier itself has directed its activity establishes a closer connection between the supplier's negligent act and the recipient's injury, thereby ameliorating the otherwise difficult concerns of causation and of credible evidence of reliance. Finally, no unfairness results to those recipients who are excluded from the class of beneficiaries because they have means of private ordering—among other things, they can establish direct communication with an auditor and obtain a report for their own direct use and benefit. For these reasons, the rule expressed in the Restatement Second of Torts represents a reasoned, not an arbitrary, approach to the problem before us.

* * *

Having determined that intended beneficiaries of an audit report are entitled to recovery on a theory of negligent misrepresentation, we must consider whether they may also recover on a general negligence theory. We conclude they may not. Nonclients of the auditor are connected with the audit only through receipt of and express reliance on the audit report. Similarly, the gravamen of the cause of action for negligent misrepresentation in this context is actual, justifiable reliance on the representations in that report. Without such reliance, there is no recovery regardless of the manner in which the audit itself was conducted.

By allowing recovery for negligent misrepresentation (as opposed to mere negligence), we emphasize the indispensability of justifiable reliance on the statements contained in the report. As the jury instructions in this case illustrate, a general negligence charge directs attention to defendant's level of care and compliance with professional standards established by expert testimony, as opposed to plaintiff's reliance on a materially false statement made by defendant. The reliance element in such an instruction is only implicit—it must be argued and considered by the jury as part of its evaluation of the causal relationship between defendant's conduct and plaintiff's injury. In contrast, an instruction based on the elements of negligent misrepresentation necessarily and properly focuses the jury's attention on the truth or falsity of the audit report's representations and plaintiff's actual and justifiable reliance on them. * * *

* * *

C. Intentional Misrepresentation

As Chief Judge Cardozo recognized in Ultramares, supra, 74 N.E. 441, the liability of auditors to third parties presents different policy considerations when intentional fraud is involved. The secondary position of the auditor in the presentation of financial statements, the moral force of the argument against unlimited liability for mere errors or oversights and the uncertain connection between investment and credit losses and the auditor's report pale as policy factors when intentional misconduct is in issue. By joining with its client in an intentional deceit, the auditor thrusts itself into a primary and nefarious role in the transaction.

In this context, the auditor's actual knowledge of the false or baseless character of its opinion is not required: "If the defendant has no belief in the truth of the statement, and makes it recklessly, without knowing whether it is true or false, the element of scienter is satisfied."

We are directed to no authority that would immunize auditors from liability to third parties for intentional misrepresentation; the general rule appears to be to the contrary. (Rest.2d Torts, § 531 ["One who makes a fraudulent misrepresentation is subject to liability to the persons or class of persons whom he intends or has reason to expect to act or to refrain from action in reliance upon the misrepresentation, for pecuniary loss suffered by them through their justifiable reliance in the type of transaction in which he intends or has reason to expect their conduct to be influenced."].)

V. *Disposition*

This case was tried on the assumption that the general negligence rule and foreseeability approach * * * represented California law. The jury was instructed in accordance with that approach. For the reasons stated above, we have rejected the [general negligence] rule * * * in favor of a negligent misrepresentation rule substantially in accord with section 552 o f the Restatement Second of Torts. As a result, plaintiffs' judgment based on the general negligence rule must be set aside. Because plaintiffs were not clients of Arthur Young, they were not entitled to recover on a general negligence theory.

* * * Because of its disposition of the appeal, the Court of Appeal did not reach the merits of the Shea plaintiffs' cross-appeal. On remand, the Court of Appeal shall decide the cross-appeal and direct judgment or further proceedings as appropriate and consistent with this opinion.

For the reasons stated above, the judgment of the Court of Appeal is reversed and this case is remanded with instructions to: (1) direct judgment in favor of defendant Arthur Young and against plaintiff Bily; and (2) decide the cross-appeal of the Shea plaintiffs and then to direct judgment or further proceedings as appropriate, consistent with our opinion.

■ PANELLI, ARABIAN, BAXTER AND GEORGE, JJ., concur.

KENNARD, JUSTICE, dissenting.

* * *

The majority recognizes that accountants acknowledge a responsibility to third parties who foreseeably rely on audit reports in their business dealings with the audited company. Yet the majority adopts a rule that betrays the expectations of third party users whose reliance makes the audit report valuable to the audited company. Under the majority's rule, the audit report is made a trap for the unwary, because only the most legally sophisticated and well advised will understand that the report will not deliver what on its face it seems to promise: a qualified professional's actual assurance that the financial statement fairly states the financial situation of the audited company. An assurance with no legal recourse is essentially a hoax. Under the rule the majority adopts, any value that third parties place on the unqualified opinion is mistaken, because the law now insists that reliance upon the opinion, no matter how reasonable and foreseeable, is unjustified.

Finally, and perhaps most important, the majority pays too little attention to the importance of negligence liability as a means of preventing bad financial data from entering and polluting the waters of commerce. Without a liability rule that enforces the reasonable expectations of third party users of audit reports and provides an adequate incentive for due care, we may expect less careful audits, inefficient allocation of capital resources, increased transaction costs for loans and investments, and delay and disruption in the processes of lending and investing.

Existing law should be preserved. Negligent accountants should be held accountable for reasonably foreseeable injuries caused by the faulty performance of their professional duties in auditing financial statements. I would affirm the judgment of the Court of Appeal.

■ MOSK, J., concurs.

NOTES

1. To summarize briefly this complex subject, accountants can face two major types of liabilities—common law liability and statutory liability. Accountants' liability usually results in monetary damages. Both private parties, such as creditors or shareholders, and administrative agencies, like the SEC, can bring lawsuits seeking damages. Intentional misconduct, however, can also result in criminal sanctions. In addition, state licensing authorities can revoke an accountant's license to practice, and the SEC can bar an accountant from participation in any proceeding before or filing with the Commission, which pretty much precludes any professional work on behalf of a publicly-traded company.

We can divide common law liability into two categories, contract and tort. In appropriate circumstances, liability can flow to both clients and third parties. As the principal case indicates, courts have recognized three separate tort causes of action against auditors—negligence, negligent misrepresentation, and intentional conduct or fraud. Under the negligence theory, courts have applied at least three different standards: (1) requiring something akin to privity of relationship for recovery, (2) allowing recovery to third parties whose reliance on the audit report was "foreseeable", and (3) limiting liability to third parties that the audit intended to benefit.

Statutory liability can flow from professional malpractice statutes, civil RICO, the federal securities laws and the blue sky laws. As an example of recent legislation affecting accountants' legal liability, Texas enacted a statute which limits the legal liability of accountants involved in issuing securities of small businesses to no more than three times their fees, provided that the accountant did not engage in intentional wrongdoing. 1997 Tex. Gen. Laws ch. 638, § 1. Other states have enacted privity statutes that raise often insurmountable obstacles to a third party's ability to maintain a professional liability action against an accountant.

2. The principal case and the subject of accountants' legal liability raise several important policy questions. Does the decision in the principal case permit accountants to profit from the value which is expected to result from third party reliance on audit opinions, while nevertheless escaping liability when negligence causes injury to relying third parties? Does the threat of liability reinforce the accountant's independence from the client, preventing loyalty to the client from affecting, either consciously or unconsciously, the auditor's professional judgment? Does potential liability of accountants

prevent harm by deterring negligent conduct? Do cases involving accountants' legal liability present an inherently legislative problem?

3. Upon the dissolution of an enterprise due to management fraud, the auditing firm often finds itself as the only solvent entity from which the shareholders can seek restitution. Aggressive auditing firms, however, have begun seeking damages from the corporate officials, particularly for amounts the auditor paid to settle shareholder claims. Notice that the mere existence of auditor claims can preclude corporate officials from settling a lawsuit against themselves because the corporate officials could still be vulnerable to litigation from the outside auditor.

4. In this era of heightened liability potential, not surprisingly auditors have sought relief, and one avenue has been so-called "liability caps", which have increasingly appeared in audit engagement letters. These provisions may eliminate the audit client's right to sue the auditor by requiring arbitration, mediation or alternative dispute resolution; bar the client from seeking punitive damages; or require the client to indemnify the auditor from any losses arising from the client's misrepresentations, willful misconduct, or fraudulent behavior. Critics complain that these restrictions compromise the auditor's independence and performance. The accounting industry has responded that such provisions allow the parties to control the costs accompanying litigation, comport with available remedies under the federal securities laws, and do not limit the extent to which investors can sue the auditors. The issue awaits final resolution, either legislative or judicial.

5. It is to be recalled that since Sarbanes-Oxley auditors must confront this array of potential liabilities while receiving substantially less revenues from its public audit clients. As noted earlier, SOx flatly prohibits auditors from providing certain types of non-audit services to audit clients. The legislative history states that three basic principles informed the list of prohibited activities that Congress established for registered public accounting firms to qualify as independent: an auditing firm (1) should not audit its own work; (2) should not function as part of client management or as a client employee; and (3) should not act as an advocate for the audit client. The "prohibited activities" for auditors include bookkeeping or other services related to the audit client's accounting records or financial statements; financial information systems design and implementation; appraisal or valuation services, fairness opinions, or contribution-in-kind reports; actuarial services; internal audit outsourcing; management functions; human resources; broker-dealer, investment adviser or investment banking services; legal services; expert services unrelated to the audit; and, subject to the SEC's approval, any other service that the PCAOB decides to prohibit via regulation. An auditor may perform services not included on the prohibited list, such as tax services, for an audit client only if the client's audit committee approves those services in advance.

6. During the hearings that ultimately led to Sarbanes-Oxley, Congress considered a total ban that would have prevented auditing firms from providing any non-audit services, including so-called "tax services," to publicly traded audit clients. Tax services can range from tax compliance work, such as preparing tax returns, to sophisticated tax minimization strategies, or "tax shelters," that aggressively seek to use quirks in the Internal Revenue Code to avoid taxes. Ultimately, Congress decided not to impose an absolute ban on non-audit services, and not to include tax services in the list of services that were expressly prohibited. Subsequently, the release that announced the SEC's final rules on auditor independence specifically reiterated the agency's "long-standing position that an accounting firm can provide tax services to its audit clients without impairing the firm's independence." Strengthening the Commission's Requirements Regarding Auditor Independence, 68 Fed. Reg. 6006, 6017 (Feb. 5, 2003). Various commentators, however, have continued to argue that conflicts of interest arise anytime an auditor offers significant tax advice to an audit client or promotes a tax shelter to anyone. *See, e.g.,* Barrett, *"Tax Services" as a Trojan Horse in the Auditor Independence Provisions of Sarbanes-Oxley,* 2004 MICH. ST. L. REV. 463 (arguing that auditors for public companies should not provide tax compliance services to audit clients or their executives). While management can no longer hire or fire the auditor, under the guise of increasing auditor independence, management can use "enhanced independence" to support a recommendation to the audit committee to hire another firm to provide tax services, other permissible non-audit services, or future audit services. Thus, if the auditor does not approve, or at least acquiesce in, certain accounting treatments or disclosures that management prefers, the auditor conceivably jeopardizes potentially significant future professional fees.

As mentioned earlier, in April 2006 the SEC approved new PCAOB ethics and independence rules concerning tax services. These rules prohibit auditors from providing non-audit services to audit clients related to (1) confidential transactions, as defined under Treasury regulations, (2) aggressive tax position transactions, described as significantly motivated by tax avoidance, unless the applicable tax laws more likely than not allow the proposed tax treatment, and (3) any tax service to any person who fills a financial reporting oversight role at an audit client, or to an immediate family member of such a person. Order Approving Proposed Ethics and Independence Rules Concerning Independence, Tax Services, and Contingent Fees, 71 Fed. Reg. 23,971, 23,971–72 (April 25, 2006).

*

CHAPTER III

THE TIME VALUE OF MONEY

A. IMPORTANCE TO LAWYERS

Any lawyer who has ever filled out a time sheet knows that "time is money." Although almost every lawyer has heard about billable hours, lawyers should also understand the time value of money, which provides an alternative application for the saying that "time is money." As a fundamental principle, lawyers must always remember that: "A dollar today is worth more than a dollar tomorrow." This chapter will discuss various situations in which the time value of money can affect the practice of law.

We can compare borrowing money to renting a car, in the sense that the borrower usually agrees to pay "rent" for the use of either asset. With money, we describe this rent as *interest*. For the borrower, the time value of money refers to the interest expense of borrowing money over a period of time. For the lender, the time value of money refers to the interest earned from lending or investing money.

The lawyer who understands the time value of money has learned a useful tool for resolving money-related issues. For instance, suppose that a lawyer represents a plaintiff who, under the terms of a settlement offer, can select either an immediate cash payment of $100,000 or five annual payments of $25,000 each, beginning one year after the plaintiff signs the settlement agreement. If the relevant interest rate is nine percent per year and in the absence of tax and other considerations, which option should the plaintiff prefer?

The time value of money can also affect defendants. The lawyer representing a defendant against a plaintiff seeking future lost profits should ask the court to reduce any such award to present value. After all, a dollar in the future is not worth as much as a dollar today. Remarkably, however, lawyers, and therefore judges and juries, sometimes do not consider this issue. If the defendant does not raise the issue at trial, an appellate court may refuse to reduce an undiscounted award.

Lawyers also use time value of money concepts for financial planning. Whether planning for their own retirements, saving for college educations for their children or grandchildren, or advising clients about these same matters, every lawyer should understand the power of compound interest. A lawyer specializing in estate planning will use time value of money concepts to advise clients in selecting payment options under life insurance policies, set up charitable remainder trusts, and estimate the value of estates. Tax lawyers use time value of money concepts to defer income and accelerate deductions. Finally, time value of money concepts provide an excellent opportunity to consider how lawyers should present accounting and financial information to juries.

Although the time value of money has a long history in finance and accounting, financial accounting standards have traditionally ignored present value, using instead the undiscounted sum of estimated future cash flows for various purposes. In February 2000, however, the Financial Accounting Standards Board issued a new Statement of Financial Accounting Concepts that establishes a framework for using future cash flows, as discounted to present value, as the basis for certain accounting measurements. USING CASH FLOW INFORMATION AND PRESENT VALUE IN ACCOUNTING MEASUREMENTS, Statement of Financial Accounting Concepts No. 7 (Financial Accounting Standards Bd. 2000). You may recall from the last chapter that Statements of Financial Accounting Concepts provide an overall framework as FASB sets accounting rules. As the Board issues new or revised accounting standards, the new concepts statement will likely increase significantly the importance of time value of money principles in financial accounting. Regardless of whether the new concepts statement significantly changes financial accounting, this chapter will acquaint you with the basics of time value analysis. By chapter's end, you will be able to analyze and resolve problems involving the time value of money.

B. INTEREST

As previously mentioned, interest represents a charge for the use of money. Borrowers agree to pay interest when they believe that the benefit they receive from spending the money outweighs the interest they must pay to borrow the money. Lenders and investors lend money when they believe that the interest income they will earn in the future outweighs the opportunity cost of spending today.

1. FACTORS DETERMINING INTEREST RATES

Numerous and complex factors affect interest rates. Financial analysts often divide a stated interest rate into various components that can help to explain the different factors which can influence the market rate. These components include a pure rate of interest, the inflation premium, the maturity premium, the default premium and the illiquidity premium.

Economists often describe the *pure rate of interest* as the rate which lenders would charge and borrowers would agree to pay if the risks which we will discuss shortly did not exist. Financial analysts generally believe that this pure rate of interest falls between two and three percent per year. The rate on short-term U.S. Treasury obligations in periods of stable prices perhaps best illustrates the risk-free interest rate. Interest rates, however, almost always exceed this pure rate of interest because various premiums compensate lenders for the different risks that they assume by lending money.

Inflation risk refers to the general loss in purchasing power from rising prices. For this reason, interest rates tend to rise when inflation increases and drop when the price level declines. The *inflation premium* compensates the lender for the inflation which the lender expects over the loan's term. Next, the *maturity premium* offsets the risks associated with committing funds for longer periods. Various general market, business and economic risks underlie the maturity premium. Historically, long-term interest rates have exceeded short-term interest rates for investments presenting similar risks. The maturity premium helps explain this difference. The difference in interest rates between long-term U.S. Treasury bonds and short-term U.S. Treasury obligations illustrates maturity premium.

The *default premium* reflects the risk that the borrower will default on the loan and that the lender will lose the loan principal and any accrued interest. As a general rule, the rates for U.S. Treasury obligations do not include a default premium. The differences in interest rates between bonds with similar maturities in different risk categories, such as U.S. Treasury bonds, high grade corporate bonds and below investment grade bonds, sometime referred to as *junk bonds*, document a default premium. Finally, the *illiquidity premium* compensates a lender for lack of marketability and the resulting price concession that the lender may have to grant if unexpected circumstances force the lender to sell the debt instrument, particularly if the lender needs to raise cash quickly. The spread between interest rates on nonpublicly traded bonds and highly marketable bonds with similar other characteristics demonstrates an illiquidity premium.

Lawyers should, but often do not, consider the various components and different factors that may determine market interest rates in contractual negotiations and litigation. Contracts and pleadings frequently use risk-free or statutory interest rates that bear no resemblance to market rates. *See, e.g.,* Medcom Holding Co. v. Baxter Travenol Laboratories, Inc., 200 F.3d 518 (7th Cir. 2000) (concluding that the district court should have awarded prejudgment interest at a market rate rather than the statutory rate of five percent simple interest).

2. COMPUTATIONS

We generally state interest as a rate over a specified period of time, such as eight percent per annum. To compute the actual dollar amount of interest, we start with the basic equation:

$$\text{Interest} = \text{Principal} \times \text{Rate} \times \text{Time}$$

where *Interest* represents the dollar amount of interest; *Principal*, the amount of money that the debtor borrows; *Rate*, the stated cost of borrowing one dollar per unit of time; and *Time*, the number of units of time that the principal remains unpaid.

We normally count one year as one unit of time because people usually express the interest rate as an annual rate. You should note, however, that when someone expresses the rate in something other than an annual rate or the time in something other than years, we can still use this equation as long as we adjust the formula for the proper units of time. For example, if someone charges interest at one percent per month, we would use months as the unit of time.

When the loan period extends over several units of time, the borrower and lender decide whether the borrower will pay *simple* interest or *compound* interest. With simple interest, the borrower pays interest on the original principal amount only, regardless of any interest that has accrued in the past. Under compound interest, the borrower pays interest on the unpaid interest of past periods, as well as on the original principal amount.

Example 1: *Simple Interest Calculation*

Betty borrows $10,000 from Larry, who charges simple interest at a rate of eight percent per year. At the end of the first year, Betty owes Larry $800 interest, calculated as follows:

$$
\begin{aligned}
\text{Interest} = \ & \text{Principal x Rate x Time} \\
= \ & \$10,000 \text{ x } .08/\text{year x 1 year} \\
= \ & \$800
\end{aligned}
$$

Now suppose that the $10,000 loan remains outstanding for another year. Under simple interest, we calculate the second year's interest based upon the original principal amount only. The $800 first year's interest does not affect the interest calculation in the second year. For the second year, therefore, Larry earns another $800 interest. Thus, at the end of the second year Betty owes Larry a total of $11,600, representing $10,000 original principal plus $1,600 simple interest at $800 per year.

Example 2: *Compound Interest Calculations*

Assume Linda deposits $10,000 in a bank account that pays interest at a rate of eight percent per year, compounded annually. At the end of the first year, the bank owes Linda $800 interest, calculated as above.

Now suppose that Linda keeps the original $10,000 plus the $800 interest in the bank account for another year. The bank adds, or compounds, the $800 first year's interest to the $10,000 original principal amount before calculating the interest for the second year. In the second year, Linda earns $864 interest, calculated as follows:

Interest = Principal x Rate x Time
    = $10,800 x .08/year x 1 year
    = $864

Thus, at the end of the second year the bank owes Linda a total of $11,664, which represents $10,000 original principal plus interest at $800 for year one, which we added to unpaid principal to compute interest for year two, and $864 for year two. Because of compounding, Linda earned $64 more interest than she would have earned under simple interest.

Example 3: *Another Compound Interest Calculation*

Same facts as **Example 2**, except that Linda deposits $100,000 instead of $10,000. At the end of the first year, the bank owes Linda $8,000 interest, and in the second year, Linda earns $8,640 interest. Thus, at the end of the second year, the bank owes Linda a total of $116,640.

Comparing the amount the bank owes Linda at the end of year two with the original principal in **Examples 2** and **3**, the ratio remains constant at 1.1664; that is, because the Rate and the Time remained constant, and only the Principal changed. We can use this ratio as a shortcut for making similar calculations involving the same Rate and Time.

Examine Table I in Appendix B, *infra,* which lists Rates across the top and Periods down the left side. Find the column with eight percent at the top and the row for two periods. They intersect at 1.1664, the same number as the ratio that we calculated above. Someone has similarly precalculated the other numbers in the body of the table for different Rates and Times, each ratio representing the shortcut for a specific combination of Rate and Time.

Appendix B contains a total of four tables, each table embodying a shortcut for four different types of compound interest calculations: future value of an amount, future value of a series of equal amounts, present value of an amount, and present value of a series of equal amounts. We will examine the concepts of both future value and present value, beginning with future value.

C. FUTURE VALUE

We can describe *future value* as the sum to which an amount or a series of periodic and equal amounts will grow at the end of a certain amount of time, invested at a particular compound interest rate. Future value, therefore, can apply either to one amount or a series of equal amounts. Accountants use the term *annuity* to refer to a sequence of periodic and equal amounts. In this section, we will discuss two different future value calculations: the first for single amounts and the second for annuities. We begin with the future value of a single amount.

1. SINGLE AMOUNTS

Examples 2 and 3 both involve the concept of *future value*. We can define *future value* as the amount to which a current Principal *p* will grow at the end of *n* periods of Time, invested at *i* compound interest Rate. Accountants sometimes refer to future value amount as the *future amount of $1* or the *amount of a given sum*. Table I lists the amounts to which one dollar invested will grow at the end of various periods of time, at various compound interest rates. Using the table, we can easily compute the future value of a current principal amount if we know the interest rate and the length of time over which the amount will remain invested. Let's continue with another simple example:

Example 4: *Future Value—Simple Illustration*

Dawn invests $10,000 in an individual retirement account ("IRA") which earns twelve percent, compounded annually. How much money will the account contain at the end of ten years? $31,058.50. Using Table I, we find the future value factor for ten periods at twelve percent compound interest. The column for twelve percent interest and the row for ten periods intersect at 3.10585, which means that one dollar will grow to approximately $3.11 at the end of ten years at twelve percent compound interest per year. We multiply Dawn's original investment of $10,000 times the 3.10585 future value factor to arrive at a $31,058.50 future value. Now let's try a more complicated calculation:

Example 5: *Future Amount—More Complicated Illustration*

In 1901, the monetary reward to Nobel Prize winners was $40,000. By 1999 the prize, actually awarded in Swedish kronor, had grown to approximately $1,000,000. If a 1901 Nobel Prize winner invested the proceeds from the award at five percent interest, compounded annually, would the 1901 winner have more or less than $1,000,000 in 1999?

If the 1901 prize winner had invested the proceeds at five percent interest, compounded annually, by 1999 the proceeds would have grown to more than $4,771,000. To answer the question, we must calculate the future value of $40,000 after 98 years at five percent, compound interest. Although Table I shows the amounts to which one dollar invested will grow at the end of various periods of time, at five percent compound interest, the Table does not list a factor for 98 periods. Nevertheless, we can use Table I to answer the question if we make a few intermediate calculations.

First, using Table I, we find the factor for 50 periods and five percent compound interest, or 11.46740. Table I tells us that one dollar would have grown to about $11.47 if invested at five percent compound interest for fifty years. Using this factor, we can compute that $40,000 would have grown to $458,696, or $40,000 times 11.46740, at the end of 50 years. Next, we use Table I to find the factor for 40 periods and five percent interest, or 7.03999.

During the next forty years, each dollar would have grown to $7.04 if invested at five percent compound interest. The $458,696 at the end of fifty years, therefore, would have increased to $3,229,215.25, or $458,696 times 7.03999, at the end of ninety years. Finally, we use Table I to find the factor for eight periods and five percent interest, or 1.47746. During the last eight years, $3,229,215.25 would have grown to $4,771,036.36, which equals $3,229,215.25 times 1.47746. To summarize:

Year	Factor	Amount
1901		$40,000.00
1951	11.46740	458,696.00
1991	7.03999	3,229,215.25
1999	1.47746	4,771,036.36

a. CONSEQUENCE OF MORE FREQUENT COMPOUNDING

You will recall from **Example 4**, that $10,000 will grow to $31,058.50 after ten years at twelve percent interest, compounded annually. But what if the investment will compound interest semiannually? To calculate future value when the lending agreement requires compounding more than once a year, we must first adjust for the length of the compounding period, as in the following examples.

Example 6: *Future Value—Interest Compounded Semiannually*

Frank invests $10,000 in an IRA earning twelve percent interest, compounded *semiannually*. How much will Frank have at the end of ten years? $32,071.40. Because the investment requires the borrower to compound interest twice a year, in ten years the borrower will have compounded interest twenty different times. Every six months, Frank will earn six percent interest or one-half the twelve percent annual rate. Using Table I, we find a future value factor of 3.20714 for $1 invested for twenty periods of time at six percent compound interest. Multiplying the $10,000 original investment times the 3.20714 future value factor yields a $32,071.40 future value.

Example 7: *Future Value—Interest Compounded Quarterly*

Sheila invests $10,000 in an IRA earning twelve percent interest, compounded *quarterly*. How much will Sheila have at the end of ten years? $32,620. Because the investment requires the borrower to compound interest four times a year, in ten years, the borrower will have compounded the interest forty different times. Every three months, Sheila will earn three percent interest or one-fourth the twelve percent annual rate. Using Table I, we find a future value factor of 3.26204 for $1 invested for forty periods of time at three percent compound interest. Multiplying the $10,000 original investment times the 3.26204 future value factor yields a future value of $32,620.40.

From **Examples 4, 6 and 7**, we can see that, assuming the same stated interest rate, in these illustrations twelve percent interest, lenders and investors prefer more frequent compounding because the compounding produces a higher effective interest rate. In contrast, at any particular interest rate, borrowers prefer simple interest or compound interest with less frequent compounding. The investors in **Examples 4, 6 and 7** all invested in accounts which earned interest at a twelve percent stated rate. At the end of ten years, however, Sheila has earned more interest on the same investment than either Frank or Dawn. Similarly, the borrowers in **Examples 4, 6 and 7** all agreed to pay twelve percent interest. Dawn's borrower paid less interest for the ten year period than Frank's borrower, and both those borrowers paid less interest than Sheila's borrower.

We can also discern a general rule to determine the future value factor from Table I when the contract requires interest compounding more than once a year. When interest is compounded c times a year, multiply the number of years the principal will be invested times c, divide the annual interest rate by c, then use the future value factor located at this adjusted Time and Rate. For example, suppose that Terry deposits $2,000 in a bank account that pays eight percent per year, compounded quarterly. How much will Terry have in five years? The bank compounds interest four times a year, or twenty times over five years. The bank calculates an adjusted rate of two percent per quarter by dividing the eight percent annual rate divided by the four quarters in a year. Using Table I, we find a future value factor of 1.48595 at the adjusted time of twenty periods and the adjusted interest rate of two percent. Multiplying the $2,000 times 1.48595, Terry will have $2,971.90 at the end of five years.

b.   RULE OF 72s: DOUBLING AN INVESTMENT

Dividing 72 by the interest rate gives us the approximate number of years in which an investment will double at compound interest. For example, an investment earning six percent interest, compounded annually, will double in approximately twelve years. To illustrate, Table I shows the future value factor for six percent and twelve periods as 2.01220. Thus, the Rule of 72s enables us to estimate quickly how soon an investment will double.

To illustrate, we can use the Rule of 72s to estimate how much money a twenty-five year old person needs to retire as a millionaire at age sixty-five, assuming a nine percent return, compounded annually. At a nine percent compounded annual return, an investment will double every eight years. Even if the twenty-five year old never saves another penny, we can work backwards as follows:

Age	Amount
65	$1,000,000
57	500,000
49	250,000
41	125,000
33	62,500
25	31,250

As the table illustrates, relative small amounts can grow to significant sums over time.

2. ANNUITIES

Suppose that instead of making a one-time deposit to her IRA, Erica decided to invest $2,000 every year. In an *annuity*, the investor makes a series of equal payments at regular time intervals, such as depositing an amount from every paycheck into a savings account or investing $2,000 in an IRA every year. In an *ordinary annuity*, which accountants sometimes refer to as an *annuity in arrears*, the investor starts making payments at the end, rather than at the beginning, of the first period. In contrast, under an *annuity due*, which accountants might call an *annuity in advance*, the investor makes payments at the beginning of each period. We can calculate the future value of both ordinary annuities and annuities due using the principles to determine the future value for a single amount.

a. ORDINARY ANNUITY

With an *ordinary annuity*, or *annuity in arrears*, the first payment occurs at the end of the first period. The future value of an ordinary annuity represents the sum accumulated at the time of the last payment. To illustrate, suppose that Dianne contributes $1,000 at the end of each year for four years to an annuity paying five percent compound interest. How much will Dianne have at the end of four years? By examining the timing of the payments, we can use Table I on the next page to compute the future value of this annuity.

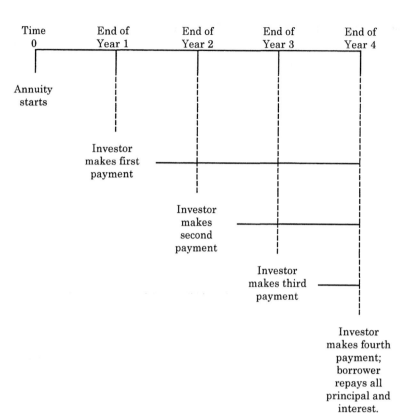

We notice that the first payment at the end of year one will compound three times before the end of year four; the second payment will compound twice; the third payment will compound once; and the fourth payment does not earn any interest, because we are determining the value as of the date of the fourth and last payment. Summarizing the future value factors from Table I for five percent interest for these periods, we get:

First payment (three periods)	1.15763
Second payment (two periods)	1.10250
Third payment (one period)	1.05000
Fourth payment (no interest)	1.00000
Total	4.31013

If Dianne contributed $1 at the end of each year, she would have $4.31 at the end of four years. But Dianne invested $1,000 each year. Multiplying Dianne's $1,000 annuity payment times this sum of future value factors, we see that Dianne will have $4,310.13 at the end of four years.

Alternatively, we could use Table II in Appendix B, *infra,* to determine the future amount of this annuity. Table II uses the future value factors from Table I for single amounts to calculate the future value factors for an ordinary annuity. Assuming the same facts as above, we find a future value factor at Table II of 4.31013 for an annuity of $1 for four payments at five percent compound interest. Multiplying the $1,000 annuity payment times the 4.31013 future value factor yields a $4,310.13 future value, the same amount that we calculated earlier, but with much less effort.

When working with Tables I and II, recall that we can adjust Table I to reflect semiannual and quarterly compounding of a stated annual rate. We cannot adjust Table II in the same way, however, because Table II would require an additional payment at the end of each semiannual or quarterly period.

Example 8: *Future Value of an Ordinary Annuity*

Paul's parents plan to invest $2,000 at the end of each year for the next fifteen years in his college fund. Assuming that the fund will earn six percent compound interest, how much will Paul have in fifteen years? $46,551.94. Using Table II, we find a future value factor of 23.27597 for an annuity of $1 for fifteen payments at six percent compound interest. Multiplying the $2,000 annuity payment times the 23.27597 future value factor yields a future value of $46,551.94.

But what if Paul's parents decide to invest $2,000 at the beginning of each year to fund his college education? How much will the college fund contain at the end of fifteen years? We turn now to the future amount of an annuity due.

b. ANNUITY DUE

Recall that with an *annuity due*, unlike an ordinary annuity, the investor makes payments at the beginning of the each period. The future value of an annuity due represents the sum accumulated one period *after* the last payment. Thus, each payment compounds for one more period than the payment would under an ordinary annuity. To illustrate, let us recalculate Dianne's annuity as an annuity due, using Table I. By examining the timing of the payments, we can use Table I to compute the future value of her annuity.

The first payment at the beginning of year one will compound four times by the end of year four; the second payment will compound three times; the third payment will compound twice; and the fourth payment will compound once, because we determine the future value of an annuity due one period after the last payment. Summarizing the future value factors from Table I for five percent for these periods, we get:

First payment (four periods)	1.21550
Second payment (three periods)	1.15763
Third payment (two periods)	1.10250
Fourth payment (one period)	1.05000
Total	4.52563

Multiplying Dianne's $1,000 annuity payment times this sum of future value factors, we see that Dianne will have $4,525.63 at the end of four years.

D. Present Value

Future value analysis tells us how much a given amount or annuity, invested at compound interest, will grow to at some time in the future. Conversely, present value analysis tells us how much a given future sum or annuity is worth today. In this section, we will again discuss present values in two different contexts: the first for single amounts and the second for annuities. We again start with the present value of a single amount.

1. Single Amounts

Present value analysis flows from the fundamental principal that a dollar today is worth more than a dollar tomorrow because you could invest that dollar today and you will have the dollar plus some small amount of interest tomorrow. Suppose that someone agrees to pay you $1,100 one year from now. Assuming a ten percent interest rate, how much is that promise worth today? Using future value analysis, we can calculate that $1,000 today will grow to $1,100 in one year at ten percent interest. In other words, we can see that a promise for $1,100 one year from now is worth $1,000 today.

We can define *present value* as the amount that will grow to a larger sum at the end of *n* periods of time in the future, at *r* compound interest rate. Accountants sometimes refer to this present value amount as the *present value of $1* or the *present value of a single sum.* Just as someone precalculated Table I for future value computations, we can also use a precalculated table for present value calculations. In fact, Table III in Appendix B, *infra,* lists the amount that will grow to one dollar at the end of *n* periods of time in the future, at *r* compound interest rate. In other words, Table III shows the present value of one dollar at the end of *n* periods, *discounted* at *r* compound interest. We say discounted because we start with a larger known amount in the future and determine the lower present value. In contrast, to calculate the future amount, we start with a known amount and add interest to determine the larger amount in the future. Several examples can illustrate the concept.

Example 9: *Present Value—Simple Illustration*

Amy promised to give David, her twelve year old brother, $10,000 on his twenty-second birthday. What is the present value, discounted at eight percent interest annually, of this promise? Using Table III, we find a present value factor of .46319 at ten periods and eight percent interest. Multiplying the $10,000 promised payment times the .46319 present value factor yields a $4,631.90 present value.

We have determined that the promise to pay $10,000 in ten years, discounted at eight percent interest each year, is worth $4,631.90 today. Using Table I, we can verify our calculation. We first find 2.15892 as the future value factor for ten periods at eight percent compound interest on Table I. That factor means that one dollar will grow to approximately $2.16 at the end of ten years at eight percent compounded annually. We then multiply the $4,631.90 we determined above times the 2.15892 future value factor to arrive at a $9,999.90 future value, which we can round to $10,000 to eliminate some slight imprecision in the tables.

Having verified our present value calculation, we can see what happens when we compound interest more frequently than annually. Recall the general rule that we derived in the future value context: when the scenario requires compounding interest c times a year, we multiply the number of years times c, divide the annual interest rate by c, then use the future value factor located at this adjusted Time and Rate. We apply the same rule in present value calculations.

Example 10: *Present Value—Interest Compounded Semiannually*

Same facts as **Example 10**, except assume that we will compound interest semiannually. Because this scenario requires us to compound interest twice a year, in ten years, we must compound interest twenty times. Every six months, we will compound interest at four percent or one half the eight percent annual rate. Using Table III, we look at twenty periods and four percent interest and find a .45639 present value factor. Multiplying the $10,000 promised payment times the .45639 present value factor yields a $4,563.90 present value.

Example 11: *Present Value—Interest Compounded Quarterly*

Same facts as **Example 10**, except that we will compound interest quarterly. At Table III, we look at forty periods and two percent interest, and find a present value factor of .45289. Multiplying the $10,000 promised payment times the .45289 present value factor yields a present value of $4,529.

Notice that the more frequently we compound interest, the lower the present value drops, because more frequent compounding produces a higher effective rate of interest. Recall **Examples 4, 6** and **7**. A higher effective rate of interest means that we can invest less now, which means a lower present value, to arrive at a given sum in the future.

2. ANNUITIES

Suppose that instead of promising to make a one-time payment, someone promises to make a *series* of equal payments, such as agreeing to pay regular amounts on a loan. In an annuity, this person promises to make these payments at regular intervals of time. The present value of an annuity represents the present value of this series of payments discounted at compound interest. You can also think of this present value as the lump sum that someone must invest now, at compound interest, to permit a series of equal withdrawals at regular intervals, and end up with nothing after the final withdrawal. In either event, we can calculate the present value of an annuity using the principles developed above.

a. ORDINARY ANNUITY

Recall that in an ordinary annuity or an annuity in arrears, the first periodic payment or investment occurs at the end of the first period. If we turn the transaction around, we could say that the first withdrawal also occurs at the end of that first period. For example, suppose that Steve enters a four-year lease on his apartment, promising to pay $1,000 at the end of each year. Steve can earn eight percent on his investments. How much would Steve have to invest now to meet his rental obligations? By examining the timing of the withdrawals, we can use Table III to compute the present value of this annuity.

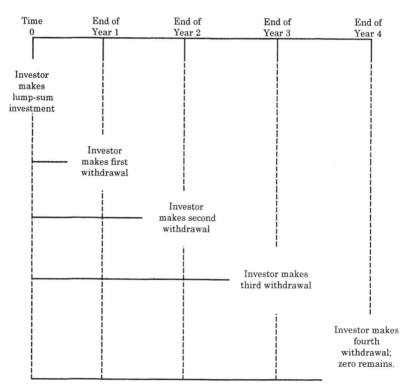

We notice that we will discount the first withdrawal at the end of year one once to the beginning of year one. Similarly, we will discount the second withdrawal twice; the third withdrawal three times; and the fourth withdrawal four times. Summarizing the present value factors from Table III for eight percent interest for these periods, we get:

First withdrawal (one period)	.92593
Second withdrawal (two periods)	.85734
Third withdrawal (three periods)	.79383
Fourth withdrawal (four periods)	.73503
Total	3.31213

Multiplying Steve's $1,000 rental payment times this sum of present value factors, we see that Steve must invest $3,312.13 at eight percent interest today to have enough money to withdraw $1,000 at the end of each of the next four years.

Alternatively, we could use Table IV in Appendix B, *infra,* to determine the present value of this annuity. Table IV uses the future value factors from Table III for one-time payments to calculate the present value factors for an ordinary annuity. Assuming the same facts as above, we find a present value factor at Table IV of 3.31213 for an annuity of $1 for four payments at eight percent compound interest. Multiplying the $1,000 annuity payment times the 3.31213 present value factor yields a $3,312.13 present value.

We can verify these calculations as follows: In the first year, the $3,312.13 initial deposit earns eight percent interest or $264.97, bringing the account balance to $3,577.10. After subtracting the first $1,000 withdrawal at the end of the first year, $2,577.10 remains available to earn interest during the second year. During the second year, that remaining balance earns $206.17 interest, which increases the balance to $2,783.27. The second withdrawal reduces the balance to $1,783.27. In the third year, the $1,783.27 earns $142.66 interest, raising the balance to $1,925.93. After subtracting the third withdrawal, $925.93 remains in the account to earn interest during the fourth year. In the final year, $74.07 interest on the previous balance increases the balance to $1,000, which the fourth withdrawal entirely consumes. Summarizing these calculations, we could develop the following chart:

Description	Interest	Principal	Balance
Initial Deposit			$3,312.13
Interest During Year 1	$264.97		3,577.10
First Withdrawal		$1,000.00	2,577.10
Interest During Year 2	206.17		2,783.27
Second Withdrawal		1,000.00	1,783.27
Interest During Year 3	142.66		1,925.93
Third Withdrawal		1,000.00	925.93
Interest During Year 4	74.07		1,000.00
Fourth Withdrawal		1,000.00	–0–

Recall that we could adjust Table I, but not Table II, to reflect semiannual and quarterly compounding of a stated annual rate. Similarly, we cannot adjust Table IV because the table would require an additional payment or withdrawal at the end of each semiannual or quarterly period.

Before continuing, let's try one more example which requires us to calculate the present value of an ordinary annuity:

Example 12: *Present Value of an Ordinary Annuity*

Suppose Victoria wins $1,000,000 in a sweepstakes, payable $100,000 at the end of each year for ten years. If the applicable interest rate is seven percent, compounded annually, what is the present value of all the sweepstakes payments? $702,358. Using Table IV, we find a present value factor of 7.02358 for an annuity of $1 for ten payments at seven percent compound interest. Multiplying the $100,000 annuity payment times the 7.02358 present value factor yields a $702,358 present value.

b. CALCULATING THE AMOUNT OF THE ANNUITY PAYMENT

So far, we have determined the present value of an annuity, given the amount of the annuity payment. Because the present value of an annuity equals the annuity payment times the factor from Table IV, we can also solve for the amount of an annuity payment, given the present value of the annuity.

To illustrate, assume that Jolanda borrows $100,000 for five years at ten percent interest. The lender requires repayment of the loan through equal, annual payments at the end of each of the next five years. The lender will credit each payment to accrued interest first, and then to principal. What annual payment will the lender require Jolanda to make?

We know that the present value of the annuity is $100,000, because the lender is giving Jolanda $100,000 cash today. We can find a 3.79079 present value factor in Table IV for an ordinary annuity of $1 for five payments at ten percent compound interest. Because the present value of an annuity equals the annuity payment times the factor from Table IV, we get:

$100,000 = Annuity Payment x 3.79079

Solving this equation, we see that the annuity payment equals $26,379.73. Therefore, Jolanda must pay the lender $26,379.73 at the end of each year for five years to repay her $100,000 loan.

Let us examine how much of each $26,379.73 payment the lender credits to interest and principal. For the first year, the interest equals the ten percent interest rate times the $100,000 original principal amount outstanding during the year, or $10,000. Of the $26,379.73 that Jolanda pays at the end of the first year, the lender credits $10,000 to interest and the remaining $16,379.73 to principal. Subtracting the $16,379.83 principal payment from the $100,000 original loan amount leaves $83,620.27 as the new principal balance which remains outstanding during the second year. At the end of the second year, Jolanda pays another $26,379.73. Interest for that year equals $8,362.03, ten percent interest times the $83,620.27 remaining principal. The lender credits the $18,017.70 difference between the $26,379.73 payment and the $8,362.03 interest to principal, which reduces the loan balance outstanding during the third year to $65,602.57. Summarizing these calculations for the five years, we get:

Year	Payment	Interest	Principal	Balance
0				$100,000.00
1	$26,379.73	$10,000.00	$16,379.73	83,620.27
2	26,379.73	8,362.03	18,017.70	65,602.57
3	26,379.73	6,560.26	19,819.47	45,783.10
4	26,379.73	4,578.31	21,801.42	23,981.68
5	26,379.73	2,398.17	23,981.56	.12

Rounding creates the twelve cent remaining balance, which we will ignore as insignificant. We can use a similar calculation to determine the amount of the periodic payments for an annuity due.

E. PERPETUAL ANNUITIES

All the annuities we have examined so far, whether in the future value or present value context, have been of limited duration. Unlike the previous annuities, with a perpetual annuity the investor intends the annuity to continue forever. For an annuity to continue forever, the investor may withdraw only the interest earned; the investor cannot withdraw any of the original principal.

To illustrate, assume that Ann, who plans to retire soon, wants to make sure she will have $60,000 per year in annual income. Assuming a five percent interest rate, how much money must Ann have in her retirement fund to guarantee $60,000 in annual income? This time, we can easily compute an answer. To determine what principal amount at five percent interest will produce $60,000 annual income, simply solve for X in the following equation, where X represents the principal amount:

$$.05X = \$60,000$$

$$X = \frac{\$60,000}{.05}$$

$$X = \$1,200,000$$

Ann, therefore, must invest $1,200,000 at five percent interest to guarantee $60,000 in annual income.

F. COMPREHENSIVE ILLUSTRATIONS

Thus far, we have examined perpetual annuities and four different types of compound interest calculations: future value of an amount, future value of a series of equal amounts, present value of an amount, and present value of a series of equal amounts. In all our previous examples, we have used one and only one of these computations. In the real world, however, we may have to apply more than one of these computations to solve a particular problem. Three common examples include evaluating payment options, valuing bonds, and retirement planning.

1. CHOOSING AMONG A PRESENT AMOUNT, A FUTURE SUM AND AN ANNUITY

Assume that under the terms of a settlement agreement, plaintiff has the option of receiving either: (1) an immediate cash payment of $200,000, (2) a deferred payment of $400,000 payable in ten years, or (3) a five-year annuity, beginning one year after the plaintiff signs the settlement agreement, which will pay $50,000 annually. Ignoring tax considerations and assuming a relevant interest rate of seven percent, compounded annually, which settlement option should plaintiff accept?

Before comparing these offers, we must find a common denominator to evaluate each offer. The $200,000 payment would give plaintiff cash immediately. The $400,000 payment would require plaintiff to wait ten years before collecting any cash. The annuity will pay $50,000 at the end of each of the next five years.

We can compare these options either: (a) at the present, (b) immediately after the last annuity payment at the end of the fifth year, (c) immediately after the $400,000 deferred payment in ten years, or (d) some other time. If we select (a), we need only: (i) discount the $400,000 future payment to its present value and (ii) compute the present value of the ordinary annuity. We already knows that Option 1, which provides an immediate $200,000 cash payment, offers a $200,000 present value. Alternatively under (b), we must: (i) compute the future amount of the single $200,000 payment in five years; (ii) discount the $400,000 to its present value at the end of the fifth year; and (iii) calculate the future amount of the ordinary annuity immediately after the last payment. If we select (c), we must calculate: (i) the future amount of the single $200,000 payment in ten years; (ii) the future amount of the ordinary annuity immediately after the last payment; and (iii) the future amount of the previous sum in another five years. Depending upon which time we select under (d), we may have to make even more computations. By selecting (a), however, we can avoid unnecessary computations.

Recall that we already know that Option 1 offers a $200,000 present value. Using Table III, we can calculate the present value of Option 2. Table

III lists .50835 as the present value of $1 for ten years at seven percent, compound interest. Multiplying the $400,000 proposed payment times the .50835 present value factor yields a $203,340 present value for Option 2. We can compute the present value of Option 3 using Table IV. In that table, we find 4.10020 as the factor for five periods and seven percent compound interest. Multiplying the $50,000 annual payments times the 4.10020 present value factor yields a $205,010 present value for Option 3.

Because Option 3 has the highest present value, we should advise the plaintiff to select that option. Under Option 3, plaintiff will receive five $50,000 payments, totaling $250,000. Assume that our engagement letter entitles us to a one-fifth contingent fee. Does the plaintiff owe us $50,000 immediately upon accepting Option 3 and signing the settlement agreement? Common sense suggests that if we want to collect our fee immediately, we can charge only one-fifth of the present value of all the future payments or approximately $41,000. As a practical matter, absent an explicit agreement to the contrary, a court may permit a client to pay legal fees attributable to an annuity as the client collects each payment.

2. CALCULATING THE MARKET VALUE OF BONDS

Bonds generally give the owner two separate rights: (1) the right to periodic interest payments and (2) the right to the repayment of principal at the bond's maturity. The periodic interest payments give rise to an annuity while the principal represents a single amount. To determine a bond's market value, we must determine the present value of the interest payments and the principal.

Assume that Starbucks Coffee Company uses bonds to borrow money at ten percent interest per year, payable semiannually. Further assume that after Starbucks issues the bonds, interest rates increase to twelve percent annual interest, compounded semiannually. If the bonds will mature in exactly three years, how much would a reasonable investor pay for such a bond with a $10,000 principal amount?

This bond gives its owner two separate rights: (1) the right to the six semiannual interest payments of $500, or one half of the ten percent annual rate times $10,000; and (2) the right to repayment of the $10,000 bond principal at maturity, or in this case after three years. The value of the bond, therefore, equals the sum of the present values of these two rights discounted at the market interest rate of twelve percent annual interest, compounded semiannually.

By contract, the bond's terms set $500 as the amount of the semiannual interest payments. As a result, the amount of the annuity does not change as the market interest rate fluctuates. The present values of the rights to those semiannual interest payments and the principal amount, however, do vary as the market interest rate changes. Consequently, we discount the semiannual interest payments and the principal amount at the market rate.

Using Table IV, we find a 4.91732 present value factor for an annuity of $1 for six payments at six percent compound interest which represents one half of the twelve percent annual market rate. Multiplying the $500 semiannual interest payment times the 4.91732 present value factor yields a $2,458.66 present value for the interest payments. Next, we turn to the present value of the $10,000 principal which the borrower will repay in three years. Because the semiannual compounding requires us to discount interest twice a year for three years, we must discount the principal amount to present value over six periods. Every six months, we will discount the principal at six percent or one half the twelve percent annual rate. Using Table III, we look at six periods and six percent interest and find a .70496 present value factor. Multiplying the $10,000 principal amount times the .70496 present value factor yields a $7,049.60 present value. Therefore, the bond should trade for $9,508.26, the sum of the $2,458.66 present value of the semiannual interest payments and the $7,049.60 present value of the principal.

Now assume the same facts as above, except that, after Starbucks issues the bonds, the market interest rate on comparable bonds falls to eight percent annual interest, compounded semiannually. Still assuming that the bond will mature in exactly three years, how much would a reasonable investor pay for this $10,000 bond?

Again, we must determine present values for both (1) the right to the six semiannual interest payments which the bond's terms still fix at $500 each and (2) the right to repayment of the $10,000 bond principal at maturity in three years. Using Table IV, we find a 5.24214 present value factor for an annuity of $1 for six payments at four percent compound interest which represents one half of the eight percent annual market rate. Multiplying the $500 semiannual interest payment times the 5.24214 present value factor yields a $2,621.07 present value.

As to the present value of the repayment of the $10,000 bond principal in three years, the semiannual compounding again requires us to discount interest twice a year, or six times. Every six months, we will discount the principal at four percent or one half the eight percent annual rate. Using Table III, we look at six periods and four percent interest and find a .79031 present value factor. Multiplying the $10,000 principal amount times the .79031 present value factor yields a $7,903.10 present value. Therefore, the bond should trade for $10,524.17, the sum of the $2,621.07 present value of the semiannual interest payments and the $7,903.10 present value of the principal.

As we have just seen, the value of bonds varies inversely with the current market interest rate. When the market interest rate rises, the value of bonds decreases. When the market interest rate falls, the value of bonds increases.

G. Cautions About Time Value Analysis

To become acquainted with basic time value analysis, we have used nothing more than a simple calculator and the Tables in the back of this book. Business calculators and electronic spreadsheets, however, can quickly perform more complex time value calculations. For example, if a lender charges interest at something other than a whole percentage point, or interest compounds weekly, or the loan term extends over many periods, then a business calculator or an electronic spreadsheet can easily make these difficult computations.

In time value analysis, notwithstanding mathematical precision, an invalid underlying assumption can yield extremely inaccurate and unreliable results. For example, although we can calculate the future value of an investment at 800 percent per year for the next 40 years, only a complete fool would assume that any investment could perform that well. Similarly, time value analysis assumes that we can reinvest the earnings of an investment at the same interest rate, period after period, when in fact, interest rates fluctuate all the time.

Moreover, time value analysis ignores taxes and other considerations, such as terminal illnesses. For instance, suppose that a plaintiff, under the terms of a settlement offer, can select either an immediate cash payment of $1,000,000 or twenty annual, but nonassignable, payments of $200,000 each, beginning one year after the plaintiff signs the settlement agreement. If the plaintiff suffers from a terminal illness, the plaintiff might select the immediate payment, even if the twenty annual payments would normally offer a greater present value. We could also explain this decision on the grounds that the illness has caused the plaintiff to use a very high discount rate which exceeds the market rate.

In conclusion, time value analysis provides one factor for lawyers and their clients to consider when making decisions. Remember to consider these other factors, and the limitations of time value analysis, before you base a decision solely on time value analysis.

PROBLEMS

Problem 3.1A. Red, White, and Blue, believing themselves to be astute investors, each deposited $5,000 in different banks on January 1, 1985. Red deposited his $5,000 in an account that paid eight percent simple interest per year; White deposited his $5,000 in an account that paid eight percent annual interest, compounded annually; and Blue deposited his $5,000 in an account that paid eight percent interest per year, compounded semiannually. How much would each person have in his savings account on January 1, 2001?

Problem 3.1B. In 1803, the United States purchased the Louisiana Territory from France for $15 million.

(1) If France had invested the $15 million in a savings account on November 1, 1803 at six percent simple interest per year, how much would France have in the account on November 1, 2000?

(2) If France had invested the $15 million in a savings account on November 1, 1803 at six percent annual interest, compounded annually, how much would France have in the savings account on November 1, 2000?

Problem 3.1C. In 1626, Native Americans sold Manhattan Island for $24. If the Native Americans had invested the $24 in a savings account on October 1, 1626, at six percent annual interest, compounded annually, how much would they have in the account on October 1, 2000?

Problem 3.2A. Molly's grandparents plan to give her $3,000 each year for her college fund. If they give her $3,000 at the end of each year for the next eighteen years, how much will she have at the end of eighteen years, assuming that she is able to earn eight percent interest per year, compounded annually?

Problem 3.2B. Martha's employment contract requires her employer, D Corp., to deposit $4,000 per year into Martha's pension plan. If, at the end of each year, D Corp. deposits $4,000 for the next twelve years, how much will Martha have at the end of the twelfth year, assuming that D Corp. is able to earn ten percent interest per year, compounded annually?

Problem 3.2C. Mary Ann's parents will celebrate their 50th anniversary in seven years, and she would like to start saving money now so that she can surprise them with a marvelous gift on their anniversary. If she can save $1,200 at the end of each year for the next seven years, how much will Mary Ann have on at the end of the seventh year, assuming that she is able to earn six percent interest per year, compounded annually?

Problem 3.3A. Under the terms of a settlement agreement, Defendant promised to pay Plaintiff $180,000 fifteen years from now. If Defendant can earn nine percent per year on his investments, compounded annually, what is the present value of his promise?

Problem 3.3B. A prestigious law school has just accepted Mark's application, and his parents are so proud that they promise to give him $20,000 upon his graduation in three years.

(1) If his parents can earn ten percent per year on their investments, compounded annually, what is the present value of their promise?

(2) What is the present value of their promise if the interest compounds semiannually?

Problem 3.3C. Beth bequeaths $300,000 in trust to pay the income at the end of each year to Mark for life, remainder to Nancy. The trust can earn eight percent per year, compounded annually. Mark has a life expectancy of 18 years.

(1) What is the present value of Nancy's remainder interest?

(2) What is the present value of Mark's income interest?

Problem 3.4A. Melanie owes the bank $25,000 from the purchase of her new sports car. The debt bears interest of twelve percent per year, payable annually. Melanie wants to pay the debt and interest in four annual installments beginning in one year. What equal annual installments will pay the debt and interest?

Problem 3.4B. Noelle won $20,000,000 in the state lottery, payable $1,000,000 a year for twenty years. The applicable interest rate is six percent per year, compounded annually. If the lottery payments are payable at the end of each year, what is the present value of all the lottery payments?

Problem 3.4C. Under the terms of a settlement agreement, Defendant must pay Plaintiff ten annual installments of $100,000 each. The applicable interest rate is four percent per year, compound annually. Assume that the Internal Revenue Service will allow the Defendant to claim a one-time deduction in the present year for the present value of the payments. If the payments are payable at the end of each year, what is the amount of Defendant's deduction?

Problem 3.5A. Disturbed about the lack of financial aid that his alma mater provides to its students, I. M. Generous decides to set up an endowment fund to provide a $15,000 annual scholarship for a needy student. Assuming a nine percent annual interest rate, how much must Generous donate to his alma mater to fund the endowment permanently?

Problem 3.5B. Planning to retire soon, Patricia wants to set up a retirement fund that will provide $80,000 in annual income. Assuming a six percent annual interest rate, how much must Patricia have in her retirement fund to guarantee $80,000 in annual income?

Problem 3.5C. Under the terms of a settlement agreement, Defendant must provide $200,000 per year for anti-smoking ads forever. Defendant wants to set up a permanent trust fund that will earn this amount. Assuming a ten percent annual interest rate, how much must Defendant put in the fund?

Problem 3.6A. Your best friend is the proud parent of a new baby girl. Your friend's parents want to pay for their granddaughter's freshman year of college. Your friend estimates that one year of college will cost $50,000 at a public university in eighteen years.

(1) If your friend's parents can earn an after-tax rate of return of five percent per year, compounded annually, how much should they set aside today to pay for their granddaughter's freshman year?

(2) If they want instead to make equal, annual payments at the end of each of the next five years, how much should they set aside each year?

Problem 3.6B. You are trying to decide whether to purchase or lease your next car. The dealer is willing to sell you a new Saturn for $18,000. At the end of six years, you estimate that the fair market value of the Saturn will be $6,000. The dealer is also willing to lease the car to you for six annual payments of $2,500 beginning in one year, plus a $3,600 "rental reduction" or non-refundable down payment at the time you accept delivery. Assume that the applicable interest rate is ten percent per year, compounded annually. Applying present value principles, which option would you choose?

*

CHAPTER IV

INTRODUCTION TO FINANCIAL STATEMENT ANALYSIS AND FINANCIAL RATIOS

A.   IMPORTANCE TO LAWYERS

In the first chapter, we discussed the three basic financial statements, the balance sheet, the income statement, and the statement of cash flows, plus some presentation of changes in owners' equity, whether or not in the form of a separate statement. A lawyer must understand the form and content of these financial statements to be able to interpret and analyze them. In this chapter we will examine how lawyers can use the basic financial statements and related information to counsel clients. As one lesson from Enron's collapse, attorneys should remember that a missing financial statement may indicate a desire to hide disappointing results, or perhaps the business lacks sufficiently complete or reliable books and records. As a starting point, therefore, a lawyer should ask probing questions any time an enterprise does not provide a complete set of financial statements.

The financial statements are almost always accompanied by notes, which explain the accounting policies that the enterprise has adopted and contain additional disclosures about important matters affecting the financial statements and the business. As a result, any knowledgeable user of financial statements will carefully read the notes, which the legal community may refer to as *footnotes*. As we discussed in Chapter II, generally accepted accounting principles often provide alternatives, and of course the accounting principles chosen and their application to particular situations can greatly influence the amounts reported in the financial statements. The notes will explain why management chose a particular accounting principle from among the acceptable alternatives. A reader should consider whether the policies and principles used by management fit the industry and whether a change in accounting policies has affected the enterprise's financial position, especially for comparative purposes. In short, the notes help a reader to assess how the applicable accounting principles and policies affected the numbers in the financial statements.

The notes also provide additional detail about items and amounts which appear in summary form in the financial statements. We will discuss many of these additional disclosure requirements in later chapters. In particular, businesses use the notes to divulge information about acquisitions, debt and borrowing arrangements, operating lease commitments, pension and retirement benefits, and financial information relating to different business segments. The notes also commonly disclose information about other commitments and contingencies. The term *commitments* generally refers to quantifiable transactions that management has affirmatively entered into on the enterprise's behalf, such as capital expenditures to expand operating facilities. In contrast, *contingencies* reflect uncertain future events, such as litigation and guarantees, whose ultimate consequences, if they do occur, will adversely affect the company.

The experienced user will also request and read financial statements for more than one accounting period. In academic terms, the financial statements and the accompanying notes represent the business's report card and cumulative grade point average. Just as a seasoned job interviewer usually prefers to evaluate grades from more than one academic term, a knowledgeable reader of financial statements favors financial statements covering more than one accounting period. As we will discuss in more detail later, a thoughtful reader will want to review a series of financial statements to assess the business's general direction. Financial statements for a single accounting period do not reveal whether the business's operating results and financial position are improving, holding steady, or declining.

Finally, an experienced reader of financial statements will look for the report, if any, from the independent accountant or auditor. If there isn't one, the reader must view the statements with considerable skepticism. If the financial statements do include a report from an independent accountant, it will indicate whether it was based upon a full audit, a review or compilation, or some other agreed-upon procedures. As we saw in Chapter II, an experienced reader will look for an unqualified audit opinion, though even an unqualified opinion does not guarantee the financial statement's accuracy. But remember, as discussed in detail at pages 157-161, *supra*, SOx now requires that in addition to the usual auditor's opinion on the financial statements, the auditor must report on management's assessment of the company's internal control over financial reporting, and investors should pay particular attention to any "material weaknesses" disclosed. However, as also noted there, investors have been urged not to overreact to disclosures of material weaknesses, and instead can take some comfort in learning that these weaknesses have been discovered and can be addressed.

A lawyer who can read and understand these documents has developed a valuable tool for understanding business transactions, appreciating investment and credit decisions, and advising clients. Of particular value in this regard is the required section in various SEC filings called

Management's Discussion & Analysis ("MD&A"), in which public companies are called upon to analyze and expound on their financial condition and results of operation: this discussion gives the reader the opportunity to see the company through the "eyes of management." MD&A's have become increasingly important of late, and the SEC has urged use of this venue to disclose important information about critical accounting policies and trends affecting the business. MD&A's are discussed further on page 233, *infra*, and reviewed in detail at pages 280 - 288.

B. ANNUAL REPORTS

As previously mentioned, most businesses, including all publicly-traded corporations, present their financial statements in an annual report. The astute reader of an annual report will want to understand the purpose behind each section. But before discussing those sections, we must understand why businesses prepare annual reports.

State corporate laws require corporations to hold annual meetings to elect directors and to conduct other business. Especially in publicly-traded corporations, shareholders live throughout the country, and maybe around the world. For various reasons, shareholders often cannot, and usually do not, attend such meetings. Corporate laws, however, require a *quorum* before the corporation can validly conduct any business. A quorum means that the holders of a certain number of shares, most often a majority, must attend a shareholders' meeting, either in person or by *proxy*. Unless shareholders that do not attend a meeting appoint proxies, or agents, to represent them at the meeting, the quorum requirement may prevent the shareholders as a group from electing new directors or transacting any other business. Therefore, a corporation's management usually solicits proxies for shareholders' meeting.

Pursuant to the regulation of proxy solicitation under federal securities law, enterprises which have securities traded on a national securities exchange, or have $10 million or more in assets *and* 500 or more owners of any class of equity securities, are required to send, either before or concurrently with the solicitation, an annual report that meets detailed requirements, with an exception allowing small business issuers to send only specified financial statements. The proxy rules also require registrants to send substantially equivalent information to security holders even if the registrant does not solicit proxies.

An annual report summarizes an enterprise's financial and operational activities for the most recent calendar or fiscal year. SEC regulations require registrants to include the following in their annual reports: (1) audited financial statements for the most recent year, plus several immediately preceding years for comparative purposes; (2) quarterly financial data; (3) a historical summary of selected financial data for the most recent five years or all of the registrant's years if less than five; (4) a description of the business; (5) business segment information, if applicable; (6) information about executive officers and directors; (7) historical data about the market prices of the company's equity securities during the past two years; and dividends on those securities during that period; (8) perhaps most importantly, management's discussion and analysis of the enterprise's financial condition and the results of its operations; and (9) the new requirement, management's report on internal controls over financial reporting, and the corresponding report from the independent auditor on management's assessment.

Research shows that most investors, on average, spend only a few minutes glancing at an annual report. As a result, registrants have used various gimmicks, including coupons for free or discounted merchandise, supermodels, and scented annual reports, to try to impress readers. Registrants typically highlight positive information in such attention-getting sections while placing negative information in technical sections that intimidate the common reader. As attorneys, we must expend the extra time and energy to read carefully the technical sections and analyze an annual report. By doing so, we can glean important information that may affect our client's business interests or investments.

In addition to supplying the financial statements, notes, and report of independent auditor discussed in the previous section, registrants usually disseminate the other required information in the following standardized sections:

Business Profile: This section describes the enterprise's business, and often contains the names of the directors, officers or senior executives: for an example, see the profile in Starbucks' SEC Form 10-K for fiscal 2005, on pages 1-8 plus 16-17 in Appendix A.

The business profile frequently contains the business's *mission statement*—a broad statement about the enterprise's purpose and future goals. The mission statement should give the reader some sense about the business's values and direction. For example, a computer software company may stress innovation in its mission statement; as a result, the reader should expect that the business will incur substantial costs to research and develop new software. Overly-broad mission statements obviously do not help in this regard, but may indicate that management has not developed a focused strategy for the business.

Financial Highlights: The contents of this section will vary among registrants, but generally contain quantitative information on sales or revenues, income or loss per ownership unit, balance sheet items, financial ratios and other information. Supporting graphs often accompany this quantitative data. We should keep in mind that management carefully selects the information presented in this section, with an eye to portraying the enterprise's financial condition and performance as favorably as possible. In addition, as we will discuss in considerable detail later in this chapter, significant fluctuations between periods may be due to nonrecurring or unusual items rather than normal operations, which would only be revealed by carefully examining the financial statements and the relevant footnotes.

Letter to the Owners: For the annual report, the highest ranking executive of the enterprise, typically the chairman of the board or the president of a corporation, usually writes the *letter to shareholders*. This letter should be read with considerable skepticism because this part of the annual report functions as another public-relations piece. Experienced readers and financial analysts watch for euphemisms, such as the word "challenging," to describe bad situations or to predict tough financial times. See the "To Our Shareholders" letter from the Starbucks 2005 Annual Report on pages ii and iii in Appendix A.

Operational Overview: This section summarizes the enterprise's normal business functions. For large, multi-segmented enterprises, such as General Electric Co. or Procter & Gamble, this part of the annual report describes each business segment's products, markets and key financial data. Consequently, experienced readers often find this section helpful in analyzing the financial statements.

Historical Summary of Financial Data: As noted earlier, the proxy rules require registrants to present five years of income statements, balance sheets and other data. Financial analysts describe this section as the business's "medical record" because the summary compares the business's financial vital signs over the years given. This selected financial data from the Starbucks Form 10-K for fiscal 2005 is on page 20 in Appendix A.

Management's Discussion and Analysis: This extremely important section should contain (1) management's "crystal ball" expectations or predictions regarding prospective results of operations, capital resources, and liquidity, and (2) pursuant to pressure by the SEC after the financial frauds in the early 2000's, identification of critical accounting policies, including those assumptions, estimates, and other judgments or uncertainties which affect the application of the chosen accounting policies to the financial statements. As indicated above, MD&As will be reviewed in greater detail later, but in the meantime, remember that the independent accountants do not audit the information contained there.

Report on Internal Control over Financial Reporting: Historically, management would include a boiler plate report acknowledging management's responsibility for: (1) the preparation, fairness and integrity of the financial statements; (2) the maintenance of a system of internal accounting controls; and (3) the establishment of an independent audit committee to oversee the financial reporting and controls. Now, however, as required by SOx, for public companies the report will include that very important assessment by management of the company's internal controls, and be accompanied by the auditor's report on that assessment.

C. ANALYTICAL PROCEDURES

Financial statements seek to provide useful information to help existing and potential investors, creditors and other users reach rational investment, credit and similar decisions. Normally, these decision-makers try to make predictions about an enterprise's financial future on the basis of its experience to date. This process calls for some analysis of the financial data available, and a number of analytical techniques and ratios have proved quite helpful. Of course, much depends upon the decision-maker's objective. A potential buyer of common stock might focus on different aspects of the financial data than those facets that will gain the attention of a banker considering a short-term loan. The holder of a twenty-year bond will contemplate yet a third set of concerns. But these decision-makers will consider some common themes, and, as to many of these, ratios derived from data collected on the financial statements can provide relevant and helpful information. In this chapter, we will look at some of these procedures and ratios, not to try to qualify as financial analysts, but to develop an understanding of the basic tools and techniques which accountants and analysts use to interpret financial statements.

Among the most common procedures utilized by accountants and financial analysts in their review of an enterprise's financial statements are trend analysis, common-sized analysis, and financial ratios. All these methods permit an analyst to look beyond the financial statements themselves to assess whether changing general economic or industry conditions, such as fluctuating interest rates, inflation, or vacillating consumer confidence, will affect the enterprise.

1.   TREND ANALYSIS

Trend analysis involves comparing financial statements for an enterprise over several periods. This comparison allows the reader to determine where the enterprise generated and spent its resources over a longer period of time. By analyzing an enterprise over a series of reporting periods, a reader may notice various patterns or trends, such as increasing sales or decreasing accounts payable.

2.   COMMON-SIZED ANALYSIS

Common-sized analysis, which accountants and financial analysts also refer to as *vertical analysis*, consists of reducing a financial statement, such as the income statement or the statement of cash flows, to a series of percentages of a given base amount, such as net sales or total cash flow for the period. In the Starbucks 2005 Form 10-K, on page 23 in Appendix A, a table sets forth the percentage which certain items in the consolidated statements of earnings bear to the company's total net revenues. A reader of financial statements can obtain useful information by comparing these percentages either to those in prior years for the same enterprise, or to the current percentages for comparable businesses. As another example, an investor may want to compare the percentage that an enterprise's cash flow from operations currently bears to its total cash flow from all sources with the counterpart percentage in earlier years.

3. FINANCIAL RATIOS

Creditors and investors frequently rely on ratios to assess the financial health of an enterprise. In general, financial ratios basically fall into four groupings. These categories include *liquidity ratios, leverage or coverage ratios, activity ratios, and profitability ratios*. Liquidity and leverage ratios provide information on an enterprise's ability to cover its anticipated operating expenses, such as payroll, to meet its debt obligations in the short and long run, and to distribute profits to owners. Coverage ratios also measure the relative claims that creditors and owners hold on the business's assets. Profitability ratios assess how effectively the business operates. Activity ratios provide information about how effectively a business uses its assets.

Lawyers will often use financial ratios in contracts and loan agreements, and to evaluate business transactions. Whether representing the borrower or the lender, lawyers should understand how to apply financial ratios and negotiate loan covenants to their client's advantage. To illustrate, most loan agreements give the lender the right to demand immediate repayment in full if the borrower defaults. Loan agreements frequently define "default" as including the borrower's failure to maintain certain financial ratios. If such a default gives a lender the right to demand immediate repayment, accounting rules require the business to treat the entire loan balance as a current liability. Reclassifying long-term debt as a current liability could cause defaults under other lending arrangements.

Lawyers representing borrowers can avoid such defaults by carefully drafting and negotiating realistic covenants or by obtaining a waiver prior to any anticipated defaults. If a lender agrees to waive a default for at least one year from a balance sheet date, the accounting rules will not require the borrower to treat the liability as a current liability, which gives the borrower the opportunity to improve its financial condition.

As a result of differences among various definitions of certain ratios, an attorney should insist that contracts or loan documents define any ratios they include. An attorney should also consult the client's accountant about these ratios, their definitions, and their applications to the client's situation. Moreover, the need to understand financial data in order to provide competent representation is no less present if litigation develops and the lawyer's role changes from advisor to advocate.

Some of these financial ratios, like some of analytical techniques more generally, utilize the figures on the balance sheet, some look to the income statement, and some to cash flow data. This calls for a closer look at each of these financial statements in turn, together with their related analytical tools and ratios.

D.   THE BALANCE SHEET

At the beginning of the twentieth century, the balance sheet dominated accounting practice, and the business community focused almost exclusively on the balance sheet. To see how a business was doing, accountants and financial analysts merely compared the change in net assets, that is, assets less liabilities, on successive balance sheets after eliminating additional investments or withdrawals. At that time, accounting practice commonly recognized income and expenses only when the business received or paid cash. With such an unrefined concept of income, an income statement did not add much, and accountants could as well have entered the income and expense items directly in a proprietorship account. Over time, however, this cash-basis method of accounting gave way to accrual accounting, and the income statement eventually presented a more refined and meaningful picture of what happened between successive balance sheet dates. As one expert described the situation at that point, "the income statement was primary and the balance sheet was the holding pen for items awaiting recognition in the income statement."

More recently, the current fundamental framework in accounting has refocused on the recognition of assets and liabilities, with the income statement reflecting changes in those assets and liabilities for the period. Thus, marked shifts in emphasis have occurred, from the balance sheet to the income statement and then back to the balance sheet, when seeking the most significant measure of a business enterprise. In addition, financial analysts today give increasing attention to the statement of cash flows.

In any event, the balance sheet supplies useful information to investors, creditors and others in reaching rational investment, credit and similar decisions.

1.   CHANGES IN OWNERS' EQUITY

To understand the role of the balance sheet in stating a business's financial position, we should reexamine the relationship between the balance sheet and the income statement. Consider, for example, what happens in the balance sheet accounts during the period which the income statement covers. In general a business earns net income by obtaining cash or other assets in excess of the amount of the assets expended or liabilities incurred. Thus, E. Tutt generated net income because the amount of cash and accounts receivable which she obtained from professional fees during the period exceeded the total of the cash expended and the liabilities incurred for expenses during the same period. Similarly, Marty Jones realized net income by obtaining a total of cash and receivables during the period which exceeded the cost of the shoes which he sold plus the expenses which he paid or became obligated to pay. Notice that whenever a business earns a profit, its net assets, i.e., assets less liabilities, will increase; conversely, a decline in net assets will accompany a loss for the period. That is another way of saying that net income or loss affects owners' equity, because net assets always equal owners' equity. But remember that owners' equity is also affected by transactions with the owners, this is, contributions from, or distributions to, the owners, which are not meaningful elements in judging how an enterprise is doing. To illustrate, look at E. Tutt's balance sheets for June 30 and July 31, on pages 76 and 85, respectively, *supra*. Net assets totaled $2,860 on June 30 and $3,670 on July 31. Because the contribution to and withdrawal from the proprietorship during the period just happened to be equal in this case, the increase in net assets during July of $810 exactly equaled the net income for that period.

Historically, there were occasions, particularly in legal settings, when the change in net assets from non-owner sources between successive balance sheet dates was used to determine net income or loss for the intervening period. An early case, *Stein v. Strathmore Worsted Mills,* 221 Mass. 86, 88-89, 108 N.E. 1029, 1039 (1915), illustrates this, in a dispute involving a bonus based on a percentage of net profits:

> The chief question presented by this case is the meaning of the words "net profits" in a contract between the plaintiff and the defendant, whereby the former became a selling agent for the defendant, a textile manufacturer, at a stated annual salary and in addition a percentage on net profits. Net profits has a fairly well-defined significance in law. Profit in a going business implies a comparison between two dates. In the contract between these parties those dates are the beginning and the end of each of the two years as to which the plaintiff seeks to recover his percentage. As applied to these two periods, net profits mean a comparison between the [net] assets of the defendant on these dates.

As another example, the Internal Revenue Service ("IRS") has long recognized that since income increases net assets, any increase in a taxpayer's net assets probably signals the presence of net income. So the IRS has often used the *net worth method* to prove that taxpayers failed to report some of their income when their net assets increased by more than the amount of income they did report, and they could not explain the difference. This approach was described with approval by the Supreme Court in Holland v. United States, 348 U.S. 121,125, 75 S.Ct. 127,130, 99 L.Ed. 150, 159 (1954):

> In a typical net worth prosecution, the Government, having concluded that the taxpayer's records are inadequate as a basis for determining income tax liability, attempts to establish an "opening net worth" or total net value of the taxpayer's assets at the beginning of a given year. It then proves increases in the taxpayer's net worth for each succeeding year during the period under examination and calculates the difference between the * * * net values of the taxpayer's assets at the beginning and end of each of the years involved. * * * [I]f the resulting figure for any year is substantially greater than the taxable income reported by the taxpayer for that year, the Government claims the excess represents unreported taxable income.

Notably, the net worth method also helped send the famous gangster Al Capone to jail in the early 1930s for tax evasion. For the years 1922, 1923, 1924 and 1925, Capone filed delinquent tax returns reporting $20,000 income for each of three years and $15,000 income for one year. During a period including those same years, Capone deposited sums totaling $1,851,840.08 in various banks under fictitious names. The Seventh Circuit affirmed the convictions. Capone v. United States, 51 F.2d 609 (7th Cir.1931).

Any effort to measure an enterprise's financial performance by computing the change in net assets between successive balance sheet dates gives rise to the question whether to take account of unrealized appreciation. To be sure, in Chapter I we saw that the historical cost principle calls for recording assets at cost, rather than current market value, on the ground that accountants can easily and objectively ascertain cost while reasonable minds can disagree about current fair market value. However, there are some who believe that the balance sheet should show the current market value of the assets, because it would thereby present a more meaningful picture of the enterprise's current condition and worth. As we shall see later, that view has prevailed to a limited extent, in connection with marketable securities which are not being held for long-term investment. In any event, the business could always disclose information about current value in the notes to the financial statements, which would allow a financial analyst to take account of any increase or decrease in the value of those assets when computing the change in net assets between particular balance sheet dates. Obviously, periodic revaluation of assets could significantly impact the picture of the enterprise's business fortunes that the financial statements portray.

Look at E. Tutt's balance sheet for July 31, on page 85, *supra*. Suppose that on July 31, E. Tutt finds that her office equipment, recorded at $775, has appreciated in value to $1,000, presumably because of an increase in the price of such equipment in the second-hand market. If despite GAAP's disapproval she recorded the asset at that figure, her net assets, and the amount in the Proprietorship account, on July 31 would increase to $3,895. Ignoring the offsetting contribution to, and withdrawal from the enterprise during July of $100 each, comparing the $3,895 to the $2,860 of net assets, or Proprietorship, on June 30 would indicate that the enterprise had gained $1,035 since June 30, rather than the $810 shown on the income statement. (We will consider shortly the implications of revaluation of assets in connection with determining the propriety of a proposed dividend under corporate law.)

In 1997 the FASB adopted new accounting rules which recognize that the change in net assets between successive balance sheets can effectively measure an enterprise's financial performance. Statement of Financial Accounting Standards No. 130, *Reporting Comprehensive Income* , calls greater attention to changes in equity resulting from non-owner sources during a period by requiring an enterprise to report all such changes in equity in a financial statement, and to display this so-called "comprehensive income" and its components with the same prominence as other financial statements. SFAS No. 130 defines "comprehensive income" as "the change in equity [net assets] of a business enterprise during a period from transactions and other events and circumstances from non-owner sources." The term, therefore, includes all increases and decreases in net assets during the period except those changes resulting from contributions by and distributions to owners.

For many companies this requirement is not likely to have much impact, because most changes in equity from non-owner sources are already being reported on the traditional income statement. However, there are some non-owner changes in equity, such as unrealized gains and loss from holding certain categories of marketable securities (referred to a few paragraphs earlier, and to be examined in more detail later when we revisit the subject of unrealized appreciation), which would have been reflected only on the balance sheet, not in the traditional income statement, but will now be included in the Statement of Comprehensive Income.

Despite the increased emphasis on statements of income, both traditional and comprehensive, plus that close relative, cash flow, users of financial statements have not yet sent the balance sheet to the financial junk heap. After all, the balance sheet still plays an important role by showing just what the business owns, what it owes, and the nature of the proprietary interests; and to whatever extent recording of unrealized appreciation or diminution in value might be called for, the balance sheet constitutes a useful vehicle. Moreover, data on the balance sheet are still used to calculate some important ratios which provide useful information in making judgments about an enterprise's financial performance, as we will see shortly.

One step that can serve to make the balance sheet more meaningful is to segregate dissimilar types of changes in net assets. Accountants have historically divided shareholders' equity into different categories, such as capital stock, additional paid-in capital and retained earnings, to reflect different sources of and changes in a corporation's net worth. Suppose, for example, that a shareholder or political subdivision donates assets to a corporation and the corporation does not issue stock or provide any other consideration in exchange for the assets. In that event, the corporation's accountant could create a separate account, perhaps called *Donated Capital*, to reflect the increase in net assets from the donation. In the alternative, the accountant could report the amount in an account which includes various types of additional paid-in capital. Segregating the additional paid-in capital between donations, or other special transactions, and amounts which shareholders paid in excess of par or stated value results in more meaningful disclosure about a corporation's financial position.

Once again, note that lawyers and corporate statutes may not use the same labels as accountants in referring to various segments of shareholders' equity. For example, the legal capital system would probably refer to the donated capital mentioned in the previous paragraph as "Donated Surplus", and would call the changes in equity resulting from operating profits and losses "Earned Surplus" (as the accountants used to do, before they switched to "Retained Earnings", to get away from the ubiquitous term "Surplus"). In situations where, despite accounting objections, assets are being revalued, for example in connection with a proposed dividend distribution, lawyers might well use the term "Revaluation Surplus". If a corporate statute, or case law interpreting a statute, distinguishes among the different types of surplus (i.e., different sources of net assets) from which the corporation can make distributions, separate identification of those various sources of surplus can become very important.

PROBLEM

Problem 4.1. Freidus, the owner of all the stock of Starrett Corporation, which had been issued for $5,000, had also made loans to the corporation totaling $430,000. After the corporation had incurred an operating deficit of $320,000, its balance sheet appeared as follows:

Assets		Liabilities & Shareholder's Equity	
Cash	$10,000	Accounts Payable	$35,000
Accounts Receivable	18,000	Loans Payable	430,000
Inventory	22,000	Stated Capital	5,000
Plant	100,000	Surplus (Deficit)	(320,000
	$150,000		$150,000

At that point Freidus forgave the corporation's debt to himself. Shortly thereafter, the corporation applied to a federal lending agency for a loan, presenting a balance sheet on which the shareholders' equity section showed simply "Stated Capital" of $5,000 and "Surplus" of $110,000. Subsequently, Freidus was indicted under a statute which prohibits the making of a false or fraudulent statement or representation to any agency of the United States. As a judge sitting without a jury, how would you decide the case?

2. ANALYTICAL TERMS AND RATIOS

In addition to showing changes in owners' equity over time, the data on the balance sheet continues to offer a basis for making some relevant judgments about an enterprise's financial condition. We now turn to some of the terms and ratios which accountants and business analysts use to interpret and evaluate the figures that appear on the balance sheet.

Consider the following balance sheet for a small corporation:

X Corp.
Balance Sheet, December 31

Assets		Liabilities & Shareholders' Equity	
Cash	$ 2,000	Accounts Payable	$10,000
Accounts Receivable	3,000	Bonds Payable	5,000
Inventory	16,000	Total Liabilities	$15,000
Plant	19,000	Shareholders' Equity	25,000
	$40,000		$40,000

Can you tell whether this corporation is in good financial shape? Because the corporation failed to subdivide the $25,000 in shareholders' equity into contributed capital and retained earnings components, we cannot tell whether the company has produced earnings, either recently or at some time in the past. But did you also notice that X Corp. may well have some trouble meeting its accounts payable in the near future? In fact, unless X raises cash through some other means, such as borrowing or issuing more stock, X cannot pay off its accounts payable until the company has sold the inventory and collected payment. This kind of information particularly interests short-term creditors, and would also benefit long-term creditors and stockholders. Indeed, because of the importance of such timing considerations, as we previously discussed in Chapter I, accountants usually arrange both assets and liabilities on the balance sheet in the order of their currentness, with the most current items at the top. Most modern balance sheets go further and expressly classify their assets and liabilities as between current and fixed (i.e., non-current), as the Starbucks consolidated balance sheets on page 41 in Appendix A illustrate. Remember that current assets usually include cash, cash equivalents, and any other assets which the business expects to convert into cash within a year, which normally means accounts receivable, inventory, probably any marketable securities, and possibly short-term prepaid expenses, even though, strictly speaking, the business will not convert the prepaids into cash. Current liabilities would encompass those obligations which the business expects to pay within one year, which would typically include accounts payable, accrued expenses payable, plus any portion of a long-term indebtedness falling due within one year. Assuming that X Corp. does not have to repay any portion of the bonds payable within a year, an accountant might recast it's balance sheet in classified form as follows:

X Corp.
Classified Balance Sheet, December 31

Assets		Liabilities & Shareholders' Equity	
Current Assets		Current Liabilities	
Cash	$ 2,000	Accounts Payable	$10,000
Accounts Receivable	3,000		
Inventory	16,000	Bonds Payable	5,000
Total	$21,000	Total Liabilities	$15,000
Plant	19,000	Shareholders' Equity	25,000
	$40,000		$40,000

a. WORKING CAPITAL

Because of the importance attached to both current assets and current liabilities, accountants and financial analysts pay special attention to the excess of current assets over current liabilities, usually referred to as *working capital*. A simple net figure, however, does not tell us a great deal. For example, if one company has $25,000,000 in current assets and $20,000,000 in current liabilities, and another has $10,000,000 in current assets and $5,000,000 in current liabilities, both have working capital of $5,000,000 but their financial conditions differ quite significantly. It is here that some of those financial ratios referred to earlier could be quite instructive.

b. FINANCIAL RATIOS

(1) *Liquidity Ratios*

For example, take the liquidity ratio called the "current ratio", which compares the amount of the current assets to current liabilities. For the two companies mentioned above, the difference between them   becomes immediately apparent, since the first one's ratio of current assets to current liabilities is 1.25 ($25,000,000/$20,000,000), while the second company's is 2.0 ($10,000,000/$5,000,000). The current ratio is one of the most common tests used to evaluate the financial condition of a business, especially its ability to pay its debts as they become due.

Financial professionals often say that a current ratio less than 1.0 heralds a problem, while a current ratio exceeding 2.0 generally indicates satisfactory liquidity, a test which X Corp. meets. However, these generalizations must be qualified according to the type of industry, seasonal business factors and similar considerations. As an example, banks usually need greater liquidity than manufacturers.

We must also keep in mind that financial professionals primarily use any ratio in comparative terms. In other words, they compare a ratio as of one date or for a particular period with the same business's ratio for an earlier date or period, or with the ratio of some other enterprise, or at least with some standard. Although creditors and investors generally prefer a higher current ratio, an abnormally high current ratio can also evidence a problem. If a business keeps too many of its resources in liquid assets, the business may not be replacing long-lived assets or making other investments necessary for long-term success.

An important variant of the current ratio is one that takes into account only the "quick assets" of the enterprise, that is, its cash plus cash equivalents, other highly-liquid assets like marketable securities held as short-term investments, and accounts receivable. This so-called "acid test" ignores inventories because short-term creditors in particular are concerned about speedy liquidity in case of sudden calamity, and it often takes a good deal of time to convert inventory into cash. Prepaid expenses are sometimes excluded from "quick assets" because prompt refunds are not always available.

Financial professionals usually consider a ratio approximating 1.0 under the acid test as satisfactory. You should observe that X Corp., with an acid test of .50 [($2,000 cash + $3,000 accounts receivable)/$10,000 current liabilities], does not come close to meeting this test, which somewhat confirms the concern expressed earlier about its liquidity. Even though X Corp.'s ratio falls below 1.0, the company will survive as long as the business can convert inventory into cash before the company's debts mature. The acid test comes close to applying a worst case analysis, in effect assuming that the business could not sell any more inventory.

(2) Leverage Ratios

As you might expect, financial professionals do not confine their analysis to current assets and liabilities. These analysts also use leverage ratios, such as debt to equity and debt to total assets, to assess the business's overall ability to pay its debts. For example, both investors and lenders usually consider the composition of a company's long-term financing, particularly the long-term debt, both in absolute and relative amounts.

Debt financing represents both a special opportunity and a significant risk. The opportunity lies in the fact that if the company can borrow at, say, seven percent interest, and earn a return of, say, ten percent on the borrowed funds by utilizing them in the business, the excess of three percent redounds to the benefit of the shareholders. Under these circumstances, the more debt the company issues, the greater the return to the shareholders. The financial community often refers to this phenomenon as *leverage*: the greater the proportion of debt, the more highly leveraged the company. But the more debt the company incurs, the greater its risk. After all, the company normally must pay interest in any event, even if the company earns less than the interest rate on the borrowed funds, or perhaps does not earn anything at all. In addition, the debtor company must repay the borrowed funds on the agreed date or face the prospect of bankruptcy.

Financial analysts most commonly use the ratio of debt to total owners' equity, which they usually call the *debt-equity ratio*, to measure the relative amount of debt in a business's financial structure. Again, the definition of "debt" can vary under this ratio. Most lenders and analysts will compare long-term debt to total equity, perhaps including the current portion of long-term debt in the debt factor. X Corp.'s balance sheet, with no indication of whether any of the $5,000 bonds payable is currently due, shows a .20 ratio of that debt to the $25,000 shareholders' equity. Other analysts will use total liabilities instead of just long-terms' debt: this variant produces a .60 debt to equity ratio ($15,000 in total liabilities to $25,000 in shareholder's equity). In any event, the relationship of the amount of a company's debt, however defined, to the amount of its equity, may provide a more relevant indication of how risky the debt is, because the amount of equity serves as somewhat of a safety net for the creditors in case of financial difficulty. Hence, the lower the ratio of debt to equity, the safer the loans are; the higher the debt to equity ratio, that is, the more highly leveraged a company is, the greater the risk that the company will not be able to repay creditors if the company encounters hard times. Of course, judgment as to how much leverage may be desirable depends upon the type of business and other circumstances. For example, financial analysts might consider a debt-equity ratio of 1.5 as quite high for a typical industrial concern, but relatively normal for many public utilities.

The 1998 financial crisis involving Long-Term Capital Management L.P. ("LTCM") illustrates both the debt to equity ratio and the danger of excessive leverage. It seems that by the time of its near collapse, LTCM had borrowed approximately 100 times its capital, which would translate to a debt-equity ratio of 100-to-1. However, this apparently did not come to light because LTCM's year-end 1997 financial statement showed a 25-to-1 assets-to-capital ratio, well within the normal range for a financial services company.

Sometimes, however, accountants and financial analysts will use the *debt to total assets ratio* to compare the business debt to the sum of the debt and equity. Once again, the definition of "debt" can vary, ranging from an all-inclusive total liabilities to just long-term debt exclusive of the current portion of long-term debt: under the former, the debt to total asset ratio is .375 ($15,000 in total liabilities to $40,000 in total assets), while under the latter the ratio is .125 ($5,000 bonds payable to $40,000 total assets).

c.   NET BOOK VALUE

Accountants, in particular, frequently use one other term, *net book value,* or simply *book value,* when discussing the balance sheet, as in the cartoon from Ben & Jerry's Homemade, Inc.'s 1992 annual report, on page C-4 in Appendix C. The term *book value* refers to the difference between an enterprise's assets and its liabilities as reflected in the business's accounting records, usually expressed as an amount per outstanding common share or other ownership interest.

If we assume that X Corp. has 100 common shares outstanding, we can readily calculate X Corp.'s net book value as $250 per share ($25,000 shareholders' equity divided by 100 outstanding shares). To determine the net book value per common share in a corporation which has also issued preferred stock, the preferred stock's liquidation preference is deducted from the total equity, and the net remaining is divided by the number of common shares.

d.   CAUTIONS

We should always remember that the balance sheet does not pretend to report the assets or liabilities at fair market value. As a result, the balance sheet figures do not necessarily tell the whole story: the assets may be worth a lot more or a lot less than the figures at which they appear in a business's accounting records. Accordingly, absent unusual circumstances a business's net book value does not reflect what a buyer might pay for the business.

We should also keep in mind that figures for working capital or net book value, and the various ratios that the accountant or financial analyst may compute, are only as good as the balance sheet from which they are derived. If, for example, a balance sheet overstates inventory, absent some offsetting additional err or the balance sheet will also overstate owners' equity, resulting in an overstatement of the working capital, the current ratio, and the net book value, as well as an understatement of the debt to equity ratio.

Notwithstanding these cautions, lawyers and their clients frequently use financial ratios derived from the balance sheet. Table 4–1 computes the terms and ratios discussed in this section from the numbers contained in Starbucks' consolidated balance sheet for fiscal 2005 on page 41 in Appendix A.

Table 4-1—Balance Sheet Terms and Ratios (000s omitted)

Term or Ratio	Formula	Starbucks for 2005	Ratio
Liquidity			
1. Working Capital	Current Assets — Current Liabilities	$(17,662) a	N/A
2. Current Ratio	$\dfrac{\text{Current Assets}}{\text{Current Liabilities}}$	$\dfrac{\$1,209,334}{\$1,226,996}$	..986
3. Acid Test	$\dfrac{\text{Cash (and Equivalents) + Short-Term Investments + Receivables}}{\text{Current Liabilities}}$	$\dfrac{\$497,798 \text{ b}}{\$1,226,996}$	.406
Leverage			
4. Debt to Equity	$\dfrac{\text{Total Liabilities}}{\text{Total Owners Equity}}$	$\dfrac{\$1,423,431 \text{ c}}{\$2,090,634}$	.681
5. Debt to Total Assets	$\dfrac{\text{Total Liabilities}}{\text{Total Assets}}$	$\dfrac{\$1,423,431 \text{ c}}{\$3,514,065}$	.405
6. Net Book Value	$\dfrac{\text{Net Book Value Attributable to Common Shares}}{\text{Common Shares Outstanding}}$	$\dfrac{\$2,090,634 \text{ d}}{794,812 \text{ shares}}$	$2.63 per share

a. $1,209,334 (Total current assets) – $1,226,996 (Total current liabilities)

b. $173,809 (Cash and cash equivalents) + $133,227 (Short-term investments) + $190,762(Accounts receivable)(net)

c. $1,226,996 (Total current liabilities) + $2,870 (Long-term debt) + $0 (Deferred income taxes, net) + $193,565 (other long-term liabilities)

d. $2,090,634 (Total shareholders' equity) – $0 (no outstanding preferred stock)

PROBLEM

Problem 4.2. Using the consolidated balance sheet and any useful miscellaneous information for Starbucks for the year ended October 2, 2005 in Appendix A, do you see any trends compared to 2004 worth noting?

E.   THE INCOME STATEMENT

As we saw in Chapter I, shareholders' equity can also be increased or decreased by transactions which do not involve operations. For example, when E. Tutt took home a chair from her law office, the net assets of her sole proprietorship decreased although the transaction did not relate to her professional activities. Similarly, if Tutt contributed law books to her law office, there would be an increase in net assets although no business activities were involved. Thus, comparing successive balance sheets does not necessarily measure an enterprise's performance. Instead, the income statement, which includes only items of increase and decrease in equity resulting from operations, is the place to look for a picture of how the enterprise performed between balance sheet dates.

1. RESULTS OF OPERATIONS

Creditors, investors and analysts are well aware that the presentation of an enterprise's performance in the income statement could help predict whether the business would be likely to generate profits in the future. A picture of the company's cash flow is also important, because businesses need cash to operate, that is, to pay expenses, to satisfy obligations as they mature, and to distribute earnings to owners. In analyzing a company's financial statements to judge its prospects, ratios derived from various numbers on the statements can provide useful information.

Before looking at some of the measures that the financial community uses to gauge an enterprise's profitability, however, we should first observe that unsophisticated readers of financial statements frequently concentrate unduly on just the net income figure on the income statement, the so-called "bottom line". This practice probably got started when, as happened all too often in the past, but is relatively rare these days, the financial press highlighted the net income figure, or the related *earnings per share* which we will discuss shortly, without paying sufficient attention to the presence of unusual or nonrecurring items. Moreover, the net income figure comes after deduction of interest on debt and income taxes, and so potentially ignores differences between enterprises financed largely by creditors, and those relying mostly on capital from owners, or between those enterprises which do pay income taxes and those which do not, like partnerships, limited liability companies, and S corporations, whose income is taxed directly to the owners of the enterprise.

In any event, whatever its shortcomings, the net income figure on the income statement will in many cases have been subjected to an audit for consistency with GAAP, pursuant to SEC requirements for all publicly-traded enterprises, but for many non-public entities as well. However, starting during the dot-com bubble in the late 1990s, many companies have been including alternative presentations, relying upon unaudited pro forma, or "as if" numbers to portray their operating results. Various terms have been used to refer to these non-GAAP metrics, such as recurring earnings, core earnings, earnings before interest and taxes ("EBIT"), and earnings before interest, taxes, depreciation, and amortization ("EBITDA"). We will take a closer look at those alternative presentations shortly.

2. UNUSUAL OR NON-RECURRING ITEMS

As noted above, trying to predict how a business will perform in the future requires paying particular attention to any unusual or nonrecurring items that affected the recent performance but are not likely to be experienced in future periods. Among the possible ways of presenting items of this kind in trying to highlight them are, in descending order of forcefulness, (1) as a separate line on the income statement, perhaps with a special caption like "extraordinary", (2) as a parenthetical on some existing line, or (3) in an explanatory note to the financial statements. In addition, the MD&A section is required to identify any unusual or infrequent events or transactions, plus any significant economic changes that materially affect the amount of reported income from continuing operations, and, in each case, to disclose the extent to which that item affected reported income. The sophisticated reader watches carefully for such information and disclosures.

Attorneys and anyone else examining financial statements must exercise caution because enterprises may broadly construe the terms "unusual" or "nonrecurring" to include particular items although such items or circumstances can be expected to occur again in the not-too-distant-future. For example, Motorola Inc. reported at least one "special" item, albeit not the same item, in fourteen consecutive earnings reports. Representatives from the company assert that failing to highlight such items, which included restructuring expenses and write-offs for bad investments and obsolete inventory, could make it more difficult to obtain a reliable prediction of future operating results from the company's financial statements. But if a company reports such items periodically, even if not every quarter, are those items really "special," or do they actually reflect normal costs of doing business? Jesse Drucker, *Motorola's Profit: 'Special' Again?*, WALL ST. J., Oct. 15, 2002, at C1.

Of course, the financial community pays a lot of attention to how enterprises present their operating results on the income statement, and GAAP attempts to resolve various questions that arise. One recurring difficulty stems from the fact that the income statement reports the operating results for a particular *period*. To take a simple illustration, how should an enterprise's current financial statements reflect a recovery in an antitrust suit for lost profit of a prior year? Obviously, the enterprise cannot recall all the copies of the income statement for the earlier year, although it is possible to restate the results for that year, and publicize the restatement in the financial press as widely as possible, an approach that has been taken regularly in recent years to disclose and correct serious, often fraudulent, misstatements of income in an earlier year. Here, however, there is no error: there simply was no income to recognize until the successful lawsuit. On the other hand, simply including in current income a material recovery having nothing to do with current operations could give a misleading impression of the enterprise's current profitability.

If an item of this kind is indeed to be included in the current income statement, it would certainly seem to call for using one of those techniques referred to above for highlighting the special character of such an item. The most dramatic of those approaches would be to include the recovery as a separate line item on the income statement, with a caption like "Income Unrelated to Current Operations" or "Extraordinary Item", and located after a figure for "Net Income from Current Operations." The latter would then provide a picture of the results of current operations, excluding the special item. This important technique will be discussed in detail shortly. However, it would still leave the special item reflected in the final Net Income figure for the period, which, as we have seen, can be troublesome because of that penchant of average, financially unsophisticated investors to concentrate unduly upon the final "Net Income" figure.

Not surprisingly, this dilemma has led to efforts to exclude such items from the current income statement entirely, and that is the subject of the next section.

a. PRIOR PERIOD ADJUSTMENTS

Notice that if the enterprise had been able to record this lost profit in the earlier year in which it really "belonged", it would have increased the net income figure for that prior year, and would now be included in retained earnings. We can reach the same end-point in the current period without affecting current income simply by offsetting the cash receipt with a direct credit to Retained Earnings, that is, by skipping the current income statement and crediting (or debiting, as the case may be) a special item directly to Retained Earnings. Accountants use the term "prior period adjustment" to refer to this process of by-passing the income statement, connoting the fact that such a direct entry to Retained Earnings in effect adjusts the results of a prior period in which an item that happened to be currently realized really "belonged".

This approach, however, presents it's own difficulties. For one thing, how would an enterprise decide whether a particular item qualified as "special" enough to be entirely omitted from the income statement, and hence from the determination of net income? After all, the desire to impress creditors and owners could tempt management to err on the side of regarding losses as special, and therefore excludible, while viewing most gains as ordinary and therefore includible; this would certainly impair the income statement's meaningfulness. In addition, as important as each individual income statement is, perhaps even more significant is an enterprise's series of consecutive income statements, and the trends they may indicate, which users of financial statements can utilize to judge more readily the enterprise's future prospects. Ideally, any series of consecutive income statements should portray as complete a picture as possible of the business's fortunes over the total period that the series covers. If an item by-passes the income statement in any period included in the series, it will be omitted from the entire series, which could cloud the picture that the series presents. Readers might be better served if an enterprise included every item of gain or loss in some year's income statement, with an appropriate disclosure if the item does not theoretically belong in that year. That way, the individual reader can assess the significance of particular special items.

Then there are those transactions which do not clearly "belong" to some prior period, but instead simply do not directly relate to operations in any period. For example, suppose an enterprise sells a manufacturing plant. Should the enterprise include the gain or loss from this relatively somewhat unusual, or at least non-operating, transaction in the income statement for the current period? If any income statement should include this transaction, it ought to be the one for the current period, since that is when the transaction occurred, although notice that the gain or loss was probably accumulated over the several periods while the item was owned. Once again, competing considerations are presented. Including the item in the income statement makes the net income figure a less meaningful reflection of the results of the enterprise's regular operations for that period. On the other hand, by-passing the income statement in favor of a direct credit, or debit, to Retained Earnings would exclude this very significant item from the series of income statements, thereby impairing the validity of the overall picture presented by the series, especially if the enterprise sells plants from time to time.

The conflict between these two objectives—making each individual income statement as meaningful a picture as possible of the enterprise's operations for that period, and having any series of income statements represent a virtually complete portrayal of the enterprise's fortunes for the time-span that the series covers—presents considerable difficulty. For many years, the accounting profession regarded the question of which way to treat any particular unusual item as pretty much a judgment call, which enterprises could resolve as they saw fit. Predictably, such flexibility caused considerable trouble, both in comparing an enterprise's current performance with its earlier years, and in making current comparisons with other businesses which may have treated similar items differently.

Over the years, the FASB's predecessors, and ultimately the FASB itself, issued pronouncements designed to provide guidance for dealing with these troublesome items, and, more particularly, to narrow the discretion available to individual companies and thus achieve more uniform treatment throughout the financial community. The trend of these rulings has been all one way – in the direction of making it ever harder for an item claimed to be unusual to qualify for any special accounting treatment. Of particular importance is the fact that the most extreme such special treatment, the prior period adjustment technique of bypassing the income statement, was ultimately virtually abolished, per SFAS No. 16, PRIOR PERIOD ADJUSTMENTS (FASB 1977), which states that "all items of profit and loss recognized during a period . . . shall be included in the determination of net income for that period", with the only exceptions being for correction of an error in the financial statement of a prior period, and certain technical tax adjustments. For this purpose, errors include mathematical mistakes, mistakes in the application of accounting principles, and oversight or misuse of facts that existed at the time the financial statements were prepared. With that limited exception for correction of errors, the final upshot is that the policy favoring inclusion of every operating item somewhere in the total series of income statements triumphed over the policy of making each year's net income figure as meaningful a picture of the company's performance that year as possible.

Let's take a closer look at the procedure for making a prior-period adjustment to deal with an error to be corrected, say, a receipt or payment of cash in the current period representing income or an expense which should have been accrued in an earlier year, but wasn't because of a misunderstanding of the facts or the relevant accounting rules. If this were not a case of error, no prior period adjustment or bypassing of the current income statement would be allowed, and the income or expense involved would simply be reflected in the current year. But this was an error, so a prior-period adjustment may be utilized in correcting it, and the income or expense involved would not be recognized in the current year. Instead, if the earlier year in which the error was made was recent enough to be one of those included with the current financial statements for comparative purposes (typically, the two most recent prior years), the financial statements for that year will be actually restated to reflect that item correctly, with appropriate adjustment of the financial statements for subsequent years, including the current one, with respect to retained earnings and the affected asset or liability accounts. If the error occurred in a year prior to those included in the current financial report, then we would just use the old bypassing procedure, consisting of a direct credit (or debit, as the case may be) to the amount in the retained earnings account (or other appropriate component of equity) in the opening balance sheet for the earliest year that is in fact included in the current financial report, to reflect the cumulative effect of the error on periods prior to those presented; there would also be a corresponding adjustment in the affected asset or liability accounts, and, again, appropriate adjustments in all succeeding years, including the current one.

To illustrate this process with a concrete case, assume a receipt of payment in the current year (year 3) for services from a customer for work which was substantially completed two years earlier (in year 1), so the income involved should have been recognized back then. Another example would be a payment made by the enterprise in the current year 3 for services received in year 1, which should have been, but wasn't, accrued as an expense back then. If year 1, in which the item should have been recognized, is included in the current report, which it would be if the two prior years are being included in the current financial report, year 1's statements would be restated to correct the error by reflecting the item: in the income example, the result would be an increase in net income and hence retained earnings for that year. The increase in retained earnings would be carried forward in all subsequent years, including the current one, with the corresponding adjustment to the affected assets or liabilities, but the income statement for the current year 3 would not be affected. If only the most recent prior year (year 2) is being included with the financial statements for the current year 3, and year 1 is not being presented, then, as noted above, the old bypassing procedure is used, with a direct credit to the opening balance of retained earnings for the earliest prior year which is presented (here, year 2), and a corresponding adjustment in the affected asset or liability accounts (here, presumably some type of receivable). Year 2, being the only prior year included, is necessarily the earliest prior year in this case, and would be the recipient of these adjustments, while current year 3 would reflect the increase in retained earnings and corresponding adjustments in affected asset or liability accounts, but it's income statement would be unaffected.

Notice that under this approach the income from this transaction will not have been reflected in any income statement as originally issued, but this technique does as a practical matter bring the income into the series of income statements as long as the series being looked at goes back far enough. In addition, as noted earlier, if the amount involved in the erroneous omission is substantial enough, the company may be called upon to issue a corrected income statement for the year of the error, and disseminate it widely through the financial press, with the resulting unwelcome adverse publicity that accompanies any restatement reflecting a significant accounting error.

We must also note the substantial downside of the exception for correction of error when it is a loss rather than a gain which the company has mistakenly failed to recognize in an earlier year. For example, consider the accounting for the company which was held liable for the anti-trust violation in the previous example. If in some earlier year that anti-trust loss had become both probable and capable of being reasonably estimated in amount, as will be discussed in detail in Chapter VII GAAP would have required recognition of the loss in that earlier year. Since the failure to do so was an error calling for correction, a prior period adjustment would be in order in the current year when the loss is actually realized, with the consequence that this very important item would not appear in any income statement, at least as originally issued. That result would be particularly ironic because a major reason for the virtual elimination of prior period adjustments under SFAS

No. 16 was the SEC's express adverse view of the practice of resorting to prior period adjustments for payments in settlement of adverse claims on the ground that they related to the operations of a prior year. Managements may now be tempted to try to continue that prior practice by relying upon the exception for correction of an error, claiming that recognition of the prospective loss in an earlier year was required under GAAP, unless dissuaded by a requirement that the earlier accounting error be publicly acknowledged and the results for the prior year restated.

Continuing its effort to converge accounting standards worldwide, the FASB has added some new disclosure requirements when an enterprise restates its financial statements to correct an error. For fiscal years beginning after December 15, 2005, an enterprise that restates must disclose: (1) the nature of the error; (2) the correction's effect on each financial statement line item and any per-share amounts affected for each prior period presented; and (3) the change's cumulative effect on retained earnings or other appropriate component of equity as of the beginning of the earliest period presented. ACCOUNTING CHANGES AND ERROR CORRECTIONS, Statement of Financial Accounting Standards No. 154, ¶¶ 25, 26 (Financial Accounting Standards Bd. 2005).

Apart from the limited circumstance related to error corrections, enterprises must include all items of profit or loss in the income statement. While this treatment may not best match expenses and losses against revenues, the approach ensures that all of these items will flow through the income statement. However, by separately identifying material items related to previous years, either on the income statement or in the notes to the financial statements, an enterprise can enable investors to interpret more intelligently the enterprise's operating results. PRIOR PERIOD ADJUSTMENTS, Statement of Financial Accounting Standards No. 16, ¶ 11 (Financial Accounting Standards Bd. 1977), *as amended by* ACCOUNTING FOR INCOME TAXES, Statement of Financial Accounting Standards No. 109, ¶ 288(n) (Financial Accounting Standards Bd. 1992).

As to items that are unusual or special for reasons other than their relation to previous years, the severe limitation on prior period adjustments puts added pressure on the other approaches to highlighting such items, particularly that most forceful alternative, labeling an item as "extraordinary" on the income statement. That approach has received even more attention historically than prior period adjustments. However, before examining it in more detail we take a brief look at the unique issues that arise when an enterprise discontinues a significant line of activity.

b. DISCONTINUED OPERATIONS

Discontinued operations refers to termination of a distinct component of a business by way of being sold or otherwise transferred, eliminated, abandoned, or designated for sale. A component comprises operations and cash flows that the enterprise can distinguish, both operationally and for financial reporting purposes, from its other operations. A segment, reporting unit, subsidiary, consolidated joint venture, division, department, or asset group can qualify as a component.

An enterprise must separately report on its income statement the results of any discontinued operations, net of any related income tax expense or benefit, if two conditions are met: (1) the disposition or sale has eliminated, or will eliminate, the component's operations and cash flows from the entity's ongoing operations, and (2) the enterprise will not have any significant continuing involvement in the component's operations. For example, assume that an entity owns and operates a number of retail stores selling household goods, each of which qualifies as a component because the entity can clearly distinguish the operations and cash flows for each store; accordingly, the complete termination of any one or more stores without more would constitute a discontinued operation. On the other hand, a decision to close two stores to open a new superstore in the same region, which would continue to sell the household goods previously sold in the retail stores as well as other related products, would not meet the requirements for reporting the closed stores' results in discontinued operations, since neither the retail operations in the region nor the related cash flows from the sale of household goods would be eliminated.

The separate listing for discontinued operations, which appears on the income statement just before any extraordinary items (the subject of the next section of this chapter), enables the reader to assess the results of continuing operations in the current period and to compare those results to prior periods on a consistent basis. Indeed, when a component is discontinued, any of its income included in the enterprise's overall income from continuing operations in prior years must be reclassified to the separate listing for discontinued operations in those same years for the purpose of presenting comparative financial statements. Although the enterprise's total net income or loss for each year remains unchanged, the shift from continuing operations to discontinued operations can affect contract drafting and interpretation.

This separate category for discontinued operations will also contain any loss (or gain for a subsequent increase in value) that the enterprise must recognize pursuant to the rules for the impairment or disposal of long-lived assets, which we will discuss later in Chapter IX, less any applicable income taxes or plus any related tax benefit. If the enterprise expects a loss from a proposed sale, then pursuant to the doctrine of conservatism the enterprise must immediately include the estimated loss on the income statement under the heading for discontinued operations. By comparison, an enterprise cannot recognize future operating losses from these discontinued operations until they occur. If the enterprise expects a net gain on the sale, both the revenue recognition principle and conservatism require the enterprise to wait until it recognizes the income, which ordinarily occurs at the actual disposal. ACCOUNTING FOR THE IMPAIRMENT OR DISPOSAL OF LONG-LIVED ASSETS, Statement of Financial Accounting Standards No. 144, ¶¶ 41–44 (FASB 2001).

c. EXTRAORDINARY ITEMS

We turn now to a closer look at the special category of items which qualify as "extraordinary" under GAAP. As noted above, these items appear in a separate section on the income statement, immediately after discontinued operations and following the figure labeled "Income before Extraordinary Items", with the special feature that extraordinary items are shown net of income tax effects, that is, after offsetting any extraordinary gains with the income tax incurred thereon, and any extraordinary losses with the resulting tax saving.

Pursuant to the earlier-referred-to steady narrowing of eligibility for special treatment for non-ordinary items, over the years the scope of the "extraordinary" category was continuously reduced. The final tightening came in 1973, in Accounting Principles Board Opinion No. 30: prior to that ruling, it was enough to qualify for the special treatment as extraordinary if the gain or loss from an event or transaction was found to be either *unusual in nature* or *infrequent in occurrence* (not that those two standards don't overlap somewhat); but APB Op. No. 30 changed the test to require that both of those standards be satisfied.

To qualify as unusual in nature, an event or transaction must possess a high degree of abnormality and either not relate to, or only incidentally relate to, the enterprise's ordinary and typical activities; to satisfy the "infrequent in occurrence" requirement, the enterprise must not reasonably expect the underlying event or transaction to recur in the foreseeable future. APB Op. 30, ¶¶ 20–23.

In determining whether an item qualifies as either unusual or infrequent, an enterprise must consider the business's operating environment, which includes industry characteristics, geographical location and governmental regulations. As a result, an event or transaction may qualify as unusual or infrequent for one enterprise but not another, given differences in their operating environments. For example, if a hail storm destroys a large portion of a tobacco manufacturer's crops, the enterprise can treat the loss as an extraordinary item if severe damage from hail storms occurs only very rarely in the locality. In contrast, because severe frosts typically occur every three or four years in Florida, frost damage to a citrus grower's crops in Florida would not qualify. After Mount St. Helens erupted in 1980, Weyerhauser Co. treated a $36 million loss arising from destroyed timber, inventory, and buildings as extraordinary on its financial statements because no eruption had occurred at the volcano in 130 years. Gullapalli, *For Annual-Report Purposes, Hurricane Katrina Is 'Ordinary,'* WALL ST. J.,Sept. 2, 2005 at C3.

APB Op. 30 also provides expressly that certain specified events and transactions do not qualify as extraordinary items, presumably because they cannot satisfy the test of being both unusual and infrequent: the list includes write-offs of receivables, losses attributable to labor strikes and "[o]ther gains and losses from sale or abandonment of property, plant, or equipment used in the business". APB Op. 30, ¶ 23.

After the terrorist attacks on September 11, 2001, the FASB Emerging Issues Task Force ultimately reached a consensus that enterprises could not treat losses or costs resulting from the attacks as extraordinary items under GAAP. Some Task Force members believed that although the terrorist attacks qualified as "unusual in nature" for many businesses, those events did not satisfy the "infrequent in occurrence" requirement, because terrorists attacks had occurred in the United States in the past and could reasonably be expected to recur in the foreseeable future. Although other members felt that the sheer magnitude of the attacks might allow certain losses and costs arising from the events to qualify as extraordinary items, in the end the Task Force decided against such treatment. Given an already weakening economy, the members agreed that no one line on a financial statement could possibly isolate the extensive and pervasive losses directly attributable to the attacks from those arising from the general economic slowdown. However, the Task Force did conclude that enterprises should, at a minimum, disclose the nature and amounts of any losses or contingencies resulting from the terrorist attacks and any related insurance recoveries in the notes to the financial statements. ACCOUNTING FOR THE IMPACT OF THE TERRORIST ATTACKS OF SEPTEMBER 11, 2001, EIT Issue No. 01-10 (Financial Accounting Standards Bd. 2001).

More recently, and in response to a question during the aftermath of Hurricane Katrina in 2005, a spokesman for the FASB issued a statement concluding that losses from the storm and subsequent flooding and evacuation did not qualify as extraordinary because "'every year many businesses across the country are affected by [hurricanes and other natural disasters] and thus they do not represent an unusual and infrequent occurrence to businesses or to insurers.'" Gullapalli, op. cit. *supra*, at C3.

Until 2002, GAAP automatically classified the aggregated gains and losses from extinguishing debt, if material, as extraordinary items without regard to the unusual and infrequent requirements. *See* REPORTING GAINS AND LOSSES FROM EXTINGUISHMENT OF DEBT, SFAS No. 4, ¶ 8 (Financial Accounting Standards Bd. 1975). In 2002, FASB rescinded the rule because many enterprises were using debt extinguishment as a risk management strategy. Enterprises can now classify gains and losses from debt extinguishment as extraordinary items only if the underlying transactions meet the *unusual* and *infrequent* criteria in APB Opinion No. 30. Therefore, enterprises that use debt extinguishment in their recurring operations can no longer classify the resulting gains and losses as extraordinary items. RESCISSION OF FASB STATEMENTS NO. 4, 44, AND 64, AMENDMENT OF FASB STATEMENT NO. 13, AND TECHNICAL CORRECTIONS, SFAS No. 145, ¶¶ 1, 6a (FASB 2002).

(1) *Unusual or Nonrecurring Operating Items*

Although an item can not qualify as extraordinary if it satisfies just one of the two tests, "unusual" and "infrequent in occurrence", users of financial statements usually want information about any such unusual or infrequent item, if material, so that they can decide whether to factor in or to ignore its effects, especially relative to future periods. For this reason, GAAP requires an enterprise to report a material event or transaction that qualifies as either unusual in nature or infrequent in occurrence, but not both, as a separate item in computing income or loss from continuing operations. However, such an item must appear at its gross amount, without adjusting for any income tax effect. In addition, the enterprise should disclose the nature and financial effects of each such event or transaction, either on the income statement itself or in the notes to the financial statements. REPORTING THE RESULTS OF OPERATIONS – REPORTING THE EFFECTS OF DISPOSAL OF A SEGMENT OF A BUSINESS, AND EXTRAORDINARY, UNUSUAL AND INFREQUENTLY OCCURRING EVENTS AND TRANSACTIONS, Accounting Principles Board Opinion No. 30, ¶26 (1973). As we will see later in this chapter, the MD&A in a public company's securities filings with the SEC also may provide information about these events or transactions. Knowledgeable readers watch carefully for such disclosures.

PROBLEMS

Problem 4.3A. A dramatic historical example of polar alternatives for the treatment of out-of-the-ordinary transactions occurred in 1962, involving two of the largest industrial enterprises in the world, General Motors Corporation ("GM"), and Standard Oil Company of New Jersey ("Jersey") as it then was (now Exxon Corporation). In 1924 the two companies had joined forces to organize a new entity, Ethyl Corporation, to produce a lead compound additive for gasoline which would eliminate so-called "engine knock" (but which, as we now know, turned out to be a serious pollutant, and has long since been banned). GM and Jersey each owned fifty percent of the stock of Ethyl, and with Ethyl's business success those holdings increased substantially in value. In 1962, the two companies sold their respective fifty percent interests to an outside buyer, and they each realized a gain of around 75 million dollars from the combination of the sale proceeds, plus a large special distribution just before the sale. (The slight difference in the amount of gain was due to some differences in internal accounting over the years.) However, the two companies accounted for this special gain in very different ways, GM recording it as a separate line item among the other sources of revenue on the income statement, and Jersey choosing instead to by-pass the income statement and credit the gain directly to earned surplus. Both of these accounting treatments were permitted at the time.

At the respective annual meetings of the two companies for 1962, the question of the accounting treatment of the gain was raised. At the GM meeting, the Chairman replied that "we have followed very consistently the practice of incorporating all these items, whether good or bad, whether pluses or minuses, through the income account, so that . . . you can tell the changes in our net worth through operations just by adding up the income" over the years. At the Jersey meeting, the response was as follows:

> "We felt that, in view of the size of this item in relation to the total earnings, if we had credited it to current earnings, the reported results for the year would have been materially distorted. We felt it would give a more realistic picture of the progress of the company from the standpoint of comparative figures from year to year if we did not have this sort of distortion in one particular year."

Could the two companies just as readily have each come out the other way, GM relying upon potential distortion to by-pass the income statement, and Jersey relying upon consistency to include the gain in income? Would it affect your answer to know that GM's net income for 1962, including this gain, amounted $1,459 million, compared with net income for 1961 of $880 million, while Jersey's net income for 1962, which did not include this gain, was $841 million, compared with $758 million in 1961?

Problem 4.3B.   Suppose that X Corp. sells its home office building, which was carried on the balance sheet at net book value (cost less depreciation) of $1,000,000, for $1,500,000 in cash. How should the company reflect the gain in its financial statements for the year of the sale? In particular, could X Corp. record the transaction in the same way as either GM or Jersey handled the gain on the sale of Ethyl stock? How should the auditor respond if the company insists upon adopting either one of those approaches? Does APB No. 30, described on pages 255-256, *supra*, provide an answer in ¶ 23 or otherwise?

The following chart may help in thinking about the foregoing questions. Assume that X Corp. had revenues of $50,000,000 (apart from the sale of the office building), and expenses of $41,000,000 (which includes income taxes, except for the capital gains taxes of $170,000 on the $500,000 gain from the sale of the office building). Here is the way the company's income statement might have looked under the three alternative methods for reporting the gain on the sale of the office building: (1) the approach followed by GM for its gain on the sale of Ethyl stock; (2) the approach followed by Jersey for its gain on the sale of Ethyl stock; or (3) the approach called for by APB Op. No. 30 for an extraordinary item.

	GM	Extraordinary Item Treatment	Jersey
Revenues	$50,000,000	$50,000,000	$50,000,000
Other Income	500,000	- -	- -
Total	50,500,000	50,000,000	50,000,000
Less: Expenses (income taxes included	41,170,000	41,000,000	41,000,000
Net Income before Extraordinary Item	- -	9,000,000	- -
Add: Extraordinary Item (net of taxes of $170,000)	- -	330,000	- -
NET INCOME	$ 9,330,000	$ 9,330,000	$ 9,000,000

Problem 4.3C. In the 1970 Annual Report of GAF Corporation, the front cover showed the following under a caption called "Highlights":

	1970	1969
Net Income per shares . .	$ .80	$ .54

The more detailed presentation later in the
report showed the following:

	1970	1969
Net Income per Share before Extraordinary Item .	$ .34	$ .85
Extraordinary Item per Share	$ .46	($ .31)
Net Income per Share	$ .80	$ .54

Does this incident tell us anything about the proper treatment of extraordinary items in financial statements?

d. CHANGES IN ACCOUNTING PRINCIPLES AND ESTIMATES

As we saw in Chapter II, GAAP does not establish a rigid rule as to how to report every type of transaction. More specifically, GAAP often allows alternative accounting methods or calls for management to exercise judgment in determining the most appropriate accounting for particular transactions or events. It addition, GAAP constantly changes and evolves.

However, that does not mean that an enterprise is free to shift from one accounting approach to another whenever it wishes, even if the two approaches are equally acceptable under GAAP. That is because switching methods can seriously interfere with comparison of current financial statements for an enterprise with its statements for prior years. Of course, the manner in which a particular transaction or event is reported can significantly affect the current period's financial statements. But for any recurring type of transaction or event, if the approach adopted currently is different from the method used earlier, the trends revealed in a series of income statements could be seriously distorted, substantially reducing their usefulness.

Accordingly, GAAP has imposed significant limitations on an enterprise's ability to change its accounting. For this purpose, the term "accounting change" connotes a change in (1) an accounting principle, (2) an accounting estimate, or (3) the reporting entity. The term "accounting change," however, explicitly does not include correction of an error made in previously issued financial statements. With respect to a change in the reporting entity, as a practical matter GAAP treats that in much the same way as a change in an accounting principle, so the text that follows discusses only changes in an accounting principle or an accounting estimate.

(1) Changes in Accounting Principles

A change in an accounting principle occurs whenever an enterprise adopts a principle that differs from the one that the enterprise previously used for financial reporting purposes. In this regard, the term *accounting principle* includes not only accounting principles and practices, but the methods that an enterprise uses to apply them. The adoption of a new principle to handle events that have occurred for the first time or that previously qualified as immaterial does not constitute a change in accounting principle. As one clear-cut example discussed in more detail in chapter VIII, a switch from first-in, first-out ("FIFO") to last-in, first-out ("LIFO") when accounting for inventory would constitute a change in an accounting principle.

Because the consistency principle requires an enterprise generally to give the same accounting treatment to similar transactions and events in different accounting periods, under GAAP an enterprise can only change an accounting principle if the new principle qualifies as "preferable." Unfortunately, GAAP does not define that term. As a practical matter, whenever FASB, or another designated body described in categories (a) through (d) of the hierarchy discussed in Chapter II on page 146, issues a pronouncement that (1) creates a new accounting principle, (2) interprets an existing principle, (3) expresses a preference for a particular principle, or (4) rejects a specific principle, GAAP may *require* an enterprise to adopt a corresponding change in accounting principle; in that event, GAAP treats the new pronouncement as "sufficient support" for the change. If GAAP does not require the change, the enterprise bears the burden to justify the switch. In any event, new pronouncements typically include specific transition provisions, which enterprises must follow.

Until 2005 the manner of reporting an accounting change was governed by Accounting Principles Board Opinion No. 20, *Accounting Changes* (1971), which required an enterprise that adopts an accounting change to include in the net income of that period the cumulative effect that retroactively changing to the different accounting principle would have had on the amount of retained earnings at the beginning of that period. In 2005, in order to bring U.S. GAAP into line with international accounting standards, the rule was changed to provide that companies should simply apply a new accounting principle in the year adopted, with no additional impact on the net income of that current year. Statement of Financial Accounting Standards No. 154, *Accounting Changes and Error Corrections* (FASB 2005). However, SFAS No. 154 does require that unless the enterprise cannot reasonably determine the period-specific effects, the financial statements for each prior year presented for comparative purposes in the current annual report must be revised to reflect the application of the newly-adopted accounting principle. If the accounting change would have affected one or more years prior to the earliest one included in the current annual report, the enterprise must (1) determine the cumulative effect of the accounting change on all those affected years prior to the earliest one presented currently, and (2) reflect that cumulative effect directly in the retained earnings account (or other appropriate equity accounts) as of the beginning of the first year that is presented currently, with appropriate adjustment in the affected asset or liability accounts in that opening balance sheet.

To illustrate the difference between APB Opinion No. 20 and SFAS No. 154, assume that a change in accounting principle adopted in year 3 would have reduced an enterprise's year 1 earnings by $300 million and year 2 earnings by $200 million, while also producing lowered earnings in year 3, the current period. Under APB Op. No. 20 the enterprise would use the newly-adopted method to compute net income for year 3 (assuming it could satisfactorily explain why that new method qualified as "preferable"); but in addition the enterprise would have been required to record the entire $500 million cumulative effect of the accounting change in prior years as a charge against income in year 3, which would be reported net of income taxes as a separate line item in the income statement immediately after extraordinary items. Notice that the financial statements for years 1 and 2 would continue to reflect the "old" accounting principle. In contrast, under SFAS No. 154, if the financial statements for both years 1 and 2 are being presented with the financial statements for year 3 for comparative purposes, the enterprise would revise the financial statements of those two years to reflect the changed accounting principle, thereby reducing year 2 earnings by $200 million and year 1 earnings by $300 million. The SFAS No. 154 approach would appear to enhance consistency in financial reporting, as well as the comparability of an enterprise's financial statements from period to period.

If only the financial statements for the most recent earlier year, here, year 2, were presented in conjunction with the financial statements for year 3, then only year 2's earnings would be revised to reflect the application of the changed accounting principle. In addition, however, under SFAS No. 154 the cumulative impact of the accounting change in all affected years prior to year 2 (here, that's just year 1) would be reflected directly in the retained earnings as of the beginning of the earliest year that is presented (here, year 2), so there would be a reduction in the retained earnings account of $300 million, with appropriate accompanying adjustments in assets or liabilities, in that opening balance sheet for year 2.

To summarize the disclosures required under SFAS No. 154 when a change in accounting principle is adopted, the enterprise must report (1) the change and the reason for it, explaining why the newly-adopted principle qualifies as preferable; (2) the change's effect on income from continuing operations, net income, any other affected line item on the financial statements, any affected per-share amounts for the current period, and any prior period retrospectively adjusted; and (3) any cumulative effect of the change on retained earnings or other components of equity as of the beginning of the earliest period presented.

As mentioned in the discussion on audit reports on page 177 *supra*, a change in accounting principle has generally called for the auditor to add explanatory language to an unqualified opinion, even though the new method qualifies as "preferable." If the new method does not so qualify and causes a material effect on the financial statements, the auditor must issue either a qualified or adverse opinion. Financial statement users should view enterprises that change accounting principles without sufficient support very skeptically.

(2) Changes in Accounting Estimates

In connection with preparing financial statements, management must estimate various items, such as useful life, salvage value, and warranty expenses, that affect the recorded amounts for various assets, liabilities, revenues, and expenses. Naturally, the actual results may differ from these estimates. When the estimate involves future projections, as for example estimating the useful life of an asset for purposes of depreciation or amortization, after a few years an enterprise's experience may indicate that the asset's originally estimated useful life no longer accurately predicts how long the asset will continue to provide benefits. By definition, estimates can and do change when new events occur, or as management acquires more information. For this reason, SFAS No. 154 reaffirms the rule in APB Opinion No. 20, limiting the accounting for changes in estimates to the period of change if the change affects that period only, or to the period of change and future periods if the change affects both; an enterprise should not restate amounts reported in financial statements for prior periods or report pro forms amounts for those periods.

e. PRO FORMA METRICS

As indicated above, the term pro forma is often used by the financial community to refer to financial presentations that do not conform to GAAP, with its fairly conservative approach to measuring an enterprise's performance. In particular, when computing net income a firm is required by GAAP to include all expenses incurred during the reporting period, and prohibited from recognizing income that is merely expected to materialize in the future. In contrast, pro forma metrics typically exclude some expenses related to an enterprise's normal activities, while sometimes including projected benefits that will not be realized until later.

Enterprises originally used pro formas to adjust GAAP financials to exclude the effects of major, nonrecurring events or to show what an enterprise's financial statements would look like if a proposed merger or other acquisition occurred. These metrics gained popularity during the internet stock surge in the 1990s, eventually becoming common in all industries because the approach allowed enterprises to present a more favorable view of earnings by minimizing large asset write-downs and other expenses that dragged down net income under GAAP. By the early 2000s, public companies were repeatedly utilizing those non-GAAP metrics referred to earlier, "recurring earnings," "core earnings," EBIT, EBITDA, and the like. These figures allowed enterprises to present a more optimistic picture of their financial results, highlight favorable financial data, and dismiss or ignore less-flattering GAAP reporting measures.

For example, assume that a newspaper publishing company generated $1 million from its business operations in 2005 before a $5 million settlement following a jury verdict for libel in an article the company published. Under GAAP, the company would report a $4 million net loss. If the company hired Legally Blonde business law expert Elle Woods to advise the company, she might recommend that the company prepare pro forma statements that ignore the "totally heinous" jury verdict and related settlement, and report $1 million as income before special items. Given the potential to mislead investors, some financial experts, including a former SEC chief accountant, routinely criticize such gauges of performance, referring to some pro forma metrics as "EBS," or "everything but the bad stuff."

While no specific definition of the term "pro forma" exists, an attorney should understand that these non GAAP numbers almost allow businesses to establish their own accounting standards and rules for reporting financial information, sometimes even presenting results "as if" certain events or transactions did not occur, or assuming that certain other things will happen exactly as planned. As a result, attorneys evaluating financial statements must distinguish between GAAP reporting measures and pro forma metrics.

(1) Advantages

Pro forma metrics can indeed serve legitimate purposes. Knowledgeable investors and analysts can find pro formas helpful in measuring an enterprise's current profitability and trying to predict its future operating results. Even the SEC has recognized that "[p]ublic companies may quite appropriately wish to focus investors' attention on critical components of quarterly or annual financial results in order to provide a meaningful comparison to results for the same period of prior years or to emphasize the results of core operations." Cautionary Advice Regarding Use of "Pro Forma" Financial Information in Earnings Releases, Financial Reporting Release No. 59, 66 Fed. Reg. 63,731, 63,732 (Dec. 10, 2001). In addition, pro forma metrics such as EBITDA can produce more useful comparisons between enterprises which finance their operations largely with borrowed funds, on which they must pay interest, and those that rely more upon equity capital contributed by owners and therefore have less interest expense.

Standard & Poors ("S&P"), an independent provider of investment data used in analyzing and valuing companies, employs a pro forma metric called "core earnings" to measure operating income. S&P introduced a new definition of core earnings in mid-2002 to enhance consistency in financial reports on different companies, and to provide greater transparency in the computations and adjustments underlying the measure. S&P's core earnings metric focuses on earnings after taxes generated from an enterprise's principal business activities, and that entails making adjustments to net income which are inconsistent with GAAP. In particular, S&P ignores certain items, such as gains from pension funds and charges for goodwill impairment or litigation settlements, which GAAP would require to be taken into account, while sometimes including items that GAAP does not require, of which the most notable example had been the cost of employee stock options, but as we have seen, now GAAP requires inclusion of this cost. Unlike most pro forma numbers, which enterprises develop using their own criteria, S&P plans to use these guidelines consistently in arriving at core earnings. Whatever the measure, however, all users of financial statements, including lawyers, need to understand how any pro forma figure differs from its counterpart GAAP reporting number.

(2) The Pitfalls

For one thing, a specific enterprise's pro formas may lack comparability to that company's prior period numbers or the results of competitors. More generally, pro forma metrics can mislead investors and other users of financial information if they obscure GAAP results, or are used to distort an enterprise's financial appearance. For example, Enron, in its 2000 fourth quarter earnings release, boasted a twenty-five percent increase in earnings per share ("EPS") for the full year 2000 when compared to 1999. On the other hand, buried in the last section of the earnings release was a very different story: Enron disclosed that EPS for 2000, including nonrecurring charges as required by GAAP, increased only from $1.10 per share in 1999 to $1.12 per share in 2000. This translated to a 1.8 percent increase, in stark contrast to the twenty-five percent increase that Enron touted at the beginning of its earnings release. Similarly, in 2001 Enron used a pro forma metric called "recurring net income" to announce a $393 million profit in its earnings release for the third quarter of 2001, just weeks before the company filed for bankruptcy protection. Later in that release Enron reported that it actually sustained a $618 million net loss for that period under GAAP. Enron turned its GAAP loss into a pro forma profit by labeling $1.01 billion in charges as "one-time" or "nonrecurring", and excluding those charges from "recurring net income." However, those charges, which included restructuring costs and write-downs of investments and other assets, arose from the company's normal business activities. These uses of pro forma metrics by Enron seem calculated to mislead the public.

The chances that a pro forma metric will give a distorted picture increases when the enterprise does not disclose where the underlying numbers come from, or does not reconcile the metric to a comparable GAAP measure. In addition, pro formas should allow for comparison to previous results for the same business and current results for competitors.

(3) Regulation G

Although some restraint on pro forma metrics was provided by the federal securities laws prohibiting material misstatements or omissions in disclosures relating to securities, Congress decided to deal more specifically with the pro forma phenomenon, and in SOx section 401(b) directed the SEC to issue regulations to protect investors from false or misleading pro forma information. In response to that mandate, the SEC issued Regulation G, which became effective on March 28, 2003 and applies whenever a public company discloses material information that includes a pro forma metric. Conditions for Use of Non-GAAP Financial Measures, Financial Reporting Release No. 65, 68 Fed. Reg. 4820 (Jan. 30, 2003). Regulation G contains two important components: (1) a general prohibition against materially false or misleading pro forma metrics; and (2) a specific requirement to reconcile any reported pro forma metric with the most closely comparable GAAP reporting measure. In addition, the accompanying release explicitly endorsed the Earnings Press Release Guidelines that the Financial Executives International ("FEI") and the National Investor Relations Institute ("NIRI") have jointly promulgated.

Consistent with the FEI/NIRI guidelines, Regulation G prohibits public companies from giving non-GAAP financial metrics greater prominence than comparable GAAP reporting measures in their earnings releases. In essence, pro forma metrics may not supplant GAAP numbers, but they may clarify current period results and future prospects. In addition, the new rules bar public companies from using "titles or descriptions of non-GAAP financial measures that are the same as, or confusingly similar to, titles or descriptions used for GAAP financial measures." Neither the final regulations nor the answers to frequently asked questions about Regulation G that the staff in the Division of Corporation Finance has posted on the SEC's web site, however, provide any examples of "confusingly similar" terms. Given their resemblance to "income from continuing operations," "income before extraordinary items," and "net income," public companies should keep in mind that labels such as "net income from operations," earnings before special items," or "recurring net income" may invite SEC scrutiny. To help users of financial information better understand the nature and relevance of any pro forma metrics reported, the SEC now requires explanations and reconciliations of pro forma metrics to GAAP reporting measures, specifically in tabular format, in any release that uses pro forma metrics. This rule seeks to ensure that public companies provide users of financial statements information detailing where the pro forma metrics come from and why management believes them useful, so that users can better determine how much weight to give them.

Regulation *G* also expressly bans companies from designating items as "special," "nonrecurring," or "unusual" in certain public filings, specifically 10-Ks and 10-Qs, if similar items have occurred in the previous two years or if the enterprise expects such events or transactions to occur again within two years. Public companies, however, may still use such designations to define pro forma metrics in other releases so long as the enterprise explains where the pro forma metric comes from and includes the necessary reconciliation to GAAP. As discussed more fully in Chapter VI, the SEC now explicitly prohibits the use of pro forma metrics to smooth earnings. Finally, because enterprises have historically used pro formas to show what an enterprise's financial statements would look like after a merger or other business acquisition, the rules contain an important exception for such disclosures, but any such disclosures remain subject to SEC regulations regarding mergers and business combinations that predate SOx.

(4) Practical Tips for Lawyers

Knowing the difference between GAAP reporting measures and pro forma metrics allows lawyers to represent and advise clients more effectively and to reach more informed investment decisions. Anyone using pro forma information would do well to follow the SEC's advice and to keep the following questions in mind:

> *What is the company assuming?* "Pro forma" financial results can be misleading, particularly if they change a loss to a profit or hide a significant fact. For example, as noted above, they may assume that a proposed transaction that benefits the company has actually occurred.

> *What is the company not saying?* Be particularly wary when you see "pro forma" financial results that only address one component of a company's financial results. These kinds of statements can be misleading unless the company clearly describes what transactions are omitted and how the numbers might compare to other periods.

> *How do the "pro forma" results compare with GAAP-based financials?* Look for a clear, comprehensible explanation of how "pro forma" results differ from financial statements prepared under GAAP rules, and make sure you understand any differences before relying on "pro forma" results.

> *Are you reading "pro forma" results or a summary of GAAP-based financials?* Remember that there is a big difference between "pro forma" financial information and a summary of a financial statement that has been prepared in accordance with GAAP. When financial statements have been prepared in compliance with regular accounting rules, a summary of that information can be quite useful, giving you the overall picture of a company's financial position without the mass of details contained in the full financial statements.

Staff of the Securities & Exchange Commission, "Pro Forma" Financial Information Tips for investors Qast modified Dec. 4, 2001), *available at* http://www.sec.gov/investor/pubs/ proformal2-4.htm.

It should also be remembered that understanding financial statements can give an attorney a great advantage in a number of legal arenas. At a minimum, therefore, lawyers should:

(1) Read earnings releases, public announcements, and annual reports in their entirety and with healthy skepticism. Decide for yourself whether any pro forma metrics accurately portray the enterprise's financial health and performance. Remember that Enron tried to hide a $1 billion loss by labeling it as "non-recurring" and leaving it out of the from pro forma metrics.

(2) Assess the quality of earnings. Gains from onetime events, such as litigation recoveries and sales of major assets, usually do not reliably predict future earnings performance. In its 10Q for the second quarter in 2001, Enron gushed: "Profits from North American power marketing operations, which increased significantly, included the sale of three peaking power plants." Are the earnings from those sales likely to recur?

(3) Watch out for "everything-but-bad stuff" reporting. Has the enterprise included in past pro formas expenses and charges similar to those being omitted now? Are the events or economic circumstances underlying these items likely to recur in the future?

PROBLEM

Problem 4.2D. Your law firm serves as outside counsel to KeoughHall Health Corp. ("Keough"), a health care provider listed on the NYSE. Keough's audit committee has asked your firm to review a proposed earnings release announcing the company's results for its most recent quarter, in which Keough posted a $55 million net loss, which included $245 million for various write-offs and restructuring charges. The first paragraph of Keough's proposed release declares, "net income from operations was $190 million, or $.40 per share." The net loss of $55 million is not mentioned until the final sentence of the tenth paragraph. From your previous work for Keough, you know that the company has used the term "net income from operations" for years. What advice would you give to the audit committee?

f. COMPREHENSIVE INCOME AND THE FUTURE

As noted at page 239, *supra*, SFAS No. 130, *Reporting Comprehensive Income* (1997), now requires enterprises to include in the financial statements a report of "comprehensive income", defined as "the change in equity (net assets) of a business enterprise during a period from transactions and other events and circumstances from nonowner sources" -- in other words, all changes in equity during a period except those resulting from investments by owners and distributions to owners. The comprehensive income report must be as prominently displayed as the other financial statements.

As discussed later in Chapter VI, the rules for reporting certain investments in debt and equity securities require enterprises to include changes in the fair values of those investments in a separate component of the equity section of the balance sheet. Similar rules apply to various adjustments arising from converting a foreign entity's financial statements to U.S. dollars, changes in the fair value of certain derivatives that qualify as hedges, and certain pension obligations that an enterprise has not yet recognized as pension costs. It is because of items like these, none of which would appear in the regular income statement, that SFAS No. 130 requires enterprises to include a report of comprehensive income and its components in the basic financial statements, and to give it the same prominence as the other statements.

SFAS No. 130 divides comprehensive income into two parts: (1) *net income*, which includes income from continuing operations, discontinued operations, extraordinary items, and effects of changes in accounting principles, and (2) *other comprehensive income*, which includes all other non-owner changes in net assets, such as the ones listed in the previous paragraph.

SFAS No. 130 does not require firms to use the term "comprehensive income" or any specific format, so enterprises may use: (i) a "statement of income and comprehensive income;" (ii) separate statements for "traditional" net income and comprehensive income; (iii) a "statement of changes in equity" or (iv) some other format to present the required information. If an enterprise does not have any items of "other comprehensive income" during an accounting period, the enterprise need not report a separate amount for comprehensive income. To date, most corporations have used a statement of changes in stockholders' equity, as Starbucks does as shown on page 43 in Appendix A.

In 2001 FASB added to its agenda a project on financial performance reporting by business enterprises that could replace or redesign the income statement and the reporting of comprehensive income, with the goal of improving both the quality and breadth of information in financial statements, so that readers can better evaluate an enterprise's financial performance, and also calculate key financial measures.

In an effort to move further toward convergent standards worldwide, in 2004 the FASB and IASB decided to combine their respective projects on financial reporting, classification and aggregation, and the display of specified items and summarized amounts on the face of all basic financial statements, but not addressing financial ratios, other than earnings per share and other per-share amounts.

As of May 2006, the FASB had tentatively decided that a business entity should report all items of revenue, expense, gain and loss in a revised single statement entitled "the statement of earnings and comprehensive income," which would show a total for all non-owner changes in financial position. In addition, enterprises would report a subtotal for net income. The statement would separately report income from at least three major categories: business activities, financing activities, and other gains and losses. This redesigned statement would presumably supplant both the income statement and the statement of comprehensive income under GAAP. While tentatively deciding to require enterprises to report earnings per share on the face of the income statement, FASB has preliminarily voted to allow the new performance measure, labeled "comprehensive income per share." These changes could mean that "net income" will lose the "bottom line" position it has held for many years. In March 2006, the IASB published an exposure draft on the first phase of the project, which addresses what constitutes a complete set of financial statements and the requirements to present comparative information. The exposure draft proposed to bring international financial reporting standards into line with SFAS No. 130, *Reporting Comprehensive Income.* FASB and IASB plan to issue an preliminary discussion document on the project's second phase, which addresses the more fundamental issues for presentation of information on the face of the financial statements in the first quarter of 2007. *Project Update, Financial Statement Presentation – Joint Project of the IASB and FASB (Formerly known as Financial Performance Reporting by Business Enterprises)* (FASB May 26, 2006).

3. RATIO ANALYSIS

As noted at pages 234-235, supra, knowledgeable users frequently analyze the income statement by converting each line to a percentage of sales; indeed, the annual report or the financial statements commonly include a breakdown showing net income, as well as the major expense categories for the period, as a percentage of net sales. Such percentages can be compared with the corresponding figures either from the same enterprise in previous years or from competitors for the current year.

Accountants and financial analysts have also developed a number of financial ratios based upon the net income or other numbers appearing in the income statement. Once again, however, keep in mind that these financial ratios are only as good as the financial statements from which they are derived. An erroneous income statement or balance sheet can produce misleading financial ratios. That caution aside, the ratios which use numbers from the income statement fall into three categories, coverage, profitability, and activity.

a. COVERAGE RATIOS

Coverage ratios measure the extent to which income, usually determined before interest and taxes, covers certain payments related to an enterprise's long-term debt. The most commonly-used coverage ratios are stated in terms of some desired (or perhaps minimum acceptable) multiple of the interest on the debt, or the sum of interest plus the amount of principal currently due. Similarly, the dividend coverage ratio measures the extent to which net income (this time, after interest and taxes) covers regular dividend payments.

b.   PROFITABILITY RATIOS

Recall that profitability ratios assess how effectively a business operates. These profitability ratios include earnings per share, the price to earnings ratio, return on sales, gross profit percentage, and the returns on assets and equity. Consider the following income statement for X Corp., which has issued 100 common shares, all of which remained outstanding during the entire year.

X Corp.
Income Statement
For the Year Ended December 31

Net Sales		$100,000
Cost of Goods Sold:		
Opening Inventory	$14,000	
Purchases	72,000	
Goods Available for Sale	$86,000	
Less: Closing Inventory	16,000	70,000
Gross Profit		$30,000
Operating Expenses		20,000
Income Before Taxes		$10,000
Income Taxes		$4,000
Net Income		$6,000

(1)   Earnings Per Share

When analyzing a corporation's income statement, lawyers will perhaps most frequently encounter the term *earnings per share*, sometimes abbreviated *EPS*, which usually refers to the net income attributable to the company's common shares. To compute the net income attributable to the common shares, the accountant or financial analyst subtracts any dividends on preferred stock, from the company's net income and then divides the remaining amount by the weighted average of common shares outstanding during the period. Because X Corp. has not issued any preferred shares and 100 common shares remained outstanding during the entire year ended December 31, we can compute $60 ($6,000 net income/100 common shares outstanding) as the earnings per share for that year.

The business community uses this ratio as an important yardstick, perhaps the most important one, for comparing an enterprise's performance in the current accounting period to that in a prior period. Although accounting standards generally require enterprises to show information regarding earnings per share or net loss per share on the face of the income statement, GAAP exempts nonpublic enterprises from this requirement. These rules state that enterprises should also show per share amounts for *Income from Continuing Operations* and *Income Before Extraordinary Items*. Finally, the rules encourage businesses to explain the numbers used in the earnings per share calculation in the notes to the financial statements.

In a collaborative effort with the International Accounting Standards body, in 1997 the FASB issued SFAS No. 128, Earnings per Share, to simplify the standards for computing earnings per share and to conform the applicable rules more closely to international accounting standards. The pronouncement requires enterprises with publicly-held common stock, or with outstanding contractual obligations that could allow holders to obtain common stock either during, or after the end of, the reporting period, to report figures for *basic earnings per share* and, if applicable, *diluted earnings per share*. The new terms "basic earnings per share" and "diluted earnings per share" replace the previously used labels "primary ea rnings per share" and "fully diluted earnings per share," respectively. Under the new rules, *basic earnings per share* describes the amount of earnings for the period available to each share of common stock outstanding during the period, computed as illustrated above, by dividing income available to common shareholders by the weighted average of common shares outstanding during the period. SFAS No. 128 defines *diluted earnings per share* as the amount of earnings for the period available to each share of common stock, taking account of not only the shares in fact outstanding during the period, but also all shares that would have been outstanding if the enterprise had issued common shares for all *dilutive potential common shares* outstanding during the period. Dilutive potential common shares are rights like options, warrants and convertible securities, which entitle the holder to acquire common shares either during, or after the end of, the reporting period; the resulting increase in the number of shares would normally reduce the earnings per share, often considerably, even after taking account of any increase in earnings resulting from the exercise of the rights, as for example the reduction in interest expense when bonds are converted into stock. Computing the amount of the dilution in earnings per share can present quite a challenge, so we need not go into the actual mechanics here.

(2)   Price to Earnings Ratio

Once determined earnings per share has been det4ermined, an analyst will usually compute the *price to earnings ratio*. This ratio, which the business community often refers to simply as the *P/E* or the *P/E ratio*, compares the market price of the common shares to the earnings per share. Although a price to earnings ratio is not available for privately-held corporations because their shares do not have a publicly-quoted price, we can illustrate the computation using X Corp. as an example. Suppose its common shares were trading at $300 per share. Using the $60 earnings per share figure which we previously computed for X Corp., we can calculate a P/E ratio of 5 ($300 per share market price/$60 earnings per share). As with the other ratios discussed in this chapter, the investor, creditor or other user must compare the P/E ratio against industry and market standards to interpret the number.

(3)   Return on Sales

Another common profitability ratio, the ratio of net income to sales for an accounting period, usually stated in percentage terms, provides some index to the enterprise's efficiency. This ratio, which financial analysts usually refer to as *return on sales*, shows the percentage of each sales dollar that becomes net income. For the year ended December 31, X Corp.'s income statement shows a 6.0 percent return on sales ($6,000 net income/$100,000 sales). The higher the return on sales, the more profitably, and presumably the more efficiently, the business sells goods or provides services.

(4)   Gross Profit Percentage

Closely related to the return on sales, the *gross profit percentage* reflects the business's profitability from selling its products, ignoring operating expenses, such as general, selling and administrative expenses. You will recall from Chapter I that gross profit represents the difference between sales and cost of goods sold. This ratio compares the gross profit to sales, again commonly expressed in percentage terms. Using the income statement, we can compute a 30.0 percent gross profit percentage ($30,000 gross profit/$100,000 sales) for X Corp. for the year ended December 31. A higher gross profit percentage usually suggests that the business's products enjoy some advantage over the competition, whether technological, legal, or marketing.

(5)   Return on Assets

The return on assets ratio measures a business's profitability relative to its total assets, usually expressed in terms of average assets, however defined. Most simply, analysts define "average assets" as the average of beginning and ending assets for the period. If X Corp.'s average assets for the year equaled the $40,000 December 31 amount, the return on assets would be 15.0 percent ($6,000 net income/$40,000 average assets). The higher the return on assets, the better job management is doing in utilizing its resources in the business.

(6) Return on Equity

Another net income test in common use is the ratio of net income to owners' equity, that is, the amounts that owners have invested in the business, whether directly as a capital contribution or indirectly by leaving accumulated earnings in the business. This ratio, which the business community sometimes refers to as *return on equity* or *ROE*, gives a measure of how successfully the management is utilizing the assets of the stockholders under its stewardship. If we subtract X Corp.'s $6,000 net income from its $25,000 total shareholders' equity on December 31, we can assume that shareholders' equity at the beginning of the year equaled $19,000. As a result, we will use $22,000 [($19,000 beginning equity + $25,000 ending equity)/2] as average equity. Thus, we can compute a 27.3 percent ROE for the year ended December 31 ($6,000 net income/$22,000 average equity). Because analysts cannot compute a P/E ratio for privately held businesses, they often use return on equity to measure their profitability.

(7) Earnings Before Interest, Taxes, Depreciation and Amortization

In recent years, the non-GAAP measure known as *EBITDA*, or earnings before interest, taxes, depreciation and amortization, which as noted above is often used as a pro forma measure of operating results, has also become increasingly important as the numerator in coverage ratios. Because depreciation and amortization do not involve the current expenditure of cash, readers of financial statements have used this measure to compare the enterprise's current operating results to those of a prior period or to its competitors' numbers, or to quantify the extent to which an enterprise's "adjusted" income, before interest and taxes, can service the enterprise's debt obligations. Although enterprises do not always include separate amounts for depreciation and amortization on the income statement, readers can find amounts for these items in the operating section of the statement of cash flows. Interest expense usually is reported separately on the income statement, though sometimes it is combined with other costs, under a general caption like "interest and other expenses"; in addition, the amount of cash paid as interest during the period may be shown on the statement of cash flows. In any event, any legal agreement using EBITDA, as is true with any other particular pro forma metric, should define exactly how the parties will compute the figure.

c. ACTIVITY RATIOS

We should also mention three activity ratios which compare amounts from the balance sheet and the income statement and measure how effectively the business utilizes its resources. In many loan transactions, often referred to as *asset-based lending*, the borrower pledges accounts receivables or inventory to secure the loan. Lenders in such transactions frequently focus on an activity ratio, such as receivables or inventory turnover, in making credit decisions.

(1) Receivables Turnover

The ratio of credit sales to average accounts receivable, however defined, for a period provides some measure of the liquidity of the accounts receivable. Thus if X Corp.'s credit sales for the year amounted to $30,000 and its average accounts receivable during the year equaled the $3,000 balance on December 31, that constitutes a *receivables turnover* ratio of 10, which is often described by saying the accounts receivable turn over 10 times a year. In effect, this means that, on average, the company collected its accounts receivable in one-tenth of a year, or 36.5 days..

Along these same lines, analysts frequently compare the terms for payment which businesses in the industry typically offer to customers against a particular enterprise's days of receivables outstanding to evaluate the enterprise's efficiency in collecting receivables. As an example, if the industry generally gives customers thirty days to pay their bills, but receivables turnover indicates that on average this business collects its receivables every fifty days, those facts may suggest inefficiencies in the enterprise's collection process and could even indicate a problem with the receivables' collectibility. In addition, analysts often compare the payment terms which a business extends to its customers against the terms that the business is allowed by its vendors. A business can face liquidity difficulties if its suppliers require satisfaction of accounts payable over a shorter period than the time it takes the business to collect accounts receivables from its customers.

(2) Inventory Turnover

Financial analysts commonly perform similar analysis regarding the relationship between the cost of goods sold for the year and the average inventory figure during the year, which they often compute by simply averaging the opening and closing inventories. Because X's average inventory amounted to $15,000 [($14,000 opening inventory plus $16,000 closing inventory)/2], a financial analyst might say that the *inventory turnover* ratio equaled 4.67 times ($70,000 cost of goods sold/$15,000 average inventory). This means that, on average, the company completely sells an amount equal to its average inventory about every 78.2 days.

F.   THE STATEMENT OF CASH FLOWS

As we saw in Chapter I, one of the basic financial statements is a statement of cash flows which can provide important insights into a business. Through careful scrutiny of this statement, a reader can assess how well an enterprise manages its cash, and here too ratios can be a useful tool. However, before looking more closely at ratios based upon cash flow information, there are three other worthwhile steps to take with respect cash flows: *examining the patterns of relationship among the cash flow from operating, investing, and financing activities; comparing the amount of cash flows from operations to the net income figure; and preparing monthly cash flow statements.*

1. PATTERNS

Because the statement of cash flows includes three separate sections, eight possible patterns of cash flows from the various sections exist. Chart 4–1 displays these possibilities.

Chart 4–1. Cash Flow Patterns								
Pattern	1	2	3	4	5	6	7	8
1. Operating Cash Flows	+	+	+	+	–	–	–	–
2. Investing Cash Flows	+	–	+	–	+	–	+	–
3. Financing Cash Flows	+	–	–	+	+	+	–	–

The first four patterns contain situations where an enterprise generated positive net cash flows from its operations, which usually denotes a healthy enterprise that can use this cash to expand operations, satisfy long-term obligations, or provide a return on investment to its owners. In fact, if the enterprise is not investing in new equipment, a reader must wonder when the existing equipment will simply wear out or become obsolete.

The second four patterns describe situations in which the enterprise generated negative net cash flow from operations, which indicates that the enterprise's cash inflows from operations do not cover operating expenses. At some point, these cash flow deficits from operations will force the venture to sell assets, borrow from creditors, or raise additional funds from the owners to continue its operations. If this pattern continues over an extended period, the business will almost assuredly go bankrupt, like the W.T. Grant Company, as described on page 104, *supra.*

In pattern one, the enterprise generated cash from all three activities. In other words, the business generated a positive cash flow from operations, sold off capital assets, and raised additional capital. Although very unusual, such an enterprise obviously wants to increase its cash on hand. An enterprise usually uses positive cash from operations to expand by buying capital assets, to satisfy creditors by paying off debt, or to distribute profits to its owners.

Pattern two, arguably the pattern that all enterprises hope to fall under, shows that the business generated cash flow from internal operations and used the cash for investing activities, such as the purchase of property, plant, or equipment, and also spent the cash on its financing activities, like paying its debts or distributing earnings to owners. Mature businesses usually fall into this scenario.

In pattern three, the enterprise generated positive cash flow from operations and investing activities, most likely from selling capital assets. The business used this cash for financing activities, such as paying its creditors, investors, or both. This pattern may suggest that the enterprise has decided to downsize or restructure by selling assets to repay its debt or to buy out owners. The cash from operations did not cover the financing needs, so the sale of long-term assets raised additional cash to cover the difference.

Pattern four, typical of a growing business, demonstrates an enterprise that generated cash from operating and financing activities to buy long-term assets, which may include investments in non-operating assets, like securities.

In pattern five, the enterprise generated a negative cash flow from its operations. To cover this deficit and stay in business, the enterprise generated positive cash flow from its investing activities, such as selling capital assets, and its financing activities, like seeking additional investments from owners or taking loans. An enterprise may endure this situation for awhile, but unless there is a turnaround eventually the venture will face bankruptcy, as occurred with the W.T. Grant Company.

In pattern six, the enterprise generated cash from its financing activities by raising capital from creditors, owners or both to cover its operating cash flow deficit and provide resources to purchase additional capital assets. Young, fast-growing businesses typically fall into this category. The negative cash flow from operations may have resulted from large increases in inventory to prepare for expanded operations and sales. Investors may invest cash in such ventures, anticipating a return in the future. An enterprise may also fall under this pattern while expecting increased future sales.

In pattern seven, the enterprise probably sold off capital assets to support its operations and to pay off its creditors, or distribute cash to investors, or both. An enterprise in the process of liquidation or down-sizing would fall under this pattern.

Finally, in pattern eight, an extremely unusual situation, the enterprise generated a negative cash flow in all of its activities. An enterprise could only survive these unusual circumstances for a short time, i.e., until any cash it initially had on hand runs out.

When an unusual pattern, such as pattern one, three, five, seven, or eight appears, an attorney should understand why the enterprise is in that situation; and of course, the comparative size of the cash inflows and outflows may be what matters most.

2. CASH FLOW FROM OPERATIONS COMPARED TO NET INCOME

While analyzing the patterns among the various activities, financial analysts also compare the cash flow from operations with the net income figure. Four possible combinations exist as shown in Chart 4–2.

Chart 4–2. Cash Flow from Operations Compared to Net Income:				
Pattern	1	2	3	4
Cash Flows from Operating Activities	+	+	−	−
Net Income	+	−	+	−

Net cash flow from operations generally correlates to net income, but significant differences between the two may exist. We have already noted that a gain or loss upon the sale of a capital asset for cash will be reflected in net income but not in cash flow from operations. For another example, a capital intensive business, such as steel manufacturing, could be operating at only a slight profit, or even showing a loss, but nevertheless generating significant cash flows from its operations, if its depreciation expense is large. This normal situation is no cause for concern; on the other hand, non-normal situations, such as net loss on the income statement coupled with negative cash flow from operations continuing for several periods, should be carefully watched.

Of course, one of the principal reasons for a divergence between net income and operating cash flows is timing differences: recognition of revenue and expense under accrual accounting may not involve an inflow or outflow of cash. For example, as noted earlier, depreciation expense will affect net income in the period, but not the cash flow; conversely, an item may affect cash in the period but not net income, such as prepayment of rent. Special note should be taken of an important new entrant on this scene: the new requirement that grants of stock options should be recognized as a current expense adds another item to the list of charges against income that are not accompanied by a current outflow of cash.

There are no particular general patterns of recurring combinations or the like in this area, so the user of the financial statements must investigate all the timing differences to see if they explain any disparity that may exist between net income and operating cash flow.

3. MONTHLY CASH FLOW STATEMENTS

To supplement annual statements of cash flows, management typically uses budgeted monthly, and sometimes weekly or daily, cash flow statements to determine the amount of cash surplus or deficit that an enterprise will generate over a short period of time. Through the use of a budgeted monthly cash flow statement, management can readily determine if an enterprise will have excess cash or a cash shortfall in the near future. Armed with this knowledge, management may decide to make accelerated payments on its outstanding debt with any excess cash, or obtain short-term financing to cover any cash shortfalls.

4. RATIO ANALYSIS

Historically, the ratios used by readers of financial statements usually related to balance sheet and income statement accounts. However, the increased attention to cash flows in today's business atmosphere has led to greater interest in ratios based on cash flow information. For example, a recent study demonstrates the importance of cash flow information in the loan assessment process. When ranking fifty-nine different ratios in order of importance to the processing of a loan, cash flow to current maturities of long-term debt ranked third behind the debt to equity ratio and the current ratio. In addition, the cash flow to total debt ratio ranked ninth. The study also concluded that over sixty percent of all loan agreements included clauses involving the rate of cash flow to current maturities of long-term debt. As the importance of the statement of cash flows increases, attorneys can expect to see and use these ratios much more frequently. Cash flow ratios typically fall into three categories: liquidity and coverage; profitability; and quality of income.

a. LIQUIDITY AND COVERAGE

You will recall that liquidity and coverage ratios help assess an enterprise's ability to meet its debt obligations in the short and long run, to pay dividends, and to cover anticipated operating expenses, such as payroll. Cash flow ratios in these categories typically provide information on the business's ability to meet its scheduled cash payments.

b. PROFITABILITY

As we have already seen, profitability ratios convey information about the ability of an enterprise to provide its investors with a return on their investment. *Cash return on investment* provides information on the cash-generating ability of an enterprise's assets, while *Cash flow per common share* furnishes the information about how much cash the enterprise generated per share of common stock outstanding. However, accounting pronouncements forbid disclosure of the latter ratio in the financial statements, to avoid confusion with earnings per share, which is based upon accrual accounting. Because these cash return ratios contain no provision for the replacement of assets or existing contractual commitments, the cash returns will usually exceed their counterparts based on net income, especially for industrial enterprises.

c.   QUALITY OF INCOME

Finally, cash flow ratios can fall into a new category called *quality of income*, or the ability of an enterprise to actually generate cash from the amount it reports as income from operations. These ratios allow the reader to assess how readily the enterprise converts net income to cash. For example, under accrual accounting, an enterprise may "book" revenues as an account receivable before the business actually receives cash from sales. The venture may also record expenses as accrued liabilities before it actually spends cash by paying the bill. An enterprise that takes a long time to receive cash from its sales and promptly pays its expenses would generate a low *cash quality of income ratio* because the net income significantly exceeds cash flow from operations. Although more difficult to calculate because of potentially unavailable information, *cash quality of income before interest, taxes and depreciation*, more accurately reflects the effect of accrual accounting on net income as mentioned above. By removing the effects of interest, taxes and depreciation on net income, this latter ratio further highlights the timing differences arising from accrual accounting.

G.   MANAGEMENT'S DISCUSSION AND ANALYSIS

As one of the essential parts of an annual report which we discussed earlier in the chapter, the proxy rules applicable to publicly-held companies require the inclusion of a discussion and an analysis of the enterprise's financial condition and results of operations. This requirement, as well as other rules which compel such companies to file periodic reports with the SEC, help furnish information about the enterprise to the investing public. The SEC has adopted Regulation S–K to provide standard instructions for registrants filing forms under the federal securities laws. Regulation S–B contains similar disclosure requirements for small business issuers, i.e., having revenues and public floats below $25 million.

Item 303 of Regulation S–K requires registrants to discuss their financial condition, including liquidity and capital resources, changes in financial condition and results of operations in both the annual report sent to shareholders and the periodic reports filed with the SEC. Item 303 of Regulation S–B imposes similar obligations on small business issuers. The financial community refers to these requirements as *Management's Discussion and Analysis*, sometimes abbreviated to *MD&A*. In particular, the MD&A rules require registrants and small business issuers to disclose narratively various events and contingencies affecting their businesses. By requiring registrants to provide both historical and prospective analysis of the financial statements, with an emphasis on the future of the business, the MD&A section strives to give investors an opportunity to view the business "through the eyes of management."

Shortly after Enron filed its bankruptcy petition in December 2001, the SEC issued a statement that encouraged public companies to explain in plain English in their MD&A their "critical accounting policies;" the assumptions, estimates, and other judgments or uncertainties affecting the application of those policies; and the likelihood that the company would report different amounts under different conditions or using different objectives. Cautionary Advice Regarding Disclosure About Critical Accounting Policies, Financial Reporting Release No. 60, 66 Fed. Reg. 65,013 (Dec. 17, 2001).

Less than six months later, the SEC issued proposed rules that would require issuers and registrants to include a separately captioned section regarding the application of critical accounting policies in the MD&A section of various securities filings. The rules would require disclosures about both the critical accounting estimates used to apply the company's accounting policies and the initial adoption of certain accounting policies. Disclosure in Management's Discussion and Analysis about the Application of Critical Accounting Policies, 67 Fed. Reg. 35,620 (proposed May 20, 2002). Although other rule-making projects that Sarbanes-Oxley directed the SEC to complete in very short time periods have prevented the commission from issuing final rules, various officials at the SEC have indicated that the Commission plans to do so.

Of particular relevance to MD&A, SOx section 401(a) directed the SEC to issue final rules to require each annual and quarterly report that registrants must file with the Commission to disclose "all material off-balance sheet transactions, arrangements, obligations (including contingent obligations), and other relationships of the issuer with unconsolidated entities or other persons, that may have a material current or future effect on financial condition, changes in financial condition, results of operations, liquidity, capital expenditures, capital resources, or significant components of revenues or expenses." Pursuant to that charge, the SEC issued final regulations in early 2003 that require registrants to explain their off-balance sheet arrangements in a separately captioned subsection of the MD&A portion of various disclosure documents. The rules also require a registrant other than a small business issuer to disclose in tabular format somewhere in the MD&A section the amounts of payments due under certain known contractual obligations, as of the latest fiscal year-end balance sheet date.

In early 2003, the SEC's Division of Corporation Finance issued a report summarizing the significant issues that its staff raised with companies in the Fortune 500 while reviewing the annual reports that those companies filed during 2002. The report listed inadequate discussions in MD&A as the staff's top concern. The staff emphasized that its review efforts would continue to focus on this section in disclosure documents and encouraged all companies to present useful and meaningful disclosures about financial condition, operating results, and liquidity.

The SEC's most recent guidance regarding MD&A sought to elicit more meaningful disclosure with regard to such key indicators of financial condition and operating performance as (i) liquidity and capital resources, (ii) material events and uncertainties that would cause reported financial information to fail to predict future operating performance or financial condition, and (iii) critical accounting estimates. In sum, the SEC wants the MD&A "to provide information about the quality and potential variability of a company's earnings and cash flow, so that readers can ascertain the likelihood that past performance is indicative of future performance." Commission Guidance Regarding Management's Discussion and Analysis of Financial Condition and Results of Operations, Financial Reporting Release No. 72, 68 Fed. Reg. 75,056 (Dec. 29, 2003).

1.   THE PURPOSE OF REQUIRED DISCLOSURE IN MD&A

After reviewing the MD&A filings of more than 200 registrants in 1988, the SEC found that nearly all of the MD&A sections did not comply with the regulations. Consequently, the SEC published Financial Reporting Release No. 36, 54 Fed. Reg. 22, 427 (1989), to clarify its position on required MD&A disclosures. The following excerpts represent the SEC's best statement of the goals and purposes of MD&A:

III.   Evaluation of Disclosure—Interpretive Guidance

A.   Introduction

The MD&A requirements are intended to provide, in one section of a filing, material historical and prospective textual disclosure enabling investors and other users to assess the financial condition and results of operations of the registrant, with particular emphasis on the registrant's prospects for the future. * * *

The Commission has long recognized the need for a narrative explanation of the financial statements, because a numerical presentation and brief accompanying footnotes alone may be insufficient for an investor to judge the quality of earnings and the likelihood that past performance is indicative of future performance. MD&A is intended to give the investor an opportunity to look at the company through the eyes of management by providing both a short and long-term analysis of the business of the company. * * *

B. Prospective Information

Several specific provisions in Item 303 require disclosure of forward-looking information. MD&A requires discussions of "known trends or any known demands, commitments, events or uncertainties that will result in or that are reasonably likely to result in the registrants' liquidity increasing or decreasing in any material way." * * * Disclosure of known trends or uncertainties that the registrant reasonably expects will have a material impact on net sales, revenues, or income from continuing operations is also required. Finally, the Instructions to Item 303 state that MD&A "shall focus specifically on material events and uncertainties known to management that would cause reported financial information not to be necessarily indicative of future operating results or future financial condition."

* * * [T]he distinction between prospective information that is required to be discussed and voluntary forward-looking disclosure is an area requiring additional attention. * * *

* * * The distinction between the two rests with the nature of the prediction required. Required disclosure is based on *currently known trends, events, and uncertainties that are reasonably expected to have material effects*, such as: a reduction in the registrant's product prices; erosion in the registrant's market share; changes in insurance coverage; or the likely non-renewal of a material contract. In contrast, optional forward-looking disclosure involves *anticipating a future trend or event or anticipating a less predictable impact of a known event, trend or uncertainty.*

* * *

IV. Conclusion

In preparing MD&A disclosure, registrants should be guided by the general purpose of the MD&A requirements: to give investors an opportunity to look at the registrant through the eyes of management by providing a historical and prospective analysis of the registrant's financial condition and results of operations, with particular emphasis on the registrant's prospects for the future. The MD&A requirements are intentionally flexible and general. Because no two registrants are identical, good MD&A disclosure for one registrant is not necessarily good MD&A disclosure for another. The same is true for MD&A disclosure of the same registrant in different years. * * *

NOTES

1. The SEC has promulgated rules which establish a safe harbor for disclosure of "forward-looking information." 17 C.F.R. §§ 230.175(c) and 240.3b–6 (1999). The rules define such "information" to include statements regarding "future economic performance contained in" MD&A. In FRR No. 36, the SEC observed that these safe harbors apply to both required statements concerning the future effect of known trends, demands, commitments, events or uncertainties and optional forward-looking statements.

2. In the Private Securities Litigation Reform Act of 1995, Congress added safe harbor provisions for forward-looking statements to both the Securities Act of 1933 and the Securities Exchange Act of 1934. Both safe harbors specifically apply to qualifying statements in MD&A unless the plaintiff can prove that the person making or the executive officer approving the statement had "actual knowledge * * * that the statement was false or misleading."

2. COMPLIANCE WITH GAAP ALONE DOES NOT SATISFY MD&A REQUIREMENTS

In recent years, the MD&A section has become a focal point for the SEC's enforcement activities. Linda Quinn, former director of the SEC's Division of Corporate Finance, called MD&A one of the "linchpin[s] of the disclosure system." She also emphasized that the SEC intends to continue to "press heavily" for companies to disclose information not reflected in their historic financial statements that likely will affect their future. In 1992 the SEC had announced the settlement of its first enforcement action against a registrant for alleged shortcomings in its MD&A, although its financial statements complied with generally accepted accounting principles. In re Caterpillar Inc., 1992 WL 71907 (S.E.C.). Caterpillar's Brazilian subsidiary, CBSA, had an unusually good year in 1989, accounting for some 23 percent of Caterpillar's net profits, though CBSA's revenues represented only 5 percent of Caterpillar's total. CBSA's success was due largely to non-operating items, many of which resulted from the hyper-inflation in Brazil and the related currency exchange rate. CBSA's financial results were presented on a consolidated basis with the remainder of Caterpillar's operations, as was entirely permissible under GAAP, but that meant that the impact of CBSA's contribution to Caterpillar's overall results was not apparent from the face of the financial statements (or from any notes thereto). However, early in 1990, political and economic developments in Brazil gave clear indications that CBSA was not only unlikely to repeat its exceptional performance of 1989 but was likely to suffer a loss, which could have a material adverse effect on Caterpillar's bottom line in 1990.

The SEC pointed out that under Item 303(a) of Regulation S-K Caterpillar was required to describe "any unusual or infrequent events or transactions . . . that materially affected the amount of reported income", and also to discuss " any known trends or uncertainties that . . . the registrant reasonably expects will have a materially favorable or unfavorable impact on net sales or revenues or income". Hence, Caterpillar should have included in its MD&A a discussion and analysis of the impact of CBSA on its 1989 results of operations, and should also have disclosed in filings with the SEC the known uncertainty as to CBSA's ability to repeat its 1989 performance.

The SEC has continued to bring enforcement actions against registrants for inadequate disclosures about their financial statements even though those financial statements complied with GAAP. These actions document the SEC's positions that (a) the disclosures must occur in the MD&A section, rather than in press releases, (b) MD&A must discuss material unusual or nonrecurring items and their effect on the "quality of [both current and expected future] earnings;" and (c) MD&A must discuss "known trends" or practices likely to affect future financial statements in a material way.

In another case involving a registrant which did not violate GAAP, Sony Corporation ("Sony") settled administrative charges arising from the company's failure to disclose losses in its Sony Pictures Entertainment Inc. subsidiary ("SPE") in the MD&A sections of its annual reports for the fiscal year ended March 31, 1994. This inadequate disclosure occurred during the several months before Sony wrote down about $2.7 billion in goodwill related to the acquisition of SPE. Despite the expressed preference of its outside auditors and own financial officers, Sony did not report SPE's results as a separate industry segment. Instead, the company reported the combined results of SPE and Sony's profitable music business as a single "entertainment" segment. This treatment obscured the approximately $967 million in net losses that SPE had incurred after the acquisition and before the close of the fiscal year ended March 31, 1994, which the SEC described as a "known trend." In addition, Sony's filings failed to disclose that the company had been considering for more than a year the possible need to write down a substantial part of the goodwill attributable to SPE.

As part of the settlement, Sony agreed among other things to engage an independent auditor to examine its MD&A presentation for the fiscal year ending March 31, 1999. In March, 1998 the AICPA issued standards setting forth the procedures that an auditor should undertake when examining a registrant's MD&A in such an engagement. 1998 WL 439898 (S.E.C.).

In 2002, the SEC initiated cease-and-desist proceedings against Edison Schools, Inc. ("Edison")because the company failed to disclose that a substantial portion of its reported revenue included payments that never reached Edison. Under a number of Edison's contracts with local school districts to manage their schools, substantial payments were made by the districts directly to teachers, who remained school district employees, or other vendors to the schools, but Edison treated those payments as though they had been received by Edison as revenues and then paid out as expenses. Although Edison's revenue recognition did not violate GAAP, the failure to fully disclose this practice distorted the realities of Edison's operations and financial results, and Edison consented to a cease-and-desist order. *In re* Edison Schools, Inc., Accounting and Auditing Enforcement Release No. 1555,[2001-2003 Accounting and Auditing Enforcement Releases Transfer Binder] Fed. Sec. L. Rep. (CCH) ¶ 75,070, 2002 WL 1315557 (S.E.C.). The new rules under Sarbanes-Oxley will almost certainly accelerate this trend.

More recently, in 2005 the SEC brought and settled cease-and-desist proceedings against The Coca-Cola Company on the grounds that the company failed to disclose certain end-of-quarter sales practices used to meet earnings expectations and that would likely affect the company's future operating results. Through a process known as "gallon pushing," between 1997 and 1999 Coca-Cola offered Japanese bottlers favorable credit terms to induce them to purchase beverage concentrate that they otherwise would not have purchased until a later fiscal period. Without admitting or denying the SEC's findings, Coca-Cola consented to an administrative order finding that the company had violated antifraud and periodic reporting requirements in the federal securities laws. The company also voluntarily implemented measures to strengthen its internal disclosure review process. *In re* Coca-Cola Co., Accounting and Auditing Enforcement Release No. 2232, 7 Fed. Sec. L. Rep. (CCH) ¶ 75,894 (Apr. 18, 2005).

3. ENFORCEMENT ISSUES ARISING FROM LIQUIDITY PROBLEMS

The SEC has brought other enforcement actions involving failures to disclose known liquidity problems. One such case is In re America West Airlines, Inc., 1994 WL 183412 (S.E.C.), where the Commission criticized the registrant to failing to disclose in the MD&A section serious financial difficulties that made continuing operations unlikely:

Specifically, America West's MD&A disclosure in its Report on Form 10–K for the year ended December 31, 1990, failed to discuss fully uncertainties related to its ability to meet its financial covenants. Instead, the MD&A discussion stated the following:

> "At December 31, 1990, the Company was not in compliance with certain of the covenants. Waivers were secured for such violations and during the first quarter of 1991, amended covenants were established. The Company anticipates to be in compliance with such amended covenants. * * *"

Such disclosure did not adequately address the known uncertainties relating to America West's liquidity position at that time. The Company had failed to comply with the leverage covenant provision in November 1990. Subsequently, management faced uncertainties about the Company's ability to comply with its covenants. These uncertainties are illustrated by management's request to the Board in January 1991 for authority to amend the Company's financial covenants as needed to avoid violating such covenants. In fact, on January 31, 1991, two days after management received authority from the Board to amend its financial covenants on an ongoing basis, the Company did fail to comply with its January $100 million cash covenant provision. Furthermore, the Company's failure to comply with its covenant provisions in November and January gave rise to events of default. Consequently, in both instances the lenders had the option of rendering the debt immediately due and payable.

Furthermore, the MD&A disclosure failed to discuss as required the known material uncertainties relating to the Company's ability to obtain the financing necessary to remedy its liquidity problems. Indeed, rather than addressing America West's liquidity position directly, the MD&A disclosure stated the following about the Company's efforts to obtain financing:

> "In spite of the net loss incurred in 1990 and the anticipated net loss for the first quarter of 1991, the Company believes that its present capital commitments can be met as they become due with existing capital resources, its ability to obtain additional financing and its anticipation of improved operating results beyond the first quarter 1991."

While the MD&A did state that the Company's ability to meet its capital commitments was, in part, dependent upon its ability to obtain additional financing, it did not disclose that the Company was primarily dependent on external financing to remedy its liquidity problems. Further, the MD&A did not discuss as required the known uncertainties related to its ability to obtain such financing.

More recently, the SEC brought separate public administrative proceedings against Terex Corporation ("Terex"), its former chairman, and others, for inadequately disclosing an accounting adjustment and its effect on the current liabilities of Terex and Fruehauf Trailer Corporation ("Fruehauf"). The accounting adjustment caused Fruehauf to fail to meet specified financial ratios in long-term loans totaling $82.7 million from various financial institutions, and to violate certain loan covenants which gave the lenders the right to accelerate the loans. In such circumstances, SFAS No. 78, *Classification of Obligations that are Callable by the Creditor* (date), requires that the borrower reclassify the underlying long-term obligation as a current liability. Because Fruehauf continued to classify the $82.7 million as long-term liabilities, both Fruehauf and its ultimate parent, Terex, understated their current liabilities. In re Terex Corp., 1999 WL 228426.

As recently as May 2006, SEC officials publicly stated that MD&A disclosure failures remain a top enforcement priority. In 2005, the SEC filed charges against Kmart's former CEO and former CFO for material misrepresentations and omissions about the company's liquidity in the MD&A section of Kmart's Form 10-Q for the third quarter and nine months ended October 31, 2001. Among other allegations, the SEC asserts that the two officers failed to disclose the reasons for a massive inventory overbuy in the summer of 2001 and the impact it had on the company's liquidity. Kmart filed for bankruptcy in early 2002. SEC v. Conaway, Accounting and Auditing Enforcement Release No. 2295 (Aug. 23, 2005); *see also* Bologna, *Firms Getting Disclosure Message, But MD&A Still Enforcement Priority*, 38 Sec. Reg. & L. Rep. (BNA) 867 (May 15, 2006).

H. The Future of Financial and Non-Financial Reporting

Investment analysts and other users of financial statements often criticize the current financial accounting model, which generally uses historical cost to present quantitative information and ignores many intangibles that have dramatically influenced the "new economy". As mentioned in Chapter I, FASB has already begun to take steps toward a fair-value-based system which could eventually require enterprises to report all financial assets and liabilities at fair value. In addition, FASB's current project on financial reporting by business enterprises could lead to a framework for a new business reporting model and replace the current income statement with a revised statement of comprehensive income.

More fundamentally, however, critics of the current model increasingly have called upon enterprises to reveal indicators that management tracks on a regular basis to assess the business's performance. For example, an enterprise might disclose key trends in operating or performance data and management's analysis of changes in such data; forward-looking information about such things as opportunities, risks and management's plans; or information about order backlogs, market share, product innovation, revenue per transaction, revenue per employee, customer acquisition costs, customer satisfaction, costs per unit, management quality, and intangible assets, especially those not currently included in financial statements. Ultimately, securities regulators or accounting rule-makers may develop a framework regarding the types of supplemental and non-financial information that enterprises should provide to investors. In the meantime, however, leadership in this area will likely come from individual companies and industries that provide voluntary disclosures. Public companies increasingly disclose such information in MD&A. *See generally* Richard I. Miller & Michael R. Young, *Financial Reporting and Risk Management in the 21st Century*, 65 FORDHAM L. REV. 1987 (1997) (discussing (1) the potential liability arising from improvements in financial reporting systems, which would presumably move away from objectively verifiable data and towards more subjective information, thereby increasing the opportunity for second-guessing and hence the enterprise's exposure to litigation, and (2) how individuals and organizations responsible for structuring financial reporting relationships can manage that liability both to facilitate honest financial reporting and to give financial reporting systems the flexibility to evolve).

Without setting a deadline, SOx section 409 directs the SEC to move towards "real-time" disclosure. That section authorizes the Commission to issue any rules requiring rapid and current disclosures regarding material changes in financial condition or operations deemed "necessary or useful for the protection of investors and in the public interest." Sarbanes-Oxley Act of 2002, Pub. L. No. 107-204, § 409, 116 Stat. 745, 791.

*

CHAPTER V

LEGAL ISSUES INVOLVING SHAREHOLDERS' EQUITY AND THE BALANCE SHEET

A. IMPORTANCE TO LAWYERS

As indicated in Chapter I, shareholders own the residual claim to a corporation's assets, which is usually termed *shareholders' equity*: the equity is shown on the corporation's balance sheet as the difference between the company's assets and liabilities, both generally recorded at historical cost. Shareholders' equity increases when the enterprise succeeds, and shrinks, or may disappear entirely, when the business struggles.

In our initial discussion of the corporate balance sheet, we saw that accountants generally divide shareholders' equity into three components: capital stock accounts, either common or preferred stock (although the term stated capital is sometimes used); additional paid-in capital; and retained earnings. Under the legal capital system, with which lawyers were traditionally most often involved, the more likely titles for these categories have been, stated capital(or perhaps legal capital), capital surplus and earned surplus, respectively. We can compare the different titles which accountants and the legal capital system assign to the various components of shareholders' equity as follows:

SHAREHOLDERS' EQUITY CATEGORIES	
ACCOUNTING NOMENCLATURE	LEGAL TERMINOLOGY
Capital Stock: Common Stock or Preferred Stock	Stated Capital or Legal Capital
Additional Paid-in Capital	Capital Surplus
Retained Earnings	Earned Surplus

As we saw in Chapter I, under the legal capital system the corporate statutes (1) require corporations to issue shares for consideration which equals or exceeds the shares' par value, and (2) restrict a company's ability to distribute assets to shareholders, using a test based upon legal or stated capital. The latter seeks to protect creditors, plus those shareholders with dividend or liquidation preferences (and even the residual shareholders, to some extent) by prohibiting distributions to shareholders which would reduce a corporation's net assets to an amount less than the legal capital safety margin. An unlawful distribution may give rise to claims against the corporation, its directors, and the shareholder recipients. However, as it turned out there were steps corporations could lawfully take to circumvent the protections that the legal capital system purportedly offered, so most modern corporate statutes have eliminated the concepts of stated capital and par value, and instead base their limitations on distributions to shareholders on the solvency of the corporation, as will be described in more detail shortly. Nevertheless, despite its shortcomings the legal capi3tal system continues to survive in about one-fourth of the states, including the commercially important jurisdictions of Delaware and New York.

In all states, whatever the test for unlawful distributions, resolving the issues raised will often involve important accounting issues. However, lawyers should remember that whether a corporation could lawfully declare and pay a dividend or repurchase shares depends upon the test imposed by the corporation statute, which may or may not be construed in accordance with GAAP. That should not be too surprising, since the legislative dividend policies embodied in the statute may be different from the meaningful disclosure objectives which underlie GAAP.

B. DISTRIBUTIONS AND LEGAL RESTRICTIONS

As savvy creditors and their lawyers came to recognize that the legal capital system did not effectively safeguard creditors' rights, those with sufficient bargaining power were no longer willing to rely on the easily avoidable statutory restrictions; instead, they began using contractual provisions, often referred to as *restrictive covenants*, to protect their interests. We have already had some discussion of covenants in Chapter IV, such as a provision requiring a corporation to conform to certain financial ratios, or one defining the term "default" in a loan agreement to include failure to comply with specified restrictive covenants. And of course one of the most common types of covenant is a prohibition against certain distributions that would deplete the corporation's net worth and ability to pay its debts, but might not be prevented by the legal capital system.

Like the dividend statutes, these covenants often present accounting issues, and here too GAAP may not be controlling. Obviously, lawyers have an important role to play in negotiating and drafting restrictive covenants, and they must appreciate the impact of accounting principles.

1. STATUTORY RESTRICTIONS

About thirteen states continue to follow the legal capital system and use the traditional par value rules, limiting distributions to *surplus* under various definitions. Recall that the legal capital system traditionally divides surplus into two components: capital surplus and earned surplus. These surplus tests basically limit the amount that a corporation can distribute to shareholders to the excess of the total shareholders' equity over the stated capital. (Sometimes, however, these surplus statutes also limit distributions from capital surplus under particular circumstances.)

Another statutory formulation which amounts to the same thing prohibits corporations from making a distribution to shareholders if it will impair stated capital. This approach, too, forbids distributions which leave the amount of a corporation's net assets at less than its stated capital. In other words, a corporation can declare and pay a dividend or redeem shares only in an amount no greater than the corporation's surplus, which illustrates stated capital's role as a "cushion" for the benefit of the corporation's creditors (and shareholders with a liquidation preference).

To illustrate how such surplus statutes operate, suppose that the balance sheet for Maledon, Inc. reflects the following:

Assets		Liabilities & Shareholders' Equity	
Cash	$13,000	Current Liabilities	$2,000
		Long-Term Debt	5,000
		Total Liabilities	$7,000
		Shareholders' Equity:	
Equipment	2,000	Stated Capital (2,000 Shares, $2 par)	4,000
		Capital Surplus	5,000
Other Assets	4,000	Earned Surplus	3,000
Total Assets	$19,000	Total	$19,000

Recall that accountants would be more likely to use such titles as Additional Paid-in Capital and Retained Earnings in place of Capital Surplus and Earned Surplus, respectively, and might well use Common Stock instead of Stated Capital. Unless Maledon's articles of incorporation provide otherwise, the company can lawfully declare a dividend which does not exceed $8,000.

2. INSOLVENCY TESTS

Most modern corporate statutes apply one or more *insolvency* tests to determine whether a corporation can lawfully distribute assets to shareholders (whether or not some other test, such as one based upon stated capital, also applies). These economic tests forbid distributions unless (1) the corporation can continue to pay its obligations as they come due (the equity insolvency test), or (2) the corporation's assets after the distribution are at least equal to its liabilities (the balance sheet insolvency test), or, most commonly (3) the corporation can satisfy both tests.

The equitable insolvency test prohibits distributions if the corporation is, or would thereby become, unable "to pay its debts as they become due in the usual course of business." Usually, if a corporation is carrying on its operations in normal fashion, that fact itself probably indicates that no issue arises under this requirement. Alternatively, if an auditor has examined the financial statements, and there is no qualification in the auditor's report about the corporation's ability to continue as a going concern, and there have been no subsequent adverse events, there would normally be no question of equity insolvency. However, if a corporation has encountered liquidity or operational difficulties, the directors may want "to consider a cash flow analysis, based on a business forecast and budget, covering a sufficient period of time to permit a conclusion that known obligations of the corporation can reasonably be expected to be satisfied over the period of time that they will mature." Model Bus. Corp. Act Ann.§6.40, Comment 2(3rd ed. 1996).

As to the balance sheet insolvency test, notice that the corporation may reduce its assets down to its liabilities, which eliminates the "cushion" for creditors that stated capital once represented. However, these statutes often provide that if the corporation has outstanding any shares with a liquidation preference, then the assets remaining after a distribution must least equal the sum of the liabilities plus the total liquidation preference, thereby coincidentally preserving some cushion for the creditors.

3. RELATIONSHIP OF GAAP TO STATUTORY RESTRICTIONS

Whenever a dividend statute uses the balance sheet to judge an enterprise's financial position, a question arises as to whether one may or should revalue the assets. For example, under corporate statutes prohibiting distributions "which impair capital", or permitting them only "out of surplus", or "out of net assets in excess of capital", all of which tests call for a balance sheet computation, should the assets be measured at present value, or rather at the balance sheet figure based on cost, often referred to as the "book value" of the assets, in determining the amount by which net assets exceed stated capital?

Up until now, we have ignored the interpretive questions of what the dividend statutes mean when they use accounting terms such as "assets" and "liabilities." Thus, in our earlier examples concerning Maledon, Inc., we simply accepted the book value figures listed on the balance sheet for the company's assets and liabilities in applying the dividend statute. Assuming that the company prepared its balance sheet in accordance with GAAP, those figures on the balance sheet would be based upon historical cost. In determining the amount available for distribution to its shareholders, however, it is a matter of statutory construction, as informed by dividend law policy, as to whether a company may write up its assets to reflect their current fair values. To illustrate, look again at the balance sheet of Maledon, Inc., on page 293, *supra*. Suppose that the value of Maledon's equipment has appreciated to, say, $5,000. If the dividend statute is construed to be consistent with GAAP, that means the accounting bar against recognition of unrealized appreciation in most circumstances would apply, so the unrealized appreciation would not be taken into account for dividend purposes either, and Maledon would be limited to a distribution of $8,000. But the statute might be interpreted not to follow GAAP and instead to allow Maledon's board of directors to increase its surplus for dividend purposes by $3,000, by writing up its equipment account to reflect the equipment's current fair market value. As illustrated by the following case, perhaps the best-known dividend decision ever, dividend statutes often fail to make clear which outcome is intended, leaving the issue for the courts to resolve.

Randall v. Bailey

Supreme Court of New York, Trial Term, New York County, 1940.
23 N.Y.S.2d 173, affirmed 288 N.Y. 280, 43 N.E.2d 43 (1942).

■ WALTER, JUSTICE.

A Lender of Bush Terminal Company, appointed in a proceeding under Section 77B of the Bankruptcy Act, 11 U.S.C.A. § 207, here sues former directors of that company to recover on its behalf the amount of dividends declared and paid between November 22, 1928, and May 2, 1932, aggregating $3,639,058.06. At the times of the declarations and payments, the company's books concededly showed a surplus which ranged from not less than $4,378,554.83 on December 31, 1927, down to not less than $2,199,486.77 on April 30, 1932. The plaintiff claims, however, that in fact there was no surplus, that the capital was actually impaired to an amount greater than the amount of the dividends, and that the directors consequently are personally liable to the corporation for the amount thereof under Section 58 of the Stock Corporation Law. Defendants claim that there was no impairment of capital and that the surplus was actually greater than the amount which plaintiff concedes as the amount shown by the books.

The claims of the plaintiff, although branching out to a multitude of items, are basically reducible to [two]:

1. It was improper to "write-up" the land values above cost and thereby take unrealized appreciation into account.

2. It was improper not to "write-down" to actual value the cost of investments in and advances to subsidiaries and thereby fail to take unrealized depreciation into account.

* * *

I next turn to the subject of unrealized appreciation and depreciation.

Until 1915 the company's land was carried upon its books at cost. In 1915 the land was written up to 80% of the amount at which it was then assessed for taxation, and in 1918 it was written up to the exact amount at which it was then so assessed. Those two writeups totaled $7,211,791.72, and the result was that during the period here in question the land was carried on the books at $8,737,949.02, whereas its actual cost was $1,526,157.30. Plaintiff claims that the entire $7,211,791.72 should be eliminated because it represents merely unrealized appreciation, and dividends cannot be declared or paid on the basis of mere unrealized appreciation in fixed assets irrespective of how sound the estimate thereof may be. That obviously and concededly is another way of saying that for dividend purposes fixed assets must be computed at cost, not value, and plaintiff here plants himself upon that position, even to the point of contending that evidence of value is immaterial and not admissible. If that contention be sound, the company indisputably had a deficit at all the times here involved in an amount exceeding the dividends here in question. The importance of the question so presented, both to this case and to corporations and corporate directors in general, is thus apparent, and it is, I think, surprising that upon a question so important to and so often occurring in the realm of business there is, not only no decision which can be said to be directly in point, but, also, no discussion in text-book or law magazine which does much more than pose the question without answering it. * * *

It is to be emphasized at the outset that the question is not one of sound economics, or of what is sound business judgment or financial policy or of proper accounting practice, or even what the law ought to be. My views of the business acumen or financial sagacity of these directors, as well as my views as to what the legislature ought to permit or prohibit, are entirely immaterial. The question I have to decide is whether or not an existing statute has been violated. The problem is one of statutory construction.

The words of the statute, as it existed during the period here involved, are: "No stock corporation shall declare or pay any dividend which shall impair its capital or capital stock, nor while its capital or capital stock is impaired * * *."

* * *

In summary, I think that it cannot be said that there is a single case in this State which actually decides that unrealized appreciation cannot be taken into consideration, or, stated in different words, that cost and not value must be used in determining whether or not there exists a surplus out of which dividends can be paid. I think, further, that such a holding would run directly counter to the meaning of the terms capital and capital stock as fixed by decisions of the Court of Appeals construing the earlier statutes, and that such construction of those terms must be deemed to have been adopted by the legislature in enacting the statute here involved. I thus obviously cannot follow decisions to the contrary in other States or any contrary views of economists or accountants. If the policy of the law be bad it is for the legislature to change it.

* * * I am of the opinion that the same reasons which show that unrealized appreciation must be considered are equally cogent in showing that unrealized depreciation likewise must be considered. In other words, the

test being whether or not the value of the assets exceeds the debts and the liability to stockholders, all assets must be taken at their actual value.

I see no cause for alarm over the fact that this view requires directors to make a determination of the value of the assets at each dividend declaration. On the contrary, I think that is exactly what the law always has contemplated that directors should do. That does not mean that the books themselves necessarily must be altered by write-ups or write-downs at each dividend period, or that formal appraisals must be obtained from professional appraisers or even made by the directors themselves. That is obviously impossible in the case of corporations of any considerable size. But it is not impossible nor unfeasible for directors to consider whether the cost of assets continues over a long period of years to reflect their fair value, and the law does require that directors should really direct in the very important matter of really determining at each dividend declaration whether or not the value of the assets is such as to justify a dividend, rather than do what one director here testified that he did, viz. "accept the company's figures." The directors are the ones who should determine the figures by carefully considering values, and it was for the very purpose of compelling them to perform that duty that the statute imposes upon them a personal responsibility for declaring and paying dividends when the value of the assets is not sufficient to justify them. What directors must do is to exercise an informed judgment of their own, and the amount of information which they should obtain, and the sources from which they should obtain it, will of course depend upon the circumstances of each particular case. * * *

NOTES

1. Other courts have shared the judicial attitude expressed in *Randall v. Bailey.* For example, in *British Printing & Communication Corporation PLC v. Harcourt Brace Jovanovich, Inc.*, 664 F.Supp. 1519 (S.D.N.Y.1987), the court approvingly cited *Randall v. Bailey* and held that, under New York law, a corporation may measure its assets at their fair market value rather than their accounting book value for purposes of determining the amount available for distribution to shareholders.

Delaware has had a somewhat checkered history on this issue, due in part to the shifting format of its dividend provision over the years. In a very early case, decided when the statute took the form of a prohibition against dividends "except from the surplus or net profits arising from the business" (language which had evolved from an earlier prohibition against dividends "except from surplus profits arising from the business"), the court, after acknowledging that it could be difficult to determine the surplus or net profits of an insurance company, concluded as follows:

"Some things seem clear, and one is that an estimated increase in the value of the building owned by the Insurance Company and occupied by its officers and employees, however accurately the increase be estimated, is not a net profit arising from the business of the company. If it is an investment of capital of the company its increased value when realized by a sale may perhaps be treated as a profit, but until realized it is surely unwise, inaccurate and wrong to so regard it and pay out money based on such an estimate, for it is only a guess, and if a correct one it may become incorrect later when the conditions which produced the estimated increase of value change."

Kingston v. Home Life Ins. Co. of America, 11 Del. Ch. 258, 101 A. 848 (1917), affirmed on other issues, 11 Del. Ch. 438, 104 A. 25 (1918).

Subsequently, the wording of the Delaware statute was changed to provide that a corporation could pay dividends "out of its net assets in excess of its capital," and it was unclear whether the Kingston prohibition against including unrealized appreciation still applied. The uncertainty continued when the statute was amended in 1967 to make the test simply "out of its surplus". But recently, the Delaware Supreme Court expressly condoned a corporation's revaluation of assets and liabilities for purposes of determining the amount available to redeem shares (presumably the same as the test for paying dividends), saying: "Balance sheets are not, however, conclusive indicators of surplus or a lack thereof". Klang v. Food & Drug Centers, Inc., 702 A. 2d 150, 154 (1997).

2. New York has also had a somewhat variegated dividend law history. Here are excerpts from the court's opinion in Hill v. International Products Co., 129 Misc. 25, 220 N.Y.S. 711 (1925), an early decision which illustrates a battle over revaluation for dividend purposes in the course of cross-examination of a witness. The purchaser of a large block of preferred stock from a corporation sought rescission on the ground of misrepresentation about the affairs of the corporation, and, as the following excerpts from the opinion indicate, got a sympathetic reaction from the court (although the defendant ultimately prevailed on laches):

The dividend declared on August 19, 1919, was, as above noted, $356,452.25, away in excess of the surplus net profits on June 30, 1919, from a very favorable calculation of defendant's assets. A careful reading, however, of the reports of Price, Waterhouse & Co. and W. S. Peat, in evidence, made on Central Products Company and International Products Company for the period to the close of the year 1918, Defendant's Exhibits H-8 and I-8, have convinced me that the assumed surplus of $349,000 did not actually exist. Plaintiffs' Exhibit 51, which is Exhibit A attached to Defendant's Exhibit H-8, shows a surplus in Central Products Company at the close of 1918 of $798,672.48, Argentine paper. The notation appearing on said Exhibit A is as follows:

"Surplus on Live Stock, etc., as per Profit and Loss Account, Exhibit B, $798,672.48."

It is this figure translated into United States gold which is the $349,000, the assumed surplus carried over from 1918. The reports of the accountants, upon even a most casual analysis, show that as a result of the operations of Central Products Company up to the close of 1918 there was no such surplus. Defendant's Exhibit H-8 is entitled:

"Report, Balance Sheet, and Profit and Loss Account, August 1, 1917, to December 30, 1918, of Central Products Company."

The report is dated August 1, 1919. This alleged surplus apparently arises almost entirely from book entries respecting the alleged increase in the value of cattle on the hoof. It is not claimed that the cattle were actually weighed. They were apparently assumed to be heavier, because they had grown older and their weight increased. At the trial, moreover, the following testimony was given by Mr. Farquhar:

"Q. Now, you realize, do you not, that in making up this estimated surplus and undivided profits of June 28, 1919, of $527,951.58, that that was composed of surplus and net earnings, December 28, 1918, of $549,000? A. Yes.

"Q. And the other figure, that makes up that total of $178,951.58, was the estimated profits for the first six months? A. Yes; on canned meat and quebracho extract.

"Q. And this item of $349,000 -- that was the item carried over to the fattening of cattle, as surplus from 1918, wasn't it? A. Breeding -- the business of the cattle department -- breeding and fattening of cattle.

"Q. Well, except for a very small portion, that was an item due, wasn't it, as you understood, to the fattening of cattle? A. And breeding.

"Q. What? A. And breeding; increased age and weight.

"Q. Exactly; increased age and weight. You didn't understand that that profit had accrued from sales actually made, but from an estimate of the increased value of the cattle? A. And inventory of the increase.

"Q. Well, an inventory of the increased value of the cattle? A. Yes.

"Q. Not from actual sales of cattle made and money taken in? A. No.

"Q. So that, in voting for this dividend in August, 1919, you regarded these inventory estimates or valuations of the profits of the cattle department as an earning actually made, didn't you? A. Breeding; increased weight; fattening inventory.

"By the Court: Q. Did you consider that as earnings of the company? A. Based on the chartered accountant's reports and the lawyers' advice.

"Q. Irrespective of what it was based on, did you yourself consider it as earnings of the company? That is what the judge wants to know. A. Yes.

"By Mr. Seabury: Q. And you realized, did you not, when you voted for this dividend, if that item of $349,000 was not properly to be regarded as earnings, that then you did not have earnings sufficient to pay the dividends of $356,000? A. But we did regard it as earnings."

It would seem to me that this alleged increase in value of cattle not realized by an actual sale of cattle is not a proper item to be taken into consideration in determing actual surplus of a going concern. Hutchinson v. Curtiss, 45 Misc. 484, 92 N.Y.S. 70; * * * Kingston v. Home Life Ins. Co. of America, 22 Del. Ch. 258, 101 A. 898.

* * * Irrespective of what causes may have been instrumental in bringing about this alleged surplus of $349,000, which was carried over from 1918, the facts indicate to me that such surplus did not exist. The representation of the company, made through the declaration of such dividend, that the surplus and net profits were at least equal to the dividend declared, was therefor, in my opinion, a material misrepresentation.* * *

3. In the *Randall* opinion the court expressly observes that among the elements that do *not* determine the question of statutory construction is "proper accounting practice". But is it really possible to ignore the accounting context from which the typical statutory terms such as "net assets" or "impairment of capital" are drawn? Is it not likely that when a legislature chooses terms of accounting rather than legal art, it meant to incorporate their accounting significance? In any event, the historical cost principle, the accounting rule which, as described on page 54, *supra*, generally requires that assets be reflected on the basis of cost (less depreciation to date), and rejects recognition of unrealized appreciation, has been firmly fixed in GAAP at least since the APB's 1965 Opinion No. 6, which stated in paragraph 6 that "property, plant and equipment should not be written up by an entity to reflect appraisal, market or current values which are above cost to the entity." Not that this principle has not gone without challenge over the years. There was a considerable groundswell for change during the 1970's, when the high level of inflation made figures based upon original cost especially unrealistic. In 1979 FASB No. 33 was issued, requiring the larger public companies to provide supplemental information regarding the effects of inflation, particularly with respect to the current replacement cost of assets, although the basic balance sheet was to continue to reflect figures based upon cost. Adherents of the traditional view argued that the change in the price level did not necessarily measure the amount that could be realized upon the sale of an asset: the realizable value, especially of operating assets, was still a matter of conjecture, and perhaps wasn't all that relevant anyway, since the enterprise usually had no intention of selling such assets.

There is also the point that while an enterprise is certainly better off if its assets are worth more than the cost-based figures at which they are recorded on the balance sheet, it is not necessary to write up the assets on the balance sheet to reflect this advantage. At least in the case of depreciable operating assets, the benefit will be reflected in the fact that the enterprise is enjoying lower annual depreciation expenses, and hence higher net income, than would be the case if the company's costs for such assets were more consistent with the current higher values; as a corollary, the company's "Return on Equity" ratio, described on page 274, *supra*, will be much more favorable, since the numerator, net income, will be higher, and the denominator, owner's equity or net assets, will be lower. On the other hand, maybe this argument proves too much, because measuring the "net assets" denominator on the basis of historic cost rather than current values seems to understate the amount that the current management actually has to work with, and hence to overstate how successful the management has been, at least as measured by the return-on-equity ratio.

In any event, as will be examined in more detail in Chapter VI, generally accepted accounting principles now make an exception for most investments in debt instruments and marketable equity securities, and call for recording such assets at current fair market value. It is easy to distinguish publicly traded shares from tangible operating property, since for marketable securities the market usually provides a reasonable determination of fair value; in addition, unless being held for control, marketable securities, unlike operating property, may well be sold in the foreseeable future. Moreover, there is no depreciation advantage associated with securities, so recording them at current value is the most direct way of reflecting the benefit of any appreciation in value. SFAS No. 115, *Accounting for Certain Investments in Debt and Equity Securities* (FASB 1993), is the authoritative accounting pronouncement which mandates that marketable securities not held for control should be carried at current value. As to where to reflect the gain (or loss) resulting from writing the securities up (or down) to fair market value, that depends upon whether the securities are being held principally for sale in the near term (so-called "trading securities"), or are merely generally "available for sale". In the former case, the amount of unrealized appreciation (or diminution in value) being recognized on the trading securities will be included in the income statement. As to available-for-sales securities, on the other hand, which will certainly be the more common case, the unrealized appreciation (or diminution) will instead appear only on the balance sheet, as a separate component of the equity section.

4. Most established corporations' balance sheets show surpluses which enable the corporation to pay its regular dividends. However, sometimes the

restructuring of a corporation, by way of a preferred stock dividend or the like, may turn on how large a regular dividend would have been lawful, making it important to know whether dividends can be declared from revaluation surplus. Moreover, in the 1980s corporations began paying large extraordinary dividends as a defense to an unwelcome takeover attempt, and there too the revaluation question can become significant.

5. Suppose that in the example involving Maledon, Inc. on page 293, *supra,* the equipment had decreased in value to $500. Would the company's board of directors have to take that into account in determining the amount available for distribution? If so, would the corresponding reduction be in earned surplus or capital surplus, and does that matter with respect to the dividend determination?

6. In *Resolution Trust Corp. v. Fleischer,* 826 F. Supp. 1273 (D. Kansas, 1993), involving the legality of dividends paid by a savings and loan association, the governing corporation statute prohibited dividends "except from the earnings and undivided profits" of the company, with a further condition that the company meet "the net worth requirement" for federal insurance of accounts, plus a provision imposing liability on the directors for "an impairment of capital". The plaintiff government agency contended that because the association's net worth determined on a fair market value basis was negative, the dividends were unlawful and the directors were liable. However, the court held that the statutory provisions did not require a fair market value determination. After noting the absence of any express statutory requirement to use fair market value, the court said:

> "The court finds that indeed such an interpretation would create severe practical problems for the industry. Every time an institution desired to pay dividends, it would be required, in effect, to conduct a liquidation analysis of its assets. Such an analysis would conceivably require separate appraisals of all the properties owned by an institution. Such appraisals can be highly subjective, with the fair market value of specified property often resting in the eyes of the appraiser. . . .

> "The Kansas statutes are phrased in accounting terms such as "earnings" and "undivided profits." This court finds it much more likely that the legislature intended net earnings and capital of an institution to be evaluated according to the institution's ability to pay as a going concern, not based on a fair market liquidation analysis. The court therefore finds that Kansas law does not require that an institution's capital, net worth and earnings be determined on a fair market value basis."

Was the court correct that adopting the fair market value interpretation would require a "liquidation analysis" of the corporation's assets?

As the foregoing cases illustrate, the applicable statutes often fail to provide any insight as to how a company should compute its assets and liabilities. The following Task Force Report from the ABA Corporate Law and Accounting Committee of the Section of Corporation, Banking and Business Law, *Current Issues on the Legality of Dividends from a Law and Accounting Perspective,*[*] 39 Bus. Law. 289, 292-94 (1983), concluded that GAAP offered the most practical answer to the question of what accounting approach directors and courts should apply in assessing issues which arise under dividend statutes:

GAAP AS A LEGAL STANDARD

Under the statutes, the accounting principles to be applied in determining net assets and liabilities are generally unspecified. What, then, are the accounting principles to be applied under these statutes prescribing a financial statement test? GAAP is by far the most practical standard for the courts.

First, with the exception of some closely regulated industries, GAAP accounting is required by the Securities and Exchange Commission for publicly held companies and is effectively required by the American Institute of Certified Public Accountants (AICPA) for both public and private companies. These requirements have resulted in a single set of accounting principles for most publicly traded and larger private companies. Thus lenders, trade creditors, and, especially important for our purposes, equity investors receive GAAP statements for such companies.

Second, the objectives of the financial accounting standards for general purpose external financial reporting, as set forth in the FASB's summary of its Statement of Financial Accounting Concepts No. 1, include:

§ 1210.34: Financial reporting should provide information that is useful to present and potential investors and creditors and other users in making rational investment, credit, and similar decisions. The information should be comprehensible to those who have a reasonable understanding of business and economic activities and are willing to study the information with reasonable diligence.

§ 1210.37: Financial reporting should provide information to help present and potential investors and creditors and other users in assessing the amounts, timing, and uncertainty of prospective cash receipts from dividends or interest and the proceeds from the sale, redemption, or maturity of securities or loans. Since investors' and creditors' cash flows are related to enterprise cash flows, financial reporting should provide information to help investors, creditors, and others assess the amounts,

---

[*]Copyright © 1983, The American Bar Association. Reprinted with permission.

timing, and uncertainty of prospective net cash inflows to the related enterprise.

§ 1210.40: Financial reporting should provide information about the economic resources of an en terprise, the claims to those resources (obligations of the enterprise to transfer resources to other entities and owners' equity) and the effects of transactions, events, and circumstances that change resources and claims to those resources.

These objectives have not been and may never be fully achieved, but they demonstrate that GAAP financial statements are designed, in part, to show the ability of a corporation that is a going concern to pay cash dividends. Such objectives are consistent in a realistic way with the purposes of the dividend statutes: the protection of creditors, shareholders, and the relationships among the shareholders. For a going concern, a basic assumption of GAAP, these objectives come far closer to carrying out these protective functions than the fair valuation standard of the Bankruptcy Law, the fair salable value standard of the Uniform Fraudulent Conveyance Act, * * * or the continuing process of valuation and revaluation such as that contemplated by *Randall v. Bailey.* For a going concern considering the declaration of dividends, it seems inappropriate to require a valuation of assets on the basis of theoretical current realization when such assets are not going to be the subject of current realization. * * *

Third, the courts are quite unequipped to choose among and revise accounting principles. It is not a question of accepting, rejecting, or revising a particular item: instead an interrelated set of principles that focus on agreed objectives must be devised. Beneath the concepts of assets, liabilities, net income, and surplus is a complex network of definitions, assumptions, and judgments which are often individually, and always collectively, complex.

Fourth, some jurisdictions implicitly recognize GAAP as the standard for accounting determinations through statutes permitting directors to rely on financial statements prepared by public accountants. Several states expressly permit the use of generally accepted accounting principles. * * *

NOTES

1. The revised Model Business Corporation Act, which is the leader of the trend toward eliminating the legal capital system and instead basing dividend restrictions upon corporate solvency, provides that the board of directors may base its determination of the amount available for distribution under that test "either on financial statements prepared on the basis of accounting practices and principles that are reasonable in the circumstances *or on a fair valuation or other method that is reasonable in the circumstances.*" Model Bus. Corp. Act Ann. § 6.40(d) (3d ed. 1998/99 Supp.) (emphasis added). As the official commentary to MBCA § 6.40 articulates,

the Act "contemplates that generally acceptable accounting principles are always 'reasonable in the circumstances' * * *."

2. In contrast, California's corporation statute, for example, requires the board of directors to use GAAP in determining the company's assets and liabilities. The provision states that all references to financial statements and accounting items "mean such financial statements or such items prepared or determined in conformity with generally accepted accounting principles then applicable," Cal. Corp. Code § 114 (West 1990), thereby presumably prohibiting the inclusion of unrealized appreciation in determining the amount of the assets of a corporation.

4. CONTRACTUAL RESTRICTIONS

The corporate statutes require, either implicitly or explicitly, that any distribution comply not only with the express statutory provisions, but also with any limits imposed in the corporation's articles of incorporation. Such a prerequisite to a distribution is one example of a contractual restriction, because the articles of incorporation serve as a contract between the shareholders and the corporation.

Given the weaknesses in the statutory restrictions limiting distributions, however, as noted earlier sophisticated creditors enjoying superior bargaining power often impose their own various contractual limitations or prohibitions on borrowers as a condition to any loan. These restrictive covenants frequently limit distributions to owners, require the borrower to maintain certain financial ratios, prohibit the debtor from incurring any additional indebtedness, and compel the borrower to pay withholding and sales taxes. Such restrictive covenants may also prohibit or limit, absent the lender's approval, pledges of assets; purchases, capital expenditures, or leases exceeding a certain amount; sales or issuance of capital stock; mergers, consolidations, or sales of assets; salaries paid to officers and directors; or management changes. Large borrowers, however, commonly refuse to accept such covenants.

Covenants restricting distributions to shareholders typically limit such distributions to an amount derived from three components: (1) all or part of the borrower's accumulated net earnings from the *peg date*, a fixed date often the beginning of the fiscal year in which the borrower issues the debt, to the end of some period preceding a distribution's declaration or payment, (2) the proceeds from the sale of stock after the peg date, and (3) the *dip*, a specified amount of existing retained earnings.

Loan agreements typically treat the borrower's failure to comply with the restrictive covenants as a "default," which may give the lender the right to demand immediate repayment or require the borrower to cure the default before a grace period expires. To illustrate, in 1996 Kmart Corp.'s creditors agreed to remove a bond provision that would have required the company to repay $548 million in real-estate-related bonds if credit rating agencies lowered Kmart's rating below investment grade. If Kmart and its creditors had not reached the agreement, the payment would have triggered covenants in other loan agreements requiring Kmart to repay an additional $3.1 billion. The agreement did not come free to Kmart. The company agreed to pay fees and higher interest rates which caused at least a $70 million charge against earnings during the quarter. More recently, Lucent Technologies, Inc. reportedly paid a $3.75 million fee to its lenders for an amendment to certain debt covenants so that the company could meet a minimum book value covenant. Michael Rapoport & Jonathan Weil, *Goodwill as a Banker's Weapon*, WALL ST. J., Sept. 23, 2002, at C1 (also quoting a Lucent spokesperson as saying the company made " 'no real concessions' ").

PROBLEMS

Problem 5.1A. Noelle Ries incorporated Ries, Inc. (the "Company") three years ago. The Company issued its 100 authorized shares, $100 par value common stock, to her in exchange for $15,000. About the same time, the Company borrowed $55,000, payable on demand, from Melanie Rubocki. The Company immediately used the loan proceeds to purchase land which cost $30,000. Although the Company has not repaid any principal on the loan, the corporation has not incurred any other indebtedness. The Company's only assets include the land, a bank account containing $25,000 and a $5,000 account receivable from a customer.

During its first year, the Company lost $4,000. The Company earned a $2,000 profit in its second year. In its third year, an uninsured tort claim against the Company caused an $8,000 loss for the year.

(1) Assuming no contractual limitations on distributions, would a $2,000 dividend at the end of the third year be lawful under any of the following statutory formulations?

(a) a surplus test?

(b) an earned surplus test?

(c) a retained earnings test?

(d) an equity insolvency test?

(e) the MBCA's balance sheet test?

(2) How, if at all, would your answers to the questions in part (1) change if the land has appreciated in value to $50,000?

Problem 5.1B. X Corp. had the following balance sheet on January 1:

X Corp.
Balance Sheet, January 1

Assets		Liabilities & Shareholders' Equity	
Cash	$ 11,000	Shareholders' Equity	
Plant	90,000	Stated Capital	$100,000
		Earned Surplus	1,000
Total	$101,000	Total	$101,000

CASH
| 300

Prepaid Inter 150
Inter Exp 150

On February 1, X borrowed $5,000, giving a note due three years later, with interest at twelve percent per year. X Corp. agreed to pay the $600 annual interest in two installments each year, $300 on April 30 and $300 on October 31. Assume for simplicity that X Corp. did not earn any income or incur any other expenses during the calendar year. How large a dividend could X Corp. properly pay at the close of the calendar year, under a statute which permits dividends only "out of net assets in excess of capital"?

Problem 5.1C. Your law firm has long represented The Cougar Company. A note from a senior partner describes the following facts:

Cougar, whose current fiscal year ends shortly, has paid dividends for many years in a row. However, last year was not a good one for the company. At the beginning, Cougar had stated capital of $1,000,000, capital surplus of $200,000, and an earned surplus of $500,000, but during the year suffered an operating loss of $600,000. Cougar has also already incurred an operating loss of $150,000 in the current year, and expects to do no better than break even during the rest of the year. However, Cougar still has some $170,000 of cash, and the Directors would like to declare the regular cash dividend of $100,000.

Some years ago Cougar invested $50,000 in LMN Corporation, and the investment is currently worth approximately $150,000, with excellent prospects for further appreciation. Cougar also owns some real estate which cost $300,000, but was recently appraised for only $200,000, although the decline is believed to be only temporary.

The governing corporation statute provides that "No dividend shall be distributed if it would reduce the corporation's net assets to less than its stated capital". Your senior partner has asked for your views as to whether the proposed dividend would be lawful.

C. Drafting and Negotiating Agreements and Legal Documents Containing Accounting Terminology and Concepts

At one time or another in every lawyer's career, a lawyer will draft or negotiate an agreement or legal document containing accounting terminology or concepts. The following practical suggestions are adapted from Terry

Lloyd, *Financial Language in Legal Documents**, distributed at a Practicing Law Institute seminar:

From time to time every attorney is called on to draft an agreement embodying some accounting concepts or principles. Such agreements might be a shareholders' agreement with a buy/sell provision based on a corporation's net worth or a supply contract with a termination provision or triggered by a party's becoming insolvent. Even litigators are occasionally required to draft settlement documents with accounting or financial provisions.

General Principles of Drafting

All too often however, the drafting process consists of going to the files, locating a similar agreement or agreements and tailoring those documents to the terms of the new transaction. Just as frequently, attorneys simply state that all accounting issues are to be governed by "generally accepted accounting principles" (GAAP) under the assumption that GAAP is only slightly less hallowed than the deity and motherhood. Although these approaches are better than providing that "all computations shall be made in accordance with good accounting standards," they are not likely to achieve the best results for your client. Set forth below is a list of principles of legal drafting which should be used in drafting any agreement involving accounting or financial concepts. The first five of these principles apply generally to all legal documents; the remaining five apply only to those embodying accounting concepts.

1. Completely Mutual Documents are Not Necessarily Even.

Attorneys often make the mistake of thinking that if all the covenants in an agreement are parallel, (i.e. the terms apply equally to both parties), the document is fairly drawn. * * * This problem arises frequently in buy/sell agreements in which there is a tendency to make clauses mutual. Assuming, for example, you represent the less wealthy of the parties, who owns 20% of a two-person venture, a mutual covenant giving each party a right of first refusal to buy the other's interest may be of great value to the other party and of little value to your client. * * *

2. When Relying On Past Agreements, Be Careful Which Document You Choose.

* * * [The fallacy of relying] heavily on what attorneys used to call the "form file." * * * is that * * * you may be using a document drawn for the benefit of your opposition [perhaps because your firm was on the other side

---

* Copyright © 1997, Terry Lloyd, CPA, CFA. Reprinted with permission.

in the earlier matter]. * * *

3. *Long Forms are Not Necessarily Superior.*

* * *As a practical matter, if your client controls a situation (such as a majority partner in a joint venture) the less said the better as your client is likely to have carte blanche unless inhibited by an agreement. Control typically includes the ability to pick accounting methods, which is discussed in more detail below, under Rule Six. On the other hand, if your client is not in control of the situation, the more matters reduced to writing, the better protected she will be . . . . [with one exception: if] there is a large disparity in bargaining power, . . . the courts often resolve ambiguities in favor of the party that did not prepare the agreement.

4. *Make Sure the Mechanics Work.*

* * *

5. *Clear the Documents with Your Client's Accountants.*

* * * While there is no shame in not knowing GAAP, it is really quite easy to have someone who does understand the implications look at the calculations.

6. *If your Client is in Control, Use a Bottom Line Concept; If the Opposing Party is in Control, Use a Top Line Concept.*

The prior discussion of Rule Three, suggested that if your client is in control of a situation, usually the less said in an agreement, the better. The corollary to that rule is that when your client isn't in control, base calculations on items not subject to judgment or manipulation by either party. In the course of preparing financial statements, numerous accounting judgments and estimates are made, such as the useful lives of depreciable assets, the collectibility of receivables, the obsolescence of inventory, the recognition of liabilities, etc. Alone, or in combination, these elections can have a profound effect on the bottom lines (net income and equity) of the resulting financial statements. On the other hand, "creative accounting" is less likely to have a significant effect on the "top lines" (revenues and cash) of those same statements. For this reason, if the accounting judgments are to be made by your client, you will want to use a bottom line concept, since she will enjoy the ability to shape the outcome by appropriate selection of accounting methods and estimates. On the other hand, if the opposing party is in charge of the accounting, you will want to key the agreement to the top lines which are less susceptible to manipulation through creative accounting. * * * You should also consider using some variation of cash flow, which is much less susceptible to manipulation.

* * *

9. GAAP May Not be Best for Your Client.

Generally accepted accounting principles are filled with assumptions, estimates and practices that may not necessarily reflect the true circumstances and economic health of an entity. GAAP accounting is, admittedly, a conservative discipline and leans heavily toward *understating* assets and profits when judgment is required. The theory is that management, who is responsible for accounting and the financial statements, tends to overstate assets and earnings, so GAAP and the auditors should be inclined in the other direction. * * *

Existing accounting principles also use historical costs (the purchase price of the asset), rather than current or fair value [,so] the numbers on the financials may bear little relationship to true economic value. This is increasingly true in an age of intellectual property and other intangible assets. * * * In too many cases, reality (true economic value) and GAAP simply do not agree. * * * In simple terms, GAAP is probably a good place to begin the calculations, but not a place to end.

10. GAAP is Not a Static Set of Principles.

* * * Reliance on an old form of agreement could have disastrous consequences if you are dealing in an area in which there has been a major change in GAAP.

More importantly, if the agreement you are preparing is to be in effect for an extended period, you must also take into consideration *which* GAAP you are adopting, that which is in effect now or that which will be in effect when the required computations are to be made. * * * Remember also that GAAP allows for elections and changes of methods. Most parties are well served by including language stating that methods and elections will be consistent throughout the agreement's period. Often lenders like some certainty in their agreements and loan covenants (such as how loan-to-value ratios are calculated), but enjoy the fact that GAAP tends to become more restrictive over time in its treatment of income and assets. This is a case where more or less specificity on accounting practices and the definitions of some calculations may help your client.

* * *

Agreements Employing Balance Sheet Items

The operative provisions of many agreements are keyed to financial balance sheet items, such as amount and quality of accounts receivable. * * * Balance sheet concepts are commonly employed in legal agreements in the following types of provisions:

● The termination provision of commercial agreements, where either party is given the right to terminate in the event the other party becomes "insolvent."

- The pricing provision of acquisition agreements, where the purchase price is based on the book value, * * * net worth or total assets of the acquired entity.

- Negative covenants in loan agreements, where the borrower is required to maintain a specified minimum working capital, current ratio, tangible assets or net worth; and

- The funding limit provision in a loan or commercial financing or factoring agreement, where the amount of available credit is limited by the reported (book) value of the borrower's inventory, machinery and equipment and/or accounts receivable.

These four types of provisions share in common the fact that one or more of their operative clauses is based on a line item in a company's balance sheet. When the determination of each line item involves complex accounting principles and estimates, an understanding of those principles and judgments is important in drafting documents that help your client.

* * * For example, if a loan agreement contains a covenant requiring the borrower to maintain a current ratio (the borrower's current assets divided by its current liabilities) of at least 2 to 1, the borrower might be placed in default under that covenant in the final year of the loan because, under GAAP, the outstanding balance of the loan would become a current liability in the final year of the loan, since any amount due in less than one year is considered "current" by accounting standards. * * *

Finally, it's important to understand the effect on accounting data that may result from the exercise of accounting estimates. One observer has called GAAP a five lane highway. For example, management is given wide latitude in determining the useful lives of its assets. If management concludes that a class of assets should be expensed over three instead of ten years, that decision will have a profound effect on both the balance sheet and income statement. * * *

Basic Considerations

An attorney drafting an agreement utilizing accounting concepts should first be aware of which financial values are relevant to the measurements called for in the agreement. For example, he should help the client decide whether or not a given payment or condition of default or termination should be based on the subject enterprise's total assets, specific assets, current assets, working capital or net worth (among other measures). In making this determination, the attorney should consult with the client about her ability (or the other party to the agreement) to manipulate the chosen accounting measurement through the selection of accounting methods and estimates, based on surrounding circumstances, such as material transactions with related parties.

* * *

Specific Accounting Concerns

As noted above, it may be appropriate to provide that certain financial determinations are to be made on a basis other than GAAP, such as the cash method or modified GAAP. * * * [For example, in] drafting contracts involving balance sheet concepts, consider whether or not it is to your client's advantage to utilize a "hard" or "realizable" asset concept. If you are drafting the default provisions in a loan agreement on behalf of the lender, you should be concerned with whether or not the borrower will have sufficient assets to repay the loan at the time a default occurs. Accordingly, you should provide maximum assurance that sufficient assets of the borrower will always exceed a specified level. * * * it would be of little comfort to your client if the borrower's entire net worth is represented by an unrealized intangible asset such as "goodwill."

* * *

Similarly, it is often advisable to specify the treatment of certain balance sheet accounts to suit your client's needs. For example,* * * [l]enders commonly place a cap on the amount they will loan on the basis of the borrower's receivables. In drafting such a loan limit provision, * * * in representing the lender, you should draft a provision specifying that, for the purposes of computing the borrower's eligible receivables, only receivables not older than a specified period (commonly 90 days) should be counted.

* * *

Individual Balances

When including *cash* in the overall asset base, be aware that all cash is not "free" or available for unrestricted use. Some restrictions include collateralized balances, security deposits made by others, escrow amounts and compensating balances. * * *

* * * There is a particular problem when receivables are for services provided. Unlike goods, services (like legal advice) cannot be repossessed and liquidated. * * * Are longer than normal or stated credit terms interest bearing? What other leverage does the service provider have to force (if necessary) payment of the receivable?

* * *

Intangibles must be evaluated individually. In liquidation, goodwill counts for nothing and, conversely, some companies may have explicit goodwill with no asset on the books to reflect this competitive advantage.

* * *

Unearned or prepaid items (such as retainers or subscriptions paid to a publisher) are booked as liabilities since the recipient has an obligation to provide goods or services in the future. Hopefully, the cost of providing that good or service is less than the amount paid, so prepaids really have an equity portion in them. GAAP requires the full amount to be carried as a liability until it is earned.

* * *

NOTES

1. Lawyers, especially those representing borrowers, should not underestimate the possibility that changing accounting principles can drastically impact restrictive co venants and other legal documents. In December 1990, the FASB issued Statement of Financial Accounting Standards No. 106, entitled "Employers' Accounting for Postretirement Benefits Other Than Pensions." Before the pronouncement, many employers used a "pay-as-you-go" basis, or cash method, to account for the costs incurred to provide postretirement health care benefits. The pronouncement, however, required employers to accrue the expected costs necessary to provide those benefits during the years that the employee renders the services required to earn the benefits. In addition, the new rule required companies to establish a reserve for previously earned benefits. *The Wall Street Journal* reported that the new rules would reduce profits, and therefore equity, by as much as $1 trillion starting in 1993, "a record for any accounting rule."

2. Given that GAAP often sanctions alternate treatments for the same transaction or event and accounting standards cannot begin to address every conceivable situation, knowledgeable lawyers have long advised borowers or sellers to avoid provisions in covenants or the like that represent or warranty the financial statements as "true, correct, and complete" or as "full and accurate presentations" of the enterprise's financial picture. However, now that SOx requires the chief executive officer and chief financial officer of each public company to certify quarterly and annually that to their knowledge the financial statements fairly present in all material respects the financial condition, operating results, and cash flows, without any limitation to GAAP, counsel for lenders and buyers will likely ask for warranties and representations containing similar language from public companies. In view of the difference in burden of proof between criminal convictions under the federal securities laws and civil judgements in contract or misrepresentation cases, borrowers and sellers will remain well advised to refuse.

3. Because of the devastating effects that changes in accounting principles can cause in restrictive covenants and other legal documents, lawyers should try to stay abreast of FASB's agenda. In that regard, we highlight several recent developments and areas to watch that potentially affect topics covered in the first five chapters.

(a) *Derivatives.* In 1998, the FASB completed its long-running project on derivatives, that is, financial contracts that derive their value from some underlying asset, and issued Statement of Financial Accounting Standards No. 133, *Accounting for Derivative Instruments and Hedging Activities*, which ultimately took effect at various points in 2001. SFAS No. 133 requires enterprises to show all derivatives as either assets or liabilities on the balance sheet, to measure those instruments at fair value, and to include in earnings, as either gains or losses, the changes in those fair values during a period. Before this pronouncement, literally trillions of dollars of derivatives contracts and changes in the value of those contracts did not appear in financial statements. Including amounts for these derivatives and their changes in value in financial statements obviously affects numerous financial ratios and could potentially cause, or cure, defaults in many contracts and lending agreements.

(b) *Distinguishing liabilities and equity.* Some financial instruments, commonly referred to as *hybrid instruments*, contain both debt and equity characteristics. For example, mandatorily redeemable preferred shares obligate the issuer to repurchase the shares at particular times or under certain conditions. In May 2003, FASB issued a new standard that will require enterprises to treat such mandatorily redeemable preferred shares and certain other financial instruments, including put options that do or may require an issuer to repurchase its own shares in exchange for cash or other assets, as liabilities, rather than as equity—the more typical result under previous accounting principles. Similarly, enterprises must treat payments or accruals of "dividends" on mandatorily redeemable preferred shares as interest on the income statement and statement of cash flows. The new rules generally became effective no later than 2004. ACCOUNTING FOR CERTAIN FINANCIAL INSTRUMENTS WITH CHARACTERISTICS OF BOTH LIABILITIES AND EQUITY, Statement of Financial Accounting Standards No. 150 ¶¶ 9, 11, 18, A5 (FASB 2003). The resulting reclassifications could affect the ratios commonly contained in loan agreements and other contracts.

In October 2000, FASB issued a proposed standard that would also require enterprises to present noncontrolling interests, including the minority interests mentioned at the end of Chapter I, as equity. Some companies currently report these amounts as liabilities, the approach adopted by Starbucks in its 2005 financial statements, as indicated in Note 11 on page 63 in Appendix A. Other companies present minority interests in the "mezzanine," that is, in a section between liabilities and equity on the balance sheet. The proposed rules would require these companies to reclassify these minority interests as equity. ACCOUNTING FOR FINANCIAL INSTRUMENTS WITH CHARACTERISTICS OF LIABILITIES, EQUITY, OR BOTH, Proposed Statement of Financial Accounting Standards (FASB 2000). Ultimately, FASB plans to issue a definitive pronouncement that provides a single comprehensive model for classifying all financial instruments. Again, any reclassifications that the new rules may potentially require could affect leverage and coverage ratios in loan agreements and other contracts.

(c) *International accounting principles*. Attention should be paid to the ongoing effort to achieve convergence between U.S. and international accounting standards as described at pages 139 - 145, *supra*, which responds to the desire of the industrialized world for some system of global accounting standards, especially in connection with cross-border securities listings. In this regard, there was an important recent development when an EU regulation took effect on January 1, 2005, requiring all listed companies to use International Financial Accounting Standards ("IFRSs") to prepare their consolidated financial statements. As a result, lawyers in the United States now need to consider IFRSs in transactions with EU companies and their subsidiaries. U.S. lawyers will also need to monitor international developments for domestic transaction purposes, as harmonization will inevitably lead to changes in U.S. GAAP. In addition, the SEC has joined the EU Internal Market Commission in a project designed to allow foreign companies to use IFRSs in securities filings in the United States, without any reconciliation to GAAP, by 2009 at the latest. These factors deserve serious consideration.

(d) *Pensions*. Under current pension accounting rules, unfunded pension liabilities can force an enterprise to record a "minimum pension liability" on its balance sheet, and as a component of "other comprehensive income." Increases in minimum pension liability directly reduce owners' equity. Companies that entered into loan agreements which did not exclude pension liability adjustments from the definition of net worth often must pay fees to amend loan covenants, pay off debt earlier, or agree to other more onerous terms. Bryan-Low, *Pension Liability Raises a Flag Among Bankers,* WALL ST. J., Nov. 26, 2002, at C1 (reporting that Delta Air Lines "paid an 'amendment' fee; of just under $1 million" to amend a line of credit).

The SEC staff urged the FASB to reconsider, preferably in collaboration with the IASB, the accounting for postretirement benefit obligations, including pensions, and in November, 2005 the FASB added such a project to its agenda. Current accounting rules allow enterprises to report important information about pensions in the notes to the financial statements, rather than on their balance sheets, and also to smooth the performance of the investments in pension plans, thereby spreading swings in value over years.

A part of the first phase in the project the FASB issued an exposure draft on March 31, 2006 that would require enterprises to recognize the overfunded or underfunded status of their defined benefit postretirement plans as an asset or a liability on the balance sheet. Enterprises would measure the asset or liability as the difference between the fair value of plan assets and projected benefit obligations, which includes assumptions about inflation, employment longevity, and employee mortality. The proposal also requires enterprises to report any changes in the net asset or liability in other comprehensive income. Currently, the net asset or liability for each plan only appears in the notes to the financial statements. For many companies, the change will increase liabilities, and could adversely affect debt-to-equity ratios, which might require the firms to renegotiate lending agreements. On January 1, 2006, *The Wall Street Journal* reported that the companies in the Standard & Poor's 500-stock index faced $461 billion in underfunded postretirement liabilities, $140 billion in pensions and $321 billion in health-care obligations. FASB has sought to implement the changes in the first phase, which would apply only to the pension obligations, as quickly as possible, planning to issue a final statement by September 30, 2006, which would make the new rules described above effective for fiscal years ending after December 15, 2006. EMPLOYERS' ACCOUNTING FOR DEFINED BENEFIT PENSION AND OTHER POSTRETIREMENT PLANS – AN AMENDMENT OF FASB STATEMENTS NO. 87, 88, 106, AND 132(R), Proposed Statement of Fin. Accounting Standards (FASB Mar. 31, 2006); *see also* Ian McDonald, *Health Benefits Ail as Pensions Heal*, WALL ST. J.,June 6, 2006, at C3; David Reilly, *FASB to Move Pension Accounting From Footnotes to Balance Sheets*, WALL ST. J.,Mar. 31, 2006, at C3.

(e) *Time value of money.* The FASB's 2000 Statement of Financial Accounting Concepts No. 7, described on page 206, *supra*, will presumably eventually lead to new or revised accounting standards that would modify the amounts at which various assets and liabilities appear on the balance sheet and establish rules for how changes in those amounts would affect the financial statements.

(f) *Fair Value.* The FASB has continued to move toward requiring that all financial assets and liabilities be reported at fair value. The concepts statement referred to in the previous paragraph could eventually lead to new or revised accounting standards that would significantly change financial reporting, thereby substantially affecting many financial ratios and, indeed, the entire framework for financial accounting.

*

CHAPTER VI

REVENUE RECOGNITION AND ISSUES INVOLVING THE INCOME STATEMENT

A. IMPORTANCE TO LAWYERS

At least since the 1930s, both existing and potential creditors and investors have turned to the income statement to try to predict an enterprise's prospects because any financial returns, whether interest, dividends, or appreciation in an investment's value, will usually flow from the business's earnings or ability to generate earnings. As mentioned in Chapter I, businesses often prefer to recognize revenue as soon as possible and to defer expenses for as long as possible. However, under the GAAP revenue recognition principle, based in large measure on the doctrine of conservatism, a business cannot recognize revenue until the enterprise has substantially completed performance in an exchange transaction. These exchange transaction and substantial completion requirements force businesses, and their accountants and lawyers, to focus on substance rather than form in analyzing various problems involving revenue recognition.

These revenue recognition requirements are normally satisfied when a business exchanges goods or services for cash, or claims to cash, and delivers the goods, or when the business substantially performs the services that entitle it to the promised consideration. However, sometimes what appears to be a completed transaction may not actually constitute an unconditional transfer. For example, the consideration received may lack a readily ascertainable value in money or money's worth, or the vendor may have failed to perform some important obligations under the contract. A seller may even offer the purchaser the right to return the item purchased with no obligation. In all these examples, the circumstances preclude revenue recognition.

Against this background, the matching principle seeks to offset expenses against related revenues wherever possible in determining an enterprise's net income. In other words, accrual accounting strives to match interrelated items of expense and income in the appropriate accounting period. For example, if Marty Jones sells shoes which cost $10,000 for $15,000, treating the $10,000 cost of goods sold as an expense in a different accounting period from that in which the sales were reflected would grossly distort Jones' operating results. If an enterprise recognizes income related to a prospective expense in the current accounting period, then the enterprise should accrue the related expense, estimating the amount (as accurately as possible) if no precise figure is available, in order to achieve the desired matching. In contrast, if an expenditure relates to revenues that an enterprise cannot yet recognize under GAAP, or the expenditure will benefit a future accounting period generally, then the expenditure represents an asset, perhaps more accurately an unexpired cost, which should not be charged against income in the current period.

This chapter, therefore, also addresses the use of some deferral and accrual techniques to achieve the most informative periodic reflection of expense and income. Although these materials generally deal with income and expense items separately, we should keep in mind that as a practical matter the problems of choosing the appropriate period for reflecting items of income and expense often arise together rather than as separate questions. After all, business operations usually involve a continuous series of transactions in which the enterprise incurs expenses to produce income. However, quite often related items of income and expense will appear to have occurred in different periods, but since they should be matched in the same period, the question is, which one. In general, it may be best to look first at whether any limitations on revenue recognition are applicable, because they are more stringent than the requirements relating to expenses: thus, for example, an enterprise may have to defer expenses because they directly relate to revenues which the enterprise cannot recognize until a subsequent accounting period.

In addition to revenue recognition and matching, several other accounting principles influence the income statement. As a practical matter, conservatism affects both revenue recognition and matching. To provide meaningful financial data, a business must also be consistent in its application of accounting treatment from period to period, and properly disclose the methods used to recognize revenues and record costs in the financial statements. Accordingly, our discussion will focus on five central themes: revenue recognition, conservatism, matching, consistency and disclosure.

Throughout this chapter we will discuss various situations in which recognition of revenue or expenses, and other issues involving the income statement, affect the practice of law, and lawyers should understand how and why. For one thing, lawyers often draft, negotiate or interpret contractual provisions that refer to "net income" in various types of agreements, e.g., employment, collective bargaining, partnership, and shareholder buy-sell. In addition, almost all financial frauds involve income measurement issues. To illustrate, an enterprise or its owners or managers can mislead investors by prematurely recognizing revenues, or by deferring expenses which the business should match against current revenues. Alternatively, the enterprise can shortchange employees entitled to profit-sharing payments by accelerating expenses or deferring revenues.

Beginning in the late 1990s, numerous financial frauds involving improper revenue recognition sent shockwaves throughout the financial markets. Enron's sudden collapse in 2001 distinctly marked an escalating accounting crisis in corporate America. In addition to the highly publicized frauds at WorldCom and Tyco, other accounting scandals occurred at well-known companies, including AOL Time Warner, Citigroup, Coca-Cola Co., Freddie Mac, IBM, KMart, Lucent Technologies, Merck, Qwest, and Xerox. In a 2003 study that the Sarbanes-Oxley Act of 2002 required, the SEC discovered that over half of the actions brought for financial reporting violations during the five-year period ended July 30, 2002 involved improper 704 OF THE S ARBANES-OXLEY A CT OF 2002 (Jan. 24, 2003), *available at* http://www.sec.gov/news/studies/sox704report.pdf.

Schemes to recognize revenue improperly take many deceptive forms, including fictitious sales, prematurely recognized revenue, unlawfully recorded reserves, "sham" sales transactions with related entities, and nonmonetary sales arrangements engineered solely to create the false appearance of revenues. In the post-Enron world, lawyers should keep in mind that although revenues generally represent the largest item on the income statement, accounting rule-makers have only recently begun to adopt specific rules governing revenue recognition. Accordingly, many commentators have observed that the smallest number of accounting rules governs the largest income statement item.

One all too common type of improper revenue recognition, known as "channel stuffing", involves a manufacturer using bargaining power or financial incentives to pressure dealers to order more goods than they want, in order to enable the manufacturer to record additional revenue in the current period and thereby reach a desired level of net income. A dramatic recent example that received a lot of notoriety involved Bristol-Myers Squibb, one of the world's major drug companies, which indulged in a practice of paying incentives to its wholesalers to buy extra products and in effect stockpile the inventory, so that Bristol-Myers could show higher current income. This practice inflated revenue from 1999 to 2001 by $2.5 billion, and earnings by $900 million. In 2005 the company entered into a settlement of the Justice Department's criminal investigation by agreeing to pay $300 million to a shareholders' restitution fund; added to previous payments of $150 million to settle the SEC's civil charges, the second-largest ever SEC settlement payment involving accounting fraud, and $339 million to settle a class-action suit over the matter, this improper revenue recognition will have cost Bristol-Myers around $800 million. Also in 2005, two former Bristol-Myers executives were indicted; the company, on the other hand, was able to avoid indictment by agreeing to a deferred prosecution arrangement, under which the company will escape a criminal charge if it complies with all the terms and conditions of the agreement, which, as usual, included appointment of an independent party to monitor the company's activities. Deferred prosecution arrangements have become popular because they make it possible to punish a corporation without causing excessive loss to the employees and shareholders. Bristol-Myers Ex-Officials Are Indicted, June 16, 2005 Wall St. J. A3, A11.

Some new wrinkles in overstating earnings received special attention in 2004-05, particularly in connection with retail enterprises. In the food business, it is common for suppliers and the retailers to agree that the stated price for goods is subject to a volume discount if the retailer's purchases exceed a specified level for the year; similarly, a retailer who advertises the supplier's products often is entitled to an allowance from the stated price for some portion of that cost – a so-called promotional allowance. But these arrangements have often tempted retailers to take larger discounts or allowances than were agreed on, perhaps hoping that the supplier will not want to make a fuss with a valued customer. More to the immediate point, retailers have sometimes just arbitrarily taken larger deductions than could possibly be justified, in order to be able to show a higher net income.

One such company was U.S. Foodservice, Inc. (USF), a subsidiary of the major Dutch food conglomerate Royal Ahold. Four of USF's executives, in an attempt to make it appear that the company had achieved certain earnings targets which would entitle the executives to virtually double their salaries, just baldly inflated the amount of its promotional allowances, and then not only supplied that false information to the company's outside auditors, but also persuaded employees at several of USF's major suppliers to provide false confirmation of the overstated promotional allowances. Criminal as well as civil charges were brought against those now-former executives, and two of them have pleaded guilty. In addition, nine employees or agents of USF suppliers who signed those false confirmations have been charge criminally and pleaded guilty. Betz and Diamond, Nine Facing Criminal, Civil Actions Over Alleged Ahold Accounting Scheme, 37 Sec. Reg. & L. Rep. 158 (Jan. 24, 2005).

Similar improprieties have turned up in the financial statements of several large department store companies. In that industry, it has long been the case that department stores have expected clothing manufacturers and other merchandise suppliers to share in their sales risk by refunding part of the price paid by the retailers when some items do not sell well at full price and have to be marked down. In addition, it is standard practice for the retailers to discount the price owed to the vendor to take account of defects in the goods received, errors in the mix of products shipped, or simply shortfall in the numbers. Here too, however, the retailers have somewhat the upper-hand, except when the vendor has a particularly high-powered name or brand, and in recent years it appears that retailers have been taking advantage of the situation by claiming larger mark-down allowances than had been agreed to, and in some cases even misstating the amount of markdowns, or defective goods, or number of items received. Obviously, the impetus for such conduct is the desire of the retailer, particularly publicly-traded companies, to shore up their earnings figure for accounting purposes, but once again, booking a claimed allowance of discount known to be unjustified would result in a false financial statement.

This issue hit the financial headlines in 2005 when it was learned that one of the best-known retailers in the country, Saks Fifth Avenue, had been sued by a giant Japanese apparel manufacturer for taking substantial deductions and credits that were not allowed under the contract between the two. Saks subsequently admitted that it "overcollected" money from its suppliers; fired three executives, including its general counsel, who were involved in the practice; and announced that it would repay vendors about $48 million in improper markdown allowances and interest. It now appears that there are many others lawsuits against major department stores over improper deductions of this kind, some of them with damage claims in the tens of millions. Both the SEC and the U.S. Attorney's office are investigating, and charges from either direction may be forthcoming.

It is ironic that these practices by retailers, at least the deductions for markdowns, may actually have gotten started as a result of sales practices by vendors, pressuring retailers to order more goods than they had really wanted, in a kind of forerunner of channel stuffing as described above. In response, retailers would agree to place the larger order as long as the vendor would guarantee that if some of the goods couldn't be sold at full price, the vendor would refund enough to protect the retailer's profit margin. That contributed to a more general expectation of vendors sharing the burden of retail markdowns, which has now been carried to these illegitimate extremes.

Another special target of regulators investigating possible financial statement abuses in 2004 was insurance companies, when it came to light that certain novel types of insurance products were being used by buyers to manage their earnings. The spotlight shone especially brightly on American International Group, Inc. (AIG), perhaps the largest insurance company in the world, and a favorite of Wall Street because of its history of continuous, steady earnings growth over many years; investors were also impressed by AIG's apparent ability to keep the ratio of its underwriting losses (payments on claims by insureds) to its premiums revenue at the lowest levels in the industry. While it is true that the accounting for the insurance business is especially complex, particularly with respect to re-insurance transactions, i.e., those in which an insurance company itself in effect buys insurance from another company, to obtain protection against the possibility of incurring a particularly large loss claim on an existing policy, some of these efforts to manage earnings were fairly obvious. The most controversial scenario involved so-called "finite insurance", developed in the 1980's and designed to limit the maximum risk of the insurance company if a covered loss did occur, while also providing both an accounting and a tax advantage for the insured. In its simplest form, finite insurance consists of a multi-year contract calling for total premiums over the period almost equal to the amount of the potential losses being covered, but with the further proviso that at the end of the contract most of the total amount of premiums paid in excess of any reimbursed losses would be refunded. Thus the insurance company's risk was limited to the difference between the maximum of losses covered by the policy and the total premiums paid by the insured. Buyers, on the other hand, were able to avoid paying lots more in premiums than their actual loss experience, as often happened to insureds with favorable loss experience. Of course self-insurance could do that too, but at a cost of much greater earnings volatility, which would not be favored by investors. In other words, with finite insurance the buyer could provide for its losses over a period of years in a stable, budgeted manner, while also securing an annual deduction for tax purposes.

However, when the risk actually being taken by the insurance company is quite small, the question arises as to whether the arrangement really constitutes insurance, or should instead be treated as a kind of loan by the customer to the insurance company, to be repaid except to the extent of losses incurred. In 1992, after intense debate, the FASB ruled that to qualify for being treated as insurance for accounting purposes there had to be a "reasonable possibility" that the insurer might "realize a significant loss". These terms were never formally defined, but in practice there was an informal guideline of at least a 10% chance of a 10% loss; however, it was management that determined the chance and possible amount of loss, and there was ample incentive for stretching to find compliance.

Finite insurance became a particularly tempting vehicle for abuse in the form of helping to cloak losses, and thereby avoid full disclosure in financial statements. In one notable early case involving AIG, a company had suffered a $29 million trading loss, and was particularly anxious to avoid disclosing the full amount because the company had earlier indicated that the loss would be between $13 million and $18 million. The company arranged to purchase from AIG a policy under which in exchange for $15 million in future premiums the company immediately received $11.9 million in "insurance" proceeds, which the company set off against its trading loss and hence avoided showing the full amount of that loss; however, since AIG never incurred any risk of loss, this was not an insurance transaction, so there was no basis for such a set-off.

The AIG transaction that has received by far the most attention (and criticism) arose at a time when investors were expressing some concern that AIG's loss reserves, the amount that AIG estimated would probably have to be paid out for losses incurred on its existing policies, might not in fact prove sufficient to cover the total of those losses. The obvious cure for this problem was to charge additional expense against income to build up the reserve, but AIG was very reluctant to incur the resulting reduction in net income.

Instead, AIG entered into a putative reinsurance deal with an insurance company called General Re, a subsidiary of Berkshire Hathaway, the company run by the fabled investor, Warren Buffet, which of course added all the more to the media attention this transaction ultimately received. AIG purported to provide reinsurance to General Re for $500 million of possible losses on which General Re was the primary insurer, and AIG received $500 million in premiums. Although obviously AIG was undertaking no risk in the transaction, AIG treated the $500 million received from General Re as income from reinsurance premiums, and coupled this with a charge against income for additional potential losses, thereby raising its loss reserve by that amount while leaving AIG's net income the same as it would have been without this transaction. General Re treated the deal not as a purchase of reinsurance, but rather as a loan to AIG which would be repaid (presumably with interest for the use of the money, or some other compensation to General Re for entering into the deal). As of mid-2005, the top management at AIG had been replaced, and the new officials acknowledged that AIG had improperly accounted for this transaction, along with a number of others. AIG has released a restatement of its operations since 2000 to correct these accounting improprieties, and the result was a reduction in the company's shareholders' equity of several billion dollars, or over 3%. In mid-2005, regulators were continuing to investigate whether former senior AIG officials should face civil, and perhaps criminal, proceedings.

In the meantime, two former senior General Re executives have pled guilty to criminal conspiracy to commit fraud. In early 2006, a federal grand jury indicted three other former senior General Re executives, including an assistant general counsel, and one former senior executive of AIG for their alleged involvement in the financial fraud at AIG. Shortly thereafter, AIG agreed, without admitting or denying wrongdoing, to pay more than $1.6 billion to resolve SEC, New York state, and Justice Department charges arising from the accounting fraud and other alleged misconduct. *See* Betz et al., *AIG to Pay $1.6B to Resolve NY, SEC, DOJ Charges Over Accounting*, 38 Sec. Reg. & L. Rep. (BNA) 263 (Feb. 13, 2006).

Throughout this chapter, we will discuss various situations in which revenue recognition and other issues involving the income statement, such as allocating and matching costs, affect the practice of law. Lawyers should understand the rules governing revenue recognition and the income statement, to be able to provide sound legal advice, both prospectively and retrospectively.

As a starting point, corporate lawyers, who often serve as critical "gatekeepers" under the federal securities laws, must understand revenue recognition methods to prevent, identify, and remedy financial frauds, because so many financial frauds involve income measurement issues. As one notable example, Enron fraudulently recognized revenue from a now infamous "Nigerian barge" agreement with Merrill Lynch, under which

Enron recorded $12 million in profit even though it promised to repurchase the barges and, therefore, retained the risk of loss. *See, e.g., Enron Corp.: Judge Refuses Defendants' Bid To Have Trials Held Separately*, WALL ST. J., Apr. 26, 2004, at C5. Other fraud possibilities include overstating net income by prematurely recognizing revenues, and deferring expenses that should be matched against current revenues. Increasingly, all lawyers, whether litigators or those in transactional practice and whether representing publicly-traded or privately-owned enterprises, risk malpractice liability if they do not recognize and r espond to "red flags" signaling potentially fraudulent revenue recognition issues.

Because investigators could find the "fingerprints" and failings of lawyers behind the recent financial frauds, lawyers can no longer avoid responsibility for such accounting shenanigans by blaming unscrupulous executives and rogue auditors. In that connection, there was a dramatic increase in the responsibility of lawyers when, in response to lawyers' involvement in the recent corporate scandals, SOx section 307 directed the SEC to issue rules establishing "minimum standards of professional conduct for attorneys appearing and practicing before the Commission in any way in the representation of issuers". The rules are to require "an attorney to report evidence of a material violation of securities law or breach of fiduciary duty or similar violation" up-the-ladder to the chief legal counsel or chief executive officer and, if those officers do not "appropriately respond", then to report the evidence to the audit committee, some other committee composed solely of independent directors, or the board of directors. 15 U.S.C.A. § 7245 (West Supp. 2004). In January, 2003 the SEC issued final rules, effective August 5, 2003, implementing SOx section 307. Implementation of Standards of Professional Conduct for Attorneys, 68 Fed. Reg. 6296 (codified at 17 C.F.R. Part 205 (2003)), *available at* http://www.sec.gov/rules/final/33-8185.htm. The SEC is considering a requirement that the attorney withdraw if there is no satisfactory response, and that the SEC be notified by the company. As a result of the SEC's action, the ABA has amended its Model Rules of Professional Conduct to move in roughly parallel fashion.

Lawyers often draft, negotiate or interpret contractual provisions that refer to "net income" in employment, collective bargaining, partnership, buy-sell and other agreements. Lawyers must grasp the concepts of revenue recognition to provide legal services competently for such prospective business transactions. *See, e.g., Margonis v. Rossi*, 253 N.E.2d 577 (Ill. App. Ct. 1969) (finding a lawyer demonstrated an "ineptness of language" by confusing the terms "net income" and "gross income" while drafting a partnership agreement).

As another example, lawyers often perform *due diligence* to determine whether a prospective transaction will further their client's best interests. Historically, approximately half of the attorney malpractice cases involving due diligence arise from an accounting failure, and some forty percent of those involve revenue recognition. In such cases, the courts typically look to see if the attorney failed to spot and investigate "red flags" indicating improper or fraudulent revenue recognition. Jackson, *Due Diligence[:]*

Careful Use of the Process Helps to Minimize Liability Exposure, CORP. COUNS. WEEKLY (BNA), May 10, 2004, at 4.

The number of companies restating prior financial statements has reached staggering levels in the past several years and continues to grow at an alarming rate. In 2005, 1,195 domestic public companies restated their financial statements, compared to 613 in 2004, 514 in 2003, 330 in 2002, and 270 in 2001. In additions, another 100 foreign filers amended their financial results in 2005, nearly tripling from thirty-seven in 2004. Observers have pointed to three major causes that have contributed to the growth in restatements in recent years: the new internal controls provision in SOx section 404 has led to testing and outside auditor scrutiny that has uncovered numerous errors and weaknesses; successor audit firms' willingness to second-guess Arthur Andersen's accounting practices following its demise; and the provisions in Sarbanes-Oxley that require executives to certify that the financial statements fairly present in all material respects the entity's financial condition and operating results. *See, e.g.,* Burkholder, *Glass, Lewis Reports New Record of Nearly 1,300 Restatements in 2005,* 38 Sec. Reg. L. Rep. (BNA) 403 (Mar. 6, 2006).

Significantly, errors in revenue recognition continue to be a top cause for restatements, with errors in accounting for reserves and contingencies not far behind. Among the reasons for the high number of restatements due to revenue misstatements, according to the chief accountant of the SEC's Division of Corporate Finance, is that not only is there no comprehensive framework for revenue recognition from the FASB, but there are not even many rules providing guidance on the matter; accordingly, this becomes an especially fertile area for SEC comment letters to issuers raising questions about a particular approach adopted, and such a letter often in and of itself leads to a restatement. Billions of dollars in previously reported revenue evaporated in the recent financial restatements, which left many investors reflecting on then SEC Chairman Arthur Levitt's prophetic speech, set out at pages 340-347, *infra,* noting "an erosion in the quality of earnings, and therefore . . . . financial reporting."' Burkholder, *Levitt Seeks Corporate Help in SEC Drive To Stem 'Erosion' in Financial Reporting,* 30 Sec. Reg. & L. Rep. 174 (1998).

Lawyers have already felt the consequences from the SEC's efforts to remedy widespread problems in revenue recognition and financial accounting reporting. In 1999, the SEC fined the former general counsel of Livent Inc. $25,000 and barred him from appearing or practicing before the SEC as an attorney for five years for his role in drafting and finalizing agreements related to a financial fraud and then concealing those agreements from the company's independent auditors. Other examples include barring an attorney who served as general counsel for Policy Management Systems Corporation from appearing or practicing before the SEC for five years, for allowing the corporation to recognize revenue on contracts that the parties did not finalize or execute until after the end of the accounting period, and a jury conviction in 2003 of Franklin Brown, Rite Aid Corp.'s general counsel and executive vice-president, for his role in the company's financial fraud. Also in 2003 Michael Munson, former outside counsel for Nicor Energy LLC, was indicted for his role in a financial fraud to inflate the company's net income by $11 million. Munson allegedly assisted corporate executives in a scheme to stretch fiscal recognition of a legal settlement payment over two years rather than treating the entire amount as an expense in accordance with GAAP. *Court Upholds Indictment Against Attorney for Alleged Role in Inflating Firm's Earnings*, 2 Corp. Accountability Rep. (BNA) 933 (Aug. 27, 2004). More recently, the growing stock-option-pricing scandals that began drawing attention in early 2006 have already ensnared lawyers: for example, McAfee Inc. fired its general counsel after one of the endless number of informal or regulatory probes of public companies which were occurring regularly during 2006.

The litigation that follows from financial frauds can impose enormous costs. To settle the class action securities fraud lawsuit that arose from Cendant's accounting irregularities, for example, the company agreed to pay at least $2.83 billion, the largest settlement in the history of class action securities fraud litigation. More recently, in 2006 Nortel Networks Corp. agreed to a settlement worth about $2.4 billion to resolve two class actions arising from the company's accounting scandal; in the same month, a federal district court approved a $960 million settlement that McKesson Corp. and its subsidiary reached in early 2005 to resolve a securities fraud class action; just two months earlier, Royal Ahold N.V. agreed to pay approximately $1.1 billion to settle a securities action arising from an accounting fraud involving inflated vendor rebates.

The SEC and other governmental regulators may also impose civil penalties in response to financial frauds: notably, for WorldCom's multi-billion dollar overstatement of net income, in 2003 the SEC imposed a $2.25 billion fine, $1.5 billion suspended, the largest civil money penalty ever imposed against a corporation not a broker-dealer. The SEC can also seek disgorgement of any benefits that officers and directors received from their fraudulent conduct; as one illustration, for fraudulently inflating revenues by approximately $3 billion, the SEC fined two former Xerox officers $1 million each, the largest fines ever imposed against individuals for financial fraud; barred four officers from serving as officer or directors for any public company (a remedy made available to the SEC by SOx); and ordered six former senior executives to pay almost $20 million in disgorgement and prejudgment interest. SEC v. Allaire, Accounting and Auditing Enforcement Release No. 1796, 7 Fed. Sec. L. Rep. (CCH) ¶ 75,456 (2003).

On the criminal law side, SOx added several new federal white-collar crimes and significantly increased the maximum potential criminal fines and imprisonment for other offenses. As one recent example of the potential criminal liability, a federal judge sentenced Jamie Olis, a lawyer and vice president for Dynegy convicted for his involvement in a scheme to overstate cash flows, to more than twenty-four years in prison under the pre-SOx guidelines, while his former boss and co-worker pleaded guilty in exchange for five-year prison sentences.

In addition, companies can incur significant legal costs for accounting investigations: some observers have estimated that in slightly more than one year Qwest spent as much as $75 million in legal fees for outside attorneys alone during an accounting investigation and continued to spend about $7 million per month, the equivalent of approximately 100 lawyers billing $350 per hour for 50 hours per week. Berman, *Qwest Is Spending Top Dollar to Defend Accounting Practices*, WALL ST. J., Mar. 10, 2003, at C1. As another example, Enron executives expect that legal and accounting fees for its bankruptcy will reach $1 billion, and, with $25 million accumulating per month, the legal fees are expected to be the largest in bankruptcy history.

Continuing a theme from Chapter V, we will again see that an enterprise may use GAAP for preparing financial statements for creditors and investors, another set of rules for tax purposes, and still another for reporting to a regulatory agency. Different standards may also apply for specific contracts. For this reason, an enterprise may keep different sets of accounting records to maintain information necessary for the various sets of rules that may apply to the enterprise. We will also see, however, that separate sets of financial records can indicate financial fraud.

B. THE BASICS OF EXPENSE RECOGNITION

Before starting the analysis of revenue recognition, let's have a quick reminder of the corresponding issues involved in recognition of expenses.

We know that as important as revenues are they do not equal profits: an enterprise cannot show a profit unless its revenues exceed its expenses. See, *e.g.*, Pashman v. Chemtex, Inc., 825 F.2d 629, 631 (2d Cir.1987) ("Perhaps the first rule of accounting is that the black ink of profit is not entered into the ledger until expenses are deducted from gross revenues."). To provide a meaningful picture about an enterprise's operations, therefore, the income statement attempts to compare revenues for an accounting period against the expenses necessary to produce those revenues.

This objective produces two consequences. First, if an enterprise reasonably expects a particular expenditure to produce revenues in a subsequent accounting period, the matching principle precludes the enterprise from treating the expenditure as an expense in the current accounting period. Instead, the enterprise should defer the expenditure to that future period. In other words, the enterprise should treat the expenditure as an asset, or, perhaps more accurately, an unexpired cost. An obvious example is an expenditure to obtain services which will not be received until a future period, as when E. Tutt paid her temporary secretary $180 in salary on July 31 for the last week in July and the first two weeks in August: Tutt debited $60 to Salary Expense for July, and postponed $120 to August as deferred salary expense. Second, and conversely, the matching principle also requires an enterprise to recognize in an accounting period any expenses which are related to revenues being recognized during that period, even if the expense has not been paid yet (and maybe even if the anticipated service or other benefit has not been received yet, if it is closely enough related to revenue being recognized).

The foregoing represent simple examples of deferral and accrual, the techniques which accountants use to match expenses and revenues. In reality, it is often a lot more difficult to judge whether an expenditure will actually benefit a future accounting period, or whether an enterprise should charge a future expected expenditure or loss against income in the current period. In resolving these questions, enterprises should consider and apply the following basic rules: (1) an enterprise should match expenditures and losses against revenues that result directly and jointly from the same transactions or events; (2) if an expenditure or loss does not directly relate to any particular revenue-producing transaction, but does generally relate to revenues earned in an accounting period, the enterprise should recognize an expense or loss for that accounting period; (3) if an expenditure does not relate to a particular transaction, but generally aids in the production of revenues in more than one accounting period, the enterprise should systematically and rationally allocate the expenditure among the different accounting periods that the enterprise expects to benefit from the expenditure; (4) if an enterprise can not relate an expenditure or loss either to a particular revenue transaction or to any future accounting period, the enterprise should recognize the item in the accounting period in which the cost was incurred or the loss was discerned. Recognition and Measurement in Financial Statements of Business Enterprises, Statement of Financial Accounting Concepts No. 5, ¶¶ 85-87 (Financial Accounting Standards Bd. 1984).

To take a closer look at deferral of expense, remember that back in Chapter I we saw that if an enterprise expects an expenditure to benefit one or more future accounting periods, the enterprise does not treat the expenditure as a current expense, but reports the item as an asset on its balance sheet: the item qualifies under the rubric that assets represent economic resources which an enterprise (1) acquired in a transaction, (2) expects to provide future benefits, (3) and controls. For most purposes we can view an asset, whether tangible or intangible, as the balance of a previous cash outlay which an enterprise has not yet allocated to current expense, because that is how much of what the enterprise acquired remains available for use or consumption in the future. To the extent that an expenditure relates to future activities, or benefits subsequent accounting periods, the expenditure represents an unexpired cost which the enterprise should defer.

1. ALTERNATIVE THEORIES FOR DEFERRING EXPENSES FOR FINANCIAL ACCOUNTING PURPOSES

In deferral, the important judgment question is the extent to which an expenditure will benefit a future accounting period, and hence should be deferred, to be matched with the benefit in that future period. Two bases for deciding whether an enterprise should defer expenditures are "cause and effect" relationships, or systematic and rational allocations.

a. "CAUSE AND EFFECT" RELATIONSHIPS

One theory for deferring expenses or losses is whether a "cause and effect" relationship exists between an expense or loss and the enterprise's revenues in a particular accounting period. For example, a sale of merchandise involves both revenue from the sale, and an expense for cost of goods sold. Other expenses that may directly relate to a sales transaction include shipping costs to deliver the item to the customer, sales commissions, costs of installation, and any other variable selling expense. Generally, a merchant recognizes revenue when it delivers the underlying goods to the customer. The cost of the goods, shipping costs and selling expenses, which we can describe as the "cause," produce an "effect," namely the sales revenue. Given this "cause and effect" relationship, the enterprise treats the cost of the goods, shipping costs, sales commissions and related selling costs as expenses in the accounting period in which the business recognizes the sales revenue.

If an enterprise has not yet recognized the revenue from a particular transaction or event, it should defer any directly related expense items to achieve the necessary matching. For an obvious example, if an enterprise cannot recognize revenue from the sale of an item yet, then the item's cost should not be included in the cost of goods sold for the period. Instead, the item, plus any sales commissions or related selling costs already incurred, should continue to appear on the enterprise's balance sheet as an asset until the accounting period in which the business recognizes the revenue.

Unfortunately, deferral on this basis can be abused: in fact, numerous financial frauds over the years have involved hiding expenses as assets, by pretending that the expenditures would provide some future benefit to the enterprise. In 2001 occurred perhaps the most dramatic example ever, when the chief financial officer of WorldCom, in a blatant effort to inflate the company's operating results, deferred an amount of expenditures, at first reported to be some $3.6 billion, but which later turned out to be around $9 billion, or maybe even $11 billion, that should have been expensed because there appeared to be no basis in generally accepted accounting principles or otherwise for deferral.

b. SYSTEMATIC AND RATIONAL ALLOCATION

Some expenditures do not relate to any particular transaction, but generally aid in the production of revenues. For example, casualty insurance represents one of the general costs of doing business. Since, as we saw back in Chapter I, the benefit of financial protection against loss is enjoyed ratably over the policy's duration, the enterprise should allocate the policy's cost ratably among the accounting periods that the policy covers. Thus, the purchase of a three-year policy for $300 on January 1 of year one would result in $100 of expense for year one, while $200 appears on the balance sheet as an asset, called Deferred Insurance Expense, or Deferred Insurance Cost, or perhaps just Prepaid Insurance, at the end of year one. The deferred expense asset would be charged off, or *amortized*, to current expense ratably over the next two years: $100 in year two, leaving $100 in the Deferred Insurance Expense account at the end of that year; then that remaining $100 in year three. Notice that this treatment mirrors the way we handled E. Tutt's prepayment of rent for three years in Chapter I. We will discuss in more detail in Chapter IX the way accountants use depreciation and amortization to allocate the costs of long-lived assets over the accounting periods expected to benefit from their use.

When an expenditure's benefit occurs as a function of time, the basis for allocation among the current period and the future periods involved is usually obvious, whether the total duration of the benefit is fixed by contract, as in the case of prepaid insurance, or, say, by statute, as in the case of a patent. So, if an enterprise purchases a two-year insurance policy on July 1 of year one for $200, $50 would be treated as an expense in the second half of year one, $100 in year two, and $50 in the first half of year three; the respective amounts not yet charged to current expense as of the end of years one and two would appear in the Deferred Insurance Expense account on the company's balance sheet at those year-ends. Occasionally, the expected period of benefit from an intangible can only be estimated, as is usually the case with respect to a tangible asset (where the period of expected benefits is referred to as the "useful life" of the asset); indeed, sometimes the benefits of an intangible may be expected to coincide exactly with the useful life of a particular tangible asset, and hence would be amortized over the same period.

It is often difficult to decide whether an expenditure, particularly one not associated with the creation of any tangible asset, is in fact sufficiently likely to benefit future periods to make it deserving of at least some deferral, with the consequent creation of an asset on the company's balance sheet. The accounting authorities have given a good deal of attention to this issue, and the subject is reviewed in section F of Chapter IX, *infra*, dealing generally with accounting for intangibles.

PROBLEMS

Problem 6.1A. The following quotation comes from the opinion in *Cox v. Leahy*, 209 A.D. 313, 204 N.Y.S. 941 (1924), an action by the trustee in bankruptcy of an insolvent company to recover from directors for an allegedly unlawful dividend:

> "The directors of a corporation may declare and pay a dividend, when the corporation has surplus profits equal to or greater than the amount of the dividend paid. The fact that the corporation has not the ready funds sufficient to pay the dividend, and therefore borrows money with which to pay the dividend, does not render the declaration and payment illegal. . . . To what extent the property capital was impaired by the payment of the dividend is the question to be determined, and the dispute is confined to a few of the items in the statement of assets and liabilities.
>
>   *   *   *
>
> "Third item - prepaid insurance and taxes. The prepaid insurance, we think, was an asset. It had an actual value belonging to the company. Not only in law is it an asset, but in practice prepaid insurance is uniformly entered as an asset in making the balance sheet of a business. The asset account should be increased by the amount of the unearned premiums, $590.04. We think prepaid taxes rest on a different basis. They are in no wise available for a refund, and are paid for past expenses of government as well as future. . . . "

Look at Problem 5.1B on pages 306-307, *supra*. In answering the question, assume that Cox v. Leahy had been decided in X Corp.'s jurisdiction.

Problem 6.1B. Assume that a company decides, upon advice of its advertising agency, on a concentrated program of radio advertising once every three years, with merely a minor sustaining program in between. The company expects that this program will best support a steady public demand for its products. The company estimates that the program will cost $1,000,000 during the first year, and $100,000 in each of the next two years. Assuming that costs coincide with the estimates, what entries should the company record at the close of each year? Are expenditures incurred for advertising or promotion simply general costs of doing business in the periods in which the services are received, or is more refined analysis called for? Does APB Op. No. 17 generally, or the AICPA staff interpretation described on page 573, *infra,* provide an answer? If the cost for the third year turns out to be $130,000, what should the entry be for that year?

Problem 6.1C. An airline company spent $1,000,000 during the year just ended to train personnel on new planes which the company had not yet put into commercial use. How should the airline treat this expenditure in its financial statements for that year? Is this other than just a general cost of doing business in that period?

Is it relevant to the inquiry here that GAAP, pursuant to Statement of Financial Accounting Standards No. 2 (FASB 1974), requires enterprises to treat all research and development costs as expenses in the period incurred? FASB No. 2 describes "research" as planned search or critical investigation seeking new knowledge in the hope that the enterprise can use that knowledge to develop a new product or service or a new process or technique or to bring about a significant improvement in an existing product or process. The pronouncement defines "development" as "the translation of research findings or other knowledge into a plan or design for a new product or process or for a significant improvement to an existing product or process whether intended for sale or use." The latter term includes formulating, designing and testing alternatives, constructing prototypes, and operating pilot plants. Appendix B to FASB No. 2 explains that the Board reached its conclusion to require treatment as an expense based on several factors, including the high degree of uncertainty that usually exists regarding the future benefits of individual research and development projects and the lack of causal relationship between expenditures and benefits. The coverage of FASB No. 2 extends to a company's costs of research and development conducted by others on the company's behalf, including any loan or advance to another if repayment depends solely on how R&D work being done for the company pans out. In addition, based on a provision in FASB Interpretation No. 4 (1975), which deals with the applicability of FASB No. 2 to acquisition transactions, an enterprise must immediately expense goodwill attributed to the in-process research and development of the acquired company in certain circumstances.

Problem 6.1D. For another illustration that first impressions may not be accurate, consider interest on borrowed funds, which normally would be thought of as a general cost of doing business. Like insurance, this looks to be a paradigm case for an annual charge to current expense for the period covered by the interest paid. But suppose the funds were borrowed to acquire (or construct) some new operating facility; as we shall see in more detail in Chapter IX, the cost of a facility includes all the expenditures needed to acquire it, and to get it ready for its intended use. Suppose further, then that the new facility had not been completed by year end, and therefore had made no contribution to the production of revenues for the year. Might the interest expenditure that year be treated as part of the cost of the facility, instead of being charged to current expense?

This issue of how to deal with interest being paid or accrued on funds to finance the development of a new program, construction of a new facility, or the like, during a period before the new element has contributed to the production of revenues, is an important enough issue to have received special attention from both the SEC and the FASB. The amounts of such interest can be very large, particularly in the real estate development field, or in the public utility business where expansion and new construction are virtually continuous. Until 1979, an enterprise's management could decide, within rather broad parameters, whether or not to defer such interest expense, though GAAP did require each enterprise to follow a consistent practice.

In the mid–1970s, the SEC, concerned about the increasing number of companies that decided to defer interest in such circumstances, in effect imposed a moratorium prohibiting any more companies, other than public utilities, from adopting the practice. Following its general, but not invariable, practice of deferring to the authoritative standard-setters for the profession, the Commission urged the FASB to consider the issue. In 1979, the FASB concluded that interest incurred during a construction period, prior to any contribution to revenues by the asset involved, should be deferred and treated as part of the historical cost of acquiring the asset, being a cost necessary to bring the asset to the desired condition for its intended use. The objective, according to the Board, was to get a better measure of the enterprise's total investment in the asset, while also charging a cost which will benefit future periods against the revenues of those periods. Statement of Financial Accounting Standards No. 34, *Capitalization of Interest Costs*, No. 34 (FASB 1979).

The Board added that enterprises should not capitalize interest costs in connection with inventories that the enterprise routinely manufactured, or for assets, including land, which are not undergoing activities to ready them for use. If an enterprise incurs interest expense in financing the acquisition of land as a site for a new facility, that interest too during the consturcution period should be capitalized as part of the cost of the facility. Three members of the Board dissented on the ground that charging interest to expense when incurred results in more meaningful financial information, particularly with respect to the overall return on capital during each period.

Now consider this situation: During its recently-ended fiscal year, Z Corp. paid $143,000 in real estate taxes, which the accounting department charged to current tax expense. Analysis at the end of the year revealed that $27,000 of this amount related to a new warehouse which the corporation built during the year, but had not placed in service by the end of the year.

(1) Which of the following year-end adjusting entries, if any, would you recommend?

a. Warehouse Building	$27,000	
Tax Expense		$27,000
b. Deferred Expenses	$27,000	
Tax Expense		$27,000
c. Prepaid Taxes	$27,000	
Tax Expense		$27,000

Is there any other information you would like to have before resolving this question?

(2) How would it affect the situation if Z Corp. had outstanding an issue of so-called "income bonds," which require the corporation to pay the specified interest only to the extent earned during the year, and the corporation had not earned the full amount of interest for the year? Would the rules applicable to changes in accounting principles, summarized on pages 259-263, *supra*, be relevant?

2. DEFERRED LOSSES

Although GAAP generally requires enterprises to recognize losses and non-temporary declines in value immediately, certain statutory or regulatory schemes may require an enterprise to defer some portion of the loss to a later accounting period for other purposes. A recent Supreme Court case, Shalala v. Guernsey Memorial Hospital, 514 U.S. 87, 115 S.Ct. 1232, 131 L.Ed.2d 106 (1995), illustrates a dispute regarding whether an enterprise should immediately recognize a loss or defer it. In that case, the hospital issued bonds in 1972 and 1982 to fund capital improvements. In 1985, the hospital refinanced the debt by issuing new bonds, which saved an estimated $12 million in future interest expense. However, the transaction resulted in a $672,581 loss for financial accounting purposes, and the hospital sought Medicare reimbursement for about $314,000 of the loss. The Secretary of Health and Human Services denied the claim, concluding that the hospital must amortize the $314,000 loss over the life of the old bonds.

Describing the issue in the case as "whether the Medicare regulations require reimbursement according to generally accepted accounting principles (GAAP)", the majority opinion answered in the negative. In discussing the differences between the objectives of financial accounting and Medicare reimbursement, the Supreme Court stated:

> Although one-time recognition in the initial year might be the better approach where the question is how best to portray a loss so that investors can appreciate in full a company's financial position, see APB Opinion 26, ¶ ¶ 4–5, the Secretary has determined in [the Regulations] that amortization is appropriate to ensure that Medicare only reimburse its fair share. The Secretary must calculate how much of a provider's total

allowable costs are attributable to Medicare services, which entails calculating what proportion of the provider's services were delivered to Medicare patients. * * * Given the undoubted fact that Medicare utilization will not be an annual constant, the Secretary must strive to assure that costs associated with patient services provided over time be spread, to avoid distortions in reimbursement. * * * Should the Secretary reimburse in one year costs in fact attributable to a span of years, the reimbursement will be determined by the provider's Medicare utilization for that one year, not for later years. This leads to distortion. If the provider's utilization rate changes or if the provider drops from the program altogether the Secretary will have reimbursed up front an amount other than that attributable to Medicare services. * * *

Contrary to the Secretary's mandate to match reimbursement with Medicare services, which requires her to determine with some certainty just when and on whose account costs are incurred, GAAP "do[es] not necessarily parallel economic reality." R. Kay & D. Searfoss, Handbook of Accounting and Auditing, ch. 5, p. 7 (2d ed. 1989). Financial accounting is not a science. It addresses many questions as to which the answers are uncertain, and is a "process [that] involves continuous judgments and estimates." Id., at ch. 5, pp. 7–8. In guiding these judgments and estimates, "financial accounting has as its foundation the principle of conservatism, with its corollary that 'possible errors in measurement [should] be in the direction of understatement rather than overstatement of net income and net assets.'" Thor Power Tool Co. v. Commissioner, 439 U.S. 522, 542, 99 S.Ct. 773, 786, 58 L.Ed.2d 785 (1979) (citation omitted). This orientation may be consistent with the objective of informing investors, but it ill-serves the needs of Medicare reimbursement . . . .

514 U.S. at 97–101, 115 S.Ct. at 1238–39, 131 L.Ed.2d at 118–20.

Four Justices dissented, concluding that the Medicare regulations had incorporated GAAP as the reimbursement default rule.

For a case which rejected the use of deferred losses, see *Fidelity-Philadelphia Trust Co. v. Philadelphia Transportation Co.,* 404 Pa. 541, 173 A.2d 109 (1961). That case arose in a dispute about income bonds which required the issuer, Philadelphia Transportation Co. ("PTC"), to pay a fixed three percent interest (of the face amount) per annum, and up to an additional three percent each year to the extent covered by the issuer's "net income" for the year. Net income was described as gross income, determined pursuant to "accepted principles of accounting", less depreciation and other expenses, determined "in accordance with sound accounting practice". For the years 1957 and 1958 PTC concluded that it did not earn any net income, and hence did not owe the bondholders any more than the fixed three percent in either year; the trustee for the bondholders brought suit, contending, among other things, that PTC had improperly deferred two losses from earlier years which provided the basis for deductions in 1957 and 1958.

One of the losses stemmed from the fact that, prior to the years in question, PTC had decided to retire certain tracks and convert to motor buses, a process which the company completed in 1956. Rather than charging off the track's $7,200,000 remaining book value as a loss at the end of 1956, PTC decided to amortize this amount, that is, write it off over future years, at the rate of $1,200,000 per year, on the ground that future years would enjoy both savings in maintenance costs and the benefits of a new bus system. Affirming the lower court's holding, the Supreme Court of Pennsylvania concluded that such "benefits are at most incidental, ancillary outgrowths of the track retirement program", and that the total "retirement loss * * * was reasonably foreseeable by the end of 1956", so it should have been entirely written off at that time. 404 Pa. at 545, 173 A.2d at 112.

The second loss resulted from the ruling of the Pennsylvania Public Utility Commission in 1953 that the remaining balance of what had been paid many years earlier to pave and repave streets, in order to install and maintain the tracks, which amount was being amortized at the rate of two percent per year, could no longer be included among the assets viewed as devoted to providing utility services, collectively referred to as the *rate base*, on which a utility company is entitled to earn a fair return from the amounts it charges its customers. For accounting purposes, however, despite the Commission's ruling, PTC had kept the balance of the paving costs on its balance sheet, and continued its amortization program. As a result, PTC had charged off $300,000 against income in both 1957 and 1958. The Court concluded that the Commission's action in removing the unamortized balance of these costs from the rate base had stripped the "asset" of its only corporate benefit, and hence it should have been written off completely for accounting purposes by the end of 1953; that meant that PTC had understated its income by another $300,000 in both 1957 and 1958.

In sharp contrast to its position on the two previous matters, when PTC incurred a substantial cost for repaving the streets in connection with that 1956 track abandonment referred to above, the company charged off a portion in 1956 and all of the remainder in 1957, despite permission from the Commission to amortize the latter amount over a five year period. After noting the inconsistency between PTC's position on this matter and on the previous two, the court held that, as a result of including this 1957 item in the rate base for five years, the company would enjoy the benefit of earning a fair return on the item for those five years, so it should have been spread out over the five year period.

PROBLEM

Problem 6.5. Niagara Power Co. is a large public utility. The public utility commission fixes the rates the company may charge at a level which can reasonably be expected to produce a fair return on the company's *rate base*, that is, the amount of the company's net assets, which is what the company has devoted to providing service to the public. One of the company's three main plants, carried on the corporation's books (at original cost less depreciation) at $10,000,000, was located at the head of Niagara Falls. During the company's most recent fiscal year, a rock slide caused that plant to collapse into the Niagara River. The company's earned surplus at the beginning of the year was $60,000,000; gross revenues for the year amounted to $180,000,000, and "regular" expenses were $150,000,000. Should the $10,000,000 book value of the plant be charged against current income for the year? Past income? Future income?

C. ESSENTIAL REQUIREMENTS FOR REVENUE RECOGNITION

Returning now to the issues involved in revenue recognition, the starting point is that under GAAP an enterprise can recognize revenue only when (1) a bona fide exchange transaction with an outsider has occurred, (2) the enterprise has received cash or the right to receive cash, or can readily convert any other consideration received into money or money's worth, and (3) the enterprise has substantially completed the earnings process. *See* Recognition and Measurement in Financial Statements of Business Enterprises, Statement of Financial Accounting Concepts No. 5, §83 (FASB 1984). However, not every authority identifies three prerequisites for revenue recognition in just this way; indeed, some cases and administrative materials identify only two, sometimes by incorporating the money or money's worth element into one of the other two requirements, or perhaps by combining the bona fide transaction requirement with the substantial completion requirement. For example, some authorities explicitly state, or at least imply, that an exchange transaction has not occurred until the seller of goods or services has received money ior money's worth, or the customer's promise to pay is very secure. *See also* Stevelman v. Alias Research Inc., 174 F. 3d 79, 83 (2d Cir. 1999) ("Industry standards and generally accepted accounting principles ('GAAP') require that a company's revenues not be recorded until such time as an *exchange* of merchandise has taken place and collection of the sales price on that merchandise is reasonably assured.") (emphasis in original).

On the other hand, the SEC lists *four* conditions which must be met for revenue to be recognized. The SEC's staff recently attempted to put together in a single document all the authoritative standards found in various literature on revenue recognition. Thereafter, the staff expressed its belief that enterprises can recognize revenue only upon satisfying the following four conditions: (1) the evidence must persuasively demonstrate that an arrangement exists; (2) the enterprise must have delivered the product or performed the services; (3) the arrangement must contain a fixed or determinable sales price; and (4) the circumstances must reasonably assure collectibility. Staff Accounting Bulletin No. 101, 64 Fed. Reg. 1,122,290

(1999). In any event, no matter how the requirements may be stated, in considering them lawyers should keep in mind that there is usually great incentive for individuals and businesses to show good operating results, and one way of doing so is to maximize the amount of revenues being recognized in the period. This can make it very tempting to stretch a point, and even to cross the fraud line by intentionally overstating revenues. For publicly-traded enterprises the tendency of the financial markets' to focus on the most recent, quarterly results can encourage managers to misstate earnings. A desire to postpone addressing financial difficulties or to avoid violating a restrictive covenant could be a motive for both publicly-traded and closely-held businesses, and in both contexts managers and accountants and other employees may feel that their job or compensation depends upon results. Some individuals commit financial frauds to qualify for larger bonuses, especially in recent years in connection with stock options. On the other hand, personal motivations lead some owners or managers in closely-held businesses to *understate* earnings, in order to reduce income taxes. Understated earnings may also minimize payments to employees under profit-sharing plans and labor agreements or to minority owners under buy-sell agreements.

The fraudulent practices undertaken to increase revenue recognition have included creating fictitious transactions, backdating transactions, prematurely shipping goods or sending items not ordered, selling goods to customers that lack the financial ability to pay, and recording "sales" when the transaction remains subject to contingencies. Side letters may attempt to hide various contingencies that can arise from return or cancellation privileges, sales that are conditioned upon resale, often referred to as *consignments*, or the vendor's agreement to provide future services.

The broad scope of inappropriate revenue recognition and even downright financial fraud was already noted above. Financial frauds often require cooperation from lower-level employees or customers to deceive auditors. In In re Kurzweil Applied Intelligence, Inc., 7 Fed. Sec. L. Rep. (CCH) ¶ 74, 207 (SEC 1995), sales representatives forged signatures on apparent sales confirmations, and also altered documents. Employees in the accounting department destroyed records relating to fraudulent sales, helped to hide inventory, and created fictitious accounts receivable collection sheets. The perpetrators also enlisted customers to sign false audit confirmations and to misrepresent the status of negotiations which the company had fraudulently recorded as sales. The participants in the scheme gave a warehouse a false list to use in completing another audit confirmation. Finally, following instructions from one of the executives, a sales person obtained an audit confirmation from a customer, signed the customer's name, and used the customer's fax cover sheet to transmit the confirmation directly to the auditors.

In response to the frequent involvement by lower-level employees and third parties in financial frauds, SOx section 303 directed the SEC to establish rules to prohibit any officer or director of an issuer, or any other person acting at the direction of an officer or director, from taking any action to fraudulently influence, coerce, manipulate, or mislead the issuer's independent auditor for the purpose of rendering a financial statement materially misleading. In May 2003, the SEC promulgated final rules, effective June 27, 2003, to implement that provision. Improper Influence on Conduct of Audits, Financial Reporting Release No. 71, 68 Fed. Reg. 31, 820 (May 28, 2003). In the release adopting the final rules, the SEC emphasized that the statute only requires "fraudulent" action with regard to conduct to "influence" the auditor. *Id.* at 31,823. At least with respect to the verbs "coerce, manipulate, or mislead," the SEC's final rules prohibit such conduct that a person "knew or should have known" could result in rendering the financial statements materially misleading. By seemingly adopting a negligence standard, the SEC arguably ignored the provision in SOx section 303 that prohibits conduct undertaken "for the purpose of rendering such financial statements materially misleading." Although the SEC admits that the language "knew or should have known" historically reflected a negligence standard, the SEC maintained that SOX's objective to restore investor confidence justifies the Commissions's interpretation. *Id.* at 31,826-27. In addition, the SEC stressed that persons "under the direction" of an officer or director encompasses a broader category than supervision or control, and could include third parties such as outside layers, customers, or vendors. Notably, the SEC specifically described "inaccurate or misleading legal analysis" as conduct that could violate Rule 13b2-2(b). *Id.* at 31,821-23. Although the new rule extends to a broad category of actors, only the SEC can enforce the provision in a civil proceeding. In essence, the new rules supplement regulations issued under the Foreign Corrupt Practices Act, which, as described at pages 155-156, *supra*, prohibits, among other things, falsifying books and accounting records, providing false or misleading statements, or omitting to state any material fact to an accountant in connection with an audit.

Often, questionable management conduct with respect to financial statement presentation falls short of actual fraud, but is nevertheless inconsistent with the goal of making the statements as objective and as meaningful as possible. One area of particular concern stems from the fact that the stock markets have historically given higher price-earnings ratios to companies that have shown an ability to report steady, predictable earnings growth. Many business executives have been far too willing to accommodate investors' desires for steady growth, and indeed see nothing wrong with the practice. In this regard, the financial community often refers to managerial actions which increase or decrease a business's current reported earnings without a real increase or decrease in economic profitability as *earnings management* or *income smoothing*. The latter term refers to efforts to keep the business growing at a steady rate. When business executives manage or smooth earnings, whether by a change in accounting method, or by an operating decision like offering customers special discounts at year-end to accelerate sales, the financial statements do not accurately reflect the enterprise's economic strength: that violates the trust which users place in financial statements and may cause users to reach decisions different from those that they might have made if they had enjoyed access to all relevant information. Understood in this context, earnings management and income smoothing raise important issues involving business and legal ethics.

Here is the speech by SEC Chairman Arthur Levitt referred to earlier, in which he identifies certain problem areas in current financial accounting and reporting, and sets forth an action plan to address the problems:

"The 'Numbers Game,'" remarks by Arthur Levitt

Chairman, Securities and Exchange Commission
NYU Center for Law and Business, September 28, 1998.

* * *

I'd like to talk to you about [a] widespread, but too little-challenged custom: earnings management. This process has evolved over the years into what can best be characterized as a game among market participants. A game that, if not addressed soon, will have adverse consequences for America's financial reporting system. A game that runs counter to the very principles behind our market's strength and success.

Increasingly, I have become concerned that the motivation to meet Wall Street earnings expectations may be overriding common sense business practices. Too many corporate managers, auditors, and analysts are participants in a game of nods and winks. In the zeal to satisfy consensus earnings estimates and project a smooth earnings path, wishful thinking may be winning the day over faithful representation.

As a result, I fear that we are witnessing an erosion in the quality of earnings, and therefore, the quality of financial reporting. Managing may be giving way to manipulation; integrity may be losing out to illusion.

Many in corporate America are just as frustrated and concerned about this trend as we, at the SEC, are. They know how difficult it is to hold the line on good practices when their competitors operate in the gray area between legitimacy and outright fraud.

A gray area where the accounting is being perverted; where managers are cutting corners; and, where earnings reports reflect the desires of management rather than the underlying financial performance of the company.

[I] want to talk about why integrity in financial reporting is under stress and explore five of the more common accounting gimmicks we've been seeing. Finally, I will outline a framework for a financial community response to this situation.

This necessary response involves improving both our accounting and disclosure rules, as well as the oversight and function of outside auditors and board audit committees. I am also calling upon a broad spectrum of capital market participants, from corporate management to Wall Street analysts to investors, to stand together and re-energize the touchstone of our financial reporting system: transparency and comparability.

This is a financial community problem. It can't be solved by a government mandate: it demands a financial community response.

THE ROLE OF FINANCIAL REPORTING IN OUR ECONOMY

Today, America's capital markets are the envy of the world. Our efficiency, liquidity and resiliency stand second to none. Our position, no doubt, has benefited from the opportunity and potential of the global economy. At the same time, however, this increasing interconnectedness has made us more susceptible to economic and financial weakness half a world away.

The significance of transparent, timely and reliable financial statements and its importance to investor protection has never been more apparent. The current financial situations in Asia and Russia are stark examples of this new reality. These markets are learning a painful lesson taught many times before: investors panic as a result of unexpected or unquantifiable bad news.

If a company fails to provide meaningful disclosure to investors about where it has been, where it is and where it is going, a damaging pattern ensues. The bond between shareholders and the company is shaken; investors grow anxious; prices fluctuate for no discernible reasons; and the trust that is the bedrock of our capital markets is severely tested.

THE PRESSURE TO "MAKE YOUR NUMBERS"

While the problem of earnings management is not new, it has swelled in a market that is unforgiving of companies that miss their estimates. I recently read of one major U.S. company, that failed to meet its so-called "numbers" by one penny, and lost more than six percent of its stock value in one day.

I believe that almost everyone in the financial community shares responsibility for fostering a climate in which earnings management is on the rise and the quality of financial reporting is on the decline. Corporate management isn't operating in a vacuum. In fact, the different pressures and expectations placed by, and on, various participants in the financial community appear to be almost self-perpetuating.

This is the pattern earnings management creates: companies try to meet or beat Wall Street earnings projections in order to grow market capitalization and increase the value of stock options. Their ability to do this depends on achieving the earnings expectations of analysts. And analysts seek constant guidance from companies to frame those expectations. Auditors, who want to retain their clients, are under pressure not to stand in the way.

ACCOUNTING HOCUS-POCUS

Our accounting principles weren't meant to be a straitjacket. Accountants are wise enough to know they cannot anticipate every business structure, or every new and innovative transaction, so they develop principles that allow for flexibility to adapt to changing circumstances. That's why the highest standards of objectivity, integrity and judgment can't be the exception. They must be the rule.

Flexibility in accounting allows it to keep pace with business innovations. Abuses such as earnings management occur when people exploit this pliancy. Trickery is employed to obscure actual financial volatility. This, in turn, masks the true consequences of management's decisions. These practices aren't limited to smaller companies struggling to gain investor interest. It's also happening in companies whose products we know and admire.

So what are these illusions? Five of the more popular ones I want to discuss today are "big bath" restructuring charges, creative acquisition accounting, "cookie jar reserves," "immaterial" misapplications of accounting principles, and the premature recognition of revenue.

"Big Bath" Charges

Let me first deal with "Big Bath" restructuring charges.

Companies remain competitive by regularly assessing the efficiency and profitability of their operations. Problems arise, however, when we see large charges associated with companies restructuring. These charges help companies "clean up" their balance sheet--giving them a so-called "big bath."

Why are companies tempted to overstate these charges? When earnings take a major hit, the theory goes, Wall Street will look beyond a one-time loss and focus only on future earnings.

And if these charges are conservatively estimated with a little extra cushioning, that so-called conservative estimate is miraculously reborn as income when estimates change or future earnings fall short.

When a company decides to restructure, management and employees, investors and creditors, customers and suppliers all want to understand the expected effects. We need, of course, to ensure that financial reporting provides this information. But this should not lead to flushing all the associated costs--and maybe a little extra--through the financial statements.

Creative Acquisition Accounting

Let me turn now to the second gimmick.

In recent years, whole industries have been remade through consolidations, acquisitions and spin-offs. Some acquirers, particularly those using stock as an acquisition currency, have used this environment as an opportunity to engage in another form of "creative" accounting. I call it "merger magic."

* * *

So what do [these acquirers] do? They classify an ever-growing portion of the acquisition price as "in-process" Research and Development, so--you guessed it--the amount can be written off in a "one-time" charge--removing any future earnings drag. Equally troubling is the creation of large liabilities for future operating expenses to protect future earnings--all under the mask of an acquisition.

Miscellaneous "Cookie Jar Reserves"

A third illusion played by some companies is using unrealistic assumptions to estimate liabilities for such items as sales returns, loan losses or warranty costs. In doing so, they stash accruals in cookie jars during the good times and reach into them when needed in the bad times.

I'm reminded of one U.S. company who took a large one-time loss to earnings to reimburse franchisees for equipment. That equipment, however, which included literally the kitchen sink, had yet to be bought. And, at the same time, they announced that future earnings would grow an impressive 15 percent per year.

"Materiality"

Let me turn now to the fourth gimmick--the abuse of materiality--a word that captures the attention of both attorneys and accountants. Materiality is another way we build flexibility into financial reporting. Using the logic of diminishing returns, some items may be so insignificant that they are not worth measuring and reporting with exact precision.

But some companies misuse the concept of materiality. They intentionally record errors within a defined percentage ceiling. They then try to excuse that fib by arguing that the effect on the bottom line is too small to matter. If that's the case, why do they work so hard to create these errors? Maybe because the effect can matter, especially if it picks up that last penny of the consensus estimate. When either management or the outside auditors are questioned about these clear violations of GAAP, they answer sheepishly[:] "It doesn't matter. It's immaterial."

In markets where missing an earnings projection by a penny can result in a loss of millions of dollars in market capitalization, I have a hard time accepting that some of these so-called non-events simply don't matter.

Revenue Recognition

Lastly, companies try to boost earnings by manipulating the recognition of revenue. Think about a bottle of fine wine. You wouldn't pop the cork on that bottle before it was ready. But some companies are doing this with their revenue--recognizing it before a sale is complete, before the product is delivered to a customer, or at a time when the customer still has options to terminate, void or delay the sale.

ACTION PLAN

Since U.S. capital market supremacy is based on the reliability and transparency of financial statements, this is a financial community problem that calls for timely financial community action.

Therefore, I am calling for immediate and coordinated action: technical rule changes by the regulators and standard setters to improve the transparency of financial statements; enhanced oversight of the financial reporting process by those entrusted as the shareholders' guardians; and nothing less than a fundamental cultural change on the part of corporate management as well as the whole financial community.

This action plan represents a cooperative public-private sector effort. It is essential that we work together to assure credibility and transparency. Our nine-point program calls for both regulators and the regulated to not only maintain, but increase public confidence which has made our markets the envy of the world. I believe this problem calls for immediate action that includes the following specific steps:

Improving the Accounting Framework

First, I have instructed the SEC staff to require well-detailed disclosures about the impact of changes in accounting assumptions. This should include a supplement to the financial statement showing beginning and ending balances as well as activity in between, including any adjustments. This will, I believe, enable the market to better understand the nature and effects of the restructuring liabilities and other loss accruals.

Second, we are challenging the profession, through the AICPA, to clarify the ground rules for auditing of purchased R&D. We also are requesting that they augment existing guidance on restructurings, large acquisition write-offs, and revenue recognition practices. It's time for the accounting profession to better qualify for auditors what's acceptable and what's not.

Third, I reject the notion that the concept of materiality can be used to excuse deliberate misstatements of performance. I know of one Fortune 500 company who had recorded a significant accounting error, and whose auditors told them so. But they still used a materiality ceiling of six percent of earnings to justify the error. I have asked the SEC staff to focus on this problem and publish guidance that emphasizes the need to consider qualitative, not just quantitative factors of earnings. Materiality is not a bright line cutoff of three or five percent. It requires consideration of all relevant factors that could impact an investor's decision.

Fourth, SEC staff will immediately consider interpretive accounting guidance on the do's and don'ts of revenue recognition. The staff will also determine whether recently published standards for the software industry can be applied to other service companies.

Fifth, I am asking private sector standard setters to take action where current standards and guidance are inadequate. I encourage a prompt resolution of the FASB's projects, currently underway, that should bring greater clarity to the definition of a liability.

Sixth, the SEC's review and enforcement teams will reinforce these regulatory initiatives. We will formally target reviews of public companies that announce restructuring liability reserves, major write-offs or other practices that appear to manage earnings. Likewise, our enforcement team will continue to root out and aggressively act on abuses of the financial reporting process.

Improved Outside Auditing in the Financial Reporting Process

Seventh, I don't think it should surprise anyone here that recent headlines of accounting failures have led some people to question the thoroughness of audits. I need not remind auditors they are the public's watchdog in the financial reporting process. We rely on auditors to put something like the good housekeeping seal of approval on the information investors receive. The integrity of that information must take priority over a desire for cost efficiencies or competitive advantage in the audit process. High quality auditing requires well-trained, well-focused and well-supervised auditors.

As I look at some of the failures today, I can't help but wonder if the staff in the trenches of the profession have the training and supervision they need to ensure that audits are being done right. We cannot permit thorough audits to be sacrificed for re-engineered approaches that are efficient, but less effective. I have just proposed that the Public Oversight Board form a group of all the major constituencies to review the way audits are performed and assess the impact of recent trends on the public interest.

Strengthening the Audit Committee Process

And, finally, qualified, committed, independent and tough-minded audit committees represent the most reliable guardians of the public interest. Sadly, stories abound of audit committees whose members lack expertise in the basic principles of financial reporting as well as the mandate to ask probing questions. In fact, I've heard of one audit committee that convenes only twice a year before the regular board meeting for 15 minutes and whose duties are limited to a perfunctory presentation.

Compare that situation with the audit committee which meets twelve times a year before each board meeting; where every member has a financial background; where there are no personal ties to the chairman or the company; where they have their own advisers; where they ask tough questions of management and outside auditors; and where, ultimately, the investor interest is being served.

The SEC stands ready to take appropriate action if that interest is not protected. But, a private sector response that empowers audit committees and obviates the need for public sector dictates seems the wisest choice. I am pleased to announce that the financial community has agreed to accept this challenge.

As part eight of this comprehensive effort to address earnings management, the New York Stock Exchange and the National Association of Securities Dealers have agreed to sponsor a "blue-ribbon" panel to be headed by John Whitehead, former Deputy Secretary of State and retired senior partner of Goldman, Sachs, and Ira Millstein, a lawyer and noted corporate governance expert. Within the next 90 days, this distinguished group will develop a series of far-ranging recommendations intended to empower audit committees [to] function as the ultimate guardian of investor interests and corporate accountability. They are going to examine how we can get the right people to do the right things and ask the right questions.

Need for a Cultural Change

Finally, I'm challenging corporate management and Wall Street to re-examine our current environment. I believe we need to embrace nothing less than a cultural change. For corporate managers, remember, the integrity of the numbers in the financial reporting system is directly related to the long-term interests of a corporation. While the temptations are great, and the pressures strong, illusions in numbers are only that--ephemeral, and ultimately self-destructive.

To Wall Street, I say, look beyond the latest quarter. Punish those who rely on deception, rather than the practice of openness and transparency.

CONCLUSION

Some may conclude that this debate is nothing more than an argument over numbers and legalistic terms. I couldn't disagree more. * * *

Our mandate and our obligations are clear. We must rededicate ourselves to a fundamental principle: markets exist through the grace of investors.

Today, American markets enjoy the confidence of the world. How many half-truths, and how much accounting sleight-of-hand, will it take to tarnish that faith?

As a former businessman, I experienced all kinds of markets, dealt with a variety of trends, fads, fears, and irrational exuberances. I learned that some habits die hard. But, more than anything else, I learned that progress doesn't happen overnight and it's not sustained through short cuts or obfuscation. It's induced, rather, by asking hard questions and accepting difficult answers.

For the sake of our markets; for the sake of a globalized economy which depends so much on the reliability of America's financial system; for the sake of investors; and for the sake of a larger commitment not only to each other, but to ourselves, I ask that we join together to reinforce the values that have guided our capital markets to unparalleled supremacy. Together, through vigilance and trust, I know, we can succeed.

NOTES

1. Chapter IX reviews "big bath" changes and creative acquisition accounting in more detail, while "cookie jar reserves" and revenue recognition will be discussed further in this chapter.

2. In a recent *Business Week* survey of chief financial officers, twelve percent admitted that "they had 'misrepresented corporate financial results' at the request of senior company executives," while fifty-five percent responded that "they had been asked to do so but 'fought off' the demand."

3. Accountants sometimes classify actions to manage earnings into two types: those which involve changing accounting methods and those which involve operating decisions. Adjusting the reserve, or the amount the enterprise has accrued as an expense to satisfy a contingency, illustrates a change in accounting method. In contrast, offering special terms to customers at year-end in an attempt to accelerate into the current accounting period sales which would normally not occur until the next accounting period exemplifies an operating decision.

4. As its most visible actions during the period beginning shortly before Chairman Levitt's speech and continuing to the present, the SEC has brought well-publicized enforcement actions against at least three registrants and their high-ranking officers for managing earnings.

About three months before the speech, the SEC moved against Venator Group, Inc., formerly known as Woolworth Corporation ("Woolworth"), and four former officers at Woolworth and two of its major subsidiaries, charging they engaged in a scheme to inflate the company's reported earnings by understating cost of sales and improperly deferring certain operating expenses that the subsidiaries incurred in the first two quarters of the company's 1993 fiscal year. This fraudulent conduct enabled Woolworth to report a profit for each of the first two quarters. The former officers then adjusted results in the third and fourth quarters, so that the company could report accurate results by year-end, when the outside auditor examined the company's financial statements.

Less than three months after Chairman Levitt's speech, the SEC brought action against W.R. Grace & Co. ("Grace") and seven former executives, including the company's former president and chief financial officer, for falsely reporting operating results between 1991 and 1995 by deferring income to smooth earnings. Rather than report the income, the company allegedly established reserves that did not conform with GAAP and then used those reserves to manipulate quarterly and annual earnings

In 1999, the SEC instituted public administrative proceedings against Terex Corporation, its former chairman, and an affiliate, for overstating Terex's pre-tax earnings by at least $77.3 million in its 1989-91 annual and quarterly reports, by improperly excluding losses from certain subsidiaries and using undisclosed reserves the company had previously established.

In late 1999, SEC Enforcement Director Richard Walker told attendees at the AICPA's annual National Conference on Current SEC Developments that the SEC plans to criminally prosecute those individuals that manage earnings. He stated: "We are turning the numbers game into a Monopoly game. That is, cook the books and you will go directly to jail."

5. The SEC continues to oversee the financial community's efforts to improve financial accounting and reporting and to work on initiatives related to the agency's agenda to curb "earnings management." The SEC has issued proposed rules to specify the discolsures that registrants must provide concerning changes in valuation and loss accrual accounts. Supplementary Financial Information, 65 Fed. Reg. 4585 (2000) (proposed Jan. 31, 2000). The SEC staff has also published a number of staff accounting bulletins on materiality, restructuring charges, and revenue recognition, while exhibiting concern about several other issues, including asset write-downs, restructuring activities, charges related to acquired research and development, and provisions for bad loans and other uncollectible accounts.

In January, 1999 the AICPA issued new guidance on revenue recognition, having earlier established a special working group on in-process research and development. Meanwhile, the FASB's agenda includes rulemaking projects on those obligations that require an enterprise to recognize a liability, especially obligations arising from the retirement of long-lived assets, and impairment and asset disposal issues.

1. A BONA FIDE EXCHANGE TRANSACTION WITH AN OUTSIDER

Returning to the first of the requirements for revenue recognition, that there be an exchange transaction, it must be observed that financial statement users do not view all exchange transactions equally. Just as a professor's letter of recommendation probably assesses your skills more objectively than a letter from your grandmother, exchange transactions between unrelated parties determine revenue more objectively than sales between related parties. Therefore, financial statement users prefer to rely upon transactions between unrelated parties to measure current revenue and to predict future revenue. Accountants and lawyers commonly use the term *arms-length* to describe transactions between unrelated parties, and they know that if the parties are related the transaction may provide little evidence of what would occur at arms length.

a. IN GENERAL

Perhaps the most often mentioned requirement of GAAP for recognition of revenue is the existence of a completed transaction. A simple analogy may help illustrate why. Imagine that you compile a brilliant law school survival guide. Because it leads to excellent grades, you want to "share" your masterpiece with your classmates. Although generous by nature, you need cash more than gratitude, and decide to sell the survival guides for ten dollars each rather than give them away. Reasoning that at least 4,800 law students nationwide seek excellent grades each year, you recognize $4,000 [(4,800 guides times $10 per guide) divided by 12 months] in revenue for the first month, say January, and head to the bank to finance the Porsche that you have dreamed about since your sixteenth birthday. However, the loan officer would not be very impressed when she learns that you have not actually sold any survival guides yet. As she shreds your loan application, she explains that the bank cannot afford to share in your optimism. Until law students actually buy the survival guide, the loan officer cannot verify that you can sell 400 survival guides each month at ten dollars each. According to the objectivity principle and conservatism, you are permitted to recognize revenue only as you sell each survival guide.

As an *a fortiori* application of the arms-length principal, it is also important that the transaction be "external", that is, the mutual transfers of value should be between separate persons or enterprises. Therefore, transferring materials between the purchasing division and the manufacturing division of a single enterprise would not qualify. For this reason, the SEC instituted cease-and-desist proceedings against a registrant which recognized revenue when the company shipped equipment to its field representatives: there was no external transaction until the equipment was sold and shipped to a customer.

And, of course, an external transaction with an unrelated party, i.e., at arms-length, makes it more likely that the amount of a cash equivalent, like a promise to pay, transferred by the buyer represents the market value for the underlying services, goods, or other assets. Until the enterprise actually sells the goods in a market transaction, accountants cannot verify the goods' market value and, therefore, cannot determine the amount that the enterprise should recognize as revenue. "Solid" external, arms-length, exchange transactions help to minimize the risk that an enterprise will recognize income prematurely or otherwise overstate revenue.

b. SHAMS

Unfortunately, here as in other contexts (notably tax), appearances may belie the true substance. In particular, a transaction can be made to appear to qualify as a bona fide exchange with an outsider, when upon closer examination it is clear that the parties have not transferred the risks that usually accompany ownership. Thus, in In re Reliance Group Holdings, Inc., 1991-1995 Fed. Sec. L. Rep (CCH) ¶73,989 (SEC 1994), a major insurance company, Reliance, owned some appreciated debt securities on which the company wanted to recognize gain to avoid showing an overall loss for the current quarter. However, at the same time the officer in charge of fixed income securities did not want to give up the company's investment in these bonds. Accordingly, a deal was worked out with a salesman at Reliance's regular brokerage firm under which the broker-dealer would purchase the bonds, and then 31 days later would sell them back to Reliance, in effect (though not in form) for the same price. The broker-dealer would receive a specified fee for this service. The SEC condemned Reliance's recognition of gain on the transaction, stating that in order to recognize revenue, an exchange transaction must take place which transfers the risks and rewards of ownership, and that never happened here.

The following case further illustrates circumstances where economic substance prevents an enterprise from recognizing income even though the transaction's form resembles a "sale."

Lincoln Savings & Loan Association v. Wall

United States District Court, District of Columbia, 1990.
743 F.Supp. 901

■ SPORKIN, DISTRICT JUDGE.

In this consolidated action, plaintiffs American Continental Corporation and Lincoln Savings and Loan Association seek to regain operational control of Lincoln Savings and Loan Association. Plaintiff American Continental Corporation ("ACC") is an Ohio corporation with its principal place of business in Phoenix, Arizona. Plaintiff Lincoln Savings and Loan Association ("Lincoln") is a California corporation chartered as a savings and loan institution by the State of California Department of Savings and Loans. Lincoln is a wholly owned subsidiary of ACC. The deposits in Lincoln were insured by the Federal Savings and Loan Insurance Corporation ("FSLIC"). Defendant Office of Thrift Supervision is the successor agency of the Federal Home Loan Bank Board ("FHLBB" or "Bank Board"). On April 14, 1989, the Bank Board pursuant to its statutory authority appointed a conservator to take over the management of Lincoln. * * *

I. BACKGROUND

* * *

Plaintiffs here contend that they at all times managed and operated Lincoln on a sound financial basis. Plaintiffs allege that defendant was not justified in seeking and obtaining their removal from control of Lincoln which was effectuated by the Bank Board's appointment of a conservator * * * for Lincoln. Plaintiffs claim that the Bank Board's actions were arbitrary and capricious and that these actions were so ill founded that they precipitated Lincoln's severe financial crisis.

* * * It is defendant's contention that plaintiffs engaged in numerous unsafe and unsound banking practices and that as a result of these and other improper practices there had been a substantial dissipation of the thrift's assets. The Bank Board asserts that it was these practices that led to Lincoln's downfall.

In the post-deprivation hearing conducted before this Court, the Board justified its actions by introducing proof on a number of specific transactions which it claims fully sustain its position. Plaintiffs have countered by alleging that the transactions enumerated were perfectly proper and have introduced expert testimony to demonstrate the accounting treatment afforded these transactions fully conformed with all the professional norms that existed at the time the transactions were effected. Plaintiffs also introduced evidence from their independent auditors which plaintiffs claim fully support the accounting treatment taken.

* * *

III. DISCUSSION

* * *

Before examining the specific transactions that were the subject of the evidentiary hearing, some background discussion is necessary. It is quite clear that the thrift industry has had a number of problems over the past two decades. In the 1970s, the limits that were placed on both the borrowing and investing activities of thrifts drove a number of savings and loan associations into financial difficulty. First, because of limits on the amount of interest thrifts could pay to investors, savings and loans became noncompetitive with other financial institutions. This resulted in Congress' removing the interest rate ceiling that limited the rate that thrifts could pay to the savings public. Later when Congress learned that the thrifts continued to face severe financial problems, it enacted certain deregulatory measures to provide additional investment opportunities for thrifts, aside from the traditional one of financing the purchase of single family homes. With the number of thrifts facing financial difficulties, Congress believed that it could stave off bailing out the thrift industry of its financial problems by deregulating it and thereby inducing investors to pour private funds into sick thrifts. Congress chose this tack to avoid having to bail out the industry with taxpayers' money. . . . As will later be seen by what happened with Lincoln, the privatization gambit failed miserably and today . . . the magnitude of the S & L debacle is probably 5 to 10 [times what it would have been]. * * *

Charles Keating, Jr., ("Keating"), the chairman and chief executive officer of ACC, was one of those entrepreneurs who was willing to enter the S & L industry once Congress lessened the regulatory restrictions. . . . [In 1976 he acquired] American Continental Corporation ("ACC"). Keating moved the company to Phoenix, Arizona and continued to focus its operations on single-family home construction and development. When Keating first took over the company, it was in a loss posture. Over the years, Keating was able to turn it around to where it was moderately successful. In the late 1970s and early 1980s, ACC became very active in building large single-family housing developments in Phoenix and Denver. In addition to the actual construction of homes, ACC started a mortgage company in 1978 to assist home buyers with financing. Building on this experience, in 1981, ACC created a system for packaging and selling groups of single family home mortgages—the investment instrument became known as mortgaged backed securities.

Toxic Loans

With the passage of the [new federal legislation in 1980 and 1982], Keating decided to look for a savings and loan association to add to his real estate empire. After analyzing various thrifts that were for sale, Keating decided to see if Lincoln Savings & Loan could be acquired. Keating was attracted to Lincoln for three primary reasons 1) he was impressed with its fine reputation in the industry; 2) the controlling block of Lincoln's stock was owned by one family; and 3) Lincoln was a California chartered savings and loan. According to Keating's testimony, this accumulation of stock in the hands of one family would make Lincoln easier to acquire if the family was interested in selling. The fact that Lincoln had a California State Charter attracted Keating because the California legislature had embarked on a course aimed at deregulating the state's thrift industry in 1982 with the passage of the Nolan Act. By removing restrictions that had previously been in place, the Nolan Act further broadened the field of direct investments that California savings and loans would be permitted to make.

Although Lincoln had not been formally offered for sale, it had been losing money and the principal owners agreed to entertain an offer from ACC. After a short negotiating period, ACC agreed to acquire Lincoln for $51 million, which represented a premium of some $17 million over the institution[']s net worth of $34 million. ACC closed the Lincoln acquisition on February 24, 1984. The financing was provided through the issuance and sale in December of 1983 of approximately $55 million in exchangeable preferred stock. This preferred stock issue was underwritten by Drexel, Burnham, Lambert, which had previously underwritten for ACC a high yield debt offering of $125 million in August of 1983.

At the time Lincoln was acquired, it was conducting a traditional savings and loan business. It was largely in the business of lending money to purchasers of single family dwelling units in Southern California. While its business was conservative, it was not thriving financially. At the time of the acquisition, Lincoln had assets of approximately $1 billion and a net worth of $34 million. When ACC took over, it was required to and did obtain approval of both the California and Federal thrift regulators. In the change of control application that ACC filed with the federal regulators prior to its acquisition of Lincoln, it stated that "While it is anticipated that the current officers of the Holding Company and the Institution [Lincoln] will remain upon consummation of the proposed transaction, the Applicant [ACC] intends to augment this management team." ACC also reaffirmed its commitment to maintain Lincoln's current level of community lending * * *.

These commitments, however, were short lived. Once ACC was given approval, it deviated from its original plan. Contrary to ACC's representations to the federal regulators that it would retain existing management, the former management team was soon replaced by ACC officials. Although virtually all of Lincoln's pre-acquisition activities had been conducted in the Los Angeles and surrounding areas, after its sale a good portion of Lincoln's business was transferred to Phoenix, Arizona, ACC's home base. Indeed, by 1986, most of Lincoln's operations were conducted out of a newly-constructed Phoenix office, which was located next to ACC corporate offices in downtown Phoenix.

After the acquisition, the mix of Lincoln's business also changed. Lincoln cut back drastically on its single-family mortgages and it began to make all kinds of non-real estate investments. It made direct investments in equity securities and also included "high yield-high risk" bonds in its investment portfolio. It took equity participations in emerging new businesses and made a number of high risk loans to individuals engaged in speculative endeavors. While ACC employed many lawyers, accountants, and other professionals to watch over and handle Lincoln's investments, an inordinate amount of business was originated by Keating himself. This was so even though Keating held no official position with Lincoln. Numerous multi-million dollar deals were negotiated by Keating personally with ACC's staff of professionals left to work out the precise details.

Although when ACC took over Lincoln its expectations were that it would be able to operate in a business environment that would not unduly limit the kinds of investments it could make, this deregulatory environment soon changed. In May 1984, approximately three months after ACC acquired Lincoln, the Bank Board proposed new rules aimed at restricting direct investments by savings and loan institutions. After notice and comment, a final rule was adopted on January 31, 1985 (hereinafter "Direct Investment Regulation").

The Direct Investment Regulation, among other things, . . . imposed a ceiling—equal to the greater of 10% of the institution's assets or twice the institution[']s "regulatory net worth"—on the amount of such investments. The Board adopted this rule because it was convinced that the deregulatory environment that was in existence . . . would be disastrous to the thrift industry and could place in jeopardy the insurance fund that backed individual savings accounts up to $100,000 per account.

* * *

The Bank Board's case is fairly straightforward. It asserts that Lincoln engaged in a number of imprudent transactions in order to improperly upstream monies to ACC, its parent, which was experiencing financial difficulties.

* * *

B. The Wescon Transaction

One of Lincoln's direct investments involved the development of 20,000 acres of land outside Phoenix known as the Estrella Project. The most remote part of the project, the southern half, consists of some 8500 acres and is referred to as Hidden Valley.

The evidence shows that on March 31, 1987, a Lincoln subsidiary sold 1000 acres of raw land in Hidden Valley to a company called West Continental Mortgage and Investment Corporation (Wescon). The terms of the sale involved a cash down payment of $3.5 million, along with a non-recourse note for the balance of $10.5 million for a total sales price of $14 million.

Since Lincoln's pro rata cost of the property sold was only $3 million, it was able to book a gain of $11 million along with $250,000 in accrued interest. * * *

Wescon never made a payment against the balance on the outstanding note. Wescon was a company of little means. It had a net worth of only $31,000, and it really had no intention of developing the property. Fernando Acosta, the President of Wescon, was quite blunt in his testimony at the hearing. He stated that his company was acting only as a "straw" for Mr. Garcia, the head of E.C. Garcia & Company. Indeed, when Wescon was being pressed to fulfill its obligations under the transaction, Acosta went to Garcia who agreed to assume Wescon's obligation under the agreement but, like Wescon, made no payments to Lincoln.

It is clear, and this Court finds, that the sole reason for the Wescon transaction was to enable the ACC complex to record an $11 million profit * * *. ACC justifies its action by stating that certain arcane accounting provisions allowed it to book the $11 million profit. Indeed a great deal of testimony at the trial was devoted to the propriety of the accounting treatment of this and a number of Lincoln's other profit-recording transactions. If ACC, its accountants and experts are correct, that $11 million can be booked as profit from this transaction * * *, then the system of accounting that exists in the United States is in a sorry state. Here we have a sham transaction from the start with the identity of the real party in interest being shielded from those who must exercise appropriate oversight of the transaction. Because of the use of a straw buyer the accounting audit trail does not disclose all the salient points associated with the transaction.

According to the appraisal obtained by Lincoln, the appraised value of the property was only $9 million, or some $5 million under the designated sales price. The purported buyer was woefully underfinanced and on the basis of its financial statements unable to repay its loan or even service the debt. Since under the terms of the transaction the seller had no recourse against the buyer for the unpaid balance of the debt and since the pay downs on the debt were to be made on a deferred basis, it is clear the seller was not looking for the debt to be repaid in any realistic time frame.

Of particular importance as to this aspect of the transaction was the fact that the actual 25% down payment ($3.5 million) emanated from a loan E.C. Garcia made to Wescon. This meant that Wescon had not invested a single dollar of its own money in the transaction. Moreover, when the entire series of transactions between the Garcia and ACC complex of companies is reviewed, it emerges that in fact the money for the down payment actually emanated from Lincoln itself. The Garcia stable of companies was a heavy borrower from Lincoln. Indeed, at about the time of the Wescon transaction approximately $30 million in loans were being finalized between the Garcia companies and Lincoln. It is also clear from the record that E.C. Garcia was really not interested in buying the Hidden Valley parcel, but was doing so because he did not want to jeopardize a loan of over $20 million he was in the process of obtaining from Lincoln that was going to be used in a transaction that was extremely important to Garcia. It is more than a coincidence that this $20–million loan from Lincoln to Garcia closed on the same day as the $14.5 million sale of the property to Wescon was concluded.

A review of the Wescon transaction demonstrates the booking of an $11 million profit by Lincoln * * *, even though when reviewed in the light most favorable to plaintiffs, Lincoln only received cash of $3.5 million. [In addition,] Lincoln itself was the indirect source of the $3.5 million Wescon down payment.

* * * The Court was quite surprised by [ACC's accounting] experts' rationalization which supported plaintiffs' position as to the appropriate accounting for this transaction. To be generous to the position expounded by plaintiffs' experts, the Court will attribute the position they took to the abstract application of accounting principles.

What it is hoped the accounting profession will learn from this case is that an accountant must not blindly apply accounting conventions without reviewing the transaction to determine whether it makes any economic sense and without first finding that the transaction is realistic and has economic substance that would justify the booking of the transaction that occurred. [Accountants must be particularly skeptical where a transaction has little or no economic substance. This is so despite the fact that the transaction might technically meet GAAP standards.] Moreover, they should be particularly skeptical of any transaction where the audit trail is woefully lacking and the audited entity has failed to comply with the record keeping requirements established by a federal regulatory body. * * *

IV. CONCLUSIONS OF LAW

Based upon the above findings, it is this Court's conclusions of law that the Bank Board acted appropriately in all respects in it * * * placing Lincoln in conservatorship * * *. * * * None of the Bank Board's material findings were arbitrary or capricious and accordingly the Court will enter judgment in favor of the Bank Board and dismiss plaintiffs' action in its entirety. Based upon the facts found by this Court, to return Lincoln to ACC, a defunct entity, would be the height of irresponsibility.

* * *

NOTES

1. Near the end of the opinion in the principal case, at 743 F. Supp. 918-20, appeared the following passage, which attracted considerable public attention and created an uproar in both the legal and accounting professions:

> There are other unanswered questions presented by this case. Keating testified that he was so bent on doing the "right thing" that he surrounded himself with literally scores of accountants and lawyers to make sure all the transactions were legal. The questions that must be asked are:

> Where were these professionals, a number of whom are now asserting their rights under the Fifth Amendment, when these clearly improper transactions were being consummated?

> Why didn't any of them speak up or disassociate themselves from the transactions?

> Where also were the outside accountants and attorneys when these transactions were effectuated?

> What is difficult to understand is that with all the professional talent involved (both accounting and legal), why at least one professional would not have blown the whistle to stop the overreaching that took place in this case.

> While we in this nation have been trying to place blame for the savings and loan crisis on the various governmental participants in the crisis and on the government's fostering of deregulation within the thrift industry, this Court believes far too little scrutiny has been focused on the private sector. * * *

Was Judge Sporkin unfairly criticizing members of the legal profession, having in mind that they owed a duty of loyalty to their client?

2. At least two prominent law firms have agreed to multimillion dollar settlements to resolve malpractice claims arising from their representation of Lincoln Savings & Loan Association, the nation's most famous failed thrift. In 1992, the New York law firm, Kaye, Scholer, agreed to pay $41 million, after federal regulators sought $275 million because the firm allegedly concealed damaging information about Lincoln. In a separate action, the Cleveland-based Jones, Day firm agreed to a $24 million settlement.

3. The number and scope of recent financial frauds invites a further look at the question Judge Sporkin rhetorically asked in the *Lincoln Savings and Loan* case: where were all the lawyers and why did they not speak up or blow the whistle to prevent or remedy the financial frauds? While the lawyers played diverse roles with varying degrees of involvement, investigators have found lawyers behind many of the recent corporate scandals. As an overview, we might divide lawyers' involvement into four broad categories.

First, some lawyers simply failed to recognize "red flags." even when whistle-blowers called the circumstances to their attention. For example, notwithstanding prior concerns about Enron's financial accounting and securities law disclosures, Vinson & Elkins LLP, Enron's principal outside law firm, concluded, after conducting only a limited inquiry, that Enron's former vice president Sherron Smith Watkin's famous memo warning of an "accounting scandal" neither raised serious alarms nor warranted a deeper investigation of financial fraud. *Limited Partners: Lawyers for Enron Faulted Its Deals, Didn't Force Issue*, WALL ST. J., May 22, 2002, at A1; *see also* Berman, *Global Crossing Board Report Rebukes Ex-Outside Counsel*, WALL ST. J., Mar. 11, 2003, at B9 (criticizing Simpson Thacher & Bartlet, Global Crossing's former outside law firm, for inadequately investigating a former employee's letter that questioned the company's multibillion dollar "capacity swaps" used to inflate revenues).

Second, when lawyers did recognize the "red Flags," they failed to express their concerns to the appropriate corporate officers or directors. Although Vinson & Elkins sometimes objected to Enron's dealings that posed conflict-of-interest concerns or disregarded Enron's best interests, the firm was content when lawyers from Enron's legal department and Andrew Fastow, Enron's chief financial officer, ignored the concerns or slightly modified the transaction to sidestep the particular concern; the law firm failed to inform Enron's general counsel or board of directors because it concluded there was no basis for such "extraordinary action."

Third, some lawyers passively facilitated, whether negligently or ignorantly, the corrupt executives with their fraudulent accounting schemes. *See e.g.,* WILLIAM C. POWERS, JR. ET AL., REPORT OF INVESTIGATION BY THE SPECIAL INVESTIGATIVE COMMITTEE OF THE BOARD OF DIRECTORS OF ENRON

CORP. 10(2002) (hereinafter "Powers"), *available* at
http://news.findlaw.com/hdocs/enron/sicreport/sicreport020102.pdf (finding
that Vinson & Elkins provided advice and drafted documents involving many
of the transactions with Enron's SPEs, including "true sales" opinion letters,
and assisted with Enron's disclosures of related-party transactions, and
concluding that the law firm failed to provide "objective and critical
professional advice").

Finally, as noted above, some lawyers have been found guilty of
knowingly and actively participating in various fraudulent accounting
schemes.

Here is another case of doubtful revenue recognition and other apparent
improprieties, and this time the auditor is the alleged villain:

Fine v. American Solar King Corp.

United States Court of Appeals, Fifth Circuit, 1990.
919 F.2d 290, *cert. dismissed* 502 U.S. 976, 112 S.Ct. 576, 116 L.Ed.2d 601 (1991).

■ KING, CIRCUIT JUDGE:
Plaintiffs-appellants (Plaintiffs) allege that the accounting firm of Main
Hurdman violated § 10(b) of the Securities Exchange Act of 1934 and Rule
10b–5 promulgated thereunder by issuing a materially false and misleading
qualified report on American Solar King's (ASK) financial statement for fiscal
year 1982. The district court * * * granted summary judgment in favor of
Main Hurdman. We reverse.

I. BACKGROUND

ASK manufactured collectors for the solar heating of water, and sold
groups of such collectors, with associated circulatory equipment and control
devices, through a network of distributors for use in the residential solar
energy market. In fiscal year 1982, ASK entered the industrial solar energy
market, which involved the sale of larger arrays of the same kind of solar
collectors to apartment complexes and other industrial users. Under ASK's
industrial sales program, the user did not actually buy the system but
guaranteed to pay for energy used, up to a maximum of eighty percent of
prior fuel costs. The system was sold to a tax-shelter, limited partnership.
The first sale was to S.E.P. No. 1 for use by a Wisconsin meat packer
(Provimi) and had a sale price of $1,750,000. The partnership paid for the
system with $20,000 cash, a short-term note for $905,000, and a long-term,
ten-year note at ten percent interest. ASK entered the transaction the day
prior to the end of its 1982 fiscal year.

In order to secure the Provimi sale in fiscal year 1982, ASK's own officers
and directors purchased about thirty-five percent of S.E.P. No. 1's
partnership interests. As a result of the Provimi sale, ASK recognized
$1,239,000 of revenue and $964,000 of profits from the Provimi transaction

in its 1982 financial statements. With this sale, ASK reported a profit for its fourth quarter and only a small loss for the year as a whole; without this sale, they would have reported a highly unprofitable year.

The Plaintiffs allege that ASK engaged in a fraudulent sch eme to overstate its financial statements for fiscal year 1982, and that the Plaintiffs purchased ASK's common stock at artificially inflated prices as a result. Specifically, the Plaintiffs allege that ASK's financial statement for fiscal year 1982 was false and misleading because it:

(1) Improperly recognized revenue from the Provimi sale;

(2) Failed to discount a below market-rate note received in payment for the Provimi system;

(3) Failed to reserve sufficient funds for uncollectible accounts; and

(4) Improperly recognized revenue from sales to Solar Heating, Inc. (Solar Heating), a company under ASK's control.

Main Hurdman violated § 10(b) and Rule 10b–5, the Plaintiffs allege, by issuing a materially false auditor's opinion on ASK's inflated 1982 financial statements. They claim that Main Hurdman's opinion was materially false because:

(1) Main Hurdman incorrectly represented, subject to qualification, that ASK's 1982 financial statements were prepared in conformity with Generally Accepted Accounting Principles (GAAP);

(2) Main Hurdman falsely qualified its opinion by stating that it was "unable to determine the adequacy of the provision for uncollectible accounts," when it knew that the provision for uncollectible accounts was inadequate by at least $200,000 to $300,000; and

(3) Main Hurdman falsely stated that it conducted its audit in accordance with Generally Accepted Auditing Standards (GAAS).

* * *

II. MAIN HURDMAN'S LIABILITY AS A PRIMARY VIOLATOR

* * *

The Plaintiffs allege that Main Hurdman acted with intent to deceive, or severe recklessness, when it issued its qualified auditor's report on ASK's financial statements for fiscal year 1982. Main Hurdman, they argue, knew that ASK improperly recognized revenue from the Provimi sale and from sales to Solar Heating, a company that ASK controlled. They allege that Main Hurdman approved the accounting for these sales in order to benefit certain of Main Hurdman's clients who invested in S.E.P. No. 1 and in order to keep ASK as a client. The Plaintiffs also argue that Main Hurdman knew that its qualification of its report, which stated that Main Hurdman could not determine the adequacy of ASK's reserve for uncollectible accounts, was false because ASK knew that the reserve was inadequate by at least $200,000 to $300,000.

The Plaintiffs observe that Main Hurdman examined the Provimi transaction both before and during their audit. A Main Hurdman planning memo stated:

> This transaction must be looked at closely to determine if it was indeed a sale, if the notes carried by ASK are at fair values or if any related parties are involved.... Due to small anticipated net income per books we need to be concerned that the client has done anything possible to record income.

The Plaintiffs argue that, despite these reservations, Main Hurdman approved ASK's accounting for the Provimi sale and that Main Hurdman knew, or should have known, that ASK's accounting for the Provimi sale violated GAAP.

The Plaintiffs' expert testified that revenue may be recognized under GAAP only when the earnings process is virtually complete and an exchange has taken place. At the end of ASK's fiscal year, however, the Provimi system had not yet been constructed or shipped to the buyer and ASK retained material maintenance and warranty obligations. GAAP also provides that revenue should not be recognized when the seller retains material obligations, or if uncertainties exist with respect to the sale. Significant uncertainties existed, the Plaintiffs' expert opined, concerning whether ASK could install the system by the end of the year as required by their contract.

GAAP also provides that the profit on a sale should not be recognized if collection of the sale price is not reasonably assured. The Plaintiffs argue that Main Hurdman knew that the transaction required completion of a working system, and also knew that the solar panels themselves had not been shipped by ASK to S.E.P. No. 1 or Provimi at year end. Main Hurdman also was aware, the Plaintiffs assert, that interest and principal on the ten-year note was to be paid from payments by Provimi for the energy actually used and would negatively amortize if such payments were inadequate. No evidence existed, the Plaintiffs argue, that the system would ever generate energy sufficient to make the payments on this note. Nor could ASK have been reasonably assured that the individual partners would be able to make up any shortfall on the note after ten or more years.

Main Hurdman argues that ASK's recognition of the Provimi sale conformed with GAAP and that Main Hurdman's conduct negated any intent to deceive. They observe that ASK disclosed the facts concerning the Provimi sale in its 1982 financial statements. They also note that Main Hurdman indicated that the sale, as originally structured, could not be recognized in fiscal year 1982. ASK restructured the sale's terms to include full transfer of title to the solar equipment, and transfer of risk of loss, delay, and other matters during the installation process, to the purchaser by the end of the fiscal year. Subsequent installation was to be supervised by ASK as agent for, and at the risk of, the purchaser. Main Hurdman also presented evidence that S.E.P. No. 1 paid for an uninstalled system and that the cost of installation was not recognized in 1982. Collection of th e notes, Main Hurdman argues, was reasonably assured because they were secured by the solar energy equipment, by the personal worth of S.E.P. No. 1's general partner, and by the individual partner's notes, due unconditionally, for their pro rata share.

The Plaintiffs also allege that ASK's accounting for the long-term note violated GAAP. GAAP requires the evaluation of the reasonableness of the interest rate on a note that is received as consideration for the sale of goods. If the note bears an unreasonably low interest rate, the purchase price must be deemed to include a portion of the interest and the actual face amount of the note must be discounted. The long-term note carried a ten percent rate of interest at a time when the prime rate was fifteen and one-half percent. The Plaintiffs argue that because S.E.P. No. 1 had no credit history, and no assets or security, it could not have obtained even a prime rate loan in the open market. The Plaintiffs argue that Main Hurdman knew, therefore, that the ten-percent rate was below market and was prima facie unreasonable.

Main Hurdman argues that the terms of the note were disclosed in ASK's financial statement and that it determined that the interest rate was reasonable because rates had been falling sharply during the year before the note was executed and were expected to continue to decline. The Plaintiffs, on the other hand, observe that Accounting Principles Board Opinion No. 21 specifically provides that considerations of subsequent changes to interest rates are to be ignored and the interest rate must be evaluated at the time the note is issued.

The Plaintiffs also allege that ASK inflated its revenue for fiscal year 1982 by entering into improper transactions with Solar Heating. Solar Heating had been a large customer of ASK, but could not pay for goods previously purchased. ASK acquired irrevocable proxies for all of Solar Heating's stock, replaced the company's directors and officers with officers of ASK, and continued to sell to Solar Heating. The Plaintiffs assert that a combined financial statement should have been issued for Solar Heating and ASK and that the intercompany sales should have been eliminated from ASK's financial statements. Even if a combined statement was not required, the Plaintiffs argue, a significant reserve should have been set aside for the possibility that Solar Heating might never make payment.

Main Hurdman argues that it determined that the control of Solar Heating was likely to be temporary and that GAAP does not require consolidation of financial statements in such instances. Control by ASK, they noted, was only until Solar Heating paid its debt to ASK, although no fixed date existed for termination of such control. The Plaintiffs, on the other hand, argue that ASK had no assurance of when, if ever, Solar Heating would be able to pay its debt, and the Plaintiffs observe that the debt was increasing because of continued sales to Solar Heating. ASK's control of Solar Heating, they argue, should have been considered indefinite rather than temporary.

The Plaintiffs' expert also opined that Main Hurdman should have realized that ASK's financial statement departed from the GAAP of conservatism, which requires that all possible errors in financial statements be in the direction of understatement rather than overstatement of net income and net assets. He also opined that Main Hurdman departed from the GAAP that requires that transactions be recorded in accordance with economic reality when the form of the transaction differs from its substance.

The Plaintiffs argue that Main Hurdman knew, or should have known, that its statement that ASK's financial statement was in accordance with GAAP was false. They also argue that Main Hurdman knew that its qualifying statement was false. Main Hur dman's qualifying paragraph stated:

> While management is of the opinion that the allowance for doubtful trade accounts and notes receivable is adequate at July 31, 1982, we [Main Hurdman] are unable to determine the adequacy of the provision for uncollectible accounts.

The Plaintiffs argue that Main Hurdman kn ew that the account was inadequate and provided this statement because ASK adamantly refused to adjust the account and because Main Hurdman did not wish to lose ASK as a client. Main Hurdman, on the other hand, argues that they could not reasonably estimate an adequate reserve.

An audit memorandum by Main Hurdman's audit manager indicates that he believed that ASK's reserve for doubtful accounts should have been increased by at least $200,000 to $300,000. He stated that because

> the client had a bad year they would not even consider the possibility of an adjustment of that size [$200,000 to $300,000]. Therefore, it was decided after several discussions with the client that a qualified opinion would be issued in regard to the A/R [accounts receivable] issue. Since we knew that we were going to qualify as to receivables, all work on W/Ps [workpapers] listed above was stopped as it would be very time consuming and was no longer necessary in light of the qualified opinion.

The Plaintiffs assert that this memorandum indicates that Main Hurdman either knew that the account was inadequate or purposely avoided determining the adequacy of that account.

* * * The district court concluded that the Plaintiffs' evidence did not raise a triable issue * * * because their evidence could not reasonably be construed as indicating that Main Hurdman departed from the standards of ordinary care.

A reasonable jury, however, could infer from the Plaintiffs' evidence that Main Hurdman knew that its statements were false when it indicated that ASK's financial statements complied with GAAP, and when it stated that ASK's financial statements fairly represented ASK's financial position. Main

Hurdman, as evidenced by their own audit working papers, formed an opinion that the provision for uncollectible accounts was inadequate by at least $200,000 to $300,000. In fact, Main Hurdman admits that their "audit team could not accept ASK's position that the existing reserve was adequate...." "The only uncertainty, it appears, was on the exact amount by which the account was inadequate. Main Hurdman, we observe, states that their engagement partner "believed that an adequate reserve might be substantially more than the $200,000—$300,000 range noted in the work papers by his subordinate." Even assuming that Main Hurdman's statement that it was "unable to determine the adequacy of the provision for uncollectible accounts" was true, "a conscious purpose to avoid learning the truthfulness of a statement is an extreme departure from the standards of ordinary care." G.A. Thompson & Co. v. Partridge, 636 F.2d 945, 962 (5th Cir.1981). The Plaintiffs' evidence, we conclude, creates a triable issue whether Main Hurdman knew that its qualification was false, or whether Main Hurdman consciously avoided learning the truthfulness of its qualification.

Main Hurdman's qualification also was misleading, the Plaintiffs' expert opined, because Main Hurdman failed to disclose that ASK's financial statements were materially affected by ASK's improper revenue recognition from the Provimi and Solar Heating sales, although Main Hurdman must have known that the accounting for these transactions was improper. * * *

Main Hurdman argues that the disagreement between the Plaintiffs' expert and their accountants indicates at most a difference of professional judgment concerning the application of GAAP * * *. See Godchaux v. Conveying Techniques, Inc., 846 F.2d 306, 315 (5th Cir.1988) ("an ethical, reasonably diligent accountant may choose to apply any of a variety of acceptable accounting procedures when that accountant prepares a financial statement."). In Godchaux, we observed that GAAP tolerates a wide range of acceptable procedures, and we concluded that in reviewing an accountant's conduct a district court may determine only whether an accountant has chosen a procedure from within that universe of acceptable practices. Id. at 315. Our rule in Godchaux does not assist Main Hurdman, however, because the Plaintiffs' expert unequivocally testified that Main Hurdman's accounting of ASK's 1982 financial statements could not be included within the universe of acceptable practices under GAAP, and his testimony suffices to create a triable issue on that question.* * *

Even were we to accept Main Hurdman's argument that the Plaintiffs must show that Main Hurdman knew the statement was misleading as well as false, we would have to conclude that the danger of misleading the public through a public accountant's knowing issuance of a false opinion is obvious. A public accountant performs an important public function and must be aware that the public places great faith in the probity of its opinions.

The Plaintiffs also adduced evidence of an improper motive that, if believed, suggests that Main Hurdman assisted ASK in a scheme to mislead the public by inflating ASK's revenues. The Plaintiffs observe, for example, that several of the investors in S.E.P. No. 1 were Main Hurdman's clients, and the Plaintiffs suggest that Main Hurdman approved ASK's accounting of the Provimi sale to ensure that these clients received tax advantages from the Provimi sale. The Plaintiffs also argue that Main Hurdman may have been motivated, in part, by a desire to keep ASK as its client. The Plaintiffs' evidence and speculation as to motive, in itself, does not suffice to create a triable issue * * *. We have noted, however, that summary judgment should be used sparingly when motive and intent are factors.

* * * A reasonable jury, we conclude, might believe the Plaintiffs' expert and find that Main Hurdman knew that it was issuing a false and misleading report, or that it was severely reckless in issuing its report.

NOTES

1. The principal case illustrates several concepts from Chapter II. First, the plaintiffs alleged that Main Hurdman's desire to ensure that certain clients who invested in the limited partnership received tax advantages, and also to keep ASK as a client, compromised the firm's intellectual honesty and independence. Second, the decision highlights the importance of working papers in cases involving accountants' legal liability. The court's opinion strongly suggests that the planning memo and the audit memorandum from the audit manager regarding the reserve for doubtful accounts which the plaintiffs uncovered in the audit working papers influenced the court's decision. Finally, near the end of the opinion Judge King mentions the "important public function" that accountants perform because "the public places great faith" in audit opinions.

2. Think about the fact that ASK sold the first system to the limited partnership for "a sale price of $1,750,000" and that "ASK recognized $1,239,000 of revenue * * * from the Provimi transaction". Is it relevant that the consideration the partnership paid for the system included a long-term, ten-year note at ten percent interest?

2. DISTINGUISHING BETWEEN SALES REVENUE AND INTEREST IN DEFERRED PAYMENT TRANSACTIONS

In the Lincoln Savings case, even if Wescon had been more financially sound, and the $3.5 million down-payment had not in effect come from Lincoln, do you think it would have been appropriate to record a gain of $11 million on the transaction? It was noted above that in the Fine case a ten-year note was included in revenue at substantially less than the face amount. There is an important issue here as to whether the face amount of a note or other obligation is indicative of the amount at which the transaction should be recorded. A promissory note exchanged for services, goods or other property represents two separate elements even though the note may not refer to both: (1) the amount equal to the bargained-for price for the services, goods or other property that the seller and the purchaser presumably at least implicitly agreed upon, and (2) interest, to compensate the seller during the promissory note's life for the delay in getting the funds that the seller would have received in a cash transaction at the closing. If the note provides either no interest or, as in the Fine case, an interest rate which differs from the market rate, the note's face amount does not reasonably represent the present value of the consideration given or received in the exchange. In order not to misstate the "real" sales price, and hence the profit to the seller, as well as the interest income in subsequent accounting periods, the parties should record the note at its present value, based upon the market interest rate, and that is what GAAP requires. APB Op. No. 21 (1971).

Note the discussion of future value in Chapter III, from page 216(at D) to 217, *supra*, particularly Example 10. Suppose that a dealer in boats sells one in exchange for the buyer's promissory note for $10,000, with payment due in exactly ten years. May the dealer recognize $10,000 in sales revenue? Of course not. The majority of the $10,000 has nothing to do with the boat's purchase price (which would presumably be equal to the present fair market value of the boat), and instead represents compensation for the ten-year delay in receiving that amount — in other words, it represents interest which will be earned over the next ten years. Upon determining the appropriate rate of interest for an obligation of this kind, say eight percent, compounded annually, we could calculate from interest tables just how much of the $10,000 represents the amount which would have been paid up front in cash (and hence the real price of the boat), and how much represents interest to be earned in the future; but we don't have to, because the example on page 216 tells us that with the assumed eight percent interest rate the present fair market value of the note (and, presumably, in an arm's length transaction the price paid for the boat) is approximately $4,632, with the remaining $5,368 representing interest to be earned in the future. Accordingly, the dealer should record no more than the $4,632 in sales revenue. The $5,368 difference between the note's face amount and its present value, representing interest to be earned in the future, is called *discount*: that is really just another name for Deferred Interest Income, which will be recognized by the seller as interest income over the note's ten-year life. (Normally, a deferred income account only arises when cash has been received in advance; but when the seller records the expected future interest payments as a receivable, accounting-wise that is the functional equivalent of receipt of cash.) At the time of the sale, the boat dealer might record the following journal entry:

Note Receivable	$10,000	
Sales Revenue		$4,632
Discount on Note Receivable		5,368

The Discount on Note Receivable serves as a contra-asset account which the seller would reflect on the balance sheet as a direct deduction from the note's face amount. The depiction of the note on the balance sheet or in a footnote to the financial statements should describe the terms, including the assumed reasonable interest rate. As a result, the promissory note might appear on the boat dealer's balance sheet as follows:

Note Receivable ($10,000 face amount, non-interest
bearing, due in ten years (less unamortized discount
of $5,368, based on eight percent per annum imputed
interest, compounded annually)) $4,632

Each year, the boat dealer would recognize as interest income eight percent of the "real" amount of the note (that is, the face amount discounted at the imputed interest rate to reflect present value -- here, initially, $4,632), and correspondingly reduce the discount by that amount. This process is referred to by accountants as "amortizing the discount." In the first year after the sale, the dealer would have earned approximately $371 in interest income, representing the $4,632 discounted amount of the note times eight percent interest. For that first year, the dealer might record the following journal entry:

Discount on Note Receivable $ 371
    Interest Income $ 371

That entry would reduce the unamortized discount to $4,997, so at the start of the second year the promissory note might appear on the boat dealer's balance sheet as follows:

Note Receivable ($10,000 face amount, non-interest
bearing, due in nine years (less unamortized discount
of $4,997, based on eight percent per annum imputed
interest, compounded annually)) $5,003

For the second year, the dealer would recognize $400 as interest income (eight percent interest times $5,003, the discounted amount of the note for the second year). In each of the following years, the dealer would recognize eight percent of the discounted amount of the note for that year as interest income, until the entire $5,368 had been recognized and the discount had been fully amortized.

A similar analysis is applicable with respect to an obligation payable in installments, what is termed in Chapter III as an annuity. Suppose a piece of property is sold for $10,000 down, and $10,000 payable at the end of each of the next four years. Is that a sale for $50,000, which the seller would be justified in recording as revenue? Again, the answer is clearly no, since, except for the down payment, a portion of each installment represents interest for the delay in paying the outstanding balance. The fact that the parties have not specified any interest — indeed, even if they have expressly specified *no* interest — is not controlling: the laws of economics apply and they call for recognition of interest when payment of a specified amount is deferred. Once we determine an appropriate rate of interest for this obligation — say, eight percent — we can calculate from the interest tables just how much of the total $40,000 payable in the future constitutes interest. The process parallels what is described in Chapter III as determining the present value of an annuity, and in fact the illustration on pages 218-220, multiplied by ten, gives us the answer here: the total interest on the four future installments amounts to $6,880, leaving $33,120 as what might be thought of as the "real", or "true" principal of the obligation. Assuming that 8% is the appropriate market rate of interest, the $33,120 figure should also approximate the current value of the note, which is the amount at which GAAP contemplates it will be recorded in the financial statements.

Actually, this obligation entitling the seller to receive $40,000, without interest, payable at the rate of $10,000 at the end of each of the next four years, is really the same as an obligation for $33,120, with express interest at eight percent, principal and interest together being paid off at the rate of $10,000 per year for four years. Thus, the obligation might be initially recorded on the balance sheet of the seller at the true principal of $33,120, just as though that was the actual face amount; the interest will be reflected (at the imputed reasonable market rate, which we have assumed to be 8%) only as it is earned and received, coincident with the receipt of each installment. On the other hand, the seller could display the obligation at the full $40,000, to make it consistent with the actual face amount; but in that event, as in the earlier example, the recorded face amount would be accompanied by an offsetting discount, here in the amount of $6,880, the total of the interest to be earned over the four years. And again, this discount is in effect a Deferred Interest Income account, but it is carried as a deduction on the left-hand side of the balance sheet, instead of on the right-hand side where deferred income accounts normally appear.

The deferred interest income, or discount, would be credited to current income as it is earned and received as part of each installment. Of course the portion of each installment that constitutes interest is not the same — there is a lot more interest in the first installment, amounting to eight percent of the balance owed during the first year (i.e., the "true" principal, $33,120), than in the installment at the end of the fourth year, since during that year the balance outstanding amounted to only approximately $926. The chart on page 219, again multiplied by ten, gives us the amount of interest in each of the four installments. The fact that the interest portion decreases in each successive installment leads to this approach being labeled as the declining-balance method of reflecting interest. More important, this method accurately assigns the interest, based upon the express or imputed rate as the case may be, among the respective accounting periods, and is commonly referred to as the "effective interest" method.

Sometimes, when the total amount of the interest on an installment obligation is readily ascertainable, it is tempting for simplicity to resort to a so-called straight-line method, under which the total interest is allocated equally among the installments. Here, that would result in allocating $1,720, one-fourth of the total interest of $6,880, to each of the four installments. However, the straight-line method does not accurately match the interest to the accounting periods, and that is why the authoritative accounting promulgation, APB Op. No. 21, favors the effective interest method.

Obviously, carrying the obligation in the Note Receivable account on the seller's balance sheet at the full face amount of $40,000, with the discount of $6,880 shown as an offset, produces the net figure of $33,120. As the imputed interest is earned each year, the Discount would be reduced (so that it always reflects the amount of interest still remaining to be earned in the future): this is another illustration of the process known as "amortizing the discount." So at the end of the first year, upon receipt of the $10,000 installment, cash would be debited and Note Receivable credited. At the same time, the interest earned during that year, $2,650, would be credited to Interest Income and debited to Discount. On the seller's balance sheet at the end of that first year, Note Receivable would reflect $30,000, offset by the amount then in the Discount account, $4,230 ($6,880-$2,650).

The simpler approach is just to record the net figure of $33,120, the true principal amount, in Note Receivable. In that event, upon receipt of the $10,000 installment at the end of the first year, the $2,650 which represents interest would be credited to Interest Income, and the remaining $7,350 would be credited to the Note Receivable, reducing it to $25,770. The receipt of $2,650 of interest would reduce the discount from $6,880 to $4,230, and the accompanying parenthetical description would disclose a remaining face amount for the obligation of $30,000, less unamortized discount of $4,230, producing the same net figure of $25,770. This process would be followed for each successive installment until the note has been paid off.

PROBLEM

Problem 6.2. Culinary Corporation (CC) is a large, publicly-owned corporation operating a chain of rapid service restaurants under the name "Chicken Counter" throughout the country. CC keeps its books of account on a fiscal year basis, and its most recent fiscal year just ended last month. After considerable growth earlier, a few years ago CC's net income leveled out at around $3,000,000, on sales revenues of approximately $50,000,000. In an effort to expand its operations, CC's management decided to embark on a franchising program, under which local entrepreneurs would be awarded a permanent franchise to operate a restaurant under the name and distinctive style of "Chicken Counter." The cost of a franchise was set at $50,000, payable $10,000 down and $10,000 at the end of each of the next four years; in case of default in such payments, CC reserved the right to cancel the franchise and treat payments made to date as liquidated damages. In addition, the franchisee is required to pay CC annual royalties in the amount of 2% of the franchisee's sales. The franchise agreements also required that the enterprise be operated in strict accordance with CC's rules and regulations, and many of the items sold in the restaurant were expected to be purchased from CC.

The new franchise program was formally adopted by CC's board of directors about fifteen months ago, with awards of the franchises to start a couple of months later, at the beginning of the fiscal year just ended. Management believed that for the foreseeable future the optimum number of franchises which CC could properly service and supervise would be about 120, and the plan was award about forty new franchises a year until that number was reached. It was expected that the cost of getting forty franchises started, consisting of such things as site selection, start-up advertising and promotion, and pre-operation training of franchise personnel, would amount to approximately $720,000.

Early last year, CC's management decided that a substantial promotional campaign should be undertaken to publicize the new franchise program. After consulting with its long-time advertising firm about the most effective promotion program for the sale of franchises, CC adopted a plan under which $800,000 was expended last year in promoting the sale of franchises, and another $400,000 is to be spent during this year just under way; no further franchise advertising is expected to be needed the following year to sell the last 40 franchises. By the end of last year, CC had sold its first forty franchises for $2,000,000, of which it had received down payments totaling $400,000.

CC's management is aware that franchise companies have been the subject of special attention in the stock market, with a good deal of concern expressed about not only the picture of current operations for such companies but also their long-term growth rate. Accordingly, management wants to be very careful about how the facts relating to the franchise program are reflected in the company's financial statements for last year, which are already in the process of preparation. CC's management has consulted the senior partner in your office, who in turn has asked for your views on the matter, particularly with regard to whether income should be recognized on the sale of the forty franchises, and, if so, in what manner.

a. DOUBT ABOUT THE ULTIMATE RECEIPT OF CASH

As noted at the outset, one of the conditions for recognition of revenue is the receipt of either cash or some consideration readily convertible into cash in a reasonably estimable amount. Often, what is received in an exchange transaction is some cash plus a right to additional cash, payable in the future, as in the example above of $10,000 down, plus $10,000 at the end of each of the next four years. Normally, such a right to cash will satisfy the above condition for recognition of revenue, since it is automatically convertible into cash, although, as we have seen, that does not necessarily mean that the full face amount of the obligation is eligible for recognition as revenue, because that figure may have to be adjusted to take account of imputed interest at a market rate. However, sometimes a transaction providing for deferred payments involves circumstances, such as a sale to a financially weak purchaser, or little if any downpayment with the future payments deferred over quite a long period, which preclude reasonable assurance that the amount of the obligation will be collected in full. In that event, it would be inappropriate to include in current revenue even the amount of the receivable as adjusted for interest, and instead one of the two alternative methods described below should be utilized. Incidentally, the Wescon deal in the Lincoln Savings case is an example of such a transaction, exhibiting all of the flaws referred to above, but the purported sale there seems to be so clearly a sham that it probably should not have been reflected in the company's financial statements on any basis. For illustrative purposes we will use the example referred to above, and assume that the obligor is financially weak, to demonstrate the two substitute methods for recognizing revenue on a deferred payment transaction when there is not reasonable assurance that the receivable will be collected in full.

(1) *Installment Method*

The installment method underscores the importance of the ultimate receipt of cash, by providing for the recognition of revenue only as, and to the extent that, cash is actually received. The seller first determines what the profit on the transaction would be if all of the promised installments are received, computed as the difference between the sales price (as adjusted for any substantial imputed interest) and the sum of the cost of whatever was exchanged by the seller plus any related expenses of the transaction. If we posit cost and expenses (hereinafter, "costs of sale") at, say, $18,000 in our illustrative example, the estimated net profit on the transaction would be $25,120, computed by deducting costs of sale of $18,000 from the sales price of $43,120 ($10,000 down payment plus the $33,120 "true" principal amount of the note). The $25,120 net profit represents 58.28% of the sales price of $43,120, so each receipt of cash representing payment of principal (rather than interest) should result in 58.28% thereof being reflected as net profit, while 41.72% is applied to recovery of the costs of sale. That means that for the downpayment, which includes no interest and is all repayment of principal, $5828 would be reflected as profit. For the installment received at the end of the first year, as we noted earlier, $2,650 would be viewed as interest; of the $7,350 representing payment of principal, 58.28%, or approximately $4,285, would be reflected as profit. The same type of calculation would be made for the non-interest portion of each of the three successive installments.

The bookkeeping mechanics to reflect this accounting treatment might be as follows. Since we only want to recognize in current revenue so much of the sales price as has been received in cash, here $10,000 at the time of the downpayment, we would defer the rest of the prospective sales revenue (which, as we have seen, is best measured by the figure equal to the face amount of the obligation less the imputed interest, i.e. the true principal of the obligation):

Cash	$10,000	
Note Receivable	33,120	
Sales Revenue		$10,000
Deferred Revenue		33,120

At the same time, we want to charge to current expense, and thereby match with that current revenue, the appropriate proportion of the costs of sale, equal to 41.72% of the principal portion of the installment, here $4,172, while the rest of the $18,000 should be deferred:

Costs of Sale	$4,172	
Deferred Costs of Sale	13,828	
Cash		$18,000

The closing of Sales Revenue of $10,000 and Costs of Sale of $4,172 to Profit and Loss will produce the desired recognition of $5,828 of net profit.

When the first deferred installment of $10,000 is received, at the end of year 1, we must initially allocate between receipt of principal (which constitutes payment of a portion of the sales price, and will of course reduce the balance of the Note Receivable account), and interest income (earned by virtue of the delay in paying the full price). As we noted earlier, the interest income portion of that first installment amounts to $2,650, so the entry would be:

Cash	$10,000	
Interest Income		$2,650
Note Receivable		7,350

Then, we want to reflect in current revenue the $7,350 principal portion of the installment, which represents payment of that much of the sales price, and we do so by transferring that amount from the Deferred Revenue account.

Deferred Revenue	$7,350
Sales Revenue	$7,350

Similarly, we want to charge to current expense the appropriate proportionate amount of the costs of sale, which again should be equal to 41.72% of the principal portion of the installment (which is also the amount of sales revenue being recognized, here $7,350); so $3,065 of costs should be matched with the $7,350 of revenue, which we do by transferring $3,065 from the Deferred Costs account.

Costs of Sale	$3,065
Deferred Costs	$3,065

These same bookkeeping mechanics would be utilized as the remaining installments are received. If the obligation is not paid in full, any remaining unrecovered costs in the Deferred Costs of Sale account would have to be written off as a loss.

(2) *Cost Recovery Method*

The cost recovery method is even more conservative than the installment method, since it requires all cash received in payment of the sales price to be applied against the costs of sale first, postponing any profit recognition until the costs have been recovered in full. Accordingly, this method is used when there is particularly large doubt about collection of the full amount of the receivable. In addition, when there is such uncertainty, it may be that until all costs have been recovered, no portion of any installment would be treated as imputed interest income, and perhaps even express interest would be ignored, in favor of first applying every penny of cash received in connection with the transaction to the recovery of the costs of sale. After all, when there is considerable doubt that the full amount of the obligation will ever be received, it is somewhat unrealistic to think of earning interest by virtue of payment deferral.

Accordingly, in cases of this kind it may make sense not to record an overall obligation at all, and instead simply defer the costs of sale: then, as each payment of cash is received it can be offset by an equal amount of the costs of sale transferred from the Deferred Costs account and charged to current expense. Thus, in our illustrative example the downpayment of $10,000 would be offset by charging off $10,000 of the costs of sale, leaving $8,000 in the Deferred Costs account. The $10,000 installment received at the end of the first year would be offset by charging off the $8,000 in the Deferred Costs account, and the excess $2,000 of the installment would be reflected in income for the year. Any subsequent amounts received on the note would be credited to income in full.

(3) *Summary Comparison of Accrual, Installment, and Cost Recovery Methods*

Notice that although if there is no default the three methods would all ultimately reflect the same total addition to income, amounting in our illustrative example to $50,000 — $18,000, or $32,000, the timing and character of the additions would vary. Under the standard accrual approach, there would be gain on the sales transaction at the time it takes place, in the amount of $25,120 ($43,120 — $18,000), while $6,880 of imputed interest income on the note would be spread over the four year duration of the note on the declining-balance schedule. Under the installment method, presumably the imputed interest income would be allocated among the four years of the note in the same manner as under the accrual method (although it is also possible that under the installment method, imputation of interest would be ignored, as suggested under the cost recovery method). If there is imputation of interest, the installment method would reflect gain on the sales transaction in the amount of $5,828 on the down payment, $4,284 on the first installment on the note, $4,628 on the second, $4,992 on the third, and $5,388 on the fourth, totaling, of course, $25,120. Under the cost recovery method, with no imputation of interest the total gain of $32,000 would all be attributed to the sales transaction, and the recognition schedule would be $0 on the down payment, $2,000 on the first installment on the note, and $10,000 in each of the other three installments.

(4) *Related Party Transactions*

As noted earlier, when a transaction is at arm's length with an unrelated party, it is likely that the consideration given by the buyer parallels the market value of whatever the seller transferred in this deal; when there is some kind of special relationship between the two, there is the possibility that factors other than the elements in the instant deal underlie the price and other terms. In other words, if an enterprise transacts business with a related party, it may be possible to manipulate revenue by selling to the related party at prices arbitrarily fixed higher or lower than fair value, especially if no cash changes hands in the transaction. The Fine case illustrates a related party transaction, in that officers and directors of the putative seller had purchased about thirty-five percent of the buyer. For a more homely example, imagine that the following events develop in the law school survival guide hypothetical on page 350, *supra*. During February, law students purchase 200 survival guides at five dollars each. After you agree to share Porsche-privileges, your younger sibling promises to pay $3,000 for 200 survival guides. With a new loan application in hand, you triumphantly return to the bank. The loan officer again commends you on selling 400 survival guides at what appears to be ten dollars each. You mention how fortunate you are that your sibling appreciates both great literature and fast cars. You watch in dismay as the loan officer again shreds your loan application. The loan officer explains that quite apart from the possibility that your sibling may have been moved simply by filial considerations to help you out, the fifteen dollar purchase price ($3,000 total consideration divided by 200 survival guides) includes the value of Porsche-privileges rather than just the survival guide's value. The loan officer further explains that, unless you grant Porsche-privileges to future purchasers, the 200 survival guides your sibling purchased do not forecast future demand for guides at a price of fifteen dollars. In contrast, the 200 guides your classmates purchased at five dollars each reflect their true market value and hence a price at which one could reasonably expect future demand. As we can see, loan officers and investors who know the nature of an enterprise's exchange transactions can better assess current revenue and predict future demand.

The Lincoln Savings case illustrates a similar type of related-party transaction, though not a classic case like a deal between siblings, or one between an enterprise and some of its managers, or between two entities owned by the same people. In Lincoln Savings, the actual maker of the note was just a straw (with only nominal net worth); and Garcia, the individual who advanced the funds used by Wescon to make the down-payment, appears to have had very little interest in Wescon, or the property being purchased from Lincoln. However, he had a great interest in preserving a good relationship with Lincoln because his various companies were heavy borrowers from Lincoln, and in fact at that very time Garcia's companies were in the midst of obtaining loans totaling $20,000,000 from Lincoln. Therefore, even if the purported purchase by Wescon had not been such a sham, it would not have provided a meaningful measure of the values involved in the transaction, or the amount of revenue earned by Lincoln, because Garcia was not dealing at arm's length. Like the sibling in the above example, he was motivated by other considerations, and no doubt some of the overpayment he was willing for Wescon to make for the land actually represented additional consideration for Lincoln making loans to his companies.

Businesses do not necessarily account for related party transactions differently than for unrelated party transactions; but if related party transactions other than compensation arrangements, expense allowances, and other similar items in the ordinary course of business, qualify as material, GAAP, per FASB No. 57, *Related Party Disclosures* (1982), requires that enterprises disclose the following information in their financial statements:

(1) The nature of any relationships involved;

(2) A description of the transactions for each period for which the financial statements present an income statement, including any information necessary to understand the transactions' effects on the financial statements;

(3) The dollar amounts of the transactions and the effects of any change in the method used to establish terms when compared to those followed in the preceding period; and,

(4) Amounts due from or to related parties on each balance sheet date and the related terms governing those amounts.

Significant related party relationships or transactions can conceivably preclude an auditor from issuing an unqualified opinion because an underlying relationship or transaction can prevent the financial statements from "fairly present[ing]" the enterprise's financial condition, operating results and cash flows. Generally accepted auditing standards require an auditor to identify related party relationships and transactions and to obtain and evaluate competent evidence regarding the purpose, nature, and extent of any relationship or transaction, plus the effect on the financial statements. Before issuing an unqualified opinion, the auditor must conclude that the financial statements adequately disclose any related party transaction or relationship. In particular, any disclosure should not imply that the enterprise consummated a transaction on terms equivalent to those that would have prevailed in an arms-length transaction unless management can substantiate the representation. If such a representation appears in the financial statements, and management cannot substantiate it, then the auditor should express either a qualified or adverse opinion, depending on materiality. Omnibus Statement on Auditing Standards—1983, SAS No. 45 (AICPA 1983).

3. EXCEPTION TO THE BONA FIDE TRANSACTION REQUIREMENT: ACCOUNTING FOR INVESTMENTS IN SECURITIES

a. PASSIVE INVESTMENTS

In the first survival guide example, the loan officer explained that the bank could not afford to share in your "optimism." In other words, the bank needed actual, bona fide transactions or sales to demonstrate that you could generate cash to repay your loan. As mentioned in Chapter I, accountants often use conservatism to avoid overly optimistic financial statements. Under conservatism, GAAP calls for accrual of all losses and expenses as soon as they appear likely, but generally waits to recognize revenues and gains until the underlying events appear virtually certain. Banks and other users of financial statements, however, cannot afford undue "pessimism." No one benefits when a bank denies a loan to a borrower who needlessly understates income, assets or equity.

In the interests of realism, GAAP authorizes an exception to the bona fide transaction requirement for recognizing revenue or gain. Actually, we have already encountered this exception, back in Chapter V, because it starts with a departure from the principle of recording assets at historical cost, in the case of most debt and publicly-traded equity securities. Since reliable valuation evidence is usually available for such securities, GAAP requires that they be carried on the balance sheet at current fair market value, unless the securities are being held long-term, which means until maturity for debt, or for control purposes in the case of stock (which will be discussed in detail shortly). FASB No. 115, *Accounting for Certain Investments in Debt and Equity Securities* (1993).

As observed on page 301, *supra*, if the debt securities, or publicly-traded shares, are held principally for sale in the short run, the unrealized gain or loss corresponding to recording the securities at fair value will appear in the enterprise's income statement, even though there has been no exchange or other transaction — a clear departure from the ordinary rules for gain recognition. As to securities falling somewhere between planned long-term holding and contemplated short-term sale, termed by FASB No. 115 as "available for sale", the recognition of the unrealized gain or loss accompanying recording the asset at current fair value is not reflected in the income statement but instead appears on the balance sheet, in a special section of the shareholders' equity. However, if changing circumstances have caused a decline in the value of an asset which is not viewed as temporary, the principle of conservatism would require the immediate recognition of the loss by a charge against current income.

As to when marketable equity securities should be designated as a long-term holding, which would usually be because of potential participation in control of the investee, the test is whether the investing company holds sufficient voting stock to have power to exercise significant influence over operating and financial policies of the investee. As discussed below, under GAAP there is a presumption that this condition is satisfied when the investing company owns twenty percent or more of the investee's voting stock. In that event, as described at pages 388-390, *infra*, the investing company must use the special form of accounting known as the "equity method", unless the investing company has actual majority control, in which event the two companies must be consolidated for accounting purposes.

For equity securities which are not long-term holdings but do not have a readily determinable market value, enterprises must account for such investments at historical cost, and to treat any dividends that the investee distributes from net accumulated earnings after the acquisition date as income. Any dividends which exceed net accumulated earnings subsequent to the acquisition date are treated as a return of investment that reduces the cost recorded on the enterprise's books.

Because dividends serve as the event for recognizing income from an investment properly accounted for at cost, investing the enterprise's financial statements may not reflect the investee's performance. The dividends that the investing enterprise includes in income during an accounting period may not mirror the investee's earnings, or losses, for that period. To illustrate, an investee may pay no dividends for several accounting periods and then pay dividends substantially in excess of earnings in that particular period. As a result, the cost method prevents the investing enterprise from adequately reflecting the earnings related to investments in common stock either cumulatively or in the appropriate periods. However, remember that if the investee incurs a series of operating losses, or other factors indicate that the investment has suffered a decrease in value which appears to be non-temporary, GAAP requires the investing company to recognize a current loss.

(1) *Available-for-Sale Securities and Comprehensive Income*

The treatment of available-for-sale securities provides a good opportunity to review and expand on the subject discussed earlier in Chapter IV, i.e., SFAS No. 130, *Reporting Comprehensive Income*, promulgated by the FASB in 1999 to require enterprises to report the amount of their "comprehensive income" in the financial statements. The pronouncement defines comprehensive income as "the change in equity [net assets] of a business enterprise during a period from transactions and other events and circumstances from nonowner sources." Previously, enterprises reported most changes in equity from nonowner sources on the income statement; some nonowner changes in equity, however, such as the unrealized gains and losses from holding "available-for-sale" marketable securities, did not affect the income statement, and appeared only in a separate component of the equity section of the balance sheet.

SFAS No. 130 divides "comprehensive income" into "net income" and "other comprehensive income." "Net income" includes income from continuing operations, discontinued operations, extraordinary items, and cumulative effects of changes in accounting principles. "Other comprehensive income" includes foreign currency items, minimum pension liability adjustments, and the unrealized gain or loss on certain investments in debt and equity securities. The new pronouncement does not require a specific format to report "comprehensive income" but does mandate that an enterprise display an amount representing total non-owner changes in equity for the period somewhere in the financial statements. As a result, enterprises may use: (i) a "statement of income and comprehensive income," (ii) separate statements for "traditional" net income and comprehensive income, (iii) a "statement of changes in equity," or (iv) some other format to present the r equired information.

To illustrate the concept of comprehensive income, assume that, as its only investment, Vogt Corporation ("Vogt"), a calender year corporation, purchases 10,000 shares of Keller, Inc. ("Keller"), a publicly traded corporation with total market value exceeding $1 billion, on March 1, Year 1 for $100,000 (i.e., $10 per share). Further assume that by the end of Year 1, the market value of each share of Keller stock has increased to $13 per share. At the end of Year 2, the market price equals $18 per share. On February 1, Year 3, Vogt sells its Keller shares for $17 per share. How much income and comprehensive income does Vogt recognize from these events?

At the time of the original investment, Vogt would make the following journal entry:

Investments	$100,000	
Cash		$100,000

As available-for-sale securities, the Keller shares will appear on Vogt's balance sheet at the end of Year 1 and 2 at their fair values of $130,000 and $180,000, respectively. The increase in value would appear in a separate section of shareholders' equity. At the end of Year 1, Vogt would make the following journal entry to reflect the increase in fair value:

Investments	$30,000	
Unrealized Gain on Marketable Equity		
Securities (an equity account)		$30,000

After the $30,000 debit to the Investments account, that account would show a $130,000 debit balance. In addition to appearing in the equity section of the balance sheet, the $30,000 unrealized gain would appear in both "other comprehensive income" and comprehensive income. Although Vogt would not recognize net income from the increase in fair value (because no exchange transaction has occurred), the financial statements would show $30,000 in "other comprehensive income" and comprehensive income of $30,000 ($-0- net income plus $30,000 in "other comprehensive income").

At the end of Year 2, Vogt would make the following journal entry to reflect the increase in the fair value of the Keller shares to $180,000 during the year:

Investments	$50,000	
Unrealized Gain on Marketable Equity Securities (an equity account)		$50,000

After the $50,000 debit to the Investments account, that account would show a $180,000 debit balance. After the $50,000 credit, $80,000 would appear as unrealized gain in the equity section of the balance sheet. In addition, the $50,000 increase in the unrealized gain during Year 2 would appear in both "other comprehensive income" and comprehensive income. Although Vogt would not recognize any net income from the increase in fair value (again because no exchange transaction has occurred), the company's financial statements would show $50,000 in "other comprehensive income" and comprehensive income of $50,000 ($-0- net income plus $50,000 in "other comprehensive income").

When Vogt sells the Keller shares on February 1, Year 3, Vogt would record the following journal entry:

Cash	$170,000	
Unrealized Gain on Marketable Equity Securities	80,000	
Investments		$180,000
Gain on Sale of Investments		70,000

Because Vogt has sold its only investment, which appeared at $180,000 in the Investment account after the $80,000 increases in value during Years 1 and 2, Vogt can no longer show the unrealized gain as a separate item in shareholder's equity and must reverse the $80,000 that previously appeared as unrealized gain. Although Vogt can recognize $70,000 in gain, representing the difference between the $170,000 sales proceeds and the $100,000 original investment, the company must also report a ($80,000) (loss) in "other comprehensive income" from eliminating the balance in the unrealized gain account that appeared in shareholders' equity. Combined with the $70,000 in net income from the sale of investments, Vogt would report a ($10,000) (loss) in comprehensive income for Year 3.

We could summarize the effects on comprehensive income as follows:

	Net Income	Other Comprehensive Income	Comprehensive Income
Year 1	$-0-	$30,000	$30,000
Year 2	$-0-	$50,000	$50,000
Year 3	$70,000	($80,000)	($10,000)
Totals	$70,000	$-0-	$70,000

Note that all $70,000 in gain appears in net income during Year 3, while that same collective amount appears in comprehensive income over the same period as $30,000 income in Year 1, $50,000 income in Year 2, and a ($10,000) (loss) in Year 3. The requirement to report comprehensive income precludes an enterprise from recognizing all the income related to the increase in the value of an investment in the year of sale. Under the previous accounting rules, enterprises could decide when to recognize gains from investments.

(2) *Held-to-Maturity Debt Securities*

Long-term debt holdings are termed held-to-maturity securities and they are defined in FASB No. 115 as debt securities that the enterprise has the positive intent and ability to hold until maturity (*i.e.*, the date when the borrower must repay any unpaid principal and accrued interest). Until one year before maturity, an enterprise normally lists held-to-maturity securities as noncurrent assets on a classified balance sheet. Changes in circumstances which can cause an enterprise to alter its intent to hold a particular security to maturity without affecting its intent to hold other debt securities to maturity in the future include a significant deterioration in the issuer's creditworthiness; modifications in tax law, and amendments in statutory or regulatory requirements affecting what qualifies as a permissible investment or the maximum level of certain kinds of investments. In addition, isolated, nonrecurring and unusual events that could not have reasonably been anticipated can cause an enterprise to sell or reclassify a held-to-maturity security without raising doubts about its intent to hold other debt securities to maturity. In contrast, an enterprise may not classify a debt security as held-to-maturity if the enterprise anticipates selling the security in response to fluctuations in market interest rates, needs for liquidity, or changes in alternative investment opportunities or the like.

Enterprises carry held-to-maturity securities on the balance sheet at *amortized cost*, which is initially equal to cost, but is adjusted annually, as described below, to reflect the proper reallocation between principal and interest when there is a difference between the stated interest rate and the current market rate for such an obligation. As noted in Chapter III, the market value of a bond moves in the opposite direction from the market interest rate. So if there is a general increase in interest rates, taking the current market interest rate for similar investments above a given bond's stated interest rate, the bond's market value will decrease: as illustrated in the example on pages 223 - 24, *supra*, when interest rates increased from ten percent to twelve percent, compounded semiannually, the market value of a $10,000 face amount bond fell to $9,508.26. The difference between the $10,000 face amount and the $9,508.26 market value represents *market discount*. In contrast, if interest rates drop, the bond's value will increase, and the bond will trade at a premium, because a reasonable investor will be willing to pay more than the $10,000 face amount as long as the yield on that price is at least equal to the current market interest rate. Whenever the interest rate stated in a debt security is different from the market rate for similar investments, the security will trade at either a discount or a premium. The purchaser will amortize any discount or premium by crediting or debiting it, as the case may be, to interest income over the debt security's remaining term to maturity, using the applicable current market interest rate. Amortized cost, therefore, represents the original cost to acquire the debt security, adjusted to reflect the amortization to date of any discount or premium.

Market discount (or premium) really just represents additional or reduced interest being earned over the life of the bond, due to the fact that at maturity the holder will receive more (or less) than the amount paid to purchase the bond. In that respect, market discount is similar to original issue discount, discussed on pages 366 - 369, *supra*, except that the purchase price in the market provides clearer evidence of the present fair market value of the obligation, and hence the "true principal", than does the constructive figure obtained by estimating the appropriate current interest rate for the obligation. In fact, when we know the current value at which a bond is trading in the market, we could determine from the interest tables the market interest rate which produces that value. And while a market purchase is normally recorded at cost, not at the face value less the discount, in effect the market discount is amortized in a manner akin to the illustration on page 367, based upon including in current interest income an amount equal to the current market rate times the adjusted cost figure for that year. However, there are two differences between the original issue discount example discussed above and the instant case: first, we are now talking about a bond which pays interest in cash twice a year, so the amortization of the discount is limited to the amount by which the current interest income, measured as indicated above, exceeds the stated interest received in cash; and second, since the note is carried at a figure which is already net of the discount, the debit corresponding to the additional interest income is made directly to the asset account, but of course that produces the same net increase in the carrying amount of the bond as would have resulted from a reduction in an offsetting discount.

To illustrate amortized cost, assume that ABC Corporation purchases a $10,000 face amount bond bearing ten percent annual interest, payable semiannually, exactly three years before maturity, at a time   when the market interest rate is around twelve percent interest, again compounded semiannually. On the basis of our previous discussion, we may assume that ABC pays $9,508.26 for the bond. At the time of the purchase, ABC might record the following journal entry:

Investments in Bonds	$9,508.26	
Cash		$9,508.26

Every six months until maturity, ABC would receive the $500 interest on the bond ($10,000 face amount times the five percent interest rate for half a year) which is due as a matter of contract. At the same time ABC would recognize as interest income for each six month period an amount equal to one-half of the current market interest rate of 12%, or 6%, times the discounted amount at which the bond is carried for that period, which is equal to the initial cost adjusted for any earlier amortization of the market discount. For the first six months ABC would be carrying the bond at the original cost of $9,508.26, so the credit to interest income for that period would be approximately $570.50. That would be offset by the debit to cash for the $500 actually received and an increase of $70.50 in the figure at which the bond is carried   (the functional counterpart of a reduction, or   amortization, of the market discount).

Cash	$500.00	
Investments in Bonds	70.50	
Interest Income		$570.50

The entry would increase the bond's amortized cost or carrying value to $9,578.76 ($9,508.26 cost plus $70.50 amortized discount).

In the second six-months and each of the following periods, ABC would recognize six percent of the bond's amortized cost amount for the particular period as interest income for that period. Thus, for the second six-month period, ABC would recognize $574.73 as interest income ($9,578.76 amortized cost times six percent interest). For that second interest payment, ABC might record the following journal entry:

Cash	$500.00	
Investments in Bonds	74.73	
Interest Income		$574.73

The entry would increase the amortized cost or carrying value of the bonds to $9,653.49 ($9,578.76 plus $74.73 amortized discount).

The following table summarizes the amortization of the market discount during the three years or six semiannual periods until maturity:

Period	Interest Income	Cash Received	Amortization of Discount	Amortized Cost
0				$9,508.26
1	$570.50	$500.00	$70.50	9,578.76
2	574.73	500.00	74.73	9,653.49
3	579.21	500.00	79.21	9,732.70
4	583.96	500.00	83.96	9,816.66
5	589.00	500.00	89.00	9,905.66
6	594.34	500.00	94.34	10,000.00

Similarly, we can illustrate the amortization of market premium by assuming that DEF Company ("DEF") purchases a $10,000 face amount bond bearing ten percent annual interest, payable semiannually, exactly three years before maturity and when the market interest rate stands at eight percent interest, again compounded semiannually. From our previous example, assume that DEF pays $10,524.17 for the bond. Every six months until maturity, DEF would recognize four percent of the bond's carrying amount as interest income. At the end of the first six months, the borrower would pay $500 interest on the bond ($10,000 face amount times the five percent contract interest rate for that six month period). Under the effective interest method, DEF would have only earned $420.97 in interest income ($10,524.17 purchase price times four percent market interest rate for this semiannual period). Accordingly, DEF might record the following journal entry for that first interest payment:

Cash	$500.00	
Interest Income		$420.97
Investments in Bonds		79.03

The entry would treat $79.03 as a return of the original investment and reduce the amortized cost or carrying value of the bonds to $10,445.14 ($10,524.17 minus $79.03 amortized premium).

In the second six-month period and following periods, DEF would continue to recognize four percent of the bond's amortized cost amount as interest income for the next period. For the second six-month period, DEF would recognize $417.81 as interest income ($10,445.14 amortized cost times four percent interest).

The following table summarizes the amortization of the market premium during the three years or six semiannual periods until maturity:

Period	Interest Income	Cash Received	Amortization of Premium	Amortized Cost
0				$10,524.17
1	$420.97	$500.00	$79.03	10,445.14
2	417.81	500.00	82.19	10,362.95
3	414.52	500.00	85.48	10,277.47
4	411.10	500.00	88.90	10,188.57
5	407.54	500.00	92.46	10,096.11
6	403.84	500.00	96.16	9,999.95

(Rounding off creates the five cent difference between the bond's amortized cost at the end of the sixth semiannual period and the bond's face amount.)

(3) *Comparison of the Accounting Treatments for the Different Categories of Debt and Marketable Equity Securities Held as Passive Investments*

The following chart summarizes the different categories of debt and marketable equity securities and their accounting treatments:

Classification of Investment	Type of Security	Balance Sheet Valuation of the Investment	Other Balance Sheet and Income Statement Effects
Held-to-Maturity	Debt	Amortized Cost	None
Trading Securities	Debt or Equity	Fair Value	Unrealized Holding Gains and Losses Included in Income Statement
Available-for-Sale	Debt or Equity	Fair Value	Unrealized Holding Gains and Losses Reported Net in Equity Section

An investing enterprise must treat any transfers between categories as a recognition event at fair value according to the previously described rules. Thus, if an enterprise transfers a debt security from the held-to-maturity category to the available-for-sale category, the enterprise must recognize the unrealized holding gain or loss on the transfer date in a separate component of shareholders' equity. Conversely, if an enterprise transfers a debt security from available-for-sale into the held-to-maturity category, the enterprise must continue to report the unrealized holding gain or loss on the transfer date in a separate component of shareholders' equity, but must amortize that amount over the security's life to maturity similar to the amortization of any market discount or premium. Given the definitions for held-to-maturity and trading securities, transfers from held-to-maturity and into or from trading securities should only rarely occur. But, if an enterprise transfers a debt security from held-to-maturity to the trading category, the enterprise must immediately recognize the unrealized holding gain or loss in income.

b. LONG-TERM HOLDINGS OF EQUITY SECURITIES

As noted above, when an enterprise owns, directly or indirectly, at least twenty percent of an investee's voting stock, GAAP presumes that the enterprise can exercise significant influence over the investee. If the holding is more than fifty percent of the voting shares, the enterprise generally must prepare consolidated financial statements, which results in recognition of gains or losses attributable to a subsidiary's operations even though the enterprise has not sold its investment in the subsidiary. As noted earlier, when the holding is at least twenty percent but not more than fifty percent, GAAP generally requires the enterprise to use the "equity method" to account for the investment, which produces a result somewhat similar to consolidated statements, as described at pages 388-390, *infra*.

(1) *Consolidated Financial Statements*

You may recall the introduction of consolidated financial statements in Chapter I. At that time, we saw that such statements combine financial data for a parent company and its majority-owned subsidiaries as if the parent and any subsidiaries represent a single accounting entity. GAAP requires an enterprise's financial statements to consolidate all majority-owned subsidiaries unless the enterprise does not hold actual control or holds only temporary control. For example, contract, court order or other circumstances may deprive a majority shareholder of actual control. In addition, bankruptcy or legal reorganization may give the majority shareholder only temporary control. *Consolidation of All Majority–Owned Subsidiaries*, Statement of Financial Accounting Standards No. 94, ¶ ¶ 10, 13 (FASB 1987).

In Chapter I, we focused solely on how accountants aggregate nonreciprocal assets and liabilities. In this chapter, we consider how the parent company should reflect a subsidiary's earnings subsequent to its acquisition in the consolidated accounts. Because the make-up of the subsidiary's balance sheet does not affect the process, for the sake of simplicity consider the following balance sheets for X and Y:

X Corp.
Balance Sheet, Immediately After Acquisition of Y Corp.

Assets		Liabilities & Equity	
Cash	$100,000	Liabilities	$250,000
Investment	200,000	Common Stock	300,000
Plant	400,000	Retained Earnings	150,000
	$700,000		$700,000

Y Corp.
Balance Sheet, Immediately After Acquisition by X Corp.

Assets		Liabilities & Equity	
Cash	$ 50,000	Common Stock	$200,000
Plant	150,000		$200,000
	$200,000		

Suppose that during the first year after the acquisition, Y earned $50,000 while X remained completely inactive. Y's balance sheet might then look like this:

Y Corp.
Balance Sheet, One Year After Acquisition

Assets		Liabilities & Equity	
Cash	$100,000	Common Stock	$200,000
Plant	150,000	Retained Earnings	50,000
	$250,000		$250,000

X's balance sheet would have remained:

X Corp.
Balance Sheet, One Year After Acquisition

Assets		Liabilities & Equity	
Cash	$100,000	Liabilities	$250,000
Investment	200,000	Common Stock	300,000
Plant	400,000	Retained Earnings	150,000
	$700,000		$700,000

Since Y's net assets now exceed X's cost of the investment in Y, the consolidation technique of replacing the asset Investment on X's balance sheet with Y's net assets appears to make the columns of the consolidated balance sheet unequal:

X Corp.
Consolidated Balance Sheet, One Year After Acquisition

Assets		Liabilities & Equity	
Cash	$200,000	Liabilities	$250,000
		Common Stock	300,000
Plant	550,000	Retained Earnings	150,000
	$750,000		$700,000

To balance, we must increase the consolidated retained earnings in an amount equal to the $50,000 increase in the subsidiary's retained earnings after acquisition. After all, we can attribute this increase to the consolidated enterprise. The increase, therefore, properly belongs in the consolidated retained earnings. The consolidated balance sheet should appear as follows:

X Corp.
Consolidated Balance Sheet, One Year After Acquisition

Assets		Liabilities & Equity	
Cash	$200,000	Liabilities	$250,000
		Common Stock	300,000
Plant	550,000	Retained Earnings	200,000
	$750,000		$750,000

Notice that if Y subsequently paid a dividend to X, the payment would not affect the consolidated balance sheet. The increase in X's net assets and retained earnings arising from the dividend would offset the corresponding decrease in Y's net assets and retained earnings.

Once again, the foregoing consolidation technique applies whenever a parent corporation owns at least a majority voting interest in a subsidiary, unless the parent does not hold actual control or maintains only temporary control. If the parent corporation owns less than complete control, you may recall from Chapter I that *minority interest* represents the ownership interest that does not belong to the parent or another subsidiary. In that circumstance, the parent must deduct the minority interest's share of the subsidiary's net income for a particular accounting period in determining consolidated net income. In calculating consolidated net income, the parent corporation must also remove the effects of any intercompany transactions. For example, if the parent sold goods to the subsidiary or vice versa, the consolidated financial statements must eliminate those transactions so that the consolidated income statement will only reflect sales to enterprises outside the consolidated group.

(2) Equity Method

Suppose, however, that X only owns fifty percent of Y's outstanding voting shares and, therefore, does not hold a controlling financial interest in Y. Recall that under recording at cost, X would simply treat the investment in Y as an asset on X's balance sheet. Under this approach, X's books would reflect Y's subsequent earnings only when and to the extent that Y actually paid dividends to X, at which time X would include the dividend in its income and ultimately in its retained earnings. There is an intermediate position between recording at cost and full consolidation, a kind of "quasi-consolidation," which accountants refer to as the *equity method.*

Under the equity method, an enterprise initially records an investment in an investee's stock at cost, but then adjusts the investment's carrying amount to recognize the investing enterprise's share of the investee's earnings or losses after the acquisition date, and includes this pro rata share in the investing enterprise's net income. This process, however, requires adjustments similar to those which an enterprise would make in preparing consolidated statements, such as eliminating intercompany gains and losses. Under the cost method, in contrast, the investing enterprise only reports income in the period in which the investee declares a dividend.

The investing enterprise also adjusts the investment in the investee to reflect its share of changes in the investee's capital. For example, any dividends that the investee pays reduce the investment's carrying amount. Once again, a series of operating losses or other factors may indicate that the investment has suffered a non-temporary decline in value. The investing enterprise must recognize this decline even though the decrease exceeds the loss that the enterprise would otherwise recognize under the equity method. Operating losses or a decline in an investment's market price below the carrying amount, however, does not necessarily indicate a non-temporary loss in value. The investing enterprise's management must evaluate all factors.

GAAP requires an enterprise to use the equity method to account for investments in common stock if an investment in voting stock enables the investing enterprise to exercise significant influence over the investee's operating or financial decisions. Under APB Opinion No. 18, *The Equity Method of Accounting for Investments in Common Stock*, it is presumed that an investment of twenty percent or more of an investee's voting stock carries the ability to exercise significant influence, while an investment of less than twenty percent does not.   However, in appropriate circumstances an investing enterprise can rebut these presumptions. Representation on the board of directors, participation in policy making processes, material intercompany transactions, interchange of managerial personnel, or technological dependency can all indicate an ability to exercise significant influence.

Under the equity method, X's balance sheet would show merely its investment in Y, rather than Y's net assets which would appear in consolidated financial statements. X's financial statements, however, will reflect Y's subsequent earnings or losses whether or not Y declares any dividends, just as would occur under consolidation.

To illustrate, assume again that Y had earned $50,000 during the first year after X acquired fifty percent of its voting stock for $200,000, while X was completely inactive. Y's balance sheet at the end of that year looked like this:

Y Corp.
Balance Sheet, One Year After Acquisition

Assets		Liabilities & Equity	
Cash	$100,000	Common Stock	$200,000
Plant	150,000	Retained Earnings	50,000
	$250,000		$250,000

Because a fifty percent ownership interest does not qualify for consolidation, under the cost method X would have to wait for Y to declare a dividend before reflecting any of Y's post-acquisition earnings on X's financial statements. Until then, X's balance sheet would remain the same as it appeared immediately after X purchased Y's stock:

X Corp.
Balance Sheet, One Year After Acquisition

Assets		Liabilities & Equity	
Cash	$100,000	Liabilities	$250,000
Investment	200,000	Common Stock	300,000
Plant	400,000	Retained Earnings	150,000
	$700,000		$700,000

Under the equity method, in contrast, X would write up the investment in Y to reflect its share in Y's earnings subsequent to acquisition. An increase in X's retained earnings would balance the increase in the investment account. As a result, X's balance sheet would appear as follows:

X Corp.
Balance Sheet, One Year After Acquisition

Assets		Liabilities & Equity	
Cash	$100,000	Liabilities	$250,000
Investment	225,000	Common Stock	300,000
Plant	400,000	Retained Earnings	175,000
	$725,000		$725,000

Notice that the equity method produces a balance sheet which resembles the consolidated balance sheet with two important exceptions. First, under the equity method the write-up is limited to X's percentage ownership, and no "minority interest" is reflected on X's books of Y's earnings. Second, X does not substitute Y's net assets for the asset "Investment" on X's balance sheet.

a) *Consolidation of Variable Interest Entities*

In response to the Enron scandal, GAAP now requires enterprises to consolidate certain entities known as variable interest entities ("VIEs"), a term which encompasses the special purpose entities ("SPEs") at root in Enron's "financial engineering." These new rules apply even if the enterprise does not own a majority of the voting shares. Recall from the discussion at pages 385-387, *supra,* that an enterprise must generally consolidate an entity if it owns a controlling financial interest, usually defined as a majority voting interest in the entity. Enron, however, illustrated that an enterprise may retain effective control or significant influence over an entity through arrangements other than voting stock, including contractual agreements, the entity's organizational documents, and other governing documents. Significantly, Enron designed its SPEs to avoid including the assets and debt on its consolidated balance sheet as the consolidation method would generally dictate. In addition, Enron created some SPEs to inflate revenues by recognizing sales on transactions with the SPEs, a treatment that both the consolidation and equity methods would otherwise disallow. In other words, Enron either evaded or disregarded such modest accounting literature regarding consolidating SPEs as there was, and also the SEC's general rule that required an independent investor with ownership of at least three percent of the SPE's assets and control over the SPE to consolidate. See Bratton, *Enron and the Dark Side of Shareholder Value,* 76 TUL. L. REV. 1275 (2002) (discussing in detail how Enron abused its extraordinarily complex web of SPEs to avoid consolidating the entities under previous accounting rules).

Notably, while accountants and lawyers alike have integrated the term SPE into their common business vernacular, the FASB recognized in its recent promulgation on the subject that no clear or generally accepted definition exists. CONSOLIDATION OF VARIABLE INTEREST ENTITIES (AN INTERPRETATION OF ARB NO. 51), FASB Interpretation No. 46 (revised December 2003), ¶ E1 ("FIN 46"), which we will review shortly. As a general starting point, a recent report on Enron's collapse defines an SPE as "an entity created for a limited purpose, with a limited life and limited activities, and designed to benefit a single company." Powers, pages 358-359, *supra,* app. A at 95. Although SPEs may take any legal form, including a corporation, partnership, or trust, the organizational documents or contractual arrangements often limit or predetermine activities and powers.

This general description may be unhelpful, but enterprises do use these SPEs for legitimate financing, investing, or leasing functions, to increase efficiency in transacting business and to limit exposure to risk. For example, enterprises often legitimately use SPEs for securitization, the process by which a business assembles a pool of financial assets, such as mortgage loans or credit card receivables, and transfers them to an SPE, potentially recognizing the transfer as a sale. While enterprises primarily benefit from securitization by isolating the risk to the financial assets within the pool, which often allows a higher credit rating and more favorable financing terms, benefits generally flow to consumers as well. *See, e.g.,* Richard, *Investors Come to the Defense of Securitization, Special Purpose Entities Tainted by Enron's Fall,* WALL ST. J., Mar. 19, 2002, at C15 (noting that securitization contributed to the increased availability of credit cards to Americans).

Because commercial lawyers often draft the organizational documents for SPEs and assist with subsequent transactions, lawyers should generally understand the form, purpose, and the accounting treatment of VIEs, including legitimate SPEs, under that FASB accounting pronouncement referred to above, FIN 46. Recent estimates indicate that trillions of dollars of assets reside in such off-balance sheet entities and the new accounting rule governing VIEs could add as much as $379 billion of assets and $377 billion of liabilities to the balance sheets of companies in the Standard & Poor's – 500 stock index. Bryan-Low, *Accounting Board Clarifies Rule,* WALL ST. J., Nov. 3, 2003, at A11.

Although SPEs can serve legitimate business purposes, after Enron popularized SPEs under such infamous names as Braveheart, Chewco, and JEDI, many lawyers and law students associate SPEs with complex transactions designed to distort an enterprise's financial condition and operating results. Enron-era SPEs often existed as highly leveraged, shell entities that enterprises exploited to inflate revenues and to move liabilities and poorly performing assets off the balance sheet. Thus, Enron conducted a joint venture investment partnership known as JEDI that involved debt totaling $1.6 billion by 1999. As another example, Enron recorded a $16 million gain by selling an interest in a Polish company to an SPE known as LJM2 for $30 million after failing to find an unrelated buyer, and, remarkably, later bought the interest back from LJM2 for $31.9 million. In a deal with the SPE code-named Braveheart, Enron reported a $111 million gain by transferring an agreement with Blockbuster Video for movies on demand after Enron determined that it would never realize any real profits from the agreement.

It was in response to the gaps in the prior consolidation rules exposed by the Enron scandal that in 2003 FASB adopted and subsequently revised interpretation FIN 46. FASB essentially adopted a substance over form approach for consolidating certain entities by focusing on the enterprise's actual variable interest in the entity, which includes contractual, ownership, or other pecuniary interests. *Id.* ¶ 2(c). Although accountants and lawyers both commonly refer to all VIEs simply as SPEs, FIN 46 substituted the former term to emphasize that the guidelines apply to a broader spectrum of entities. Simply stated, FIN 46 specifies two general inquiries to determine whether an investing enterprise must consolidate an entity that might otherwise escape consolidation under the voting stock analysis.

First, FIN 46 treats any entity, including SPEs, that meet *any of the following conditions* as a VIE, and hence subject to consolidation:

(1) The entity's total equity investment at risk does not permit the entity to finance its activities without additional financial support (with a rebuttable presumption that an entity qualifies as a VIE if its equity investments fall below ten percent of its total assets).

(2) The equity investors as a group *lack* any one of the following characteristics of a controlling financial interest:

(a) the ability through voting rights to make decisions about the entity's activities; or

(b) the obligation to absorb the entity's expected loss; or

(c) the right to receive the entity's expected returns.

(3) Some equity investors have voting rights disproportionate to their obligation to absorb the entity's expected losses, their right to receive the entity's expected returns, or both, and substantially all of the entity's activities either involve or are conducted on behalf of the equity investor that has disproportionately few voting rights.

Second, FIN 46 generally considers an investing enterprise the primary beneficiary of a VIE, and, therefore, it must consolidate the VIE, if the enterprise or related parties own interests in the VIE that will absorb a majority of the VIE's expected losses, receive a majority of the VIE's expected returns, or both.

FIN 46 also imposes disclosure requirements on the primary beneficiary of a VIE, such as (1) the VIE's nature, purpose, size, and activities; (2) the consolidated assets that serve as collateral for the VIE's obligations; and (3) the lack of recourse if the consolidated VIE's creditors have no claim to the primary beneficiary's general credit. Alternatively, even if an enterprise does not qualify as the primary beneficiary, an enterprise that owns a significant interest in a VIE must disclose: (1) the nature of the enterprise's involvement with the VIE and when that involvement began; (2) the VIE's nature, purpose, size, and activities; and (3) the enterprise's maximum exposure to loss from its involvement with the VIE. Id. ¶ 24.

c. LOSSES

As previously noted, GAAP requires an enterprise to treat any "other than temporary" decline in an investment's value as a loss. In Staff Accounting Bulletin No. 59, the SEC's staff expressed its belief that the phrase "other than temporary" does not mean permanent.

SAB No. 59 lists various factors, which singularly or collectively can suggest that an investment has experienced a non-temporary decline. The factors include the length of time and the extent to which market value has remained less than cost, the investing enterprise's intent and ability to hold the investment for such time as to allow for any anticipated recovery in market value, and the investee's financial condition and near-term prospects.

d. PERSONAL FINANCIAL STATEMENTS

One other commonly encountered situation deviates from the historical cost principle and the exchange transaction requirement. Banks and other lenders frequently rely on personal financial statements for making credit decisions about individuals, focusing on the individual's assets and liabilities. Similarly, attorneys consider current values in estate, gift and income tax planning for clients. Elected public officials and candidates for public offices often disclose personal financial information. In all these situations, current fair values, even if estimated, usually provide more relevant information than historical costs.

Statement of Position 82–1, *Accounting and Financial Reporting for Personal Financial Statements*, establishes GAAP for personal financial statements. That pronouncement states that personal financial statements should present all assets and liabilities at their estimated current values or amounts. In addition, a personal balance sheet should treat any estimated income taxes on the differences between the assets' current values and costs as a liability in determining net worth.

4. SALE OR EXCHANGE WITH A RIGHT OF RETURN

To be contrasted with an obvious sham transaction is a sale or exchange which is subject to an express provision giving the buyer a right to return the item and receive a full refund or credit. In such cases there has clearly been an exchange transaction, including a transfer of legal title, so the transaction is real enough; but in terms of economic substance, the seller seems to have retained the risks of ownership, which certainly suggests that revenue should not yet be recognized.

In Statement of Financial Accounting Standards No. 48, *Revenue Recognition When Right of Return Exists* (FASB 1981), the Financial Accounting Standards Board established accounting and reporting standards for sales in which either the contract or existing practice gives the buyer the right to return the product. Under that pronouncement, a seller can recognize revenue immediately only if the surrounding circumstances satisfy the following six conditions:

> (1) The underlying agreement substantially fixes or determines the price to the buyer on the date of sale;

(2) The buyer has paid the seller, or the underlying agreement obligates the buyer to pay   the seller whether or not the buyer resells the product;

(3) The product's theft, physical destruction or damage will not change the buyer's obligation to the seller;

(4) The buyer acquiring the product for resale has economic substance apart from any resources that the seller has provided;

(5) The underlying agreement does not impose significant obligations on the seller for future performance directed to bringing about the product's resale; and

(6) The seller can reasonably estimate future returns.

If a sales transaction satisfies all six requirements, SFAS No. 48 specifies that the seller recognize the sales revenue and the costs of the sale in the income statement (but with appropriate adjustment to reflect estimated returns).

In many cases, an exchange transaction satisfies the first five requirements, and revenue recognition hinges on whether the seller can reasonably estimate future returns. That determination, in turn, depends on many factors and circumstances which vary from case to case. SFAS No. 48, however, provides that the following factors may impair the seller's ability to establish a reasonable estimate:

(a) The product's susceptibility to significant external factors, such as technological obsolescence or changes in demand;

(b) A relatively long return period;

(c) Insufficient or no historical experience with similar sales or similar products;

(d) Changing circumstances, such as modifications in the seller's marketing policies or relationships with customers, which preclude the enterprise from applying historical experience; or

(e) Inadequate volume of relatively homogeneous transactions.

If the seller cannot reasonably estimate returns, or fails to satisfy one of the other five requirements necessary for revenue recognition at the time of sale, the enterprise should not recognize sales revenue and cost of sales until either: (1) the return privilege has substantially expired, or (2) the underlying circumstances subsequently satisfy the six conditions, whichever occurs first.

5. NON-MONETARY TRANSACTIONS

Recall that one of the requirements for recognition of revenue is that the enterprise actually receive cash or have a right to receive cash, or be able readily to convert the consideration received into money or money's worth. In most exchange transactions, a business provides or transfers services, goods or other assets for cash, or claims to cash-like notes receivable or accounts receivable; and the monetary amount of the cash or claim to cash usually provides an objective basis for measuring revenue, or the gain or loss from the exchange. But there are plenty of transactions which involve only non-monetary assets, such as inventories, investments, or long-lived assets on both sides, and some such transactions may represent another instance when it is inappropriate to recognize revenue or gain, despite the presence of a bona fide exchange with an outside party.

Nevertheless, the starting point is with the rule that gain or loss generally *should* be recognized on an exchange of non-monetary assets, based upon the difference between the cost of the asset surrendered and the fair market value of the asset received (or, if it is more readily determinable, of the asset surrendered, since in an arm's length transaction the two would normally be equal). APB Opinion No. 29, *Accounting for Non-Monetary Transactions* (1973). But gain or loss should not be recognized if fair market values cannot be determined within reasonable limits, and under APB Op. No. 29 that includes any situation in which there are major uncertainties about the ability to realize value from the asset obtained in a non-monetary exchange; instead, the asset acquired should be accounted for at the recorded amount for the asset surrendered.

In addition, even when fair market values can be readily determined, revenue or gain should not be recognized if a non-monetary exchange "is not essentially the culmination of an earning process." Op. No. 29 identifies two types of transactions which fall under this rule: (1) the exchange of an inventory item for an inventory item that the enterprise will sell in the same line of business to a customer other than the other party to the exchange, and (2) the exchange of a productive asset other than inventory for a similar asset or an equivalent interest in the same or a similar asset. Transactions in this second category would include a trade of player contracts by professional sports franchises, the exchange of leases on mineral properties, or a swap of one parcel of real estate for another. Again, if nonrecognition applies, the enterprise should account for the asset acquired at the recorded amount for the asset relinquished.

Problem 6.3. Wootton Real Estate, Inc., a concern which traded in real estate, owned some obsolete housing in East Cambridge. It desired to expand its operations by acquiring land suitable for new residential construction. Paulus and Company, a manufacturing concern, owned some land in Lincoln on which it had intended to erect a factory if the zoning boundaries could be changed. When a citizens' committee in Lincoln was formed to oppose the Paulus project, Paulus deci ded to build in East Cambridge. An even exchange was arranged between Wootton and Paulus. Wootton estimated the value of the Lincoln land at $50,000. The East Cambridge property had cost Wootton $40,000.

Wootton's book entry was:

Lincoln Land	$50,000
East Cambridge Property	$40,000
Income	10,000

Wootton's auditors questioned the credit to income where there had been no "receipt of cash or its equivalent, to evidence earnings." They argued that since Wootton's risk was the same as before — the risk of loss of value of land held in portfolio — there had been no "realization."

Wootton replied that if all its holdings were liquidated the next day the transaction would show a profit of at least $10,000. Wootton had already received a bid of $27,000 for half of the Lincoln property. Who is right, Wootton or the auditors?

Assuming that the Lincoln land cost Paulus and Company $35,000, how should Paulus treat the transaction? Would your conclusion differ if Paulus had made the swap with Wootton because it had abandoned plans for a new plant and was instead interested in the East Cambridge property as a land speculation?

6. EARNINGS PROCESS SUBSTANTIALLY COMPLETE

In addition to satisfying the requirement of a bona fide transaction with an outsider, an enterprise must substantially complete the earnings process before recognizing revenue. To satisfy this substantial completion requirement, an enterprise must normally deliver the underlying goods or render the contemplated services; an exchange of promises is not enough. However, even delivery does not automatically satisfy the substantial completion requirement: recall the earlier discussion of the sale or exchange with a right of return. In addition, there can be less formal arrangements or understandings which give customers the right to refuse to pay for the goods, and hence preclude current recognition of revenue.

a. RECEIPT OF CASH IN ADVANCE: DEFERRED INCOME

The fact that payment for the goods or services has been received in advance does not lessen the need to deliver the goods or render the services before recognizing revenue. Remember that back in Chapter I Ms. Tutt could not include in July's revenues a retainer she received for work to be done in August because she had not earned the income yet. As important as the ultimate receipt of cash is, and as beneficial and reassuring as it is to have the cash in hand at the outset, it does not override the requirement that the earning process be substantially complete before revenue is recognized. Instead, an enterprise must defer the prospective revenue until the required performance has been at least substantially completed. The following case further illustrates income deferral and also explains how and why financial accounting rules can differ from tax rules.

Boise Cascade Corporation v. United States

United States Court of Claims, 1976.
530 F.2d 1367, *cert. denied* 429 U.S. 867, 97 S.Ct. 176, 50 L.Ed.2d 147 (1976).

■ PER CURIAM:

These are consolidated cases, in which plaintiffs seek the recovery of nearly $2,400,000 in income taxes plus interest thereon, paid for the years 1955 through 1961. They now come before the court on exceptions by the parties to the recommended decision filed by Trial Judge Lloyd Fletcher, on September 20, 1974, * * * having been submitted to the court on the briefs and oral argument of counsel. He held for the plaintiffs on all the significant issues. After briefing and oral argument, the court agrees with the trial judge in part, and disagrees in part.

* * *

We agree substantially with the portions of the recommended opinion that hold the Commissioner of Internal Revenue to have abused his discretion under IRC § 446(b), in determining that Ebasco's method of accounting failed to reflect income clearly for Federal Income Tax purposes and in requiring a change in such method as set forth below. The portions of the said trial judge's opinion that deal with this subject are set forth below and are adopted as our opinion with some modifications made by the court.

* * *

Trial Judge Fletcher's opinion, as modified by the court, follows:

The plaintiffs are Boise Cascade Corporation and several of its subsidiary companies. The original petition was filed by Ebasco Industries Inc. and its subsidiary companies which . . . [later] merged with Boise Cascade. Ebasco Industries was engaged in holding various investments . . . [including] ownership interests in various operating subsidiaries which were (and continue to be) engaged primarily in rendering engineering, construction, architectural, and consulting services. . . .

The plaintiffs' annual shareholder reports included a certification by independent accountants that the financial statements were prepared in conformity with generally accepted accounting principles applied on a basis consistent with that of the preceding year.

In its business, Ebasco Services enters into contracts to perform engineering and similar services. Under the various terms of these contracts, Ebasco is entitled to bill fixed sums either in monthly, quarterly, or other periodic installments, plus such additional amounts as may be provided for in a particular contract. Depending on the terms of the different contracts, payments may in some cases be due prior to the annual period in which such services are to be performed, and in some cases subsequent thereto.

For a number of years prior to 1959 and continuing to the time of trial, Ebasco included in its income for both book and tax purposes amounts attributable to services which it performed during the taxable year, a procedure accepted by the Internal Revenue Service on prior audits. Ebasco determined the amounts so earned by dividing the estimated number of service hours or days required to complete the particular contract into the contract price. The resulting quotient represents an hourly or daily rate which is then multiplied by the number of hours or days actually worked on the contract during the taxable year. As the contract is performed, the rate is adjusted to reflect revised estimates of the work required to complete the contract.

Where Ebasco billed for services prior to the tax year in which they were performed, it credited such amounts to a balance sheet account called "Unearned Income[."] Where the services were performed in a subsequent period, the "Unearned Income" account was debited, and such amounts were included in an income account called "Service Revenues." The amount recorded in the latter account was included in income for both book and tax purposes. In determining the amount which was to be included in the "Unearned Income" account, the costs of obtaining the [contract, which included the cost of preparing bids, proposals, and estimates, advertising, selling and other expenses,] were not taken into account; and, with the exception of prepaid insurance and similar items, all such amounts were expensed in the tax year during which they were incurred. The amounts in the "Unearned Income" account were treated as liabilities and were excluded from gross income for each tax year consistently in Ebasco's books, records, and shareholder reports, as well as in its tax returns. All of the amounts included in the account during one tax year were earned through the performance of services during the following year and were included in income for such following tax year. When the amounts credited to the "Unearned Income" account were collected, Ebasco had an unrestricted right to the use of such funds.

During the three tax years in issue, an average of over 94 percent of the amounts included in the "Unearned Income" account was received by Ebasco under contracts which obligated it to perform engineering services in connection with the design and construction of electric generating plants. These contracts either required that services be performed by a specified date or required that Ebasco should perform those services "with all reasonable dispatch and diligence," as "expeditiously as possible," or some comparable requirement. The small remaining amounts in the account were received either under contracts which required Ebasco to perform specific services in connection with a specific project of a client, or required Ebasco to provide consultation and advice on an annual basis for an annual fee.

In addition to its "Unearned" account, Ebasco maintained an "Unbilled Charges" account computed in the same manner as the "Unearned Income" account. The balance in such account represented amounts earned through the rendering of services, or on partially completed contracts, or earned prior to contracting under all of which payment was not then due by the terms of a contract or was not billable and due prior to execution of a future contract. Stated another way, the amounts included in this account were those which Ebasco was not entitled to bill or receive until a year subsequent to the year in which the services were actually rendered. Such amounts were recorded in "Service Revenues" and included in income for tax as well as book purposes in the taxable year in which the services were rendered. Likewise, the costs attributable to the rendering of services which produced the year-end balance in the "Unbilled Charges" account were deducted from gross income in the year such services were rendered. In 1959, 1960, and 1961 there were approximately $405,000, ($56,000), and $179,000 of such net amounts, respectively, carried in the "Unbilled Charges" account.

Plaintiffs' consolidated income tax returns for 1959 through 1961 were audited by the Government, and the amounts in the "Unearned Income" account were included in taxable income for Federal tax purposes. These adjustments were made pursuant to section 446(b) of the 1954 Code under which the Commissioner determined that plaintiffs' deferral method of accounting did not clearly reflect income. During the same examination for the same tax years, no adjustments were made to the "Unbilled Charges" or the "Service Revenues" accounts.

At trial Ebasco presented expert testimony related solely to the accounting practices described above. The sole witness was a qualified certified public accountant and a partner in a major accounting firm. Based on his broad experience with comparable service companies and his personal familiarity with the accounting practices of Ebasco, he expressed his expert opinion with respect to the accounts in issue and the changes made by the Commissioner.

He testified that the method of accounting used by Ebasco which employs both an "Unearned Income" account and an "Unbilled Charges" account and is based on [recognizing] amounts as income at the time the related services are performed is in accordance with * * * generally accepted accounting principles and clearly reflects Ebasco's income. He indicated that this method properly matched revenues with costs of producing such revenues and is particularly appropriate in this case because almost all of Ebasco's income is derived from the performance of services by its own personnel. He further testified that this method of accounting was widely used by companies engaged in rendering engineering and similar services, and that such method clearly reflected the income of Ebasco.

With respect to costs incurred in obtaining contracts, such as bid preparation, overhead, advertising, and other selling expenses, the witness considered them to be properly deducted in the year incurred as continuing costs of doing and developing business. [The witness distinguished such costs from commissions which in some instances may properly be amortized where they relate directly to the contract involved and thus reduce the amount realizable under such contract.] He explained that these costs should not properly be amortizable over the life of any particular contract since they were costs connected with new business development and were unrelated to performance of the contract.

The accounting method proposed by the Commissioner requires Ebasco to accrue as income the amounts included in the "Unearned Income" account and also requires the accrual, consistent with plaintiffs' accounting method, of amounts in the "Unbilled Charges" account. In the opinion of plaintiffs' expert, this method of accounting was not in accordance with generally accepted accounting principles and did not clearly reflect Ebasco's income. To him, the Commissioner's method was erroneous in that it required the inclusion in income of amounts billed but not yet earned on contracts in one accounting period without at the same time acknowledging the obligations and costs to be incurred by Ebasco in the future performance of such contractual commitments. He termed such method as "hybrid" in that while it recognized the accrual method with respect to unbilled charges which were earned but not yet billable, it had the effect of imposing a cash basis method as to the billed but unearned charges in the "Unearned Income" account.

Finally, the witness testified that if Ebasco were to use a method of accounting under which amounts in the "Unearned Income" account would be accrued as income and amounts in the "Unbilled Charges" account would *not* be accrued as income, such method would more clearly reflect the income of Ebasco than the method of accounting proposed by the Commissioner. He stated that, while such method was not technically in accordance with generally accepted accounting principles, it was a more logical and consistent approach to use in determining the income of Ebasco than the Commissioner's method.

* * *

These issues present but another facet in the continuing controversy over the proper timing for Federal income tax purposes of various income and expense items incurred by an accrual basis taxpayer. Based on expert accounting testimony presented by Ebasco at trial, it can hardly be disputed that Ebasco's system for deferral of unearned income is in full accord with generally accepted accounting principles as that phrase is used in financial or commercial accounting. But such a showing alone is not determinative for income tax purposes. The taxpayer must also show that its method clearly reflects income for the purposes of the Internal Revenue Code. Thus, while generally accepted methods of accounting are of probative value and are treated with respect by Treas. Reg. § 1.446–1(a)(2), they are not necessarily synonymous with the proper tax accounting to be afforded an accrual item in a given situation.

This variance is especially noticeable in cases where the taxpayer's accounting method results in the deferment of income. The taxpayer in such a situation is generally relying on well-known accounting principles which essentially focus on a conservative matching of income and expenses to the end that an item of income will be related to its correlative expenditure. Tax accounting, on the other hand, starts from the premise of a need for certainty in the collection of revenues and focuses on the concept of ability to pay. Thus, under this theory, where an item of income has been received even though as yet unearned, it should be subject to taxation because the taxpayer has in hand (or otherwise available) the funds necessary to pay the tax due.

(The Court then reviewed three important Supreme Court decisions.)

* * *

It seems clear to me that, despite defendant's vigorous contention to the contrary, this trilogy of Supreme Court decisions cannot be said to have established an unvarying rule of law that, absent a specific statutory exception, a taxpayer may never defer recognition of income received or accrued under a contract for the performance of future services, no matter whether such deferral clearly reflects income.

Defendant persuasively argues, however, that its interpretation of the cases is justified by the Court's additional ground for decision in [two of the cases, in which] the Court's majority and minority opinions gave close consideration to the legislative history of sections 452 and 462 of the 1954 Code. These sections contained the first explicit legislative sanctions of deferral of income (§ 452) and deduction of future estimated expenses (§ 462). In the next year, however, both sections were retroactively repealed. To the majority in [one of the cases,] this repealer action constituted "clearly a mandate from the Congress that petitioner's system was not acceptable for tax purposes." The dissent, of course, viewed the legislative history in different perspective.

To me, the dilemma and its likely solution, have been gracefully and accurately stated by the able and comprehensive opinion of the Fifth Circuit Court of Appeals in *Mooney Aircraft, Inc. v. United States*, 420 F.2d 400, 408–409 (5th Cir., 1969) where the court observed:

> This alternative ground, based on legislative intent, would seem to dispose of the entire question: *all* deferrals and accruals are bad unless specifically authorized by Congress. But the Court was careful to discuss the legislative history as dictum and restricted its holding to a finding that the Commissioner did not abuse his discretion in rejecting the *AAA*'s accounting system. It specifically refrained from overruling *Beacon* [*Beacon Publishing Co. v. Commissioner of Internal Revenue*, 218 F.2d 697 (10th Cir.1955) (deferral of prepaid subscriptions)] and *Schuessler* [*Schuessler v. Commissioner of Internal Revenue*, 230 F.2d 722 (5th Cir.1956) (accrual of expenses of 5–year service period)], distinguishing them on the ground that future performance was certain. . . .

The *Mooney Aircraft* approach was foreshadowed by the Seventh Circuit's decision in *Artnell Company v. Commissioner of Internal Revenue*, 400 F.2d 981 (7th Cir., 1968). There, Chicago White Sox, Inc. had received and accrued in a deferred unearned income account amounts attributable to advance ticket sales and revenues for other services related to baseball games to be played thereafter during the 1962 season. Prior to such performance, however, Artnell acquired Chicago White Sox, Inc., liquidated it, and continued operation of the team. In the final short-year return filed as transferee by Artnell in behalf of White Sox, Inc., Artnell excluded the deferred unearned income previously received by White Sox. The Commissioner required such amounts to be accrued as income to White Sox on receipt, and the Tax Court sustained him. In reversing and remanding, the Seventh Circuit analyzed the Supreme Court's trilogy, *supra*, and said at 400 F.2d 984–985:

* * *

It is our best judgment that, although the policy of deferring, where possible, to congressional procedures in the tax field will cause the Supreme Court to accord the widest possible latitude to the commissioner's discretion, there must be situations where the deferral technique will so clearly reflect income that the Court will find an abuse of discretion if the commissioner rejects it.

Prior to 1955 the commissioner permitted accrual basis publishers to defer unearned income from magazine subscriptions if they had consistently done so in the past. He refused to allow others to adopt the method. In 1955 his refusal was held, by the tenth circuit, in *Beacon*, to be an abuse of discretion. In *Automobile Club of Michigan,* the Supreme Court distinguished Beacon, on its facts, because "performance of the subscription, in most instances, was, in part, necessarily deferred until the publication dates after the tax year." The Court, however, expressed no opinion upon the correctness of *Beacon*. In 1958, Congress dealt specifically with the *Beacon*, problem. It is at least arguable that the deferral as income of prepaid admissions to events which will take place on a fixed schedule in a different taxable year is so similar to deferral of prepaid subscriptions that it would be an abuse of discretion to reject similar accounting treatment. . . .

Judicial reaction to *Artnell* has been mixed. . . . Defendant's reaction, of course, is simply that "*Artnell* was wrongly decided."

Out of this mélange, one must choose a path. To use one of Justice Holmes' favorite expressions, I "can't help" but conclude that what Ebasco is pleased to call its "balanced and symmetrical" method of accounting does in fact clearly reflect its income. It achieves the desideratum of accurately matching costs and revenues by reason of the fact that the costs of earning such revenues are incurred at the time the services are performed. *See, Mooney Aircraft, supra*, 420 F.2d at 403. Entirely unlike the factual situations before the Supreme Court in the automobile club and dance studio cases, Ebasco's contractual obligations were fixed and definite. In no sense was Ebasco's performance of services dependent solely upon the demand or request of its clientele.

Based upon the foregoing considerations, it is necessary to conclude that Ebasco's method of accounting under which income is accrued as the related services are performed clearly reflects its income, and, accordingly, the Commissioner is not authorized by § 446(b) to impose another method of accounting. That this is true becomes particularly obvious when it is realized that the accounting method imposed upon Ebasco by the Commissioner is a classic example of a hybrid system combining elements of the accrual system with a cash system, a mixture generally viewed with disfavor. Thus, where Ebasco's billing precedes the rendition of its contracted-for services, the Commissioner proposes to tax as income amounts billed even though such amounts have not then been earned by performance. On the other hand, where the performance of services precedes billing, the commissioner would tax amounts as income at the time the services are rendered even though, under such contracts, Ebasco has no present right to bill, or receive payment of such amounts. The inconsistency within the Commissioner's method is strident.

His method would appear to the ordinary mind to distort income instead of clearly reflecting it. Judging both by what he has rejected and what he would impose he has abused his discretion within the meaning of the authority cited, *Mooney Aircraft and Artnell*. Ebasco has demonstrated not only that its method of accounting is in accordance with generally accepted accounting principles but, in addition, clearly reflects its income, treating these issue to be discrete, as we must. Therefore, the amounts accrued in Ebasco's "Unearned Income" account are not taxable until the year in which Ebasco performs the services which earn that income. *   *   *

NOTES

1. The principal case involved income taxes for the years 1955 through 1961. In Revenue Procedure 71-21, 1971-2 C.B. 549, the Internal Revenue Service announced an administrative decision to allow accrual method taxpayers to defer prepaid income for services as long as the taxpayer will perform the services before the end of the following taxable year. The deferral, however, applies no longer than to the end of that following year. Similarly, Treasury Regulations permit an accrual method taxpayer to elect to defer advance payments for goods and long term contracts. Treas. Reg. § 1.451-5 (as amended in 1985). Neither authority, however, authorizes an accrual method taxpayer to defer prepaid interest or rent.

2. In the principal case, Ebasco expensed the costs for obtaining the contracts, which included the cost of preparing bids, proposals and estimates, advertising, and other expenses, and the Commissioner did not challenge that treatment. Notice, this treatment technically does not match those expenses with the revenues that they produced.

Problem 6.4. E Corp. is engaged in rendering engineering and architectural services. Early in its most recent fiscal year, which ended on August 31, E learned that a large utility, P Co., might be interested in obtaining engineering and consulting services in connection with construction of a new generating plant. One of E's three sales representatives, who work full-time soliciting this kind of business for E, on a straight salary of $60,000 per year each, without commissions, spent all of his time for four months trying to land a contract with P. In addition, since P was considering a number of unusual features for its new plant, E retained a well-known scientist to work with its regular staff on the preparation of a proposal to P Corp., for which the scientist was paid $39,000. In March E got the contract, which called for specified engineering and other consulting services over the following fifteen to eighteen months in connection with building the new plant. Under the contract, E was to receive a total of $500,000, payable at the rate of $100,000 every three months, starting on May 15, regardless of when E's services were actually performed. Due to delays in P's construction schedule, E had in fact performed no services for P by the close of the fiscal year, and E had received only the first $100,000 payment. How should these facts be reflected in E's financial statements for the year?

b. DELIVERY, PASSAGE OF TITLE, OR OVERALL PERFORMANCE

When a customer orders goods from a manufacturer, with or without a down payment, we know that the manufacturer cannot recognize revenue at that time: at a minimum, it must wait until completing the manufacturing process because production represents the principal requirement that the manufacturer must perform under the contract. In most cases, full performance requires the seller to deliver the goods, either to the buyer, or to a carrier destined for the buyer. Some sales contracts will require other necessary steps as well, such as labeling the goods, installing the products at the buyer's premises, or the like. Keep in mind, however, that substantial performance is enough to justify revenue recognition, the seller need not complete every element of performance. Thus, the real question often becomes: "At what point does the seller achieve substantial performance?" The answer often requires professional judgment. Although accountants typically view the passage of title to the goods from the seller to the buyer as a sensible demarcation, lawyers cannot always agree when that has occurred. As a general rule, any reasonable cut-off point, *consistently applied*, should qualify. If an enterprise must still complete some steps, presumably insubstantial, the enterprise should accrue the estimated costs to perform at the same time, so that the income statement will match the entire expense of performance against the revenue from the transaction.

The following case illustrates these issues in a tax setting:

Pacific Grape Products Co. v. Commissioner

United States Court of Appeals, Ninth Circuit, 1955.
219 F.2d 862.

■ POPE, CIRCUIT JUDGE.

Petitioner is a canner of fruit and fruit products. It regularly billed its customers for all goods ordered by them, but not yet shipped and remaining in petitioner's warehouse, on December 31 in each year. It accrued upon its books the income from the sales of such unshipped goods in the taxable years ending on the days of such billing. On the same date it also credited to the accounts of brokers the brokerage due on account of sales of such unshipped goods, and accrued the cost of such unshipped goods including therein the anticipated cost of labeling, packaging and preparing the same for shipment. For many years the petitioner reported its income accordingly. (It filed its returns on the calendar year, accrual basis.)

The Commissioner, in determining deficiencies for the years 1940 to 1944, held petitioner's method of accounting did not clearly reflect its income and made adjustments by excluding from the computation of income for the years 1939, 1940 and 1941, the sales prices of unshipped goods billed on December 31 of those years, and included such amounts in the computations of income for the years 1940, 1941 and 1942 respectively. He likewise transferred to these later years the brokerage fees and the estimated costs mentioned which related to these goods. The result was a deficiency in income tax for the years 1940 and 1943, and in excess profits tax for the years 1940, 1941, 1942 and 1944, and in declared value excess profits tax for the year 1944. The determinations mentioned were upheld by the Tax Court on petition for redetermination.

Since its organization in 1926 petitioner has operated its cannery at Modesto, California. Its product was limited to fruit and fruit products. Its canning season in each year extends from about July 1st to November 1st. During such season it enters into numerous contracts for the sale of its current pack. * * *

The contracts described the quantity, price, grade, size of cans, and variety of fruit or fruit products to be sold. Some provided for labels bearing petitioner's name; others provided for the use of labels bearing the buyer's trade name, in which case the labels were furnished by the buyer to whom an allowance was made for the labels. A large portion of the goods covered by the contracts are shipped during the calendar year in which the fruits are packed. On occasion some buyers request petitioner to withhold shipment of all or part of their contract amounts until the following year and petitioner normally complies with such request. In that connection the contract form used provides: "Goods to be shipped in seller's discretion as soon as practicable after packing. * * * If seller shall elect to withhold shipment at buyer's request, then the goods unshipped shall be billed and paid for on the following dates respectively hereinafter specified. * * * Fruits, Fruit Products or Sundry Vegetables, December 31." Accordingly goods remaining unshipped on December 31 of each year were billed by the petitioner to their respective buyers on that date.

On December 31 of each year the petitioner always has on hand a sufficient quantity of goods of every variety, grade and size of can to fill all contracts. * * * The fruits of different varieties, grades and sizes of cans were separately arranged in separate stacks with no commingling of variety, grade or size in any one stack. It was stipulated in the Tax Court that all of the canned fruits and fruit products here involved were fungible goods within the meaning of the Uniform Sales Act * * *. The evidence showed that in accruing and entering upon its books in these years the expense of brokerage fees, petitioner calculated the amount of such fees in accordance with the customary trade practice of the California canning industry. That practice was to accrue the expenses of such fees as of the dates the unshipped goods were billed. With respect to the expenses of shipment of the goods, that is, the cost of labeling, packing and freight, it accrued and entered upon its books as an item of deduction the anticipated cost of these items. What the cost would be was known from the petitioner's past experience with such expenditures.

The Tax Court, six judges dissenting, upheld the Commissioner's determination that the method employed by the petitioner of computing accrued income from its sales did not clearly reflect its income. The court based its conclusion entirely upon its determination that title to the goods in question did not pass to the buyers on the billing dates. * * *

* * * In this we think that the Tax Court was in error.

* * *

It is true that the goods here had to be labeled, packed and shipped at a subsequent date. Such a circumstance is a matter to be taken into consideration in ascertaining the intention of the parties as to when the property in the goods is to pass under Rule 2 of the California Civil Code, § 1739, § 19 of the Uniform Sales Act. But that circumstance is not controlling, for all of the rules specified in that section are subject to the initial qualification of the section,—"unless a different intention appears", etc. Not only is the different intention indicated by the proof of the custom here referred to, but the language of the contract provides that the goods unshipped shall be billed and paid for on December 31. While there is no evidence to show that the buyers actually paid for those goods on December 31 (the implication is quite otherwise), yet the contract clearly specifies that payment was due on that date, which would further confirm an understanding that title had then passed.

Since title had thus passed to the buyers, it is plain that petitioner's method of accounting and accruing in such years its gross income from sales of such merchandise clearly reflected its income. Consistently, and to make reflection of income complete, it properly accrued its shipping expenses relating to this merchandise as part of its cost of goods sold in the respective years billed. The record shows that the items making up these expenses were either precisely known or determinable with extreme accuracy. Labels and cases for packing were on hand. The expenses of labor in labeling and casing were determinable on the basis of petitioner's past experience. Freight costs were available from published rate schedules. * * *

We think also that petitioner correctly treated the brokerage fees relating to the goods billed on the December 31 dates as deductible expenses in those years. The Tax Court disapproved this procedure on the ground that it thought there was a failure to introduce evidence of the contracts with the brokers to show that there was any fixed liability for the brokerage fees prior to the payment of the purchase price for the goods. The evidence, however, showed that the brokers doing business with the industry contracted in accordance with the established trade practice of considering that title to the unshipped goods passed on the billing dates, and that the brokerage fees accrued to the broker on those dates. In our view the finding that there was want of proof on this point is clearly erroneous.
       * * *

Finally, we are of the view that the petitioner's method of accounting clearly and accurately reflected its income wholly apart from the question whether title to the goods did or did not pass to the buyers on the dates of billing. Upon this aspect we are agreed with what the six dissenting judges said in this case.[10]

---

[10]"Opper, J. dissenting: The practice of disapproving consistent accounting systems of long standing seems to me to be exceeding all reasonable bounds. Methods of keeping records do not spring in glittering perfection from some unchangeable natural law but are devised to aid business men in maintaining sometimes intricate accounts. If reasonably adapted to that use they should not be condemned for some abstruse legal reason, but only when they fail to reflect income. There is no persuasive indication that such a condition exists here. On the contrary, a whole industry apparently has adopted the method used by petitioner."

"It will not do to say that respondent should not have disturbed petitioner's accounting method, but that since he has done so, we are powerless to do otherwise. As long as we continue to approve the imposition of theoretical criteria in so purely practical a field, respondent will go on attempting to seize on such recurring fortuitous occasions to increase the revenue, even though he may actually accomplish the opposite. I think it evident that petitioner's generally recognized accounting system did not distort its income and that it should be permitted to continue to use it. * * *"

Not only do we have here a system of accounting which for years has been adopted and carried into effect by substantially all members of a large industry, but the system is one which appeals to us as so much in line with plain common sense that we are at a loss to understand what could have prompted the Commissioner to disapprove it. Contrary to his suggestion that petitioner's method did not reflect its true income it seems to us that the alterations demanded by the Commissioner would wholly distort that income. It is reasonable that both the taxpayer and the Government should be able accurately to ascertain the income accruing to the taxpayer on account of each annual pack. The Commissioner would break up the petitioner's product for the year 1940 and throw the receipts from the portion shipped before December 31 into gross income for that year and the receipts from the unshipped portion into the following year. If in a succeeding year there arose a market shortage which led to a demand which brought about almost complete shipment of the pack before December 31, the Commissioner's accounts for that succeeding year would cover one nearly complete pack and portions of the income and deductions relating to the preceding pack. We see no reason for any such requirement on the part of the Commissioner.

The judgment of the Tax Court is reversed and the cause is remanded with directions to modify the judgment in accordance with this opinion.

NOTES

1. The substantial completion requirement finds support in the *matching principle* emphasized throughout these materials: when recognition of revenue is delayed pursuant to the substantial completion rule, the enterprise will have rendered most, if not all, of the required performance. By waiting until substantial completion, the enterprise will have already incurred most related costs, thus removing any doubt about whether performance will occur and eliminating the need to estimate most expenses.

2. As previously mentioned, when the seller delivers goods to a buyer the revenue recognition principle generally treats the goods as sold because the seller has substantially completed its obligations. When some relatively minor uncertainty remains, such as a warranty obligation, the seller could theoretically defer a portion of the revenue until the warranty period expires. In the real world, however, most enterprises estimate the likely costs to honor the warranties for the goods sold and accrue those estimated expenses at the time of the sale to achieve the desired matching.

PROBLEMS

Problem 6.5A. Suppose that in year 1 the O'Hara Company entered into a contract calling for the manufacture and delivery of goods in year 2 for $1,000,000. The company estimated that it would cost $612,000 to perform the contract. What entries would the company make at the close of year 1 if it wanted to reflect the profit on this contract in year 1? Would that be proper? What if the issue was how large a dividend O'Hara Company could pay?

Problem 6.5B. Assume that at the close of its fiscal year just ended the Pacific Grape Products Company had on hand $300,000 of completed canned goods inventory which had been ordered by customers but not yet labeled or shipped; the sales price of these goods was $420,000, the brokers' commissions were five percent of sales price, and the estimated cost of labeling and shipping the goods was $15,000. Assume further that if the company had treated these goods as not having been sold during the year just ended, and hence had not recognized the income and related expenses during that year, its balance sheet as of the close of that year would have appeared as follows:

Pacific Grape Products Company

Assets		Liabilities & Equity	
Cash	$90,000	Liabilities	
Accounts Receivable		Note Payable	$500,000
(net of $14,000		Accounts Payable	334,000
allowance for		Expense Payable	75,000
doubtful accounts)	686,000	Estimated Liabilities	12,000
Inventory	580,000	Total Liabilities	$921,000
		Equity	
Fixed Assets (after		Common Stock	$1,500,000
depreciation)	1,634,000	Retained Earnings	579,000
Deferred Expenses	10,000	Total Equity	$2,079,000
Total Assets	$3,000,000	Total Liabilities & Equity	$3,000,000

How would the balance sheet look if the company treated these goods as sold during the year just ended? How would that treatment have affected the company's income statement? Which approach do you favor?

c. EXCEPTIONS TO THE SUBSTANTIAL COMPLETION REQUIREMENT

We have already seen one important exception to the substantial completion requirement, when the transaction involves granting the right to use an asset, i.e., the enterprise leases property or lends money, and the corresponding revenues are earned in accordance with the passage of time.

Another significant exception involves the accounting for a substantial contract, other than for the production of fungible inventory, which extends over more than one period. When such a contract, say, for the construction of a large bridge, spans several accounting periods, application of the traditional view barring recognition of any revenue until the period in which the project reaches substantial completion, referred to in this context as the completed-contract method, does not provide a very meaningful picture of how the enterprise is doing in the earlier periods, particularly if this contract represents a considerable proportion of the total activities of the business. Accordingly, GAAP sanctions the use of the *percentage-of-completion* method for such contracts: that method allows an enterprise to reflect in each period an a mount of the total revenues expected from the contract which is proportionate to the percentage of performance on the contract during the period, to be matched with those costs of performance during that period, thereby reflecting in the period the proportionate amount of the total estimated profit on the contract.

The following article examines the percentage-of-completion method and compares it with the completed-contract method.

CLIFFORD E. GRAESE & JOSEPH R. DEMARIO, *REVENUE RECOGNITION FOR LONG TERM CONTRACTS**

142 J. Accountancy 53 (Dec. 1976).

In recent years the forms of contracts under which goods and services are delivered have become markedly more complex, and the range of products and services delivered under contractual arrangement has greatly expanded. At one time contracting transactions were limited to the physical construction of major goods, such as an office building or large ship, and did not generally include services. However, the range of items that is delivered under contractual arrangements today includes research, computer software services, sophisticated weapons delivery systems and space hardware and software. . . . This article examines the problems of revenue recognition on long term contracts and provides guidelines for using the percentage-of-completion method (percentage method) of revenue recognition.

Scope of This Article

The accounting concepts addressed in this article apply to those contracting transactions where (a) revenue recognition at the time the contract is entered into is not appropriate because the earning process is incomplete and (b) the individual contract serves as the basis for revenue recognition, cost accumulation and cost estimation because the earning process and costs incurred are inextricably bound up with the seller's obligations under the contract.

---

*Reprinted with permission from the *J. Accountancy,* © 1976 by the AICPA. Opinions of the authors do not necessarily reflect policies of AICPA.

Such contracting situations are frequently referred to as "long term," but the distinguishing feature of the transactions to which this article applies is not any specific duration of the period of performance under the contract. ... Accordingly, the term "long term contracts" as used in this article is not restricted to contracts with a specified minimum performance period .

The Basic Accounting Issue

The principal problem in accounting for long term contracts is determining the period in which revenue should be recognized. A key consideration in the determination of the appropriate accounting period for revenue recognition is an evaluation of the uncertainties which arise because performance on a given contract extends over a period of time. The uncertainties include the buyer's ability to make the payments required by the contract, the seller's ability to complete his performance obligations under the contract and the seller's ability to make reasonable estimates of the stage of completion and of future costs to complete the contract at the end of any accounting period.

The need to make estimates is present in many aspects of the accounting process, but it is of particular concern in contract accounting. The fact that performance extends over a period of time makes predictions of future costs and estimates of the stage of completion difficult. This difficulty tends to increase as the length of the performance period increases, although even in relatively shorter term contracts, circumstances can be such that estimates of the percentage of completion and of future costs can be difficult to make.

The nature of work to be performed under the contract also contributes to the difficulty of making estimates. For example, it may be a relatively simple matter to estimate the percentage of completion and the costs to complete where the contract calls for the construction of a type of equipment normally constructed by the contractor. A more difficult estimating problem would be involved in a contract for the construction of an underwater tunnel where unforeseen technical problems could arise, including those resulting from inaccurate geological surveys. Still more difficulty is encountered in estimates involving a new product, particularly one involving technology that extends beyond the present state of the art. Examples of this are frequently found in the aerospace-defense industry.

Authoritative literature provides for two acceptable methods for recognizing revenue on long term contracts, one of which recognizes revenue over the period of contract performance based on estimates where such estimates are reasonably reliable and the other of which postpones revenue recognition until the ultimate profit is known, thereby recognizing all the revenue in the period when the performance is completed or substantially completed. Both of these methods are widely employed in accounting practice. They are the percentage-of-completion method and the completed-contract method.

The Two Methods of Revenue Recognition

Accounting literature states that revenue is generally recognized when the earning process is complete or virtually complete and an exchange has taken place. The completed-contract method conforms to this realization principle in that income is recognized only when the contract is completed, or substantially so. (However, consistent with generally accepted accounting principles, anticipated losses are recognized as soon as they become evident.) The percentage-of-completion method, also provided for in authoritative accounting literature, is an acknowledged exception to the realization principle; revenue is recognized as work progresses, i.e., before the earning process is complete.

The principal advantage of the completed-contract method is that it does not rely on estimates for revenue recognition purposes and therefore eliminates the risk of recognizing revenue that does not materialize or that is subject to substantial subsequent adjustment. A major disadvantage of the method is that periodic reported income can be erratic when, for example, a few large contracts are completed in one accounting period but no contracts are completed in the previous or subsequent period even though the level of performance activity has been relatively constant throughout. When numerous contracts are regularly completed in each accounting period, periodic income may not be erratic, but there is a continuous lag between the time when work is performed and when the related revenue is recognized.

The disadvantage of the percentage-of-completion method is that it is subject to the risk of error in estimating the portion of contract performance completed and the costs to be incurred. When conditions are present that permit reasonable estimates to be made, the percentage-of-completion method has the advantage of recognizing revenue each period, based on the contracting efforts that took place in that period.

The AICPA committee on accounting procedure indicated in Accounting Research Bulletin No. 45 that the advantage of reflecting in the financial statements the revenue from business activity on long term contracts in periods prior to their completion should take precedence over the greater degree of certainty of results reported under the completed-contract method—provided the estimates necessary to apply the percentage method are sufficiently dependable. This all-important caveat enables us to redefine the basic issue in accounting for long term contracts: What are the circumstances that indicate that the estimates necessary to apply the percentage method will be sufficiently dependable to produce reliable results?

* * *

Requirements for Use of the Percentage Method

The percentage method produces reliable results if there is available adequate evidence of ultimate proceeds and if the estimates of future costs and the extent of contract performance completed are reasonably dependable. Compliance with these key requirements for each contract is essential to justify the use of the percentage method for that contract. Thus, certain contracts could appropriately be accounted for by the use of the percentage method while others are appropriately accounted for only by the completed-contract method. We believe the requirements for the use of the percentage method on long term contracts can be presumed to be fulfilled if all of the following conditions are present:

☐ There is a written contract executed by the parties that clearly specifies [all the relevant terms.]

☐ The buyer has the ability to satisfy his obligations under the contract.

☐ The seller has the ability to perform his contractual obligations.

☐ The seller has an adequate estimating process and the ability to estimate reliably both the cost to complete and the percentage of contract performance completed.

☐ The seller has a cost accounting system that adequately accumulates and allocates costs in a manner consistent with the estimates produced by the estimating process.

* * *

Ability to estimate. The seller must have the ability to reliably estimate costs to complete and should also have established methods to provide reasonable assurance of a continuing ability to estimate. . . .   Under the percentage method, the seller must not only be able to estimate that costs will not exceed contract revenues but he must also be able to reasonably determine the amount of profit that will result. Previous reliability of a seller's estimating process can be indicative of continuing estimating ability, particularly if the circumstances in the situation in question are similar to those of the past. However, new or changing circumstances may raise doubts about the continuing reliability of a previously demonstrated estimating ability. . . .

Measurement of the Percentage of Completion

Authoritative literature, such as the AICPA's *Audits of Construction Contractors*, provides for the use of the ratio of aggregate cost to date to the most recent estimate of total costs at completion (cost-to-cost) for the measurement of the percentage of completion. However, it also recognizes the possibility of using other methods of measuring the percentage of completion where such methods appropriately measure the portion of work performed. For example, labor hours, labor dollars, machine hours or architectural estimates may provide an appropriate measure of work performed.

In measuring contract performance, the method used must, because of the nature of contracting, give recognition to the risks of contract performance. Inherent in the seller's obligation under the contract are risks of performance which can affect the cost of the contract. For example, suppose a contract calls for the construction of a machine that the seller has had previous experience in manufacturing but requires that the machine perform a function which is not provided for by the existing design and requires that the contractor develop modifications in design which enable the machine to perform that function. In this case, an appropriate measure may be manufacturing labor hours since contract revenue recognition should not begin until the performance risks inherent in developing modifications (e.g., all engineering design costs) have been eliminated. The seller's risks of performance should be carefully evaluated and taken into account in selecting the measure of contract performance and in determining the percentage of completion appropriate in the circumstances.

In practice the predominant method of measurement of the percentage-of-contract performance completed is the cost-to-cost method. In applying the cost-to-cost method, adjustments must be made for the following:

☐ Materials purchased that have not been installed or used during the contract performance, if such materials are significant to costs incurred to date.

☐ Subcontractor costs, to the extent that the timing of payments to the subcontractor differs significantly from the amount of work performed under the subcontract.

☐ Types of costs included in costs incurred to date but not included in the total cost estimate.

* * *

Care must be exercised to ensure that costs included in contract costs to date are appropriately reflected in both the numerator and the denominator of the cost-to-cost calculation of the percentage of completion. Examples of the types of cost that might be found in the numerator on a total-to-date basis and not fully estimated in the denominator are general and administrative costs associated with contract effort and certain purchased services. If such costs are included as contract costs to date for the purpose of the cost-to-cost computation, . . . failure to include the estimated amount of these costs in the total estimated contract costs results in an erroneous determination of contract performance and a disproportionate recognition of profit.

Certain sellers, although using the percentage method for contract revenue recognition, defer any recognition of revenue until a specified percentage-of-contract performance is complete (in practice the percentages noted ranged from 5 percent to 40 percent). Those sellers who defer revenue recognition under the percentage method until a specified level of performance is reached take the position that, although they generally meet all the criteria for the application of the percentage method at the outset of the contract, completion to the specified level gives additional assurance of the dependability of the estimating process. We believe that the practice of deferring revenue recognition until a specified contract performance level is reached is acceptable if the specified performance level is reasonable in the circumstances, if the practice is applied consistently to all contracts and if full disclosure of the method is made in the financial statements.

Deferral of Costs in Anticipation of Future Sales

* * *

In some instances, sellers incur precontract costs (e.g., the cost of engineering, estimating or architectural effort or other costs for work begun on goods or services before any contracts are received). The decision to incur these costs may be based on commitments or other indications of interest in negotiating a contract. We believe that precontract costs, whether based on a commitment or not, should not be included in contract costs or inventory prior to receipt of the contract. Such costs, however, may be deferred subject to evaluation as to probable recoverability. We believe that such precontract costs may be deferred only if the costs can be directly associated with a specific anticipated future contract and it is probable that the costs will be recovered from that contract.

* * *

In some cases, sellers will produce goods in excess of the amounts required by a contract in anticipation of future orders. The costs that are appropriately related to producing those goods may be deferred if it is probable that the costs deferred will be recovered. In considering recovery, special consideration must be given to the uniqueness of the goods involved.

Frequently, learning or startup costs are incurred in connection with the performance of a contract. In some circumstances, the seller anticipates that follow-on or future contracts will be received for the same goods or services. He therefore considers it appropriate to spread such costs over both existing and anticipated future contracts. . . .

Such learning or startup costs are generally labor, overhead, rework or other unique costs that must be incurred in order to complete the existing contract in progress. It is difficult to establish a direct relationship between such costs and the anticipated future contracts. More importantly, because receipt of future contracts cannot reasonably be anticipated, we believe it is not appropriate to aggregate revenues and costs from both existing and anticipated future contracts. Further, because future revenues and the related incremental costs generally cannot be estimated, the recovery of such costs from anticipated contracts is in such doubt that we believe they should not be deferred but should be charged to the contracts under which they were incurred.

Costs that were expensed when incurred because their recovery was not considered probable should not be reinstated by a credit to earnings if a contract is subsequently obtained. Costs that were appropriately deferred may be included in contract costs upon receipt of the contract. . . .

NOTES

1. Under the completed-contract method, until the contract is substantially completed the enterprise defers all construction costs in an asset account, usually referred to as *Construction in Process,* and records any payments plus amounts due but not collected in a liability account, *Billings on Construction in Process*. If the costs incurred exceed the billings, the enterprise reports the excess on the balance sheet as a current asset, in the nature of a deferred expense; if billings exceed costs, the excess appears as a current liability, in the nature of deferred income. In the year in which the enterprise substantially completes the contract, it would report all revenues and all expenses attributable to the contract on the income statement for that year.

Under the percentage-of-completion method, on the other hand, the enterprise recognizes estimated revenues based on the progress that it made on the contract during the accounting period. For each period, the income statement shows the actual expenses incurred on the contract during the period and an amount of estimated revenue which bears the same ratio to the total expected revenue as the costs incurred during the period bear to the total estimated costs to perform the contract (subject to any adjustments to reflect changes in estimated costs).

To illustrate, assume that in the first year of a $1 million contract an enterprise incurs $90,000 in expenses, and that the enterprise expects to spend another $510,000 performing the contract. Because the enterprise has incurred fifteen percent of the total $600,000 expected costs on the contract, under the percentage-of-completion method the enterprise would recognize gross profit in the first year equal to fifteen percent of the total expected gross profit of $400,000, or $60,000.   Although the actual bookkeeping mechanics get quite complex, one way of approaching it is to recognize fifteen percent of the total expected revenues of $1,000,000, or $150,000, to offset the $90,000 in costs incurred, producing the gross profit figure of $60,000.

2. If an enterprise expects to incur a loss on a contract under either method, conservatism technically requires the enterprise to recognize the loss immediately. If a close relationship exists, however, between profitable and unprofitable contracts and those contracts constitute parts of the same project, an enterprise may treat the group as a unit when determining whether to recognize a loss immediately.

3. Statement of Position 81–1, which qualifies as category (b) authority in the GAAP hierarchy, states that the percentage-of-completion and completed-contract methods do not offer "acceptable alternatives for the same circumstances." As the above article observes, an enterprise should use the percentage-of-completion method when the total contract revenues can be determined, and the enterprise can reasonably and reliably estimate total costs and progress towards completion, and the other conditions noted are satisfied; otherwise, the enterprise must use the completed-contract method.

4. The excerpt from the article also briefly mentions, and criticizes, what is often termed the *program method*, under which an enterprise estimates (1) the aggregate total revenues from the product or service under both existing and anticipated future contracts, (2) the aggregate total number of units of product or service expected to be sold to obtain those revenues, and (3) the aggregate total costs to produce those units. Then the enterprise matches the average cost per unit, based on aggregate total costs in the "program," against current contract revenues. Through this process, the enterprise averages the net profit from both current and *anticipated* future contracts, even though there has been no transaction relating to the future contracts.

To illustrate, assume that a defense contractor builds a prototype aircraft which costs $100 million to develop, design and build, and which the contractor sells to the government for $80 million, with the expectation that the government will order at least five more aircraft at that same price, but which will only cost $40 million each to produce. Accordingly, aggregate total revenues are expected to equal $480 million (six aircraft at $80 million each), and aggregate total costs $300 million ($100 for the first unit and $40 million each for the next five units), for a $50 million average cost per unit. Under the program method, the contractor matches the $50 million average cost per unit against the $80 million initial contract price and reports a $30 million gross profit on the sale of the prototype. In contrast, if the contractor had matched the $100 million in costs necessary to develop, design and build the prototype against the $80 million initial contract price, the contractor would have recognized a $20 million loss.

As a result, the program method generates a higher profit, or smaller loss, for the current contract than if the enterprise accounted for the contract separately. Of course, if the anticipated future contracts do not materialize, the enterprise must then recognize larger losses, or smaller profits, in subsequent years, making the enterprise a riskier investment. *See, e.g.*, Polin v. Conductron Corp., 552 F.2d 797 (8th Cir.1977) (affirming the district court's conclusion that defendant did not commit securities fraud because the proxy statement and annual report warned that recovery of various costs related to aircraft simulators would depend upon future contracts).

PROBLEMS

Problem 6.6A. Your law firm represents Data Control Inc. ("DCI"), a company with a fiscal year ending August 31 that manufactures and sells computer tape and tape cartridges. DCI is considering an initial public offering and has retained your firm to prepare the registration statement necessary for the public offering. During your preparation of the registration statement, you learn that during the last week of August 19X1, Year One, John Ward, the company's chief financial officer, convinced Fred Engel, who currently owns sixty-percent of DCI's outstanding shares, to accept a $100,000 shipment of computer cartridges to enable DCI to meet sales projections for the fiscal year ending August 31, Year One. Engel also owns and operates Engel Enterprises, a sole proprietorship which sells computer cartridges. Engel agreed to accept the shipment on credit with the understanding that he would have no obligation to pay for the shipment unless he could resell the cartridges and that he could return the shipment at any time within ninety days for full credit. On October 30, Year One, Engel resold the last portion of the shipment to an unrelated third party. Can DCI recognize revenue on the transaction during its fiscal year ending August 31, Year One, if it complie s with the related party disclosure requirements in Statement of Financial Accounting Standards No. 57? If so, what information must DCI disclose to satisfy GAAP. If not, explain briefly.

Problem 6.6B. Crimson Company began operations on January 1, Year One. On December 31, Year One, Crimson Company owned the following investments in marketable securities:

	Cost	Fair Value
Best Company Bonds	$20,000	$17,000
Domers Ltd. Common Stock	100,000	82,000
Falcon, Inc. Common Stock	35,000	49,000

Best Company Bonds are classified as a held-to-maturity security. Domers Ltd. common stock is a trading security. Falcon, Inc. common stock is an available-for-sale security. Crimson Company reasonably determines that the changes in fair value are temporary in nature.

(a) How much income or loss, if any, should Crimson Company report to reflect the changes in value of the investments? Explain briefly.

(b) Would your answer differ if the changes are "other than temporary," and if so, how? In any event, explain briefly.

Problem 6.6C. In problem 6.4 on page 404, *supra*, suppose instead that by the end of that recently ended fiscal year E had incurred costs of $45,000 in performing under the contract with P, having originally estimated that the total cost of its performance under the contract would amount to $300,000. How should E reflect the transaction in its financial statements for that year (a) assuming, as before, that P has paid $100,000 of the total contract price by the end of the fiscal year, or (b) assuming instead that P has not made any payment by the end of the year because the contract did not require any payment until E finished the job?

D. ACCRUAL OF EXPENSES AND LOSSES

Returning now to the subject of recognition of expenses, we have seen that whenever an enterprise recognizes income in the current accounting period, any related expense must also be reflected currently to achieve the necessary matching. That requires a debit to the appropriate current expense account, and if the expense is not actually paid during the period the corresponding credit is to an Expense Payable or Accrued Expense liability account, reflecting the fact that the enterprise faces an obligation to pay the amount in the future. Even if the enterprise cannot determine the precise amount of the expense, as long as it belongs in the current period it should be estimated as accurately as possible and accrued in the usual manner.

In reality, such estimation serves as the norm rather than the exception, as businesses commonly estimate unpaid expenses. When the Pacific Grape company, in problem 6.5B on page 409, *supra*, estimated that shipping and labeling costs would total $15,000 under the contracts for the goods ordered but not yet shipped at the end of a calendar year, upon recognizing the income from those sales contracts in the current year the company also had to accrue those estimated expenses in the current year.

There is, however, a significant distinction between this Pacific Grape situation and, say, the accrual of the $25 telephone expense in the practice problem involving E. Tutt. In the latter case, the telephone company had already supplied the services for which E. Tutt accrued the expense, and, by using the telephone during July, she had enjoyed the benefits from those services in the current accounting period. In addition, no uncertainty existed regarding the obligation which the Expense Payable represented. The same would apply to the $50 worth of janitorial services that E. Tutt would accrue to reflect services performed during June on page 51, *supra*. Under the accrual method, E. Tutt would accrue the expense so that June would bear the burden of the janitorial services which aided the production of revenues during the month. In Pacific Grape, on the other hand, the shippers would not have performed any of their expected services by the end of the year in which the company recognized the revenues. As a result, Pacific Grape would not have enjoyed any of the benefit of these services as yet, and presumably Pacific Grape's actual liability to pay for the services would depend upon their actual performance.

In effect, however, an accountant could view Pacific Grape as having enjoyed the benefit of these expenses, even though the shippers had not yet performed the services involved, because the services function as a necessary condition precedent to earning the income being recognized. As a corollary, an accountant might say that Pacific Grape became obligated to pay for these services in an accounting sense, even if not legally speaking, thus justifying the creation of an Expense Payable type of liability account.

Nevertheless, the fact that the business has not yet performed the services representing the expense in question does make accountants a little more reluctant to accrue the expense. Among other things, businesses usually encounter greater difficulty in estimating the cost of unperformed services, as compared with those that the vendor has already completed. Fortunately, the rule that a business should not recognize the income from a transaction until the enterprise has substantially completed the required performance greatly reduces this problem. By hypothesis, when an enterprise has substantially completed overall performance, not many related services can remain unperformed. In other words, delaying income recognition until the enterprise has substantially completed the work assures not only that the business will not prematurely record revenue, but also that the enterprise will have completed practically all services necessary to be entitled to the income. Accordingly, most expenses the business accrues will relate to services already performed, so the corresponding liability will represent an unconditional obligation, which probably facilitates any needed estimation.

However, there will be some instances when a business may need to accrue expenses for services before they have been performed. For example, assume that a manufacturer of machinery has completed the machines for a particular order and shipped them to the customer by the end of the current period, but the manufacturer has not totally completed performance because it remains responsible for installing the machines in the customer's plant. In such a case, a judgment question arises as to whether the manufacturer has completed performance to such an extent that the enterprise can recognize income on the transaction. If the enterprise can recognize the income, that normally means, as we have seen, that the enterprise will report all the income from the transaction. As a corollary, the enterprise will also accrue all related expenses, including those like the costs of installation, which have not been performed yet, to achieve a proper matching with the underlying income.

1. THE CAPTION FOR THE LIABILITY CREATED UPON ACCRUAL OF AN EXPENSE

We should also briefly mention one other point about accrued expenses at this time. Some accountants have suggested that in any case in which an enterprise must estimate the amount of an accrued expense, the enterprise should use a different name, such as "Estimated Liability", for the liability created. Such nomenclature would presumably allow a reader to separate such liabilities from those which are unconditional, whether or not due yet, and certain in amount. Thus, an enterprise might call the liability created when accruing an expense for future installation of machines "Estimated Liability for Installation" rather than "Installation Expense Payable" or "Accrued Installation Expense." No uniform practice exists on this matter, however, and many enterprises lump all their accrued expense liabilities under a single heading like "Accrued Expenses."

Because lawyers will often encounter various terminology to describe accrued liabilities, we should also mention some history about this vocabulary. At one time, accountants used the term "Reserve," as in "Reserve for Installation Expense," to signify estimated or conditional liabilities. However, that term suggests that something, presumably assets, has been set aside to satisfy the underlying liability, so an unsophisticated reader could easily be mislead. Admittedly, anytime an enterprise accrues an expense, the accrual lowers net income for the accounting period, which in turn reduces retained earnings, and net assets, at the end of the period. As a result, any such accrual adversely affects the amount that a corporation could lawfully distribute to its shareholders. In this sense, a more sophisticated reader might view recording the expense and the corresponding liability as preserving assets in a general way.

An enterprise can, however, actually set aside cash or other assets and specifically earmark those assets for a particular purpose, such as discharging a debt or paying for a new plant. For example, the enterprise might establish a formal escrow arrangement or, less formally, simply open a special bank account. The term "Reserve," unfortunately, suggests that the enterprise has established some such arrangement. In fact, however, calling the liability a "Reserve" means nothing more than that the enterprise created a liability and estimated the amount, in conjunction with accruing an expense.

Loose terminology has often accompanied the term "Reserve" in related contexts. Particularly in judicial opinions, you may encounter references, for example, to "deducting the reserve from income," or "reserves out of income." Presumably, this language seeks to express the fact that the enterprise created a Reserve account in conjunction with a charge against income in exactly the same amount. Such phrases, however, can confuse a reader, because the term "Reserve" actually connotes a liability which appears on the balance sheet, and liabilities themselves do not affect the determination of net income.

Given these concerns, Accounting Terminology Bulletin No. 1 urged that the accounting profession narrowly confine the word "Reserve" and recommended that enterprises discontinue the term's use to describe the liability accompanying an accrued expense. Even so, the term "Reserve" still appears in this context in secondary materials, and even occasionally in financial statements, to describe the liability resulting fromaccruing estimated expenses, environmental costs, and the like.

Note that we have now developed a hierarchy of credits that can accompany the recognition of an expense in the current period. An enterprise credits:

a.   a Prepaid or Deferred Expense account . . . .   if the expense was prepaid in a prior period.

b.   Cash . . . .   if the expense was paid for in the current period.

c.   an Expense Payable (Or Accrued Expense) account . . . .   if the expense hasn't been paid for, but a fixed liability to pay a fixed amount of money exists.

d.   an Estimated Liability account (or, sometimes, particularly in the past, a Reserve account). . . .   if the expense has not been paid for, but there is a liability to pay an uncertain, but estimable, amount of money or to perform or provide services, and the enterprise desires to show such liabilities separately.

Whatever the name given to the liability when an enterprise accrues an expense, payment of the expense is treated the same as payment of any other liability, with a debit to the liability account to record the reduction in the liability, and a credit to cash. As we have seen, when the payment or other discharge of the liability occurs in a subsequent period, the income statement for that period does not reflect the expense, since it had already been recognized in the earlier period.

When an enterprise can only estimate the size of the liability at the time the expense is accrued, the amount actually required to discharge the liability will rarely exactly equal the figure originally estimated and charged against income. The difference between the amount originally estimated and the actual cost is a normal recurring adjustment to be reflected in the income statement for the period in which the enterprise discharges the liability. So, if in the foregoing hypothetical Pacific Grape had accrued an estimated $25,000 in shipping expenses in the year of revenue recognition, with an accompanying credit to an Estimated Liability account, and in the later year of performance the shipping actually cost $28,000, Pacific Grape would record the following entry in the latter year:

Estimated Liability for Shipping $25,000
Shipping Expense   3,000
    Cash $28,000

If instead the actual cost turned out to be only $23,000, the $2,000 difference would be included in income (or perhaps as a reduction in related expenses) for the year paid.

2. ALTERNATIVE THEORIES FOR ACCRUING EXPENSES AND LOSSES FOR FINANCIAL ACCOUNTING PURPOSES

Having revisited the mechanics for accruing an expense before it has been paid or accrued, thereby charging a future expected expenditure or loss against income in the current period, we turn to the important judgment question of when to do so. As we know, GAAP basically requires an enterprise to record an expense when the enterprise in effect uses or consumes economic resources to deliver or produce goods, render services, or engage in other activities that constitute the enterprise's primary or central operations. In addition, an enterprise must recognize a loss when it expects previously recognized assets to provide reduced benefits, or no more at all.

As indicated in the discussion of deferral at the beginning of this chapter, perhaps the most common basis for reflecting an expense or loss in the current period is the existence of a cause and effect relationship between the item in question and revenues being recognized currently. In particular, expenses which result directly from the same transaction as the current revenues, such as cost of goods sold, shipping charges, and sales commissions, must be charged off currently, regardless of whether they have been paid yet, and even if the performance or the benefit has not been received yet.

Then there are costs that cannot be related directly to any specific revenue, but do aid generally in the production of current revenues, like compensation to executives, office rent, and utility costs. These expenditures represent general costs of doing business in the current period; they must be recognized as current expenses, and if they have not yet been paid, accrual is the way of accomplishing it. Sometimes these expenditures which do not relate to any particular transaction provide general assistance to the operations of the business in more than one accounting period. For example, an enterprise may enter into a multi-year lease, sign a long-term loan, or purchase a long-lived asset. An enterprise should charge the underlying costs, regardless of when they are actually paid, against the revenues for the periods in which the costs contribute generally to the enterprise's ability to produce revenues.

To illustrate, recall that when E. Tutt signed a three-year lease for office space under which she was not required to pay any of the total rent of

$15,000 until the end of the third year, we nevertheless debited $5,000 to Rent Expense for the first year, with an offsetting credit to an accrued Rent Payable liability, then in the second year, again $5,000 was debited to Rent Expense, with the Rent Payable liability correspondingly increased to $10,000; finally, at the end of year three $5,000 would be debited to Rent Expense for that year, and the Rent Payable liability would be momentarily increased to $15,000, but of course would promptly be debited to close it out, offsetting the credit to cash for the payment of the $15,000 at year-end as agreed. (In year three the bookkeeper could skip the step of increasing the Rent Payable liability to $15,000, and simply treat $5,000 of the $15,000 payment of cash as the offset to Rent Expense for the third year with the remaining $10,000 of the credit to cash offsetting the debit closing out what would then be only a $10,000 balance in the Rent Payable liability account.)

Sometimes, the benefits in succeeding periods do not correspond ratably to the passage of time. That would be true of the interest expense on, say, a three-year loan of $10,000, at 10% compound interest, all payable at maturity: as we have seen, under the effective interest method the total interest of $3,310 cannot be allocated equally among the loan's three years, because the interest expense actually increases over the three years, as the amount owed goes up to reflect the unpaid interest each year.

As we also saw in connection with deferral, if an expenditure or loss cannot be related either to a particular future revenue transaction, or generally to production of revenues in a future period, the item should be recognized in the period when the obligation was incurred or the loss was discerned, and again accrual is the way to do so if payment has not been made. So, for example, an obligation incurred to resolve a litigation, whether pursuant to a settlement or an adverse judgment, does not generally provide future benefits to an enterprise, so unless an expense or loss was already accrued in an earlier period (a subject which will be further examined in the next chapter), any such amount should be immediately expensed and, if not yet paid, an offsetting liability must be credited. Similarly, enterprises immediately recognize a loss when a cost recorded as an asset in a prior period is no longer expected to provide discernible future benefits. Finally, enterprises sometimes recognize costs as expenses in the period incurred because the enterprise either cannot determine the period to which the costs otherwise relate or concludes that the added cost of making such a determination is not justified by the potential benefit.

3. OTHER ISSUES INVOLVING ACCRUAL OF EXPENSE AND DEFERRAL OF INCOME

The issues which we have been discussing, namely whether a prospective expenditure should be charged to the current period, in part or in whole, or whether instead it should be left to future recognition because the benefits occur after the end of the current period, illustrate the kinds of judgment questions that accountants constantly face and which concern lawyers. In the attempt to match related revenues and expenses, close questions can arise as to the accounting period in which to do the matching, when it appears that the related items occurred in different periods. One guideline stems from the fact that income recognition is subject to more stringent imitations than recognition of expense: hence, if payment of an expense comes before recognition of the related income is appropriate, the enterprise must defer the expense until it can recognize the income. If, on the other hand, income is earned before a related expense has been incurred, the expense should be accrued to be matched with the income.

For an example of a judgment call, suppose an enterprise has received certain revenue, but it is a borderline question as to whether it has been earned yet because some performance remains to be done, which usually means that some related expenses have not yet been incurred. In such a case, a business can accomplish matching either by treating the amount received as deferred income until the related expenses have been incurred, or by recognizing the advance receipts in current income and accruing the estimated related future expenses into that year (with a credit to an Expense Payable account). Note the kinship between expenses payable and deferred income: whenever the liability account created to accrue an expense represents an obligation to perform or provide services, the liability bears resemblance to a Deferred Income account, which also reflects an obligation to perform services (or perhaps to deliver goods). However, accruing the related future expenses often requires estimating the amount of those expenses, and the more estimation that is needed, the less reliable the enterprise's financial reporting. Thus, an important advantage of the general rule, that a business should not rec ognize the income from a transaction until the required performance has been at least substantially completed, becomes clear: by the time of substantial completion, the business will have incurred most of the related expenses, reducing the need to estimate future expenses.

Occasionally, even though the matching of an expected expenditure will not occur until a future period when the related revenue is recognized, there may be reason to reflect the liability in the current period, which would involve combining accrual and deferral in the same transaction. To illustrate, suppose an enterprise signs a more expensive three-year lease than the one referred to above — say, for $50,000 per year, with the whole $150,000 not due until the end of the third year. Of course $50,000 should be charged to expense for the first year, with a credit to an offsetting liability. But the whole three-year lease liability may be regarded as highly significant in the portrayal of the present financial condition of the enterprise(quite apart from those cases where what is a lease in form is really an installment purchase of an asset, to be discussed in Chapter 9). If so, the total lease commitment could be recorded as a liability on the balance sheet, even though only a portion of the obligation is chargeable to current expense because the rest of the benefit remains to be enjoyed in the future.

To the extent that the liability recorded exceeds the amount being charged to current expense, as indicated on page 70, *supra*, the only sensible debit to offset it would be to some kind of deferred expense asset. Though usually a deferred expense asset is only created when an advance payment of cash has been made, for accounting purposes the current recognition of the liability to pay cash constitutes the functional equivalent, and hence supports recording the asset.

For another example, take the brokers' commissions in Problem 6.5B on page 409, *supra*. If Pacific Grape treats the $300,000 in goods which customers ordered, but which the company had not shipped by the end of the year, as not sold during that year, then the principles of matching dictate that the company should not charge these commissions to expense for that year. In this circumstance, the company would normally not create an Expense Payable account, and the liability for the brokers' commissions would not appear on the balance sheet at the close of that year. If, however, as suggested in the *Pacific Grape* case, the brokers had earned their commissions as of the end of the year, so that there was an existing, enforceable legal obligation to them, the balance sheet could be viewed as misleading if this liability did not appear; that would be resolved by recording the liability, which in turn would require a corresponding debit to a deferred expense asset.

Similar issues may arise regarding decisions to reflect receivables prior to recognizing the related income. For example, take the $420,000 which the customers had contracted to pay Pacific Grape for the goods which they had ordered, but that the company had not shipped by year end. Although traditional accounting would seem to suggest that Pacific Grape should not record the right to receive this amount until the company recognizes the income from the transaction, notice that Ebasco, in the *Boise Cascade* case, accounted for amounts billed for services not yet performed by reflecting a receivable and crediting "Unearned Income", a deferred income account, as described on page 398, *supra*.

Problem 6.7. X Corp. sells and services computers, mostly to individuals for personal use. As a feature of its general sales policy, X provides to each buyer a right to have the computer thoroughly checked and serviced on one occasion during the calendar year following the purchase. X adds $60 to the computer's selling price to cover this feature, because its experience has confirmed that the average cost of fulfilling this commitment to check and service has averaged about $50 per computer. For the year of sale, how should X account for the $60 cash received and the prospective $50 cost to be incurred in the following year?

4.   THE PROBLEM OF UNCOLLECTIBLE ACCOUNTS

As we saw in the earlier discussion of revenue recognition, unless some special doubt exists about the buyer's ability to pay, a seller normally recognizes revenue from a sales transaction at the point when the seller has substantially completed the required performance. The fact that the buyer has not yet paid for the goods does not matter. If L Corp. completes a sale of goods in year 1 to Jones Company for $1,000 on credit, L Corp. would record the following entry:

Accounts Receivable: Jones Co.	$1,000	
Sales Income		$1,000

Suppose that L Corp. learns in year 2 that Jones Company has filed for bankruptcy and that the company's insolvency means that L Corp. will not collect any amount on the account receivable. Since that account receivable has become worthless, L Corp. should "write off" the account, that is, eliminate the receivable from its books. To do so, L Corp. can simply credit the asset Accounts Receivable: Jones Co. As for the corresponding debit, unless L Corp. has taken some earlier steps to pave the way for a different treatment, it must charge a current loss or expense account. But query, does charging the loss due to an uncollectible account against the year in which the account happens to become uncollectible meaningfully match expenses against the related income? Realistically, any losses stemming from uncollectible accounts are part of the cost of selling goods on credit, so L Corp. should match those losses, like all other related expenses, against the revenues from the sales which gave rise to the losses. L Corp., therefore, needs an entry each year to reflect the likely future losses resulting from credit sales made during that year. Of course, as already noted, if there is special reason to think that any particular customer who bought on credit will not be able to pay for the goods, the seller should not recognize income until payment actually occurs. But, in fact, in the great majority of credit sales the seller expects to and does collect the receivable in the ordinary course of business. Moreover, based on prior experience or other factors, the seller can usually reasonably predict the amount of defaults which will occur. Accordingly, each year a seller should estimate and accrue the expected amount of losses on credit sales made during the year, which thereby matches those losses with the revenues to which they relate.

The technique for reflecting these future expected losses as an expense in the current year resembles the process for accruing any other expense before the enterprise pays the underlying amount. The seller debits a current expense account, often called "Bad Debt Expense", or perhaps "Uncollectible Accounts Expense," for the amount of the estimated future losses on credit sales for that year. Paralleling the normal practice of crediting a liability account when an enterprise accrues an expense or loss prior to payment, the seller here too might credit a liability — presumably an estimated liability, because the amount is uncertain. Two important differences, however, distinguish this account from other estimated liability accounts. First, this estimated-liability-type account does not constitute an obligation to pay money, or perform services, but rather represents the fact that the business will not collect some money which, by recording its receivables, the enterprise had projected it would receive in the future. Second, the account created to reflect estimated losses on credit sales usually appears on the balance sheet as an offset to Accounts Receivable, or, in accounting terminology, as a contra-asset account, rather than separately as a liability, to give a more accurate picture about how much cash the enterprise actually expects to obtain from the receivables. Perhaps for these reasons, enterprises usually do not use an "Estimated Liability" caption for this account, preferring to call it something like "Allowance for Doubtful Accounts."

As we saw, accountants often referred to estimated-liability-type accounts created when accruing a conditional expense (or one requiring estimation of the amount) as a "Reserve." Thus, the term "Reserve for Bad Debts", which appears very often in the older literature and judicial opinions, means exactly the same thing as "Allowance for Doubtful Accounts."

An Allowance for Doubtful Accounts enables an enterprise to handle an account receivable which becomes uncollectible in a later period without affecting current income in that period. Upon determining that a particular account receivable has become either wholly or partly uncollectible, the enterprise can debit the Allowance for Doubtful Accounts to balance the credit to the account receivable which has become uncollectible. This entry does not affect the income statement, any more than paying off a liability does: the only difference is that the enterprise credits the worthless account receivable rather than cash. As a result, if L Corp. in the example above had previously created an Allowance for Doubtful Accounts, upon discovering in year 2 that the account receivable from Jones had become totally uncollectible, L would record the following entry:

Allowance for Doubtful Accounts	$1,000	
Accounts Receivable: Jones Co.		$1,000

Occasionally, an enterprise receives some payment on an account receivable which the enterprise previously wrote off. Suppose, for example, that in year 3 Jones Company experienced some unexpected good fortune and paid $100 on its account with L Corp. Since the write-off of the account receivable did not affect current income when it occurred, such a recovery should not affect current income when it happens either. Instead, L Corp. would view this collection as an indication that it was incorrect to write off the entire account receivable. As a result, L Corp. would partially reverse that earlier entry and reflect the cash receipt as follows:

Accounts Receivable: Jones Co.	$100	
Allowance for Doubtful Accounts		$100
Cash	$100	
Accounts Receivable: Jones Co.		$100

In practice, L Corp. might well combine the two entries into a single entry, which reaches the same end point, as follows:

Cash	$100	
Allowance for Doubtful Accounts		$100

This single entry, however, would not reflect the fact that Jones Company eventually paid a portion of its account.

Incidentally, the Allowance for Doubtful Accounts does not attempt to isolate the credit losses from different years in separate accounts. Instead, enterprises use a single continuing Allowance for Doubtful Accounts. An enterprise increases the Allowance account during the year by credits, corresponding to the debits to Bad Debt Expense, based upon the percentage of the year's credit sales that the enterprise estimates will become uncollectible. As we noted, the Allowance account is also increased by any collections on accounts receivable that the enterprise had previously written off as worthless. And of course, the Allowance account is decreased by the amount of the accounts receivable written off because they became worthless during the year.[*]

In estimating the percentage of credit transactions during a period which will result in uncollectible accounts, experience normally serves as the best guide, just as is true with ordinary estimated liabilities. For a new enterprise, or one which has not previously extended credit to customers,

---

[*]We should mention one mechanical bookkeeping refinement at this point. An enterprise may write off worthless accounts receivable directly against the Allowance for Doubtful Accounts, and likewise credit directly to that account any rececipts from accounts previously written off. But bookkeepers often prefer to keep both a separate account to reflect the amount of accounts receivable which have become uncollectible during the period and one to show any collections on accounts receivable previously written off. That requires setting up special temporary subaccounts for the Allowance account, typically called "Bad Debts Charged Off" and "Bad Debts Collected," respectively, to reflect these items. Then, when an account receivable is written off as uncollectible, the bookkeeper debits the Bad Debts Charged Off account. At the end of the period, the bookkeeper would close that account to the left-hand side of the Allowance for Doubtful Accounts. Similarly, if a payment is received on an account receivable previously written off as uncollectible, the bookkeeper credits the Bad Debts Collected account, and at the end of the period the total in that account is closed to the right-hand side of the Allowance account. While management may find these subaccounts useful in anlyzing the enterprise's overall credit picture, they represent mechanical refinements which we can ignore.

information from similar enterprises can help the enterprise reach a fairly accurate estimate. However derived, that estimated percentage is then applied to every credit sale during the period, i.e., that percentage of each credit sale is charged to Bad Debt Expense for the period and credited to the Allowance account, and the total might be considered the *prima facie* cost of doing business on credit for the period.

But the Allowance for Doubtful Accounts performs a second important function not served by ordinary estimated liability accounts. In terms of liquidity, the accounts receivable on a balance sheet rank second only to cash, and perhaps marketable securities, so all kinds of investors, and particularly short-term creditors, pay particular attention to accounts receivable. Accordingly, in reflecting the asset Accounts Receivable on the balance sheet an enterprise must give special consideration to the amount that it actually expects to collect — in other words, the asset's real value. If an enterprise lists the gross amount of outstanding accounts receivables without in some way indicating the likelihood that not all of those receivables will prove collectible, the enterprise will mislead both current and potential investors and creditors. It is to make the situation as clear as possible that GAAP requires the Allowance for Doubtful Accounts to appear on the balance sheet as a deduction from Accounts Receivable, rather than on the right-hand side of the balance sheet as a liability. APB Opinion No. 12, ¶3 (1967).

Since the Allowance account serves this vital function of reducing the gross amount of accounts receivable to the net amount the enterprise actually expects to collect, the size of the Allowance account should not be left entirely to the process of annual additions based upon the percentage of credit sales during the period which previous experience indicates will become uncollectible (plus any collections on accounts previously written off), minus the accounts written off during the period. Instead, an enterprise should carefully analyze the existing accounts receivable at the end of each year to determine the figure which represents the best possible estimate of the amount of the receivables that will prove uncollectible. As a practical matter, business experience confirms that the "age" of the outstanding receivables significantly affects their collectibility. As a receivable becomes progressively overdue, the likelihood of non-payment increases dramatically. An enterprise, therefore, should pay careful attention to how old the existing accounts receivable are. For example, an enterprise may divide receivables among such categories as, say, less than three months old, between three and six months, between six and twelve months, and more than twelve months old, and make a separate estimate of the likely percentage of uncollectible accounts in each category. An enterprise should also consider any other special circumstances that may affect particular accounts. The figure that this process produces may well be the soundest estimate of the amount that is likely not to be collected, and this is the figure that should appear in the Allowance account at the end of the year. To set the amount in the Allowance account at the desired level typically requires a corresponding increase or decrease in the charge to the Bad Debt Expense account for the year.

The current significance of "Allowance" accounting is illustrated by the fact that SEC Chairman Arthur Levitt specifically listed "loan losses" as an example of the "miscellaneous 'cookie jar reserves'" in his description of the "third [accounting] illusion," on page 343, *supra*. These loan losses are nothing more than the "Bad Debt Expense" for the estimated uncollectible amounts in the loan portfolio of a bank or other financial institution. As one of the financial reporting initiatives following Chairman Levitt's "The 'Numbers Game'" remarks, the SEC expressed concern that financial institutions have intentionally created and maintained large reserves, or allowances, for loan losses in good economic times, to pad against potential losses during economic downtu rns. In its 1998 acquisition of Crestar Financial Corp., SunTrust Banks, Inc. agreed with the SEC to revise its reported earnings and reduce its expenses for loan losses by $100 million for the three-year period from 1994 to 1996. On the other hand, banking regulators, anxious to avoid another savings-and-loan-type crisis, have repeatedly cautioned banks to manage credit risk exposure prudently, and have warned that the SEC's efforts to limit what appear to be unnecessarily large reserves could cause banks to ignore conservatism and set reserves for loan losses too low. There are ongoing efforts by the SEC and federal bank regulators to develop new guidance to ensure that loan loss reserves remain adequate, while guarding against inappropriate earnings manipulation.

PROBLEMS

Problem 6.8A. Suppose that it was the practice of Pacific Grape Products to charge Bad Debt Expense each month in the amount of one-quarter percent of the credit sales made during the month, with a corresponding credit to Allowance for Doubtful Accounts. On $5,000,000 of sales during the year (not including, it will be recalled, the $420,000 relating to the goods ordered but not shipped at year end), this practice produced $12,500 of Bad Debt Expense for the year. The $14,000 in the Allowance account was the product of $12,000 in the account at the beginning of the year, plus the $12,500 charged to current expense and $1,000 received during the year on accounts previously written off, less $11,500 of accounts receivable written off during the year and charged against the Allowance account.

The company follows the practice of fixing the amount in the Allowance account at year end on the basis of "aging" its account receivables. Under the company's credit terms, payment is due within thirty days, and the company's experience is that once thirty days has passed without payment the percentage of loss rises steeply, the older the accounts. This past experience indicates that the figure in the Allowance account should be at least equal to the sum of the following percentages of the respective age categories: one-quarter percent of the existing receivables less than one month old; two percent of the receivables between one and three months; seven percent of the receivables between three and six months old; twenty-five percent of those between six and twelve months old; and seventy-five of those over a year old. The following table shows the breakdown of the company's receivables among the various age categories at the end of its recent fiscal year, and the percentage of each category which should be reflected in the allowance account:

Age Category	Amount of Receivables	Percentage
Less than one month old	$440,000	¼%
One to three months	220,000	2%
Three to six months	40,000	7%
Six to twelve months	16,000	25%
Over twelve months	4,000	75%

(a) What entry should the company make at the close of the year as a result of this aging procedure? 15,300

(b) Would your answer change if the issue arose in the context of applying an employee bonus provision based upon "annual net profits from operations?"

(c) What if the issue was the amount the company could lawfully pay as a dividend under a statute which provides that a corporation may "declare and pay dividends out of its surplus"?

(d) If the company recognizes in the year just ended the sale of those goods ordered but not shipped at year end, how, if at all, would that treatment affect the Allowance account?

Problem 6.8B.   Suppose that a couple of months after the close of the year in problem 6.8A, while the financial statements for the year are being prepared, Pacific Grape learns that a customer who had purchased goods for $10,000 on credit in the next to the last month of the year has unexpectedly become insolvent, and there is substantial doubt about collecting any of the amount due. How, if at all, should this information be reflected in those financial statements?

E. DRAFTING AND NEGOTIATING LEGAL ARRANGEMENTS IMPLICATING THE INCOME STATEMENT

At the end of Chapter V we reviewed in some detail accounting terminology and concepts involving the balance sheet, in agreements and other legal documents. Attorneys also frequently deal with legal arrangements implicating the income statement, such as an employment agreement, or a labor contract with a bonus provision based upon the business's net income. The following excerpts, adapted from written materials distributed at a Practicing Law Institute seminar, offer some very practical suggestions focusing on terminology and concepts underlying the income statement.

Terry Lloyd, *Financial Language in Legal Documents*[*]

adapted from Accounting for Lawyers (1994) at 261, 276–77, 283, 290–322.

Specific Accounting Concerns

* * *

Although reliance on GAAP has advantages, in some cases it may be appropriate to disregard or modify GAAP and use a different basis of accounting. GAAP is based on accrual accounting, [which] is believed to more accurately portray the financial status and results of operations of an economic enterprise—and is less susceptible to distortion. There are, nevertheless, circumstances in which it may be more appropriate to utilize cash basis accounting — [for example,] in connection with the sale of a professional practice which typically operates on a cash basis accounting system.

The notion that GAAP "is what it is" is wrong and should not be used as an excuse for not making the effort to devise accounting provisions which more appropriately carry out the intentions of the parties.

Agreements Employing Revenue and Earnings Concepts

Many agreements utilize an enterprise's revenues or earnings as the basis of determining the amount of a payment or payments to be received by one or more of the parties. Attorneys drafting such agreements should be mindful of the various possible accounting choices so that their clients will not be deprived of their rightfully anticipated compensation. Revenue or earnings formulas are typically found in the following types of agreements:

- acquisition agreements where the purchase price is based in whole or in part on the future earnings of the acquired business;

- employment or consulting agreements providing for the payment of a bonus based on the revenues or earnings of the employing enterprise;

- license, royalty and franchise agreements where the compensation paid to the licensor or franchisor is based on the revenues or earnings of the licensee or franchisee;

- partnership or joint venture agreements providing for distributions to partners to be based on the earnings of the partnership/venture during each accounting period;

---

[*]Copyright © 1997, Terry Lloyd, CPA, CFA. Reprinted with permission.

- preferred stock provisions which provide for the payment of dividends out of the earnings (as defined) of the corporation; and

- pension or other employment termination benefits based on the earnings of the employing business enterprise.

Primary Considerations

Perhaps the first question faced in drafting a revenue or earnings formula is to determine which of these measurements is more appropriate. A revenue concept is generally best suited in situations where the party to be compensated makes a direct or indirect contribution to the enterprise's revenues but has little or no control over the enterprise's overall operations. For this reason, sales and marketing personnel as well as independent contractors and trademark and patent licensors are typically compensated on the basis of their employer's or licensee's revenues (top line), as opposed to its earnings (bottom line) which can be manipulated. Franchise agreements also tend to utilize a revenue concept, especially where the franchisor's business format has a proven track record. However, where the business format is relatively untried, the results of the franchisee's operations is likely to be as much a reflection of the franchisee's managerial skills as the franchisor's operating formula. In such circumstances, the franchisor should not be entitled to any compensation unless the franchisee is generating a profit.

A second primary consideration is to determine the nature of the revenues or earnings to be utilized as the basis for determining the compensation to be paid. For example, will the determining revenues or earnings be those of a single company or those of the consolidated group; will the earnings be before or after income taxes; will they be computed on a cash basis or on an accrual basis; and will they include or exclude extraordinary items? The answers to each of these questions will materially affect the amount of compensation payable under the formula.

* * *

Normally computations of earnings are made on an after-tax basis; however, where the subject company has a net loss carry forward or is a part of a consolidated group which includes companies generating losses, the after-tax earnings may not fairly represent the results of operations of the subject company. In such circumstances, it may be preferable to base payments on pretax earnings. Extraordinary items may similarly distort the earnings of an enterprise. Unlike the issues presented above, extraordinary revenues and expenses do not necessarily result from the subject company's operations during the measuring period. For example, a substantial portion of the subject company's assets or operations might be sold during the measuring period, the proceeds of which might reflect wealth accumulated over many accounting periods. Conversely, the subject company's earnings might be reduced by reason of an uninsured casualty loss. Neither of these events may accurately reflect the value of the subject enterprise or the efforts of the formula's beneficiary. On the other hand, if extraordinary gains are excluded, the purchaser of a business could sell off parts, thereby reducing its earnings capacity and the resulting payments required to be made under the earnings formula. For these reasons, the effect of extraordinary items should be carefully considered before adopting any revenues or earnings formula.

In normal usage, "earnings" or "net income" includes extraordinary items, while "operating income" does not. Under GAAP, extraordinary items are defined as "events and transactions that are distinguished by their unusual nature and the infrequency of their occurrence." This definition is quite restrictive and would exclude a number of items which a layman might view as being "extraordinary". . ..

Specific Accounts

There is a great tendency in drafting any earnings or revenue formula to merely utilize the subject enterprise's revenues or earnings (as the case may be) "as determined in accordance with generally accepted accounting principles consistently applied." Doing so, however, ignores the fact that GAAP leaves to business enterprises a wide latitude in selecting accounting methods as well as operational decisions which could materially affect the magnitude of their reportable earnings. For this reason, it's absolutely essential to consider the various available accounting elections and make those choices at the outset that will benefit your client. These elections need only be for the purpose of computing payments under the agreement and need not prevent the enterprise from making different choices for other purposes.

* * *

Changes in Accounting Methods and Estimates. Most agreements for determining payments using earnings or income formulas require that the generally accepted accounting principles applied will be consistent with those previously applied. Although this simple restriction will eliminate many questions, it may not answer all important accounting choices. For example, the determination of cost allocations or useful lives of assets or the percentage of allowance for bad debts are referred to in accounting language as "estimates" and are not considered generally accepted accounting principles. It takes little imagination to see that changes in "estimates" can have an equal, if not greater, impact on reportable earnings than changes in principles. As a result, the consistency clause should, at a very minimum, encompass accounting estimates. Changes in the company's operations could mandate the application of different accounting principles. For example, if the reporting company (heretofore only a manufacturing company) decided to open retail outlets, it might be required (or at least permitted) to compute its finished goods inventory under a different generally accepted accounting principle. Similarly, if it changed the terms on which it sold its products (for example, by adopting a liberal return policy), it might be required under GAAP to alter the method by which it recognized its revenues.

Lastly, there is the ever-present possibility that GAAP itself might change, raising the issue of whether earnings are to be computed in accordance with GAAP or on a basis consistent with past accounting practices. This is not merely an academic consideration. The FASB is constantly rethinking previously established generally accepted accounting principles (including those established by the FASB itself) and every such change could have a serious effect on an outstanding contractual arrangement.

Unfortunately, there is no simple answer to the problems posed by operational changes or changes in GAAP. Nevertheless, attorneys drafting agreements in situations where such changes may be likely should try to deal with these issues by at least setting general guidelines as to how they should be handled.

* * *

Operational Changes. One potentially plaguing problem is that posed by expansion of operations which are likely to generate losses during the measurement periods. . . . In order to protect the would-be recipient under such circumstances, her attorney may wish to employ one or more of the following covenants:

- No changes in the operations of the acquired company during the payout period without the consent of the seller;

- No losses from new operations will be offset against the earnings of the operations in existence at the time of the sale; or

* * *

Repairs and Maintenance. A variation on the expanded operations ploy is for the new owner of an acquired business to embark on a campaign of extensive repairs and preventive maintenance during the measuring period, with the result that reportable "earnings" and the seller's contingent payment will be sharply reduced. To protect against this possibility, seller's counsel might seek to place a cap on repair and maintenance costs either in dollar or percentage terms. Rather than concern himself with every potential area of distortion, the lawyer drafting the agreement may avoid this detail (and potential for oversight) by dealing with an appropriate [revenue rather than earnings approach].

Related Party Transactions. Related party transactions come in numerous forms and always carry the potential of distorting financial results. Accordingly, where the reporting company buys or sells goods or services from or to an affiliated company or will likely do so during the measuring period, an understanding should be reached regarding the pricing of such goods or services to insure that earnings are not diverted to another enterprise. Similarly, where the reporting company shares resources with an affiliate, the allocation of those shared costs could have a profound effect on reportable earnings. To guard against such pricing and allocation abuses, payee's counsel might wish to specify that the subject company will buy goods and services from affiliated companies at their cost or on a "most-favored nation" basis and all cost allocations must be expressly approved by the payee.

* * *

NOTES

You may recall from the discussion in Chapter V that given the devastating effects that changes in accounting principles can cause in restrictive covenants and other legal documents, lawyers should try to stay abreast of the FASB's activities and agenda. With that suggestion in mind, here are several recent developments and areas to watch regarding the income statement.

(a) *Derivatives*. As described earlier, at page 314, *supra*, SFAS No. 133, *Accounting for Derivative Instruments and Hedging Activities*, (FASB 1998), has required enterprises to include the changes in the fair values of various derivatives contracts during an accounting period in either "net income" or "comprehensive income." Including these changes in value in the income statement obviously affects numerous financial ratios and could potentially cause, or cure, defaults in many contracts and lending agreements.

(b) *Comprehensive Income*. Now that SFAS No. 130 requires enterprises to report and display "comprehensive income" to reflect all nonowner changes in equity, will or should "comprehensive income" replace the terms "income" or "net income" in various financial contracts? Do references to "income" or "net income" in existing contracts really mean "comprehensive income" as the new "bottom line?" For example, can management include increases in unrealized holding gains on securities when computing bonuses based upon a certain percentage of "income?" Can management exclude unrealized losses on derivatives contracts that only affect "comprehensive income?"

(c) *Earnings Per Share*. How will the new requirements in SFAS No. 128 that enterprises compute "basic earnings per share" and "diluted earnings per share" for fiscal periods ending after December 15, 1997 affect references to "primary earnings per share" and "fully diluted earnings per share" particularly in previously existing contracts that do not address changes in generally accepted accounting principles?

(d) *Consolidation Policy*. Since 1982, the FASB has been working on new guidelines for enterprises to follow when deciding whether to consolidate the activities of subsidiaries or affiliates for financial reporting purposes. As you may recall from the discussion earlier in this chapter, at page 385, current accounting rules generally require consolidation if one enterprise owns more than fifty percent of the other entity's voting shares. This bright-line test, however, has allowed enterprises to use various techniques, such as maintaining fifty percent or less ownership, to avoid consolidating poorly-performing subsidiaries or reporting research and development expenses on the income statement. Under the revised proposal, a control test would trigger the consolidation requirement, which would continue to apply until the parent ceases to control the other enterprise. The proposed standard defines "control" as a nonshared decision-making ability of an entity to direct the policies and management that guide the ongoing activities of another entity so as to increase its benefits and limit its losses from that other entity's activities. Such changes could obviously affect an enterprise's balance sheet, income statement, and financial ratios and could potentially cause, or cure, defaults in many contracts and lending agreements.

(e) *Stock Options.* As discussed on page 138, *supra*, in 2004 the FASB adopted the controversial rules requiring public companies to treat the fair value of any employee stock options as an expense. As these new rules become effective pursuant to the schedule there described, they will produce a reduction in net income, which can be quite substantial for companies awarding many options.

PROBLEMS

Problem 6.9A. Assume that the B Bank was organized on January 1 last year with $2,000,000 of paid in capital. B immediately began to accept deposits from the public and had accumulated $3,000,000 in deposits by the end of the year. On July 1 of that year B made a loan of $500,000 to the Y Corp., taking a one-year note with interest of eight percent payable at maturity (on the following June 30). On August 1, B invested $1,000,000 in six percent, twenty year, $1,000 government bonds. The annual interest of $60 per bond was payable in quarterly installments, represented by 80 coupons in the face amount of $15 each, attached to each bond and maturing serially every three months. The first of these coupons matured on October 31 of that year, and B collected $15,000. B also invested $2,800,000 in listed marketable securities, on which B received $250,000 in cash dividends during the year. B's total expenses for the year, including interest on its deposits, amounted to $180,000, and all but $40,000, representing accrued interest owed to depositors, was paid in cash during the year.

(1) To how much additional compensation is the president of B entitled under a contract which provides for a bonus of "ten percent of annual net profits, computed without deduction of the bonus"?

(2) Representing the bank in negotiating an employment contract with the next president, what contractual language would you recommend?

*

CHAPTER VII

CONTINGENCIES

A. IMPORTANCE TO LAWYERS

Perhaps the most troublesome questions involving accrual arise regarding conditional expenses and losses, which may or may not ever occur and which accountants refer to as *contingencies*. Should an enterprise reflect such items in the financial statements despite their uncertainty? This question poses a real dilemma, particularly when the contingent loss or expense contributed to revenue production in the current period, because the matching principle requires an enterprise to match expenses with the revenues that they helped to produce. If the enterprise does not charge the loss or expense against income in the earlier period and the loss or expense subsequently occurs, the business will regret the failure to charge the item against income in the earlier period to which it "belonged." On the other hand, if the enterprise accrues the loss or expense and then it never actually materializes, the company will rue having accrued it in the earlier period. In most cases, the enterprise cannot tell exactly how the future will turn out. If the business decides to accrue the expense or loss in the current period, then the enterprise will debit a current expense or loss account and credit an accrued liability. The business might give the liability a special name, such as "Contingent Liability," to distinguish that type of item on the balance sheet from unconditional liabilities.

Suppose that Neiers Company ("Neiers"), a corporation engaged in the shipbuilding business, usually builds and sells one cruise ship a year. Neiers warrants that each ship can maintain a certain speed for a specified number of years and agrees to refund $250,000 of the purchase price if the ship does not live up to the warranty. If Neiers must make good on such a warranty in some future period, the matching principle would treat that cost as an expense to offset against revenue in the year of sale. At the same time, Neiers may never incur this cost. A question of judgment, therefore, arises: Does the likelihood that Neiers will ultimately incur the cost justify a charge against income in the year of sale? If so, Neiers might record the following entry:

Warranty Expense	$250,000	
Contingent Liability on Warranty		$250,000

If the chances that Neiers will incur this cost do not rise to the level which justifies a charge against income, a question remains whether Neiers should reflect the contingent liability in some other way in the financial statements, perhaps simply by disclosing the contingent liability's existence in a footnote. If Neiers does not record a charge against income in the year of sale and the company actually incurs the cost in some later year, Neiers must charge the refund against income in that later year; it could not qualify as a prior period adjustment, as a result of the virtual elimination of that approach described in Chapter IV on pages 251-252, *supra*.

Notice the difference between a contingent liability, where uncertainty exists as to whether the enterprise will incur any expense or loss, and an unliquidated liability, where the enterprise has incurred an expense or loss attributable to the current period but uncertainty remains as to the exact amount. As we have seen, accountants usually handle the latter by trying to estimate the likely amount. Occasionally, however, management cannot ascertain the amount with any reasonable accuracy. In this situation, enterprises have hesitated to record any charge against current income, preferring instead to disclose the liability, perhaps in a footnote. Of course, uncertainty can also exist as to the amount for a contingent expenditure or loss. That uncertainty presents another reason against trying to reflect the contingent item in the current income statment.

Sometimes a number of related contingent expenses or losses arise in the same year. Actually, this fact serves to simplify the accounting treatment. Suppose, for example, that Neiers sells many ships per year, each with the same warranty described above. Although each particular warranty remains entirely contingent, assume it is statistically certain that Neiers will ultimately issue some refunds. In these circumstances, the previous experience of Neiers or some similar shipbuilder likely provides a fairly sound guide as to what percentage of the total possible refunds Neiers will eventually have to pay. In other words, the situation becomes more like a fixed liability which remains uncertain as to amount, rather than a truly contingent liability. Therefore, if, as is often the case, the enterprise can estimate the amount with reasonable accuracy, the business should record a charge against income in the current period, with a corresponding credit to an estimated liability account.

All lawyers should recognize the various legal issues that can arise regarding contingent liabilities. As an initial matter, GAAP includes rules that require enterprises to accrue, disclose, or both accrue and disclose contingent losses and liabilities in certain circumstances. If an enterprise's financial statements do not follow these requirements, the enterprise may find itself defending a lawsuit alleging fraud. *See, e.g., In re* Corning, Inc. Securities Litigation, No. 92 Civ. 345 (TPG), 1997 WL 235122 (S.D.N.Y. May 7, 1997), where the court found that the class action complaint sufficiently alleged that Corning's consolidated financial statements and periodic reports failed to reveal information about the potential liabilities that a subsidiary may have incurred in manufacturing and selling breast implants to approximately 800,000 women, although the district court ultimately granted Corning's motion for summary judgment, more than seven years later, 349 F.Supp. 2d, 698 (S.D.N.Y. 2004); SEC v. Trans Energy, No. 1-01-CV-02060, 2002 SEC LEXIS 465 (D.D.C. Feb. 27, 2002) (entering permanent injunction against registrant and two officers and imposing civil penalties against the officers for failing to disclose in its 1998 through 2000 SEC filings the existence of material lawsuits that resulted in over $1 million in consent judgments against the company. In addition, issues about whether or how to disclose information about contingencies frequently perplex securities lawyers, particularly given the SEC's recent emphasis on the Management's Discussion and Analysis ("MD&A") requirements, which are discussed in Chapter IV on pages 280–288, *supra*, and should be reviewed at this point. The GAAP financial accounting standards and the MD&A requirements may differ, and if the MD&A rules in fact impose a higher standard for disclosure, a registrant could theoretically observe the GAAP requirements but still violate the federal securities laws. In that event, a lawyer who relied on GAAP in advising a registrant about disclosure obligations for securities law purposes could end up liable for malpractice.

The Enron crisis illustrates the importance of disclosing financial guarantees in the notes to the financial statements. When various Enron affiliates—commonly referred to as SPEs, which Enron formed to keep debt off its books—sought credit, the lenders often required that Enron guarantee the debt. On several occasions, Enron's guarantee took the form of a promise to pay cash, or to issue additional common shares, to repay an SPE's debt if the market price of Enron's common shares dropped under a certain amount or if Enron's bond rating fell below investment grade. While the notes to Enron's financial statements disclosed guarantees of the indebtedness of others, Enron did not mention that its potential liability on those guarantees totaled $4 billion. *See* Bratton, *Enron and the Dark Side of Shareholder Value*, 76 TUL. L. REV. 1275 (2002). When material, GAAP specifically requires an enterprise to disclose the nature and amount of guarantees of the indebtedness of others. Again, inadequate disclosure can subject enterprises to liability and lawyers to malpractice claims.

Issues involving contingencies can also arise when drafting, negotiating and interpreting contracts. To repeat an earlier theme, although an enterprise almost always uses GAAP to prepare financial statements for creditors and investors, different rules may apply for specific contracts, establishing rates for public utilities, or tax purposes. *See, e.g.*, Commonwealth Transp. Commissioner v. Matyiko, 253 Va. 1, 481 S.E.2d 468 (1997) (concluding that even though the corporation did not need to record a contingent liability in the financial statements, the directors could not vote to distribute all the corporation's assets to shareholders without making arrangements for the potential need to pay the liability and holding the directors personally liable when the liability materialized). In particular, transactional lawyers should always consider how to treat contingent liabilities when working on mergers and acquisitions, partnership agreements, or buy-sell agreements.

Perhaps most importantly, however, all attorneys, whether litigators or transactional lawyers, who represent enterprises that undergo financial statement audits must respond to inquiries from independent auditors about litigation, claims and assessments involving their clients. As indicated in

Chapter II, *supra*, financial statements present various assertions, including that reported liabilities actually exist; expenses and losses occurred during the particular accounting period; the financial statements record the enterprise's liabilities, expenses and losses at appropriate amounts; and the financial statements contain any necessary disclosures. In every audit engagement, therefore, the auditor must obtain evidence about contingent liabilities arising from litigation, claims, assessments and other uncertainties to determine whether the enterprise has properly treated those items in the financial statements. In particular, the auditor must use reasonable efforts to determine whether any material unrecorded or undisclosed liabilities exist. In addition to requesting information and representations from an enterprise's management about contingencies, the auditor must request corroborating information from the enterprise's outside counsel. To satisfy this second obligation, the auditor typically requests the client to send an audit inquiry letter directing and authorizing outside counsel to provide information about litigation, claims and assessments to the auditor. Inquiry of a Client's Lawyer Concerning Litigation, Claims, and Assessments, Statement of Auditing Standards No. 12 (AICPA 1976). If the enterprise's lawyers fail or refuse to reply to these inquiries, presumably under some theory of confidentiality arising from the attorney-client privilege, the auditor may qualify the audit opinion. In other circumstances, the auditor may issue an adverse opinion or disclaim an opinion. As we noted in Chapter II on page 126, *supra*, any report other than an unqualified opinion can adversely affect the enterprise's ability to attract capital, borrow funds, or even to continue in business.

If the auditor issues an unqualified opinion with respect to financial statements which do not appropriately treat contingencies, the auditor, as well as the enterprise, can face substantial legal liability. *See, e.g.*, Endo v. Albertine, 863 F.Supp. 708 (N.D.Ill.1994) (denying motions for summary judgment by issuer and auditor in class action presenting claims for alleged failure to disclose material facts regarding contingent tax deficiencies exceeding $100 million and environmental liabilities over $60 million). Such potential liability, plus a desire to maintain their professional reputations, motivates auditors to seek as much information about contingent liabilities as possible from an enterprise's outside counsel.

As you might surmise, lawyers must exercise great care in responding to these audit inquiry letters. A lawyer may not disclose confidential information to the auditor without the client's consent. If the client authorizes the lawyer to disclose information to the auditor, lest the auditor refuse to render an unqualified opinion, the client potentially waives the attorney-client privilege, at a minimum as to any information disclosed. Although numerous states have enacted an accountant-client privilege, the common law did not recognize such a privilege and no such privilege exists under federal law.

For this reason, the disclosure requirements may present discovery opportunities for litigators and pitfalls for attorneys representing businesses which need audited financial statements. Litigators should recognize the discovery possibilities of obtaining accounting information and supporting data regarding contingencies. Sophisticated litigators will carefully examine the opponent's financial statements for information about any contingency related to the dispute. In appropriate circumstances, savvy litigators will seek information about relevant contingent liabilities during discovery, by examining the opponent's books, records and tax returns or requesting such information from the opponent's auditor.

To put these issues in some perspective, assume that your law firm represents Ace Oil Corporation ("Ace"), a small publicly-traded company which distributes heating oil from four storage and distribution facilities located in Pacioli, the fictional fifty-first state. Various federal, state and local laws and regulations govern the operation of the company's facilities. You and your law firm have advised Ace that, beginning in the coming year, regulations will go into effect in stages over the next seven years that will require the company to remove, replace or modify the storage tanks and various other equipment which the company currently uses in its operations. In addition, the company faces an existing legal obligation to decontaminate the soil near its largest facility.

At your firm's suggestion, Ace hired an environmental consultant with whom you have worked in the past to evaluate the applicable technological, regulatory and legal factors involved. The consultant estimated that the total environmental expenditures over the next seven years related to the tanks and equipment will total approximately $5 million. Of that amount, about $4.75 million represents capital expenditures which the company expects to recover through operations. The existing tanks and equipment currently appear on the company's books with net book values of $500,000 and $475,000 respectively. The consultant estimates that the soil decontamination costs will exceed $1 million, an amount material to the company's operations, and could reach $3 million. The company has filed an insurance claim regarding the contaminated soil, but the insurance company, which faces insolvency from similar claims, has denied coverage. In addition, the insurance policy has a $500,000 deductible. *See* Disclosure of Certain Significant Risks and Uncertainties, Statement of Position 94–6 (AICPA 1994). The following questionnaire from the Audit Inquiry Committee is addressed to you and a number of other lawyers in the firm:

CONFIDENTIAL QUESTIONNAIRE—Please return as soon as possible

Client: Ace Oil Co.   Insert "None"
                                                      where appropriate

1. Please identify any lawyer in our firm (other than those listed above) who performed services for the client since December 31, 200X   _____

2. If we have represented the client in any litigation or administrative proceeding pending or settled since December 31, 200X, please attach a description including (A) the court or agency; (B) case style and number; (C) nature of claim; and (D) amount in controversy or nature of relief sought.

                _____

3. Please attach a description of any of the following matters as to which we have been specifically engaged by the client to provide legal advice or representation since December 31, 200X: (A) threats of litigation; (B) assessments or threatened assessments of additional taxes; and (C) other asserted claims.

                _____

4. Please attach a brief description of any unasserted possible claim or assessment by or against the client, but only if (A) you have recognized it in the course of performing legal services for the client since December 31, 200X, and (B) it is more likely than not that it will be asserted.

                _____

5. Please attach a brief description of any advice you have given the client concerning disclosure or non-disclosure either in financial statements or to the SEC of any unasserted possible claim or assessment since December 31, 2000X.

Date: _____   _____
                                             Responding Attorney

How should you respond? What legal consequences can result from your firm's response? Although this example involves an environmental contingency, similar issues often arise in antitrust, government contract, intellectual property, product liability, securities, tax and other matters.

B. THE FINANCIAL ACCOUNTING RULES

Statement of Financial Accounting Standards No. 5, *Accounting for Contingencies* (FASB 1975) ("SFAS No. 5"), establishes a framework for recording and reporting contingencies for financial accounting purposes. Subject to a general, but specific, exception for immaterial items, the pronouncement provides as follows:

STATEMENT OF FINANCIAL ACCOUNTING STANDARDS NO. 5,
ACCOUNTING FOR CONTINGENCIES*

Financial Accounting Standards Board, 1975.

INTRODUCTION

1. For the purpose of this Statement, a contingency is defined as an existing condition, situation, or set of circumstances involving uncertainty as to possible gain (hereinafter a "gain contingency") or loss[1] (hereinafter a "loss contingency") to an enterprise that will ultimately be resolved when one or more future events occur or fail to occur. Resolution of the uncertainty may confirm the acquisition of an asset or the reduction of a liability or the loss or impairment of an asset or the incurrence of a liability.

2. Not all uncertainties inherent in the accounting process give rise to contingencies as that term is used in this Statement. Estimates are required in financial statements for many on-going and recurring activities of an enterprise. The mere fact that an estimate is involved does not of itself constitute the type of uncertainty referred to in the definition in paragraph 1. For example, the fact that estimates are used to allocate the known cost of a depreciable asset over the period of use by an enterprise does not make depreciation a contingency; the eventual expiration of the utility of the asset is not uncertain. Thus, depreciation of assets is not a contingency as defined in paragraph 1, nor are such matters as recurring repairs, maintenance, and overhauls, which interrelate with depreciation. Also, amounts owed for services received, such as advertising and utilities, are not contingencies even though the accrued amounts may have been estimated; there is nothing uncertain about the fact that those obligations have been incurred.

3. When a loss contingency exists, the likelihood that the future event or events will confirm the loss or impairment of an asset or the incurrence of a liability can range from probable to remote. This Statement uses the terms *probable, reasonably possible*, and *remote* to identify three areas within that range, as follows:

   a. *Probable*. The future event or events are likely to occur.

   b. *Reasonably Possible*. The chance of the future event or events occurring is more than remote but less than likely.

---

[1]The term *loss* is used for convenience to include many charges against income that are commonly referred to as *expenses* and others that are commonly referred to as *losses*.

c. *Remote.* The chance of the future event or events occurring is slight.

4. Examples of loss contingencies include:

a. Collectibility of receivables.

b. Obligations related to product warranties and product defects.

c. Risk of loss or damage of enterprise property by fire, explosion, or other hazards.

d. Threat of expropriation of assets.

e. Pending or threatened litigation.

f. Actual or possible claims and assessments.

* * *

h. Guarantees of indebtedness of others.

* * *

STANDARDS OF FINANCIAL ACCOUNTING AND REPORTING

Accrual of Loss Contingencies

8. An estimated loss from a loss contingency (as defined in paragraph 1) shall be accrued by a charge to income if *both* of the following conditions are met:

a. Information available prior to issuance of the financial statements indicates that it is probable that an asset had been impaired or a liability had been incurred at the date of the financial statements.[4] It is implicit in this condition that it must be probable that one or more future events will occur confirming the fact of the loss.

b. The amount of loss can be reasonably estimated.

Disclosure of Loss Contingencies

9. Disclosure of the nature of an accrual made pursuant to the provisions of paragraph 8, and in some circumstances the amount accrued, may be necessary for the financial statements not to be misleading.

10. If no accrual is made for a loss contingency because one or both of the conditions in paragraph 8 are not met, or if an exposure to loss exists in excess of the amount accrued pursuant to the provisions of paragraph 8, disclosure of the contingency shall be made when there is at least a reasonable possibility that a loss or an additional loss may have been

---

[4]*Date of the financial statements* means the end of the most recent accounting period for which financial statements are being presented.

incurred.[6] The disclosure shall indicate the nature of the contingency and shall give an estimate of the possible loss or range of loss or state that such an estimate cannot be made. Disclosure is not required of a loss contingency involving an unasserted claim or assessment when there has been no manifestation by a potential claimant of an awareness of a possible claim or assessment unless it is considered probable that a claim will be asserted and there is a reasonable possibility that the outcome will be unfavorable.

11. After the date of an enterprise's financial statements but before those financial statements are issued, information may become available indicating that an asset was impaired or a liability was incurred after the date of the financial statements or that there is at least a reasonable possibility that an asset was impaired or a liability was incurred after that date. * * * In [these] cases * * * the condition for accrual in paragraph 8 (a) is * * * not met. Disclosure of those kinds of losses or loss contingencies may be necessary, however, to keep the financial statements from being misleading. If disclosure is deemed necessary, the financial statements shall indicate the nature of the loss or loss contingency and give an estimate of the amount or range of loss or possible loss or state that such an estimate cannot be made. Occasionally, in the case of a loss arising after the date of the financial statements where the amount of asset impairment or liability incurrence can be reasonably estimated, disclosure may best be made by supplementing the historical financial statements with pro forma financial data giving effect to the loss as if it had occurred at the date of the financial statements. * * *

12. Certain loss contingencies are presently being disclosed in financial statements even though the possibility of loss may be remote. The common characteristic of those contingencies is a guarantee, normally with a right to proceed against an outside party in the event that the guarantor is called upon to satisfy the guarantee. Examples included * * * guarantees of indebtedness of others * * *. The board concludes that disclosure of those loss contingencies, and others that in substance have the same characteristic, shall be continued. The disclosure shall include the nature and the amount of the guarantee. Consideration should be given to disclosing, if estimable, the value of any recovery that could be expected to

---

[6]For example, disclosure shall be made of any loss contingency that meets the condition in paragraph 8(a) but that is not accrued because the amount of loss cannot be reasonably estimated (paragraph 8(b)). Disclosure is also required of some loss contingencies that do not meet the condition in paragraph 8(a)—namely, those contingencies for which there is a *reasonable possibility* that a loss may have been incurred even though information may not indicate that it is *probable* that an asset had been impaired or a liability had been incurred at the date of the financial statements.

result, such as from the guarantor's right to proceed against an outside party.

* * *

General or Unspecified Business Risks

14. * * * General or unspecified business risks do not meet the conditions for accrual in paragraph 8, and no accrual for loss shall be made. No disclosure about them is required by this statement.

* * *

Gain Contingencies

17. [The following general principles apply to gain contingencies:]

a. Contingencies that might result in gains usually are not reflected in the accounts since to do so might be to recognize revenue prior to its realization.

b. Adequate disclosure shall be made of contingencies that might result in gains, but care shall be exercised to avoid misleading implications as to the likelihood of realization.

* * *

Appendix A
EXAMPLES OF APPLICATION OF THIS STATEMENT

21. This appendix contains examples of application of the conditions for accrual of loss contingencies in paragraph 8 and of the disclosure requirements in paragraphs 9–11. * * * It should be recognized that no set of examples can encompass all possible contingencies or circumstances. Accordingly, accrual and disclosure of loss contingencies should be based on an evaluation of the facts in each particular case.

Collectibility of Receivables

22. The assets of an enterprise may include receivables that arose from credit sales, loans, or other transactions. The conditions under which receivables exist usually involve some degree of uncertainty about their collectibility, in which case a contingency exists as defined in paragraph 1. Losses from uncollectible receivables shall be accrued when both conditions in paragraph 8 are met. Those conditions may be considered in relation to individual receivables or in relation to groups of similar types of receivables. If the conditions are met, accrual shall be made even though the particular receivables that are uncollectible may not be identifiable.

23. [If, based on current information and events, it is probable that the enterprise will be unable to collect all amounts due a ccording to the contractual terms of the receivable, the condition in paragraph 8(a) is met.

As used here, *all amounts due according to the contractual terms* means that both the contractual interest payments and the contractual principal payments will be collected as scheduled according to the receivable's contractual terms. However, a creditor need not consider an insignificant delay or insignificant shortfall in amount of payments as meeting the condition in paragraph 8(a).] Whether the amount of loss can be reasonably estimated (the condition in paragraph 8(b)) will normally depend on, among other things, the experience of the enterprise, information about the ability of individual debtors to pay, and appraisal of the receivables in light of the current economic environment. In the case of an enterprise that has no experience of its own, reference to the experience of other enterprises in the same business may be appropriate. Inability to make a reasonable estimate of the amount of loss from uncollectible receivables (i.e., failure to satisfy the condition in paragraph 8(b)) precludes accrual and may, if there is significant uncertainty as to collection, suggest that the installment method, the cost recovery method, or some other method of revenue recognition be used * * *; in addition, the disclosures called for by paragraph 10 of this statement should be made.

Obligations Related to Product Warranties and Product Defects

24. A warranty is an obligation incurred in connection with the sale of goods or services that may require further performance by the seller after the sale has taken place. Because of the uncertainty surrounding claims that may be made under warranties, warranty obligations fall within the definition of a contingency in paragraph 1. Losses from warranty obligations shall be accrued when the conditions in paragraph 8 are met. Those conditions may be considered in relation to individual sales made with warranties or in relation to groups of similar types of sales made with warranties. If the conditions are met, accrual shall be made even though the particular parties that will make claims under warranties may not be identifiable.

25. If, based on available information, it is probable that customers will make claims under warranties relating to goods or services that have been sold, the condition in paragraph 8(a) is met at the date of an enterprise's financial statements because it is probable that a liability has been incurred. Satisfaction of the condition in paragraph 8(b) will normally depend on the experience of an enterprise or other information. In the case of an enterprise that has no experience of its own, reference to the experience of other enterprises in the same business may be appropriate. Inability to make a reasonable estimate of the amount of a warranty obligation at the time of sale because of significant uncertainty about possible claims (i.e., failure to satisfy the condition in paragraph 8(b)) precludes accrual and, if the range of possible loss is wide, may raise a question about whether a sale should be recorded prior to expiration of the warranty period or until sufficient experience has been gained to permit a reasonable estimate of the obligation; in addition, the disclosures called for by paragraph 10 of this

statement should be made.

26. Obligations other than warranties may arise with respect to products or services that have been sold, for example, claims resulting from injury or damage caused by product defects. If it is probable that claims will arise with respect to products or services that have been sold, accrual for losses may be appropriate. The condition in paragraph 8(a) would be met, for instance, with respect to a drug product or toys that have been sold if a health or safety hazard related to those products is discovered and as a result it is considered probable that liabilities have been incurred. The condition in paragraph 8(b) would be met if experience or other information enables the enterprise to make a reasonable estimate of the loss with respect to the drug product or the toys.

Risk of Loss or Damage of Enterprise Property

27. At the date of an enterprise's financial statements, it may not be insured against risk of future loss or damage to its property by fire, explosion, or other hazards. The absence of insurance against losses from risks of those types constitutes an existing condition involving uncertainty about the amount and timing of any losses that may occur, in which case a contingency exists as defined in paragraph 1. Uninsured risks may arise in a number of ways, including * * * noninsurance of certain risks or co-insurance or deductible clauses in an insurance contract * * *. Some risks, for all practical purposes, may be noninsurable, and the self-assumption of those risks is mandatory.

28. The absence of insurance does not mean that an asset has been impaired or a liability has been incurred at the date of an enterprise's financial statements. Fires, explosions, and other similar events that may cause loss or damage of an enterprise's property are random in their occurrence. With respect to events of that type, the condition for accrual in paragraph 8(a) is not satisfied prior to the occurrence of the event because until that time there is no diminution in the value of the property. There is no relationship of those events to the activities of the enterprise prior to their occurrence, and no asset is impaired prior to their occurrence. Further, unlike an insurance company, which has a contractual obligation under policies in force to reimburse insureds for losses, an enterprise can have no such obligation to itself and, hence, no liability.

Risk of Loss From Future Injury to Others, Damage to the Property of Others, and Business Interruption

29. An enterprise may choose not to purchase insurance against risk of loss that may result from injury to others, damage to the property of others, or interruption of its business operations. Exposure to risks of those types constitutes an existing condition involving uncertainty about the amount and timing of any losses that may occur, in which case a contingency exists as defined in paragraph 1.

30. Mere exposure to risks of those types, however, does not mean that an asset has been impaired or a liability has been incurred. The condition for accrual in paragraph 8(a) is not met with respect to loss that may result from injury to others, damage to the property of others, or business interruption that may occur after the date of an enterprise's financial statements. Losses of those types do not relate to the current or a prior period but rather to the *future* period in which they occur. Thus, for example, an enterprise with a fleet of vehicles should not accrue for injury to others or damage to the property of others that may be caused by those vehicles in the future even if the amount of those losses may be reasonably estimable. On the other hand, the conditions in paragraph 8 would be met with respect to uninsured losses resulting from injury to others or damage to the property of others that took place prior to the date of the financial statements, even though the enterprise may not become aware of those matters until after that date, if the experience of the enterprise or other information enables it to make a reasonable estimate of the loss that was incurred prior to the date of its financial statements.

* * *

Threat of Expropriation

* * *

Litigation, Claims, and Assessments

33. The following factors, among others, must be considered in determining whether accrual and/or disclosure is required with respect to pending or threatened litigation and actual or possible claims and assessments:

a. The period in which the underlying cause (i.e., the cause for action) of the pending or threatened litigation or of the actual or possible claim or assessment occurred.

b. The degree of probability of an unfavorable outcome.

c. The ability to make a reasonable estimate of the amount of loss.

34. As a condition for accrual of a loss contingency, paragraph 8(a) requires that information available prior to the issuance of financial statements indicate that it is probable that an asset had been impaired or a liability had been incurred at the date of the financial statements. Accordingly, accrual would clearly be inappropriate for litigation, claims, or assessments whose underlying cause is an event or condition occurring after the date of financial statements but before those financial statements are issued, for example, a suit for damages alleged to have been suffered as a result of an accident that occurred after the date of the financial statements. Disclosure may be required, however, by paragraph 11.

35. On the other hand, accrual may be appropriate for litigation, claims, or assessments whose underlying cause is an event occurring on or before the date of an enterprise's financial statements even if the enterprise does not become aware of the existence or possibility of the lawsuit, claim, or assessment until after the date of the financial statements. If those financial statements have not been issued, accrual of a loss related to the litigation, claim, or assessment would be required if the probability of loss is such that the condition in paragraph 8(a) is met and the amount of loss can be reasonably estimated.

36. If the underlying cause of the litigation, claim, or assessment is an event occurring before the date of an enterprise's financial statements, the probability of an outcome unfavorable to the enterprise must be assessed to determine whether the condition in paragraph 8(a) is met. Among the factors that should be considered are the nature of the litigation, claim, or assessment, the progress of the case (including progress after the date of the financial statements but before those statements are issued), the opinions or views of legal counsel and other advisers, the experience of the enterprise in similar cases, the experience of other enterprises, and any decision of the enterprise's management as to how the enterprise intends to respond to the lawsuit, claim, or assessment (for example, a decision to contest the case vigorously or a decision to seek an out-of-court settlement). The fact that legal counsel is unable to express an opinion that the outcome will be favorable to the enterprise should not necessarily be interpreted to mean that the condition for accrual of a loss in paragraph 8(a) is met.

37. The filing of a suit or formal assertion of a claim or assessment does not automatically indicate that accrual of a loss may be appropriate. The degree of probability of an unfavorable outcome must be assessed. The condition for accrual in paragraph 8(a) would be met if an unfavorable outcome is determined to be probable. If an unfavorable outcome is determined to be reasonably possible but not probable, or if the amount of loss cannot be reasonably estimated, accrual would be inappropriate, but disclosure would be required by paragraph 10 of this statement.

38. With respect to unasserted claims and assessments, an enterprise must determine the degree of probability that a suit may be filed or a claim or assessment may be asserted and the possibility of an unfavorable outcome. For example, a catastrophe, accident, or other similar physical occurrence predictably engenders claims for redress, and in such circumstances their assertion may be probable; similarly, an investigation of an enterprise by a governmental agency, if enforcement proceedings have been or are likely to be instituted, is often followed by private claims for redress, and the probability of their assertion and the possibility of loss should be considered in each case. By way of further example, an enterprise may believe there is a possibility that it has infringed on another enterprise's patent rights, but the enterprise owning the patent rights has not indicated an intention to take any action and has not even indicated an

awareness of the possible infringement. In that case, a judgment must first be made as to whether the assertion of a claim is probable. If the judgment is that assertion is not probable, no accrual or disclosure would be required. On the other hand, if the judgment is that assertion is probable, then a second judgment must be made as to the degree of probability of an unfavorable outcome. If an unfavorable outcome is probable and the amount of loss can be reasonably estimated, accrual of a loss is required by paragraph 8. If an unfavorable outcome is probable but the amount of loss cannot be reasonably estimated, accrual would not be appropriate, but disclosure would be required by paragraph 10. If an unfavorable outcome is reasonably possible but not probable, disclosure would be required by paragraph 10.

39. As a condition for accrual of a loss contingency, paragraph 8(b) requires that the amount of loss can be reasonably estimated. In some cases, it may be determined that a loss was incurred because an unfavorable outcome of the litigation, claim, or assessment is probable (thus satisfying the condition in paragraph 8(a)), but the range of possible loss is wide. For example, an enterprise may be litigating an income tax matter. in preparation for the trial, it may determine that, based on recent decisions involving one aspect of the litigation, it is probable that it will have to pay additional taxes of $2 million. Another aspect of the litigation may, however, be open to considerable interpretation, and depending on the interpretation by the court the enterprise may have to pay taxes of $8 million over and above the $2 million. In that case, paragraph 8 requires accrual of the $2 million if that is considered a reasonable estimate of the loss. Paragraph 10 requires disclosure of the additional exposure to loss if there is a reasonable possibility that additional taxes will be paid. Depending on the circumstances, paragraph 9 may require disclosure of the $2 million that was accrued.

* * *

NOTES

1. SFAS No. 5 sets forth the analytical framework for analyzing the accounting treatment for loss contingencies, including both pending litigation, claims, and assessments, and unasserted claims and assessments. Because application of the rules imposed by SFAS No. 5 necessarily involves some measure of judgment, an enterprise's management may have considerable discretion in determining whether the enterprise should actually accrue a loss contingency in its accounts, that is, debit a current expense and credit a (contingent) liability, or, if not, at least disclose the possibility of a loss, presumably in the notes to the financial statements; hence accounting for such items is more of an art than a science. In addition, when accrual is called for, paragraph 9 of SFAS No. 5 may require disclosure of the nature or identity of the particular accrual, and perhaps the specific amount accrued for that purpose, to prevent the financial statements from

being misleading. So, an enterprise faced with a loss contingency may have to choose among: (a) fully accruing and specifically identifying the potential loss; (b) fully accruing but not specifically disclosing the particular potential loss; (c) accruing a part and disclosing the possibility of more; (d) merely disclosing the contingency; or (e) if the contingency is sufficiently unlikely to occur, not even disclosing it.

2. Paragraph 8 of SFAS No. 5 requires an enterprise to accrue an estimated loss if (a) information available prior to the issuance of the financial statements indicates it is probable that an asset has been impaired or a liability incurred by the date of the financial statements, and that the fact of the loss will be confirmed by one or more future events; and (b) the enterprise can reasonably estimate the amount of the loss. As to the first set of conditions (keeping in mind that condition (b) must also be satisfied to make accrual required), notice that the event that gave rise to the probability of a loss must have occurred by the date of the end of the period covered by the financial statements, thus ruling out, for example, a lawsuit seeking damages on account of an accident that occurred after the date of the financial statements; nevertheless, under paragraph 11 of SFAS No. 5 the enterprise might be required to disclose the existence of a potential loss incurred after the financial statement date, to make the presentation of the financial status of the enterprise as complete as possible. On the other hand, it is not a requirement for accrual or disclosure that the enterprise learn of the occurrence of the underlying event and the resulting probability of loss by the date of the financial statements: paragraph 8 makes clear that as long as the underlying event occurred by the date of the financial statements, any information available prior to the issuance of the financial statements can be taken into account in determining the appropriate accounting treatment, if any, of the loss contingency in those financial statements.

3. Turning to the requirement in paragraph 8 that it be probable that a loss has been incurred and will be confirmed by one or more future events, notice that in paragraph 3 of SFAS No. 5 "probable" is in effect defined as "likely"; the other two categories in the spectrum of likelihood adopted by SFAS No. 5 are "reasonably possible" and "remote". SFAS No. 5 provides almost no additional guidance as to the meaning of "probable" or "likely," so about all we have to go on is that those terms must surely contemplate something less than virtual certainty, probably a fair amount less. One obvious possibility, especially to a litigator, is "more likely than not", or "anything greater than fifty percent." The "clear preponderance" test sometimes used by courts of equity is another possibility, which would step up the level some. Mundstock, A FINANCE APPROACH TO ACCOUNTING FOR LAWYERS 227 N. 3 (2d ed. 2006), asserts that "on average, accountants interpret 'probable' as more than 75% likely," up from "say, 60 to 70 percent" in the 1999 edition.   A leading accounting text sets the level even higher: "most accountants and auditors appear to use *probable* to mean 80 to 85 percent or larger". Stickney & Weil, FINANCIAL ACCOUNTING[:] AN INTRODUCTION TO CONCEPTS, METHODS AND USES 520 n.5 (8th ed. 1997).

In recent documents and deliberations involving the treatment of uncertain tax positions, the FASB indicated its belief that "more likely than not" conveys a lower percentage threshold than "probable." A 2005 exposure draft took the view that for accounting purposes enterprises could only recognize the projected benefits from a particular tax position if it met the test, "*probable* of being sustained on audit by taxing authorities based solely on the technical merits of the position." Accounting for Uncertain Tax Positions, an interpretation of FASB Statement No. 109, Proposed Interpretation ¶ 6 (Fin. Accounting Standards Bd. July 14, 2005) (emphasis added). The interpretation explicitly described th e term "probable" as "consistent with its use in [SFAS No. 5] to mean that 'the future event or events are likely to occur.' " *Id*. After various comments, the Board changed course and tentatively decided to adopt a "more likely than not" standard, thereby converging with the IASB, which essentially equates "probable" with "more likely than not." *See* Burkholder, *FASB Makes it Easier for Firms to Record Tax Benefits from Uncertain Positions*, 3 Corp. Accountability Rep. (BNA) 1177 (Dec. 2, 2005). Compare the SEC's interpretation of the "reasonably likely" test for MD&A disclosure, described on page 470, *infra*.

At the other end of the spectrum from "probable" is "remote", which SFAS No. 5 in effect defines in terms of when "[t]he chance of the future event or events occurring is slight." SFAS No. 5's third category, "reasonably possible", lies between the other two on the spectrum and is more or less defined just that way in paragraph 3(c); sometimes referred to in terms of "realistic possibility", it is viewed by most commentators as the default category, when neither of the other two applies.

In trying to judge the likelihood of a loss stemming from a pending claim or existing litigation, an enterprise should consider factors such as the following: (a) progress of the case — whether the claimant has filed a complaint or initiated proceedings, and, if so, the current stage of the claim or litigation, such as discovery or trial; (b) opinion of legal counsel – even if counsel cannot give a favorable opinion, the loss may still not be sufficiently likely to call for accrual; (c) prior experience of the enterprise, or other enterprises, in similar matters; and (d) management's intended response — whether management intends to settle or defend the case.

4. As to the second condition for accrual under paragraph 8 of SFAS No. 5, the ability to reasonably estimate the potential loss, in many situations where a loss has probably been incurred, the enterprise cannot reasonably estimate any single amount, but can only identify a wide range of possible losses. When some amount within a range seems like a better estimate than any other amount within the range, an enterprise should accrue that amount. If the enterprise cannot determine a best estimate within the range, under FASB Interpretation No. 14, Reasonable Estimation of the Amount of a Loss (1976), the enterprise should accrue the minimum amount in the

range *and* disclose any reasonably possible additional loss that satisfies the other requirements in SFAS No. 5.

ACCOUNTING TREATMENT FOR ASSERTED CLAIMS			
		Ability to Reasonably Estimate the Potential Loss	
		Reasonable Estimate	No Reasonable Estimate
Likelihood of an Unfavorable Outcome	Probable	Accrue and, if necessary, disclose to avoid misleading financial statements	Disclose contingency and range of possible loss or state that no reasonable estimate possible
	Reasonably Possible	Disclose contingency and estimated amount of possible loss	Disclose contingency and range of possible loss or state that no reasonable estimate possible
	Remote	Neither accrue nor disclose, unless guarantee	Neither accrue nor disclose, unless guarantee

Once again, recall that an enterprise must also disclose information about (1) contingencies from underlying events that occurred after the date of the financial statements, but before the enterprise issued the financial statements which could have a material effect on the financials and (2) guarantees.

5. In the case of unasserted claims, a business must first assess the probability of assertion. If the enterprise concludes that assertion is not probable, SFAS No. 5 does not require accrual or disclosure. On the other hand, if assertion seems probable, then the enterprise must proceed in exactly the same manner as if someone had asserted the claim. You should note that weird outcomes can result from applying the rules regarding unasserted claims. Assume that an enterprise assigns a fifty-one percent chance to the probability that the claimant will assert a $100 million claim and a fifty-one percent chance to an unfavorable outcome on the full claim. Under a broad construction of "probable", the enterprise might have to accrue, and perhaps identify, a $100 million potential loss even though the overall chance that the enterprise will incur the loss equals 26.01 percent (fifty-one percent times fifty-one percent).

6. Paragraph 14 of SFAS No. 5 prohibits enterprises from recording accruals for general or unspecified business risks. Such "general" reserves

illustrate the "cookie jar reserves" that then-SEC Chairman Arthur Levitt listed as one of the five most popular accounting illusions, in his famous "The 'Numbers Game'" speech. See pages 340-348, *supra*. In 2002, the SEC initiated cease-and-desist proceedings against Microsoft Corporation because the company maintained between about $200 million and $900 million in unsupported and undisclosed reserves, accruals, allowances, and liability accounts during its fiscal years ended June 30, 1995 through June 30, 1998, which understated the company's income for that period. Although not related to any litigation, these reserves lacked properly documented support and substantiation. Microsoft consented to a cease-and-desist order to resolve the proceedings. *In re* Microsoft Corp. Accounting and Auditing Enforcement Release No. 1563 [2001 - 2003 Accounting and Auditing Enforcement Release Transfer Binder] Fed. Sec. L. Rep. (CCH) ¶ 75,078,2002 WL 1159487. (June 3, 2002); *see also* SEC v. Bennett, Accounting and Auditing Enforcement Release No. 2281, 7 Fed, Sec, K, Reo, (CCH) ¶ ____ (July 26, 2005) (defendant consented to injunction, $25,000 civil penalty, and officer or director bar for five years for approving the use of reserves without a specific contingency or insufficient support).

Emerging Issues Task Force Topic No. D-77, *Accounting for Legal Costs Expected to Be Incurred in Connection with a Loss Contingency*, expresses the belief that most enterprises have expensed such legal costs as incurred, but recognizes that some companies have accrued estimated legal costs. ACCOUNTING FOR LEGAL COSTS EXPECTED TO BE INCURRED IN CONNECTION WITH A LOSS CONTINGENCY, (Fin. Accounting Standards Bd. Jan. 23, 1997; Mar. 24-25, 1999). Pursuant to APB Opinion No. 22, *Disclosure of Accounting Policies*, enterprises should disclose any material accounting policies, as well as the methods used to apply those policies, and apply those policies consistently. Presumably pursuant to this authorization and in response to litigation arising from the drug Vioxx, Merck & Co., Inc. ("Merck") first disclosed an accounting policy regarding "Legal Defense Costs" in th company's 2004 annual report. According to this policy, Merck accrues "[l]egal defense costs expected to be incurred in connection with a loss contingency . . . when probable and reasonably estimable." MERCK& CO., 2004 ANNUAL REPORT 4- (2005). As of December 31, 2004, the company had established a reserve of $675 million solely for its future legal defense costs related to the Vioxx litigation. Note 11 to the financial statements states: "This reserve is based on certain assumptions and is the *minimum amount* that the Company believes at this time it can reasonably estimate will be spent *over a multi-year period*." *Id*. At 48 (emphasis added). During 2005, Merck spent $285 million in legal defense costs related to Vioxx-related litigation. In the fourth quarter, Merck recorded a $295 million charge to increase the reserve solely for its future legal defense costs related to the Vioxx litigation to $685 million on December 31, 2005. Note 11 to the financial statements continues: "This reserve is based on certain assumptions and is the *best estimate* of the amount that the Company believes, at this time, it can reasonably estimate will be spent *through 2007*."

MERCK & CO., 2005 ANNUAL REPORT 54 (2005)(emphasis added). In addition, the same note states that, as of December 31, 2005, "[t]he Company has not established any reserves for any potential liability relating to the {Vioxx litigation]." *Id.*

7. In November, 2002 the FASB issued an interpretation on disclosing and accounting for financial guarantees. FASB Interpretation No. 45 (Financial Accounting Standards Bd. 2002). The interpretation clarifies that, at the inception of a guarantee, the guarantor must recognize a liability for the fair value of the obligation undertaken. *Id.* ¶ *9.* The interpretation also elaborates on the disclosures that a guarantor must provide in interim and annual financial statements about its obligations under certain guarantees. In particular, they include: (1) the nature of the guarantee, including how it arose, the approximate term, and the events or circumstances that would require the guarantor to perform under the guarantee; (2) the maximum potential amount of future payments under the guarantee; (3) the carrying amount of the liability, if any, for the guarantor's obligations under the guarantee; and (4) the nature and extent of any recourse provisions or available collateral that would enable the guarantor to recover any amounts paid under the guarantee. *Id.* ¶13. However, in the case of product warranties there are special disclosure rules. Rather than disclose information about the maximum potential amount of future payments under the guarantee, a guarantor must disclose its accounting policy plus the methodology used to determine its liability for product warranties, and provide a tabular reconciliation that sets forth the changes in the guarantor's product warranty liability for the reporting period. *Id.* ¶14.

8. With respect to gain contingencies, two general principles apply. First, pursuant to the conservatism doctrine an enterprise should not record gain contingencies which the enterprise may never in fact realize. Second, an enterprise must adequately disclose gain contingencies, but should exercise care to avoid overstating the likelihood that a gain will materialize.

The following excerpts from financial statements for E.I. du Pont de Nemours and Company and JLG Industries for calendar year 1994, taken from *Accounting Trends & Techniques* (49th ed., AICPA 1995), illustrate how enterprises treat contingencies:

E.I. DU PONT DE NEMOURS AND COMPANY
NOTES TO FINANCIAL STATEMENTS

(Dollars in millions, except per share)

1 (In Part): Summary of Significant Accounting Policies

Environmental Liabilities and Expenditures

Accruals for environmental matters are recorded in operating expenses when it is probable that a liability has been incurred and the amount of the liability can be reasonably estimated. Accrued liabilities are exclusive of claims against third parties and are not discounted.

In general, costs related to environmental remediation are charged to expense. Environmental costs are capitalized if the costs increase the value of the property and/or mitigate or prevent contamination from future operations.

28. Commitments and Contingent Liabilities

The company has various purchase commitments for materials, supplies and items of permanent investment incident to the ordinary conduct of business. In the aggregate, such commitments are not at prices in excess of current market.

The company is subject to various lawsuits and claims with respect to such matters as product liabilities, governmental regulations and other actions arising out of the normal course of business. While the effect on future financial results is not subject to reasonable estimation because considerable uncertainty exists, in the opinion of company counsel, the ultimate liabilities resulting from such lawsuits and claims
will not materially affect the consolidated financial position of the company.

The company is also subject to contingencies pursuant to environmental laws and regulations that in the future may require the company to take action to correct the effects on the environment of prior disposal practices or releases of chemical or petroleum substances by the company or other parties. The company has accrued for certain environmental remediation activities consistent with the policy set forth in Note 1. At December 31, 1994, such accrual amounted to $616 and, in management's opinion, was appropriate based on existing facts and circumstances. Under the most adverse circumstances, however, this potential liability could be significantly higher. In the event that future remediation expenditures are in excess of amounts accrued, management does not anticipate that they will have a material adverse effect on the consolidated financial position of the company.

The company has indirectly guaranteed various debt obligations under agreements with certain affiliated and other companies to provide specified minimum revenues from shipments or purchases of products. At December 31, 1994, these indirect guarantees totaled $13. In addition, at December 31, 1994, the company had directly guaranteed $832 of the obligations of certain affiliated companies and others. No material loss is anticipated by reason of such agreements and guarantees.

JLG INDUSTRIES, INC.

NOTES TO CONSOLIDATED FINANCIAL STATEMENTS

Commitments and Contingencies (In Part)

The Company is a party to personal injury and property damage litigation arising out of incidents involving the use of its products. Annually the Company sets its product liability litigation insurance program based on the Company's current and historical claims experience and the availability and cost of insurance. The combination of these annual programs constitutes the Company's aggregate product liability insurance coverage. The Company's program for fiscal year 1994 was comprised of a self-insurance retention of $5 million and catastrophic coverage of $10 million in excess of the retention.

Cumulative amounts estimated to be payable by the Company with respect to pending product liability claims for all years in which the Company is liable under its self-insurance retention have been accrued as liabilities, including $2.2 million for incidents the Company believes may result in claims. Estimates of such accrued liabilities are based on an evaluation of the merits of individual claims and historical claims experience; thus, the Company's ultimate liability may exceed or be less than the amounts accrued. Amounts accrued are paid over varying periods, which generally do not exceed 5 years. The methods of making such estimates and establishing the resulting accrued liability are reviewed continually, and any adjustments resulting therefrom are reflected in current earnings.

C. SECURITIES DISCLOSURE ISSUES

Various legal issues involving contingencies, particularly environmental liabilities, product liability cases and tax disputes, can arise as an enterprise seeks to comply with disclosure requirements under the federal securities laws. Starting in the 1970s, businesses have spent increasing amounts to comply with various federal and state environmental standards. Perhaps more significantly, however, both federal and state statutes often impose liabilities on businesses that own or operate, or once owned or operated, properties which contain environmental contamination. Due to these liabilities' sheer size, issues related to accounting for environmental cleanup liabilities have pushed to the forefront in the accounting and securities fields. Today, environmental contingencies present some of the most difficult, and important, applications of SFAS No. 5.

Businesses in the United States currently face massive liabilities for environmental clean-up costs. For example, a recent Congressional Budget Office study estimates that costs to clean up only non-government sites under the Comprehensive Environmental Response, Compensation and Liability Act, as reauthorized and amended, range up to $463 billion. *AICPA Issues Proposed Guidelines for Environmental Liabilities Accounting*, 27 Sec. Reg. & L. Rep. 1123 (1995). In addition, businesses spend enormous amounts each year to comply with the various federal environmental laws and related regulations, and similar state legislation and administrative rules, in part because noncompliance can cause both civil and criminal penalties.

Lawyers can encounter accounting issues involving environmental contingencies in at least three different ways. First, both the SEC and the accounting profession have recently focused on environmental accounting and disclosure because many businesses, especially publicly-traded enterprises, did not properly accrue or disclose their environmental clean-up liabilities in their financial statements. Staff Accounting Bulletin No. 92, which follows below, illustrates the Commission's commitment to improving accounting and disclosure practices in this area. Second, SEC rules require registrants to discuss their environmental obligations in Management's Discussion and Analysis. Finally, lawyers must increasingly consider environmental contingencies in responding to audit inquiry letters, because they fear legal liability for improperly reported or disclosed environmental liabilities.

Of late, asbestos liabilities have received widespread attention. In 2001, the Rand Institute conducted a study that estimated that the U.S. courts have already adjudicated $30 billion in asbestos claims. The study anticipated that the courts will need to resolve another $200 billion in pending or future claims. Steven Harras, *Asbestos Reform Summit Held on Capitol Hill; Congress, Business, Lawyers Seek Solutions*, CORP. L. DAILY (BNA), Apr. 4, 2003.

STAFF ACCOUNTING BULLETIN NO. 92

Securities and Exchange Commission, 1993.
58 Fed. Reg. 32,843.

[It was noted in Chapter II on page136, *supra*, that Staff Accounting Bulletins (SABs) present interpretations and practices which the Office of the Chief Accountant and the Division of Corporation Finance follow in administering the disclosure requirements in the federal securities laws. The statements in SABs, however, do not bear the SEC's official approval. SAB No. 92 provides the following guidance regarding accounting and disclosures relating to loss contingencies:]

Facts: A registrant believes it may be obligated to pay material amounts as a result of product or environmental liability. These amounts may relate to, for example, damages attributed to the registrant's products or processes, clean-up of hazardous wastes, reclamation costs, fines, and litigation costs. The registrant may seek to recover a portion or all of these amounts by filing a claim against an insurance carrier or other third parties.

Paragraph 8 of *Statement of Financial Accounting Standards No. 5*, "Accounting for Contingencies," ("SFAS 5") states that an estimated loss from a loss contingency shall be accrued by a charge to income if it is probable that a liability has been incurred and the amount of the loss can be reasonably estimated. The Emerging Issues Task Force ("EITF") of the Financial

Accounting Standards Board reached a consensus on EITF Issue 93–5, "Accounting for Environmental Liabilities," that an environmental liability should be evaluated independently from any potential claim for recovery. Under that consensus, any loss arising from the recognition of an environmental liability should be reduced by a potential claim for recovery only when that claim is probable of realization. The EITF also reached a consensus that discounting an environmental liability for a specific clean-up site to reflect the time value of money is appropriate only if the aggregate amount of the obligation and the amount and timing of the cash payments are fixed or reliably determinable for that site. * * *

Because uncertainty regarding the alternative methods of presenting in the balance sheets the amounts recognized as contingent liabilities and claims for recovery from third parties was not resolved by the EITF and current disclosure practices remain diverse, the staff is publishing its interpretation of the current accounting literature and disclosure requirements to serve as guidance for public companies. * * *

Question 1: Does the staff believe that it is appropriate to offset in the balance sheet a claim for recovery that is probable of realization against a probable contingent liability, that is, report the two as a single net amount on the face of the balance sheet?

Interpretive Response: Not ordinarily. The staff believes that separate presentation of the gross liability and related claim for recovery in the balance sheet most fairly presents the potential consequences of the contingent claim on the company's resources and is the preferable method of display. Recent reports of litigation over insurance policies' coverage of product and environmental liabilities and financial failures in the insurance industry indicate that there are significant uncertainties regarding both the timing and the ultimate realization of claims made to recover amounts from insurance carriers and other third parties. The risks and uncertainties associated with a registrant's contingent liability are separate and distinct from those associated with its claim for recovery from third parties.

* * *

Question 2: If a registrant is jointly and severally liable with respect to a contaminated site but there is a reasonable basis for apportionment of costs among responsible parties, must the registrant recognize a liability with respect to costs apportioned to other responsible parties?

Interpretive Response: No. However, if it is probable that other responsible parties will not fully pay costs apportioned to them, the liability that is recognized by the registrant should include the registrant's best estimate, before consideration of potential recoveries from other parties, of the additional costs that the registrant expects to pay. Discussion of uncertainties affecting the registrant's ultimate obligation may be necessary if, for example, the solvency of one or more parties is in doubt or responsibility for the site is disputed by a party. A note to the financial statements should describe any additional loss that is reasonably possible.

Question 3: Estimates and assumptions regarding the extent of environmental or product liability, methods of remedy, and amounts of related costs frequently prove to be different from the ultimate outcome. How do these uncertainties affect the recognition and measurement of the liability?

Interpretive Response: The measurement of the liability should be based on currently available facts, existing technology, and presently enacted laws and regulations, and should take into consideration the likely effects of inflation and other societal and economic factors. Notwithstanding significant uncertainties, management may not delay recognition of a contingent liability until only a single amount can be reasonably estimated. If management is able to determine that the amount of the liability is likely to fall within a range and no amount within that range can be determined to be the better estimate, the registrant should recognize the minimum amount of the range * * *. The staff believes that recognition of a loss equal to the lower limit of the range is necessary even if the upper limit of the range is uncertain.

* * *

Question 5: What financial statement disclosures should be furnished with respect to recorded and unrecorded product or environmental liabilities?

Interpretive Response: Paragraphs 9 and 10 of SFAS 5 identify disclosures regarding loss contingencies that generally are furnished in notes to financial statements. The staff believes that product and environmental liabilities typically are of such significance that detailed disclosures regarding the judgments and assumptions underlying the recognition and measurement of the liabilities are necessary to prevent the financial statements from being misleading and to inform readers fully regarding the range of reasonably possible outcomes that could have a material effect on the registrant's financial condition, results of operations, or liquidity.

* * *

Registrants are cautioned that a statement that the contingency is not expected to be material does not satisfy the requirements of SFAS 5 if there is at least a reasonable possibility that a loss exceeding amounts already recognized may have been incurred and the amount of that additional loss would be material to a decision to buy or sell the registrant's securities. In that case, the registrant must either (a) disclose the estimated additional loss, or range of loss, that is reasonably possible, or (b) state that such estimate cannot be made.

* * *

NOTES

1. In 1996, the AICPA issued Statement of Position 96–1, *Environmental Remediation Liabilities* ("SOP 96–1"), effective for fiscal years beginning after December 15, 1996, to provide authoritative guidance on specific accounting issues regarding the recognition, measurement, display and disclosure of such liabilities. Because the FASB cleared the document for release, SOP 96–1 qualifies as Category (b) authority under the GAAP hierarchy.

SOP 96–1 provides that enterprises should accrue environmental remediation liabilities when the underlying facts and circumstances satisfy the criteria in SFAS No. 5. In addition, the statement of position contains benchmarks to help determine whether SFAS No. 5 requires accrual. The document further provides that any accrual should include (1) incremental direct costs for the remediation effort and (2) an allocable portion of the compensation and benefits for those employees that the enterprise expects to devote a significant amount of time directly to the remediation effort.

Incremental direct costs include amounts paid to complete the remedial investigation and feasibility study, fees to outside engineering and consulting firms for site investigations and to develop remedial action plans and remedial designs, amounts paid to contractors performing remedial actions, government oversight costs and past costs, amounts paid for machinery and equipment which the enterprise dedicates to the remedial action, but that does not offer an alternative use, and legal fees to outside counsel for services related to determining the remedial actions required and the allocation of costs among potentially responsible parties. This last category has proved controversial. Some accountants believe that enterprises should separately expense such legal fees and not include them among the total remediation costs. These accountants argue that legal expenses do not contribute to a site's actual cleanup. The Accounting Standards Executive Committee, however, ultimately concluded that such legal fees, which often represent one of the largest expenditures incurred in cleaning up a site and allocating the costs among the site's potentially responsible parties, constitute a direct cost for the site.

When measuring a liability, an enterprise should include its allocable share of the liability for a specific site and the enterprise's share of those costs related to the site which neither the government nor other potentially responsible parties will pay. The SOP directs enterprises to use enacted laws, existing regulations and policies, the remediation technology that the enterprise expects to use to complete the remediation, and the reporting enterprise's estimates of the costs necessary to complete the remediation at the time that the enterprise will incur those costs in the liability calculation. If the reporting enterprise can fix or reliably determine the amount and timing of the cash payments for the underlying liability, the enterprise can discount the payments to reflect the time value of money.

2. In Chapter IV on page 283, *supra*, it is observed that Item 303 of Regulation S–K requires MD&A disclosure of certain forward-looking information, including any "currently known trends, events, and uncertainties" that the registrant reasonably expects will have a material impact on its liquidity, financial condition or results of operation. In Financial Reporting Release No. 36, 54 Fed. Reg. 22,427 (1989), the SEC sets forth the following two-part test for mandatory disclosure regarding forward-looking information and gives an example involving an environmental contingency:

> Where a trend, demand, commitment, event or uncertainty is known, management must make two assessments:

> (1) Is the known trend, demand, commitment, event or uncertainty likely to come to fruition? If management determines that it is not reasonably likely to occur, no disclosure is required.

> (2) If management cannot make that determination, it must evaluate objectively the consequences of the known trend, demand, commitment, event or uncertainty, on the assumption that it will come to fruition. Disclosure is then required unless management determines that a material effect on the registrant's financial condition or results of operations is not reasonably likely to occur.

> * * *

> Application of these principles may be illustrated using a common disclosure issue which was considered in the review of a number of Project registrants: designation as a potentially responsible party ("PRP") by the Environmental Protection Agency (the "EPA") under The Comprehensive Environmental Response, Compensation, and Liability Act of 1980 ("Superfund").

> *Facts*: A registrant has been correctly designated a PRP by the EPA with respect to cleanup of hazardous waste at three sites. No statutory defenses are available. The registrant is in the process of preliminary investigations of the sites to determine the nature of its potential liability and the amount of remedial costs necessary to clean up the sites. Other PRPs also have been designated, but the ability to obtain contribution is unclear, as is the extent of insurance coverage, if any. Management is unable to determine that a material effect on future financial condition or results of operations is not reasonably likely to occur.

> Based upon the facts of this hypothetical base, MD&A disclosure of the effects of the PRP status, quantified to the extent reasonably practicable, would be required. For MD&A purposes, aggregate potential cleanup costs must be considered in light of the joint and several liability to which a PRP is subject. Facts regarding whether insurance coverage may be contested, and whether and to what extent potential sources of contribution or indemnification constitute reliable sources of recovery may be factored into the determination of whether a material future effect is not reasonably likely to occur.

Id. at 22,430. FRR No. 36, therefore, purportedly establishes a "reasonably likely to have a material effect" standard for disclosing forward-looking information and specifically applies that standard to an environmental contingency. At least one important issue, however, remains unresolved. Does the "reasonably likely" standard differ from the "reasonably possible" likelihood which would otherwise require disclosure under SFAS No. 5?

In *Greenstone v. Cambex Corporation*, 975 F.2d 22 (1st Cir.1992), the Court of Appeals for the First Circuit explicitly recognized, but did not decide, the issue. In that case, the court affirmed the district court's decision dismissing a securities fraud claim because the investor did not plead "with particularity" any specific factual allegations supporting the conclusion that Cambex or its officers knew that the company faced a significant possibility of loss arising from certain IBM Credit leases prior to the time that IBM Credit filed the lawsuit. In the opinion's last paragraph, then Chief Judge, now Justice, Breyer wrote:

> We need not * * * decide whether the appropriate standard is knowledge (1) that an IBM Credit lawsuit was "probable" or (2) that the lawsuit (or some similar loss) was "reasonably likely[."] Whether the standard is one or the other or yet some third similar standard (such as "reasonably expects"), we should reach the same result.

975 F.2d at 28.

More recently, in January 2002, the SEC indicated its view that the words "reasonably likely" express a lower disclosure threshold than "more likely than not." Commission Statement about Management's June 30, 2006 Discussion and Analysis of Financial Condition and Results of Operations, Financial Reporting Release No. 61, 67 Fed. Reg. 3746, 3748 (Jan 25, 2002), available at *http://www.sec.gov/rules/other/33-8056.htm*. Unfortunately, the SEC did not compare "reasonably likely" and "reasonably possible." In the years ahead, we can expect lawyers and the court to face this potentially important issue. In addition, to the extent that the "reasonably likely to have a material effect" standard in the MD&A requirements mandates disclosure in situations which would not qualify as "material" for accounting purposes, compliance with GAAP may once again not satisfy disclosure obligations under the federal securities laws. Compare the discussion of the relationship between MD&A and GAAP at pages 286 - 288, *supra*.

3. After its 1994 bankruptcy, Orange County filed a lawsuit on January 12, 1995 seeking more than $2 billion from Merrill Lynch & Co., Inc. for the brokerage firm's role in the risky derivatives-based investment scheme that ultimately led to the nation's largest municipal bankruptcy. On June 2, 1998, Orange County and Merrill Lynch announced a $400 million settlement to end the lawsuit. In one of the ensuing press releases, Merrill Lynch "announced that it was fully reserved for the settlement and 'that the payment will have no financial impact on earnings reported in the 1998 second quarter or subsequent quarters.'" *Merrill Lynch to Pay $400 Million to Settle Orange County Bankruptcy Suit*, 30 Sec. Reg. & L. Rep. (BNA) 846 (1998). A close examination of the supplemental table for "Non-Interest Expenses" in the MD&A in Merrill Lynch's Form 10-K for the fiscal year ended December 27, 1996 (filed March 21, 1997) reveals that other non-interest expenses increased from $697 million in fiscal 1995 to $859 million in fiscal 1996. At the very end of the textual discussion in that section, the following statement appears: "Other expenses rose 23% due in part to provisions related to various business activities and goodwill amortization." The same supplemental table in the MD&A in Merrill Lynch's Form 10-K for the fiscal year ended December 26, 1997 (filed March 3, 1998) also reveals that other non-interest expenses increased from $859 million in fiscal 1996 to $1,136 million in fiscal 1997. At the end of the third paragraph in textual discussion for that section, the MD&A comments: "Other expenses increased 32% from 1996 due to increases in provisions for various business activities and legal matters, and higher office and postage costs." The very last sentence in that section repeats the statement that appeared in the 1996 MD&A: "Other expenses rose 23% due in part to provisions related to various business activities and goodwill amortization." As counsel for Orange County would you find this information helpful? How might you use those disclosures to gather additional information, financial or other, that might help your client?

See Matthew J. Barrett, *Opportunities for Obtaining and Using Litigation Reserves and Disclosures*, 63 OHIO ST. L. J. 1017 (2002) (illustrating how the disclosures in the MD&A section of various securities filings and several other sources of accounting-related information could provide, or lead to, information about litigation reserves related to the underlying litigation); Matthew J. Barrett, *New Opportunities for Obtaining and Using Litigation Reserves and Disclosures*, 64 OHIO ST. L.J. 1183 (2003) (describing how new MD&A requirements regarding certain contractual obligations, effective for fiscal years ending on or after December 15, 2003, and new tax shelter regulations that took effect on February 28, 2003 could provide additional opportunities).

Press reports and securities filings repeatedly document that public companies continue to record accruals for estimated amounts that management consider necessary to resolve pending or expected litigation, especially in matters involving accounting fraud, asbestos, health-care fraud or product liability, and tax disputes. Recently settled cases offer the following examples (website citations available in the fourth unabridged edition):

• In June 2005, Citigroup Inc. ("Citigroup") agreed to pay $2.0 billion to resolve class action litigation involving certain purchasers of the publicity traded debt and equity securities that Enron Corp. and Enron-related entities issued before Enron's bankruptcy. In announcing the settlement, the company's press release stated:

The settlement is fully covered by Citigroup's existing litigation reserves. The company does not plan to adjust its remaining reserves, which it considers adequate to meet all of the company's remaining exposure to the additional pending Enron and research-related cases.

The company continues to evaluate its reserves on an ongoing basis.

Press Release, Citigroup Inc., Citigroup Agrees to Settle Enron Class Action for $2.0 Billion (June 10, 2005).

• Within a week, JPMorgan Chase & Co. ("JPM") agreed in principle to pay $2.2 billion to settle its portion of the same class action. In announcing the settlement, the company stated that "it expects to take a charge to earnings of approximately $2 billion (pre-tax) or approximately $1.25 billion (after-tax) this quarter to cover this settlement and to increase its litigation reserves for its other remaining legal matters. Of the approximately $2 billion addition to the litigation reserves, approximately one half is associated with the potential costs of Enron-related matters, including the cost of settling this class action. The balance represents management's current best estimate, after consultation with counsel, of the anticipated additional costs under a prudent view of the current legal environment associated with the remaining legal actions, proceedings and regulatory inquiries pending against the firm. The firm believes that its litigation reserves, after today's reserving action, are adequate to meet its remaining litigation exposures, although the reserve may be subject to revision in the future." JPM Press Release, JPMorgan Chase Agrees to Settle Enron Class Action (June 14, 2005). The statement in the press release that approximately half of the $2 billion addition to the litigation reserves is associated with Enron means that JPM had previously reserved $1.2 billion attributable to the Enron litigation.

• Less than three months earlier, JPM also agreed to pay $2 billion to settle another class action involving litigation that investors in WorldCom brought after they lost billions when the telecommunications company filed for bankruptcy in 2002 following its massive accounting scandal. In its press release announcing the settlement, JPM revealed plans to take a $900 million charge against earnings in the first quarter. JPM Press Release, JPMorgan Chase Reaches Agreement to Settle WorldCom Class Action Litigation (Mar. 16, 2005). Again, that disclosure indicates that JPM had previously reserved $1.1 billion attributable to the WorldCom litigation. Indeed, as early as January 2003, JPM announced that it had established a $900 million reserve related to regulatory inquiries and other private litigation involving Enron and other material legal actions, proceedings and investigations. In 2004, the company announced it had set aside $2.3 billion to increase its reserves to cover potential litigation costs arising from its role in the collapses of Enron and WorldCom. Sidel, *J.P. Morgan to Pay $2 Billion As Street's Bill for Bubble Soars*, WALL ST. J., Mar. 17, 2005, at A1.

• In May 2004, Citigroup agreed to pay $2.65 billion to settle its WorldCom litigation. At the same time, the company announced that it had added $5.25 billion to its litigation reserves and that the payment of the WorldCom settlement would leave $6.7 billion in litigation reserves remaining to resolve claims related to Enron's collapse and other regulatory matters involving investment research and initial public offerings. Press Release, Citigroup Inc., Citigroup Reaches Settlement on WorldCom Class

Action Litigation for $1.64 Billion After-Tax (May 10, 2004). Scannell & Pacelle, *Wall Street Gets Sticker Shock From Citigroup*, WALL ST. J., May 12, 2004, at C1.

• Bristol-Myers Squibb Company agreed in July 2004 to pay $300 million to settle a securities class action lawsuit related to wholesaler inventory and other accounting matters and the company's investment in and relationship with ImClone Systems Inc. In the press release announcing the settlement, Bristol-Myers stated that it would charge the entire amount against its litigation reserves, which the company had increased during the second quarter of 2004 by approximately $320 million to approximately $470 million. The company cautioned that the agreement did "not resolve the pending governmental investigations and other private litigation (both ERISA and derivative litigation) related to wholesaler inventory issues and other accounting matters." Bristol-Myers Press Release, Bristol-Myers Squibb To Settle Securities Class Action Litigation (July 30, 2004).

• Halliburton Company reached an agreement in December 2002 to pay about $4 billion in cash and stock to settle more than 300,000 asbestos claims. When Halliburton announced its results for the 2002 fourth quarter in February 2003, *The Wall Street Journal* reported that those results included only a $214 million charge for asbestos liability, suggesting that the company had previously established reserves for the uninsured balance. Indeed, Halliburton's Form 10-K for the fiscal year ended December 31, 2002 discloses that the company used a $2.2 billion estimate, the low end of an outside expert's range of liabilities, to accrue liability and defense costs for various asbestos claims during the second quarter of 2002 and, then, $3.5 billion, the upper end of that range, during that year's fourth quarter.

• In March 2005, Time Warner Inc. agreed to pay a $300 million penalty to the SEC and to restate its financial results for 2000 and 2001 to resolve an investigation into accounting at America Online. Previously, the company announced that it had created a $500 million reserve during its 2004 third quarter to resolve the federal probes, but that it had not set aside any reserves to settle the various civil lawsuits that it faced related to its accounting.

• MetLife Inc. resolved a tax audit with the IRS during the 2004 second quarter. The resolution allowed the company to reduce its liabilities by $105 million, thereby increasing the company's net income for that period by the same amount. *MetLife, Inc.*, WALL ST. J., Aug. 2, 2004, at B6.

An earlier illustration suggests that the Internal Revenue Service may have failed to review publicly available financial statements before resolving a tax dispute with Wabash National Corporation ("Wabash"), a company that designs, manufactures and markets truck trailers and whose shares trade on the New York Stock Exchange. In the notes to Wabash's financial statements in the company's Form 10-K for the fiscal year ended December 31, 1999, the following discussion appears in note 14 on commitments and contingencies:

> On December 24, 1998, the Company received a notice from the Internal Revenue Service that it intended to assess federal excise tax on certain used trailers restored by the Company during 1996 and 1997. Although the Company strongly disagreed with the IRS, it recorded a $4.6 million accrual in 1998 for this loss contingency in Other, net in the accompanying Consolidated Statements of Income. During 1999 the Company reached a settlement with the IRS of approximately $1.1 million, net of interest, of which less than $1.0 million was related to the restoration of used trailers. Accordingly, during the fourth quarter 1999 the Company reflected a $3.5 million reversal in Other, net [thereby recognizing that amount in Other Income] in the accompanying Consolidated Statements of Income.

4. As discussed in the MD&A materials at pages 281-282, *supra*, Sarbanes-Oxley section 401(a) directed the SEC to issue final rules that require disclosures about all material off-balance sheet transactions and similar arrangements, obligations, and other relationships. Accordingly, in early 2003, the SEC issued final regulations that require new disclosures about off-balance sheet arrangements and aggregate contractual obligations. Even though those regulations specifically exclude "[c]ontingent liabilities arising out of litigation, arbitration or regulatory actions" from the definition of off-balance sheet arrangements, separate rules apply to contractual obligations. At a minimum, those rules would reach any obligations arising from settlement agreements that registrants reach in similar cases. Using categories including "Other Long-Term Liabilities Reflected on the Registrant's Balance Sheet under GAAP," which may well apply to any liability, including a litigation reserve, that a registrant does not expect to satisfy within a year, the final rules require certain registrants to disclose in tabular format the amounts due within specified time periods, as of the latest fiscal year-end balance sheet date. The rules apply to filings that must include financial statements for fiscal years ending on or after December 15, 2003. Disclosure in Management's Discussion and Analysis About Off-Balance Sheet Arrangements and Aggregate Contractual Obligations, 68 Fed. Reg. 5982 (Feb. 5, 2003) (http://www.sec.gov/rules/final/33-8182.htm).

Although the proposed rules would have imposed additional disclosure requirements for contingent liabilities and commitments, the SEC decided to delete those provisions from the final regulations. The release that accompanied the final regulations, however, stated that the SEC would continue to assess the costs and benefits of an MD&A disclosure requirement for aggregate contingent liabilities and commitments during the Commission's ongoing review of MD&A.

D. AUDIT INQUIRIES AND RELEVANT PROFESSIONAL STANDARDS

Any business requiring audited financial statements must provide information regarding legal claims against the enterprise to its auditors. An enterprise must send a letter, which accountants usually refer to as the *management letter*, to its auditor regarding asserted and unasserted claims against the business. In addition, the enterprise requests its lawyer to send a letter to the enterprise's auditor regarding asserted and usually specified unasserted legal claims against the business. Lawyers regularly receive these *audit inquiry letters* directly from clients that require audited financial statements.

While many small businesses do not require audited financial statements, many mid-sized and most larger businesses do. Remember that all publicly traded enterprises must provide audited financial statements to the Securities and Exchange Commission. In addition, many privately held companies must supply audited financial statements to lenders or to shareholders. Finally, even governmental entities, not-for-profit organizations, churches and other organizations frequently undergo audits.

In December 1975, the American Bar Association (the "ABA") issued the following Statement of Policy to set forth the legal profession's official policy on audit inquiry letters:

Statement of Policy Regarding Lawyers' Responses to Auditors' Requests for Information[*]

American Bar Association, 1975. 31 Bus. Law. 1709 (1976) (emphasis in original).

Preamble
The public interest in protecting the confidentiality of lawyer-client communications is fundamental. The American legal, political and economic systems depend heavily upon voluntary compliance with the law and upon ready access to a respected body of professionals able to interpret and advise on the law. The expanding complexity of our laws and governmental regulations increases the need for prompt, specific and unhampered lawyer-client communication. The benefits of such communication and early consultation underlie the strict statutory and ethical obligations of the lawyer to preserve the confidences and secrets of the client, as well as the long-recognized testimonial privilege for lawyer-client communication.

---

[*]Copyright © 1975 by the American Bar Association. Reprinted with permission. [Editor's note in original: * * * A Statement on Auditing Standards, which coordinates with the approach set forth in the revised ABA Statement, was approved on January 7, 1976, by the AICPA Auditing Standards Executive Committee. * * *]

Both the Code of Professional Responsibility and the cases applying the evidentiary privilege recognize that the privilege against disclosure can be knowingly and voluntarily waived by the client. It is equally clear that disclosure to a third party may result in loss of the "confidentiality" essential to maintain the privilege. Disclosure to a third party of the lawyer-client communication on a particular subject may also destroy the privilege as to other communications on that subject. Thus, the mere disclosure by the lawyer to the outside auditor, with due client consent, of the substance of communications between the lawyer and client may significantly impair the client's ability in other contexts to maintain the confidentiality of such communications.

Under the circumstances a policy of audit procedure which requires clients to give consent and authorize lawyers to respond to general inquiries and disclose information to auditors concerning matters which have been communicated in confidence is essentially destructive of free and open communication and early consultation between lawyer and client. The institution of such a policy would inevitably discourage management from discussing potential legal problems with counsel for fear that such discussion might become public and precipitate a loss to or possible liability of the business enterprise and its stockholders that might otherwise never materialize.

It is also recognized that our legal, political and economic systems depend to an important extent on public confidence in published financial statements. To meet this need the accounting profession must adopt and adhere to standards and procedures that will command confidence in the auditing process. It is not, however, believed necessary, or sound public policy, to intrude upon the confidentiality of the lawyer-client relationship in order to command such confidence. On the contrary, the objective of fair disclosure in financial statements is more likely to be better served by maintaining the integrity of the confidential relationship between lawyer and client, thereby strengthening corporate management's confidence in counsel and encouraging its readiness to seek advice of counsel and to act in accordance with counsel's advice.

Consistent with the foregoing public policy considerations, it is believed appropriate to distinguish between, on the one hand, litigation which is pending or which a third party has manifested to the client a present intention to commence and, on the other hand, other contingencies of a legal nature or having legal aspects. As regards the former category, unquestionably the lawyer representing the client in a litigation matter may be the best source for a description of the claim or claims asserted, the client's position (e. g. denial, contest, etc.), and the client's possible exposure in the litigation (to the extent the lawyer is in a position to do so). As to the latter category, it is submitted that, for the reasons set forth above, it is not in the public interest for the lawyer to be required to respond to general inquiries from auditors concerning possible claims.

It is recognized that the disclosure requirements for enterprises subject to the reporting requirements of the Federal securities laws are a major concern of managements and counsel, as well as auditors. It is submitted that compliance therewith is best assured when clients are afforded maximum encouragement, by protecting lawyer-client confidentiality, freely to consult counsel. Likewise, lawyers must be keenly conscious of the importance of their clients being competently advised in these matters.

Statement of Policy

NOW, THEREFORE, BE IT RESOLVED that it is desirable and in the public interest that this Association adopt the following Statement of Policy regarding the appropriate scope of the lawyer's response to the auditor's request, made by the client at the request of the auditor, for information concerning matters referred to the lawyer during the course of his representation of the client:

(1) *Client Consent to Response.* The lawyer may properly respond to the auditor's requests for information concerning loss contingencies * * * to the extent hereinafter set forth, subject to the following:

(a) Assuming that the client's initial letter requesting the lawyer to provide information to the auditor is signed by an agent of the client having apparent authority to make such a request, the lawyer may provide to the auditor information requested, without further consent, unless such information discloses a confidence or a secret or requires an evaluation of a claim.

(b) In the normal case, the initial request letter does not provide the necessary consent to the disclosure of a confidence or secret or to the evaluation of a claim since that consent may only be given after full disclosure to the client of the legal consequences of such action.

(c) Lawyers should bear in mind, in evaluating claims, that an adverse party may assert that any evaluation of potential liability is an admission.

(d) In securing the client's consent to the disclosure of confidences or secrets, or the evaluation of claims, the lawyer may wish to have a draft of his letter reviewed and approved by the client before releasing it to the auditor; in such cases, additional explanation would in all probability be necessary so that the legal consequences of the consent are fully disclosed to the client.

(2) *Limitation on Scope of Response.* It is appropriate for the lawyer to set forth in his response, by way of limitation, the scope of his engagement by the client. It is also appropriate for the lawyer to indicate the date as of which information is furnished and to disclaim any undertaking to advise

the auditor of changes which may thereafter be brought to the lawyer's attention. *Unless the lawyer's response indicates otherwise, (a) it is properly limited to matters which have been given substantive attention by the lawyer in the form of legal consultation and, where appropriate, legal representation since the beginning of the period or periods being reported upon, and (b) if a law firm or a law department, the auditor may assume that the firm or department has endeavored, to the extent believed necessary by the firm or department, to determine from lawyers currently in the firm or department who have performed services for the client since the beginning of the fiscal period under audit whether such services involved substantive attention in the form of legal consultation concerning those loss contingencies referred to in Paragraph 5(a) below but, beyond that, no review has been made of any of the client's transactions or other matters for the purpose of identifying loss contingencies to be described in the response.*

(3) *Response may be Limited to Material Items.* In response to an auditor's request for disclosure of loss contingencies of a cl ient, it is appropriate for the lawyer's response to indicate that the response is limited to items which are considered individually or collectively material to the presentation of the client's financial statements.

(4) *Limited Responses.* Where the lawyer is limiting his response in accordance with this Statement of Policy, his response should so indicate (see Paragraph 8). If in any other respect the lawyer is not undertaking to respond to or comment on particular aspects of the inquiry when responding to the auditor, he should consider advising the auditor that his response is limited, in order to avoid any inference that the lawyer has responded to all aspects; otherwise, he may be assuming a responsibility which he does not intend.

(5) *Loss Contingencies.* When properly requested by the client, it is appropriate for the lawyer to furnish to the auditor information concerning the following matters if the lawyer has been engaged by the client to represent or advise the client professionally with respect thereto and he has devoted substantive attention to them in the form of legal representation or consultation:

(a) *overtly threatened or pending litigation*, whether or not specified by the client;

(b) *a contractually assumed obligation* which the client has specifically identified and upon which the client has specifically requested, in the inquiry letter or a supplement thereto, comment to the auditor;

(c) *an unasserted possible claim or assessment* which the client has specifically identified and upon which the client has specifically requested, in the inquiry letter or a supplement thereto, comment to the auditor.

With respect to clause (a), overtly threatened litigation means that a potential claimant has manifested to the client an awareness of and present intention to assert a possible claim or assessment unless the likelihood of litigation (or of settlement when litigation would normally be avoided) is considered remote. With respect to clause (c), where there has been no manifestation by a potential claimant of an awareness of and present intention to assert a possible claim or assessment, consistent with the considerations and concerns outlined in the Preamble and Paragraph 1 hereof, the client should request the lawyer to furnish information to the auditor only if the client has determined that it is probable that a possible claim will be asserted, that there is a reasonable possibility that the outcome (assuming such assertion) will be unfavorable, and that the resulting liability would be material to the financial condition of the client. Examples of such situations might (depending in each case upon the particular circumstances) include the following: (i) a catastrophe, accident or other similar physical occurrence in which the client's involvement is open and notorious, or (ii) an investigation by a government agency where enforcement proceedings have been instituted or where the likelihood that they will not be instituted is remote, under circumstances where assertion of one or more private claims for redress would normally be expected, or (iii) a public disclosure by the client acknowledging (and thus focusing attention upon) the existence of one or more probable claims arising out of an event or circumstance. In assessing whether or not the assertion of a possible claim is probable, it is expected that the client would normally employ, by reason of the inherent uncertainties involved and insufficiency of available data, concepts parallel to those used by the lawyer (discussed below) in assessing whether or not an unfavorable outcome is probable; thus, assertion of a possible claim would be considered probable only when the prospects of its being asserted seem reasonably certain (i.e., supported by extrinsic evidence strong enough to establish a presumption that it will happen) and the prospects of non-assertion seem slight.

It would not be appropriate, however, for the lawyer to be requested to furnish information in response to an inquiry letter or supplement thereto if it appears that (a) the client has been required to specify unasserted possible claims without regard to the standard suggested in the preceding paragraph, or (b) the client has been required to specify all or substantially all unasserted possible claims as to which legal advice may have been obtained, since, in either case, such a request would be in substance a general inquiry and would be inconsistent with the intent of this Statement of Policy.

The information that lawyers may properly give to the auditor concerning the foregoing matters would include (to the extent appropriate) an identification of the proceedings or matter, the stage of proceedings, the claim(s) asserted, and the position taken by the client.

In view of the inherent uncertainties, the lawyer should normally refrain from expressing judgments as to outcome except in those relatively few clear cases where it appears to the lawyer that an unfavorable outcome is either "probable" or "remote;" for purposes of any such judgment it is appropriate to use the following meanings:

(i) *probable*—an unfavorable outcome for the client is probable if the prospects of the claimant not succeeding are judged to be extremely doubtful and the prospects for success by the client in its defense are judged to be slight.

(ii) *remote*—an unfavorable outcome is remote if the prospects for the client not succeeding in its defense are judged to be extremely doubtful and the prospects of success by the claimant are judged to be slight.

If, in the opinion of the lawyer, considerations within the province of his professional judgment bear on a particular loss contingency to the degree necessary to make an informed judgment, he may in appropriate circumstances communicate to the auditor his view that an unfavorable outcome is "probable" or "remote," applying the above meanings. No inference should be drawn, from the absence of such a judgment, that the client will not prevail.

The lawyer also may be asked to estimate, in dollar terms, the potential amount of loss or range of loss in the event that an unfavorable outcome is not viewed to be "remote." In such a case, the amount or range of potential loss will normally be as inherently impossible to ascertain, with any degree of certainty, as the outcome of the litigation. Therefore, it is appropriate for the lawyer to provide an estimate of the amount or range of potential loss (if the outcome should be unfavorable) only if he believes that the probability of inaccuracy of the estimate of the amount or range of potential loss is slight.

The considerations bearing upon the difficulty in estimating loss (or range of loss) where pending litigation is concerned are obviously even more compelling in the case of unasserted possible claims. In most cases, the lawyer will not be able to provide any such estimate to the auditor.

As indicated in Paragraph 4 hereof, the auditor may assume that all loss contingencies specified by the client in the manner specified in clauses (b) and (c) above have received comment in the response, unless otherwise therein indicated. The lawyer should not be asked, nor need the lawyer undertake, to furnish information to the auditor concerning loss contingencies except as contemplated by this Paragraph 5.

(6) *Lawyer's Professional Responsibility*. Independent of the scope of his response to the auditor's request for information, the lawyer, depending upon the nature of the matters as to which he is engaged, may have as part of his professional responsibility to his client an obligation to advise the client concerning the need for or advisability of public disclosure of a wide range of events and circumstances. The lawyer has an obligation not knowingly to participate in any violation by the client of the disclosure requirements of the securities laws. The lawyer also may be required under the Code of Professional Responsibility to resign his engagement if his

advice concerning disclosures is disregarded by the client. The auditor may properly assume that whenever, in the course of performing legal services for the client with respect to a matter recognized to involve an unasserted possible claim or assessment which may call for financial statement disclosure, the lawyer has formed a professional conclusion that the client must disclose or consider disclosure concerning such possible claim or assessment, the lawyer, as a matter of professional responsibility to the client, will so advise the client and will consult with the client concerning the question of such disclosure and the applicable requirements of FAS 5.

(7) *Limitation on Use of Response. Unless otherwise stated in the lawyer's response, it shall be solely for the auditor's information in connection with his audit of the financial condition of the client and is not to be quoted in whole or in part or otherwise referred to in any financial statements of the client or related documents, nor is it to be filed with any governmental agency or other person, without the lawyer's prior written consent. Notwithstanding such limitation, the response can properly be furnished to others in compliance with court process or when necessary in order to defend the auditor against a challenge of the audit by the client or a regulatory agency, provided that the lawyer is given written notice of the circumstances at least twenty days before the response is so to be furnished to others, or as long in advance as possible if the situation does not permit such period of notice.*

(8) *General.* This Statement of Policy, together with the accompanying Commentary (which is an integral part hereof), has been developed for the general guidance of the legal profession. In a particular case, the lawyer may elect to supplement or modify the approach hereby set forth. If desired, this Statement of Policy may be incorporated by reference in the lawyer's response * * *.

NOTES

1. Two major problems arise in the lawyer's letters area. First, auditors and lawyers have different concerns related to the disclosure of information about legal claims. Auditors primarily want to encourage public disclosure of more information, to ensure that investors receive all potentially relevant information. Full disclosure helps to protect the auditor from liability if the client experiences future financial problems. Lawyers, on the other hand, strive to protect the attorney-client privilege. These goals conflict, because a lawyer's disclosure of information to auditors can waive the attorney-client privilege.

A second problem regarding lawyer's letters arises because attorneys and auditors may use different standards to determine the likelihood that a claim will result in a loss. The two professions define "remote" and "probable" in different terms, which may result in divergent standards for disclosure. Kenneth E. Harrison & Thomas C. Pearson, *Communications Between Auditors and Lawyers for the Identification and Evaluation of Litigation, Claims, and Assessments*, Acct. Horizons, June 1989, at 76. In

SFAS No. 5, the FASB defines a loss as "probable" if the future events confirming the loss are "likely to occur." In contrast, the foregoing ABA Statement of Policy describes an unfavorable outcome as "probable" when "the prospects of the claimant not succeeding are judged to be extremely doubtful and the prospects for success[ful defense] are judged to be slight." Moreover, the FASB classifies a loss contingency as "remote" if the chance of future events confirming the loss are "slight," while the ABA considers the possibility of an unfavorable outcome as "remote" when "the prospects of the client['s defense] not succeeding * * * are judged to be extremely doubtful and the prospects of success by the claimant are judged to be slight."

The following chart illustrates these different standards:

DIVERGENCE BETWEEN FASB AND ABA PROBABILITY REGIONS

Chances of an Unfavorable Outcome

ABA

	inferential		
0% remote	reasonably possible	probable 100%	
remote	reasonably possible	probable	

FASB

Note, *Attorney Responses To Audit Letters: The Problem of Disclosing Loss Contingencies Arising From Litigation and Unasserted Claims*, 51 N.Y.U. L. Rev. 838, 877 (1976).

The standards for unasserted claims similarly diverge. An auditor must determine whether the enterprise has properly treated any unasserted claims. If the likelihood of assertion is "probable," SFAS No. 5 may require the enterprise to accrue, disclose, or both accrue and disclose the claim. Although the definition in paragraph 3 of SFAS No. 5 does not expressly apply to this determination, presumably the term "probable" still means "likely to occur." In contrast, the ABA Statement of Policy considers an unasserted claim "probable only when the prospects of its being asserted seem reasonably certain * * * and the prospects of non-assertion seem slight."

These different definitions and standards can obviously cause problems. For example, the ABA definition of "probable" could lead lawyers to consider fewer unasserted claims than auditors, thereby revealing fewer claims. This creates difficulties for auditors in determining whether to accrue or disclose a claim. The ABA also has a narrower definition of remote than the FASB, so lawyers may consider fewer losses remote than auditors.

These conflicting standards can leave clients caught in the middle. Public companies generally need an unqualified opinion from their auditors for their creditors and shareholders. The client also ultimately bears responsibility for any improper disclosures. In this latter regard, the client may face lawsuits from disgruntled shareholders or the SEC if the company does not properly disclose contingencies. *See, e.g., In re* Westinghouse Securities Litigation, 90 F.3d 696 (3d Cir.1996) (reinstating class action securities fraud claims alleging that a $975 million pre-tax accrual for loan losses did not adequately cover estimated losses).

2.   In an attempt to preserve the attorney-client privilege regarding unasserted possible claims or assessments, some lawyers refuse to respond to general inquiries relating to the existence of such items in auditors' requests for information. In a recent interpretation, the Auditing Standards Board concluded that such refusals do not thereby limit the scope of the audit. The ASB, however, reiterated that the lawyer should confirm the assumption underlying the understanding between the legal and accounting professions that the lawyer, under certain circumstances, will advise the client concerning the client's obligation to make financial statement disclosures regarding unasserted possible claims or assessments. Use of Explanatory Language Concerning Unasserted Possible Claims or Assessments in Lawyers' Responses to Audit Inquiry Letters, Auditing Interpretation No. 10 of Section 337 (Auditing Standards Bd. 1997), codified at 1 Professional Standards (CCH) AU § 9337.31-.32 (AICPA, Feb. 1997).

PROBLEMS

Problem 7.1. X Corp., a closely held company that uses the calendar year for financial accounting purposes, publishes a magazine which until a few years ago was a rather placid periodical. Several years earlier, the company borrowed money from a local bank to expand its printing facilities and the loan agreement requires X Corp. to submit audited financial statements to the bank each year.

Four years ago (year 1), in an effort to boost lagging sales, X adopted a new policy of featuring more exciting, even sensational articles. The following year (year 2), the magazine published an alleged exposé in which the coach of a major football team was accused of fixing a game. A year later (year 3), the coach brought suit for libel, claiming damages of $5,000,000. X was advised by counsel that (1) there was a good chance X would be held liable, and (2) if so, the damages were most likely to run between $50,000 and $100,000, with an outside possibility that the amount would be much greater, perhaps even in seven figures. During X's most recent fiscal year (year 4), which ended a couple of months ago, the case was tried before a jury, which found against X and awarded general damages of $60,000 plus punitive damages of $3,000,000. The trial court reduced the total damages to $460,000. Pursuant to the advice of counsel, X appealed, primarily on the ground that it was error to award the plaintiff any punitive damages; but just last week the judgment of $460,000 was affirmed, and that amount was paid by X.

X has faced libel suits from time to time in the past, but never one as large as this. In all of the prior actions, X either defended successfully or settled for some modest amount, the largest settlement being some $30,000 two years ago.

X's earnings for the past four years, without taking any account of this lawsuit, have been as follows:

Year
1	Year 2	Year 3	Year 4 (recently ended)
$375,000	$600,000	$700,000	$750,000

X's balance sheet at the close of year 4 (recently-ended) was as follows:

X Corp.

Assets		Liabilities & Equity	
Current Assets		Accounts Payable	$1,250,000
Cash	$ 800,000	Note Payable	600,000
Accounts Receivable	1,100,000	Total Liabilities	$1,850,000
Inventory	1,300,000	Shareholders' Equity	
Total	$3,200,000	Stated Capital	$4,000,000
Fixed Assets		Earned Surplus	3,150,000
Plant	5,800,000	Total	$7,150,000
Total Assets	$9,000,000	Grand Total	$9,000,000

How, if at all, should the events relating to the coach's libel claim have been reflected in X's financial statements in each of the last four years?

Problem 7.2. Scary Air Airlines, Inc., a small publicly traded corporation that uses the calendar year for financial accounting purposes, publishes its audited annual financial statements in mid-March each year. On March 1, Year 2, a Scary Air turboprop plane crashed while flying on a sunny, warm day. The crash did not kill anyone, but all twelve passengers suffered injuries requiring medical treatment. The pilot, Sleepy Joe, escaped unharmed. A hospital near the crash site treated and released nine passengers for relatively minor injuries. The hospital admitted the other three passengers and they remained hospitalized for periods which did not exceed two weeks.

Scary Air had never had a crash until this accident, so management did not have any first hand experience at predicting potential losses. Scary Air's Chief Financial Officer ("CFO") estimated, however, based on industry experience, that if the company was liable for the accident it would likely end up paying between $20,000 and $50,000 to each of the nine passengers who were not hospitalized. The CFO also estimated that the company may have to pay between $100,000 and $250,000, but most likely about $150,000, to each of the three passengers who were hospitalized.

After the accident, the National Transportation Safety Board ("NTSB") immediately opened an investigation into the crash. In September,

Year 2, Scary Air learned that several passengers, including two passengers that had been hospitalized, had been meeting with a personal injury attorney.

On January 15, Year 3, the NTSB announced its findings that pilot error caused the accident. The NTSB concluded that Sleepy Joe had fallen asleep in the cockpit. The NTSB's investigation also revealed Sleepy Joe had flown 30 hours more than the monthly maximum under the applicable safety regulations of the Federal Aviation Administration ("FAA"). After the NTSB's announcement, counsel advised management that the FAA could fine Scary Air $250,000 and suspend its license for ninety days.

Management immediately decided to offer $25,000 to the nine passengers that were not hospitalized and $100,000 to the three passengers that were hospitalized. Shortly after Scary Air issued its financial statements for Year 2, the company agreed to pay six passengers that were not hospitalized $35,000 each and $190,000 to one of the passengers that was hospitalized in exchange for their releases of any and all claims arising from the accident. When the company refused to increase the settlement offers to the remaining five passengers, they filed suit, collectively seeking $2.5 million in compensatory damages and $5 million in punitive damages. Counsel advised management that (1) there was about a ninety percent chance that Scary Air would be held liable, and (2) if so, the damages were most likely to run between $500,000 and $1,500,000, with an outside possibility that the amount could reach $5 million. Later in Year 3, Scary Air consented to a $200,000 fine after the FAA agreed not to suspend the company's license.

During Scary Air's most recent fiscal year (year 4), which ended a couple of months ago, the company decided to accept a settlement offer from the five passengers to settle the case for a total of $2 million.

Scary Air's earnings for the past four years, without taking any account of this crash, have been as follows:

Year 1	Year 2	Year 3	Year 4 (recently ended)
$2,000,000	$1,750,000	$2,600,000	$3,250,000

How, if at all, should the events relating to the accident have been reflected in Scary Air's financial statements in each of the last four years?

Problem 7.3. Assume that you are a senior associate in a large law firm, and you received from the accounting firm that audits your publicly-traded client, Gunn Products, Inc., the standard audit inquiry letter requesting your reply regarding the company's litigation, claims and assessments.

You recall that about six months ago an investigator from the Federal Trade Commission visited the company   and asked some presumably routine questions about the company's pricing policies, particularly with respect to several profitable products which have enjoyed no price competition for several years. Upon doing some checking, you learn from the marketing vice president that she and several peers from competitors met each winter to discuss product pricing. She denied fixing prices, but admitted that the company's competitors charge the same prices for their products. You counseled her not to attend such meetings in the future, and the president decided that the company should wait and see if the FTC takes any further action.

The company's treasurer has warned you not to disclose the investigator's visit to the company's auditors. You are not certain whether the matter qualifies as a material contingency which could require disclosure in the financial statements. How should you respond to the audit inquiry letter?

E. DISCOVERY ISSUES

Contingencies raise several important legal issues in a litigation context. If an enterprise accrues an expense or loss for a pending claim or assessment under SFAS No. 5, can the enterprise's opponent in litigation involving the contingency obtain information about the accrual during discovery? Would any such accrual constitute an admission against interest? Will the accrual become a de facto "floor" which the litigation opponent will refuse to drop below in any settlement negotiations?

What can an enterprise do if it wants to avoid these problems but needs audited financial statements, and the independent auditor refuses to issue an unqualified opinion unless the enterprise accrues a contingent liability? Remember that an auditor must determine whether the financial statements properly treat any material contingent liabilities. Even if the auditor decides that SFAS No. 5 does not require accrual of a contingent liability, can the litigation opponent discover underlying facts which led to, but which may not entirely support, the auditor's conclusion? Presumably, the auditor asked the enterprise's lawyer about any contingent liabilities: can the litigation opponent discover the attorney's response to that audit inquiry? As you can imagine, disclosure to a litigation opponent could place the enterprise's lawyer in a very uncomfortable situation. Can a litigation opponent use any information produced to discover other relevant facts, or to gather insights about the enterprise's litigating strategy? Can an enterprise protect any information relating to its contingencies by invoking the attorney-client or accountant-client privileges? Does the work product doctrine exempt such information from discovery?

1. AUDIT INQUIRY LETTERS

The Preamble to the ABA Statement of Policy emphasizes that a lawyer must consider whether a response to an audit inquiry letter will waive the attorney-client privilege. The few courts that have addressed the issue in the last twenty years have split on the question of whether or not parties can discover the lawyer's response to these letters for use in litigation. One such case is Tronitech, Inc. v. NCR Corporation, 108 F.R.D. 655 (S.D. Ind. 1985), involving an anti-trust complaint that NCR had unfairly interfered with Tronitech's business. NCR's auditor had asked for a legal opinion by NCR's legal counsel covering the financial implications of that law suit, and Tronitech sought discovery of that audit letter. After reviewing the document in camera and determining that it did not contain any factual references which would be discoverable, the court concluded that since such an opinion by an attorney as to liability or the settlement value of a case would not be admissible at trial, it was not legally relevant and was not within the scope of discovery.

The court also determined that the audit letter was protected from discovery by the work product doctrine, which under Fed. R. Civ. P. 26(b)(3) precludes discovery of "opinion" work product reflecting the mental impression, conclusions, opinions and theories of attorneys. While work product protection under Rule 26(b)(3) is only for materials "prepared in anticipation of litigation or for trial", and does not apply to materials prepared in the ordinary course of business or otherwise for some purpose not primarily concerned with litigation, the court determined that an "audit letter is not prepared in the ordinary course of business but rather arises only in the event of litigation", and represents the attorney's conclusions and legal theories concerning that litigation.

Tronitech also argued that any privilege from discovery was waived by the disclosure of the letter to the accountants, which ended the confidentiality, but the court pointed out that "communications between accountant and client are privileged under Indiana law, * * * and audit letters are produced under assurances of strictest confidentiality".

On the other hand, United States v. Gulf Oil Corporation, 760 F. 2nd 292 (Temp. Emerg. Ct. App., 1985), took the opposite view with regard to protection under the work product doctrine for documents prepared for, and at the request of, a company's auditors. Although conceding the question was close, the Court of Appeals decided that documents prepared to allow the auditor to do its job were not "prepared in anticipation of litigation or for trial", but neither were created primarily for the business purpose of compiling appropriate financial statements. The court rejected the argument that its holding would lead lawyers to be less candid when responding to auditors: "there is no reason to believe that attorneys will violate their legal and ethical obligations to render candid and complete opinions".

NOTES

1. In most discovery disputes over accounting information regarding contingencies generally and audit inquiry letters in particular, the attorney-client privilege does not apply. In the first place, no confidential communication between an attorney and the client may exist. Second, disclosing such a communication to a third party, such as the client's

auditor, normally waives the privilege. Remaining legal issues, however, typically involve legal relevancy, the work product doctrine, and in some states, the accountant-client privilege.

While the conclusion in the Tronitech case that an audit inquiry letter from an attorney "arises only in the event of litigation" seems highly doubtful, not all courts have adopted the "primarily to assist in pending or impending litigation" standard when applying the work product doctrine. In United States v. Adlman, 134 F.3d 1194 (2nd Cir. 1998), the Second Circuit recently rejected that test and instead applied a "because of" standard that has been used in other Circuits. Under this "because of" formulation, the work product doctrine protects documents that "'can fairly be said to have been prepared or obtained because of the prospect of litigation.'" Id. at 1202 (quoting Charles Alan Wright, Arthur R. Miller & Richard L. Marcus, 8 Federal Practice & Procedure § 2024, at 343 (1994). Under this standard, a document does not lose protection merely because it was created to assist with a business decision. In dicta, however, the *Adlman* court observed that the "because of" formulation would withhold work product protection from "documents that are prepared in the ordinary course of business or that would have been created in essentially similar form irrespective of the litigation." A recent law review article takes the view that the work product doctrine has historically protected most of the materials that litigators produce, but typically not the legal work of corporate or transactional lawyers, and that the Second Circuit's decision "threatens to disrupt this traditional dichotomy." Charles M. Yablon & Steven S. Sparling, *United States v. Adlman: Protection for Corporate Work Product*, 64 Brook. L. Rev. 627 (1998).

2. In recent years, several courts have refused to protect audit inquiry letters from discovery. For example, *In re* Subpoena Duces Tecum Served on Willke Farr & Gallagher, No. M8-85 (JSM), 1997 WL 118369 (S.D.N.Y. Mar. 14, 1997), involved documents relating to an investigation that a leading New York law firm conducted on behalf of a corporation's audit committee. The audit committee had disclosed the results of the investigation to Ernst & Young, the company's auditing firm, to obtain an unqualified audit opinion, and the court held that this disclosure waived the attorney-client privilege.

As to an accountant-client privilege for audit inquiry letters, in *In re Hillsborough Holdings Corporation*, 132 B.R. 478 (Bankr.M.D.Fla.1991), the court concluded that the privilege does not apply to information which a client intends to disclose or make available to the public, and held that since the audit inquiry letters supplied representations which the client knew that the auditor would use to prepare, or more accurately to audit, public financial statements, the privilege did not apply.

3. An attorney cannot simply avoid the issues arising from audit inquiry letters by refusing to respond, since that could cause a client to receive a qualified opinion from its auditors. For example, the outside counsel to

Advanced Monitoring Systems, Inc. apparently refused to respond to requests for information regarding pending litigation or unasserted claims. As a result, the auditor issued a qualified opinion, as illustrated by the "except for" language in the second paragraph below, which, as discussed earlier in Chapter II, could adversely affect the enterprise:

> We were unable to obtain a response from legal counsel representing the Company in the lawsuit described in note 8 to the consolidated financial statements regarding the current status of the suit or other pending or threatened litigation or unasserted claims and assessments at September 30, 1993 and 1992. Therefore, we were unable to obtain sufficient competent evidential matter supporting the Company's representations regarding the contingent liability discussed in note 8 to the consolidated financial statements.

> In our opinion, except for the effects of such adjustments at September 30, 1993 and 1992, if any, as might have been determined to be necessary had a response from the Company's legal counsel been obtained as discussed in the preceding paragraph, the consolidated financial statements referred to above present fairly, in all material respects, . . . [etc.].

4.   As discussed on page 339, *supra*, SOx section 303 directed the SEC to prescribe rules or regulations to prohibit any officer or director of an issuer, or any other person acting under the direction of an officer or director, from taking any action to fraudulently influence, coerce, manipulate, or mislead the issuer's independent auditor for the purpose of rendering the issuer's financial statements materially misleading, and in the final rules implementing that provision. The SEC seems to be trying to impose a negligence standard with respect to the statutory terms "coerce, manipulate, or mislead." Some lawyers have expressed concerns about the effects of the new rules on the accord between the ABA and the AICPA (the "Accord") that led to the ABA's Statement of Policy. These lawyers worry that if law firms become overly concerned about violating Rule 13b2-2, they may begin to disclose more information in audit responses for public companies than they have in the past. As we have already suggested and will explain in more detail in the next section, disclosure to the auditor typically destroys the attorney-client privilege as to the subject matter under federal law.

2.   Accountant-Client Privilege

According to a recent decision by the Supreme Court of Colorado, at least "thirty states have codified some form of protection for communications between an accountant and a client". Colorado State Board of Accounting v. Raisch, 960 P. 2d 102, 106 n. 3 (1998). When there is no statutory privilege, businesses have sought to persuade the courts to create some barrier to prevent litigation opponents from discovering work papers and other documents prepared by employees or independent auditors, which could reveal the enterprise's estimate of a contingent liability, or other information gathered by the auditor to verify the appropriateness of the enterprise's treatment. There is also the IRS Restructuring and Reform Bill of 1998 which creates an accountant-client privilege in civil tax matters before the Internal Revenue Service or in federal courts, but that legislation will not protect accountant-client communications from disclosure in other contexts and does not change the "ability of any other body, including the [SEC], to gain or compel information." Conf. Rep. to accompany H.R. 2676, 105th Cong., 2d Sess. 88.

In FMC Corp. v. Liberty Mutual Assurance Company, 236 Ill. App. 3d 355, 603 N.E. 2d (1992), FMC sought a declaratory judgment against several insurance companies that it was entitled under certain policies to defense and indemnity coverage for prospective environmental liabilities. The insurance companies sought to subpoena from FMC's long-time auditor its workpapers relating to FMC's contingent environmental liabilities. Relying upon an earlier decision of the Illinois Supreme Court that the statutory accountant's privilege did not apply to documents or information turned over to an accountant in connection with the preparation of a tax return, because the client could reasonably expect they would be disclosed to third parties, the appellate court required the production of any documents that related to FMC's tax return; also required were any other material or communications between FMC and its auditor regarding FMC's potential environmental liabilities if received from or by, or given to, third parties. However, any materials, or communications between FMC and its auditor, not conveyed to or received from third parties, were held to be protected by the accountants privilege statute.

On the federal side, the Supreme Court has held that no confidential accountant-client privilege exists under federal law, and no state-created privilege has been recognized in cases involving a federal claim. United States v. Arthur Young & Company, 465 U.S. 805, 104 S. Ct. 1495, 79 L. Ed. 2d 826 (1984). In that case the Internal Revenue Service sought to obtain from a taxpayer's auditor the tax accrual workpapers prepared by the auditor in analyzing and evaluating the taxpayer's reserves for contingent tax liabilities. Such workpapers sometimes contain information pertaining to the taxpayer's financial transactions, identify questionable positions taken on the tax return, and reflect the auditor's opinions regarding the validity of such positions. The District Court ordered production of the workpapers pursuant to Code §1602, which authorizes the IRS to summon and "examine any books, papers, records, or other data, which may be relevant or material" to a particular tax inquiry. The Court of Appeals reversed, holding that the public interest in promoting full disclosure to auditors, and in turn enhancing the integrity of the securities markets, required protection for the work of the auditor, which called for a kind of work-product immunity doctrine for the tax accrual workpapers prepared by the auditor.

The Supreme Court reversed, finding in the Code provision no legislative intention to restrict the broad summons power of the IRS. The Court viewed the limitation imposed by the Court of Appeals as less a work-product immunity than a sort of testimonial accountant-client privilege, which was not recognized under federal law. But the Court also rejected the analogy between work-product immunity for accountants' tax accrual workpapers and the attorney work-product immunity. The Court pointed out that, unlike the attorney, who is the client's confidential advisor and advocate, the auditor "assumes a public responsibility" and "owes ultimate allegiance to the corporation's creditors and stockholders, as well as to the investing public". Accordingly, in the Court's view, even if there were some risk that the absence of work-product immunity would lead some managements to consider being less forthcoming with their auditors, the auditors could not and would not accept a lack of candor and completeness and would instead respond with qualified opinions; indeed, the Court expressed concern that work-product immunity for auditors could interfere with the appearance of independence, creating the impression that the auditor is an advocate for the client.

NOTES

1. The Supreme Court has consistently directed federal courts to construe privileges narrowly in an effort to avoid suppressing probative evidence. *See, e.g.*, Univ. of Pennsylvania v. EEOC, 493 U.S. 182, 189 (1990). In applying the Illinois accountant-client privilege at issue in *FMC Corp. v. Liberty Mutual Insurance Co.*, a federal court of appeals recently held that the privilege did not protect documents that an accountant generated while rendering nonfinancial consulting services. Pepsico, Inc. v. Baird, Kurtz & Dobson, LLP, 305 F.3d 813 (8th Cir. 2002).

2. An accountant can generally rely upon the attorney-client privilege when an attorney employs the accountant to assist in rendering legal services. Although courts initially rejected this argument, recent cases regularly recognize the attorney-client privilege in appropriate situations. The cases, however, often draw subtle distinctions, based on who retained and paid the accountant or exactly what services the accountant performed. In addition, where the accountant uses the client's books and records to prepare a report for the lawyer, the privilege protects the report, but not the books and records. The mere delivery of pre-existing accounting records to the lawyer cannot create a privilege.

3. Assuming an accountant-client privilege does not apply, does disclosing to an accountant a communication that would otherwise qualify for the attorney-client privilege generally waive the attorney-client privilege? The attorney-client privilege does not usually apply to communications that are disclosed to others for purposes other than to enable the recipient to assist the attorney in rendering legal services. *See, e.g., In re* Horowitz, 482 F.2d 72, 81 (2d Cir.1973), *cert. denied* 414 U.S. 867, 94 S.Ct. 64, 38 L.Ed.2d 86 (1973) (subsequent disclosure to accountant waived the attorney-client privilege); First Federal Savings Bank of Hegewisch v. United States, 55 Fed. Cl. 263 (2003) (concluding that the disclosure of unredacted board minutes to an accounting firm during the performance of special accounting procedures for a law firm did not waive the attorney-client privilege, but that the disclosure of those same minutes to the accounting firm during annual audits did waive the privilege).

At least one recent decision, *In re Pioneer Hi-Bred Int'l, Inc.*, 238 F.3d 1370 (Fed. Cir. 2001), suggests that proxy statement disclosures waive the attorney-client privilege. In that case, Pioneer asked outside counsel to provide an opinion concerning the tax consequences of a proposed merger, which Pioneer intended to include in its proxy statement. The court held that Pioneer's reliance on and disclosure of outside counsel's opinion in its proxy statement waived the attorney-client privilege, but only with respect to the documents that formed the basis for the advice, the documents that outside counsel considered when it rendered that advice, and all reasonably contemporaneous documents that reflected discussions concerning that advice. The *Pioneer* court did not rule on the issue of work product protection, finding the record insufficient to make such a ruling. The court did, however, rule that Pioneer's disclosure of confidential information to expert witnesses waived both the attorney-client privilege and work product protection to the same extent as any other disclosure.

On the other hand, transmission to third parties, including accountants, may not waive work product protection, courts having split on this question as to disclosures to independent auditors. Recall that the Tronitech case, page 457, *supra,* relied in part on the work product doctrine in denying the motion to produce an audit inquiry letter. *See also In re* Pfizer Inc. Securities Litigation, 1993 WL 561125 (S.D.N.Y.1993) (disclosure to independent auditor did not waive work product protection, b ut does eliminate the attorney-client privilege). *But see In re Diasonics Securities Litigation*, 1986 WL 53402 (N.D.Cal.1986), involving a motion to compel Arthur Young & Co. to produce documents prepared by or disclosed to a company's auditor so that it could assess how pending litigation, including the underlying lawsuit, would affect the company's financial condition. The court granted the motion, finding that neither the attorney-client privilege nor the work product doctrine excused production. The court found, first, that the attorney-client privilege did not apply because Arthur Young prepared or obtained the documents for accounting purposes rather than for securing legal advice. The documents also did not qualify for work product protection because they "were generated for the business purpose of creating financial statements which would satisfy the requirements of the federal securities laws and not to assist in litigation." The court reasoned that although disclosure to someone sharing a common interest under a guarantee of confidentiality does not necessarily waive the work product protection, an independent accountant's responsibilities to creditors and the investing public transcend any such guarantee.

3. When a litigant requests the production of documents from an adversary's auditor, whether the request seeks responses to audit letters to attorneys, information about specific contingencies or working papers generally, numerous tensions arise. First, the auditor must decide how to respond. As a practical matter, in most cases the auditor wants to keep the client happy so that the client remains a client. Because working papers usually provide the easiest roadmap to the client's business organization and financial statements, the client almost always prefers that the auditor not produce the working papers. In addition, the client normally does not want the auditor to release any responses to audit inquiry letters or information relating to specific contingencies. At the same time, the auditor must fulfill conflicting legal and professional responsibilities. These obligations require the auditor to comply with legitimate discovery requests, preserve client confidences, protect possible proprietary information about the auditor's procedures and maintain independence. In such situations, auditors often ignore the production request. At that time, the litigation opponent must decide whether to incur the costs necessary to serve and then to enforce a third party subpoena in an action usually separate from the underlying litigation.

If the litigation opponent decides to try to enforce a third party subpoena, unless and until the court allows the client to intervene the client does not become a party in that dispute and must view the proceedings as a spectator. To illustrate, if litigation opponent B tries to enforce a subpoena against accountant A to obtain documents relating to client C, legally speaking the enforcement action does not involve C. This situation also creates some practical concerns for C's counsel. Even if C intervenes in the dispute between B and A, C's counsel does not represent A. As a result, any communications between C's counsel and A or A's counsel do not qualify for the attorney-client privilege.

4. Some courts have explicitly rejected the argument that a defendant waives the right to deny liability by accruing an expense or loss on a claim. *See, e.g.*, Continental Ins. Co. v. Beecham, Inc., 836 F.Supp. 1027, 1047 n. 12 (D.N.J.1993) (ruling that an insurer's establishment of a reserve did not constitute an admission in a policy coverage dispute). Other courts have refused to permit a party to discover information pertaining to reserves that enterprises, especially insurance companies, may have set aside to satisfy future claims. *See, e.g.*, National Union Fire Ins. Co. v. Stauffer Chemical Co., 558 A.2d 1091 (Del.Super.1989) (denying request to produce information related to reserves on relevancy grounds because the fact that insurance company had established reserves did not necessarily mean that insurer believed applicable policies would cover hazardous waste claims). Several courts, however, have concluded that communications concerning individual case reserves qualified for work product protection, while ordering defendants to produce information regarding aggregate reserve figures. Finally, dicta from at least one court suggests that information about litigation reserves might even qualify as admissible evidence. In *In re Amino Acid Lysine Antitrust Litigation*, 1996 WL 197671 (N.D. Ill. Apr. 22,

1996), Senior District Judge Shadur ordered disclosure of any reserves that defendant Archer-Daniels-Midland Company had established for the underlying antitrust litigation before the court would rule that the proposed settlement in the class action fell within the range of fairness, reasonableness and adequacy. The judge wrote: "In this Court's experience in representing public companies, or in separately representing the outside directors of public companies, it has found such reserves to be a material indicium of the fair value of a liability, estimated by those who are presumably in the best position to make such an evaluation." *Id.* at *5.

*

CHAPTER VIII

INVENTORY

A. IMPORTANCE TO LAWYERS

Review the introductory materials on accounting for inventories in Chapter I. As those materials suggest, inventory accounting presents another deferral issue. Under generally accepted accounting principles, a business must allocate certain costs related to goods purchased or produced for sale in the ordinary course of business between the current period and future accounting periods. We can express this process in the form of an equation, as follows:

1		2		3
Total inventory costs incurred	=	Costs allocable to current period	+	Costs deferred to later periods

The difficulty lies in the fact that items 2 and 3 represent unknown amounts. While a business could determine the costs allocable to the current period by keeping a careful record of the cost of each item sold during the period, such record keeping normally would prove too time-consuming and expensive. Instead, most businesses attempt to ascertain item 3 by "taking inventory" at the end of an accounting period.

Pricing the ending inventory serves two important functions. First, the procedure calculates the amount that the business should defer as ending inventory to match against revenues in some later period. Second, the process determines what amount of the total inventory costs for the period the business should treat as an expense of the current period to match against current revenues. In effect, we could rewrite the equation above as follows:

1		2		3
Total inventory costs incurred	−	Costs deferred to later period	=	Costs allocable to current periods

In this form, the restated equation helps to explain the operation of the Cost of Goods Sold account under a periodic inventory system.

The Cost of Goods Sold account portrays the expense for goods "used up" (presumably sold) during an accounting period. To calculate this expense, a business first adds together on the debit, or left hand, side of the Cost of

Goods Sold account the opening inventory and the purchases for the period: that represents the total cost of goods which could have been sold during the period. From that total cost of goods which could have been sold, the amount of goods which were not sold and are still on hand, i.e., the closing inventory, is subtracted, by a credit, or right-hand entry, in the Cost of Goods Sold Account, and the net balance in that account constitutes the cost of goods used up (presumably sold) during the period. As noted in Chapter 1, this is really just a special example of deferral, and we could appropriately refer to the ending inventory as Deferred Cost of Goods Sold Expense.

With respect to the income statement, inventory accounting attempts to match the cost of goods sold during an accounting period with the corresponding revenues from those sales. Without matching revenues with corresponding costs, a business cannot accurately determine its net profit or loss for a particular accounting period. As a practical matter, the cost of goods sold often represents the largest deduction from revenues on the income statement.

Note the direct relationship between the ending inventory and net income. As ending inventory increases (with everything else held constant), cost of goods sold decreases, which increases net income for the current period; conversely, the lower the ending inventory, the higher the cost of goods sold, and the lower the net income for the current period. (Notice also that errors in ending inventory will carry over to the next accounting period: if we overstate ending inventory, we will also overstate beginning inventory in the following period.) Assuming we properly determine ending inventory in that following period, we will necessarily overstate cost of goods sold in that period, which will produce lower earnings. In contrast, if we understate ending inventory in the earlier period, we will understate beginning inventory in the next accounting period, thereby understating cost of goods sold and overstating net income for that next period.

As to the balance sheet, inventory appears there as a current asset, which makes it of special significance to users of financial statements, like short-term creditors, who may be particularly concerned about the business's immediate financial resources. Under the conservatism principle, a business should not carry inventory, or any other current asset, at an amount greater than the asset's current realizable value. That balance sheet objective may sometimes pull in the opposite direction from the income statement goal of a fair picture of the results of operations year to year. In this chapter, we shall consider how to try to resolve such conflicts in different situations.

Throughout this chapter, we will discuss various situations in which inventory accounting and reporting affect the practice of law. Lawyers should understand the importance of inventory accounting and reporting for various reasons. For example:

● Lawyers often draft, negotiate or interpret employment contracts, labor agreements, and partnership agreements which contain profit-sharing provisions. In addition, buy-sell agreements often require shareholders to sell their shares back to the corporation at a set price, based on earnings or net book value, upon certain events. An entity or its owners or managers can manipulate the entity's profit or loss to shortchange employees or minority investors by expensing costs which properly belong in inventory, thus increasing the entity's expenses and decreasing its profit and equity. Alternatively, management could overstate inventory, thus overstating the venture's profits, to qualify for a larger bonus.

● An enterprise's method of accounting for inventories may affect the taxes which the business or its owners owe. Closely-held businesses often understate closing inventory to keep taxable income, and hence income taxes, as low as possible. In contrast, publicly traded businesses may overstate inventory to show higher earnings. Improperly including various expenses in ending inventory, for example, would decrease the business's cost of goods sold and thereby increase its income. Like other financial frauds, intentionally misstating inventory can create criminal liability.

● As we saw in Chapters IV and V, loan agreements often contain clauses that require the borrower to maintain certain financial ratios. For example, a loan agreement may require the borrower to maintain a specified ratio of current assets to current liabilities. As a current asset, the amount of inventory can determine whether the borrower continues to satisfy such a covenant.

● Pursuant to the various legal limitations on distributions to shareholders discussed in Chapter V, a corporation's valuation of inventories can affect the amount that the entity can distribute to its owners.

● Inventory issues sometimes arise in securities fraud actions. Investors, for example, may allege that an issuer fraudulently overstated inventories, ignored losses from obsolescent goods, or failed to disclose material information related to inventories. Federal prosecutors have asserted that executives at HealthSouth Corp. inflated inventories to boost earnings artificially.

● The cost allocation issues present in accounting for inventories can also affect the computation of damages in breach of contract disputes, utility rate cases, payments under government contracts, and the allocation of environmental clean-up costs under federal and state environmental laws.

● Inventory accounting can impact antitrust litigation. The Robinson–Patman Act effectively outlaws quantity discounts unless differences in the cost of manufacture, sale or delivery justify such discounts. The method which a business uses to allocate costs to inventories directly impacts the cost of manufacture, sale and delivery.

● An entity's method of valuing inventory can also influence international trade disputes. Antidumping laws prohibit foreign manufacturers from selling goods in the United States at less than their full cost. The antidumping laws specify costs that companies must include in their calculation of inventory cost to ensure a fair playing field in U.S. markets.

In addition to the basic objective of matching the cost of goods which a business sold during an accounting period with the corresponding revenues from those sales, several other accounting principles influence inventory accounting. Under the conservatism principle, a business should not carry inventory at any amount greater than the asset's current realizable value. Occasionally, businesses must "write down" inventories to reflect circumstances which have impaired the realizable value.

Finally, to provide meaningful financial data, a business must consistently apply the same accounting treatment from period to period and properly disclose the methods used to determine inventories for the financial statements. Accordingly, our discussion will focus on four central themes: matching, conservatism, consistency and disclosure.

B. DETERMINING ENDING INVENTORY

As we have already seen, inventory accounting seeks to allocate certain costs between the present accounting period and future accounting periods. For more than forty years, Chapter 4 (entitled "Inventory Pricing") of Accounting Research Bulletin No. 43, *Restatement and Revision of Accounting Research Bulletins*, has served as the accounting profession's principal authoritative promulgation regarding inventory pricing.

When calculating its closing inventory, a business must focus on two considerations: (1) what goods, and which costs in addition to the actual purchase prices paid to acquire the goods, to include; and (2) when acquisition prices vary during the period, what flow of goods assumption to make to determine which prices should be assigned to the goods that are still on hand.

1. WHAT GOODS TO INCLUDE IN INVENTORY

In making the determination of what goods to include in inventory, a recurring question is which items purchased or sold late in a period should be counted as part of the company's inventory at the end of the period. In order for the closing inventory figure to play its role of distributing inventory costs between the present and the future, by reducing the cost of goods sold expense charged to the current period and deferring that amount to future periods in the form of an asset on the balance sheet, an accurate physical count is needed (plus, of course, an appropriate pricing of the items).

To calculate the quantity of closing inventory, a business *takes inventory*, that is, physically counts its goods on hand. As to what items should be included in the count, we noted in connection with the *Pacific Grape Products* problem on page 409, *supra*, that the balance sheet is supposed to reflect the assets owned by the company, so the test should presumably relate to whether the company has title to the goods. But lawyers in particular know how uncertain that test can be, and inevitably questions arise as to whether to include in the count goods "belonging" to the company but in the possession of someone else, or goods in the company's possession which "belong" to someone else. For example, as we saw, if a firm recognizes income from the "sale" of goods which however remain on hand, they cannot be counted as closing inventory.

The following excerpt from a leading accounting treatise discusses accepted inventory practice regarding which goods an enterprise should count in inventory. Although legal title generally controls for these purposes, we will see that accountants sometimes adopt certain rules of convenience

Lee J. Seidler & D. R. Carmichael, eds.

Accountants' Handbook 18.36–18.39 (6th ed. 1981)[*]

SPECIAL INVENTORY ITEMS. At the end of an accounting period, questions often arise as to what constitutes proper treatment of the following items:

1. Goods in transit on the inventory date, either from vendors or to customers.

2. Goods on hand that have been segregated for certain customers, or goods on order that have been segregated by the vendor.

3. Goods on order and advances on orders.

4. Merchandise either acquired or delivered on approval or under conditional sales contracts.

5. Goods consigned to agents or acquired on consignment.

6. Pledged or hypothecated merchandise.

Whether such items should be included in, or excluded from, inventory is usually determined by applying a legal test—the **passage of title**. There are a number of limitations to the legal test as a practical solution to inventory questions, and other more practical criteria are often employed. It is important, however, for the accountant to remember that use of a criterion other than the legal test rests on the assumption that no significant information is concealed by failure to apply the legal test.

Goods in Transit. Where goods are shipped f.o.b. [freight on board] shipping point and are in the hands of a common carrier on the last day of the period, strict application of the legal test requires inclusion in inventory of in-transit purchases and exclusion of customer shipments. Occasionally, however, accountants object to the application of this rule to purchases on the grounds that it is impractical, preferring instead to employ the **criterion of receipt** on or before the last day of the period. Although the use of the receipt criterion, consistently applied, does not in most instances seriously distort the statement of financial position, the ease with which in-transit purchases can ordinarily be segregated by reviewing the receiving reports for the first few days of the new period leaves little support for the use of any method other than the legal criterion. * * *

In the case of goods shipped f.o.b. destination, application of the legal test requires exclusion of in-transit purchases and inclusion of in-transit merchandise sold to customers. Common accounting procedure, however, while adhering to the legal test for purchases, employs the more practical **criterion of shipment** to exclude the merchandise shipped. Consistent application of the shipment rule causes little distortion of income and its usage eliminates the difficult task of locating merchandise en route to customers.

Segregated Goods. Where goods for filling customers' orders have been segregated by the vendor, title may pass upon segregation. If title has passed and the purchaser is aware of it, cost of the goods should be included in the purchaser's inventory and the payable recognized. Obviously, however, if the purchaser is unaware of the passage of title, such goods will be overlooked in the compilation of his inventory. The small error caused by failure to include these goods in inventory is usually considered preferable to the adoption of a procedure for surveying vendors to determine the legal status of goods on order. The effect of segregation on the passage of title is often dependent on legal technicalities difficult for even a lawyer to decide. For this reason many accountants are inclined to adopt the practice of recognizing revenue on shipment of goods, a practice resulting in the inclusion of segregated goods in the inventory of the vendor.

Purchase Orders and Advances. In general, goods on order are not included in inventory. Although the purchase contract is binding on both parties, the goods either do not exist or, if they do, title has not passed. Ordinarily, no entry should be made upon the books of the purchaser until actual delivery takes place. This, however, should not be construed as prohibiting the use of **financial statement notes** to call attention to any unusual conditions with respect to purchase commitments. The AICPA (ARB no. 43) calls for the recognition of a loss on purchase commitments when the current "market" price of the goods falls below the contract price. * * *

Advances on purchase contracts are not inventory items. They are more in the nature of **prepayments**, being cash payments in advance for services (i.e., goods) to be received in the future. Since the advance is realized in the form of goods, not cash, it is the first step in the **working capital cycle**. It constitutes the working capital element furthest removed from the cash realization point: that is, it must pass through the successive phases of inventory and accounts receivable before disinvestment. For this reason, treatment of the item as a receivable is as poor a practice as considering it inventory. Cashin and Owens (*Auditing*) state that advances on purchase contracts and any other noninventory items not properly classifiable as raw materials and supplies, work in process, or finished goods should be segregated and appropriately shown in the financial statements. Care should be taken by vendors receiving advances to see that they are properly recorded as liabilities.

Conditional and Approval Transactions. The treatment accorded approval and other conditional sales is largely a matter of expediency. A great deal depends on the probability of the return of such goods. Legally, title to the goods is vested in the vendor until the customer accepts, makes payment, or otherwise performs on the contract in the manner specified for the passage of title. As a matter of convenience, when returns of goods sold on approval are small proportionate to total shipments, the **simplest procedure** is to consider shipment equivalent to sale. When the more conservative practice of deferring revenue recognition until receipt of the customer's approval is adopted, the cost of the goods shipped conditionally and now in the hands of customers should be displayed in the financial statement as a separate inventory element.

Where goods are sold conditionally on **installment contracts**, the cost of the goods held on such contracts, less the buyers' equity in such goods, should be carried as a special inventory account. * * *

Consignments. The title to goods shipped or received on consignment remains with the consignor while possession of such goods is transferred to the consignee who acts as the agent of the consignor. Goods on consignment should be included in the inventory of the consignor as a special type of inventory and should be excluded from the inventory of the consignee. Where arbitrary mark-ons are added to the cost of goods shipped on consignment, they must be deducted from the dollar amount of consigned goods before inclusion in the final inventory. Shipping and other appropriate charges for transfer of the goods to the consignee are legitimate additions to the cost of goods shipped on consignment and are therefore a proper portion of inventory. Care should be taken to see that shipping and other charges added to the manufacturing cost of the goods on consignment are reasonable and do not include charges for double freight, etc. The probability of eventual sales of these goods is an important consideration in assigning dollar amounts to them.

Pledged or Hypothecated Goods. When goods have been pledged or hypothecated as security on a contract, title is not transferred by the pledge or hypothecation. Such goods should be included in the inventory of the owner, with the special conditions indicated in a note to the financial statements.

NOTE ON INVENTORY FRAUD

Throughout history, unscrupulous individuals have cunningly devised schemes involving inventories either to disguise theft, enhance a business's financial position, or evade taxes. Because management and auditors can typically verify the accuracy of an inventory account by taking a physical count of the goods included in ending inventory, the perpetrators must devise elaborate sche mes to evade the auditors' watchful eyes. The following examples illustrate fraudulent inventory swindles.

Hieron II, King of Syracuse, commissioned an artist to create a crown of pure gold, but upon receiving the crown, the King suspected that the artist substituted less precious metals for the gold. Archimedes, a Greek mathematician, physicist, and inventor, validated the King's suspicion by calculating the ratio of the weight of the crown to the weight of the water that the crown displaced when completely immersed. After comparing the gravity of the material in the crown with the gravity of pure gold, Archimedes concluded the crown did not contain pure gold. Physicists recognize Archimedes for this aptly named "Archimedes' Principle," while accountants recognize him as one of the first auditors.

We have already noted, in Chapter II, the massive inventory fraud committed by McKesson & Robbins, Inc. ("McKesson"), which became the driving force behind modern audit procedures requiring the verification of physical inventory. Auditors did not detect the fraud because they failed to confirm physical inventory. After regulators and the auditing profession recovered from the McKesson & Robbins scandal, the "Great Salad Oil Swindle" emerged, prompting further concern. Like Archimedes, Anthony "Tony" DeAngelis utilized the laws of physics, but in a more devious fashion. When auditors visited the site where his company, "Allied," stored oil, seeking to verify the physical inventory, they inserted dip sticks into the oil tanks to measure the level of oil present. Unfortunately, the auditors did not verify that the tanks contained only oil; DeAngelis had created phantom inventory records with forged warehouse receipts, and there was in fact only a small portion of oil floating on top of the water-filled tanks. Further, Allied reported owning more holding tanks than actually existed. During the audit, as the auditors moved from tank to tank, company employees repainted numbers on the tanks. Not only did auditors count water as oil, but they counted the same water as oil more than once.

Crazy Eddie, Inc. exemplifies another company that inventory fraud destroyed. Eddie Antar ran the company, which operated a chain of consumer electronic stores. Antar and his associates allegedly altered inventory records to inflate fraudulently the company's inventory. From 1980 to 1983, they also allegedly skimmed millions of dollars in cash from sales. By skimming less each year, they allegedly led investors to believe the company's sales and earnings were growing faster than in reality they were, which in turn inflated the company's stock price. The fraudulent schemes allegedly inflated Crazy Eddie's 1985 $12.6 million pretax income by approximately $2 million dollars, and helped turn a substantial loss into $20.6 million pretax profit in 1987. In 1996, Antar pled guilty to racketeering conspiracy.

More recently, management misappropriation involving inventory occurred at Phar–Mor, Inc. ("Phar–Mor"), the discount drug-store chain. In 1995, the company emerged from bankruptcy after enjoying above average growth and earnings during its early years. Michael I. Monus, co-founder of the chain, masterminded a $1.1 billion fraud and embezzlement scheme which has been described as " 'the largest financial fraud to have come before a bankruptcy court in the modern era.'" *Phar-Mor: Anatomy of a Financial Fraud*, Bankr. Ct. Dec. (LRP), Mar. 3, 1994, at 1. After an outside company physically counted inventory, Monus and other executives altered the figures to create more inventory, contributing to an overstatement of the company's earnings by an estimated $340 million. A jury convicted Monus of 109 felonies, and he was sentenced to nearly 20 years in prison and fined a $1 million.

2. ADDITIONAL COSTS INCLUDABLE IN INVENTORY

As a preliminary matter, we should note that inventories include not only a merchandiser's goods available for resale, but also, in the case of a manufacturer, raw materials and supplies acquired for use in the production process, plus partially completed goods, as well as finished goods awaiting sale. Inventories do not include long-lived assets, such as manufacturing plants, machinery, equipment, and office furniture, which a business enterprise does not hold for sale in the regular course of business.

Both merchandisers and manufacturers use historical cost to account for inventories, but they use slightly different rules to determine which costs to include in inventory. Accountants use the term *period costs* to refer to those costs incurred by both merchandisers and manufacturers, such as administrative salaries, advertising costs, and selling expenses, that contribute to generating revenues only in the current accounting period. As the name *period costs* suggests, a business should expense these costs in the accounting *period* in which they are incurred. In contrast, accountants treat all costs incurred to purchase or manufacture goods for sale as part of the cost of those goods and refer to these costs as *product costs*. Product costs, therefore, include all expenditures "directly or indirectly incurred in bringing [inventory] to its existing condition and location." Accounting Research Bulletin No. 43, Chapter 4, Statement 3 (Committee on Accounting Procedure, American Inst. of Certified Pub. Accountants 1953). Attaching all product costs to inventory more accurately allocates the total cost of goods sold among the appropriate accounting periods.

Berkowitz v. Barron, 428 F. Supp.1190 (S.D. N.Y. 1977), is an example of why the distinction between period costs and product costs matters. In that case the plaintiffs purchased all the stock of a small manufacturer of children's clothing which had fallen on hard times. The business failed shortly after the purchase, and the plaintiffs complained that there were material misstatements in the company's April 30, 1970 financial statements, which the defendants had warranted as fully and fairly reflecting that company's financial picture. In holding for the plaintiffs the court said:

> The most troublesome aspect of the financial statement is the treatment accorded certain items reported therein. One such item is shipping cost and expenses totaling $145,281.76 [and which include shipping salaries, the costs of supplies and charges incurred for express and parcel post]. This sum was included as a component of manufacturing overhead. Expert testimony established that this method of presentation was not in accord with generally accepted accounting principles of the time. The appropriate procedure would have been to treat such shipping costs as an operating expense, as was done in the 1969 financial statement, and take it as a deduction against gross profit, instead of including it in cost of goods sold, above the gross profit line.

The effect of this treatment was to cast a false picture of the companies' net income and inventory value. Because manufacturing overhead is a component of cost of goods sold, which in turn is one element of inventory value, improper incorporation of shipping costs and expenses in manufacturing overhead resulted in an overstatement of inventory computed to be approximately $44,560 by plaintiffs' expert witness. The enlarged inventory entry had a direct effect on the net loss/net income figure reported in the financial statement. Had the shipping costs and expenses been treated according to generally accepted accounting principles, the companies would have shown a net loss of approximately $24,960 (less the tax effect) for the fiscal year ending April 30, 1970, instead of a net income of $19,603, as was reported.

*   *   *

Without going into detail, it can be seen that these charges created a financial picture for the companies that was inaccurate. The slightly inflated inventory figure gave rise to an over optimistic estimate by plaintiffs of the revenues anticipated from liquidation of the inventory. Reporting the items above the gross profit line altered the gross profit percentage. The appearance of a small net income instead of a small net loss falsely supported the view that with good management a profit could be made.

Given these conditions, a finding that the financial statement is "materially misleading" is fully supported * * * [T]he net income/net loss and inventory value entries on a corporate financial statement are of material importance to parties interested in purchasing all of the outstanding shares of the company. This is especially true where, as here, little other information about the business is transmitted to the purchasers prior to the consummation of the sale.

NOTES

1. As a result of treating the shipping costs as manufacturing overhead, rather than operating expenses, the defendants overstated both inventory and net income. Publicly traded corporations, which must report their results of operations to the public, occasionally overstate earnings in this manner. Inflated inventories increase the apparent worth of a business and can give rise to securities fraud. Overstated inventories may also enable a business to obtain a loan or qualify for a lower interest rate than a lender would otherwise approve. Insurance companies may pay inflated claims for lost or destroyed inventories when insureds base claims on overstated rather than actual inventory values. *See, e.g.,* Cenco Inc. v. Seidman & Seidman, 686 F.2d 449, 451 (7th Cir.1982). Finally, exaggerated inventories can qualify management for larger bonuses based on net income.

In contrast, federal income tax laws provide an equally strong incentive for businesses, especially those privately owned, to understate inventories, and therefore, to understate profits and their tax liabilities. *See, e.g.,* D. Loveman & Son Export Corp. v. Commissioner, 34 T.C. 776 (1960), *affirmed* 296 F.2d 732 (6th Cir.1961), *cert. denied* 369 U.S. 860, 82 S.Ct. 950, 8 L.Ed.2d 18 (1962) (holding that the taxpayer could not deduct "freight-in" as a current expense and requiring the taxpayer to treat the expenditures as part of the cost of acquiring merchandise). Another temptation to under-state inventory, and hence net income, comes from profit-sharing agreements or buy-sell agreements which require the entity or its owners to pay amounts based on earnings or net book value to employees or other owners under certain circumstances. By expensing costs which properly belong in inventory, those in control of an entity can increase the entity's expenses and decrease its profit and equity, thereby reducing the required payments.

2. Because the company's financial statement in the Berkowitz case used a different accounting treatment for the shipping costs than in the previous period, the financial statement violated the consistency requirement.

a. MERCHANDISER

A merchandiser's inventory usually includes goods offered for resale in the ordinary course of business. In addition to the actual price paid to acquire the goods, the merchandiser should include the costs of bringing the goods to their existing condition and location in inventory. A merchandiser may include charges directly connected with bringing the goods to the place of business and the costs of converting the goods to a salable condition. These charges include freight, hauling, and other costs directly related to the acquisition of the goods. A merchandiser, however, cannot include selling expenses in product costs. To repeat, all businesses must treat selling expenses as period costs. As to shipping and handling expenses billed to customers, EITF recently reached a consensus that certain of such fees should be treated as revenues rather than as reductions in shipping expenses.

b. MANUFACTURER

For a manufacturer, product costs include the expenditures for raw materials and labor, plus the normal indirect expenses of operating the factory, such as light, heat, depreciation, insurance and property taxes, often referred to as *factory overhead costs*, which a business incurs to manufacture a product. Accounting for the inventory of a manufacturing business can be troublesome because of the three separate components: raw materials, goods in process, and finished goods ready for sale. While the raw materials inventory creates no particular difficulty, goods in process and finished goods present special problems. Obviously, the cost of these assets at the end of an accounting period must, at a minimum, include not only the raw materials used but also the cost of the labor employed to bring the goods to their present condition. Manufacturing concerns can often determine from the manufacturing records the costs of materials and the expense of labor directly involved in the production process, which accountants usually refer to together as *direct*, or *prime*, costs. These records typically show the amount and kind of raw materials used and the number of hours and type of labor expended.

In addition, accountants view those factory overhead costs, like depreciation and insurance, as just as much a part of production expense as the prime costs of raw material and labor. However, there has been a nagging question as to whether such treatment is appropriate for such factory overhead items as idle facility expenses, excessive spoilage, double freight, or rehandling costs, if they occur in particularly large amounts. That question has now been definitively resolved: in November 2004, the FASB, as part of its efforts to converge accounting standards worldwide, issued a new standard on inventory costs to clarify that enterprises which incur abnormal amounts of such expenses must treat them as period costs rather than as product costs. In addition, this standard requires enterprises to allocate fixed overhead costs based on their production facilities' normal capacity. The new rules apply to inventory costs incurred during fiscal years beginning after June 15, 2005. INVENTORY COSTS – AN AMENDMENT OF ARB NO. 43, CHAPTER 4, Statement of Financial Accounting Standards No. 151 (FASB 2004).

Even though a manufacturing business cannot readily assign any of the normal overhead costs to particular goods, the appropriate amount of overhead expense must be deferred and added to the goods in process and finished goods included in ending inventory. There is no more justification for treating as a period expense the overhead costs allocable to the goods in process and finished goods on hand at the end of the period than there would be for charging off the raw material, or direct labor, incorporated in that inventory. However, it is not so easy to decide how much of the total factory overhead for the period a manufacturer should allocate to the goods in process and finished goods on hand at the end of the period.

Accountants describe raw materials and direct labor as variable costs, meaning they are directly dependent upon the amount of production; as production levels increase or decrease, costs for raw materials and direct labor change accordingly. Fixed costs, on the other hand, such as factory overhead, usually do not change within the normal production range. But remember that some fixed costs are not allocated at all to inventory: general administrative expenses, like executive salaries, or interest on debt, are treated entirely as expenses of the period in which they were incurred.

Cost accounting attempts to allocate overhead, or indirect, costs. Like most accounting processes, cost accounting is an art, not a science, and strives to find a reasonable and practical approach rather than a precisely accurate solution. Especially when a business produces a number of different products in various processing stages, cost accounting can become quite complicated. Even for a relatively simple, one-product business, difficult questions arise in the allocation of costs between goods in process and those completed during the period (most of which, of course, have presumably been sold by the end of the period).

The following chart illustrates a sample statement of cost of goods sold for a manufacturing concern:

Statement of Cost of Goods Sold
XYZ Company, Inc.
For the Year Ended December 31, 1996

Beginning Inventory, Finished Goods			$10,000
Cost of Goods Manufactured			
Beginning Inventory, Goods in Process		$1,000	
Raw Materials			
Beginning Inventory, Raw Materials	$3,000		
Net Purchases	$19,000		
Raw Materials Available for Use	$22,000		
Less: Ending Inventory,			
Raw Materials	5,000		
Cost of Raw Materials Consumed	$17,000		
Direct Labor	$30,000		
Manufacturing Overhead			
Supervisors' Salaries			
$3,000			

Supervisors' Salaries $3,000
Depreciation on Plant
  and Factory Equipment   2,600
Factory Rent   1,400
Utilities   1,200
Indirect Labor   900
Factory Supplies   500
Miscellaneous Factory Expense   400

Total Overhead		$10,000	
Total Manufacturing Costs for Period		$57,000	
Subtotal		$58,000	
Less: Ending Inventory, Goods in Process		9,000	
Cost of Goods Manufactured			$49,000
Cost of Goods Available for Sale			$59,000
Less: Ending Inventory, Finished Goods			15,000
Cost of Goods Sold			$44,000

The following case involves understatement of inventory and consequent understatement of income and tax liability

Photo-Sonics, Inc. v. Commissioner

United States Court of Appeals, Ninth Circuit, 1966.
357 F.2d 656.

■ ELY, CIRCUIT JUDGE:

We face a petition for review of a Tax Court decision upholding the assessment of a deficiency in the payment of income taxes.

The controversy stems from taxpayer's method of accounting for its inventory of goods which it manufactured. Under the method, generally described as "prime costing" or "prime cost", only the cost of direct labor and materials were allocated to inventory value. No portion of factory-overhead expense, variable or fixed, was included.

The key to validity of an accounting method is, in accounting terms, a matching of costs and revenues and, in terms of the taxing statute, a clear reflection of income * * *. The Government urges that, just as labor and materials cannot be expensed in the year in which such expenses are incurred without giving due regard to whether the manufactured product remains on hand, factory-overhead expenses which constitute a portion of the cost of unsold manufactured products cannot be expensed as they are incurred but rather should be allocated to the manufactured products and deducted, as a cost of sale, when the goods are sold. It contends that proper allocation of factory-overhead expenses, both fixed and variable, to the inventory is the only manner by which the taxpayer's income for a given period may be clearly reflected.

It may be that "direct costing", the allocation to inventory of labor, materials, and variable factory overhead, is an accurate method by which to account for inventory. If consistently applied, it would not seem to be less satisfactory than the method advanced by the Government, *i.e.*, the "absorption costing" method under which labor, material, and both fixed and variable factory overhead are allocated. Both methods are accepted, although "absorption costing" seems now to be preferred by most American accountants. The Tax Court arrived at its determination "without attempting to lay down any broad principles applicable to inventories." 42 T.C. at 936. We, exercising similar restraint, are concerned with a particular accounting method only as it relates to the particular facts which are before us.

Here, the taxpayer allocated no portion of its factory-overhead expense to inventory. The regulations clearly specify that such be done. Treas. Reg. § 1.471–3(c) (1964). A method which excludes all factory-overhead costs is not an acceptable accounting practice. See American Institute of Certified Public Accountants, Accounting Research Bull. No. 43. The significance of failure to allocate any of such costs to inventory is emphasized by looking in this case, as an example, to one of the items of unallocated factory overhead, shop and tool expense. This expense represented items purchased during the year which were either too inexpensive to depreciate or were consumed during the year. The Tax Court found that it amounted to $8,215.34 in 1958, $40,397.22 in 1959, and $103,896.18 in 1960. Thus, in an expanding business in which some of the products manufactured in one fiscal period are sold in a subsequent fiscal period, the expenses which are attributable to the cost of sales in a subsequent year are matched against the lower sales revenues of a prior year. The effect of such a practice, if allowed, would obviously permit taxpayer to report less income than the amount which was truly earned. It would not be an "accounting practice * * * clearly reflecting the income" as required by section 471.

In reviewing the proceedings below, it is seen that certain testimony of accountants produced by the taxpayer cast doubt upon the validity of taxpayer's accounting method. One such witness admitted, in the Government's cross examination, that an opinion given by a Certified Public Accountant as to the accuracy of financial statements prepared by taxpayer's method would require qualification if factory-overhead expense were material; otherwise, an examiner of the financial statement would be misled. It cannot be denied that, here, factory-overhead expense was significantly material.

We are not persuaded that the Commissioner's determination was arbitrary. It follows that the Tax Court's decision, not clearly erroneous, must be Affirmed.

c. OTHER ILLUSTRATIONS OF "COST ACCOUNTING"

Lawyers often need to understand cost accounting issues and their relevance to the practice of law. For example, lawyers may encounter cost accounting concepts in a simple breach of contract action brought by a seller against a defaulting buyer. In calculating damages, a lawyer for the seller should recognize that each potential sale contributes to paying the seller's fixed overhead costs. Any amount of the selling price in excess of variable costs will offset the seller's fixed costs. By losing a sale, the seller loses not only the profit from that particular sale, but also that sale's contribution to the total fixed costs for the period. Failing to recognize the contribution to fixed overhead would understate the seller's damages. *See, e.g.,* Sure–Trip, Inc. v. Westinghouse Eng'g & Instrumentation Servs. Div., 47 F.3d 526 (2d Cir.1995) (instructing that under Pennsylvania law a plaintiff can recover lost profits equal to the difference between (i) the revenue that the plaintiff would have derived under the contract and (ii) any variable costs that the plaintiff would have incurred in performing the contract).

A case from early this century, L.P. Larson, Jr., Company v. William Wrigley, Jr., Company, 20 F.2d 830 (7th Cir.1927), *reversed in part on other grounds* 277 U.S. 97, 48 S.Ct. 449, 72 L.Ed. 800 (1928), illustrates cost accounting concepts in an infringement action. Although Larson proved that Wrigley's "Doublemint" gum had infringed Larson's "Wintermint" gum, Larson could not calculate the lost profits attributable to the infringement and instead requested that all the net profits arising from "Doublemint" sales be awarded as damages. In determining Wrigley's "Doublemint" profits, counsel and the court used cost accounting to establish what costs Wrigley should allocate to "Doublemint" for the period in question. Both parties appealed the district court's decision finding the "Doublemint" net profits to be $1.4 million, and the court of appeals was left to weigh the cross-contentions that too much, or not enough, had been allowed as deductions for advertising expenses, unredeemed profit-sharing coupons, and certain other expenses.

There are many other areas where cost accounting is legally relevant. One of particular current importance is in the environmental context. In *United States v. R.W. Meyer, Inc.*, 889 F. 2d 1497 (Sixth Cir. 1987), *cert. denied*, 494 U.S. 1057, 110 S. Ct. 1527, 108 L. Ed. 2d 767 (1990), the EPA was seeking reimbursement for the cost of cleaning up a site, as authorized by the federal statute. The EPA included in its claim not only the direct costs incurred by the agency for its personnel plus the actual on-site expenses of the cleanup, totaling approximately $181,000, but also another almost $53,000 for "indirect costs", representing an allocable share of the indirect administrative and other costs inherent in operating the environmental cleanup program. These "overhead costs" included rent and utilities for site and non-site office space, plus payroll and benefits for program managers, clerical support, and other administrative staff. The defendant argued that the EPA was entitled only to reimbursement for the costs incurred in the cleanup at the defendant's site, but the district court concluded that EPA should be able to recover all of its costs, including indirect overhead. The court of appeals affirmed, saying:

> [T]he statute contemplates that those responsible for hazardous waste at each site must bear the full cost of cleanup actions and that those costs necessarily include both direct costs and a proportionate share of indirect costs attributable to each site. In essence then, the allocation of the indirect costs to specific cleanup sites effectively renders those costs direct costs attributable to a particular site. We are confident that had Meyer or the other defendants undertaken the cleanup operation by contracting with another company to perform the cleanup, the costs of that cleanup, whether characterized as costs, direct costs plus indirect costs, or otherwise, would include the type of indirect costs challenged here.

In the public utility context, rate regulation cases frequently involve cost accounting issues. To illustrate, regulators frequently approve different rates for different service classifications, such as commercial and industrial versus residential, peak versus off-peak, etc. To establish and justify different rates, regulators need to allocate costs among the different service classifications.

Cost accounting issues also arise in antitrust disputes. The Robinson–Patman Act essentially bars manufacturers from giving price discounts unless "differences in the cost of manufacture, sale or delivery" justify the discounts. Businesses may pass reductions in direct costs on to customers. A business relies on cost accounting to determine its costs to manufacture, sell and deliver goods. Improperly treating product costs as period expenses would lower the cost of manufacturing the goods, which could invite an unjustified discount.

PROBLEMS

Problem 8.1A. A large cotton mill company contemplated a public issue of its securities, and the prospective underwriters wanted their auditors to make an immediate audit of the company's books. The company's own time accounting firm assisted in the audit. Although there were no disputes either as to the physical counts of goods on hand upon this sudden closing of the books, or as to methods of pricing, the underwriters' auditors concluded that the company's inventories were overstated by more than one million dollars. On the other hand, the company's accountants asserted that the new auditors were understating accounts payable by the same amount.

The dispute turned on the analysis of the transactions whereby the company acquired its raw cotton. In essence they were as follows: the company's cotton buyer would place an order for a firm amount and grade of cotton at a certain price (based on the New York cotton market) with one of several firms of cotton brokers in Boston. The broker would promptly segregate specific cotton in warehouses in the South and direct its shipment to the company. Title to this cotton was in the broker, subject to pledge evidenced by warehouse receipts in the hands of banks. The cotton arrived at the company's facility, but the shipping documents, including the receipts or bills of lading, went to the bank in Boston. By arrangement with the bank, the company unloaded the cotton, mingled it in its warehouse and sometimes started to process part of it immediately upon arrival. The company "classed" the cotton to see if it was up to contract specifications, and on the ninth day after its arrival would give a check to the broker. The broker then paid the bank, received the documents, and turned them over to the company.

The question was whether cotton in the company's warehouse, or, in some cases, tumbling through its opening machinery, should or should not have been included in inventory while "title" to it remained in the bank.

Should title be the test for whether this cotton should be recorded in the company's inventory?

The auditors for the underwriters insist that the opening inventory was overstated by $900,000 and closing inventory was overstated by $1,100,000, and they proposed the following journal entries to implement their view:

> Purchases $900,000
> Opening Inventory $900,000

> (To record as purchases in the current year goods previously treated as purchased in the prior year.)

Accounts Payable$1,100,000

    Purchases $1,100,000

(To reverse an earlier entry which erroneously treated these goods as purchased in the current year.)

Assuming that the price of cotton has remained constant throughout, to what extent would the change in policy affect the net income of the company for the period involved?

Problem 8.1B. On December 24 of year 1, X Corp. ordered goods in the amount of $10,000 from one of its suppliers for delivery in late January of year 2. In accordance with its business practice with its suppliers, X included a check in the amount of 10% of the purchase price with its order. On December 29, X learned that its order had been accepted and its check cashed. How should this transaction be recorded in the financial statements of X for year 1?

Problem 8.1C. M Corp., a manufacturer of electronic business equipment, and D Co., which operates a large department store, have reached a tentative agreement that M will design and build a special computer for D to provide better inventory control. Because of D's unique requirements, the machine will be different from any that M has built before, and hence the parties have agreed that the price for the new machine should be equal to M's costs of building it plus a flat fee of $50,000. Your law firm serves as general counsel for D Co. and you have been asked to consider how the computation of M's costs should be approached in the formal contract, and whether there are any problems calling for special attention.

M maintains the following expense accounts:

Employment Costs
    Wages & salaries, including
        vacation pay and sick leave
    Social security taxes

Plant and Machinery Costs
    Depreciation
    Repair and maintenance
    Plant protection

Selling
    Advertising expense
    Bad debt expense
    Sales force compensation

General and Administration
    Insurance
    Property taxes
    Utilities expense
    Legal and accounting fees
    Stockholder relations
        (meetings, annual
        reports, etc.)
    Contributions & donations
    Amortization of patents

Financing
    Interest expense

3. HOW TO PRICE INVENTORY

Once a business has determined what items to include in ending inventory for the particular year, the business must decide how to price those items. Remember that the business likely purchased merchandise or raw materials at several different prices during the year, and so it must choose which of the different prices to use for the items in ending inventory.

Conceptually, a business would most accurately match inventory expenses to revenues by specifically identifying the cost of each item it sells during the period. In most cases, however, in a business selling any substantial number of items it is not practical to try to use specific identification. Instead, most businesses choose, and consistently apply, one of several cost flow assumptions.

a. ALTERNATIVE FLOW ASSUMPTIONS

Generally accepted accounting principles recognize several different cost flow assumptions for pricing inventory. These assumptions establish a set pattern of inventory flow and eliminate the need to specifically account for each piece of inventory as it is sold. However, keep in mind that these are *cost flow* assumptions; there is no requirement that they track the actual physical flow of the goods. Nor does a business have to use the same flow assumptions for all the categories of its inventory; but the consistency and disclosure principles mandate that the business maintain the same assumptions from period to period and properly disclose its method of inventory pricing in the financial statements.

To illustrate the different accounting methods for pricing inventories, assume that the Jones Shoe Company sells shoes at wholesale in a single style and price line. During its first year of operations, Jones Shoe purchases 8,000 pairs of shoes in four different lots at different prices and sells 5,000 pairs at $40 per pair. Accordingly, 3,000 pairs remain in inventory. At the end of the year, Jones Shoe's purchase records show the dates and prices of the various lots as follows:

Date	Amount	Unit Price	Total Price
January 1	2,000	$20.00	$40,000
March 1	3,000	22.00	66,000
June 1	2,000	23.00	46,000
November 1	1,000	21.00	21,000
Totals	8,000		$173,000

We will use this data to illustrate the computation of ending inventory under the four basic methods of inventory pricing: specific identification; first-in, first out; weighted average; and last-in, first out. (Remember that in each year after the first, there would also be an opening inventory to deal with, priced of course on the same basis, and hence at the same amount, as the ending inventory for the prior period, and that opening inventory becomes part of the goods available for sale in the current period.)

(1) Specific Identification

As previously mentioned, specific identification of goods sold can be the most accurate way to reflect the costs of inventory, but the added effort and expense would usually be disproportionate to the benefit. However, when a business can readily separate and identify each individual item in inventory, as, for example, in the case of a car dealer, jeweler, or furrier, specific identification would be used.

Assume that at the end of the year, Jones Shoe's inventory records show that the company purchased the 3,000 pairs of shoes remaining in inventory on the following dates and at the previously given prices:

Pairs	Date	Unit Price	Total Price
300	January 1	$20.00	$6,000
1,100	March 1	22.00	24,200
900	June 1	23.00	20,700
700	November 1	21.00	14,700
Totals 3,000			$65,600

Using the specific identification method, the company would compute its gross profit (i.e., sales less cost of goods sold) as follows:

Sales (5,000 pairs at $40 per pair)		$200,000
Less: Cost of Goods Sold		
Opening Inventory	$ –0–	
Purchases	173,000	
Goods Available for Sale	$173,000	
Less: Closing Inventory (from above)	65,600	$107,400
Gross Profit		$ 92,600

(2) Average Cost

The average cost method of inventory pricing eliminates the need to specifically identify the items of inventory sold. Businesses holding relatively homogeneous items in inventory often find the average cost inventory pricing administratively convenient and particularly effective. Under the weighted average cost method, a business prices all items of inventory based upon the average cost of all similar goods available during the whole period. Jones Shoe Company would compute the average cost per unit based upon the total units available as follows:

$$\text{Weighted average cost} = \frac{\text{Total cost}}{\text{Total units purchased}}$$

$$= \frac{\$173,000}{8,000 \text{ Units}}$$

$$= \$21.625 \text{ per unit}$$

Based upon the weighted average cost per unit, Jones Shoe Company would value the 3,000 pairs of shoes left in the inventory at $21.625 a pair, for a total of $64,875. Under the weighted average cost method, Jones Shoe would compute its gross profit as follows:

Sales (5,000 pairs at $40 per pair)		$200,000
Less: Cost of Goods Sold		
Opening Inventory	$ –0–	
Purchases	173,000	
Goods Available for Sale	$173,000	
Less: Closing Inventory (from above)	64,875	$108,125
Gross Profit		$ 91,875

(3) First-In, First-Out

To minimize spoilage and obsolescence, businesses normally expect to sell their oldest goods first. One flow assumption assumes that a business sells the goods in the order of their purchase. In other words, this alternative assumes that only the most recently purchased or produced goods remain unsold at the end of the period. Accountants refer to this method as *FIFO*, which serves as shorthand for the "first-in, first-out" flow assumption that underlies the method. Under the FIFO method, Jones Shoe carries its ending inventory of 3,000 pairs of shoes at $67,000, based upon including the last lot of 1,000 pairs which the company purchased at $21.00 per pair plus the 2,000 pairs from the next to the last lot purchased at $23.00 per pair.

If Jones Shoe adopts the FIFO inventory method, the company would report $94,000 in gross profit as follows:

Sales (5,000 pairs at $40 per pair)		$200,000
Less: Cost of Goods Sold		
Opening Inventory	$ –0–	
Purchases	173,000	
Goods Available for Sale	$173,000	
Less: Closing Inventory (from above)	67,000	$106,000
Gross Profit		$ 94,000

Like merchandisers, manufacturers may also use the FIFO method in pricing their inventories. Of course, because a manufacturer's cost includes not only the purchase price of the component raw materials, but also labor expense and a portion of the overhead expenses for the period, manufacturers face additional challenges in determining the cost of various lots of manufactured goods. But once the manufacturer computes the costs of the various lots, it prices the closing inventory based on the assumption that the unsold items were the ones manufactured most recently.

(4) Last-In, First-Out

While FIFO matches the oldest inventory costs with current revenues, the "last-in, first-out" flow assumption, referred to as *LIFO*, adopts the exact opposite assumption. Regardless of the actual physical movement of goods, LIFO assumes that a business sells the most recently acquired goods first. Accordingly, the goods on hand in closing inventory are viewed as the ones that were in opening inventory, plus, to the extent that inventory has grown, those acquired earliest during the current period.

Note that the LIFO assumption is generally unrealistic with respect to the actual physical flow of goods; it would accurately reflect that flow only when, for example, a business piles goods as they arrive and sells or uses them from the top of the pile, as might be true in the case of a coal dealer. And even a coal dealer could not actually have sold during the period goods which it had not purchased until after the date of the last sale in that period. But LIFO presumes that the physical flow does not matter and stresses the importance of matching related current costs with current revenues. In any event, LIFO does not depart from the principle of using cost as the primary basis for pricing inventory.

Under the LIFO method, Jones Shoe would price its ending inventory of 3,000 pairs of shoes at $62,000. The company treats the ending inventory as including the first lot of 2,000 pairs which the company purchased at $20.00 per pair and 1,000 pairs from the second lot purchased at $22.00 per pair. If Jones Shoe Company adopts the LIFO inventory method, the company would report $89,000 in gross profit as follows:

Sales (5,000 pairs at $40 per pair)		$200,000
Less: Cost of Goods Sold		
Opening Inventory	$ –0–	
Purchases	173,000	
Goods Available for Sale	$173,000	
Less: Closing Inventory (from above)	62,000	$111,000
Gross Profit		$ 89,000

(5) Retail Method

Retailers may find cost flow assumptions cumbersome in connection with lower cost items, like candy bars, canned vegetables and gallons of milk. The retail method of accounting for inventory eliminates the need to differentiate between products, and allows the retailer to calculate the business's inventory by first using retail prices and the sales figures for the period, which are readily available, and then converting back to cost, based on the ratio of inventory costs to their retail prices.

The retail method requires a business to keep records of the inventory priced at both cost and retail, and to compute the ratio of inventory cost to retail price. The enterprise calculates the ending inventory at retail by subtracting the sales figure for the period (which are of course at retail price) from the total of goods available for sale, also at retail price. The retailer then converts the ending inventory figure from retail to cost by multiplying the retail figure by the cost/retail ratio.

For example, assume Jones Shoe also operates an outlet store which sells shoes at retail. Further assume that the company owns inventory at the beginning of an accounting period which cost $100,000 but has a retail selling price of $150,000. During the period, Jones Shoe manufactures or purchases additional shoes which cost $1,100,000 and which the company prices to sell for $1,850,000. That gives us a cost figure of $1,200,000 for the total inventory for sale, but the retail selling figure is $2,000,000. Using these figures, Jones Shoe can calculate the ratio of cost to retail as follows:

$$\text{Ratio of cost to retail} \quad = \quad \frac{\text{Inventory at cost}}{\text{Inventory at retail}}$$

$$= \quad \frac{\$1,200,000}{\$2,000,000}$$

$$= \quad .60 \text{ or } 60\%$$

So the cost of the inventory on average constitutes sixty percent (60%) of the retail price. If we can compute the ending inventory at retail we can use that recent age to convert to a cost figure. Assuming that Jones Shoe's sales during the period total $1,800,000, the company can estimate the ending inventory using the retail method as follows:

	Cost	Retail
Inventory at beginning of period	$100,000	$150,000
Purchases during the period	1,100,000	1,850,000
Totals	$1,200,000	$2,000,000
Sales during the period		1,800,000
Estimated ending inventory at retail:		$200,000

That means the ending inventory figure at cost should equal $120,000 (60% of $200,000).

(6) Combination

Businesses may, and often do, use different cost flow assumptions for different categories of their inventories. For example, a department store may use specific identification for its fine jewelry, while selecting an alternative flow assumption, LIFO or FIFO, for its sock inventory. However, the business must then apply those assumptions consistently from period to period and properly discloses them in the financial statements.

b. CRITIQUE AND BASIS FOR SELECTION

The different inventory flow assumptions offer various advantages and disadvantages. Again, we must remember that the actual physical flow may differ from the flow assumption which a business adopts.

(1) Illustration of the Effects of Alternative Methods

To recap, the different inventory methods produce different amounts for ending inventory, cost of goods sold, and gross profit. The following chart summarizes those differences.

Method	Ending Inventory	Cost of Goods Sold	Gross Profit
Specific Identification	$65,600	$107,400	$92,600
Weighted Average	64,875	108,125	91,875
FIFO	67,000	106,000	94,000
LIFO	62,000	111,000	89,000

(2) First-In, First Out

One advantage of FIFO is that it prices ending inventory at approximately its current cost, so the amount shown for inventory on the balance sheet usually reflects current market price. In addition, FIFO mirrors the actual physical movement of goods in most businesses. Finally, FIFO does not allow the manipulation of profits which can occur under LIFO, as we will see below.

The disadvantage of FIFO is that it matches current sales revenues with cost of goods sold based upon earlier, lower inventory costs rather than current costs, so that during inflationary periods FIFO tends to understate the cost of goods sold, which can create an inflated view of the business's earnings.

(3) Last-In, First-Out

Unlike FIFO, the last-in, first-out approach does match current costs with current sales, thereby producing higher cost of goods sold and lower profits in times of rising prices. That made LIFO particularly attractive for income tax purposes, and ultimately for general accounting because LIFO was accepted for federal income tax purposes only if the taxpayer also used it for its general financial reporting.

However, there may be independent reasons for preferring LIFO for financial accounting. For one thing, LIFO produces a lower, and hence more conservative balance sheet figure for inventory (though maybe in some circumstances too conservative to be a fair presentation). In addition, LIFO results in a more meaningful presentation on the income statement, by matching the current inventory costs with current sales revenues.

To illustrate, suppose that in year 1 the Jones Shoe Company's inventory and purchase records show the following:

Date	Quanity	Unit Price	Total
Opening Inventory	3,000	FIFO	$67,000
February	2,000	$22	44,000
April	2,000	23	46,000
July	2,000	24	48,000
October	2,000	26	52,000
December	2,000	28	56,000
Totals	13,000		$313,000

Suppose further that Jones sold 4,000 pairs of shoes during the first half of the year at an average price of $30 per pair, and 4,000 pairs during the second half of the year at an average price of $35 per pair, for total sales revenues of $260,000. If Jones Shoe continued to carry closing inventory on the FIFO basis, the company would compute its gross profit as follows:

Sales		$260,000
4,000 pairs at $30 per pair	$120,000	
4,000 pairs at $35 per pair	140,000	
Less: Cost of Goods Sold		
Opening Inventory	$67,000	
Purchases	246,000	
Goods Available for Sale	$313,000	
Less: Closing Inventory at FIFO		
2,000 pairs at $28 per pair	$56,000	
2,000 pairs at $26 per pair	52,000	
1,000 pairs at $24 per pair	24,000	
Total Closing Inventory	$132,000	
Cost of Goods Sold		$181,000
Gross Profit		$ 79,000

Because Jones Shoe matched some of the lower inventory costs incurred before the middle of the year with the higher revenues obtained in the latter part of the year, the company derived a substantial part of the gross profit simply from the rising price level rather than from improvement in its competitive position or increased efficiency of operations.

In contrast, applying LIFO in the previous example would result in a closing inventory of $111,000, arrived at by pricing 3,000 pairs at the opening inventory figure of $67,000 and the remaining 2,000 pairs at the cost of the first 2,000 pairs purchased during the year, or $44,000. Jones Shoe would compute its gross profit under LIFO as follows:

Sales		$260,000
Less: Cost of Goods Sold		
Opening Inventory	$ 67,000	
Purchases	246,000	
Goods Available for Sale	$313,000	
Less: Closing Inventory at LIFO		
3,000 pairs from Op. Inv.	$67,000	
2,000 pairs at $22 per pair	44,000	
Total Closing Inventory	$111,000	
Cost of Goods Sold		$202,000
Gross Profit		$ 58,000

As we see, the increase in the current cost of goods sold expense which results from pricing the closing inventory on LIFO produces a lower gross profit figure, which probably better indicates the business's success in the rising price market.

However, LIFO's critics point to several potential disadvantages. For one thing, the lower amounts usually shown as ending inventory under LIFO, reflecting those early costs of inventory, can adversely affect financial ratios based on current assets, total assets, or equity, such as the current ratio or the debt to equity ratio, which loan agreements frequently use. For an example of how far below current replacement cost the LIFO inventory figure on the balance sheet can be, look at the following excerpts from the Notes to the fiscal 1994 financial statement for Oxford Industries, Inc. (whose fiscal years end around May 31), showing inventory under Current Assets (in thousands of $) at $114,465 for 1994 and $102,593 for 1993.

NOTES TO CONSOLIDATED FINANCIAL STATEMENTS

Summary of Significant Accounting Policies (In Part):

6. Inventories

Inventories are principally stated at the lower of cost (last-in, first out method, "LIFO") or market.
B. Inventories:

The components of inventories are summarized as follows:

$ in thousands	June 3, 1994	May 28, 1993
Finished goods	$59,784	$55,733
Work in process	22,549	19,931
Fabric	24,967	20,484
Trim and supplies	7,165	6,445
	$114,465	$102,593

The excess of replacement cost over the value of inventories based upon the LIFO method was $35,644,000 at June 3, 1994 and $36,667,000 at May 28, 1993.

For fiscal year 1994, net income was increased by approximately $609,000 ($.07 per share) as a result of using the LIFO method as compared to using the first-in, first-out method. During 1993 and 1992, net income was reduced by approximately $757,000 ($.09 per share) and $683,000 ($.08 per share), respectively, as a result of using the LIFO method.

During fiscal 1993 and 1992, inventory quantities were reduced, which resulted in a liquidation of LIFO inventory layers carried at lower costs which prevailed in prior years. The effect of the liquidations for 1993 was to decrease cost of goods sold by approximately $124,000 and to increase net earnings by $75,000 or $.01 per share. The effect of the liquidations for 1992 was to decrease cost of goods sold by $1,205,000 and to increase net earnings by $735,000 or $.08 per share. There were no significant liquidations of LIFO inventories in 1994. If Oxford Industries, Inc. had used FIFO rather than LIFO to price inventories, the company's balance sheet would have reported those inventories at approximately $35,600,000 more than actually shown on the June 3, 1994 balance sheet. In certain circumstances, the lower inventory amounts can significantly and adversely affect those financial ratios which use current assets, total assets or equity.

As previously noted, a taxpayer can use LIFO for federal income tax purposes only if the taxpayer uses LIFO for general financial reporting purposes, which means applying LIFO to report earnings in its financial statements. However, as a practical matter, businesses can disclose the excess of FIFO cost over LIFO cost, and thereby give an indication of what the earnings would have been if FIFO had been used. In fact, the SEC requires registrants to disclose the excess of the replacement or current cost over stated LIFO value.

As indicated above, LIFO gives management the opportunity to manipulate reported profits. If a business voluntarily or involuntarily depletes its inventories, that is, it acquires less inventory during a period than it sells, so that its closing inventory is less than its opening inventory, some of those older, lower costs preserved by the LIFO system will be part of the cost of goods sold for that period, to be matched with what in periods of inflation would be disproportionately higher revenues, resulting in gross profits that exceed normal sales margins. To see why this is so, recall that under LIFO, the earliest inventory costs of the period in which the business adopted LIFO, starting with the opening inventory of that period, if any, determine the original LIFO cost figure. As long as the physical quantity of inventory at year-end in subsequent periods does not fall below the quantity at the end of the year in which the business adopted LIFO, that original LIFO cost figure remains frozen on the balance sheet as a part of the asset Inventory. For example, if in the year an enterprise adopts LIFO its closing inventory contains ten units, and the cost attributable to those ten units pursuant to LIFO that year is $10 each, then as long as the enterprise owns at least ten units at the end of each succeeding year, the closing inventory will include ten units priced at that original LIFO cost of $10. If the physical quantity on hand at year-end expands, the business will price the excess over ten according to the LIFO principle as applied in the respective years in which the increase in volume occurred.

For a business which has used LIFO for many accounting periods, this treatment can cause inventory to be carried on the balance sheet at some very out-of-date costs, far below the inventory's current market value. This very conservative representation of inventory on the balance may not bother creditors, who could only be pleasantly surprised to find, in case of financial difficulty, that inventory can be sold for more than the amount shown on the balance sheet; but, as we have noted, undue conservatism may present to existing or prospective investors a misleadingly pessimistic view of the state of the business's affairs.

Note, this preservation of old costs on the balance sheet does not affect the income statement, so long as the quantity of goods in the inventory at the end of each year equals or exceeds the quantity on hand at the close of the prior year: Those old costs will be included in both opening inventory on the left-hand side of the Cost of Goods Sold account, and in closing inventory on the right-hand side, netting to a zero impact on cost of goods sold expense, and hence net income. But as noted above, if the quantity on hand at the end of the year falls below quantity at the beginning, perhaps because the business voluntarily reduced operations, or war, strikes, or the like caused an involuntary shortage, then some of those old LIFO costs imbedded in the Opening Inventory figure will necessarily come into play in the calculation of cost of goods sold expense, and will be matched against current revenues. In the typical case where current costs exceed LIFO costs, this will create a higher (maybe much higher) current net income figure than the business would have reported if the inventory quantity at year end had not fallen below the quantity at the beginning of the year.

To illustrate this problem which the liquidation of LIFO inventory can cause, suppose that Jones Shoe had adopted LIFO at the time of its organization and that shoes cost $10 per pair throughout that year. Suppose further, for simplicity, that the company bought 3,000 more pairs of shoes than it sold during that year, but that in each of the next eight years it purchased exactly as many pairs of shoes as the company sold. Accordingly, closing inventory for year 9, and of course opening inventory for year 10, would equal $30,000, or 3,000 pairs of shoes priced under LIFO at $10 per pair. If Jones' purchases and sales for year 10 were exactly the same as indicated in the comparison of LIFO and FIFO above, gross profit for the year computed under LIFO would equal the same $58,000 shown in that illustration:

Sales		$260,000
Less: Cost of Goods Sold		
Opening Inventory (on LIFO)	$ 30,000	
Purchases	246,000	
Goods Available for Sale	$276.000	
Less: Closing Inventory at LIFO		
3,000 pairs at $10 per pair	$30,000	
2,000 pairs at $22 per pair	44,000	
Total Closing Inventory	$74,000	
Cost of Goods Sold		$202,000
Gross Profit		$ 58,000

This result should cause no surprise: because the closing inventory in both cases equals the sum of opening inventory, either 3,000 pairs at $10 per pair in this example or 3,000 pairs at a $67,000 total cost in the illustration above, plus $44,000 (the cost of the first 2,000 pairs of shoes purchased during the year), the cost of goods sold remains the same.

But suppose that Jones Shoe did not make any purchases in October and December, so that total purchases for the year amounted to only 6,000 pairs. In that event, the gross profit would be computed as follows:

Sales		$260,000
Less: Cost of Goods Sold		
Opening Inventory (on LIFO)	$ 30,000	
Purchases	138,000	
Goods Available for Sale	$168,000	
Less: Closing Inventory of		
1,000 pairs on LIFO	$10,000	
Cost of Goods Sold		$158,000
Gross Profit		$102,000

Thus, although the company still sold 8,000 pairs of shoes for $260,000, a much higher net income is reflected. This higher income figure results from the fact that under LIFO, current revenues in the higher price-level era were matched with the older, much lower, LIFO inventory costs, which would not have entered into the determination of net income if the quantity of inventory at year-end had not dropped below the quantity in opening inventory.

Because LIFO liquidations can significantly affect reported results of operations, the SEC requires registrants to disclose any material amount of income that they realize from such an inventory liquidation. In Staff Accounting Bulletin No. 40, the SEC gives the following guidance:

F. LIFO Liquidations

Facts: Registrant on LIFO basis of accounting liquidates a substantial portion of its LIFO inventory and as a result includes a material amount of income in its income statement which would not have been recorded had the inventory liquidation not taken place.

Question: Is disclosure required of the amount of income realized as a result of the inventory liquidation?

Interpretive Response: Yes. Such disclosure would be required in order to make the financial statements not misleading. Disclosure may be made either in a footnote or parenthetically on the face of the income statement.

Staff Accounting Bulletin No. 40, Topic 11 (1981), *reprinted in* 7 Fed. Sec. L. Rep. (CCH) ¶ 75,751 (Aug. 31, 1994). Special rules apply to interim financial reports when an enterprise using LIFO liquidates a base period inventory during the fiscal year, but expects to replace the base period inventory by the end of the annual period. In that event, the interim reporting should avoid giving effect to the LIFO liquidation, by including as an expense the cost of writing down some currently-acquired inventory to the old LIFO cost.

Again, you should note that the 1994 annual report for Oxford Industries, Inc. reveals that the company liquidated LIFO inventory layers in fiscal 1993 and 1992. These liquidations increased net earnings by $75,000 or $.01 per share in fiscal 1993 and $735,000 or $.08 per share in fiscal 1992.

LIFO critics have argued that to show such an inflated net income figure for the period in which LIFO inventory was liquidated distorts the picture of both current operations and the trend of the business's fortunes. We must recognize this argument's merits, regardless of whether the business involuntarily reduced the inventory, as for example in the case of war scarcity, inadvertently decreased the inventory, or intentionally decided to liquidate the inventory, as for example if the business chose to reduce the scope of its operations. In any event, GAAP requires the business to include this extra net income from selling the low-cost LIFO inventory in the current income statement unless the liquidation was involuntary, the taxpayer intends to replace the liquidated inventory (though has not done so before year-end), and the taxpayer does not recognize gain for income tax reporting purposes. Accounting for Involuntary Conversions of Nonmonetary Assets to

Monetary Assets, an interpretation of APB Opinion No. 29, FASB Interpretation No. 30, ¶ 11 (Financial Accounting Standards Bd. 1979).

c.   LOWER OF COST OR MARKET

Accounting standards require a departure from the cost basis for pricing inventory when damage, physical deterioration, obsolescence or other circumstances cause the utility of goods, and hence their market value, to fall below their cost. In such circumstances, ARB No. 43 requires the business to recognize a loss in the current period to reflect the decline in value.

To illustrate, suppose that a drop in the price level or some other reason has caused prices to decline at the end of an accounting period to a figure below the FIFO or average cost figure for closing inventory. As we have seen, under the conservatism principle a business should not carry any current asset on the balance sheet at an amount greater than its current market value or realizable value. Historically, this balance sheet aspect of pricing inventory became paramount, leading to the classic doctrine of *lower of cost or market*, which ordains that businesses should carry inventory on the balance sheet at market value, as of the balance sheet date, if that figure is below original cost. By pricing closing inventory at the lower value figure, the business increases the cost of goods sold expense for the period. While this means that the cost of goods sold expense for the period exceeds the cost of the inventory which the business actually sold or used during the period, which arguably interferes with the matching of related costs and revenues, a diminution in the value of items on hand at year end in closing inventory represents at least a probable loss which the business should recognize in the current period under traditional principles of conservatism (or perhaps pursuant to FASB No. 5 dealing with contingencies).

Although one often encounters the term "writing down" inventory from cost to market, you should realize that accrual accounting does not require a separate journal entry reducing closing inventory from the FIFO or average cost figure to market. The business simply prices the closing inventory at the lower market figure at the time the accountant or bookkeeper records the entry debiting the Inventory account for the amount of the closing inventory and crediting the Cost of Goods Sold account for that same amount. The write-down notion arises from the fact that the business originally included the goods at cost either in Opening Inventory or in Purchases, both of which will be closed to the debit side of the Cost of Goods Sold account: so when those goods are included in closing inventory at a lower figure, the result is to increase the cost of goods sold expense, and accordingly reduce net income, by the amount of the difference between cost and market. Nevertheless, there may be occasions when management does want a separate write-down entry, to highlight a significant inventory loss, in which event the business prices closing inventory at cost in the first instance, and then does indeed write down the closing inventory with a credit while debiting a Loss on Inventory account.

Adopting the lower of cost or market basis for pricing closing inventory leads immediately to the question of what constitutes "market," or realizable, value. Where a business can obtain an actual market price quotation for the goods, businesses most often use the *current replacement cost* as the appropriate quotation for "market" at the close of the period. Thus, in the case of the Jones Shoe Company, if shoes cost $20 per pair at the end of year one, the company would carry the 3,000 pairs in closing inventory at $60,000 on the basis of lower of cost or market.

The use of replacement cost as the measure of "market" ignores the fact that in most cases the enterprise will not be selling its inventory back into the replacement market; rather, the enterprise will sell the goods to customers in the usual course of its business. For this reason, some accountants have argued that a business should look to the market in which it operates, rather than the replacement market, to value the goods. Under this view, the business should determine the appropriate "market" figure by estimating the prices at which the goods will be sold, and subtracting any necessary costs of readying the goods for sale. For example, assume that Jones Shoe estimates that the company can sell the shoes included in closing inventory for at least $25 per pair, after spending an additional $2 per pair for expenses such as packaging and shipping. The figure for estimated selling price less costs of sale, often called *net realizable value,* may offer a more meaningful guide to market value than replacement cost. In the above example, because the $23 net realizable value exceeds actual cost, as determined by either FIFO or average cost, there is no need to carry the shoes at less than actual cost.

The premise of net realizable value is that a business has not incurred a loss on closing inventory as long as the venture can sell its inventory during the following year at a price which will at least cover the original cost plus any additional expenses to complete the sale. On the other hand, if the selling price will most likely not cover that sum, then the business should recognize loss by pricing the closing inventory at net realizable value, thereby charging the loss to the current period while reflecting inventory on the balance sheet at a figure no higher than the amount that the business actually expects to realize from the inventory's eventual sale. To illustrate, assume that Jones Shoe estimates that the shoes in its closing inventory at the end of year one will eventually be sold for $20 per pair, after the company has incurred an additional $2 per pair in expenses. If the company uses net realizable value as the controlling "market," Jones Shoe would carry the shoes in inventory at $18 per pair (even if replacement cost equals or exceeds historical cost).

However, the argument for using net realizable value as the test for market value is not all one way. Since historically balance sheet conservatism is the principal reason for following lower of cost or market, there is much to be said for basing the calculation of "market" upon a forced and speedy liquidation, and for that purpose, replacement cost may be the better measure.

One other school of thought as to the "market" value of inventory stems from the view that the economic significance or utility of inventory lies in the fact that it can be sold for a profit: hence, a business should ask whether it can still realize the profit that it expected when it acquired the goods. For example, assume that Jones Shoe originally acquired a pair of shoes for $20, and expected to sell the shoes for $25 after spending an additional $2 per pair. If the estimated selling price for such shoes still on hand at the end of the year had dropped to $23, the company would have to purchase such shoes for $18 to produce the same profit-making or economic utility. According to this approach, the company should treat the "market" value of the shoes as $18; that is, a business should subtract not only any additional expenses but also the normal profit from the estimated selling price to determine the inventory's market value: hence the caption, *net realizable value less normal profit*.

In an effort to standardize the computation of "market" for inventory, many years ago ARB No. 43, the accounting profession's principal authoritative pronouncement on inventory pricing, set up a formula which incorporates all three bases discussed above. ARB No. 43 defines market value as presumptively equal to current replacement cost, so long as that figure lies somewhere between a maximum of net realizable value and a minimum of net realizable value less expected or normal profit. We could graphically illustrate these limitations as follows:

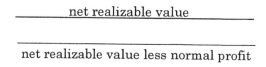

net realizable value

net realizable value less normal profit

In other words, net realizable value serves as a ceiling which the figure for market value may not exceed, while net realizable value less normal profit constitutes a floor, i.e., the market value figure may not be lower. So long as replacement cost falls somewhere between the ceiling and the floor, ARB No. 43 treats replacement cost as the proper measure of market value; but if replacement cost exceeds net realizable value, then net realizable value is the appropriate figure, and if replacement cost is below net realizable value less normal profit, then the latter is the figure for market value. Of course, the doctrine of lower of cost or market does not come into play unless the market value as so determined is below the cost.

An enterprise can use at least three different ways to apply lower of cost or market, but whichever technique is adopted must be used consistently from accounting period to period. First and most commonly, an enterprise can apply the lower of cost or market to each item in inventory. Second, the business may compare aggregate cost to aggregate lower of cost or market on a category-by-category basis. Third, an enterprise can apply lower of cost or market to the entire inventory.

(1) *Evaluation Of Lower Of Cost Or Market*

As we have already observed, the historical emphasis on balance sheet "conservatism" greatly influenced the principle that businesses should price inventory at the lower of cost or market. The more recent stress on the income statement, however, invites reconsideration of the lower of cost or market doctrine. Some commentators have expressed concern that while pricing closing inventory at the lower of cost or market does produce a conservative balance sheet, it may result in a less meaningful or even misleading periodic income picture of a business's operations. Before pursuing that point, there is the issue of consistency, since lower of cost or market requires an enterprise to recognize unrealized losses on inventory items, while unrealized gains in a rising market are ignored. There is also the difficulty of measuring net realizable value with any certainty. How should the business determine expected additional expenses? And how does the business determine a normal profit? Clearly, the lower or cost or market approach presents some serious practical problems.

However, by far the most important objection is that using lower of cost or market can distort the income statement — or, more particularly, the picture presented by the consecutive income statements for the year of the inventory writedown and the succeeding year. To illustrate, assume that, at the beginning of Year One, Russ Company purchased merchandise for $100,000. Further assume that the enterprise sold half the goods during the year for $80,000; that the remaining half of the goods, constituting the closing inventory at the end of Year One, which cost $50,000, could have been replaced at year end for $40,000; and that the goods in closing inventory were sold in Year Two for $75,000. The table that follows compares the gross profit for the two years under lower of cost or market, versus sticking to cost:

	Lower of Cost or Market	Cost
Year One:		
Sales	$ 80,000	$ 80,000
Cost of Goods Sold		
Purchases	$100,000	$100,000
Less: Ending Inventory	40,000	50,000
Cost of Goods Sold	$60,000	$50,000
Gross Profit	$20,000	$30,000

Year Two:

Sales	$75,000	$75,000
Cost of Goods Sold (Ending Inventory from Year One)	40,000	$50,000
Gross Profit	$35,000	$25,000

It is true that ending inventory and gross profit for Year One under the lower of cost or market method are more conservative than under cost. But is it really conservative to show more gross profit in Year Two than in Year One? Is it conservative to give the impression that the company's gross profit is increasing, when in fact revenues are declining, and the growth in profit is due merely to the inventory writedown, which effectively transferred $10,000 in profits from Year One to Year Two.

The lower of cost or market method assumes that a decrease in selling prices will parallel a decrease in replacement cost: otherwise, there is no loss in prospect. In the previous illustration, the initial decline in selling price was less than the fall in replacement cost, and that is often true in the real world. Indeed, that is the basis for the argument that any writedown of inventory to market should be based upon an estimated decline in the sales price, i.e. that net realizable value represents a more meaningful measure of the market value of inventory than replacement cost.

Even if we assume that the selling prices decreased in an amount equal to the decrease in inventory valuation, $10,000, so that sales revenues in Year Two total only $70,000, we still encounter potentially misleading income statements:

	Lower of Cost or Market	Cost
Year One:		
Sales	$ 80,000	$ 80,000
Cost of Goods Sold		
Purchases	$100,000	$100,000
Less: Ending Inventory	40,000	50,000
Cost of Goods Sold	$60,000	$50,000
Gross Profit	$20,000	$30,000
Year Two:		
Sales	$70,000	$70,000
Cost of Goods Sold (Ending Inventory from Year One)	40,000	$50,000
Gross Profit	$30,000	$20,000

The figures in the Cost column still seem to reflect the facts more accurately. The decrease in selling prices caused Russ Company to earn less profit in Year Two than in Year One. The Lower of Cost of Market column continues to tell the strange story that the company generated more gross profit in Year Two than in Year One, despite the decrease in selling prices during Year Two. Hence, accountants have often exercised judgment and not followed ARB No. 43 literally. Donald E. Kieso & Jerry J. Weygandt, Intermediate Accounting 404 n.6 (6th ed. 1989).

ARB No. 43 instructs businesses to measure net losses on firm purchase commitments for additional inventory in the same way as losses on inventory already owned. If material, a net loss on firm purchase commitments should be recognized and separately disclosed in the income statement.

An early dividend case illustrates the need to recognize a decline in the value of inventory, whether the goods are already on hand or merely on order, at least when the prospective loss is absolutely large and highly material. Branch v. Kaiser, 291 Pa. 543, 140 A. 498 (1928), involved a corporation which operated as a wholesaler of groceries. All of the stockholders were retail grocery stores which were customers of the corporation. The company was quite successful until 1920, when it suffered a disastrous loss of around $1,000,000, due to a sudden and dramatic decline in the market price of a number of grocery items the company handled. For example, the market price of sugar fell from around 27 cents per pound to as low as 5½ cents, and on the basis of the company's inventory on hand and future purchase commitments the loss on this item alone was $500,000. Although they were not to blame, the directors decided to conceal the calamity that had befallen the company, in the hope that future business would enable the company to recoup its losses. The directors continued to carry its inventories at cost and to pay dividends, while giving no notice of the loss in the company's financial reports. This went on for four years, with the directors "inflating" their purchases of new inventory to carry it at the old high 1920 prices (thus in effect adopting a kind of informal LIFO system), but the company ultimately ended up in bankruptcy, and the directors were held personably liable for the dividends paid by the corporation after the losses occurred.

For 2001, Ford reported a $5.07 billion fourth-quarter net loss and a $5.45 billion fiscal-year loss, arising in part from a $1 billion write-down to the company's inventory of palladium and other precious metals. Ford uses palladium in catalytic converters and began stockpiling the metal in 2000, anticipating a rise in prices. Ford purchased much of its palladium inventory at $1,000 an ounce. Prices subsequently fell to below $400 an ounce. Ford blamed the loss on unsophisticated purchasing department employees, who specialized in less-volatile metals, for enlarging the palladium inventory without hedging the company's investment. Ironically, these purchases came at the same time the company's engineers were searching for ways to use less palladium in new vehicles. A disgruntled investor filed a securities fraud lawsuit against Ford, alleging that the company failed to disclose the company's exposure to speculative losses in the palladium market. Gregory L. White, *Precious Commodity: How Ford's Big Batch of Rare Metal Led to $1 Billion Write-Off*, WALL ST. J., Feb. 6, 2002, at A1; *Ford Shareholder Files Suit, Alleging Mistake in Company's Hedging*, WALL ST. J., Feb. 6, 2002, at A1.

Although SFAS No. 5, discussed in Chapter VII, allows enterprises to accrue reserves for asset impairments, including inventory obsolescence, any such loss must qualify as both "probable" as of the balance sheet date and reasonably estimable. In the cease-and-desist proceedings instituted by the SEC against Microsoft Corporation in 2002 for unsupported and undisclosed reserves, referred to in Chapter VII at page 459, *supra*, Microsoft maintained at the parent corporation level a reserve account for inventory obsolescence that did not comply with SFAS No. 5 because the company's senior financial officials did not properly assess whether inventory losses had occurred and did not reasonably estimate any losses. In fact, together the combined parent corporation reserve and factually supported inventory reserve accounts at the operating level created a negative inventory amount for Microsoft at the end of fiscal 1997. To resolve the proceedings, Microsoft consented to a cease-and-desist order that found that the parent corporation reserves during the four fiscal years at issue did not comply with GAAP.

Special rules apply to inventory losses from market declines for interim financial reporting purposes. As a general rule, an enterprise should not defer these losses beyond the interim period in which the loss occurs. If thereafter the market goes back up, the business should recognize the gains from recovery of such losses on the same inventory in a later interim period of the same year. Such gains, however, should not exceed previously recognized losses. If an enterprise reasonably expects a market decline to recover before the end of the fiscal year, there is no need to recognize such a temporary market decline in the interim period.

We have already noted that important differences exist between GAAP and federal income tax law. Another example is Thor Power Tool Co. v. Commissioner, 439 U.S. 522, 99 S. Ct. 773, 58 L. Ed.2d 785 (1979), where the Supreme Court held that the taxpayer could not write down its spare parts inventory for tax purposes even though GAAP required a writedown in order to qualify for an unqualified opinion. In its most significant case to date involving inventory methods for federal income tax purposes, the Supreme Court explained the very different objectives of tax and financial accounting:

> The primary goal of financial accounting is to provide useful information to management, shareholders, creditors, and others properly interested; the major responsibility of the accountant is to protect these parties from being misled. The primary goal of the

income tax system, in contrast, is the equitable collection of revenue; the major responsibility of the Internal Revenue Service is to protect the public fisc. Consistently with its goals and responsibilities, financial accounting has as its foundation the principle of conservatism, with its corollary that "possible errors in measurement [should] be in the direction of understatement rather than overstatement of net income and net assets." In view of the Treasury's markedly different goals and responsibilities, understatement of income is not destined to be its guiding light. Given this diversity, even contrariety, of objectives, any presumptive equivalency between tax and financial accounting would be unacceptable.

* * *

* * * [A] presumptive equivalency between tax and financial accounting would create insurmountable difficulties of tax administration. Accountants long have recognized that "generally accepted accounting principles" are far from being a canonical set of rules that will ensure identical accounting treatment of identical transactions. "Generally accepted accounting principles," rather, tolerate a range of "reasonable" treatments, leaving the choice among alternatives to management. Such, indeed, is precisely the case here. Variances of this sort may be tolerable in financial reporting, but they are questionable in a tax system designed to ensure as far as possible that similarly situated taxpayers pay the same tax. If management's election among "acceptable" options were dispositive for tax purposes, a firm, indeed, could decide unilaterally—within limits dictated only by its accountants—the tax it wished to pay. Such unilateral decisions would not just make the Code inequitable; they would make it unenforceable.

PROBLEMS

Problem 8.2A. The Jesse James Company ("JJC") was formed on June 1. The following information is available from JJC's inventory records for the quarter ended September 30, for a particular product which JJC purchases and resells to customers:

	Units	Unit Cost
Beginning inventory, July 1	800	$9.00
Purchases		
July 5	1,500	10.00
July 25	1,200	10.50
August 16	600	11.00
September 26	900	11.50

A physical inventory on September 30 reveals 1,600 units remaining in inventory. Compute the amount of the ending inventory at September 30 under each of the following inventory methods:

1. Specific identification assuming that the ending inventory includes 100 units from the beginning inventory, 200 units purchased on July 5, 300 units from those purchased on July 25, 400 units purchased on August 16, and 600 units from the September 26 purchase.

2. Weighted average
3. FIFO
4. LIFO

Problem 8.2B. Assume that Company X, in its first year of operation, purchased three units of inventory in a rising market, at prices of $5, $6 and $7 successively, and sold two of them during the year for a total of $16.

(a) Compute X's gross profit under both FIFO and LIFO.

(b) Assuming that X adopted LIFO in year 1, and that during its second year X purchased two more units of inventory, at $8 and $9 successively, while selling two units for a total of $20, how much gross profit would X report in year 2?

(c) Would the gross profit differ if X purchased a third unit during that year, also at $9, while still selling only two items for a total of $20?

(d) How about if X purchased only one item during the year, at $8, while still selling two for $20?

(e) Now suppose that in year 3, X, still on LIFO, starts with a single item of inventory, at a cost of $5, and during the year prices peak and turn downward, so that X purchases three items during the year, at successive costs of $10, $8, and $6, while selling two items for a total price of $18. Compute X's gross profit for the year.

Problem 8.2C. Dischord Music ("Dischord") was formed on January 1. The following information is available from Dischord's inventory records for the quarter ended March 31 for compact discs which Dischord purchases and resells to customers:

	Units	Unit Cost
Beginning inventory, January 1	2,000	$4.00
Purchases		
January 31	1,000	4.20
February 15	1,500	4.40
February 26	3,000	4.60
March 7	2,500	4.80
March 28	1,000	5.00

A physical inventory on March 31 reveals 4,800 compact discs remaining in inventory. If Discord sells compact discs for $75,000 during the year, calculate the gross profit for the quarter ending March 31 under each of the following inventory methods:

1. Specific identification assuming that the ending inventory includes 300 units from the beginning inventory, 500 units purchased on January 31, 700 units from those purchased on February 15, 1,400 units purchased on February 26, and 1,200 units from the March 7 purchase, and 700 units from those purchased on March 28.

2. Weighted average
3. FIFO
4. LIFO

Problem 8.3A. Assume the following facts as to an item to be included in a closing inventory:

Cost	$500
Replacement Cost	$350
Estimated Selling Price	$600
Additional Cost of Disposal	$200
Normal Profit	$100

At what figure should this item should be carried under the formula in ARB No. 43?

Problem 8.3B. Is there a lower of cost or market problem lurking in Problem 8.2B(e)?

Problem 8.3C. Assume that the appropriate market value of the goods ordered in Problem 8.1B, on page 509, *supra*, is only $9,200 at the end of year 1. In the light of the requirements of ARB No. 43, which of the following entries would you make to reflect this fact in X's financial statements for year 1?

(a) No entry
(b) Loss on Inventory Commitment $800
        Advance on Inventory Commitment $800
(c) Loss on Inventory Commitment $800
        Estimated Loss on Inventory Commitment $800

C. CONSISTENCY

As we have seen, the consistency principle generally requires enterprises to treat the same economic events in the same way from accounting period to accounting period; otherwise, users of financial statements could not meaningfully compare a company's financial statement with statements for previous periods. The following case involves the consistency requirement, while also illustrating that unjustified writedowns of inventory are just as improper as failure to take writedowns that are called for.

Chick v. Tomlinson
Supreme Court of Idaho, 1975.
96 Idaho 483, 531 P.2d 573.

■ DONALDSON, JUSTICE.

In 1963, Carlyle Chick and H. Lowell Hatch, hereinafter called respondents, began working at appellant Lewis Korth Lumber Company for K. D. Tomlinson, appellant. . . .

In return for their efforts at Lewis Korth Lumber Company, respondents were to each receive $500 per month salary, certain expenses, and bonuses [equal to] 40% of all net profits above the first $25,000. The dispute is found in the determination and distribution of those funds.

Although the respondents were employed at Lewis Korth from 1963 to 1971, profits sufficient to fund the bonus program were made only in 1963, 1967, and 1968. The bonus for 1963 was $8,500 each while the 1967 figure was $6,500 each. Neither of these amounts is in question. However 1968 was an excellent year for the lumber business and the relatively large profits for that year are the basis for this dispute.

Appellant Tomlinson contends that the 1968 net profit figure was $77,326.82, which resulted in $20,930.72 available for distribution by the bonus plan, i.e. 40% of profits after the first $25,000.00. The trial court amended the net profit figure to $194,323.96, with $67,729.58 for distribution. The trial court arrived at this sum by disallowing deductions of $25,000 for Tomlinson's salary and of $20,000 for a bonus reserve fund taken by Tomlinson from the net profit. The trial court also disallowed an accounting procedure utilized by Tomlinson wherein the closing lumber inventory of Lewis Korth Lumber Company was intentionally understated by over one million board feet. This procedure had the effect of reducing the profit by $71,997.14, which was subsequently added back in by the trial court in arriving at its figure of $67,729.58, net profit for distribution.

*   *   *

The trial court's determination that Tomlinson's salary deduction and the bonus reserve deduction from the 1968 net profits be disallowed as contrary to the bonus agreement is * * * assigned as error. * * * During the several years of the respondents' employment at Lewis Korth Lumber Company, only in 1968 were these deductions taken. This unilateral, one-time attempt is sufficient evidence to support the trial court's determination that the deductions were not in accord with the agreement.

The trial court's revaluation of the 1968 lumber inventory is assigned as error. As we noted above, 1968 was a bumper year in the industry. Lewis Korth Lumber Company earned record profits. Tomlinson testified that traditionally such years are followed by large increases in costs as workers seek wage increases. In order to 'hedge' against this, Tomlinson continued, he ordered the closing inventory of the lumber lowered by over one million board feet. This was done allegedly to compensate for the lower price the then green lumber would demand the following spring, and had the net effect of lowering the 1968 profit figure by $71,997.14.

Appellant Tomlinson argues that the trial court disregarded the only expert testimony as to the acceptability of that accounting procedure. Victor Wakefield, a CPA, did testify as a witness for the appellant, and a segment of that testimony was as follows:

"Q: (By Mr. Givens) Now, do you, is the inventory based in board feet and dollar volume contained in your report, your inventory and adjusted inventory?

"A: (By Mr. Wakefield) It is an adjusted inventory.

"Q: And does that meet normal and accepted accounting practices?

"A: Well, the technical word, probably not, but by and large most any business has a tendency to put these hedges in in those years." * * *

The trial court elected to place greater weight on the first part of the second answer and found the accounting procedure to be unacceptable.

In this the trial court was correct. Assuming arguendo that inventory adjustment was called for, placing one million board feet 'under the rock,' as Tomlinson termed it, is hardly the correct way to go about it. The position of the American Institute of Certified Public Accountants is as follows:

STATEMENT 5

A departure from the cost basis of pricing the inventory is required when the utility of the goods is no longer as great as its cost. Where there is evidence that the utility of goods, in their disposal in the ordinary course of business, will be less than cost, whether due to physical deterioration, obsolescence, changes in price levels, or other causes, the difference should be recognized as a loss of the current period. This is generally accomplished by stating such goods at a lower level commonly designated as Market.

Discussion

.08 Although the cost basis ordinarily achieves the objective of a proper matching of costs and revenues, under certain circumstances cost may not be the amount properly chargeable against the revenues of further periods. A departure from cost is required in these circumstances because cost is satisfactory only if the utility of the goods has not diminished since their acquisition; a loss of utility is to be reflected as a charge against the revenues of the period in which it occurs. Thus, in accounting for inventories, a loss should be recognized whenever the utility of goods is impaired by damage, deterioration, obsolescence, changes in price levels, or other causes. The measurement of such losses is accomplished by applying the rule of pricing inventories at Cost or Market, whichever is lower. This provides a practical means of measuring utility and thereby determining the amount of the loss to be recognized and accounted for in the current period.
APB Accounting Principles, § 5121.08.

By failing to adopt the procedure traditionally called "cost or market, whichever is lower" Tomlinson went beyond accepted accounting procedures, and the trial court correctly rejected the devaluation of the inventory.

NOTES

1. As we saw earlier, GAAP requires a business to disclose the accounting principles that the business uses, and the methods it applies to those principles, and that requirement specifically applies to "inventory pricing." In addition, the rule of APB Op. No. 20 and FSAS No. 154, which, as described at pages 260-262, *supra*, generally prevents an enterprise from changing from one accounting principle to another unless the new principle qualifies as "preferable" to the old, is applicable to the principles and procedures which an enterprise adopts to state inventories. If an enterprise alters the basis for stating inventories, the enterprise must disclose the change's nature and effect, if material, as well as the justification, in the financial statements for the accounting period in which the change occurs.

2. In applying the requirement that in order to adopt a new accounting principle it must be "preferable", income tax savings alone will not qualify. The new accounting principle must constitute an improvement in financial reporting. Accounting Changes Related to the Cost of Inventory, Interpretation of APB Opinion No. 20, FASB Interpretation No. 1 (FASB 1974).

3. Given the relatively low inflation rates in recent years, some businesses have switched from LIFO to FIFO. In 1994, for example, Coca–Cola Enterprises Inc. changed its method of accounting for inventories from LIFO to FIFO because businesses in the company's industry predominantly use the FIFO method.

4. Lawyers frequently draft or negotiate contracts which present issues regarding inventories. Since LIFO tends to minimize net income and current assets in an inflationary environment, while FIFO maximizes current assets and earnings in that same setting, if an agreement will give your client rights based upon an enterprise's income for some period you should consider specifying that the parties will use FIFO to compute income for purposes of the contract.

*

CHAPTER IX

LONG-LIVED ASSETS AND INTANGIBLES

A. INTRODUCTION

In Chapter I, we saw that a close relationship exists between deferred expenses and assets. Many assets which an enterprise uses in its operations benefit several, or even many, accounting periods. For example, a manufacturing enterprise may purchase production equipment that should last at least five years, or a building to use as a sales office that should last even longer. The same manufacturing enterprise may also develop or purchase a patent for use in its operations. When such assets benefit several accounting periods, accountants increasingly refer to these assets, both tangible and intangible, as *long-lived assets*. The term long-lived assets, therefore, includes both tangible *fixed assets*, such as property, plant and equipment, which accountants sometimes refer to as *capital assets*, and *intangibles* like copyrights, patents and trademarks.

Long-lived assets function in the same way as other deferred expenses. The very reason why E. Tutt spent $2,000 for computer equipment for her law office, namely that the expenditure will provide benefit in future accounting periods, requires that she not treat the entire expenditure as an expense in the month she bought the computer. Rather, the expenditure reflects an unexpired cost, which E. Tutt should record as an asset. We also noted, however, that such an asset, like most tangible fixed assets other than land, will not last forever. Ultimately, E. Tutt will retire the computer. The computer may physically wear out or become technologically obsolescent. In any event, the $2,000 which E. Tutt paid to purchase the computer, less any salvage value, represents an expense which under the matching principle E. Tutt should offset against revenues during the computer's estimated useful life. Depreciation refers to the systematic allocation of a tangible asset's cost over its expected life.

An enterprise may also acquire natural resources, including timber rights, mineral interests and oil and gas reserves, or intangible assets such as a patent, for use in its business operations. In addition, enterprises often purchase other businesses, and when the purchase price exceeds the cumulative fair market values of the acquired business's individually identifiable assets, the acquiring enterprise treats the excess as *goodwill*. Goodwill reflects the fact that a business's value frequently exceeds the sum of its parts.

537

Since a fixed asset provides benefits for more than one accounting period, an enterprise should allocate the asset's cost among the different periods in a systematic and rational manner. Depreciation assigns the costs of capital assets to the future periods which an enterprise expects to benefit from the services that those assets provide. Because land does not experience wear or tear, or undergo functional or economic obsolescence, however, businesses cannot depreciate land. The term *depletion* refers to a similar cost allocation process for natural resources found on or below land, such as timber or oil reserves, which accountants often describe as *wasting assets*. Unlike depreciation, depletion attempts to measure these assets' physical consumption.

Intangibles, such as goodwill and patents, do not possess physical substance, but they do provide benefits over more than one accounting period, so their cost should be allocated among those periods. Accountants use the term *amortization* to describe this process for intangibles.

Allocating the costs of long-lived assets among the different accounting periods expected to benefit from them helps to present accurately the enterprise's financial results and condition. After all, accrual accounting seeks to match revenues with the expenses incurred to produce the revenues. To provide meaningful comparative financial data, an enterprise must consistently apply the same depreciation, depletion and amortization methods from period to period and disclose the methods used.

Obviously, before reaching issues of depreciation or amortization we must ask whether the expenditure involved actually created an asset. In other words, there is the following threshold question: Does this financial outlay represent an expense, requiring immediate income statement recognition, or should the enterprise treat some or all of the expenditure as an asset which will appear on the balance sheet and subsequently flow through one or more income statements by way of systematic cost allocation or as an offset to some particular revenue? The answers to the following questions generally help an enterprise to decide whether to treat an expenditure as an asset or expense:

- Does the expenditure create a new asset?

- Does the outlay restore an underlying asset to its original condition?

- Does the expenditure enable the enterprise to produce greater quantity or better quality products?

- Does the outlay extend an existing asset's useful life?

- How often does the expenditure recur?

In addition, the expenditure's materiality can affect the determination.

1. REPAIRS VS. CAPITAL EXPENDITURES

One important recurring example of the asset/expense dichotomy is posed by expenditures for work on an already existing tangible property, which presents the issue of repairs versus capital expenditures. Accountants define *repairs* as costs incurred to maintain an asset's operating efficiency and expected useful life. Usually small in amount and recurrent in nature, accountants treat repairs as expenses because these expenditures predominately benefit only the current accounting period. Examples of repairs include maintaining buildings, changing machine oils, and replacing minor equipment parts. As current expenses, these costs reduce current net income when incurred. The enterprise debits an expense account, such as Repair Expense, upon incurring such a cost.

Capital expenditures, on the other hand, generally increase operational efficiency and productive capacity or extend an underlying asset's useful life. Usually more significant in amount than repairs, these costs add to an enterprise's investment in the underlying asset. The enterprise debits the appropriate asset account upon incurring a capital expenditure. The resulting depreciation, depletion or amortization will reduce net income in those accounting periods that benefit from the use of the asset.

Accountants sometimes divide capital expenditures into three categories: *additions*, *improvements* and *replacements*. Additions generally increase an asset's productive capacity. For example, constructing a new wing on an existing plant may increase the enterprise's ability to manufacture products. Although theoretically these expenditures create a new asset, the enterprise may debit the underlying asset, such as the Building account, upon incurring such expenditures. Both improvements and replacements involve substituting one asset for another. An improvement, which some accountants call a *betterment,* substitutes a better asset for an existing asset. In a replacement, in contrast, the enterprise supplants an existing asset with a like asset. To illustrate, installing a concrete floor in an area where a dirt floor previously existed would constitute an improvement, while substituting one wooden floor for another demonstrates a replacement. In both situations, however, the substitutions must extend or enhance the asset's useful life.

B. IMPORTANCE TO LAWYERS

Accounting for fixed assets and intangibles affects lawyers because the methods used to recognize and recover capital expenditures can directly impact an enterprise's financial position and results. Remember that lawyers frequently draft, negotiate or litigate contracts that contain profit-sharing provisions, and accounting for long-lived assets and intangibles can affect these provisions in at least three different ways. First, accounting rules may determine whether an enterprise can treat an expenditure as an asset or must treat the cost as an expense. If what should be reflected as a current expense in the income statement is treated as a capital expenditure and recorded as an asset on the balance sheet, both the enterprise's assets and its income would be overstated. Conversely, if unexpired costs which will provide substantial benefits to subsequent accounting periods are expensed currently, assets and profits will be understated. Second, the schedule for charging depreciation, depletion and amortization expenses can significantly impact profit computations. Finally, write downs of long-lived assets and intangibles can greatly affect net income. Large write downs in recent years have prompted the business community to use the term "Big Bath" to describe an enterprise's one-time recognition of expense or loss for supposedly worthless assets. As detailed later in this chapter, while such write downs significantly reduce current income, they improve the possibility of future income by negating the allocation to future periods of expenses which would have resulted from amortization or depreciation of those assets if they had not been written down or off.

A current variant of this practice stems from the GAAP rule, noted in Chapter VI, on page 332, *supra*, requiring the immediate write off of all research and development costs, including any portion of the purchase price in an acquisition transaction which is allocable to the acquired company's "in-process research and development". That has led some acquirors to seek to allocate large portions of the acquisition cost to the acquired company's on-going research and development, in order to write it all off at the time of the acquisition and spare future accounting periods the burden of the amortization of such amounts. Commentators have observed the irony inherent in the current rules that recognize in-process research and development as an intangible asset acquired in the transaction, thereby requiring its value to be measured to see how much of the purchase price should be allocated to it, and then allow obliteration of the intangible from the balance sheet. More important, the SEC staff, noting that charges for in-process research and development during 1998 rose to 247 instances totaling $19.6 billion, has been carefully reviewing these writeoffs. During a one-year period in the late 1990s, the SEC investigated about $10 billion of the charges and forced companies to reclassify $5 billion. In the words of Lynn Turner, the agency's Chief Accountant, the SEC has challenged valuations of purchased research and development "when the amounts assigned are disconnected from reality." America Online, for example, reportedly needed to postpone the release of its fiscal 1998 earnings for almost two months so that the company could settle an accounting dispute with the SEC's staff on this subject.

However, even before then SEC Chairman Arthur Levitt's speech in 1998 highlighting "merger magic" as one of five "illusions" in accounting practice, see page 343, *supra*, FASB had begun to consider additional standards on accounting for purchased intangibles, including purchased in-process research and development. In 2003, the Board tentatively decided to eliminate the requirement in FASB Interpretation No. 4, *Applicability of*

FASB Statement No. 2 to Business Combinations Accounted for by the Purchase Method (1975), that enterprises expense certain in-process research and development ("IPR&D") acquired in a business combination. Financial Accounting Standards Board, Action Alert No. 03-32 (Aug. 13, 2003). Under a staff summary that the FASB issued in 2004, acquirors would recognize and measure this IPR&D at fair value; thereafter this intangible like other intangibles discussed below, would be periodically tested for impairment. FASB, Summary of Tentative Decisions on Business Combinations of July 27, 2004, at vi.

Another very topical issue involving the expense/asset dichotomy relates to the fact that over the next thirty years businesses in the United States will likely spend hundreds of billions of dollars to clean up environmental problems. Should businesses treat these costs as expenses, or as capital expenditures which will benefit future periods? Similarly, as the Internet emerges, enterprises have spent, and will continue to spend, enormous amounts to develop the content and the graphics on their Web sites. How should firms treat these costs for financial accounting purposes?

The influence of accounting for long-lived assets on both the income statement and the balance sheet can be very large. From a balance sheet perspective, long-lived assets often represent a substantial part of an enterprise's total assets. For example, in 1994 Sprint Corporation reported a $10,878,600,000 net balance for fixed assets, representing 72.83 percent of total assets, and Anheuser-Busch reported fixed assets of $7,547,700,000, representing 68.33 percent of total assets. The income statements of these companies also displayed the impact of depreciation accounting, reporting depreciation expenses of $1,478,400,000 which approximates 13.6 percent of total operating expenses, and $627,500,000 or almost 6.2 percent of total operating expenses, respectively.

As noted in Chapter II, an enterprise's management is often called upon to exercise judgment when applying generally accepted accounting principles. Accounting for long-lived assets requires managerial judgment involving significant estimates. As discussed below in greater detail, accounting for long-lived assets requires estimating both the assets' useful lives and any expected salvage values remaining after productive service ends. And remember, depreciation, depletion and amortization expenses represent non-cash expenditures, an important point for income statement and cash flow analysis.

That the asset versus expense determination can be a judgment call, and the decision can have such a significant impact on net income for a period, explains why, as was noted in Chapter VI, hiding expenses as assets has often been a technique for manipulating financial statements. E.g., In re Valley Systems, Inc., 7 Fed. Sec. L. Rep. (CCH) ¶74,222 (SEC 1995), involving a public company which was held to have violated the federal securities laws when its CFO sought to conceal deteriorating financial results by causing the company arbitrarily to capitalize what were clearly current period expenses, on the purported ground that they were incurred in the construction of capital equipment. See also In re Star Technologies, Inc., 1991-95 Fed. Sec. L. Rep. (CCH) ¶ 73, 964 (SEC 1993) (among a number of accounting improprieties which violated the securities laws, the company had taken no depreciation prior to the current year on computer equipment apparently purchased four years earlier, and since the asset should have been fully depreciated by the end of the current year it had to be entirely written off, substantially increasing the loss for the year).

NOTES

1. Several recent accounting pronouncements supply new guidance on the expense vs. asset issue, in an effort to eliminate inconsistencies in financial reporting. *See, e.g.,* Reporting on the Costs of Start-Up Activities, Statement of Position 98-5 (AICPA 1998) (mandating that enterprises expense organization costs and costs related to start-up activities as incurred); Accounting for the Costs of Computer Software Developed or Obtained for Internal Use, Statement of Position 98-1 (AICPA 1998) (requiring enterprises to expense computer software costs incurred in preliminary project stages, similar costs stemming from research and development, training costs, maintenance costs, and many costs related to data conversion, while specifying capitalization for external direct costs of materials and services used to develop or acquire internal use software, payroll costs for employees who work directly on tasks related to the internal use software, and interest costs incurred while developing such software); Accounting for Web Site Development Costs (Emerging Issues Task Force Issue No. 00-2, Financial Accounting Standards Bd. 2000) (concluding that enterprises should capitalize initial development costs for Web graphics, but can expense changes in the graphics).

2. Questions about whether to treat an expenditure as an expense or a capital expenditure can arise in various contexts. *See, e.g.,* Pashman v. Chemtex, Inc., 825 F. 2d 629 (2d Cir. 1987) (costs incurred by an employer to purchase a worthless ownership interest in a paint plant were not "capital expenditures," so the employer could deduct that amount from revenues in determining net profits under employment agreement which awarded salesman ten percent of pretax profits on sales); Lege v. Lea Exploration Co., Inc., 631 So.2d 716 (La. App.1994) (holding that trial court properly treated amounts lessee incurred in reworking oil and gas well, and in constructing a saltwater disposal system, as capital costs, rather than as operating expenses, in determining whether well was producing in paying quantities, so as to preclude lease cancellation).

These questions often arise in tax cases. *See, e.g.,* Indopco, Inc. v. Commissioner, 503 U.S. 79, 88, 112 S. Ct. 1039, 1045, 117 L. Ed.2d 226,236 (1992) (holding that legal, investment banking, and other fees that the taxpayer incurred to facilitate its own acquisition in a friendly takeover represented "capital expenditures," rather than deductible expenses, because the payments produced "significant benefits that extended beyond the tax year in question"); Von-Lusk v. Commissioner, 104 T.C. 207 (1995) (upholding the Commissioner's determination that the taxpayer must capitalize as development costs property taxes, and amounts incurred in meeting with government officials, obtaining building permits and zoning variances, performing engineering and feasibility studies, and drafting architectural plans related to raw land which the taxpayer planned to subdivide and use as lots upon which to build houses).

Problem 9.1A. The Americans with Disabilities Act of 1990 ("ADA") generally requires businesses classified as "public accommodations" to remove architectural barriers which prevent access to their facilities, or at least to make their services physically accessible to persons with disabilities to the extent "readily achievable." 42 U.S.C. § 12182. Assume that a corporation which operates a chain of fast-food restaurants spends $10 million to comply with the ADA. This amount includes costs to install ramps at doorways, remodel restrooms by widening toilet stalls and lowering sinks, and relocate drinking fountains at each restaurant. The expenditures do not extend the restaurants' estimated useful lives and actually reduce seating capacity in the restaurants. The corporation's labor agreement requires the corporation to contribute ten percent of its pretax income to a profit-sharing plan for certain employees. Can the business treat these costs of compliance with the ADA as expenses?

C. ALLOCATION OF CAPITALIZED COSTS

In Chapter I, we introduced depreciation accounting during our discussion regarding deferral. You may want to review those materials at this time. In a nutshell, depreciation accounting attempts to distribute the costs to acquire a fixed asset, less any estimated salvage value, systematically and rationally among the accounting periods that span the asset's expected useful life, i.e., that the enterprise expects to benefit from the assets. Such cost allocation roughly relates to the matching principle—offsetting costs against the revenues that those costs generate.

Note that GAAP does not require an enterprise to apportion the cost of a fixed asset, less salvage value, *ratably* over the asset's useful life. In other words, depreciation accounting need not allocate an equal amount to each accounting period of the useful life. Similarly, enterprises which use activity, such as operating hours or units produced, rather than time, to measure useful life, need not assign an equal amount to each operating hour or unit produced. Systems involving non-ratable allocation of cost, for example, deducting larger amounts in the early years than in the later years, can also qualify as "rational." Nevertheless, ratable allocation, which accountants usually refer to as *straight-line depreciation*, connoting the fact that the enterprise apportions cost evenly over an asset's useful life, remains the most common practice.

We should also emphasize two other preliminary points about depreciation. First, depreciation does not value fixed assets, and depreciation accounting does not attempt to measure the decline in market value which the company's assets are typically undergoing as they age. Second, although accountants usually use the term *accumulated depreciation*, depreciation accounting does not "accumulate" anything. Similarly, depreciation accounting does not guarantee that the enterprise will have sufficient resources to replace the fixed assets at the end of their useful lives. To illustrate, assume that an investor organizes X Corp. on January 1 of Year 1 and contributes a plant in exchange for 1,000 shares of $100 par value common stock. X Corp.'s balance sheet would reflect the following:

X Corp.
Balance Sheet, After Plant Acquisition

Plant	$100,000	Stated Capital	$100,000

If X Corp. assigns a fifty-year estimated useful life, without salvage value, to the plant, depreciation expense for Year 1 under the straight-line method would equal $2,000 ($100,000 cost/50 years estimated useful life). If X Corp. does not generate any income or incur any other expenses for the year, the Profit and Loss account for the year would show a $2,000 loss, and the balance sheet at the end of Year 1 would appear as follows:

X Corp.
Balance Sheet, End of Year 1

Plant	$100,000	Stated Capital	$100,000
Less: Accumulated Depreciation	2,000	Deficit	(2,000)
Total	$98,000	Total	$98,000

Given forty-nine similar years, even the most scrupulous application of depreciation accounting would not provide any "funds" to replace the plant at the end of its useful life. Only receipts that exceed expenditures can provide the funds necessary to replace fixed assets, or for any other purpose. What depreciation accounting does do is illustrate a very important type of expense which must be deducted in the current period even though there was no cash expenditure.

As we saw in the introduction to depreciation accounting in Chapter I, accumulated depreciation is carried as an offset to the asset account to which it relates, and the net figure, cost less accumulated depreciation to date, is often referred to as the *book value* of the asset. In an earlier day, the common caption for accumulated depreciation was Reserve for Depreciation, an even more misleading application of the term "Reserve" than its use as a substitute for an Estimated Expense Payable; at that time, the Reserve for Depreciation sometimes appeared on the right-hand side of the balance sheet, along with other "Reserve" accounts (including the one which in those days was called "Reserve for Bad Debts" but is now termed Allowance for Uncollectibles, and, like Accumulated Depreciation, is carried on the left-hand side of the balance sheet, as an offset to the asset).

Problem 9.2.   A state statute required that the directors of every corporation file annually a "report of condition" of the corporation, which must include a statement of assets and liabilities as of the end of the corporation's most recent fiscal year, in the form prescribed by the secretary of state. That form, as described by the court in one reported case, was a balance sheet, showing, on one side, "Assets," subdivided according to their nature, and on the other side, "Liabilities," including indebtedness of various kinds, "Capital Stock," "Reserves", and "Surplus." The statute also provided that if directors make any required statement or report "which is false in any material representation and which they know to be false," they shall be liable "to persons who shall have relied upon such false report to their damage."

Some years ago E. Transport Corp. filed a report of condition which included a balance sheet showing on the asset side, "Autos, trucks and teams," carried at $15,000. The liability side showed "Reserves" at $13,500. The $15,000 represented the original purchase price of the equipment, which had been purchased about seven years before and was currently worth about $2,000. The $13,500 in "Reserves" represented the amount charged to depreciation expense over the years on the equipment.

A creditor who extended credit to E after the above report of condition had been filed brought an action against the directors of E on the ground that the report of condition was false in a material representation "with reference to the value of the autos, trucks and teams owned by the corporation." How should the case be decided? In considering your answer, suppose that E's balance sheet, leaving out for a moment the $13,500 for "Reserves," appeared as follows in the report of condition:

Assets			Liabilities	
Cash	$	500	Accounts Payable	$8,000
Accounts Receivable		2,500		
Autos, Trucks, and Teams		15,000	Capital Stock	7,000
Goodwill		12,000	Surplus	1,500

Could a judgment about whether to lend, say, $1,000, to, E Corp., or invest that amount, be affected by where the figure for Reserves was carried on the balance sheet?

D. COMPUTATION OF ANNUAL DEPRECIATION

To properly calculate depreciation during an accounting period, an enterprise must start with the following factors: (1) costs to acquire the asset, (2) projected salvage value, and (3) estimated useful life.

1. COSTS TO ACQUIRE AND RETIRE AN ASSET

As we have seen repeatedly, enterprises use the historical cost principle to record fixed asset acquisitions, so historical cost provides the usual basis for determining depreciation. Similar to accounting for inventories, historical cost represents the cash or cash equivalent price to acquire a fixed asset and bring the item to the location and condition of its intended use. Examples of expenditures considered part of a fixed asset's historical cost include, in addition to the purchase price, freight costs and installation charges. Once an enterprise determines an asset's historical cost, that cost figure appears on the balance sheet and also becomes the starting point for depreciation calculations.

a. SPECIFIC COSTS: DIRECT AND OVERHEAD COSTS

The costs to acquire property include not only any amounts necessary to acquire the asset, but also expenditures which ready the asset for its intended use. These expenditures can include both direct and certain indirect costs.

Thus, in the case of land the historical cost includes, in addition to the purchase price paid to the seller, any other expenditures by the purchaser to acquire the land, such as the amount of any mortgages assumed, any real estate commissions, title insurance, legal fees, accrued property taxes, or surveyor fees. Although less obvious, the cost of land also includes any amounts incurred to bring the land to the condition necessary for its intended use, such as for clearing, grading or draining the property, or expenditures incurred to demolish old buildings before constructing a new facility on the property.

Buildings or improvements on the land are treated separately, and their cost includes all expenditures to acquire the facility and prepare the structure for its intended use. Construction-related costs, such as expenditures for materials and labor, attorney's fees, architect's charges and building permits, often dominate building acquisition expenditures. When an enterprise constructs facilities for its own use, the cost also includes indirect or overhead charges, including reasonable amounts for utilities, insurance, and depreciation of machines used to construct the facility. Remember too that, pursuant to FASB No. 34, as noted on page 333, *supra,* one of the expenditures to prepare property for its intended use is interest on funds borrowed to finance the acquisition or construction, to the extent that the interest is paid or accrued during the period of development of the new property, before it has contributed to the production of revenues.

For equipment too, the purchase price, freight charges and installation costs all enter into the historical cost. In addition, the cost for equipment includes any other expenditures necessary to bring the equipment to its operating location and to prepare the equipment for its productive use, such as insurance premiums during transit, amounts paid to build special foundations, and outlays for trial runs.

b. SPECIAL ISSUES IN ASSET ACQUISITIONS

The form of the transaction in which an enterprise acquires an asset can raise special accounting issues. For example, an enterprise may issue an ownership interest in the enterprise, such as stock in the corporation, in exchange for one or more assets. If the ownership interest is actively traded, its market value establishes the property's historical cost; if not, the enterprise uses the best estimate of the acquired property's fair market value as the fairest indication of its cost.

Enterprises often acquire fixed assets through long-term financing and credit contracts, using notes, mortgages or bonds. In that case, the enterprise can use the obligation's present value on the acquisition date as the asset's cost for depreciation purposes (or, if it more clearly appears, here too the fair market value of the property acquired can be used).

Enterprises sometimes acquire a group of assets in a single transaction. Such acquisitions require the acquiring enterprise to allocate the lump sum purchase price to the various assets purchased. In this situation, the general practice is to allocate the total purchase price first to current assets and noncurrent investments in marketable securities, to the extent of their respective fair market values; the remaining balance of the purchase price is then allocated among the other noncurrent assets, based on their relative fair values, as long as the price allocated to any asset does not exceed its fair value.

To illustrate, assume that ABC Co. pays $90,000 for several long-lived assets, which have the following characteristics:

	Seller's Book Value	Fair Value
Asset 1	$15,000	$ 10,000
Asset 2	10,000	20,000
Asset 3	20,000	30,000
Asset 4	30,000	40,000
	$75,000	$100,000

ABC Co. would allocate the $90,000 purchase price among the assets based on the relative fair values in the following manner.

	Cost
Asset 1	$ 9,000
Asset 2	18,000
Asset 3	27,000
Asset 4	36,000
	$90,000

By comparison, if ABC purchases the four assets for any amount which exceeds their $100,000 cumulative fair value, the excess represents goodwill, which we will discuss later in this chapter.

When an enterprise acquires an asset through a gift or nonreciprocal transfer, a strict application of the historical cost principle would call for the enterprise to assign a zero cost to the asset. Accountants, however, typically use the asset's estimated fair market value as the cost for subsequent depreciation calculations. In conjunction with debiting the particular asset account, the credit might be to a Donated Capital account.

c. ASSET RETIREMENT OBLIGATIONS

Some tangible long-lived assets, such as nuclear power plants, strip and other mines, oil and gas wells and other production platforms, and landfills, require substantial decommissioning, clean-up, or removal costs when an enterprise retires such assets from service. Until a new accounting standard became effective, diverse accounting practices existed for these asset retirement obligations (AROs). Some enterprises accrued such obligations ratably over the related asset's useful life, either as a component of depreciation expense, or as a liability. Other enterprises did not recognize liabilities for AROs until the enterprise retired the underlying asset. These divergent accounting practices left it very difficult to compare the financial statements of enterprises that faced similar obligations but accounted for them differently.

Under SFAS No. 143, *Accounting for Asset Retirement Obligations* (FASB 2001), an enterprise must record the fair value of a liability arising from a legal obligation associated with the retirement of a tangible long-lived asset in the period in which the enterprise can reasonably estimate the liability, capitalize the related costs as part of the long-loved asset's carrying amount, and allocate those costs to expense over the asset's useful life. The pronouncement defines a legal obligation as one that an existing law, written or oral contract, or the doctrine of promissory estoppel requires the enterprise to fulfill. The pronouncement, however, does not apply to obligations that arise when an enterprise improperly operates an asset or decides to sell or otherwise dispose of an long-lived asset, and to certain lessee obligations. When the enterprise satisfies the obligation subject to the new rules, the enterprise either discharges the liability for its recorded amount or recognizes a gain or a loss on the satisfaction. In addition, the enterprise must describe ARO's and reconcile changes in the components of such obligations. Subsequently, the FASB issued an interpretation clarifying that an enterprise must immediately recognize a liability for a conditional asset retirement obligation when incurred, generally upon acquisition, construction, development, or normal operation, even though uncertainty about the timing or method of settlement may exist. Although an enterprise may consider the uncertainty in measuring the liability, the enterprise must recognize the ARO if it can be reasonably estimated. ACCOUNTING FOR CONDITIONAL ASSET RETIREMENT OBLIGATIONS, FASB Interpretation No. 47 (2005).

2. SALVAGE VALUE

As outlined above, depreciation accounting is based on the asset's historical cost less *salvage value*. Salvage value reflects the residual amount that an enterprise expects to receive upon the asset's disposition at the end of its useful life — that is, the asset's estimated future trade-in value or selling price. If an enterprise expects disposal to involve additional removal or selling costs other than retirement obligations of the sort discussed in the previous paragraph, it uses "net" salvage value to determine the amount to be depreciated over the asset's useful life. To illustrate, assume that Z Corp. purchases an asset for $100,000 and expects to sell the asset for $15,000 at the end of the asset's useful life in ten years. Further assume that Z Corp. expects to incur $1,000 in costs to remove the assets from its manufacturing facility, and to pay a $1,500 commission on the sale. In these circumstances, Z Corp. would use a $12,500 net salvage value ($15,000 estimated selling price minus the $1,000 removal costs and the $1,500 selling commission),leaving a balance of $87,500 to be allocated among the ten accounting periods that the enterprise expects to benefit from the asset's use.

3. USEFUL LIFE

Unlike many deferred expenses, such as prepaid insurance, an enterprise usually cannot precisely ascertain a tangible fixed asset's useful life or *service life* for several reasons. First, service lives often differ from physical lives. An asset may possess the physical capability to continue production for years longer than the estimated useful life, but most enterprises will not continue to use facilities when asset inefficiencies cause production costs to increase, so that is taken into account when assessing useful lives. Fixed assets may become inadequate when an enterprise's production characteristics change or when a product's nature changes over time. In addition, new technologies may afford faster or more efficient production, rendering current facilities obsolete. In some situations, an accountant may employ statistical methods and engineering studies in an attempt to estimate an asset's useful life. An entity's past experience with similar assets, and perhaps the experiences of other businesses in the same industry, can also assist in estimating the useful service lives of assets. As a practical matter, however, an enterprise is often faced with a fairly arbitrary choice.

Most businesses express a fixed asset's useful life in units of accounting periods, such as years or months. Occasionally, however, a different measure may prove more convenient: as noted above, an enterprise may express a machine's useful life in terms of estimated hours of running time, in which event the amount which the enterprise treats as depreciation expense during any accounting period will depend upon the number of hours that the machine actually operated during the period. Alternatively, an enterprise might use the estimated total number of items that the machine will produce in its lifetime to measure useful life. In that event, the number of items produced in a particular accounting period will determine depreciation expense for the period.

If an enterprise expects to use a capital asset for less than its normal life, the enterprise will use that shorter period for depreciation purposes. For example, an automobile rental company which rents cars for only one or two years and then sells them to a used car dealer would allocate the difference between its cost and the established resale price to the accounting periods of actual use.

Although enterprises cannot depreciate land for financial accounting purposes, they can depreciate *land improvements*, such as parking lots, fences, sidewalks and street lights, because these assets have limited useful lives.

4. COMPUTATION OF DEPRECIATION EXPENSE

As indicated earlier, depreciation accounting is designed to allocate the cost of an asset less salvage value among the benefitted accounting periods in a "systematic and rational manner", which has normally meant the straight-line method, that is, apportioning the depreciable amount ratably among the periods of the asset's useful life. Enterprises almost always use this approach to amortize the cost of intangibles, and quite often for tangible assets also, because basing depreciation on the passage of time is simple and easy to understand. So if Trahan Co. acquired an asset at a cost of $12,000, with an estimated salvage value of $2,5000, and an estimated useful life of four years, the annual depreciation expense would presumably be $2,5000. However, unless the asset happened to be acquired on or about the first day of a fiscal year, it would be necessary to adjust the depreciation calculation to take account of the fact that the asset was not in use for the entire year. If the asset was put into service on, say, July 1 of the first year, the depreciation expense for that year would be only one-half of the annual charge, or $1,250; correspondingly, the fifth year would also be charged with one-half of a year's expense, or $1,250.

Suppose that instead the depreciation expense is to be based upon the use or productivity of the asset. For example, if, in the case of the asset described above as purchased for $12,000 and having an expected salvage value of $2,000, it was more feasible to estimate the useful life on the basis of hours of productive use, say, 20,000, than simply in terms of the passage of time, then the depreciation expense each year would be computed by multiplying the number of hours of use that year times the hourly depreciation rate of 50 cents ($10,000 depreciation base divided by 20,000, the estimated total number of hours of use).

PROBLEMS

Problem 9.3A. On August 1, Year 1, Bambi Corporation ("Bambi") purchased a new machine on a deferred payment basis. Bambi made a down payment of $1,000 and agreed to make four $2,500 quarterly installments beginning on November 1, Year 1. The cash equivalent price of the machine was $9,500. Bambi incurred and paid installation costs amounting to $300. Bambi estimates that the machine will produce 10,000 widgets over its useful life, and that there will be no salvage value. During the quarter ended October 31, Year 1, the machine produced 300 widgets. What should Bambi record as depreciation expense for the quarter ended October 31, Year 1 under the units of production method? Explain briefly, showing your computations.

a. CHANGES IN DEPRECIATION PRINCIPLES AND ESTIMATES

Suppose partway through the life of an asset it becomes clear that the original estimate of the useful life or the expected salvage value was not correct. The question affords an opportunity to illustrate the way a change in an accounting estimate, as distinguished from a change in accounting principle, is handled, per SFAS No. 154, reaffirming APB Op. No. 20, at pages 262-263, *supra*. Like other estimates, estimated useful lives and salvage value should be periodically reviewed, and if either one is no longer sound, management can, and generally should, make appropriate revision. On the other hand, recall that a change in accounting principle, for example, a shift from straight-line depreciation to an accelerated system (which will be examined in detail shortly) is permitted only if the new method qualifies as "preferable".

If management decides to revise estimated salvage values or useful lives, the enterprise will reflect those changes in the financial statements for the current and future periods only; there is no attempt to compensate or adjust for what have turned out to be erroneous figures in the previous periods. Most significantly, as just noted, revisions of useful life or salvage value, being only changes in accounting estimates, need not satisfy the "preferability" requirement.

To illustrate, if management decides that an asset's useful life will last beyond the original estimate, the enterprise computes current and future depreciation calculations on the basis of allocating the then remaining depreciable amount over the remaining newly estimated useful life. For example, suppose that an enterprise spends $100,000 to purchase a machine which the enterprise expects to sell for $10,000 at the end of its expected six-year useful life. Assuming straight-line depreciation, the enterprise would treat $15,000 per year as depreciation expense [($100,000 cost less $10,000 salvage value) divided by six-year estimated useful life]. Then suppose that in the fourth year, having accumulated $45,000 as depreciation expense during the first three years, management estimates that while salvage value will still be at $10,000, the machine will last five more years, meaning that the machine will have a useful life totaling eight years rather than the six years originally estimated. Although the enterprise has overestimated depreciation and understated income for the first three years by treating $15,000 rather than $11,250 [($100,000 cost less $10,000 salvage value) divided by eight-year revised estimated useful life] as depreciation expense each year, GAAP precludes the enterprise from adjusting the previously reported results. Instead, the enterprise will calculate depreciation for the current and subsequent periods by allocating the asset's remaining book value less any salvage value over the asset's remaining estimated life. Depreciation expense for years four through eight, therefore, would equal $9,000 per year ([($100,000 cost less $45,000 accumulated depreciation for the first three years) less $10,000 salvage value] divided by five years). Under APB Opinion No. 20 and SFAS No. 154, the enterprise should disclose any material changes in estimates in the notes to the financial statements.

5. GROUP METHOD

As a practical matter, treating every fixed asset as a separate unit for depreciation and retirement purposes can produce rather onerous bookkeeping burdens, at least for large enterprises. Enterprises, therefore, often treat a number of individual items together as a group and apply a single depreciation rate to the total cost of the assets in the group, less the total estimated salvage value. Accountants refer to this as the *group method* or sometimes as the *composite method*.

This depreciation method often involves assets with small individual values, such as small tools, or homogeneous groups of assets. For example, an obvious case for using the group method would be a cab company which purchased ten identical cabs at the beginning of year one for $22,000 each. Assume that the company expects each cab to last five years and have a $2,000 estimated salvage value at the end of that period. In such a case, the cab company could much more conveniently treat the ten cabs as a group, viewing the group in essence as a single unit which cost $220,000 and had a five-year estimated useful life, plus a $20,000 estimated salvage value. Assuming the straight-line method, the annual depreciation on this group of cabs would be $40,000.

If the company purchases more cabs, it would simply add them to the group and apply the group depreciation rate to the new total cost, again less salvage value. For example, suppose at the beginning of year two, the company buys five more cabs for $25,000 apiece. This purchase would represent a $125,000 addition to the Cabs asset account. Assuming that the company estimates that these cabs will each have a five-year useful life, and a $2,500 salvage value, the company could treat the group of fifteen cabs as a single asset which originally cost $345,000 and has a $32,500 estimated salvage value. In that event, the depreciation charge for the second year under the straight-line method would equal one-fifth of the $312,500 depreciable amount, ($345,000 cost less the $32,500 salvage value), or $62,500. The cab company, therefore, could record the following entry to record depreciation for the second year:

Depreciation Expense	$62,500	
Accumulated Depreciation		$62,500

The group method offers an advantage over the so-called unit method because it eliminates the need to reflect gain or loss upon the retirement of each individual asset. For example, assume that the cab company retires one of the ten original cabs in the group at the end of the fourth year and sells the cab for $5,000. Applying the unit method, the company's books would show a $6,000 book value for the cab at the end of the fourth year, reflecting the $22,000 original cost less $16,000 accumulated depreciation (four years at $4,000 per year). Accounting for the retirement consists of (1) closing out the Accumulated Depreciation account with a debit, (2) debiting cash for the net salvage proceeds, and (3) eliminating the asset account with a credit. If the estimates of useful life and salvage value were right on target, the net proceeds would equal the book value (original cost less accumulated depreciation to date). But often that is not the case, and any difference must be charged, or credited, to net income. So, in the foregoing example, sale proceeds of only $5,000 would have required the cab company to recognize a $1,000 loss in that year. The group method, however, operates on the theory that overdepreciation on some of the assets in a group of related assets will balance, or offset, any underdepreciation on other assets in the group. In other words, while an enterprise may retire some assets prematurely, or upon retirement obtain less than the anticipated salvage value, other assets in the group will last longer than the estimated useful life, or will bring more than the expected salvage value. Accordingly, when an asset is retired from a group, the enterprise will charge or credit, as the case may be, the difference between the asset's book value and the salvage proceeds to the Accumulated Depreciation account, with no effect upon the current income statement. That is accomplished by simply charging the asset's original cost to the Accumulated Depreciation account and crediting that account with any disposition proceeds. So, in the above example the cab company might record the following entries under the group method:

Accumulated Depreciation	$22,000	
Cabs		$22,000
Cash	$5,000	
Accumulated Depreciation		$5,000

Of course, the cab company could combine those entries:

Accumulated Depreciation	$17,000	
Cash	5,000	
Cabs		$22,000

Note that under the group method the figure in the Accumulated Depreciation account at any point in time does not necessarily reflect, as it does under the unit method, the exact amount of the depreciation to date, because that account also includes gains and losses upon previous asset retirements from that group. But because the enterprise expects that the gains will balance the losses in the long run, the accounting profession does not consider it inappropriate to continue to use the caption "Accumulated Depreciation" for the account.

Incidentally, the group method is not confined to identical assets, or assets having the same useful life. A group can include a diverse set of assets, with quite different lives: for example, all of the machinery and equipment at a plant might be included in one group. In that event, the average useful life of the asset mix is computed, and applied to the group total cost less the total estimated salvage (which may often be ignored in such cases).

PROBLEMS

Problem 9.4A. Upon its organization at the beginning of year one, Red Cab, Inc. acquired five identical cabs for $27,500 apiece. The estimated useful life of the cabs was five years, and the expected salvage value was $2,500 per cab. At the close of year two, Red Cab sold one of its cabs for $10,000, and obtained a new cab for $30,000. Since the corporation used the group method of depreciation for its cabs, it charged the entire cost of the old cab less the cash proceeds to Accumulated Depreciation. After the sale of the old cab and the purchase of the new one, Red Cab's balance sheet at the close of year two appeared as follows:

Red Cab, Inc.
Balance Sheet

As of the End of Year Two

Assets		Liabilities & Equity	
Cash	$30,000	Accounts Payable	$17,500
Supplies	2,000		
Cabs	140,000		
Less: Accumulated		Common Stock	100,000
Depreciation	(32,500)	Retained Earnings	22,000
Total	$135,500	Total	$139,500

Under a statute which permits dividends "only out of net assets in excess of capital," how large a dividend could Red Cab, Inc. legally pay? (Consider what Red Cab's balance sheet would have looked like if the company had used the unit method of depreciation, and whether that is relevant in answering the foregoing question.)

Problem 9.4B. Consider whether each of the following statements is true or false:

(1) Under the group method of depreciation, an asset may be depreciated for longer than its useful life.

(2) Under the group method of depreciation, an asset may be depreciated for more than its actual cost.

Problem 9.4C. AB Co. uses the group method of depreciation. One group consists of 100 machines, with no expected salvage value, depreciated at a rate of ten percent per annum. The total cost of the group is $200,000. At the end of the most recent fiscal year, twenty of the machines were one year old, twenty were five years old, thirty were ten years old, and thirty were fifteen years old. What entry should the company record for depreciation on this group for the year? Would you have any comment to make to the company? In considering the latter question, assume for simplicity that (1) all of the machines in this group are identical, (2) the cost of these machines has remained stable at $2,000 throughout the fifteen year period, and (3) the units in the group are all the machines of this type that the company has ever owned. In these circumstances, what amount would appear in the Accumulated Depreciation account? Can you determine what that figure would be if instead the company had started with 100 such machines in the group fifteen years ago and had maintained 100 machines in operation continuously throughout the fifteen year period?

6. ACCELERATED METHODS

Way back in 1947, the Committee on Accounting Procedure suggested in ARB No. 33, which in 1953 became Chapter 9 of ARB No. 43, that enterprises could use depreciation methods other than straight-line if the asset's expected economic usefulness justified the method. This pronouncement led numerous companies to experiment with accelerated depreciation, which allocates a greater share of an asset's total cost to the earliest years of its life when the asset enjoys the greatest, or at least most predictable, usefulness. These efforts ultimately led to more formal "declining charges" methods, under which the depreciation charge is highest in the first year and declines progressively each year thereafter.

The initial incentive for accelerated depreciation seems to have stemmed in large part from the inflation that followed World War II. Since straight-line depreciation on original cost would total far less than the cost of replacing the tangible assets when the time came, some businesses sought to base their annual depreciation charges on the current replacement cost of the asset. While there was some suggestion that this would produce a more meaningful "bottom line", or net income figure, it is quite likely that a primary goal was to obtain a larger depreciation deduction for tax purposes, thereby lowering the amount of taxable income and hence the tax burden. However, the effort to deduct depreciation based upon current replacement costs failed on both fronts. The formal rejection for GAAP came in the above ARB No. 33, which insisted upon "adhering to the generally accepted concept of depreciation on cost", while proposals to amend the tax laws never got off the ground. However, the apparent invitation to use accelerated depreciation was enthusiastically received, since that too leads to larger depreciation charges, though based upon newly acquired assets rather than older assets purchased at the lower costs of an earlier day.

A number of reasons were advanced in support of accelerated depreciation methods. One was the fact that annual maintenance costs usually rise as an asset grows older. Therefore, declining depreciation charges result in the total expenses associated with an asset remaining reasonably level over the asset's useful life. Another justification suggested is that heavier depreciation charges at the outset tend to correspond with the decline in the realizable value of the asset, which is usually greatest in the earliest years of use: having the book value figures on the balance sheet correspond as closely to value as possible is viewed as desirable, though of course it is acknowledged that depreciation accounting does not seek to reflect diminution in realizable value as such. Finally, there is the point that most decisions about expansion of capacity, and maybe even ordinary replacement, are made on the basis of relatively short-term needs, because projections beyond that are regarded as too speculative to be useful. Since the anticipated benefits are more certain in the earliest years, it is appropriate to allocate a greater portion of the total cost of the asset to those years.

Accelerated depreciation received a substantial boost in 1954, and provided the much-desired tax relief, when Congress approved declining charges methods for tax purposes in the Internal Revenue Code. Shortly thereafter, the Committee on Accounting Procedure added its official imprimatur of approval to declining charges methods of depreciation as follows:

> The declining-balance method is one of those which meets the requirements of being "systematic and rational." In those cases where the expected productivity or revenue-earning power of the asset is relatively greater during the earlier years of its life, or where maintenance charges tend to increase during the later years, the declining-balance method may well provide the most satisfactory allocation of cost. The conclusions of this bulletin also apply to other methods, including the "sum-of-the-years'-digits" method, which produce substantially similar results.

Accounting Research Bulletin No. 44, *Declining-Balancing Depreciation,* ¶

2 (Committee on Accounting Procedure, AICPA 1954) (revised in 1958 and superseded in 1987 in connection with accounting for differences in tax treatment not here material).

The two most commonly used accelerated depreciation systems are the "sum-of-the-years'-digits" method, and the "declining-balance" method.

a. SUM-OF-THE-YEARS'-DIGITS

The sum-of-the-years'-digits method produces a decreasing depreciation charge as a function of a decreasing fraction of the depreciation base (historical cost minus salvage value). The denominator of the fraction remains constant throughout, being equal to of the sum of the useful life years: for example, for an asset with a four year useful life, the denominator for the fraction is 10 (4+3+2+1); for longer useful lives a helpful formula is n(n+1)/2, which in our instant case would produce 4(4+1)/2 = 10.

For the numerator, the fraction uses the number of remaining years of useful life (including the then current one). For example, in year 1 of a four-year useful life the numerator is four. So the fraction for year 1 is 4/10ths, for year 2 its 3/10ths, year 3 is 2/10ths, and year 4 gets the remaining 1/10th. The applicable depreciation charge is the product of the appropriate fraction for the year times the depreciation base (historical cost minus salvage value). Upon making the final calculation in year 4, the end of the asset's useful life, the balance remaining (cost less accumulated depreciation) should equal the estimated salvage value. For that four-year asset acquired by the Trahan Co., back on page 550, *supra*, the sum-of-the-years'-digits calculations for depreciation over the four year useful life would be $4,000 for year 1, $3,000 for year 2, $2,000 for year 3, and $1,000 for year 4.

b. DECLINING-BALANCE METHOD

The declining-balance method also involves decreasing depreciation charges, this time utilizing a constant depreciation rate, one substantially higher than the straight-line rate, but applied to a declining depreciation base. For example, a common declining-balance rate is 150% of the straight-line rate: for an asset with a four year useful life that would be 1.5 times 25%, or 37.5%. Similarly, the so-called double-declining, or 200 percent, rate for the same asset would be twice the 25% straight-line rate, or 50%. While the rate remains constant, the depreciation base declines each year, by the amount of depreciation taken that year. In other words, each year's recognized depreciation reduces the depreciation base, so the constant rate produces lower depreciation charges in each successive year.

An important special feature of the declining-balance method is that, unlike the previously described methods, the depreciation base of the asset, to which the declining-balance rate is applied, is equal to the full original cost, unreduced by salvage value. The declining-balance calculation continues until that depreciation base has been reduced to the estimated salvage value, at which time depreciation accounting ceases with respect to that asset.

Applying the 150 percent declining depreciation rate (37.5%) to that four-year-asset acquired by the Trahan Co., which cost $12,000, and had an estimated salvage value of $2,000, we get the following:

Year	Calculation	Depreciation Expense	Remaining Balance
Starting Point: Cost			$12,000.00
1	$12,000.00 x 37.5%	$4,500.00	7500
2	$7,500.00 x 37.5%	2812.5	4687.5
3	$4,687.50 x 37.5%	1757.82	2929.68
4	$2,929.68 x 37.5%	929.68	2000
	Total	$10,000.00	

You will note that because depreciation cannot reduce the remaining balance below the $2,000 salvage value, depreciation expense for Year 4 is limited to $929.68, rather than the $1,098.63 which $2,929.68 x 37.5% would have produced.

Similarly, we could apply the double-declining depreciation rate (50%) to Trahan Co. as follows:

Year	Calculation	Depreciation Expense	Remaining Balance
Starting Point: Cost			$12,000.00
1	$12,000.00 x 50%	$6,000.00	6000.00
2	$6,000.00 x 50%	3000.00	3000.00
3	$3,000.00 x 50%	1000.00	2000.00
4	$2,000.00 x 50%	-0-	2000.00
	Total	$10,000.00	

Once again, note that because depreciation cannot drop the remaining balance below the $2,000 salvage value, depreciation expense for Year 3 is limited to $1,000, rather than the $1,500 which $3,000 x 50% would have produced. And, of course, because the entire depreciation base of $10,000 has been used up in Years 1, 2 and 3, Trahan Co. cannot take any depreciation on this asset in Year 4.

PROBLEMS

Problem 9.5A. On January 1, Year 1, the Evans Corporation purchased a new machine for $350,000. The new machine has an estimated useful life of five years and an estimated salvage value of $50,000. Determine the amount of depreciation for Years 1 through 5 and show supporting computations under each of the following depreciation methods:

(1) Straight-line   (2) Sum-of-the-Years'-Digits
(3) 150% Declining Balance   (4) 200% Declining Balance

Problem 9.5B. On January 1, Year 1, Action Corporation purchased a new machine for $160,000. The new machine has an estimated useful life of ten years and an estimated salvage value of $10,000. Determine the amount of depreciation for Years 1 through 3 and show supporting computations under each of the following depreciation methods:

    (1) Straight-line   (2) Sum-of-the-Years'-Digits
    (3) 150% Declining Balance   (4) 200% Declining Balance

7. ILLUSTRATION OF THE EFFECTS OF THE DIFFERENT DEPRECIATION METHODS ON DEPRECIATION EXPENSE

To recap, the different depreciation methods produce different amounts for depreciation expense in the accounting periods of the asset's useful life. The following chart summarizes the timing differences in our relatively simple example:

Year	Straight Line Method	Sum-of-the-Years'-Digits Method	150% Declining Balance	200% Declining Balance
1	$2,500	$ 4,000	$ 4,500	$ 6,000
2	2500	3000	2813	3000
3	2500	2000	1758	1000
4	2500	1000	929	-0-
Totals	$10,000	$10,000	$10,000	$10,000

As you can as see, the selection of a depreciation method can significantly affect the financial statements and especially net income for a particular accounting period.

     As a general rule, an enterprise's management prefers to report as much net income as possible to the enterprise's owners for financial accounting purposes, which means that we would expect enterprises to use the straight-line method to avoid having the larger depreciation expenses which a declining charges method would produce in the accounting periods immediately following a capital expenditure. The AICPA's annual survey of the accounting practices followed in 600 annual reports confirms that almost all of the companies in the study used the straight-line depreciation method for financial accounting purposes. As the following chart indicates, however, some companies used more than one method:

Number of Companies

	1994	1993	1992	1991
Straight-line.................................	573	570	564	558
Declining balance............................	27	26	26	28
Sum-of-the-years'-digits..................	9	9	12	8
Accelerated method–not specified...	49	56	62	70
Units-of-production........................	49	46	47	50
Other...	11	9	5	7

American Institute of Certified Public Accountants, Accounting Trends & Techniques 386 (49th ed. 1995).

When drafting and negotiating agreements and legal documents implicating the income statement, the accounting estimates and method or methods for computing depreciation will likely represent very important variables. A lawyer should keep in mind that, in management's discretion, a single enterprise could use a number of different methods for computing depreciation for financial accounting purposes and, as described below, still others for tax purposes. To illustrate, an enterprise may depreciate some assets on an accelerated basis, while using the straight-line method to depreciate others. As another example, an enterprise could assign disparate useful lives to similar leasehold improvements located in different premises, based upon the length of the company's leases. In addition, management may revise various accounting estimates. As a result, an agreement does well to establish some basic guidelines for computing depreciation. So, a profit-sharing agreement might require the enterprise to compute depreciation on a straight-line basis, using useful lives based upon a specified schedule, such as five years for motor vehicles, ten years for machinery and equipment, and forty years for buildings. In addition, the agreement could restrict the enterprise's ability to change accounting estimates. Many agreements attempt to address this issue by stating that the enterprise will compute depreciation on a basis consistent with past practices. Such language, however, does not adequately resolve issues which may arise when the enterprise purchases assets different in kind from those which the enterprise has previously utilized.

Problem 9.6. D Corp. is a manufacturer of pollution control equipment, with its plant located in the Northeast. A couple of years ago, in anticipation of a likely increase in demand for its products, at least in the near term, D decided to expand its operations and undertook construction of a new facility in the Southeast, which would have approximately half the capacity of its existing plant . The new plant cost $2,500,000 and was expected to have a twenty-year life, with no salvage value; it was completed just in time for operations to get underway in earnest at the beginning of D's most recent fiscal year, which ended about one month ago. D's Northeastern plant was built fifteen years ago, at a cost of $3,000,000, and its estimated useful life was twenty years, with no salvage value.

D's management has taken note of the sixty-seven percent increase in the cost of adding to its plant capacity, and has accordingly decided that the depreciation on the Northeastern plant for the year just ended should be based on the estimated current replacement coast of $5,000,000 rather than its $3,000,000 actual cost, producing depreciation expense for the year on that plant of $250,000 instead of $150,000. In addition, the management decided to charge extra depreciation on the new plant of three percent per year for each of the first three years of useful life, because of the expected intensive use of the new plant for at least that long; that made the depreciation expense on the new plant $200,000 for the year just ended.

Partly as a result of this additional depreciation expense, D's operating results for the year were somewhat disappointing, with net income at only $600,000, down from almost $1,000,000 the year before. However, there were other reasons for this sharp decline in profitability. Although D's production during the year was at record levels, fully utilizing the added capacity of the new plant, there was a distinct softening in the price for D's products, engendered by a considerable increase in competition from the entry of a number of new firms into the industry. Thus D was able to maintain its share of a growing market only by accepting significantly lower prices and profit margins.

D has outstanding 100,000 shares of preferred stock, which are subject to an Article provision calling for dividends of up to $8 per share to be paid each year, but only if, and to the extent, earned. The Article provision also recites that D's "earnings shall be determined for each year in accordance with currently accepted accounting principles, after making all necessary charges for consumption of resources and other costs accrued and losses incurred during the year."

Assume that D's figures for the year would show the following:

Income before Depreciation		$1,050,000
Less:		
Regular Depreciation on Old Plant	$150,000	
Regular Depreciation on New Plant	125,000	275,000
Income before Extra Depreciation		$ 775,000
Less:		
Extra Depreciation on Old Plant	$ 100,000	
Extra Depreciation on New Plant	75,000	175,000
Net Income		$ 600,000

(1) The directors of D have announced that the dividend on the preferred stock for the year just ended will be $6 per share, and a group of preferred stockholders has consulted your law office as to whether they are

entitled to a larger dividend. (In advising them, keep in mind the possible implications of GAAP rules on accounting changes, noted earlier in this Chapter, and discussed more fully at pages 259-263, *supra*.)

(2) Suppose that instead of attempting to charge extra depreciation expense on both of its plants, D charged only the normal depreciation on the old plant, but adopted the declining balance method of depreciation (using double the straight-line rate) on the new plant. How would the preferred stockholders make out in those circumstances?

E.   TAX DEPRECIATION AND DEFERRED INCOME TAXES

Consistent with its desire to report as much net income as possible to the enterprise's owners for financial accounting purposes, management wants to keep taxable income, and hence income taxes, as low as possible. By using accelerated depreciation for tax purposes and straight-line depreciation for financial accounting purposes, an enterprise's management can usually accomplish these twin objectives. Unlike the Internal Revenue Code's conformity requirement which requires an enterprise to use LIFO for financial accounting purposes if it wants to be able to adopt that method for tax purposes, no such rule limits the selection of different depreciation methods for tax and financial accounting purposes.

For federal income tax purposes, the Modified Accelerated Cost Recovery System ("MACRS") in section 168 of the Internal Revenue Code sets forth the current rules for depreciating most tangible assets used in a trade or business or held for investment. Section 168(b)(4) treats the salvage value for all such property as zero; establishes its own set of useful lives for various types of assets, under the rubric of "applicable recovery period;" and adopts certain conventions for dealing with the acquisition and retirement of assets in the midst of a taxable year. To encourage economic growth and investment, section 168(c)(1) specifies recovery periods significantly shorter than most assets' expected useful lives. Those periods range from three years for certain race horses to fifty years for railroad grading or tunnel bores. Under section 168(b), the applicable recovery period generally determines the depreciation method. As a general rule, taxpayers can depreciate property having recovery periods which do not exceed ten years under the 200 percent declining-balance method, switching to the straight-line method when straight-line produces a larger deduction. If the recovery period does not exceed twenty years, taxpayers can use the 150 percent declining balance method, again switching to straight line when advantageous to do so. MACRS requires taxpayers to use the straight-line method to depreciate real property and related improvements. Finally, the applicable convention determines how much depreciation a taxpayer may claim in the years in which the taxpayer places an asset in service and retires the property from service. As a general rule, MACRS requires that for personal property taxpayers use the half-year convention, which treats all property placed in service during any taxable year as having started on the mid-point of the year, thus giving taxpayers a half-year's depreciation on any depreciable personal property placed in service or sold during the year. Real property is subject to the mid-month convention, which gives a taxpayer a half-month's depreciation on any real property placed in service or sold during the month.

An important complication, however, arises from using accelerated depreciation for tax purposes and straight-line for financial accounting. As we have seen, in the early years the depreciation expense for tax purposes will be larger than for financial accounting; but since the total depreciable amount for any asset is obviously the same for both, necessarily in later years the depreciation expense for tax purposes under the accelerated method will be less than for financial accounting under straight-line. For example, assuming that Trahan Co.'s four-year asset referred to earlier was acquired at the very beginning of a year, we know that the straight-line depreciation each year would be $2,500, whereas under the sum-of-the-years'-digits for tax purposes (ignoring, for arithmetic simplicity, the half-year convention referred to in the previous paragraph), the annual depreciation expense would be $4,000, $3,000, $2,000 and $1,000 successively. So the excess of accelerated depreciation over straight-line in the first two years is reversed in the last two. The differences each year are even more dramatic under the declining-balance method, particularly when using 200% of straight-line, which we saw would produce depreciation expense of $6,000, $3,000, $1,000 and $0 for the four years successively.

The more important point is the effect this difference in depreciation rates can have on the reported net income figure for financial accounting purposes. To illustrate, assume that the four-year asset Trahan Co. acquired generates $7,500 of income each year, after deduction of all expenses other than depreciation and taxes, and that the company pays income taxes at a forty percent rate. In the following table, the first column shows the net income from the asset for the first year for financial accounting purposes, assuming that straight-line depreciation is used for tax as well as financial accounting, so that the company's taxable income would be $5,000 ($7,500 minus depreciation of $2,500),and its tax expense at the 40% rate would be $2,000. The second column shows the net income for financial accounting if the company uses sum-of-the-years'-digits depreciation for tax purposes, so that its taxable income would be $3,500 ($7,500 minus depreciation of $4,000), and its tax expense at 40% would be $1,400.

	Straight-Line Deprec. For Tax	Accel. Deprec. for Tax
Income before Depreciation and Taxes	$7,500	$7,500
Less: Depreciation	2,500	2,500
Income before Taxes	$5,000	$5,000
Less: Income Taxes	2,000	1,400
Net Income	$3,000	$3,600

At first blush, the second column would seem to be perfectly sensible, because that is what actually happened -- the company's tax bill for the year was only $1,400. But remember that in the future, years 3 and 4 to be specific, the company's taxable income will exceed its accounting income, so the company will be paying more tax than it would have in those years if straight-line depreciation had been adopted for tax purposes from the beginning. In effect, by allowing a taxpayer to use accelerated depreciation for tax purposes while the taxpayer is applying straight-line for financial accounting, the Government is enabling the enterprise to defer some of its income tax expense to a later accounting period — really the equivalent of an interest-free loan. Accordingly, we must consider whether for financial accounting purposes the additional taxes which are expected in later years would more appropriately be reflected in the earlier years, where they would have been incurred but for the legislative policy decision allowing the taxpayer to defer payment, and where they would be consistent with the lower depreciation and higher net income being shown on the company's accounting statements in those earlier years. It is no bar to an affirmative answer that the company does not actually owe any additional tax in those earlier years, since, as we have often seen, the accrual process is readily available for recognizing an expense not only before it is paid but even before it has been incurred. On the other hand, we must also take into account the possibility that because of changes in the tax law, or other circumstances which will be described shortly, those additional taxes will never in fact be incurred.

1. INTRA-PERIOD TAX ALLOCATION

It may help to lay a basis for dealing with the question of allocating tax expense from a later period to an earlier one to look first at the simpler issue involved in allocating tax expense within the same period. Consider the case of L Corp., with income before taxes for the year in the amount of $5,000,000. Assuming a tax rate of forty percent, L's taxes for the year would be $2,000,000, and its net income would be $3,000,000. Suppose that during the year L suffers a catastrophe resulting in the loss of property carried on L's books at $1,000,000, for which there is no insurance. This loss would be reflected by a credit eliminating the property and a debit to some "Loss" account, which, as we have seen, is akin to an expense account and would be closed to Profit and Loss. As a result, L's income before taxes for the year would be $4,000,000, and, assuming the loss would also be deductible for tax purposes, L's taxes would be $1,600,000. But suppose that for accounting purposes this catastrophic loss qualified for extraordinary item treatment under APB No. 30: then on L's income statement the loss should be shown separately from the income from regular operations, so that a user of the financial statements can get a picture of how the enterprise would have fared without this unusual and non-recurring item. The theory of separating out such extraordinary items, it may be recalled, is that the user may be helped to make a more meaningful comparison of this year's performance with that of prior years (in which, presumably, such a loss did not occur), or to make a judgment about the prospects of the enterprise in future years (in which in all likelihood such a loss will not occur).

How should L's income statement portray this data? There are two obvious possibilities:

(a)

Income before Extraordinary Loss and Taxes	$5,000,000
Less: Extraordinary Loss	1,000,000
Income before Taxes	$4,000,000
Less: Taxes	1,600,000
Net Income	$2,400,000

(b)

Income before Extraordinary Loss and Taxes	$5,000,000
Less: Taxes	1,600,000
Income before Extraordinary Loss	$3,400,000
Less: Extraordinary Loss	1,000,000
Net Income	$2,400,000

Both of these approaches appear to separate out the extraordinary loss, and both of course reach the appropriate net income figure. In fact, however, neither one completely disengages the extraordinary item from the results of ordinary operations. Under alternative (a), the extraordinary loss is combined with the pretax income from ordinary operations, to produce the penultimate "Income before Taxes," from which the tax figure is then deducted. But the investor who wants to make some judgments about the future on the basis of how the enterprise fared during the current year in its ordinary operations will presumably want an after-tax figure in that regard, and will not find it readily available if alternative (a) is used.

Alternative (b) is even more troubling. Although it does purport to provide an after-tax figure for income before extraordinary items (which in effect is income from regular operations), that figure is of doubtful significance, if not downright misleading, because it is based upon a tax figure which is substantially affected by the existence of the extraordinary loss, being $400,000 lower than it would have been had no such loss occurred. In other words, the extraordinary item, though reflected separately itself, is still exerting a significant impact upon the after-tax income from regular operations because of the tax effects of the extraordinary loss; the result is a figure for after-tax income from regular operations which is not indicative of how the company would have performed in the absence of such an extraordinary loss.

What seems called for is an approach which will separate out not only the extraordinary loss itself but also its related tax effect, and associate that tax effect directly with the extraordinary item. As already mentioned on page 255, *supra*, that is exactly what GAAP does, in requiring that extraordinary items be listed on the income statement "net of tax" — that is, in the case of a loss, decreased by the tax saving, and if a gain, decreased by the tax burden. Thus, L Corp.'s income statement would appear as follows:

(c)

Income before Taxes and Extraordinary Loss	$5,000,000
Less: Taxes	2,000,000
Income before Extraordinary Loss	$3,000,000
Less: Extraordinary Loss, net of tax	600,000
Net Income	$2,400,000

But, perhaps not surprisingly, even this approach has its drawbacks. For example, looking just at presentation (c), would a reader readily discern what the gross loss suffered by L Corp. was? Is that an important figure? How about L's actual tax for the year?

2. INTER-PERIOD TAX ALLOCATION

Now let us return to the issue of whether the additional tax expense expected in later years under accelerated depreciation should be accrued to the earlier years. The argument is that, in a sense, from an accounting point of view that is where the added taxes belong, to be consistent with the straight-line depreciation and resulting higher net income being reflected for accounting purposes, and that is where the added taxes would have been incurred were it not for the legislative policy allowing deferral of these taxes, through the medium of accelerated depreciation. As we saw, the company only owes $600 in tax for year 1, although its financial accounting net income of $5,000 (on the basis of depreciation expense of $2,500, rather than the $4,000 taken for tax purposes) would seem to call for income tax of $2,000. Similarly, in year 2 the company will take $3,000 of depreciation expense for tax purposes, but only $2,500 for financial accounting, so its actual tax bill will be $200 (40% tax rate x $500) less than might be expected. However, in some future year or years the company's taxable income will exceed its income for financial accounting purposes by a total of $2,000, due to depreciation expenses for tax purposes in those future years totaling less than depreciation expenses for financial accounting. Assuming for simplicity that the current forty percent tax rate will apply to all future periods, that will result in additional tax of $800. But that amount of tax was really postponed from Years 1 and 2, and to be consistent with the lower depreciation expense and higher net income shown on the financial accounting statements in those years, $600 in additional taxes really "belongs" in Year 1, and $200 belongs in Year 2. Accordingly, it makes sense for the company to accrue those amounts as income tax expense, just as the company would record any other expense which it has in effect incurred but not paid. In other words, for financial accounting purposes the income tax expense for Year 1 should reflect not only the $1,400 in income taxes that Trahan Co. actually owes now, but also the $600 in additional taxes which the tax laws allow the company to defer currently, but which the company faces in future years when depreciation for financial accounting purposes exceeds tax depreciation; and similarly, the income tax expense for Year 2 should reflect an additional $200. So, Trahan Co. would record the following entry to reflect income tax expense and income taxes payable for Year 1:

Income Tax Expense	$2,000	
Income Taxes Payable		$1,400
Deferred Income Tax Liability		600

The credit to a Deferred Income Tax Liability account is necessary to offset the added debit to tax expense of $600, but this liability does not reflect a present obligation to pay taxes to the Government. The enterprise's future taxable income (and the then applicable tax rate) will determine the amount the enterprise will actually owe as income taxes in the future. But it is important to note that if the enterprise continues to purchase new assets, either to expand its operations or to replace older property, with the resulting much higher depreciation on those new assets for tax purposes during the earliest years of useful life, the total depreciation for financial accounting purposes may never exceed tax depreciation, and the income tax deferral may never reverse itself. When that appears likely to be true, it is fair to question whether the additional tax expense and the deferred tax liability should have been reflected in the first place, but the current GAAP answer seems to be yes.

In the converse case, when taxable income exceeds income for financial accounting purposes, the enterprise in effect prepays taxes. That can occur because some expenses which can be accrued for financial accounting purposes cannot be deducted for tax purposes by virtue of stricter limitations under the tax laws. One example is the estimated cost of warranties which a manufacturer gives in connection with sales of its products. To illustrate, assume that Neiers Company earns $750,000 in income, after deduction of all expenses except for warranties and income taxes, but management concludes it is probable that in the future the company will incur warranty expenses of $250,000 related to that income. Assuming a forty percent tax rate, in the following table the first column shows the company's taxable income, without the warranty expenses, and the amount of income tax, while the second column shows the company's net income for financial accounting purposes, after deduction of both the warranty expenses and the income taxes:

	Tax Purposes	Financial Accounting
Income Before Warranty Expense	$750,000	$750,000
Less: Warranty Expense	–0–	250,000
Income Before Taxes	$750,000	$500,000
Income Taxes	300,000	300,000
Net Income		$200,000

The tax laws require Neiers Company to pay $300,000 in income taxes to the government even though the company's financial statements only seem to call for $200,000 of income tax expense. Should there be some special treatment for that extra $100,000? Remember that it is probable the company will incur the warranty expenses at some time in the future (since otherwise the contingent expense would not be recognized for financial accounting purposes either), and when that happens the company's income for financial accounting will exceed its taxable income, because the company has already subtracted the warranty expenses for financial accounting purposes. Assuming for simplicity that the forty percent tax rate continues indefinitely, and that Neiers Company will ultimately incur the entire $250,000 of warranty expenses, those expenses will be deductible for tax purposes, reducing the company's future income tax liability by $100,000. In other words, the tax laws that prevent deduction of the warranty expenses in the earlier year have, from a financial accounting point of view, forced the company to prepay $100,000 in income taxes. Therefore, to achieve the proper matching for financial accounting purposes the company should defer this amount, just as the company would defer any prepaid expense item. In other words, for financial accounting purposes, the $300,000 in income taxes payable for the year should reflect that $200,000 is a current income tax expense, and $100,000 is a prepayment of taxes, which accountants often describe as a *deferred tax asset*. Under these assumptions, Neiers Company would record the following entry to reflect income tax expense and income taxes payable for the current year:

Income Tax Expense	$200,000	
Deferred Tax Asset	100,000	
Income Taxes Payable		$300,000

Notice that this deferred income tax asset is rather soft, a far cry from, say, a deferred insurance expense asset, which represents the right to continued insurance protection, as well as a right to a refund if the insurance is canceled. Here, the projected prepayment of tax may never be realized, perhaps because the accrued contingent warranty expenses do not actually materialize, or the tax rates change. At this point, it is enough for us to observe that accounting for deferred income taxes represents one of the most complex and controversial issues in accounting. *See generally, Accounting for Income Taxes*, Statement of Financial Accounting Standards No. 109 (FASB 1992).

Problem 9.7. Suppose the following in Problem 9.6 on page 560-561, *supra*: (1) D Corp. had leased the building housing its new plant, and had spent the $2,500,000 on the purchase and installation of new machinery and equipment, which was to be depreciated as a group with an average useful life of ten years, and no expected salvage value; (2) D adopted 200% declining-balance depreciation for tax purposes, while using the straight-line method for regular financial accounting; (3) D's overall corporate income tax rate is 40%; and (4) D's income before any income taxes, and before depreciation on the new machinery and equipment, but after deduction of regular depreciation on the old plant plus all other expenses for the year, is $1,400,000. How much would be due the preferred stockholders for the year? How much would D's dividend-paying ability be increased for the year, under a corporate statute which permits dividends "out of net assets in excess of capital"?

NOTE ON DEPLETION

Accounting for depletion is a complicated and specialized subject and no attempt at full treatment will be made here. In a nutshell, as defined earlier, depletion allocates the costs of natural resources among the accounting periods in which an enterprise consumes those wasting assets such as oil and gas reserves, mineral deposits and timber rights. Like depreciation of long-lived assets, depletion seeks to spread the costs of the assets among the future accounting periods that will benefit from those expenditures. However, since the natural resources are physically consumed, depletion uses a system akin to the units-of-production depreciation method described above, with the capitalized costs allocated among the periods in proportion to the amount of the resources consumed. The enterprise estimates the total number of recoverable units from the particular wasting asset and divides that number into the total of the capitalized costs, which includes acquisition, exploration costs in some cases, and development costs, to obtain a per unit depletion cost. Each period's depletion expense is computed by multiplying the number of units withdrawn during the period by the unit depletion cost.

For enterprises like oil and gas companies which must undertake exploration or other costly activity in order to locate desired wasting assets, there is a special problem in dealing with the costs of unsuccessful efforts, like drilling wells which produce no oil. The choice is between capitalizing expenditures for unsuccessful exploration or development as part of the costs of successful endeavors, often referred to as the "full cost" method, or writing off unsuccessful efforts immediately, called the "successful efforts" method.

F. INTANGIBLES

As we have seen, accounting for intangible assets like deferred expenses can be the same as for tangibles: allocation of the cost over the asset's useful life, i.e., the duration of the expected future benefits from the underlying expenditure (though for intangibles this process is called "amortization" rather than depreciation). Indeed, accounting for intangibles may be easier, because, it maybe recalled, for many intangible assets the useful life is a specific period, fixed either by contract, as in the case of a deferred expense asset like insurance, or by statute, as for a patent, so no estimation is necessary (and there is usually no need to worry about a salvage value at the end). But when that is not true - when the useful life of a possible intangible asset cannot be readily determined as a function of the passage of time or otherwise, whether because it is not clear that the prospective future benefits will last beyond the current period at all, and if so, for how long, or, at the opposite end of the spectrum, because the benefits might last indefinitely since no foreseeable termination date appears – the accounting treatment becomes more problematical.

To understand the current accounting treatment of intangibles, we need to review Accounting Principles Board Opinion No. 17, *Intangible Assets* (1970), which divided intangible assets between the two categories, "identifiable" and "unidentifiable". Identifiable intangibles include intellectual property like patents and trademarks; deferred expense assets like prepaid insurance; computer software developments; and similar items that exist separately from a business's other assets, and have a definable and measurable relation to the company's operations. Most of these rights and property interests could be transferred in a sale apart from the other assets of the business, or perhaps surrendered for a refund. Unidentifiable intangibles, in contrast, include those elements of value which are inherent in a continuing enterprise or relate to it generally, and cannot normally be separated from the business as a whole. The prototype, and most important, unidentifiable intangible is goodwill: traditionally, goodwill has included any one or more of the many amorphous factors which contribute to the competitive advantage that a business may enjoy. Examples would be strong product acceptance, effective management, solid relationships with suppliers, and a loyal employee base. We will take a closer look at the current status of goodwill shortly.

The primary object of APB Op. No. 17 was to posit two important elements in the accounting treatment of unidentifiable intangibles, particularly goodwill: (1) any costs incurred internally in developing or enhancing an unidentifiable intangible can not be capitalized, that is deferred, to create an asset, but must instead be treated as current expenses; and (2) the cost of acquiring an unidentifiable intangible from a third party should be recorded as an asset, and then amortized over its estimated useful life if one could be determined, but in any event no more than forty years.

Op. No. 17 also dealt with specifically identifiable intangible assets, providing that the costs of developing them internally can be either capitalized or charged to current expense, in the company's discretion (subject to the principle of consistency). As to any identifiable intangible asset so created, or resulting from an acquisition from a third party, here too amortization over the useful life was required, with a maximum period of forty years.

In 2001 the accounting treatment of intangible assets was substantially rewritten by two FASB Statements of Financial Accounting Standards: SFAS Nos. 141, *"Business Combinations"*, and 142, *"Goodwill and Other*

Intangible Assets". To comprehend the significance of these rulings, we need to backtrack briefly to review the previous treatment of combination transactions, which SFAS No. 141 defines as transactions in which one entity acquires the net assets that constitute a business, or a controlling ownership in another enterprise. Of particular significance in this respect are transactions involving the acquisition of one enterprise by another where the consideration for the acquired assets consists of stock of the acquiror rather than cash (or debt): in effect, the owners of the formerly separate enterprises end up as shareholders of the resulting single corporation. The cost of the acquisition would be the fair market value of the stock issued in exchange for the acquired assets, which can be readily ascertained if the stock is publicly traded. (Otherwise, as in the case of a privately-held acquiror, especially a new or start-up enterprise, an effort could be made to determine the value of the business acquired, which in most arm's length deals should approximate the value of the consideration exchanged, and hence could serve as the cost figure.) No matter how the total cost of the acquisition is determined, it must then be allocated among the various types of assets acquired; since each type of assets plays a different role in the accounting process, each must have its own starting figure. For example, the amount allocated to inventory will likely turn into cost of goods sold expense in the current year; costs assigned to machinery and equipment will be expensed much more slowly, through depreciation over the useful life; and the same is true of any costs assigned to specifically identifiable intangible assets like the prepaid insurance or the intellectual property referred to above. The most sensible approach in allocating the costs is to rely upon the respective fair market values of the various assets acquired, since, at least in theory, it may be reasonable to assume that in an arm's length transaction the acquiror paid a price approximating the sum of the fair market values of the assets included. But of course in practice only rarely would the total price paid to acquire a going business equal the sum of the fair market values of the listed assets. When the price paid is less, the total is allocated among the assets on the basis of their relative fair market values, as illustrated on pages 547-548, *supra*. However, more commonly, the total price paid for an enterprise exceeds thetotal of the fair market values of the listed assets, including the identifiable intangible assets, and that is when that the paradigm unidentifiable intangible asset, goodwill, typically made its appearance: any excess of the total price paid over the sum of the fair market values of the tangible assets and identifiable intangibles constituted goodwill. Because goodwill is the most amorphous of assets (and usually the one quickest to evaporate if financial difficulty develops), the practice has been to allocate to each of the other assets the highest defensible market or replacement value, so that any excess of the total price paid will be as small as possible, allowing goodwill to be stated conservatively on the balance sheet.

Prior to SFAS No. 141, GAAP allowed combination transactions which met certain tests to be accounted for by a different method, under which the assets and liabilities of the acquired enterprise would be carried over to the joint balance sheet at the same figures at which they appeared on the acquired corporation's balance sheet — in other words, the figures for the acquired corporation's assets and liabilities were simply "pooled" with those of the acquiring company, and hence this method was known as "pooling of interests". The idea was to present the assets and liabilities of the acquired enterprise as they would have appeared if that company had been part of the acquiror from the outset, instead of recording them at current value as under the purchase method. The pooling of interests approach was much favored by most acquisition-minded enterprises, because it avoided the write-up of the assets of the acquired company plus the recognition of goodwill, which would have produced higher depreciation or amortization charges on the assets written up, plus a new asset, goodwill, which would have been subject to amortization. This put considerable pressure on the tests for eligibility for the pooling method, with acquirors straining to qualify, and the FASB formally concluded that pooling should be eliminated, with all combination transactions accounted for as purchases of one (or more) enterprises by another. As a corollary, probably designed mostly to make the elimination of pooling more palatable to prospective acquirors, SFAS No. 141 ended the mandatory amortization of any goodwill that might emerge in a combination transaction: instead, goodwill may be presumed at the outset to be of indefinite duration, but it must be analyzed at least annually to see if there has been any impairment in its value; if so, a write-down of the goodwill is required, with a change to current expense.

SFAS No. 141 also sought to distinguish more sharply between goodwill and other intangibles which might be recognized in connection with a combination transaction. In paragraph 39 the ruling sets out a twofold test which states that an intangible should be recognized as an asset on the balance sheet apart from goodwill (1) "if it arises from contractual or other legal rights (regardless of whether those rights are transferable or separable from the acquired entity or from other rights and obligations)", or (2) "if it is separable, that is, it is capable of being separated or divided from the acquired entity and sold, transferred, licensed, rented, or exchanged". Any acquired intangible that does not meet one of those two tests is to be included in the amount recognized as goodwill in the combination transaction.

SFAS No. 142 largely supersedes APB Op. No. 17, addressing the accounting at acquisition for intangible assets acquired individually, or with a group of assets (other than in a combination transaction since that was covered in SFAS No. 141), as well as the accounting after acquisition for all intangible assets, including goodwill. However, the new ruling does not affect the provisions of APB No. 17 dealing with accounting for the costs of internally developed intangible assets: those provisions were not "reconsidered", and paragraph 10 of SFAS 142 expressly reconfirms APB No. 17 to the effect that "[C]osts of internally developing, maintaining, or restoring intangible assets (including goodwill) that are not specifically identifiable, that have indeterminate lives, or that are inherent in a continuing business and related to an entity as a whole, shall be recognized as an expense when incurred". As to costs incurred in internally developing specifically identifiable intangibles, SFAS No.142, in paragraphs 5 and B23, SFAS, follows, APB No. 17, accepts the existing practice under which such costs are capitalized by some entities, and expensed by others as incurred.

With respect to recognition of intangible assets upon acquisition, SFAS 142 provides flatly in paragraph 9 that the intangible asset known as goodwill can only arise in a combination transaction. At the same time, in paragraph B28 the ruling encourages focusing more types of intangible assets in non-combination transactions, relying in paragraphs B 34-36 particularly upon the same two categories referred to above as separate from goodwill in combination transactions, namely, intangibles which either arise from contractual or other legal rights, or can be separated from the entity by way of sale, exchange, etc. However, SFAS 142 also expressly contemplates in paragraph 37 the possibility that an intangible acquired either individually or with a group of assets (other than in a combination transaction) might qualify for recognition as an asset even if it does not meet either the contractual-legal criterion or the separability criterion, giving as one example specially-trained employees.

Going back to the accounting for costs incurred in the internal development of intangibles, since SFAS No. 142 provides no new guidance perhaps some could be found in prior pronouncements on the subject. The earliest one in point seems to be the "Interpretation" under Op. No. 17 published by the AICPA staff, which concluded that "the Opinion does not encourage capitalizing the costs of a large initial advertising campaign for a new product or capitalizing the costs of training new employees". AICPA Accounting Interpretation No. 1 of APB Opinion No. 17(1971). To be sure, such an Interpretation ranks only in the fourth level of the hierarchy of authoritative pronouncements on accounting principles summarized on page 146, *supra*, well below the top category (a) occupied by a formal FASB opinion; and anyway, the Interpretation of APB No. 17, as well as the Opinion itself, is said in paragraph D of SFAS 142 to be "superseded". On the other hand, there is nothing really inconsistent on this subject in SFAS 142, since the Statement did not reconsider the treatment of internally developed intangibles. Hence, an Interpretation of APB No. 17 could shed some useful light; but unfortunately, this one raises as many questions as answers. Was the language of the Interpretation meant at least to cast some doubt on the propriety of capitalizing costs of the type referred to, or should it be taken more literally, leaving the Opinion neutral on the subject and hence allowing the inference that capitalization of such costs is okay? And what about those two tests in SFAS No. 142 for recognizing intangibles separate from goodwill in a combination transaction: neither of the two types of expenditures referred to in the Interpretation would seem to satisfy either the contractual-legal test or the separability test. However, as noted in the preceding paragraph, SFAS 142 does recognize that an intangible acquired in a non-combination transaction might qualify for recognition even if it does not meet either of those two tests, and the example given of specially-trained employees is certainly reminiscent of the employee training costs mentioned in the Interpretation.

On the other hand, that suggestion of a possible third category of intangibles qualifying for asset recognition is made in reference to *acquisition* of intangibles, so the question is whether the same test might be applicable in determining when an intangible is sufficiently identifiable to allow deferral of costs incurred in developing it internally. A negative answer may be inferred from the observation in SFAS 142 that "bargained exchanges that are conducted at arms length provide reliable evidence about the existence and fair value of acquired intangible assets", evidence that is "not generally available" in the case of intangible assets developed internally. To be sure, the special training itself for employees might be "acquired" from an outside source, at a bargained-for cost, but that is a harder case for recognizing of specially trained employees as an intangible than say, purchasing the services of previously-trained and presumably experienced employees.

Advertising costs, the other item addressed in the APB Op. 17 interpretation, are the subject of a much more recent promulgation, the 1993 AICPA Statement of Position (SOP) 93-7, "Reporting on Advertising Costs", which took the view that advertising costs should not be deferred because the lack of certainty as to future benefits and the difficulty of measuring them made it inappropriate to record an asset. Instead, the ruling stated, advertising costs should be promptly expensed, either as soon as they are incurred or when the advertising is first displayed, that is, aired on television or run in a magazine or the like, whichever the enterprise prefers (and applies consistently). The costs of producing advertising are incurred during production, but the costs of communicating the advertising are not incurred until the enterprise has received the relevant item, like a film or video tape, or the service, like the actual use of television air time. The latter point seems designed to avoid expensing payments made in advance of production or receipt of the service; such an advance payment would seem to qualify readily for deferral until either production occurs or the service is rendered.

The fact that advance payment for such services as employee training or advertising which had not yet been rendered would be eligible for treatment as a deferred expense asset is certainly no surprise; indeed, it had already been expressly confirmed back in 1985, in FASB Concepts Statement No. 6 (SFAC No. 6), *Elements of Financial Statements*, paragraph 249. The provision also recognized the possibility that such costs might be accounted for as assets even after the services have been received, if there is sufficient promise of measurable future benefits (which is the key element in the definition of assets in paragraph 25 of SFAC No. 6):

> Costs incurred for service such as . . . training or advertising relate to future economic benefits in one of two ways. First, costs may represent right to unperformed services yet to be received from other entities. For example, advertising costs incurred may be for a series of advertisements to appear

in [the future]. Those kinds of costs incurred are similar to prepaid insurance or prepaid rent. They are payments in advance for services to be rendered to the entity by other entities in the future. Second, they may represent future benefit that is expected to be obtained within the entity by using assets. . . . For example, prerelease advertising of a motion picture may increase the future economic benefits of the product. . . .

Those kinds of costs can be accounted for as assets either by being added to other assets or by being disclosed separately.

However, SFAC No. 6, particularly in paragraphs 175 and 176, serves the warning that treatment as an asset maybe barred by uncertainty about the future benefits, and gives advertising and training, along with research and development, start-up activities, and goodwill, as examples where "assessments of future economic benefits may be especially uncertain". SOP 93-7 relies upon the uncertainty element noted in SFAC No. 6 (plus the related inability to demonstrate or measure those benefits with sufficient reliability, one of the required criteria for recognition of an item in the financial statements) in concluding that most advertising costs should not be carried as an asset after the services have been received. (There is also the general reminder in paragraph 255 of SFAC No. 6 that its examples "are intended to illustrate the definitions and related concepts, not to establish standards for accounting practice", which depend upon not only concepts but also practical considerations; hence, Statements of Financial Accounting Concepts rank near the bottom of the hierarchy of sources for Accounting standards.)

The emphasis in the 1971 Interpretation of APB No.17 on a "large, *initial* advertising campaign for a *new* product" could implicate another possible basis for creation of a deferred expense asset even though neither the contract-legal test nor the separability test is satisfied. When an enterprise makes expenditures in support of a new line of activity which has not yet actually been launched by the end of the period, and hence no revenues from it have yet been received, there is certainly an argument for not charging such costs to expense in the current period which has enjoyed no benefits, in favor of charges to future periods when the benefits of the new activity will be received. Such costs are often referred to as "start-up", and they present the usual questions about how certain it is that the expected future benefits will be received, and for how long they will last.

Hence, the argument for deferral would be strongest when the new activity has not only produced no revenues yet, but also involves creation of a tangible asset like a new plant, along with related collateral costs which could be amortized over the tangible asset's useful life. Perhaps that is the explanation for the suggestion in SFAC No. 6 that prerelease advertising for a movie could qualify for deferral, since any advertising prior to release obviously precedes any possible benefit byway of revenue, and the movie represents an asset to which the advertising costs can be attached. In any event, unless the new activity represents a major event in the life of the enterprise, going well beyond the new developments that regularly occur in all businesses, or is clearly directed to an identifiable expected future benefit, deferral would be inconsistent with the general principle from APB No. 17 that costs of self-developed intan gibles which are inherent in a going business can not be deferred.

There may also be a category of possible start-up costs which occur after the entity has started operating, but during the initial period of operation, when there are excess costs, especially for labor, in getting under way, such as for testing, debugging, training, etc. More recently, start-up costs were subjected to a stronger, express limitation by SOP 98-5, *Reporting on the Costs of Start-up Activities* (AICPA 1998), referred to in Note 1 on page 542, *supra*. This pronouncement rules out deferral of start-up costs, defined as those incurred in "one-time activities related to opening a new facility, introducing a new product or service, conducting business in a new territory [or] with a new class of customer, initiating a new process in an existing facility, or beginning some new operation"; specifically excepted, as might be expected, are such costs as acquiring or developing tangible assets, costs of acquiring intangible assets from third parties, and costs that are eligible to be capitalized as part of inventory, long-lived assets, or some internally- developed intangible asset.

Turning now to the accounting for an intangible asset after it is created, whether that occurs in an acquisition or pursuant to a permissible capitalization of the costs of internal development, under paragraph 11 of SFAS No. 142 the proper treatment turns on whether the asset has a finite life, that is, a reasonably estimable future period of contributing economic benefit: if it does, the intangible asset must be amortized over that life; if the life of the intangible asset is indefinite, that is, could last for the indefinitely foreseeable future, the asset is not subject to amortization, and instead, under paragraph 17, just like goodwill under SFAS 141, the intangible must be reviewed regularly for the possibility of impairment in value, i.e., a decline in current value to below the carrying figure for the asset. Although the process for determining the current value of the intangible for this purpose is somewhat different from the one used for testing goodwill for impairment, the end result is the same: the intangible is written down if the current value is below the carrying figure, with the loss recognized currently. An intangible asset originally determined to have an indefinite life must also be periodically checked to see if the life has become finite, in which case amortization should commence.

Intangible assets which are determined to have a finite life are also subject to periodic review to see if there has been an impairment in value below the current book value; if so, the asset is written down to the current value, the loss is recognized currently, and the new figure is amortized over the remainder of the asset's estimated useful life. (The process for measuring impairment in value of an intangible being amortized is slightly different from both the one used in connection with intangibles having an indefinite life and hence not being amortized, and the one used for goodwill, but these variations are not here material.) In addition, intangible assets being amortized must be regularly checked to see if the original finite life determination is no longer sound, either because of a change in the estimated life, in which event the amortization schedule must be adjusted, or because the life no longer appears to be finite, in which event amortization must cease, and the accounting treatment applicable to intangibles having an indefinite life would become applicable

PROBLEMS

Problem 9.8. Bio-Med, Inc. incurred $175,000 of research and development costs in its laboratory to develop a patent which the U.S. Patent Office granted on January 31, Year One. Legal fees and other costs associated with registration of the patent totaled $35,000. On October 31, Year One, Bio-Med, Inc. paid $50,000 for legal fees in a successful defense of the patent.

Through November 1, Year One, how much should Bio-Med capitalize for the patent? Explain briefly.

Problem 9.9. Ivy Clothes, a small successful haberdashery proprietorship, had the following balance sheet at the close of its most recent fiscal year.

[handwritten annotations: Goodwill 20K; Building Fixtures 75K; Inventory 105K; CASH 200K]

Ivy Clothes

Assets		Liabilities & Proprietorship	
Cash	$50,000	Accounts Payable	$50,000
Inventory	105,000		
Building Fixtures	65,000	Proprietorship	170,000
Total	$220,000	Total	$220,000

Suppose the proprietor pays off her liabilities and sells all the rest of the assets of her business to a newly-organized corporation, Ivy Corp., for $200,000. Ivy Corp. pays the $200,000 in cash, out of the proceeds of its initial stock issue of $240,000. How should Ivy Corp. record this acquisition on its books? If relevant, assume that an investigation would reveal that the inventory's current replacement cost approximates the $105,000 figure at which the inventory was carried on the proprietorship's books, but that it would cost $75,000 to replace the building fixtures in their current condition. How do these accounting decisions at the corporation's outset affect the determination of net income in the future?

Until SFAS No. 142, accounting literature identified two separate views about the nature of goodwill. The first view described goodwill as an intangible resource arising from a business's competitive advantages. Under the second view, goodwill reflected expected earnings which exceed a fair return on the assets invested in the business. Accounting for Business Combinations and Purchased Intangibles, FASB Discussion Memorandum 46-50 (1976).

These different viewpoints lead to distinct approaches for measuring goodwill. Lawyers should recognize that these alternative methods exist because the circumstances surrounding a particular legal problem may suggest using one approach rather than the other to resolve the matter, even though SFAS No. 142 has adopted the first approach. Under that method, which accountants have historically referred to as the *residual method*, if X Corp. pays $250,000 to acquire a business that owns identifiable assets worth $240,000, X would treat the residual amount, or the $10,000 difference between those two figures, as goodwill.

G. Lease Accounting

You will recall from our discussion of revenue recognition in Chapter VI that accountants focus on substance, rather than on form, in deciding how to treat various kinds of transactions. Questions about substance often arise when an enterprise obtains the right to use another's property in exchange for consideration. Even though a lessor-lessee relationship may be established legally by the agreement, if the transaction actually transfers substantially all the benefits and risks that accompany ownership, then GAAP may require that for financial accounting purposes the parties treat the "lease" as a purchase by the lessee, and either a sale or a financing by the lessor.

If an enterprise purchases an asset on credit, both the asset and the related liability appear on the balance sheet, and that is what treating a lease as a purchase would entail. If a "lessee" must include the underlying asset and corresponding liability on its balance sheet, such treatment can adversely affect various financial ratios, such as the debt-equity ratio, and could conceivably cause the enterprise to violate a financial covenant based on that ratio, or on tangible net book value. As we will see, lease accounting can also affect the lessee's net income in various accounting periods, particular the periods immediately after the parties sign the "lease."

1. CLASSIFICATION

Accountants generally classify leases into two basic categories for financial accounting purposes: *operating leases* and *capital leases*. Operating leases represent "true" leases, in which the lessor conveys the right to use property, whether land, machinery, equipment or other, for a stated period in exchange for some consideration. In contrast, capital leases represent an installment purchase in substance, that is, a transfer of substantially all the benefits and risks that accompany ownership, in which event the parties should treat the transaction as though the lessee acquired the property and incurred an offsetting liability. There have been a number of accounting pronouncements on lease accounting, which have been codified in an FASB publication, entitled "Accounting for Leases," as of 1998.

GAAP requires enterprises to classify leases at their inception. If, at that time, a noncancelable lease meets one or more of the following criteria, Statement of Financial Accounting Standards No. 13, *Accounting for Leases* (FASB 1976), requires the lessee to treat the arrangement as a capital lease:

(1) The lease transfers ownership of the property to the lessee.

(2) The lease contains a bargain purchase option.

(3) The lease term equals or exceeds seventy-five percent or more of the leased property's estimated economic life.

(4) The present value of the minimum lease payments, excluding insurance, maintenance, taxes and similar items, equals or exceeds ninety percent of the leased property's fair value.

If the beginning of the lease term occurs during the last twenty-five percent of the leased property's estimated economic life, GAAP does not use either the third or fourth criteria to classify the lease. In addition, the lessee generally uses its *incremental borrowing rate*, defined as the rate lenders would charge the lessee for a secured loan containing repayments terms similar to the payment schedule in the "lease," to determine the present value of the minimum lease payments under the fourth criterion.

2. TREATMENT OF LESSEES

If the transaction does not satisfy any of the four tests described above, then the lease qualifies as an operating lease. Lessees generally prefer to treat leases as operating leases for two reasons. First, an operating lease does not affect the lessee's balance sheet; for this reason, the business community sometimes refers to operating leases as "off-balance sheet financing." Second, under an operating lease the lessee simply charges rent payments to expense as incurred. With a capital lease, in contrast, the lessee must recognize depreciation expense as an "owner", *plus* interest expense as an installment "obligor" in connection with the deferred payments of the "purchase price" represented by the annual payments of rent, and the total of those two expenses will often be greater than the annual rent figure in the early years of the lease.

A lessee which wants to keep a lease off the balance sheet has a good deal of room for maneuver under the criteria used to decide between an operating lease and a capital lease. For example, the lessee could "overestimate" the asset's economic life, which reduces the chance that the lease term will exceed seventy-five percent of the asset's economic life. Alternatively, the lessee could overestimate the asset's fair market value, reducing the chance that the transaction will satisfy the "ninety percent test." And of course, the lessee may request a shorter lease term, making it less likely that the lessee will satisfy either the seventy-five or the ninety percent tests.

In the post-Enron effort to improve accounting standards, observers have increasingly criticized the accounting principles that govern leases, arguing that the ninety and seventy-five percent tests are examples of arbitrary accounting rules that obscure financial statements. In 2004, *The Wall Street Journal* reported that "off-balance sheet" commitments for operating leases totaled $482 billion for companies in the Standard & Poor's 500 stock index alone, an amount equal to eight percent of the $6.25 trillion that those same companies reported as debt on their balance sheets. In addition to keeping these obligations off balance sheets, operating leases increase returns on assets and typically boost earnings by lowering depreciation expenses. Shortly after *The Wall Street Journal* article, the International Accounting Standards Board unveiled plans to overhaul its rules on accounting for leased assets; query if the FASB will follow suit. *Group to Alter Rules on Lease Accounting*, WALL ST. J., Sept. 23, 2004, at C4.

As noted, GAAP requires lessees to account for capital leases following the rules applicable to purchases of assets on an installment payment basis. To illustrate, suppose for simplicity that the lease of an automobile for four years, with annual rent of $10,000 payable at the end of each of the next four years, is characterized as a capital lease. The transaction would be treated as though the vehicle has been purchased for consideration consisting of installment payments of $10,000 for each of the next four years. As we saw at pages 367-368, *supra,* that is not a purchase for $40,000, but rather a purchase for the present value of $10,000 per year for four years, at an appropriate rate of interest. Assuming the same interest rate as in that Chapter VI example, it would mean the real purchase price was $33,120, and the straight-line depreciation expense, on the basis of a four-year life and no salvage value, would be $8,280. In addition, there would be interest of $2,650 applicable to the first year of the lease, representing the interest portion of the first installment (the imputed interest rate of 8% x $33,120, the "true" principal balance outstanding during the first year). Thus, the total of the lessee's expenses for that year from the transaction would be $10,930, almost ten percent more than the annual rent of $10,000 which the lessee's expense for the year would be under operating lease characterization.

3. TREATMENT OF LESSORS

From the lessor's standpoint, accountants divide leases into three categories: *operating leases*, *sales-type leases* and *direct financing leases*. The initial rule governing lease accounting applicable to lessors is the same as for lessees, so if the lessor really has not transferred the risks and benefits related to ownership, it is not a capital lease, and the lessor should not remove the asset from its books. On the other hand, in some situations which do require capital lease treatment for the lessee, such treatment for the lessor is subject to additional barriers which mirror the revenue recognition requirements discussed in Chapter VI: GAAP requires the lessor to classify the lease as an operating lease if collectibility does not appear reasonably certain, or if the lessor has not substantially completed performance. For lessors, then, operating lease treatment is called for not only when the transaction does not satisfy any of the four criteria described in FASB No. 13, but also when collectibility is uncertain or performance has not been substantially completed.

If the transaction satisfies the requirements for capital lease treatment by the lessor, then the lessor will treat the lease as either a sales-type lease or a direct financing lease. The distinction between the two turns on whether a difference exists between the lessor's cost or book value and the leased property's fair market value at the lease's inception, which is presumably equal to the present value of the agreed-upon "rental" payments. The presence of a difference evidences a manufacturer's or dealer's profit or loss, which calls for treatment as a sales-type lease, whereas if there is no such difference, then there is no gain or loss, and that makes it a direct financing lease.

In a sales-type lease, the "lessor" recognizes revenue from the sale of the leased property, treating the annual rent as installment payments and allocating those receipts between periodic interest income and principal payments. In a direct financing lease, the lessor in effect becomes a lender, who simply recognizes interest income over the lease's term, using the effective interest method.

PROBLEMS

Problem 9.10A. The Loebl Corporation has signed an agreement to lease a $20,000 automobile from Fitzgerald Leasing Company for five years. Under the lease agreement, which implicitly contains a twelve percent annual interest rate, Loebl will make a $1,500 down payment and annual payments of $2,500 at the end of each year. At the end of the lease, Loebl can purchase the vehicle for $10,000. Fitzgerald estimates that the vehicle will last for eight years and will be worth $8,000 at the end of the lease. Can Loebl treat this lease as an operating lease? Explain briefly.

Problem 9.10B. On January 31, Year One, Morris Company leased a new machine from Graham Corp. At the inception of the ten year lease, which assumes a ten percent interest rate, compounded annually and requires $50,000 annual rental payments at the beginning of each year, the parties estimated that the machine had a fifteen year economic life and a

$400,000 fair market value. The lease did not contain a renewal option and provides that possession of the machine reverts to Graham Corp. when the lease terminates. At what amount, if any, should the machine appear on Morris Company's balance sheet? Explain briefly.

H. WRITE–DOWNS AND THE "BIG BATH"

Until now, our discussion of long-lived assets has focused on the historical cost model. Under that model, the balance sheet presents long-lived assets at net book value, usually their actual cost or fair market value at the date of acquisition less accumulated depreciation, depletion, or amortization. Recall that accumulated depreciation, depletion, or amortization reflect that portion of a long-lived asset's original cost that the enterprise has allocated to the accounting periods that already have benefitted from the asset's use. To this point, we have assumed a certain stability in long-lived assets.

In the historical cost system, an enterprise's balance sheet reflects an adherence to decades of reliance on basic historical cost principles and the modifying conventions, objectivity, consistency, and conservatism. Under this framework, long-lived assets remained on a balance sheet based on their original historic costs, unless an other-than-temporary decline in value occurred. For such non-temporary declines, an enterprise recorded an impairment in the asset's carrying value by debiting a loss account, such as *Loss Due to Equipment Obsolescence*, usually reported on the income statement in the Other Expenses and Losses section, and crediting either the asset account or the accumulated depreciation account for the asset involved. The enterprise would then allocate the remaining book value, less any estimated salvage value, to the future accounting periods that the enterprise then expected to benefit from the asset's use or consumption.

1. THE PROBLEM

Such write-downs appeared straightforward, except that no standards existed to determine when an impairment had occurred, and, if so, to assess whether it would last, or to measure the impairment. This subjective "I'll know it when I see it" standard lacked consistency and comparability, giving an enterprise and its management much latitude and discretion when deciding impairment issues. As a result, enterprises followed diverse practices.

Based on this latitude, the expression "big bath" came to refer to situations in which an enterprise announced a enormous write-down or write-off during one accounting period. In 2002, AOL Time Warner Inc., which has subsequently changed its name to Time Warner Inc., reported a $98.7 billion net loss, at the time the largest annual loss in corporate history and more than twice what analysts on Wall Street expected, after taking a $45.5 billion charge in the fourth quarter to write down the carrying value of its America Online unit. The huge fourth-quarter charge followed a $54 billion write-down in the first quarter, which had earlier generated the largest quarterly net loss in U.S. history, when the company reduced the carrying value of assets in the Time Warner businesses. *The Wall Street Journal* described the charges as "an effort by the company to get as much bad news as possible out of the way." Peers & Angwin, *AOL Reports Record Annual Loss and Says Ted Turner Will Resign*, WALL ST. J., Jan. 30, 2003, at A1.

Less than five years before the disastrous 2001 merger between America Online Inc. and Time Warner, in October 1996, AOL announced a $385 million charge to reverse an accounting policy that had enabled the company to post quarterly profits by capitalizing massive marketing costs and amortizing them over up to two years rather than treating them as expenses. *The Wall Street Journal* described the 1996 charge as "more than five time as large as the total pretax earnings that AOL had reported for the past five fiscal years combined." Sandberg, *America Online Plans $385 Million Charge*, WALL ST. J., Oct. 30, 1996, at A3.

Such write-offs obviously can distort an enterprise's income statements, lumping losses into one quarter or year while improving past and future earnings. These items can also lead to lawsuits alleging securities fraud. Following AOL's 1996 announcement, disappointed investors filed a class action lawsuit against the company, alleging that the company and its officers violated federal securities laws. In June, 1998 the company agreed to pay up to $35 million to settle the lawsuit, noting that insurance would cover a substantial portion of the settlement. In 2000, AOL consented to a cease-and-desist order and agreed to pay a $3.5 million civil penalty to resolve administrative proceedings alleging that the company improperly accounted for its advertising costs. The company did not admit or deny the charges. SEC v. America Online, Inc., Accounting and Auditing Enforcement Release No. 1258, Fed. Sec. L. Rep. (CCH) ¶ 74,765 (2000).

For years, critics attributed less than honorable motives to such announcements and often alleged that enterprises orchestrated the timing of these large, "one-time" losses. These critics claimed that, rather than recognizing the expense or loss when incurred, enterprises used the broad discretion allowed under then-existing standards governing accounting for impairments to accumulate such expenses or losses and to manipulate the stock market's reaction to such announcements. Investor Warren Buffet compared the financial statements that followed these write-offs to bogus golf scores. Imagine a golfer reporting an atrociously high score for his first round, say a 140, and then shooting in the eighties "for the next few rounds by drawing down against the 'reserve' established in the first round. 'On Wall Street, * * * they will ignore the 140—which after all, came from a "discontinued" swing—and will classify our hero as an 80 shooter (and one who never disappoints).' " Richard A. Oppel Jr., *Buffet Deplores Trend of Manipulated Earnings*, N.Y. TIMES, Mar. 15, 1999, at C2.

As a variation, repeated write-downs can also muddy an enterprise's income statements. In 1996, *The Wall Street Journal* observed that AT&T

Corp.'s $14.2 billion in restructuring charges during the previous decade actually exceeded the $10.3 billion in total net income that the company reported during that same period. Smith & Lipin, *Odd Numbers[:] Are Companies Using Restructuring Costs To Fudge the Figures?*, WALL ST. J., Jan. 30, 1996, at A1. Another article reported that among the thirty companies in the Dow Jones industrials, the most commonly watched barometer of stock market performance, seven took material write-offs in four of the past five years, and that ten of the thirty companies reported charges that eliminated at least a quarter of their earnings over that period. Galarza & Ozanian, *Forgive Nothing; Here's How to Deal with All Those Huge "Nonrecurring" Charges*, FIN. WORLD, Mar. 11, 1996, at 18.

With such drastic and dramatic expense recognitions, one might expect shareholders and the market to look unfavorably upon these announcements. After all, both shareholders and the market usually view losses as undesirable. On balance, however, investors found a silver lining, no longer viewing these charges as admissions of corporate mismanagement. Most investors considered these charges as an effort to remove unproductive assets from the balance sheet and to enable future earnings gains. Keep in mind that the write-offs did not involve any cash payment, but instead attempted to bring future in come closer to future cash flows by reducing future depreciation, one of the largest non-cash expenses. As non-cash charges, these write-offs theoretically would not affect an enterprise's ability to pay dividends or its bills.

The SEC, FASB, and AICPA all realized that "big baths" represented an area needing increased regulation. As early as 1995, the FASB had announced new rules in the area. ACCOUNTING FOR THE IMPAIRMENT OF LONG-LIVED ASSETS AND FOR LONG-LIVED ASSETS TO BE DISPOSED OF, SFAS No. 121. SFAS No. 121 sought to provide standards for when enterprises should recognize impairment losses, and how they should measure such losses, to increase comparability and uniformity. Unfortunately, SFAS No. 121 did not address those situations in which an enterprise decided to discontinue a portion of its operations. Although the pronouncement limited management's discretion, opportunities remained for management to manipulate write-offs and reported earnings. Staff accountants at the SEC soon questioned the way that registrants reported restructuring and asset impairment charges, and suggested that firms were recognizing losses prematurely. Restructuring and Impairment Charges, Staff Accounting Bulletin No. 100, 64 Fed. Reg. 67,154 (1999). About two years later, the SEC initiated public administrative proceedings against Kimberly-Clark Corp., alleging that after its merger with Scott Paper Co. in 1995 Kimberly-Clark improperly recorded $354 million in restructuring charges while creating corresponding reserves. In subsequent years, Kimberly-Clark used a portion of those restructuring reserves to offset expenses, which increased the company's pretax income by about eleven percent in 1996 and lesser percentages in subsequent fiscal years. In 1999, the company voluntarily restated its financial statements after discussions with the SEC's Division of Corporation Finance. Without admitting or denying the SEC's allegations, the company consented to a cease-and-desist order. *In re* Kimberly-Clark Corp., Accounting and Auditing Enforcement Release No. 1533, [2001-2003 Transfer Binder] Fed. Sec. L. Rep. (CCH) ¶ 75,048 (Mar. 27, 2002).

2. THE NEW RULES

For more than ten years, the FASB has been working to improve the accounting standards involving the impairment of long-lived assets. Two recent pronouncements further limit an enterprise's ability to record large up-front write-downs and also require firms to recognize disposal or exit costs only as actually incurred.

In 2001, the FASB issued SFAS No. 144, *Accounting for the Impairment or Disposal of Long-Lived Assets*, to supersede SFAS No. 121 while still retaining many of its underlying rules. In addition to addressing the accounting for impairment of long-lived assets other than goodwill and other indefinite-lived intangibles, SFAS No. 144 establishes a single accounting model for all disposals of long-lived assets. In that regard, the pronouncement expands the rules in SFAS No. 121 to apply also to those disposals of segments of a business that APB Opinion No. 30, previously covered.

More recently, in 2002 the FASB issued new rules governing exit and disposal actions. In SFAS No. 146, *Accounting for Costs Associated with Exit or Disposal Activities*, the Board decided that future expenses arising from a plan to sell or abandon a fixed asset, such as a factory or corporate headquarters, must meet the definition of a liability before an enterprise can recognize them for financial accounting purposes. This rule nullifed EITF Issue No. 94-3, *Liability Recognition for Certain Employee Termination Benefits and Other Costs to Exit an Activity (including Certain Costs Incurred in a Restructuring)*.

a. GENERAL RULES ON IMPAIRMENTS

SFAS No. 144 reaffirms the requirements for recognizing an impairment loss that originally appeared in SFAS No. 121, but specifically does not apply to goodwill, indefinite-lived intangibles, and unproved oil and gas properties for which an enterprise has elected to use the successful-efforts accounting method. In addition, SFAS No. 144 establishes a single accounting model for assets that an enterprise plans to sell. Accordingly, SFAS No. 144 creates specific rules for long-lived assets that an enterprise holds (1) for use, (2) for disposal by other than sale, and (3) for disposal by sale.

(1) Assets Held for Use

SFAS No. 144 requires that assets an enterprise plans to hold and use in operations be reviewed periodically, especially whenever events or changes in circumstances indicate that the enterprise may not recover the asset's carrying amount. For purposes of this review, "the asset" may actually represent a group of assets, specifically the smallest group of related assets for which the enterprise can estimate identifiable future cash flows independent from those attributable to other groups of assets and liabilities. When events or changing circumstances suggest that the expected cash flows arising from the use and eventual disposition of "the asset," undiscounted and without interest charges, will not enable the enterprise to recover the asset's carrying amount, the enterprise must determine the asset's fair value and, if necessary, recognize an impairment loss. The impairment loss, if any, will equal the difference between asset's carrying amount and its fair value. Although the balance sheet has never represented a current value statement, SFAS No. 144 essentially embraces that approach for impaired assets held for use in operations.

a) IMPAIRMENT REVIEW

SFAS No. 144 dictates the circumstances in which an enterprise shall recognize an impairment loss on an asset or group of assets that the enterprise holds for use in its operations. As a starting point, the pronouncement lists various events or changes in circumstances that indicate that an enterprise should conduct an impairment review. These events and changes in circumstances include:

- A significant decrease in the asset's market value, for example, through technological obsolescence;

- A significant change in the extent or manner in which an enterprise uses the asset;

- A significant physical change in the asset;

- A significant adverse change in the legal factors or business climate that affects the asset's value;

- An adverse action or assessment by a regulator;

- An accumulation of costs that significantly exceeds the amount originally expected to be needed to acquire or construct the asset, for example, through cost overruns;

- A current period operating or cash flow loss combined with a history of such losses;

- A projection or forecast demonstrating continuing operating or cash flow losses; and

- A current expectation that the enterprise will more likely than not sell or otherwise dispose of the asset significantly before the end of its previously estimated useful life.

The pronouncement recognizes, at least implicitly, that an enterprise need not evaluate all assets every year, much less every quarter. As a result, enterprises retain some discretion in deciding when to conduct an impairment review.

b) CASH FLOWS ANALYSIS

Once an enterprise has identified events or circumstances that suggest that an impairment may have occurred, a cash flows analysis follows to determine whether an impairment actually exists. The enterprise must conduct this inquiry at the "lowest level" of identifiable cash flows. In the inquiry, an enterprise must estimate the future cash flows that the enterprise expects during the remaining useful life of the asset or asset group and upon its ultimate disposition. For this purpose, SFAS No. 144 establishes a "primary asset" approach that requires the enterprise to identify the principal long-lived tangible asset being depreciated or intangible being amortized. As the most significant component from which the asset group derives its cash-flow generating capacity, the primary asset determines the group's remaining useful life for evaluating cash flows.

Ultimately, a cash flows analysis seeks to determine the expected future cash inflows from the asset in question, and then subtracts the expected future cash outflows necessary to obtain the inflows. If the enterprise develops alternative courses of action to recover the carrying amount or identifies a range for the amount of estimated future cash flows, SFAS No. 144 endorses a probability weighted estimation approach to consider the alternative courses of action or range of estimates. If the asset's carrying amount exceeds the sum of the expected net cash flows, undiscounted and without interest charges, the enterprise must recognize an impairment loss. If the sum of the expected net cash flows exceeds the asset's carrying amount, the enterprise cannot recognize an impairment loss.

The requirement that an enterprise use the "lowest level of identifiable cash flows" to test for impairment significantly affects accounting for natural resources. Prior to SFAS No. 121, for example, oil companies typically used a country-by-country grouping to evaluate assets for impairments. Under this method, profitable wells offset unsuccessful wells, reducing or eliminating any write-offs. SFAS No. 121, however, required these companies to evaluate wells on field-by-field basis or even an individual basis if the enterprise considers a well's cash flow "identifiable." This separation may differ from the methodology that an enterprise uses to amortize various costs related to the wells. For example, an enterprise may group assets by region or product for amortization purposes, whereas SFAS No. 144 continues the rule in SFAS No. 121 that requires an enterprise to separate these assets for impairment analysis depending upon the "lowest level of identifiable cash flows."

The oil and gas industries appear susceptible to volatile earnings under SFAS No. 144 for several reasons, one of which is the virtual elimination of the prior practice that often applied country-by-country or worldwide groupings to measure impairments. A second reason is that in periods of strong oil prices, oil companies often pay premium prices to acquire properties, and then face a problem when oil and gas prices subsequently fall. In the 1995 fourth-quarter, Chevron Corp., Texaco Inc., and Mobil Corp. announced after-tax charges of $800 million, $640 million, and $487 million, respectively, to comply with SFAS No. 121. Holden, *Chevron to Take an $800 Million Charge*, WALL ST. J., Jan. 5, 1996, at B9. Given the sharp increase in oil and gas prices in the early 2000s, that situation could repeat itself later in this decade. Keep in mind, however, that the write-offs reduced subsequent depletion and amortization charges, thereby allowing higher earnings in the following years.

Notice that management enjoys considerable discretion in estimating expected future cash flows both from using an asset and from its disposition. In addition, the "lowest level of identifiable cash flows" raises some interesting possibilities. If net expected cash flows for some assets exceed their carrying amounts, can an enterprise use that excess to offset impairment losses attributable to other assets? The answer involves the proper grouping of assets. Specifically, enterprises must analyze assets, either individually or in small groups, at the "lowest level" at which the enterprise can separately identify independent cash flows. To illustrate, in response to the then newly adopted rules in SFAS No. 121, PepsiCo Inc. wrote-off approximately $520 million, or seven percent of the assets related to the company's Taco Bell, Pizza Hut, and KFC restaurants, during the fourth quarter in 1995 even though the value of the restaurants as a group exceeded their combined book values. Because PepsiCo chose to identify cash flows on a restaurant-by-restaurant basis, the company could take the charge, which will boost earnings in subsequent accounting periods. When questioned, the company conceded that another restaurant operator might group its stores by regions which could result in a lower charge. Lowenstein, *Earnings Not Always What They Seem*, WALL ST. J., Feb. 15, 1996, at C1.

c) IMPAIRMENT LOSS

If the cash flow analysis requires an enterprise to recognize an impairment loss, SFAS No. 144 requires the enterprise to determine the asset's fair value and to write down the asset to that amount. The resulting write-down represents the impairment loss. After an impairment loss has been recognized, SFAS No. 144 requires the enterprise to treat the reduced carrying amount as the asset's new cost, and forbids the enterprise to reverse or recover that loss if the impairment subsequently disappears. For a depreciable asset, the enterprise must then depreciate the asset's new cost over its remaining useful life.

As in other areas, SFAS No. 144 defines "fair value" as the amount at which the asset would change hands between a willing buyer and a willing seller in a current transaction other than a forced or liquidation sale. The pronouncement considers quoted market prices in active markets as the best evidence of fair value. For those assets without active markets, SFAS No. 144 requires an enterprise to estimate fair value based on the best information available in the circumstances. In this regard, the enterprise must consider the prices for similar assets and available valuation techniques. SFAS No. 144 specifically authorizes the discounted cash flows method as long as the enterprise uses a discount rate that reflects the risks involved.

Once again, SFAS No. 144 allows an enterprise's management to exercise consid erable discretion in estimating expected cash flows and selecting the appropriate discount rate. Note also that while an enterprise compares an asset's carrying amount to the asset's fair value to determine the amount of the impairment loss, the enterprise does not use the asset's fair value to determine whether an impairment exists initially.

(2) Assets Held for Disposal by Other than Sale

Apart from sale, an enterprise can dispose of long-lived assets via exchange; distribution to its owners, perhaps in a spinoff; or abandonment. SFAS No. 144 requires an enterprise to treat any asset that it holds for disposal by other than sale as held for use until actually abandoned or transferred, so in the meantime, the rules in the previous section apply.

An enterprise abandons an asset when there is a non-temporary cessation of use. If an enterprise commits to a plan to abandon an asset before the end of its previously estimated useful live, however, the enterprise must revise the depreciable life in accordance with the rules for changes in accounting estimates in SFAS No. 154 and APB No. 20, as described at pages 262-263, *supra*, to reflect the asset's use over its shortened useful life.

With regard to exchanges or spinoffs, SFAS No. 144 amends APB Opinion No. 29, *Accounting for Nonmonetary Transactions*, to require that an enterprise immediately recognize an impairment loss if, on the date of the exchange or spinoff, the transferred asset's carrying amount exceeds its fair value (which, by the way, in an arms length transaction could presumably be measured by the fair market value of the asset received in exchange).

(3) Assets Held for Disposal by Sale

SFAS No. 144 requires an enterprise to report all long-lived assets that it holds for disposal by sale, whether previously held and used or newly acquired, at the lower of the asset's carrying amount or fair value less the cost to sell. You may recall from the discussion in Chapter IV on pages 254-255, *supra*, that SFAS No. 144 specifically applies to discontinued operations, a term accountants use to describe components that an enterprise decides to sell or eliminate. An enterprise holds a long-lived asset for sale when, among other criteria, management commits to a plan to sell the asset, makes the asset available for immediate sale in its present condition subject only to usual and customary terms, and, subject to certain exceptions, expects the transfer to qualify for recognition as a completed sale within one year.

Unlike the treatment for assets that an enterprise plans to hold for use in operations, SFAS No. 144 requires an enterprise to subtract the cost to sell from the amount that would otherwise appear on the enterprise's balance sheet. The cost to sell an asset generally includes the incremental direct costs necessary to transact the sale, such as broker commissions, legal and title transfer fees, and closing costs. Costs to sell would not include expected future losses arising from the asset's operation pending sale. In addition, once an enterprise decides to hold an asset for disposal by sale, the pronouncement precludes the enterprise from depreciating or amortizing the asset. Finally, the new rules prohibit an enterprise from retroactively reclassifying assets as held for sale when the enterprise does not meet the requisite criteria until after the balance sheet date, but the enterprise must disclose certain information about the decision to hold for sale in the notes to the financial statements. SFAS No. 144, ¶¶ 30–40.

b. GENERAL RULES ON DISPOSAL ACTIVITIES

Under SFAS No. 146, *Accounting for Costs Associated with Exit or Disposal Activities*, an enterprise can only recognize and measure a liability arising from a restructuring, discontinued operation, plant closing, or other exit or disposal action, including obligations arising from lease terminations and employee severances, once the enterprise has actually incurred the liability. These rules, however, do not apply to exit activities that involve an entity newly acquired in a business combination or to costs to terminate a capital lease.

Previously, EITF Issue No. 94-3, allowed an enterprise to recognize liabilities and record associated expenses on the date the enterprise announced an exit plan, even though the "commitments" did not meet the definition of a liability in FASB Statement of Financial Accounting Concepts No. 6: "probable future sacrifices of economic benefits arising from present obligations of a particular entity to transfer assets or provide services to other entities in the future as a result of past transactions or events." SFAC No. 6, ¶ 35 (FASB 1985). Accordingly, enterprises could record large expenses at the time they announced a plant closing or corporate restructuring, even though circumstances might reduce the actual amounts paid for such items as consolidation of facilities or relocation of employees. However, in SFAS No. 146, FASB concluded that an enterprise's commitment to an exit or disposal plan by itself does not create a present obligation to others that satisfies SFAC No. 6's definition. When a commitment satisfies that definition, an enterprise should use fair value to measure the liability. The pronouncement defines "fair value" as "the amount at which that liability could be settled in a current transaction between willing parties." In the unusual circumstance in which the enterprise cannot reasonably estimate the fair value, it must wait until it can, before recognizing the liability. If the disposal activity does not involve a component of the entity that qualifies for treatment as a discontinued operation, the enterprise must treat costs such as employee termination benefits and the like as expenses related to continuing operations. In other words, a disposal activity should be reported as past of continuing operations before income taxes unless the activity involves a discontinued operation.

The pronouncement also establishes rules for treating the liability for, and compensation expense related to, one-time termination benefits. If an employee must perform services during a legal notification period, often sixty days, or otherwise in the future to qualify for termination benefits, SFAS No. 146 requires the enterprise to allocate the liability's fair value, estimated as of the date that an employee will stop rendering services, ratably over the future service period. Consequently, the underlying liability will accumulate during the future service period, until the obligation reaches an amount equal to the estimated fair value on the date that the required services end. As a result, enterprises will often now recognize these exit and disposal costs in one or more accounting periods following a commitment to a plan, rather than at the date of commitment.

Finally, the new rules in SFAS No. 146 require disclosures about any exit or disposal activity initiated during the current period and any subsequent one, until the enterprise completes the activity. For each major type of cost, an enterprise must: (1) report by business segment the total amount that it expects to incur in connection with the exit, the amount incurred in the period, and the cumulative amount incurred to date; (2) reconcile the beginning and ending balances in the liability accounts, showing separately the changes during the period attributable to costs incurred and charged to expense, costs paid or otherwise settled, and any adjustments to the liability, explaining the reasons for any adjustments; and (3) identify the line items in the income statement in which the costs appear.

Although the new rules do not apply to exit activities that involve an entity freshly acquired in a business combination, the FASB has tentatively decided to adopt revised standards that would apply these same rules to exit activities that arise from business combinations. Such standards, in essence, would level the playing field for restructuring costs, whether originating from an existing operating activity or an acquisition. The proposed rules would presumably preclude companies like Cendant Corp., which allegedly intentionally overstated merger reserves and then reversed those amounts in later periods to overstate pretax operating income by more than $500 million between 1995 and 1997, from using acquisition reserves to hide subsequent poor performance from investors. Wei, *Merger Loophole May Be Plugged*, WALL ST. J., Aug. 13, 2004, at C3.

*

APPENDIX A

ILLUSTRATIVE FINANCIAL REPORTS AND STATEMENTS

To Our Shareholders,

The human connection – it's the foundation of everything we do at Starbucks. One customer, one barista, one community, one great cup of coffee at a time. That seemingly simple relationship, which today develops in more than 10,500 Starbucks stores around the world, inspires millions of people to embrace us as their neighborhood gathering place. That same connection is at the heart of our passion to innovate and grow in new markets, with new tastes, new sounds and new experiences.

Every day, more than 100,000 Starbucks partners (employees) strive to exceed the expectations of every one of our customers – to achieve that delicate balance between touching people's daily lives while building a thriving and multifaceted business. Regardless of our individual differences, people around the world share a common desire to be treated with respect and dignity, and to feel a sense of community, belonging and inclusion. We believe that Starbucks helps fulfill these needs by providing a welcoming environment and a place of comfort, while serving the world's finest coffees. This has resulted in Starbucks establishing a unique *third place* between home and office: first in North America and now around the world.

In fiscal 2005, we made new connections around the world as we continued our dynamic growth. We opened 1,672 net new stores on a global basis this year, ahead of our target of 1,500 new stores; Starbucks can now be found in 37 countries. With 20 percent revenue growth resulting in record revenues of $6.4 billion and earnings per share growth of 30 percent resulting in $0.61 per share, we again demonstrated our outstanding ability to achieve our financial targets while growing our core business and building the foundation for future success, both strategies that we believe are key to increasing long-term shareholder value. Our pace has been exceptionally strong and steady, and this year we celebrated 14 consecutive years of comparable store sales growth of 5 percent or greater – a truly landmark achievement.

We feel very fortunate that the *Starbucks Experience* resonates around the world, as we have increased customer depth and awareness in existing markets. We have also been warmly accepted in new countries, including Jordan, the Bahamas and the Republic of Ireland. We are especially excited by our progress in China, and we believe this will ultimately represent one of our largest markets outside the United States. We now have more than 200 locations in mainland China and Hong Kong, with more than 150 additional locations in Taiwan. These include our first Company-operated stores in Qingdao, Dalian and Chengdu, and we are very optimistic about our continued expansion into the broader Chinese market. While we plan to focus our attention on the abundant opportunities in China, we will continue to explore new countries for future growth of our international business, including Brazil, India and Russia. We should also note that our existing market portfolio represents substantial growth potential.

Even as we expand, we know the time-honored traditions of the neighborhood merchant still hold true – we must constantly create new tastes and temptations to surprise and delight our customers. In fiscal 2005, we presented a variety of exciting innovations around the world. As part of our Global Consumer Products business, we leveraged our success from North America in Japan and Taiwan, and introduced a fresh Starbucks-branded premium ready-to-drink chilled-cup coffee called Starbucks Discoveries™ in convenience stores. Starbucks Discoveries™ received an enthusiastic reception from multitudes of customers from the moment it hit the shelves.

As a global company, we know that cultures influence one another, and the *Starbucks Experience* has been translated in many ways in different countries throughout the world. As a great example of cross-market learning, this summer we introduced a new handcrafted beverage in North America – our Green Tea Frappuccino® blended beverage, made with Tazo® green tea, which was originally created in conjunction with our Taiwanese partner.

We also constantly seek new ways to share unique elements of the coffeehouse experience with the communities we serve. In 2005, Starbucks Entertainment introduced new artists and offerings, continuing the historical connection

iii

between music and coffeehouses. Leveraging our momentum from the astounding eight GRAMMY® awards for Ray Charles' *Genius Loves Company*, Hear Music – the Sound of Starbucks, went on to co-release Herbie Hancock's terrific new album, *Possibilities*, which has been nominated for two GRAMMY® awards. Another highlight includes *Live at the Gaslight 1962*, a highly anticipated album from legendary artist Bob Dylan that is available exclusively at Starbucks. We also created a fresh approach to the familiar: this year, Starbucks helped launch an emerging band with Antigone Rising's *From the Ground Up*, our first in the Hear Music™ Debut CD series. The sum of these and many other efforts in Entertainment have helped transform the way people discover and experience music.

We know that the success of our business is not measured strictly in financial terms. We believe we have built trust with our partners, customers, suppliers and communities, and with that trust comes a responsibility to continue our growth in a sustainable way for coffee farmers, our neighborhoods and the environment. The process can be challenging, but the rewards are tremendous. For instance, Starbucks worked for four years with our suppliers to develop the first paper drinking cup to include post-consumer recycled content. Our suppliers received approval from the U.S. Food and Drug Administration in November 2004, after extensive quality and safety testing, we will roll out the new cup to our U.S. stores in fiscal 2006. The switch to 10 percent post-consumer recycled fiber in our cups will reduce our use of new tree fiber by more than five million pounds in calendar 2006 alone. This single project exemplifies our commitment to be both responsible business owners as well as responsible citizens of the world.

We bring that same sentiment to our relationships in the broader world community. We have worked for several years to develop and implement comprehensive standards for fair, ethical and sustainable coffee purchasing – specifically our C.A.F.E. (Coffee and Farmer Equity) Practices, which continued to evolve and expand in fiscal 2005. We have also reached out to new communities in need and broadened our commitment to global social issues. In April 2005, we acquired Ethos Water and adopted its mission to provide access to clean water in developing countries. For a detailed examination of our activities in social responsibility, please refer to our fiscal 2005 Corporate Social Responsibility Annual Report, which will be available online at www.starbucks.com/csr in early February.

We know that we cannot afford to rest on our past accomplishments, and we are extremely excited about our prospects for the future. In fiscal 2006, we plan to open approximately 1,800 net new stores globally – more stores than we had during the first 25 years of Starbucks history. We expect annual total net revenue growth of approximately 20 percent and annual earnings per share growth of approximately 20 percent to 25 percent for the next three to five years, demonstrating our belief in the opportunities that await us worldwide and our confidence in executing our strategy.

This is the first letter to shareholders that we have co-authored, and we hope that we have expressed our shared passion for our business and for maintaining the human connection in a way that resonates with you. We are proud of our accomplishments, made possible by the dedication and commitment of Starbucks partners, customers, suppliers and the coffee farmers with whom we have built lasting relationships. We know that the people whose lives we touch are the cornerstone of our Company's success and our future, and we owe them our deepest gratitude.

A single cup of coffee. A connection. A sense of place. It is where we began our journey and, after 34 years, it remains the heart and soul of our Company.

Warm regards,

Howard Schultz
chairman

Jim Donald
president and chief executive officer

UNITED STATES SECURITIES AND EXCHANGE COMMISSION
Washington, DC 20549

Form 10-K

ANNUAL REPORT PURSUANT TO SECTION 13 OR 15(d) OF THE SECURITIES EXCHANGE ACT OF 1934

For the fiscal year ended October 2, 2005

Starbucks Corporation

(Exact name of registrant as specified in its charter)

Washington	91-1325671
(State or other jurisdiction of incorporation or organization)	*(IRS Employer Identification No.)*
2401 Utah Avenue South Seattle, Washington 98134	98134 *(Zip Code)*
(Address of principal executive offices)	

(Registrant's telephone number, including area code): (206) 447-1575

Securities Registered Pursuant to Section 12(b) of the Act: None

Securities Registered Pursuant to Section 12(g) of the Act:

Common Stock, $0.001 Par Value Per Share

Indicate by check mark if the registrant is a well-known seasoned issuer, as defined in Rule 405 of the Securities Act.   Yes ☑   No ☐

Indicate by check mark if the registrant is not required to file reports pursuant to Section 13 or Section 15(d) of the Act.   Yes ☐   No ☑

Indicate by check mark whether the registrant: (1) has filed all reports required to be filed by Section 13 or 15(d) of the Securities Exchange Act of 1934 during the preceding 12 months (or for such shorter period that the registrant was required to file such reports), and (2) has been subject to such filing requirements for the past 90 days.   Yes ☑   No ☐

Indicate by check mark if disclosure of delinquent filers pursuant to Item 405 of Regulation of S-K is not contained herein, and will not be contained, to the best of the registrant's knowledge, in definitive proxy or information statements incorporated by reference in Part III of this Form 10-K or any amendment to this Form 10-K.   ☐

Indicate by check mark whether the registrant is an accelerated filer (as defined in Rule 12b-2 of the Exchange Act):   Yes ☑   No ☐

Indicate by check mark whether the registrant is a shell company (as defined in Rule 12b-2 of the Exchange Act).   Yes ☐   No ☑

The aggregate market value of the voting stock held by non-affiliates of the registrant as of the last business day of the registrant's most recently completed second fiscal quarter, based upon the closing sale price of the registrant's common stock on April 1, 2005 as reported on the National Market tier of The NASDAQ Stock Market, Inc. was $19,997,624,194.

As of December 14, 2005, there were 764,103,540 shares of the registrant's Common Stock outstanding.

DOCUMENTS INCORPORATED BY REFERENCE

Portions of the definitive Proxy Statement for the registrant's Annual Meeting of Shareholders to be held on February 8, 2006 have been incorporated by reference into Part III of this Annual Report on Form 10-K.

STARBUCKS CORPORATION
FORM 10-K
For the Fiscal Year Ended October 2, 2005
TABLE OF CONTENTS
PART I

PART I

Item 1. *Business*
General

Starbucks Corporation (together with its subsidiaries, "Starbucks" or the "Company"), formed in 1985, purchases and roasts high-quality whole bean coffees and sells them, along with fresh, rich-brewed coffees, Italian-style espresso beverages, cold blended beverages, a variety of complementary food items, coffee-related accessories and equipment, a selection of premium teas and a line of compact discs, primarily through Company-operated retail stores. Starbucks also sells coffee and tea products and licenses its trademark through other channels and, through certain of its equity investees, Starbucks produces and sells bottled Frappuccino® coffee drinks and Starbucks DoubleShot® espresso drink and a line of superpremium ice creams. All channels outside the Company-operated retail stores are collectively known as "Specialty Operations." The Company's objective is to establish Starbucks as the most recognized and respected brand in the world. To achieve this goal, the Company plans to continue rapid expansion of its retail operations, to grow its Specialty Operations and to selectively pursue other opportunities to leverage the Starbucks brand through the introduction of new products and the development of new channels of distribution.

Segment Financial Information

Starbucks has two operating segments, United States and International, each of which includes Company-operated retail stores and Specialty Operations. Information about Starbucks total net revenues, earnings before income taxes, depreciation and amortization, income from equity investees, equity method investments, identifiable assets, net impairment and disposition losses and capital expenditures by segment is included in Note 19 to the consolidated financial statements included in Item 8 of this Annual Report on Form 10-K ("Form 10-K" or "Report").

The following table shows the Company's revenue components for the fiscal year ended October 2, 2005:

Revenues	% of Total Net Revenues	% of Specialty Revenues
Company-operated retail	85 %	
Specialty:		
Licensing:		
Retail stores	6 %	42 %
Grocery and warehouse club	4 %	24 %
Branded products	<1 %	2 %
Total licensing	10 %	68 %
Foodservice and other:		
Foodservice	4 %	29 %
Other initiatives	1 %	3 %
Total foodservice and other	5 %	32 %
Total specialty	15 %	100%
Total net revenues	100%	

Company-operated Retail Stores

The Company's retail goal is to become the leading retailer and brand of coffee in each of its target markets by selling the finest quality coffee and related products and by providing each customer a unique *Starbucks Experience*. The *Starbucks Experience*, or third place experience, after home and work, is built upon superior customer service as well as clean and well-maintained Company-operated retail stores that reflect the personalities of the communities in which they operate, thereby building a high degree of customer loyalty. Starbucks strategy for expanding its retail business is to increase its market share in existing markets primarily by opening additional stores and to open stores in new markets where the opportunity exists to become the leading specialty coffee retailer. In support of this strategy, Starbucks opened 735 new Company-operated stores during the fiscal year ended October 2, 2005 ("fiscal 2005"). Starbucks Company-operated retail stores, including 11 Seattle's Best Coffee® ("SBC") stores and 2 Hear Music retail stores, accounted for 85% of total net revenues during fiscal 2005.

The following table summarizes total Company-operated retail store data for the periods indicated:

	Net Stores Opened During the Fiscal Year Ended		Stores Open as of	
	Oct 2, 2005 (52 Wks)	Oct 3, 2004 (53 Wks)	Oct 2, 2005	Oct 3, 2004
United States	574	514	4,867	4,293
International:				
United Kingdom	45	49	467	422
Canada	62	56	434	372
Thailand	14	11	63	49
Australia	14	4	58	44
Germany[1]	9	10	44	35
Singapore	(3)	–	32	35
China[1]	18	3	24	6
Chile[1]	1	8	10	9
Ireland	1	–	1	–
Total International	161	141	1,133	972
Total Company-operated	735	655	6,000	5,265

[1] International store data has been adjusted for the acquisitions of the Germany, Southern China and Chile operations by reclassifying historical information from Licensed stores to Company-operated stores.

Starbucks retail stores are typically located in high-traffic, high-visibility locations. Because the Company can vary the size and format, its stores are located in or near a variety of settings, including downtown and suburban retail centers, office buildings and university campuses. While the Company selectively locates stores in shopping malls, it focuses on locations that provide convenient access for pedestrians and drivers. With the flexibility in store size and format, the Company also locates retail stores in select rural and off-highway locations to serve a broader array of customers outside major metropolitan markets and further expand brand awareness. To provide a greater degree of access and convenience for nonpedestrian customers, the Company has increased development of drive-thru retail stores. At the end of fiscal 2005, the Company operated approximately 1,100 drive-thru locations.

All Starbucks stores offer a choice of regular and decaffeinated coffee beverages, a broad selection of Italian-style espresso beverages, cold blended beverages, iced shaken refreshment beverages, a selection of teas and distinctively packaged roasted whole bean coffees. Starbucks stores also offer a selection of fresh pastries and other food items, sodas, juices, bottled water, coffee-making equipment and accessories, a selection of compact discs, games and seasonal novelty items. Each Starbucks store varies its product mix depending upon the size of the store and its location. Larger stores carry a broad selection of the Company's whole bean coffees in various sizes and types of packaging, as well as an assortment of coffee and espresso-making equipment and accessories such as coffee grinders, coffee filters, storage containers, travel tumblers and mugs. Smaller Starbucks stores and kiosks typically sell a full line of coffee beverages, a limited selection of whole bean coffees and a few accessories such as travel tumblers and logo mugs. In the United States and in International markets, approximately 2,850 stores and 950 stores, respectively, carry a selection of prepared sandwiches and salads.

In addition to providing a selection of compact discs in Company-operated stores, the Company has created new and convenient ways for consumers to discover, experience and acquire all genres of music through Starbucks Hear Music™ media bars, a service that offers custom CD burning at select Starbucks retail locations in Seattle, Washington and Austin, Texas, and the Starbucks Hear Music™ Coffeehouse, a first-of-its-kind music store in Santa Monica, California. The Company has plans to open two additional Hear Music Coffeehouses in Miami, Florida and San Antonio, Texas in fiscal 2006.

The Company's retail sales mix by product type during fiscal 2005 was as follows: 77% beverages, 15% food, 4% whole bean coffees and 4% coffee-making equipment and other merchandise.

Specialty Operations

Specialty Operations strive to develop the Company's brands outside the Company-operated retail store environment through a number of channels. Starbucks strategy is to reach customers where they work, travel, shop and dine by establishing relationships with prominent third parties that share the Company's values and commitment to quality. These relationships take various forms, including licensing arrangements, foodservice accounts and other initiatives related to the Company's core businesses. In certain situations, Starbucks has an equity ownership interest in licensee operations. During fiscal 2005, specialty revenues (which include royalties and fees from licensees, as well as product sales derived from Specialty Operations) accounted for 15% of total net revenues.

Licensing

In its licensed retail store operations, the Company leverages the expertise of its local partners and shares Starbucks operating and store development experience. Licensee partners are typically master concessionaires, which can provide improved access to desirable retail space, or prominent retailers with in-depth market knowledge and access. As part of these arrangements, Starbucks receives license fees and royalties and sells coffee, tea, CDs and related products for resale in licensed locations. Employees working in licensed retail locations are required to follow Starbucks detailed store operating procedures and attend training classes similar to those given to Company-operated store managers and employees.

Starbucks opened 596 new licensed retail stores in the United States during fiscal 2005, and as of October 2, 2005, operated 2,435 licensed stores. During fiscal 2005, Starbucks opened 341 new International licensed stores, including the first stores in Jordan and The Bahamas. At October 2, 2005, the Company's International operating segment had a total of 1,806 licensed retail stores. Product sales to and royalty and license fee revenues from U.S. and International licensed retail stores accounted for 42% of specialty revenues in fiscal 2005.

At fiscal year end 2005, Starbucks total licensed retail stores by region and specific location were as follows:

Asia Pacific		Europe/Middle East/Africa		Americas	
Japan	572	Spain	39	United States	2,435
China	185	Saudi Arabia	38	Canada	118
Taiwan	153	Greece	38	Mexico	60
South Korea	133	United Arab Emirates	37	Hawaii	51
Philippines	83	Kuwait	32	Puerto Rico	11
Malaysia	62	Turkey	24	Peru	6
New Zealand	41	Switzerland	21	The Bahamas	2
Indonesia	32	France	16		
		Lebanon	10		
		Austria	9		
		Qatar	8		
		Bahrain	8		
		Cyprus	7		
		Oman	4		
		Jordan	4		
		UK	2		
Total	1,261	Total	297	Total	2,683

In grocery and warehouse club stores throughout the United States, the Company sells a selection of Starbucks® whole bean and ground coffees, as well as Seattle's Best Coffee® and Torrefazione Italia® branded coffees and a selection of premium Tazo® teas through a licensing relationship with Kraft Foods Inc. ("Kraft"). Kraft manages all distribution, marketing, advertising and promotion. In International markets, Starbucks also has licensing arrangements with other grocery and warehouse club stores. By the end of fiscal 2005, the Company's coffees and teas were available in approximately 31,300 grocery and warehouse club stores, with 30,000 in the United States and 1,300 in International markets. Revenues from this category comprised 24% of specialty revenues in fiscal 2005.

The Company has licensed the rights to produce and distribute Starbucks branded products to two partnerships in which the Company holds 50% equity interests. The North American Coffee Partnership with the Pepsi-Cola Company develops and distributes bottled Frappuccino® coffee drinks and Starbucks DoubleShot® espresso drink. The Starbucks Ice Cream Partnership with Dreyer's Grand Ice Cream, Inc., develops and distributes superpremium ice creams.

Starbucks and Jim Beam Brands Co., a unit of Fortune Brands, Inc., manufacture and market Starbucks-branded premium coffee liqueur products in the United States. The Company introduced a coffee liqueur product nationally during the fiscal second quarter of 2005, and will launch a coffee and cream liqueur product in fiscal 2006 in restaurants, bars and retail outlets where premium distilled spirits are sold. The Company does not and will not sell the liqueur products in its Company-operated or licensed retail stores.

In September 2005, the Company launched Starbucks Discoveries™, a ready-to-drink chilled cup coffee beverage in refrigerated cases of convenience stores in Japan, through a manufacturing and distribution agreement with Suntory Limited, and in Taiwan, through separate co-packing and distribution agreements with Uni-President Enterprises Corporation and the Company's equity investee, President Starbucks Coffee

Taiwan Ltd. In fiscal 2006, the Company plans to enter the ready-to-drink coffee category in South Korea through a licensing agreement with Dong Suh Foods Corporation to import bottled Starbucks Frappuccino® coffee drinks produced in the United States.

Collectively, the revenues from these branded products accounted for 2% of specialty revenues in fiscal 2005.

Foodservice

The Company sells whole bean and ground coffees, including the Starbucks, Seattle's Best Coffee and Torrefazione Italia brands, as well as a selection of premium Tazo teas, to institutional foodservice companies that service business, industry, education and healthcare accounts, office coffee distributors, hotels, restaurants, airlines and other retailers. Beginning in fiscal 2003, the Company transitioned the majority of its direct distribution accounts to SYSCO Corporation's and U.S. Foodservice's™ national broadline distribution network and aligned foodservice sales, customer service and support resources with those of SYSCO Corporation and U.S. Foodservice. Starbucks and Seattle's Best Coffee are the only superpremium national-brand coffees actively promoted by SYSCO Corporation. The Company's total worldwide foodservice operations had approximately 15,500 accounts at fiscal year end 2005, and revenues from these accounts comprised 29% of total specialty revenues.

Other Initiatives

Included in this category is the Company's emerging entertainment business, which encompasses multiple music and technology based initiatives designed to appeal to new and existing Starbucks customers. Among these initiatives are strategic marketing and co-branding arrangements, such as the 24-hour Starbucks Hear Music™ digital music channel 75 available to all XM Satellite Radio subscribers, and the availability of wireless broadband Internet service in Company-operated retail stores located in the United States and Canada. Additionally, the entertainment business includes Starbucks Hear Music's innovative partnerships with other music labels for the production, marketing and distribution of both exclusive and nonexclusive music, music programming for Starbucks stores worldwide, and CD sales through the Company's website at Starbucks.com/hearmusic.

The Company also maintains a website at Starbucks.com where customers may purchase, register or reload Starbucks stored value cards, as well as apply for the Starbucks Card Duetto™ Visa® (the "Duetto Card"), issued through the Company's agreement with Chase Bank USA, N.A. and Visa. The Duetto Card is a first-of-its-kind card, combining the functionality of a credit card with the convenience of a reloadable Starbucks Card. Additionally, the website contains information about the Company's coffee products, brewing equipment and store locations. Collectively, the operations of these other initiatives accounted for 3% of specialty revenues in fiscal 2005.

Product Supply

Starbucks is committed to selling only the finest whole bean coffees and coffee beverages. To ensure compliance with its rigorous coffee standards, Starbucks controls its coffee purchasing, roasting and packaging, and the distribution of coffee to its retail stores. The Company purchases green coffee beans from coffee-producing regions around the world and custom roasts them to its exacting standards for its many blends and single origin coffees.

The supply and price of coffee are subject to significant volatility. Although most coffee trades in the commodity market, coffee of the quality sought by the Company tends to trade on a negotiated basis at a substantial premium above commodity coffee prices, depending upon the supply and demand at the time of purchase. Supply and price can be affected by multiple factors in the producing countries, including weather, and political and economic conditions. In addition, green coffee prices have been affected in the past, and may be affected in the future, by the actions of certain organizations and associations that have historically attempted to influence prices of green coffee through agreements establishing export quotas or by restricting coffee supplies.

The Company depends upon its relationships with coffee producers, outside trading companies and exporters for its supply of green coffee. With green coffee commodity prices at relatively low levels in recent years, the Company has used fixed-price purchase commitments in order to secure an adequate supply of quality green coffee, bring greater certainty to the cost of sales in future periods, and promote sustainability by paying a fair price to coffee producers. As of October 2, 2005, the Company had $375 million in fixed-price purchase commitments which, together with existing inventory, is expected to provide an adequate supply of green coffee through fiscal 2006. The Company believes, based on relationships established with its suppliers, the risk of non-delivery on such purchase commitments is remote. During the first few months of fiscal 2005, green coffee commodity prices increased significantly. Since then, commodity prices have moderated but still remain above the historically low levels experienced in recent years. Based on its market experience, the Company believes that fixed-price purchase commitments are less likely to be available on favorable terms when commodity prices are high. The Company therefore expects to return to its previous practice of entering into price-to-be-fixed purchase contracts to meet at least some of its demand. These types of contracts state the quality, quantity and delivery periods but allow the price of green coffee over a market index to be established after contract signing. The Company believes that, through a combination of fixed-price and price-to-be-fixed contracts it will be able to secure an adequate supply of quality green coffee. However, an increased use of price-to-be-fixed contracts instead of fixed-price contracts would decrease the predictability of coffee costs in future periods.

During fiscal 2004, Starbucks established the Starbucks Coffee Agronomy Company S.R.L., a wholly owned subsidiary located in Costa Rica, to reinforce the Company's leadership role in the coffee industry and to help ensure sustainability and future supply of high-quality green coffees from Central America. Staffed with agronomists and sustainability experts, this first-of-its-kind Farmer Support Center is designed to proactively respond to changes in coffee producing countries that impact farmers and the supply of green coffee.

In addition to coffee, the Company also purchases significant amounts of dairy products to support the needs of its Company-operated retail stores. Fluid milk is purchased from multiple suppliers who have processing facilities near concentrations of Company-operated retail stores. Dairy prices in the United States, which closely follow the monthly Class I fluid milk base price as calculated by the U.S. Department of Agriculture, rose significantly in fiscal 2004. Although the Company's dairy costs rose only slightly in fiscal 2005 compared to fiscal 2004, Starbucks profitability could be adversely affected should prices increase significantly. Management continues to monitor published dairy prices on the related commodities markets, but cannot predict with any certainty future prices to be paid for dairy products.

The Company also purchases a broad range of paper and plastic products, such as cups, lids, napkins, straws, shopping bags and corrugated paper boxes from several companies to support the needs of its retail stores as well as its manufacturing and distribution operations. The cost of these materials is dependent in part upon commodity paper and plastic resin costs, but the Company believes it mitigates the effect of short-term raw material price fluctuations through strategic relationships with key suppliers.

* * *

usually under long-term supply contracts. Food products, such as fresh pastries and lunch items, are generally purchased from both regional and local sources. Coffee-making equipment, such as drip and French press coffeemakers, espresso machines and coffee grinders, are generally purchased directly from their manufacturers. Coffee-related accessories, including items bearing the Company's logos and trademarks, are produced and distributed through contracts with a number of different suppliers.

Competition

The Company's primary competitors for coffee beverage sales are restaurants, specialty coffee shops and doughnut shops. In almost all markets in which the Company does business, there are numerous competitors in the specialty coffee beverage business, and management expects this situation to continue. Although competition in the beverage market is currently fragmented, a major competitor with substantially greater financial, marketing and operating resources than the Company could enter this market at any time and compete directly against Starbucks.

The Company's whole bean coffees compete directly against specialty coffees sold through supermarkets, specialty retailers and a growing number of specialty coffee stores. Both the Company's whole bean coffees and its coffee beverages compete indirectly against all other coffees on the market. The Company believes that its customers choose among retailers primarily on the basis of product quality, service and convenience, and, to a lesser extent, on price.

Starbucks believes that supermarkets are the most competitive distribution channel for specialty whole bean coffee, in part because supermarkets offer customers a variety of choices without having to make a separate trip to a specialty coffee store. A number of coffee manufacturers are distributing premium coffee products in supermarkets that may serve as substitutes for the Company's coffees. Regional specialty coffee companies also sell whole bean coffees in supermarkets.

In addition to the competition generated by supermarket sales of coffee, Starbucks competes for whole bean coffee sales with franchise operators and independent specialty coffee stores. In virtually every major metropolitan area where Starbucks operates and expects to expand, there are local or regional competitors with substantial market presence in the specialty coffee business. Starbucks Specialty Operations also face significant competition from established wholesale and mail order suppliers, some of whom have greater financial and marketing resources than the Company.

Starbucks faces intense competition from both restaurants and other specialty retailers for suitable sites for new stores and qualified personnel to operate both new and existing stores. There can be no assurance that Starbucks will be able to continue to secure adequate sites at acceptable rent levels or that the Company will be able to attract a sufficient number of qualified personnel.

Patents, Trademarks, Copyrights and Domain Names

The Company owns and/or has applied to register numerous trademarks and service marks in the United States and in more than 150 additional countries throughout the world. Rights to the trademarks and service marks in the United States are generally held by a wholly owned affiliate of the Company and are used by the Company under license. Some of the Company's trademarks, including Starbucks®, the Starbucks logo, Frappuccino®, Seattle's Best Coffee® and Tazo® are of material importance to the Company. The duration of trademark registrations varies from country to country. However, trademarks are generally valid and may be renewed indefinitely as long as they are in use and/or their registrations are properly maintained.

The Company owns numerous copyrights for items such as product packaging, promotional materials, in-store graphics and training materials. The Company also holds patents on certain products, systems and designs. In addition, the Company has registered and maintains numerous Internet domain names, including "Starbucks.com" and "Starbucks.net."

Research and Development

Starbucks research and development efforts are led by food scientists, engineers, chemists and culinarians in the Research and Development department. This team is responsible for the technical development of food and beverage products and new equipment. The Company spent approximately $10.5 million, $8.3 million and $5.4 million during fiscal 2005, 2004 and 2003, respectively, on technical research and development activities, in addition to customary product testing and product and process improvements in all areas of its business.

Seasonality and Quarterly Results

Starbucks business is subject to seasonal fluctuations. Significant portions of the Company's net revenues and profits are realized during the first quarter of the fiscal year, which includes the December holiday season. In addition, quarterly results are affected by the timing of the opening of new stores, and the Company's rapid growth may conceal the impact of other seasonal influences. Because of the seasonality of the business, results for any quarter are not necessarily indicative of the results that may be achieved for the full fiscal year.

Employees

As of October 2, 2005, the Company employed approximately 115,000 people worldwide. In the United States, Starbucks employed approximately 97,500 people, with 91,200 in Company-operated retail stores and the remainder in the Company's administrative and regional offices, and store development, roasting and warehousing operations. Approximately 17,500 employees were employed in International Company-operated retail stores, regional support facilities, roasting and warehousing operations. At fiscal year end, employees at 10 of the Company's Canadian stores were represented by a union. Starbucks believes its current relations with its employees are good.

Item 1A. *Risk Factors*   * * *

• *Failure of the Company's internal control over financial reporting could harm its business and financial results.*

The management of Starbucks is responsible for establishing and maintaining adequate internal control over financial reporting. Internal control over financial reporting is a process to provide reasonable assurance regarding the reliability of financial reporting for external purposes in accordance with accounting principles generally accepted in the United States of America. Internal control over financial reporting includes maintaining records that in reasonable detail accurately and fairly reflect the Company's transactions; providing reasonable assurance that transactions are recorded as necessary for preparation of the financial statements; providing reasonable assurance that receipts and expenditures of the Company's assets are made in accordance with management authorization; and providing reasonable assurance that unauthorized acquisition, use or disposition of the Company assets that could have a material effect on the financial statements would be prevented or detected on a timely basis. Because of its inherent limitations, internal control over financial reporting is not intended to provide absolute assurance that a misstatement of the Company's financial statements would be prevented or detected. The Company's rapid growth and entry into new, globally dispersed markets will place significant additional pressure on the Company's system of internal control over financial reporting. Any failure to maintain an effective system of internal control over financial reporting could limit the Company's ability to report its financial results accurately and timely or to detect and prevent fraud.

Executive Officers of the Registrant

The executive officers of the Company are as follows:

Name	Age	Position
Howard Schultz	52	chairman of the Board of Directors
James L. Donald	51	president, chief executive officer and director
James C. Alling	44	president, Starbucks Coffee U.S.
Martin Coles	50	president, Starbucks Coffee International
Michael Casey	60	executive vice president, chief financial officer and chief administrative officer
Paula E. Boggs	46	executive vice president, general counsel and secretary
Dorothy J. Kim	43	executive vice president, Supply Chain Operations
David A. Pace	46	executive vice president, Partner Resources

Howard Schultz is the founder of the Company and the chairman of the board. From the Company's inception in 1985 to June 2000, he served as chairman of the board and chief executive officer. From June 2000 to February 2005, Mr. Schultz also held the title of chief global strategist. From 1985 to June 1994, Mr. Schultz was the Company's president. From January 1986 to July 1987, Mr. Schultz was the chairman of the board, chief executive officer and president of Il Giornale Coffee Company, a predecessor to the Company. From September 1982 to December 1985, Mr. Schultz was the director of retail operations and marketing for Starbucks Coffee Company, a predecessor to the Company. Mr. Schultz also serves on the board of directors of DreamWorks Animation SKG, Inc.

James L. Donald joined Starbucks in October 2002 and has been president and chief executive officer and a director of the Company since April 2005. From October 2004 to April 2005, Mr. Donald served as ceo designate. Prior to that, Mr. Donald served as president, North America from the time he joined the Company in October 2002. From October 1996 to October 2002, Mr. Donald served as chairman, president and ceo of Pathmark Stores, Inc. and prior to that time he held a variety of senior management positions with Albertson's, Inc., Safeway, Inc., and Wal-Mart Stores, Inc.

James C. Alling joined Starbucks in September 1997 as senior vice president, Grocery and was promoted to president, Starbucks Coffee U.S. in October 2004. Mr. Alling held a number of positions as senior vice president from September 1997 until November 2003, when he was promoted to executive vice president, Business and Operations — United States. Prior to joining Starbucks, Mr. Alling held several senior positions at Nestlé from 1985 to 1997 and served as vice president and general manager of several divisions, including ground coffee.

Martin Coles joined Starbucks in April 2004 as president, Starbucks Coffee International. Prior to joining Starbucks, Mr. Coles served as an executive vice president of Reebok International, Ltd. from December 2001 to February 2004, including as president and chief executive officer of the Reebok® brand from June 2002 to February 2004 and executive vice president of Global Operating Units from December 2001 to May 2002. From February 2001 to December 2001, Mr. Coles was senior vice president, International Operations for

16

Gateway, Inc. From February 2000 to January 2001, Mr. Coles was president and chief executive officer of Letsbuyit.com. From September 1992 to February 2000, Mr. Coles held several executive level general management, sales and operations positions for NIKE Inc.'s Global and European operations.

Michael Casey joined Starbucks in August 1995 as senior vice president and chief financial officer and was promoted to executive vice president, chief financial officer and chief administrative officer in September 1997. Prior to joining Starbucks, Mr. Casey served as executive vice president and chief financial officer of Family Restaurants, Inc. from its inception in 1986. During his tenure there, he also served as a director from 1986 to 1993, and as president and chief executive officer of its El Torito Restaurants, Inc. subsidiary from 1988 to 1993. Mr. Casey serves on the board of directors of The Nasdaq Stock Market, Inc.

Paula E. Boggs joined Starbucks in September 2002 as executive vice president, general counsel and secretary. Prior to joining Starbucks, Ms. Boggs served as vice president, legal, for products, operations and information technology at Dell Computer Corporation from 1997 to 2002. From 1995 to 1997, Ms. Boggs was a partner with the law firm of Preston Gates & Ellis. Ms. Boggs served in several roles at the Pentagon, White House and U.S. Department of Justice between 1984 and 1995.

Dorothy J. Kim joined Starbucks in November 1995 and was promoted to executive vice president, Supply Chain Operations in December 2004. From April 2003 to December 2004, Ms. Kim was senior vice president, Global Logistics, Planning and Procurement. From April 2002 to April 2003, Ms. Kim was vice president, Supply Chain and Coffee Operations, Logistics, and from October 2000 to April 2002, Ms. Kim was vice president, Supply Chain and Coffee Operations, Finance and Systems. Prior to becoming a vice president, Ms. Kim held several positions in retail planning and operations.

David A. Pace joined Starbucks in July 2002 as executive vice president of Partner Resources. From 2000 to 2002, Mr. Pace was the president of i2 Technologies. From 1999 to 2000 Mr. Pace served as the chief human resources officer for HomeGrocer.com. From 1995 to 1999, he served as senior vice president of human resources for Tricon Restaurants International (now YUM! Brands, Inc.).

There are no family relationships between any directors or executive officers of the Company.

17

PART II

Item 5. *Market for the Registrant's Common Equity, Related Shareholder Matters and Issuer Purchases of Equity Securities*

The following table provides information regarding repurchases by the Company of its common stock during the 13-week period ended October 2, 2005, as adjusted to give effect to the Company's two-for-one stock split completed on October 21, 2005:

Issuer Purchases of Equity Securities

Period[1]	Total Number of Shares Purchased	Average Price Paid per Share	Total Number of Shares Purchased as Part of Publicly Announced Plans or Programs[2]	Maximum Number of Shares That May Yet Be Purchased Under the Plans or Programs[2]
Jul 4, 2005 - Jul 31, 2005	6,705,000	$ 25.69	6,705,000	18,516,080
Aug 1, 2005 - Aug 28, 2005	4,144,002	$ 25.41	4,144,002	14,372,078
Aug 29, 2005 - Oct 2, 2005	2,276,550	$ 24.00	2,276,550	22,095,528
Total	13,125,552	$ 25.31	13,125,552	

[1] Monthly information is presented by reference to the Company's fiscal months during the fourth quarter of fiscal 2005.

[2] The Company's share repurchase program is conducted under authorizations made from time to time by the Company's Board of Directors. The shares reported in the table are covered by Board authorizations to repurchase shares of common stock, as adjusted to give effect for the two-for-one stock split completed on October 21, 2005, as follows: 18 million shares announced on September 23, 2004; and 20 million shares announced on May 5, 2005. On September 22, 2005, the Board authorized the repurchase of 10 million shares. Shares remaining for repurchase relate only to the authorizations announced on May 5, 2005 and September 22, 2005. Neither of these authorizations has an expiration date.

18

* * *

Item 6. *Selected Financial Data*

In thousands, except earnings per share and store operating data

The following selected financial data are derived from the consolidated financial statements of the Company. The data below should be read in conjunction with "Management's Discussion and Analysis of Financial Condition and Results of Operations," "Risk Factors," and the Company's consolidated financial statements and notes.

As of and for the Fiscal Year Ended[1]	Oct 2, 2005 (52 Wks)	Oct 3, 2004 (53 Wks)	Sept 28, 2003 (52 Wks)	Sept 29, 2002 (52 Wks)	Sep 30, 2001 (52 Wks)
RESULTS OF OPERATIONS					
Net revenues:					
Company-operated retail	$5,391,927	$4,457,378	$ 3,449,624	$ 2,792,904	$ 2,229,594
Specialty:					
Licensing	673,015	565,798	409,551	311,932	240,665
Foodservice and other	304,358	271,071	216,347	184,072	178,721
Total specialty	977,373	836,869	625,898	496,004	419,386
Total net revenues	6,369,300	5,294,247	4,075,522	3,288,908	2,648,980
Operating income	780,615	606,587	420,850	313,304	277,745
Internet-related investment losses[2]	—	—	—	—	2,940
Gain on sale of investment[3]	—	—	—	13,361	—
Net earnings	$ 494,467	$ 388,973	$ 265,355	$ 210,463	$ 178,794
Net earnings per common share — diluted[4]	$ 0.61	$ 0.47	$ 0.33	$ 0.26	$ 0.23
Cash dividends per share	—	—	—	—	—
BALANCE SHEET					
Working capital[5]	$ (17,662)	$ 604,636	$ 335,767	$ 328,777	$ 165,045
Total assets	3,514,065	3,386,541	2,776,112	2,249,435	1,807,746
Short-term borrowings[6]	277,000	—	—	—	—
Long-term debt (including current portion)	3,618	4,353	5,076	5,786	6,483
Shareholders' equity	$2,090,634	$2,470,211	$ 2,068,689	$ 1,712,456	$ 1,366,355
STORE INFORMATION					
Percentage change in comparable store sales:[7]					
United States	9%	11%	9%	7%	5%
International	6%	6%	7%	1%	3%
Consolidated	8%	10%	8%	6%	5%
Stores opened during the year:[8][9]					
United States					
Company-operated stores	574	514	506	503	498
Licensed stores	596	417	315	264	268
International					
Company-operated stores	161	141	124	117	151
Licensed stores	341	272	256	293	291
Total	1,672	1,344	1,201	1,177	1,208
Stores open at year end:[9]					
United States[10]					
Company-operated stores	4,867	4,293	3,779	3,209	2,706
Licensed stores	2,435	1,839	1,422	1,033	769
International					
Company-operated stores	1,133	972	831	707	590
Licensed stores	1,806	1,465	1,193	937	644
Total	10,241	8,569	7,225	5,886	4,709

(1) The Company's fiscal year ends on the Sunday closest to September 30.

(2) During fiscal 2001, the Company recognized losses of $2.9 million for impairments of Internet-related investments determined to be other-than-temporary.

(3) On October 10, 2001, the Company sold 30,000 of its shares of Starbucks Coffee Japan, Ltd. at approximately $495 per share, net of related costs, which resulted in a gain of $13.4 million.

(4) Earnings per share data for fiscal years presented above have been restated to reflect the two-for-one stock splits in fiscal 2006 and 2001.

(5) Working capital deficit as of October 2, 2005 was primarily due to lower investments from the sale of securities to fund common stock repurchases and increased current liabilities from short term borrowings under the revolving credit facility. See (6) below.

(6) In August 2005, the Company entered into a $500 million five-year revolving credit facility and had borrowings of $277 million outstanding as of October 2, 2005.

(7) Includes only Starbucks Company-operated retail stores open 13 months or longer. Comparable store sales percentage for fiscal 2004 excludes the extra sales week.

(8) Store openings are reported net of closures.

(9) International store information has been adjusted for the fiscal 2005 acquisitions of Germany, Southern China and Chile licensed operations by reclassifying historical information from Licensed stores to Company-operated stores.

(10) United States stores open at fiscal 2003 year end included 43 SBC and 21 Torrefazione Italia Company- operated stores and 74 SBC franchised stores.

Item 7. *Management's Discussion and Analysis of Financial Condition and Results of Operations*

General

Starbucks Corporation's fiscal year ends on the Sunday closest to September 30. The fiscal years ended on October 2, 2005 and September 28, 2003, included 52 weeks. The fiscal year ended October 3, 2004, included 53 weeks, with the 53rd week falling in the fiscal fourth quarter.

Management Overview

During the fiscal year ended October 2, 2005, all areas of Starbucks business, from U.S. and International Company-operated retail operations to the Company's specialty businesses, delivered strong financial performance. Starbucks believes the Company's ability to achieve the balance between growing its core business and building the foundation for future growth is the key to increasing long-term shareholder value. Starbucks fiscal 2005 performance reflects the Company's continuing commitment to achieving this balance.

The primary driver of the Company's revenue growth continues to be the opening of new retail stores, both Company-operated and licensed, in pursuit of the Company's objective to establish Starbucks as the most recognized and respected brand in the world. Starbucks opened 1,672 new stores in fiscal 2005 and plans to open approximately 1,800 in fiscal 2006. With a presence in 37 countries, management continues to believe that the Company's long-term goal of 15,000 Starbucks retail locations throughout the United States and at least 15,000 stores in International markets is achievable.

In addition to opening new retail stores, Starbucks works to increase revenues generated at new and existing Company-operated stores by attracting new customers and increasing the frequency of visits by current customers. The strategy is to increase comparable store sales by continuously improving the level of customer service, introducing innovative products and improving the speed of service through training, technology and process improvement. Global comparable store sales for Company-operated markets increased by 8%, making fiscal 2005 the 14th consecutive year with comparable store sales growth of five percent or greater. Comparable store sales for fiscal 2006 are expected to be in the range of three to seven percent.

In licensed retail operations, Starbucks leverages the expertise of local partners and shares its operating and store development experience to help licensees improve the profitability of existing stores and build new stores. Internationally, the Company's strategy is to selectively increase its equity stake in licensed international operations as these markets develop.

The combination of more retail stores, higher revenues from existing stores and growth in other business channels in both the United States and International operating segments resulted in a 20% increase in total net revenues for the 52 weeks of fiscal 2005, compared to the 53 weeks of fiscal 2004. Excluding the impact of the extra week in fiscal 2004, total net revenues increased 23%. Both of these revenue growth measures were at or above the Company's three to five year target of approximately 20%.

The Company's International operations delivered improved operating results, primarily due to leverage gained on most operating expenses distributed over an expanded revenue base. In recent fiscal years, the Company made substantial infrastructure investments in corporate and regional support facilities and personnel, as well as established more efficient distribution networks. Such investments have been and will continue to be necessary to support the Company's planned international expansion, which is now realizing substantial benefit from this foundation. Since both additional International and U.S. retail stores can leverage existing support organizations and facilities, the Company's infrastructure can be expanded more slowly than the rate of revenue growth and generate margin improvement. In fiscal 2005, operating income as a percentage of total net revenues increased to 12.3% from 11.5% in fiscal 2004, and net earnings increased by 27%, compared to fiscal 2004. These results demonstrated the Company's ability to improve operating margin while at the same time making strategic investments in the core retail business and in emerging specialty channels.

Acquisitions

During fiscal 2005, Starbucks increased its equity ownership in its licensed operations in Germany, Southern China and Chile, to 100%, 51% and 100%, respectively, for a combined purchase price of $41 million. Previously, the Company owned less than 20% in each of these operations, which were accounted for under the cost method. These increases in equity ownership resulted in a change of accounting method, from the cost method to the consolidation method, on the respective dates of acquisition. This accounting change also included adjusting previously reported information for the Company's proportionate share of net losses in Germany, Southern China and Chile. The cumulative effect of the accounting change for previously reported information resulted in a reduction of net earnings of $0.1 million for the 39 weeks ended July 3, 2005, and a reduction of retained earnings of $4.0 million prior to fiscal 2005.

In April 2005, Starbucks acquired substantially all of the assets of Ethos Brands, LLC, ("Ethos"), a privately held bottled water company based in Santa Monica, California, for $8 million. The earnings of Ethos are included in the accompanying consolidated financial statements from the date of acquisition.

ULTS OF OPERATIONS — FISCAL 2005 COMPARED TO FISCAL 2004

ollowing table presents the consolidated statement of earnings as well as the percentage relationship to total net revenues, unless otherwise indicated, of items ded in the Company's consolidated statements of earnings *(amounts in thousands)*:

Year Ended	Oct 2, 2005 (52 Wks)	% of Revenues	Oct 3, 2004 (53 Wks)	% of Revenues	Sept 28, 2003 (52 Wks)	% of Revenues
TEMENTS OF EARNINGS DATA						
evenues:						
ompany-operated retail	$ 5,391,927	84.7%	$ 4,457,378	84.2%	$ 3,449,624	84.6%
ecialty:						
Licensing	673,015	10.5	565,798	10.7	409,551	10.1
Foodservice and other	304,358	4.8	271,071	5.1	216,347	5.3
tal specialty	977,373	15.3	836,869	15.8	625,898	15.4
net revenues	6,369,300	100.0	5,294,247	100.0	4,075,522	100.0
of sales including occupancy costs	2,605,212	40.9	2,191,440	41.4	1,681,434	41.3
operating expenses	2,165,911	40.2[1]	1,790,168	40.2[1]	1,379,574	40.0[1]
operating expenses	197,024	20.2[2]	171,648	20.5[2]	141,346	22.6[2]
eciation and amortization expenses	340,169	5.3	289,182	5.5	244,671	6.0
ral and administrative expenses	357,114	5.6	304,293	5.7	244,550	6.0
btotal operating expenses	5,665,430	88.9	4,746,731	89.7	3,691,575	90.6
ne from equity investees	76,745	1.2	59,071	1.1	36,903	0.9
erating income	780,615	12.3	606,587	11.5	420,850	10.3
est and other income, net	15,829	0.2	14,140	0.2	11,622	0.3
ings before income taxes	796,444	12.5	620,727	11.7	432,472	10.6
ne taxes	301,977	4.7	231,754	4.4	167,117	4.1
et earnings	$ 494,467	7.8%	$ 388,973	7.3%	$ 265,355	6.5%

Shown as a percentage of related Company-operated retail revenues.

Shown as a percentage of related total specialty revenues.

olidated Results of Operations Net revenues for the fiscal year ended 2005 increased 20% to $6.4 billion from $5.3 billion for the 53-week period of fiscal 2004, n by increases in both Company-operated retail revenues and specialty operations. Net revenues increased 23% when calculated on a comparative 52-week basis for fiscal 2005 and 2004. Net revenues are expected to grow approximately 20% in fiscal 2006 compared to fiscal 2005.

ng the fiscal year ended 2005, Starbucks derived 85% of total net revenues from its Company-operated retail stores. Company-operated retail revenues increased 21% .4 billion for the fiscal year ended 2005, from $4.5 billion for the 53-week period of fiscal 2004. Company-operated retail revenues increased 23% when calculated on a comparative 52-week basis for both fiscal 2005 and 2004. This increase was primarily due to the opening of 735 new Company-operated retail stores in the last 12 months and comparable store sales growth of 8% for the 52 weeks ended October 2, 2005. The increase in comparable store sales was due to a 4% increase in the number of customer transactions and a 4% increase in the average value per transaction. Comparable store sales growth percentages were calculated excluding the extra week of fiscal 2004. Management believes increased customer traffic continues to be driven by new product innovation, continued popularity of core products, a high level of customer satisfaction and improved speed of service through enhanced technology, training and execution at retail stores. The increase in the average value per transaction was primarily due to a beverage price increase in October 2004 in the Company's U.S. and Canadian markets.

The Company derived the remaining 15% of total net revenues from channels outside the Company-operated retail stores, collectively known as "Specialty Operations." Specialty revenues, which include licensing revenues and foodservice and other revenues, increased 17% to $977 million for the fiscal year ended 2005, from $837 million for the 53-week period of fiscal 2004. Excluding the impact of the extra week in fiscal 2004, total specialty revenues increased 19%.

Licensing revenues, which are derived from retail store licensing arrangements, as well as grocery, warehouse club and certain other branded-product licensed operations, increased 19% to $673 million for the 52 week period of 2005, from $566 million for the 53-week period of fiscal 2004. Excluding the impact of the extra week in fiscal 2004, total licensing revenues increased 21%, primarily due to higher product sales and royalty revenues from the opening of 937 new licensed retail stores in the last 12 months.

Foodservice and other revenues increased 12% to $304 million for the 52-week period of fiscal 2005, from $271 million for the 53-week period of fiscal 2004. Excluding the impact of the extra week in fiscal 2004, foodservice and other revenues increased 15%, primarily attributable to growth in new and existing U.S. and International foodservice accounts and, to a lesser extent, growth in the Company's emerging entertainment business.

Cost of sales including occupancy costs decreased to 40.9% of total net revenues in the 52-week period of fiscal 2005, from 41.4% in the 53-week period of 2004. The decrease was primarily due to higher average revenue per retail transaction, offset in part by higher initial costs associated with the continued expansion of a lunch program in Company-operated retail stores. Approximately 3,800 Company-operated stores had the lunch program at the end of fiscal 2005, compared to approximately 2,600 at the end of fiscal 2004.

Store operating expenses as a percentage of Company-operated retail revenues were 40.2% for both the 52-week period of fiscal 2005 and the 53-week period of fiscal 2004, primarily due to higher average revenue per retail transaction in fiscal 2005, offset by higher payroll-related expenditures, as well as higher maintenance and repair expenditures to ensure a consistent *Starbucks Experience* in existing stores. In order to facilitate ongoing retail store revenue growth, the Company opened a higher number of drive-thru locations over the past year and extended store operating hours, which contributed to the higher payroll-related expenditures.

Other operating expenses (expenses associated with the Company's Specialty Operations) decreased to 20.2% of specialty revenues in the 52-week period of fiscal 2005, compared to 20.5% in the 53-week period of fiscal 2004. The decrease was primarily due to lower expenditures within the grocery, warehouse club and foodservice businesses, partially offset by higher payroll-related expenditures to support the Company's emerging entertainment business and to support the growth of Seattle's Best Coffee licensed café operations.

Depreciation and amortization expenses increased to $340 million in the 52-week period of fiscal 2005, from $289 million in the 53-week period of fiscal 2004. The increase was primarily from the opening of 735 new Company-operated retail stores in the last 12 months. As a percentage of total net revenues, depreciation and amortization decreased to 5.3% for the 52 weeks ended October 2, 2005, from 5.5% for the corresponding 53-week fiscal 2004 period.

General and administrative expenses increased to $357 million in the 52-week period of fiscal 2005, compared to $304 million in the 53-week period of fiscal 2004. The increase was primarily due to higher payroll-related expenditures in support of both domestic and international business growth and increased charitable donations to support multi-year corporate commitments. As a percentage of total net revenues, general and administrative expenses decreased to 5.6% for the 52 weeks ended October 2, 2005, from 5.7% for the 53 weeks ended October 3, 2004.

Income from equity investees increased to $77 million in the 52-week period of fiscal 2005, compared to $59 million in the 53-week period of fiscal 2004. The increase was primarily due to volume-driven operating results for The North American Coffee Partnership, which produces bottled Frappuccino® coffee drinks and Starbucks DoubleShot® espresso drink, and improved operating results from international investees, particularly in Japan and Korea, mainly as a result of new store openings.

Operating income increased 29% to $781 million in the 52-week period of fiscal 2005, from $607 million in the 53-week period of fiscal 2004. The operating margin increased to 12.3% of total net revenues in the 52-week period of fiscal 2005, compared to 11.5% in the 53-week period of fiscal 2004, primarily due to strong revenue growth.

Net interest and other income, which primarily consists of interest income, increased to $16 million in the 52-week period of fiscal 2005, from $14 million in the 53-week period of fiscal 2004. The increase was primarily due to higher interest income earned due to higher interest rates in fiscal 2005 compared to fiscal 2004 and to foreign exchange gains in fiscal 2005 compared to losses in fiscal 2004. Partially offsetting these increases were higher realized losses on sales of available-for-sale securities. Starbucks funded the majority of its share repurchases during fiscal 2005 through sales of its available-for-sale securities.

Income taxes for the 52 weeks ended October 2, 2005, resulted in an effective tax rate of 37.9%, compared to 37.3% in fiscal 2004. The effective tax rate differs from the statutory rate of 35% due to a variety of factors, including state income taxes, the impact from foreign operations, tax credits and other provision adjustments. The effective tax rate for fiscal 2006 is expected to be approximately 38%, with quarterly variations.

25

Operating Segments

Segment information is prepared on the same basis that the Company's management reviews financial information for operational decision-making purposes. The following tables summarize the Company's results of operations by segment for fiscal 2005 and 2004 *(in thousands)*:

52 Weeks Ended October 2, 2005	United States	% of United States Revenue	Inter-national	% of Inter-national Revenue	Unallocated Corporate	% of Total Net Revenue	Consolidated
Net revenues:							
Company-operated retail	$4,539,455	85.1%	$ 852,472	82.4%	$ —	—%	$ 5,391,927
Specialty:							
Licensing	514,932	9.7	158,083	15.3	—		673,015
Foodservice and other	280,073	5.2	24,285	2.3	—	—	304,358
Total specialty	795,005	14.9	182,368	17.6	—		977,373
Total net revenues	5,334,460	100.0	1,034,840	100.0	—	—	6,369,300
Cost of sales including occupancy costs	2,086,707	39.1	518,505	50.1	—		2,605,212
Store operating expenses	1,848,836	40.7[1]	317,075	37.2[1]	—	—	2,165,911
Other operating expenses	162,793	20.5[2]	34,231	18.8[2]	—		197,024
Depreciation and amortization expenses	250,415	4.7	56,705	5.5	33,049	0.5	340,169
General and administrative expenses	85,362	1.6	53,069	5.1	218,683	3.4	357,114
Income from equity investees	45,579	0.9	31,166	3.0	—	—	76,745
Operating income/(loss)	$ 945,926	17.7%	$ 86,421	8.4%	$ (251,732)	(3.9)%	$ 780,615

53 Weeks Ended October 3, 2004	United States	% of United States Revenue	Inter-national	% of Inter-national Revenue	Unallocated Corporate	% of Total Net Revenue	Consolidated
Net revenues:							
Company-operated retail	$3,800,367	84.6%	$657,011	81.8%	$ —	—%	$ 4,457,378
Specialty:							
Licensing	436,981	9.7	128,817	16.0	—		565,798
Foodservice and other	253,502	5.7	17,569	2.2	—	—	271,071
Total specialty	690,483	15.4	146,386	18.2	—		836,869
Total net revenues	4,490,850	100.0	803,397	100.0	—	—	5,294,247
Cost of sales including occupancy costs	1,782,584	39.7	408,856	50.9	—		2,191,440
Store operating expenses	1,546,871	40.7[1]	243,297	37.0[1]	—	—	1,790,168
Other operating expenses	144,853	21.0[2]	26,795	18.3[2]	—		171,648
Depreciation and amortization expenses	210,448	4.7	46,196	5.8	32,538	0.6	289,182
General and administrative expenses	80,221	1.8	48,206	6.0	175,866	3.3	304,293
Income from equity investees	37,453	0.8	21,618	2.7	—	—	59,071
Operating income/(loss)	$ 763,326	17.0%	$ 51,665	6.4%	$ (208,404)	(3.9)%	$ 606,587

[1] Shown as a percentage of related Company-operated retail revenues.
[2] Shown as a percentage of related total specialty revenues.

United States

The Company's United States operations ("United States") represent 84% of Company-operated retail revenues, 81% of total specialty revenues and 84% of total net revenues. United States operations sells coffee and other beverages, whole bean coffees, complementary food, coffee brewing equipment and merchandise primarily through Company-operated retail stores. Specialty Operations within the United States include licensed retail stores and other licensing operations, foodservice accounts and other initiatives related to the Company's core business.

United States total net revenues increased 19% to $5.3 billion for the fiscal year ended 2005, compared to $4.5 billion for the 53-week period of fiscal 2004. Excluding the impact of the extra week in fiscal 2004, United States total net revenues increased 21%.

United States Company-operated retail revenues increased 19% to $4.5 billion for the fiscal year ended 2005, compared to $3.8 billion for the 53-week period of fiscal 2004. Excluding the impact of the extra week in fiscal 2004, United States Company-operated retail revenues increased 22%, primarily due to the opening of 574 new Company-operated retail stores in the last 12 months and comparable store sales growth of 9% for the 52-week period of fiscal 2005. The increase in comparable store sales was due to a 5% increase in the average value per transaction, including 3% attributable to a beverage price increase in October 2004, and a 4% increase in the number of customer transactions. Management believes increased customer traffic continues to be driven by new product innovation, continued popularity of core products, a high level of customer satisfaction and improved speed of service through enhanced technology, training and execution at retail stores.

Total United States specialty revenues increased 15% to $795 million for the fiscal year ended 2005, compared to $690 million in the 53-week period of fiscal 2004. Excluding the impact of the extra week in fiscal 2004, United States specialty revenues increased 18%. United States licensing revenues increased 18% to $515 million, compared to $437 million for the 53-week period of fiscal 2004. Excluding the impact of the extra week in fiscal 2004, United States licensing revenues increased 20%, primarily due to increased product sales and royalty revenues as a result of opening 596 new licensed retail stores in the last 12 months. Foodservice and other revenues increased 10% to $280 million from $254 million for the 53-week period of fiscal 2004. Excluding the impact of the extra week in fiscal 2004, United States foodservice and other revenues increased 13%, primarily due to growth in new and existing foodservice accounts, as well as growth in the emerging entertainment business.

United States operating income increased by 24% to $946 million for the fiscal year ended 2005, from $763 million for the fiscal year ended 2004. Operating margin increased to 17.7% of related revenues from 17.0% in the 53-week period of fiscal 2004. The increase was primarily due to leverage from strong revenue growth, partially offset by higher retail store operating expenses primarily due to higher payroll-related expenditures to facilitate ongoing retail store revenue growth.

International

The Company's international operations ("International") represent the remaining 16% of Company-operated retail revenues, 19% of total specialty revenues and 16% of total net revenues. International operations sells coffee and other beverages, whole bean coffees, complementary food, coffee brewing equipment and merchandise through Company-operated retail stores in the United Kingdom, Canada, Thailand, Australia, Germany, Singapore, China, Chile and Ireland. Specialty Operations in International primarily include retail store licensing operations in more than 25 other countries and foodservice accounts in Canada and the United Kingdom. Certain of the Company's International operations are in various early stages of development that necessitate a more extensive support organization, relative to the current levels of revenue and operating income, than in the United States.

International total net revenues increased 29% to $1.0 billion for the fiscal year ended 2005, compared to $803 million for the 53-week period of fiscal 2004. Excluding the impact of the extra week in fiscal 2004, International total net revenues increased 31%. International Company-operated retail revenues increased 30% to $852 million for the fiscal year ended 2005, compared to $657 million for the 53-week period of fiscal 2004. Excluding the impact of the extra week in fiscal 2004, International Company-operated revenues increased 32%, primarily due to the opening of 161 new Company-operated retail stores in the last 12 months, comparable store sales growth of 6% for the 52-week period of fiscal 2005, and the weakening of the U.S. dollar against both the Canadian dollar and British pound sterling. The increase in comparable store sales resulted from a 4% increase in the number of customer transactions and a 2% increase in the average value per transaction.

Total International specialty revenues increased 25% to $182 million for the fiscal year ended 2005, compared to $146 million for the 53-week period of fiscal 2004. Excluding the impact of the extra week in fiscal 2004, International specialty revenues increased 27%. International licensing revenues increased 23% to $158 million for the fiscal year ended 2005, compared to $129 million in the 53-week period of fiscal 2004. Excluding the impact of the extra week in 2004, International licensing revenues increased 25%, primarily due to higher product sales and royalty revenues from opening 341 new licensed retail stores in the last 12 months, volume driven growth in the Canadian grocery and warehouse club businesses, and, to a lesser extent, the launch of new ready-to-drink coffee beverages in Japan and Taiwan. International foodservice and other revenues increased 38% to $24 million for the fiscal year ended 2005, compared to $18 million in the 53-week period of fiscal 2004. Excluding the impact of the extra week in 2004, international foodservice and other revenues increased 41%, primarily due to growth in new and existing foodservice accounts.

International operating income increased to $86 million for the fiscal year ended 2005, compared to $52 million in the 53-week period of fiscal 2004. Operating margin increased to 8.4% of related revenues from 6.4% in the 53-week period of fiscal 2004, primarily due to leverage gained on most fixed costs distributed over an expanded revenue base.

Unallocated Corporate

Unallocated corporate expenses pertain to certain functions, such as executive management, accounting, administration, tax, treasury and information technology infrastructure, that support but are not specifically attributable to the Company's operating segments, and include related depreciation and amortization expenses. Unallocated corporate expenses increased to $252 million for the fiscal year ended 2005, from $208 million in the 53-week period of fiscal 2004, primarily due to increased charitable commitments as well as higher payroll-related expenditures. Total unallocated corporate expenses as a percentage of total net revenues remained unchanged at 3.9% for the fiscal year ended 2005 and the 53-week period of fiscal 2004.

28

* * *

LIQUIDITY AND CAPITAL RESOURCES

The following table represents components of the Company's most liquid assets *(in thousands):*

Fiscal Year Ended	Oct 2, 2005	Oct 3, 2004
Cash and cash equivalents	$ 173,809	$ 145,053
Short-term investments — available-for-sale	95,379	483,157
Short-term investments — trading securities	37,848	24,799
Long-term investments — available-for-sale securities	60,475	135,179
Total	$ 367,511	$ 788,188

Starbucks has reclassified its auction rate securities of $154.1 million, previously classified in "Cash and cash equivalents," as "Short-term investments — available-for-sale securities" on the consolidated balance sheet as of October 3, 2004. The Company had historically classified these securities as cash equivalents based on management's ability to liquidate its holdings during the predetermined interest rate reset auctions, which generally occurred within 90 days of acquiring the securities. Although management had determined the risk of failure of an auction process to be remote, the definition of a cash equivalent in Statement of Financial Accounting Standards No. 95, "Statement of Cash Flows," required reclassification to short-term investments. The Company has made corresponding adjustments to its consolidated statement of cash flows for the prior fiscal years of 2004 and 2003 to reflect the gross purchases, sales and maturities of auction rate securities as investing activities rather than as a component of cash and cash equivalents. There was no impact on previously reported cash flows from operating activities as a result of the reclassification.

The Company manages its cash, cash equivalents and liquid investments in order to internally fund operating needs. The $421 million decline in total cash and cash equivalents and liquid investments from October 3, 2004 to October 2, 2005, was nearly all due to the sale of securities to fund common stock repurchases. The Company intends to use its available cash resources, including any borrowings under its revolving credit facility described below, to invest in its core businesses and other new business opportunities related to its core businesses. The Company may use its available cash resources to make proportionate capital contributions to its equity method and cost method investees, as well as purchase larger ownership interests in selected equity method investees, particularly in international markets. Depending on market conditions, Starbucks may repurchase shares of its common stock under its authorized share repurchase program. Management believes that strong cash flow generated from operations, existing cash and investments, as well as borrowing capacity under the revolving credit facility, should be sufficient to finance capital requirements for its core businesses for the foreseeable future. Significant new joint ventures, acquisitions, share repurchases and/or other new business opportunities may require additional outside funding.

Other than normal operating expenses, cash requirements for fiscal 2006 are expected to consist primarily of capital expenditures for new Company-operated retail stores and the remodeling and refurbishment of existing Company-operated retail stores, as well as for additional share repurchases, if any. For fiscal 2006, management expects capital expenditures to be in the range of $700 million to $725 million, related to opening approximately 850 Company-operated stores on a global basis, remodeling certain existing stores and enhancing its production capacity and information systems.

In August 2005, the Company entered into a $500 million unsecured five-year revolving credit facility (the "Facility") with various banks, of which $100 million may be used for issuances of letters of credit. The Facility is scheduled to expire in August 2010 and is available for working capital, capital expenditures and other corporate purposes, which may include acquisitions and share repurchases. The Company may request an increase up to an additional $500 million under the credit facility, provided there is no existing default, which would increase total availability to $1 billion.

The interest rate for borrowings under the Facility ranges from 0.150% to 0.275% over LIBOR or an alternate base rate, which is the greater of the bank prime rate or the Federal Funds Rate plus 0.50%. The specific spread over LIBOR will depend upon the Company's performance under specified financial criteria. The Facility contains provisions that require the Company to maintain compliance with certain covenants, including the maintenance of certain financial ratios. As of October 2, 2005, the Company was in compliance with each of these covenants. There were borrowings of $277 million outstanding under the Facility as of October 2, 2005, with a weighted average contractual interest rate of 4.0%.

Cash provided by operating activities totaled $924 million in fiscal 2005 and was generated primarily by net earnings of $494 million and noncash depreciation and amortization expenses of $367 million.

Cash used by investing activities totaled $221 million in fiscal 2005. Net capital additions to property, plant and equipment used $644 million, primarily from opening 735 new Company-operated retail stores and remodeling certain existing stores. Gross capital additions for fiscal 2005 were $668 million and were offset by impairment provisions and foreign currency translation adjustments totaling $24 million. During fiscal 2005, the Company increased its equity ownership in its licensed operations in Germany, Southern China and Chile and also acquired substantially all of the assets of Ethos Brands, LLC, which together used $22 million, net of cash acquired. Partially offsetting these uses of cash, the net activity in the Company's portfolio of available-for-sale securities provided $452 million for the fiscal year ended October 2, 2005.

Cash used by financing activities in fiscal 2005 totaled $674 million. During fiscal 2005, the Company repurchased 45 million shares of its common stock at an average price of $25.26 per share, using $1.1 billion. Share repurchases, up to the limit authorized by the Board of Directors, are at the discretion of management and depend on market conditions, capital requirements and other factors. The total remaining amount of shares authorized for repurchase as of October 2, 2005 was 22 million. Partially offsetting cash used for share repurchases were borrowings of $277 million under the Facility and $164 million of proceeds from the exercise of employee stock options and the sale of the Company's common stock from employee stock purchase plans. As options granted are exercised, the Company will continue to receive proceeds (financing activity) and a tax deduction (operating activity); however, the amounts and the timing cannot be predicted.

The following table summarizes the Company's contractual obligations and borrowings as of October 2, 2005, and the timing and effect that such commitments are expected to have on the Company's liquidity and capital requirements in future periods *(in thousands)*:

| Contractual Obligations | Total | Payments Due by Period | | | |
		Less Than 1 Year	1-3 Years	3-5 Years	More Than 5 Years
Debt obligations[1]	$ 280,618	$ 277,748	$ 1,537	$ 1,127	$ 206
Operating lease obligations[2]	3,097,493	423,564	804,055	690,838	1,179,036
Purchase obligations	384,588	279,076	82,887	20,449	2,176
Total	$3,762,699	$ 980,388	$ 888,479	$ 712,414	$ 1,181,418

[1] Debt amounts include principal maturities only. The amount due in less than one year includes $277 million of short term borrowings under the Facility.

[2] Amounts include the direct lease obligations, excluding any taxes, insurance and other related expenses.

Starbucks expects to fund these commitments primarily with operating cash flows generated in the normal course of business.

Off-Balance Sheet Arrangement

The Company has unconditionally guaranteed the repayment of certain Japanese yen-denominated bank loans and related interest and fees of an unconsolidated equity investee, Starbucks Coffee Japan, Ltd. ("Starbucks Japan"). The guarantees continue until the loans, including accrued interest and fees, have been paid in full, with the final loan amount due in 2014. The maximum amount is limited to the sum of unpaid principal and interest amounts, as well as other related expenses. These amounts will vary based on fluctuations in the yen foreign exchange rate. As of October 2, 2005, the maximum amount of the guarantees was approximately $9.0 million. Since there has been no modification of these loan guarantees subsequent to the Company's adoption of Financial Accounting Standards Board ("FASB") Interpretation No. 45, "Guarantor's Accounting and Disclosure Requirements for Guarantees, Including Indebtedness of Others," Starbucks has applied the disclosure provisions only and has not recorded the guarantees on its balance sheet.

Product Warranties

Coffee brewing and espresso equipment sold to customers through Company-operated and licensed retail stores, as well as equipment sold to the Company's licensees for use in retail licensing operations, are under warranty for defects in materials and workmanship for a period ranging from 12 to 24 months. The Company establishes an accrual for estimated warranty costs at the time of sale, based on historical experience. The following table summarizes the activity related to product warranty reserves during fiscal 2005 and 2004 *(in thousands)*:

Fiscal Year Ended	Oct 2, 2005	Oct 3, 2004
Balance at beginning of fiscal year	$ 3,091	$ 2,227
Provision for warranties issued	7,494	5,093
Warranty claims	(8,827)	(4,229)
Balance at end of fiscal year	$ 1,758	$ 3,091

COMMODITY PRICES, AVAILABILITY AND GENERAL RISK CONDITIONS

The Company manages its exposure to various risks within the consolidated financial statements according to an umbrella risk management policy, which was approved in May 2005 by the Company's Board of Directors. Under this policy, market-based risks, including commodity costs and foreign currency exchange rates, are quantified and evaluated for potential mitigation strategies, such as entering into hedging transactions. Additionally, this policy restricts, among other things, the amount of market-based risk the Company will tolerate before implementing approved hedging strategies and does not allow for speculative trading activity.

The Company purchases significant amounts of coffee and dairy products to support the needs of its Company-operated retail stores. The price and availability of these commodities directly impacts the Company's results of operations and can be expected to impact its future results of operations. For additional details see "Product Supply" in Item 1, as well as "Risk Factors" in Item 1A of this Form 10-K.

FINANCIAL RISK MANAGEMENT

The Company is exposed to market risk related to foreign currency exchange rates, equity security prices and changes in interest rates.

Foreign Currency Exchange Risk

The majority of the Company's revenue, expense and capital purchasing activities is transacted in U.S. dollars. However, because a portion of the Company's operations consists of activities outside of the United States, the Company has transactions in other currencies, primarily the Canadian dollar, British pound sterling, Euro and Japanese yen. Under the Company's umbrella risk management policy, the Company frequently evaluates its foreign currency exchange risk by monitoring market data and external factors that may influence exchange rate fluctuations. As a result, Starbucks may engage in transactions involving various derivative instruments, with maturities generally not exceeding five years, to hedge assets, liabilities, revenues and purchases denominated in foreign currencies.

As of October 2, 2005, the Company had forward foreign exchange contracts that qualify as cash flow hedges under Statement of Financial Accounting Standard ("SFAS") No. 133, "Accounting for Derivative Instruments and Hedging Activities," to hedge a portion of anticipated international revenue and product purchases. In addition, Starbucks had forward foreign exchange contracts that qualify as a hedge of its net investment in Starbucks Japan. These contracts expire within 31 months.

Based on the foreign exchange contracts outstanding as of October 2, 2005, a 10% devaluation of the U.S. dollar as compared to the level of foreign exchange rates for currencies under contract as of October 2, 2005, would result in a reduced fair value of these derivative financial instruments of approximately $11.3 million, of which $4.6 million may reduce the Company's future earnings. Conversely, a 10% appreciation of the U.S. dollar would result in an increase in the fair value of these instruments of approximately $11.3 million, of which $5.8 million may increase the Company's future earnings. Consistent with the nature of the economic hedges provided by these foreign exchange contracts, increases or decreases in their fair value would be mostly offset by corresponding decreases or increases in the dollar value of the Company's foreign investment, future foreign currency royalty fee payments and product purchases that would occur within the hedging period.

Equity Security Price Risk

The Company has minimal exposure to price fluctuations on equity mutual funds within its trading portfolio. The trading securities approximate a portion of the Company's liability under the Management Deferred Compensation Plan ("MDCP"). A corresponding liability is included in "Accrued compensation and related costs" on the consolidated balance sheets. These investments are recorded at fair value with unrealized gains and losses recognized in "Interest and other income, net" in the consolidated statements of earnings. The offsetting changes in the MDCP liability are recorded in "General and administrative expenses."

Interest Rate Risk

The Company's available-for-sale securities comprise a diversified portfolio consisting mainly of fixed income instruments. The primary objectives of these investments are to preserve capital and liquidity. Available-for-sale securities are investment grade and are recorded on the balance sheet at fair value with unrealized gains and losses reported as a separate component of "Accumulated other comprehensive income/(loss)." The Company does not hedge the interest rate exposure on its available-for-sale securities. The Company performed a sensitivity analysis based on a 10% change in the underlying interest rate of its interest bearing financial instruments, including its short-term borrowings and long-term debt, as of the end of fiscal 2005, and determined that such a change would not have a significant effect on the fair value of these instruments.

SEASONALITY AND QUARTERLY RESULTS

The Company's business is subject to seasonal fluctuations. Historically, significant portions of the Company's net revenues and profits were, and may continue to be realized during the first quarter of the Company's fiscal year, which includes the December holiday season. In addition, quarterly results are affected by the timing of the opening of new stores, and the Company's rapid growth may conceal the impact of other seasonal influences. Because of the seasonality of the Company's business, results for any quarter are not necessarily indicative of the results that may be achieved for the full fiscal year.

APPLICATION OF CRITICAL ACCOUNTING POLICIES

Critical accounting policies are those that management believes are both most important to the portrayal of the Company's financial condition and results, and require management's most difficult, subjective or complex judgments, often as a result of the need to make estimates about the effect of matters that are inherently uncertain. Judgments and uncertainties affecting the application of those policies may result in materially different amounts being reported under different conditions or using different assumptions.

Starbucks considers its policies on impairment of long-lived assets and accounting for self insurance reserves to be the most critical in understanding the judgments that are involved in preparing its consolidated financial statements.

Impairment of Long-Lived Assets

When facts and circumstances indicate that the carrying values of long-lived assets may be impaired, an evaluation of recoverability is performed by comparing the carrying values of the assets to projected future cash flows, in addition to other quantitative and qualitative analyses. For goodwill and other intangible assets, impairment tests are performed annually and more frequently if facts and circumstances indicate goodwill carrying values exceed estimated reporting unit fair values and if indefinite useful lives are no longer appropriate for the Company's trademarks. Upon indication that the carrying values of such assets may not be recoverable, the Company recognizes an impairment loss as a charge against current operations. Property, plant and equipment assets are grouped at the lowest level for which there are identifiable cash flows when assessing impairment. Cash flows for retail assets are identified at the individual store level. Long-lived assets to be disposed of are reported at the lower of their carrying amount or fair value, less estimated costs to sell. Judgments made by the Company related to the expected useful lives of long-lived assets and the ability of the Company to realize undiscounted cash flows in excess of the carrying amounts of such assets are affected by factors such as the ongoing maintenance and improvements of the assets, changes in economic conditions and changes in operating performance. As the Company assesses the ongoing expected cash flows and carrying amounts of its long-lived assets, these factors could cause the Company to realize material impairment charges.

Self Insurance Reserves

The Company uses a combination of insurance and self-insurance mechanisms, including a wholly owned captive insurance entity and participation in a reinsurance pool, to provide for the potential liabilities for workers' compensation, healthcare benefits, general liability, property insurance, director and officers' liability insurance and vehicle liability. Liabilities associated with the risks that are retained by the Company are not discounted and are estimated, in part, by considering historical claims experience, demographic factors, severity factors and other actuarial assumptions. The estimated accruals for these liabilities, portions of which are calculated by third party actuarial firms, could be significantly affected if future occurrences and claims differ from these assumptions and historical trends.

NEW ACCOUNTING STANDARDS

In November 2005, the FASB issued Staff Position No. FAS 115-1, "The Meaning of Other-Than-Temporary Impairment and Its Application to Certain Investments" ("FSP 115-1"). FSP 115-1 provides accounting guidance for identifying and recognizing other-than-temporary impairments of debt and equity securities, as well as cost method investments in addition to disclosure requirements. FSP 115-1 is effective for reporting periods beginning after December 15, 2005, and earlier application is permitted. The Company has adopted this new pronouncement in its fourth quarter of fiscal 2005. The adoption of FSP 115-1 did not have an impact on the Company's consolidated financial statements. The required disclosures are presented in Notes 4 and 7 of this Report.

In March 2005, the FASB issued Interpretation No. 47, "Accounting for Conditional Asset Retirement Obligations, an interpretation of FASB Statement No. 143" ("FIN 47"). FIN 47 requires the recognition of a liability for the fair value of a legally-required conditional asset retirement obligation when incurred, if the liability's fair value can be reasonably estimated. FIN 47 also clarifies when an entity would have sufficient information to reasonably estimate the fair value of an asset retirement obligation. FIN 47 is effective for fiscal years ending after December 15, 2005, or no later than Starbucks fiscal fourth quarter of 2006. The Company has not yet determined the impact of adoption on its consolidated statement of earnings and balance sheet.

In December 2004, the FASB issued SFAS No. 123R, "Share-Based Payment" ("SFAS 123R"), a revision of SFAS 123. SFAS 123R will require Starbucks to, among other things, measure all employee stock-based compensation awards using a fair value method and record the expense in the Company's consolidated financial statements. The provisions of SFAS 123R, as amended by SEC Staff Accounting Bulletin No. 107, "Share-Based Payment," are effective no later than the beginning of the next fiscal year that begins after June 15, 2005. Starbucks will adopt the new requirements using the modified prospective transition method in its first fiscal quarter of 2006, which ends January 1, 2006. In addition to the recognition of expense in the financial statements, under SFAS 123R, any excess tax benefits received upon exercise of options will be presented as a financing activity inflow rather than as an adjustment of operating activity as currently presented. Based on its current analysis and information, management has determined that the impact of adopting SFAS 123R will result in a reduction of net earnings and expects diluted earnings per share to be reduced by approximately $0.09 on a full year basis for fiscal 2006.

In December 2004, the FASB issued Staff Position No. FAS 109-1, "Application of SFAS No. 109, Accounting for Income Taxes, to the Tax Deduction on Qualified Production Activities provided by the American Jobs Creation Act of 2004" ("FSP 109-1"). FSP 109-1 states that qualified domestic production activities should be accounted for as a special deduction under SFAS No. 109, "Accounting for Income Taxes," and not be treated as a rate reduction. The provisions of FSP 109-1 are effective immediately. The Company will qualify for a benefit beginning in fiscal 2006, which is not expected to be material to the Company's consolidated financial statements.

In December 2004, the FASB issued Staff Position No. FAS 109-2, "Accounting and Disclosure Guidance for the Foreign Earnings Repatriation Provision within the American Jobs Creation Act of 2004" ("FSP 109-2"). The American Jobs Creation Act allows a special one-time dividends received deduction on the repatriation of certain foreign earnings to a U.S. taxpayer (repatriation provision), provided certain criteria are met. The law allows the Company to make an election to repatriate earnings through fiscal 2006. FSP 109-2 provides accounting and disclosure guidance for the repatriation provision. Although FSP 109-2 was effective upon its issuance, it allows companies additional time beyond the enactment date to evaluate the effects of the provision on its plan for investment or repatriation of unremitted foreign earnings. The Company continues to evaluate the impact of the new Act to determine whether it will repatriate foreign earnings and the impact, if any, this pronouncement will have on its consolidated financial statements. As of October 2, 2005, the Company has not made an election to repatriate earnings under this provision. The Company may or may not elect to repatriate earnings in fiscal 2006. Earnings under consideration for repatriation range from $0 to $75 million and the related income tax effects range from $0 to $5 million. As provided in FSP 109-2, Starbucks has not adjusted its tax expense or deferred tax liability to reflect the repatriation provision.

In November 2004, the FASB issued Statement No. 151, "Inventory Costs, an amendment of ARB No. 43, Chapter 4" ("SFAS 151"). SFAS 151 clarifies that abnormal inventory costs such as costs of idle facilities, excess freight and handling costs, and wasted materials (spoilage) are required to be recognized as current period charges. The provisions of SFAS 151 are effective for fiscal years beginning after June 15, 2005. The adoption of SFAS 151 in fiscal 2006 is not expected to have a significant impact on the Company's consolidated balance sheet or statement of earnings.

Item 7A. *Quantitative and Qualitative Disclosures About Market Risk*

The information required by this item is incorporated by reference to the section entitled "Management's Discussion and Analysis of Financial Condition and Results of Operations — Commodity Prices, Availability and General Risk Conditions" and "Management's Discussion and Analysis of Financial Condition and Results of Operations — Financial Risk Management" in Item 7 of this Report.

Item 8. *Financial Statements and Supplementary Data*

CONSOLIDATED STATEMENTS OF EARNINGS

In thousands, except earnings per share

Fiscal Year Ended	Oct 2, 2005	Oct 3, 2004	Sept 28, 2003
Net revenues:			
Company-operated retail	$ 5,391,927	$ 4,457,378	$ 3,449,624
Specialty:			
Licensing	673,015	565,798	409,551
Foodservice and other	304,358	271,071	216,347
Total specialty	977,373	836,869	625,898
Total net revenues	6,369,300	5,294,247	4,075,522
Cost of sales including occupancy costs	2,605,212	2,191,440	1,681,434
Store operating expenses	2,165,911	1,790,168	1,379,574
Other operating expenses	197,024	171,648	141,346
Depreciation and amortization expenses	340,169	289,182	244,671
General and administrative expenses	357,114	304,293	244,550
Subtotal operating expenses	5,665,430	4,746,731	3,691,575
Income from equity investees	76,745	59,071	36,903
Operating income	780,615	606,587	420,850
Interest and other income, net	15,829	14,140	11,622
Earnings before income taxes	796,444	620,727	432,472
Income taxes	301,977	231,754	167,117
Net earnings	$ 494,467	$ 388,973	$ 265,355
Net earnings per common share — basic	$ 0.63	$ 0.49	$ 0.34
Net earnings per common share — diluted	$ 0.61	$ 0.47	$ 0.33
Weighted average shares outstanding:			
Basic	789,570	794,347	781,505
Diluted	815,417	822,930	803,296

See Notes to Consolidated Financial Statements.

CONSOLIDATED BALANCE SHEETS

In thousands, except share data

Fiscal Year Ended	Oct 2, 2005	Oct 3, 2004
ASSETS		
Current assets:		
Cash and cash equivalents	$ 173,809	$ 145,053
Short-term investments — available-for-sale securities	95,379	483,157
Short-term investments — trading securities	37,848	24,799
Accounts receivable, net of allowances of $3,079 and $2,231, respectively	190,762	140,226
Inventories	546,299	422,663
Prepaid expenses and other current assets	94,429	71,347
Deferred income taxes, net	70,808	63,650
Total current assets	1,209,334	1,350,895
Long-term investments — available-for-sale securities	60,475	135,179
Equity and other investments	201,461	167,740
Property, plant and equipment, net	1,842,019	1,551,416
Other assets	72,893	85,561
Other intangible assets	35,409	26,800
Goodwill	92,474	68,950
TOTAL ASSETS	$ 3,514,065	$ 3,386,541
LIABILITIES AND SHAREHOLDERS' EQUITY		
Current liabilities:		
Accounts payable	$ 220,975	$ 199,346
Accrued compensation and related costs	232,354	208,927
Accrued occupancy costs	44,496	29,231
Accrued taxes	78,293	62,959
Short-term borrowings	277,000	—
Other accrued expenses	198,082	123,684
Deferred revenue	175,048	121,377
Current portion of long-term debt	748	735
Total current liabilities	1,226,996	746,259
Deferred income taxes, net	—	21,770
Long-term debt	2,870	3,618
Other long-term liabilities	193,565	144,683
Shareholders' equity:		
Common stock ($0.001 par value) and additional paid-in-capital — authorized, 1,200,000,000 shares; issued and outstanding, 767,442,110 and 794,811,688 shares, respectively, (includes 3,394,200 common stock units in both periods)	90,968	956,685
Other additional paid-in-capital	39,393	39,393
Retained earnings	1,939,359	1,444,892
Accumulated other comprehensive income	20,914	29,241
Total shareholders' equity	2,090,634	2,470,211
TOTAL LIABILITIES AND SHAREHOLDERS' EQUITY	$ 3,514,065	$ 3,386,541

See Notes to Consolidated Financial Statements.

[There is no page 42 in Appendix A because the Consolidated Statements of Cash Flows was moved to page 109 of the text.]

CONSOLIDATED STATEMENTS OF SHAREHOLDERS' EQUITY

In thousands, except share data

	Common Stock Shares	Amount	Additional Paid-In Capital	Other Additional Paid-In Capital	Retained Earnings	Accumulated Other Comprehensive Income/(Loss)	Total
Balance, September 29, 2002	776,457,184	$ 776	$ 890,264	$ 39,393	$ 790,564	$ (8,541)	$ 1,712,456
Net earnings	—	—	—	—	265,355	—	265,355
Unrealized holding losses, net	—	—	—	—	—	(4,426)	(4,426)
Translation adjustment	—	—	—	—	—	27,241	27,241
Comprehensive income							288,170
Exercise of stock options, including tax benefit of $35,547	16,039,208	16	129,092	—	—	—	129,108
Sale of common stock, including tax benefit of $1,043	1,486,680	1	14,664	—	—	—	14,665
Repurchase of common stock	(6,598,000)	(6)	(75,704)	—	—	—	(75,710)
Balance, September 28, 2003	787,385,072	$ 787	$ 958,316	$ 39,393	$ 1,055,919	$ 14,274	$ 2,068,689
Net earnings	—	—	—	—	388,973	—	388,973
Unrealized holding losses, net	—	—	—	—	—	(4,925)	(4,925)
Translation adjustment	—	—	—	—	—	19,892	19,892
Comprehensive income							403,940
Exercise of stock options, including tax benefit of $62,415	15,416,982	16	172,016	—	—	—	172,032
Sale of common stock, including tax benefit of $990	1,968,144	2	28,961	—	—	—	28,963
Repurchase of common stock	(9,958,510)	(10)	(203,403)	—	—	—	(203,413)
Balance, October 3, 2004	794,811,688	$ 795	$ 955,890	$ 39,393	$ 1,444,892	$ 29,241	$ 2,470,211
et earnings	—	—	—	—	494,467	—	494,467
Unrealized holding gains, net	—	—	—	—	—	350	350
Translation adjustment	—	—	—	—	—	(8,677)	(8,677)
Comprehensive income							486,140
Exercise of stock options, including tax benefit of $108,428	16,169,992	16	239,012	—	—	—	239,028
Sale of common stock, including tax benefit of $1,550	1,563,964	1	34,504	—	—	—	34,505
Repurchase of common stock	(45,103,534)	(45)	(1,139,205)	—	—	—	(1,139,250)
Balance, October 2, 2005	767,442,110	$ 767	$ 90,201	$ 39,393	$ 1,939,359	$ 20,914	$ 2,090,634

See Notes to Consolidated Financial Statements.

NOTES TO CONSOLIDATED FINANCIAL STATEMENTS

Fiscal years ended October 2, 2005, October 3, 2004, and September 28, 2003

Note 1: Summary of Significant Accounting Policies

Description of Business

Starbucks Corporation (together with its subsidiaries, "Starbucks" or the "Company") purchases and roasts high-quality whole bean coffees and sells them, along with fresh, rich-brewed coffees, Italian-style espresso beverages, cold blended beverages, a variety of complementary food items, coffee-related accessories and equipment, a selection of premium teas and a line of compact discs, primarily through its Company-operated retail stores. Starbucks sells coffee and tea products and licenses its trademark through other channels and, through certain of its equity investees, Starbucks also produces and sells bottled Frappuccino® coffee drinks and Starbucks DoubleShot® espresso drink and a line of superpremium ice creams. All channels outside the Company-operated retail stores are collectively known as "Specialty Operations." The Company's objective is to establish Starbucks as the most recognized and respected brand in the world. To achieve this goal, the Company plans to continue rapid expansion of its retail operations, to grow its Specialty Operations and to selectively pursue other opportunities to leverage the Starbucks brand through the introduction of new products and the development of new channels of distribution.

Principles of Consolidation

The consolidated financial statements reflect the financial position and operating results of Starbucks, which include wholly owned subsidiaries and investees controlled by the Company.

Investments in entities that the Company does not control, but has the ability to exercise significant influence over operating and financial policies, are accounted for under the equity method. Investments in entities in which Starbucks does not have the ability to exercise significant influence are accounted for under the cost method.

All significant intercompany transactions have been eliminated.

Fiscal Year End

Starbucks Corporation's fiscal year ends on the Sunday closest to September 30. The fiscal years ended on October 2, 2005 and September 28, 2003, included 52 weeks. The fiscal year ended October 3, 2004, included 53 weeks, with the 53rd week falling in the fiscal fourth quarter.

Reclassifications

Certain reclassifications of prior year's balances have been made to conform to the current format. Specifically, Starbucks has reclassified its auction rate securities of $154.1 million, previously classified in "Cash and cash equivalents," as "Short-term investments — available-for-sale securities" on the consolidated balance sheet as of October 3, 2004. The Company had historically classified these securities as cash equivalents based on management's ability to liquidate its holdings during the predetermined interest rate reset auctions, which generally occurred within 90 days of acquiring the securities. Although management had determined the risk of failure of an auction process to be remote, the definition of a cash equivalent in Statement of Financial Accounting Standards ("SFAS") No. 95, "Statement of Cash Flows" ("SFAS 95"), requires reclassification to short-term investments.

The Company has made corresponding adjustments to its consolidated statement of cash flows for the fiscal years ended 2004 and 2003 to reflect the gross purchases, sales and maturities of auction rate securities as investing activities rather than as a component of cash and cash equivalents. There was no impact on

44

previously reported net earnings, cash flows from operating activities or shareholders' equity as a result of this reclassification.

Additionally, the Company has reclassified its distributions received from equity investees on the consolidated statement of cash flows, from investing activities to operating activities, for the fiscal years ended 2004 and 2003. These distributions represented returns on the underlying equity investments, and therefore have been reclassified to be in accordance with the provisions of SFAS 95. There was no impact on the previously reported consolidated statements of earnings or consolidated balance sheets as a result of this reclassification.

Collectively, these adjustments increased net cash used by investing activities in the consolidated statements of cash flows by $91.0 million and $96.5 million for the fiscal years ended 2004 and 2003, respectively.

Estimates and Assumptions

The preparation of financial statements in conformity with accounting principles generally accepted in the United States of America requires management to make estimates and assumptions that affect the reported amounts of assets, liabilities, revenues and expenses. Actual results may differ from these estimates.

Cash and Cash Equivalents

The Company considers all highly liquid instruments with a maturity of three months or less at the time of purchase to be cash equivalents. The Company maintains cash and cash equivalent balances with financial institutions that exceed federally insured limits. The Company has not experienced any losses related to these balances, and management believes its credit risk to be minimal.

Cash Management

The Company's cash management system provides for the reimbursement of all major bank disbursement accounts on a daily basis. Checks issued but not presented for payment to the bank are reflected as a reduction of cash and cash equivalents on the consolidated financial statements.

Short-term and Long-term Investments

The Company's short-term and long-term investments consist primarily of investment-grade marketable debt securities as well as bond and equity mutual funds, all of which are classified as trading or available-for-sale. Trading securities are recorded at fair value with unrealized holding gains and losses included in net earnings. Available-for-sale securities are recorded at fair value, and unrealized holding gains and losses are recorded, net of tax, as a separate component of accumulated other comprehensive income. Available-for-sale securities with remaining maturities of less than one year and those identified by management at time of purchase for funding operations in less than one year are classified as short-term, and all other available-for-sale securities are classified as long-term. Unrealized losses are charged against net earnings when a decline in fair value is determined to be other than temporary. Management reviews several factors to determine whether a loss is other than temporary, such as the length of time a security is in an unrealized loss position, extent to which fair value is less than amortized cost, the impact of changing interest rates in the short and long term, the financial condition and near term prospects of the issuer and the Company's intent and ability to hold the security for a period of time sufficient to allow for any anticipated recovery in fair value. Realized gains and losses are accounted for on the specific identification method. Purchases and sales are recorded on a trade date basis.

Fair Value of Financial Instruments

The carrying value of cash and cash equivalents approximates fair value because of the short-term maturity of those instruments. The fair value of the Company's investments in marketable debt and equity securities, as well as bond and equity mutual funds, is based upon the quoted market price on the last business day of the fiscal year. For equity securities of companies that are privately held, or where an observable quoted market price does not exist, the Company estimates fair value using a variety of valuation methodologies. Such methodologies include comparing the security with securities of publicly traded companies in similar lines of business, applying revenue multiples to estimated future operating results for the private company and estimating discounted cash flows for that company. Declines in fair value below the Company's carrying value deemed to be other than temporary are charged against earnings. For further information on investments, see Notes 4 and 7. The carrying value of short-term and long-term debt approximates fair value.

Derivative Instruments

The Company manages its exposure to various risks within the consolidated financial statements according to an umbrella risk management policy. Under this policy, Starbucks may engage in transactions involving various derivative instruments, with maturities generally not longer than five years, to hedge assets, liabilities, revenues and purchases.

The Company follows SFAS No. 133, "Accounting for Derivative Instruments and Hedging Activities," as amended and interpreted, which requires that all derivatives be recorded on the balance sheet at fair value. For a cash flow hedge, the effective portion of the derivative's gain or loss is initially reported as a component of other comprehensive income ("OCI") and subsequently reclassified into net earnings when the hedged exposure affects net earnings. For a net investment hedge, the effective portion of the derivative's gain or loss is reported as a component of OCI.

Cash flow hedges related to anticipated transactions are designated and documented at the inception of each hedge by matching the terms of the contract to the underlying transaction. The Company classifies the cash flows from hedging transactions in the same categories as the cash flows from the respective hedged items. Once established, cash flow hedges are generally not removed until maturity unless an anticipated transaction is no longer likely to occur. Discontinued or derecognized cash flow hedges are immediately settled with counterparties, and the related accumulated derivative gains or losses are recognized into net earnings in "Interest and other income, net" on the consolidated statements of earnings.

Forward contract effectiveness for cash flow hedges is calculated by comparing the fair value of the contract to the change in value of the anticipated transaction using forward rates on a monthly basis. For net investment hedges, the spot-to-spot method is used to calculate effectiveness. Under this method, the change in fair value of the forward contract attributable to the changes in spot exchange rates (the effective portion) is reported in other comprehensive income. The remaining change in fair value of the forward contract (the ineffective portion) is reclassified into net earnings. Any ineffectiveness is recognized immediately in "Interest and other income, net" on the consolidated statements of earnings.

Allowance for doubtful accounts

Allowance for doubtful accounts is calculated based on historical experience and application of the specific identification method.

Inventories

Inventories are stated at the lower of cost (primarily moving average cost) or market. The Company records inventory reserves for obsolete and slow-moving items and for estimated shrinkage between physical inventory counts. Inventory reserves are based on inventory turnover trends, historical experience and application of the specific identification method. As of October 2, 2005 and October 3, 2004, inventory reserves were $8.3 million and $5.7 million, respectively.

Property, Plant and Equipment

Property, plant and equipment are carried at cost less accumulated depreciation. Depreciation of property, plant and equipment, which includes assets under capital leases, is provided on the straight-line method over estimated useful lives, generally ranging from two to seven years for equipment and 30 to 40 years for buildings. Leasehold improvements are amortized over the shorter of their estimated useful lives or the related lease life, generally 10 years. For leases with renewal periods at the Company's option, Starbucks generally uses the original lease term, excluding renewal option periods to determine estimated useful lives. If failure to exercise a renewal option imposes an economic penalty to Starbucks, management may determine at the inception of the lease that renewal is reasonably assured and include the renewal option period in the determination of appropriate estimated useful lives. The portion of depreciation expense related to production and distribution facilities is included in "Cost of sales including occupancy costs" on the consolidated statements of earnings. The costs of repairs and maintenance are expensed when incurred, while expenditures for refurbishments and improvements that significantly add to the productive capacity or extend the useful life of an asset are capitalized. When assets are retired or sold, the asset cost and related accumulated depreciation are eliminated with any remaining gain or loss reflected in net earnings.

Goodwill and Other Intangible Assets

Goodwill and other intangible assets are tested for impairment annually in June and more frequently if facts and circumstances indicate goodwill carrying values exceed estimated reporting unit fair values and if indefinite useful lives are no longer appropriate for the Company's trademarks. Based on the impairment tests performed, there was no impairment of goodwill in fiscal 2005, 2004 and 2003. Definite-lived intangibles, which mainly consist of contract-based patents and copyrights, are amortized over their estimated useful lives. For further information on goodwill and other intangible assets, see Note 9.

Long-lived Assets

When facts and circumstances indicate that the carrying values of long-lived assets may be impaired, an evaluation of recoverability is performed by comparing the carrying values of the assets to projected future cash flows in addition to other quantitative and qualitative analyses. Upon indication that the carrying values of such assets may not be recoverable, the Company recognizes an impairment loss by a charge against current operations. Property, plant and equipment assets are grouped at the lowest level for which there are identifiable cash flows when assessing impairment. Cash flows for retail assets are identified at the individual store level.

The Company recognized net impairment and disposition losses of $21.2 million, $18.8 million and $15.9 million in fiscal 2005, 2004 and 2003, respectively, primarily from renovation and remodeling activity and, to a lesser extent, from underperforming Company-operated retail stores, in the normal course of business. Depending on the underlying asset that is impaired, these losses may be recorded in any one of the operating expense lines on the consolidated statements of earnings: for retail operations, these losses are recorded in "Store operating expenses"; for Specialty Operations, these losses are recorded in "Other operating expenses"; and for all other operations, these losses are recorded in either "Cost of sales including occupancy costs" or "General and administrative expenses."

Insurance Reserves

The Company uses a combination of insurance and self-insurance mechanisms, including a wholly owned captive insurance entity and participation in a reinsurance pool, to provide for the potential liabilities for workers' compensation, healthcare benefits, general liability, property insurance, director and officers' liability insurance and vehicle liability. Liabilities associated with the risks that are retained by the Company are not discounted and are estimated, in part, by considering historical claims experience, demographic factors, severity factors and other actuarial assumptions. The estimated accruals for these liabilities, portions of which are calculated by third party actuarial firms, could be significantly affected if future occurrences and claims differ from these assumptions and historical trends. As of October 2, 2005, and October 3, 2004, these reserves were $91.6 million and $77.6 million, respectively, and were included in "Accrued compensation and related costs" and "Other accrued expenses" on the consolidated balance sheets.

Revenue Recognition

Consolidated revenues are presented net of intercompany eliminations for wholly owned subsidiaries and for licensees accounted for under the equity method, based on the Company's percentage ownership. Additionally, consolidated revenues are recognized net of any discounts, returns, allowances and sales incentives, including coupon redemptions and rebates.

Retail Revenues

Company-operated retail store revenues are recognized when payment is tendered at the point of sale. Revenues from stored value cards are recognized upon redemption. Until the redemption of stored value cards, outstanding customer balances on these cards are included in "Deferred revenue" on the consolidated balance sheets.

Specialty Revenues

Specialty revenues consist primarily of product sales to customers other than through Company-operated retail stores, as well as royalties and other fees generated from licensing operations. Sales of coffee, tea and related products are generally recognized upon shipment to customers, depending on contract terms. Shipping charges billed to customers are also recognized as revenue, and the related shipping costs are included in "Cost of sales including occupancy costs" on the consolidated statements of earnings.

Specific to retail store licensing arrangements, initial nonrefundable development fees are recognized upon substantial performance of services for new market business development activities, such as initial business, real estate and store development planning, as well as providing operational materials and functional training courses for opening new licensed retail markets. Additional store licensing fees are recognized when new licensed stores are opened. Royalty revenues based upon a percentage of reported sales and other continuing fees, such as marketing and service fees, are recognized on a monthly basis when earned.

Other arrangements involving multiple elements and deliverables as well as upfront fees are individually evaluated for revenue recognition. Cash payments received in advance of product or service delivery are recorded as deferred revenue.

Advertising

The Company expenses most advertising costs as they are incurred, except for certain production costs of advertising that are expensed the first time the advertising campaign takes place and direct-response advertising, which is capitalized and amortized over its expected period of future benefits. Direct-response advertising consists primarily of customer acquisition expenses including applications for customers to apply for the Starbucks Card Duetto™. These capitalized costs are amortized over the life of the credit card which is estimated to be three years.

Total advertising expenses, recorded in "Store operating expenses", "Other operating expenses" and "General and administrative expenses" on the consolidated statements of earnings totaled $87.7 million, $67.2 million and $49.6 million in fiscal 2005, 2004 and 2003, respectively. As of October 2, 2005, and October 3, 2004,

$11.8 million and $5.8 million, respectively, of capitalized advertising costs were recorded in "Prepaid expenses and other current assets" on the consolidated balance sheets.

Store Preopening Expenses

Costs incurred in connection with the start-up and promotion of new store openings are expensed as incurred.

Operating Leases

Starbucks leases retail stores, roasting and distribution facilities and office space under operating leases. Most lease agreements contain tenant improvement allowances, rent holidays, lease premiums, rent escalation clauses and/or contingent rent provisions. For purposes of recognizing incentives, premiums and minimum rental expenses on a straight-line basis over the terms of the leases, the Company uses the date of initial possession to begin amortization, which is generally when the Company enters the space and begins to make improvements in preparation of intended use.

For tenant improvement allowances and rent holidays, the Company records a deferred rent liability in "Accrued occupancy costs" and "Other long-term liabilities" on the consolidated balance sheets and amortizes the deferred rent over the terms of the leases as reductions to rent expense on the consolidated statements of earnings.

For premiums paid upfront to enter a lease agreement, the Company records a deferred rent asset in "Prepaid expenses and other current assets" and "Other assets" on the consolidated balance sheets and then amortizes the deferred rent over the terms of the leases as additional rent expense on the consolidated statements of earnings.

For scheduled rent escalation clauses during the lease terms or for rental payments commencing at a date other than the date of initial occupancy, the Company records minimum rental expenses on a straight-line basis over the terms of the leases on the consolidated statements of earnings.

Certain leases provide for contingent rents, which are determined as a percentage of gross sales in excess of specified levels. The Company records a contingent rent liability in "Accrued occupancy costs" on the consolidated balance sheets and the corresponding rent expense when specified levels have been achieved or when management determines that achieving the specified levels during the fiscal year is probable.

Stock-based Compensation

The Company maintains several stock equity incentive plans under which incentive stock options and nonqualified stock options may be granted to employees, consultants and nonemployee directors. Starbucks accounts for stock-based compensation using the intrinsic value method prescribed in Accounting Principles Board ("APB") Opinion No. 25, "Accounting for Stock Issued to Employees," and related interpretations. Accordingly, because the grant price equals the market price on the date of grant, no compensation expense is recognized by the Company for stock options issued to employees.

If compensation cost for the Company's stock options had been recognized based upon the estimated fair value on the grant date under the fair value methodology allowed by SFAS No. 123 "Accounting for Stock-Based Compensation" ("SFAS 123"), as amended, the Company's net earnings and earnings per share would have been as follows *(in thousands, except earnings per share)*:

Fiscal Year Ended	Oct 2, 2005	Oct 3, 2004	Sept 28, 2003
Net earnings	$ 494,467	$ 388,973	$ 265,355
Deduct: stock-based compensation expense, net of tax	(58,742)	(45,056)	(37,436)
Pro forma net income	$ 435,725	$ 343,917	$ 227,919
Net earnings per common share — basic:			
As reported	$ 0.63	$ 0.49	$ 0.34
Deduct: stock-based compensation expense, net of tax	(0.08)	(0.06)	(0.05)
Pro forma	$ 0.55	$ 0.43	$ 0.29
Net earnings per common share — diluted:			
As reported	$ 0.61	$ 0.47	$ 0.33
Deduct: stock-based compensation expense, net of tax	(0.08)	(0.05)	(0.04)
Pro forma	$ 0.53	$ 0.42	$ 0.29

The above pro forma information regarding net income and earnings per share has been determined as if the Company had accounted for its employee stock options under the fair value method. The fair value for these stock options was estimated at the date of grant using a Black-Scholes option pricing model with the following weighted average assumptions:

	Employee Stock Options		
Fiscal Year Ended	2005	2004	2003
Expected life (years)	1 - 6	1 - 6	2 - 5
Expected volatility	23% - 43%	22% - 50%	37% - 55%
Risk-free interest rate	2.4% - 4.2%	1.1% - 4.5%	0.9% - 4.0%
Expected dividend yield	0.00%	0.00%	0.00%

	Employee Stock Purchase Plans		
Fiscal Year Ended	2005	2004	2003
Expected life (years)	0.25 - 3	0.25 - 3	0.25 - 3
Expected volatility	20% - 40%	19% - 43%	30% - 50%
Risk-free interest rate	1.9% - 3.5%	0.9% - 2.3%	0.9% - 2.3%
Expected dividend yield	0.00%	0.00%	0.00%

The Company's valuations are based upon a multiple option valuation approach, and forfeitures are recognized as they occur. The Black-Scholes option valuation model was developed for use in estimating the fair value of traded options, which have no vesting restrictions and are fully transferable. In addition, option valuation models require the input of highly subjective assumptions, including the expected stock-price volatility. The Company's employee stock options have characteristics significantly different from those of traded options, and changes in the subjective input assumptions can materially affect the fair value estimate. Because Company stock options do not trade on a secondary exchange, employees do not derive a benefit from holding

50

stock options under these plans unless there is an increase, above the grant price, in the market price of the Company's stock. Such an increase in stock price would benefit all shareholders commensurately.

For option grants made in November 2003 and thereafter, the Company may provide for immediate vesting for optionees who have attained at least 10 years of service and are age 55 or older. For purposes of the pro forma presentation of stock-based compensation expense, the Company currently amortizes the expense over the related vesting period with acceleration of expense upon retirement. When the Company adopts SFAS No. 123R, "Share-Based Payment" ("SFAS 123R") in its first quarter of fiscal 2006, the accounting treatment for retirement features will change. Expense for awards made prior to adoption of SFAS 123R will continue to be amortized over the vesting period until retirement, at which point any remaining unrecognized expense will be immediately recognized. For awards made on or after October 3, 2005, the related expense will be recognized either from grant date through the date the employee reaches the years of service and age requirements, or from grant date through the stated vesting period, whichever is shorter.

As required by SFAS 123, the Company has determined that the weighted average estimated fair values of options granted during fiscal 2005, 2004 and 2003 were $8.10, $5.30 and $4.15 per share, respectively.

Foreign Currency Translation

The Company's international operations generally use their local currency as their functional currency. Assets and liabilities are translated at exchange rates in effect at the balance sheet date. Income and expense accounts are translated at the average monthly exchange rates during the year. Resulting translation adjustments are recorded as a separate component of accumulated other comprehensive income/(loss).

Income Taxes

The Company computes income taxes using the asset and liability method, under which deferred income taxes are provided for the temporary differences between the financial reporting basis and the tax basis of the Company's assets and liabilities.

Stock Split

On October 21, 2005, the Company effected a two-for-one stock split of its $0.001 par value common stock for holders of record on October 3, 2005. All applicable share and per-share data in these consolidated financial statements and related disclosures have been retroactively adjusted to give effect to this stock split.

Earnings per Share

The computation of basic earnings per share is based on the weighted average number of shares and common stock units that were outstanding during the period. The computation of diluted earnings per share includes the dilutive effect of common stock equivalents consisting of certain shares subject to stock options.

Common Stock Share Repurchases

The Company is allowed to repurchase shares of its common stock under a program authorized by its Board of Directors pursuant to a contract, instruction or written plan meeting the requirements of Rule 10b5-1(c)(1) of the Securities Exchange Act of 1934. Share repurchases are not displayed separately as treasury stock on the consolidated balance sheets or consolidated statements of shareholders' equity in accordance with the Washington Business Corporation Act. Instead, the par value of repurchased shares is deducted from "Common stock" and the remaining excess repurchase price over par value is deducted from "Additional paid-in capital." See Note 13 for additional information.

Recent Accounting Pronouncements

In November 2005, the FASB issued Staff Position No. FAS 115-1, "The Meaning of Other-Than-

Temporary Impairment and Its Application to Certain Investments" ("FSP 115-1"). FSP 115-1 provides accounting guidance for identifying and recognizing other-than-temporary impairments of debt and equity securities, as well as cost method investments in addition to disclosure requirements. FSP 115-1 is effective for reporting periods beginning after December 15, 2005, and earlier application is permitted. The Company has adopted this new pronouncement in its fourth quarter of fiscal 2005. The adoption of FSP 115-1 did not have an impact on the Company's consolidated financial statements. The required disclosures are presented in Notes 4 and 7 of this Report.

In March 2005, the FASB issued Interpretation No. 47, "Accounting for Conditional Asset Retirement Obligations, an interpretation of FASB Statement No. 143" ("FIN 47"). FIN 47 requires the recognition of a liability for the fair value of a legally-required conditional asset retirement obligation when incurred, if the liability's fair value can be reasonably estimated. FIN 47 also clarifies when an entity would have sufficient information to reasonably estimate the fair value of an asset retirement obligation. FIN 47 is effective for fiscal years ending after December 15, 2005, or no later than Starbucks fiscal fourth quarter of 2006. The Company has not yet determined the impact of adoption on its consolidated statement of earnings and balance sheet.

In December 2004, the FASB issued SFAS 123R, a revision of SFAS 123. SFAS 123R will require Starbucks to, among other things, measure all employee stock-based compensation awards using a fair value method and record the expense in the Company's consolidated financial statements. The provisions of SFAS 123R, as amended by SEC Staff Accounting Bulletin No. 107, "Share-Based Payment," are effective no later than the beginning of the next fiscal year that begins after June 15, 2005. Starbucks will adopt the new requirements using the modified prospective transition method in its first fiscal quarter of 2006, which ends January 1, 2006. In addition to the recognition of expense in the financial statements, under SFAS 123R, any excess tax benefits received upon exercise of options will be presented as a financing activity inflow rather than as an adjustment of operating activity as currently presented. Based on its current analysis and information, management has determined that the impact of adopting SFAS 123R will result in a material reduction of net earnings and diluted earnings per share.

In December 2004, the FASB issued Staff Position No. FAS 109-1, "Application of SFAS No. 109, Accounting for Income Taxes, to the Tax Deduction on Qualified Production Activities provided by the American Jobs Creation Act of 2004" ("FSP 109-1"). FSP 109-1 states that qualified domestic production activities should be accounted for as a special deduction under SFAS No. 109, "Accounting for Income Taxes," and not be treated as a rate reduction. The provisions of FSP 109-1 are effective immediately. The Company will qualify for a benefit beginning in fiscal 2006, which is not expected to be material to the Company's consolidated financial statements.

In December 2004, the FASB issued Staff Position No. FAS 109-2, "Accounting and Disclosure Guidance for the Foreign Earnings Repatriation Provision within the American Jobs Creation Act of 2004" ("FSP 109-2"). The American Jobs Creation Act allows a special one-time dividends received deduction on the repatriation of certain foreign earnings to a U.S. taxpayer (repatriation provision), provided certain criteria are met. The law allows the Company to make an election to repatriate earnings through fiscal 2006. FSP 109-2 provides accounting and disclosure guidance for the repatriation provision. Although FSP 109-2 was effective upon its issuance, it allows companies additional time beyond the enactment date to evaluate the effects of the provision on its plan for investment or repatriation of unremitted foreign earnings. The Company continues to evaluate the impact of the new Act to determine whether it will repatriate foreign earnings and the impact, if any, this pronouncement will have on its consolidated financial statements. As of October 2, 2005, the Company has not made an election to repatriate earnings under this provision. The Company may or may not elect to repatriate earnings in fiscal 2006. Earnings under consideration, or repatriation range from $0 to $75 million and the related income tax effects range from $0 to $5 million. As provided in FSP 109-2, Starbucks has not adjusted its tax expense or deferred tax liability to reflect the repatriation provision.

In November 2004, the FASB issued Statement No. 151, "Inventory Costs, an amendment of ARB No. 43, Chapter 4" ("SFAS 151"). SFAS 151 clarifies that abnormal inventory costs such as costs of idle facilities, excess freight and handling costs, and wasted materials (spoilage) are required to be recognized as current period charges. The provisions of SFAS 151 are effective for fiscal years beginning after June 15, 2005. The adoption of SFAS 151 in fiscal 2006 is not expected to have a significant impact on the Company's consolidated balance sheet or statement of earnings.

[Ed. Note—For publication convenience, notes 2 and 3 appear after note 4.)

Note 4:   Short-term and Long-term Investments

The Company's short-term and long-term investments consist of the following *(in thousands)*:

October 2, 2005	Amortized Cost	Gross Unrealized Holding Gains	Gross Unrealized Holding Losses	Fair Value
Short-term investments — available-for-sale securities:				
State and local government obligations	$ 47,960	$ 1	$ (179)	$ 47,782
Mutual funds	25,000	34	—	25,034
U.S. government agency obligations	11,327	—	(21)	11,306
Corporate debt securities	4,000	—	—	4,000
Asset-backed securities	7,373	—	(116)	7,257
Total	$ 95,660	$ 35	$ (316)	$ 95,379
Short-term investments — trading securities	35,376			37,848
Total short-term investments	$ 131,036			$ 133,227
Long-term investments — available-for-sale securities:				
State and local government obligations	$ 61,236	$ 7	$ (768)	$ 60,475

October 3, 2004	Amortized Cost	Gross Unrealized Holding Gains	Gross Unrealized Holding Losses	Fair Value
Short-term investments — available-for-sale securities:				
State and local government obligations	$ 436,754	$ 20	$ (583)	$ 436,191
U.S. government agency obligations	6,655	—	(4)	6,651
Corporate debt securities	27,275	—	—	27,275
Asset-backed securities	13,020	50	(30)	13,040
Total	$ 483,704	$ 70	$ (617)	$ 483,157
Short-term investments — trading securities	24,769			24,799
Total short-term investments	$ 508,473			$ 507,956
Long-term investments — available-for-sale securities:				
State and local government obligations	$ 130,810	$ 67	$ (348)	$ 130,529
Corporate debt securities	4,000	—	—	4,000
Asset-backed securities	658	—	(8)	650
Total long-term investments	$ 135,468	$ 67	$ (356)	$ 135,179

For available-for-sale securities, proceeds from sales were $626 million, $452 million and $141 million, in fiscal years 2005, 2004 and 2003, respectively. Gross realized gains from sales were $0.1 million, $0.2 million and $0.3 million in fiscal years 2005, 2004 and 2003, respectively, and gross realized losses from sales were $1.7 million in 2005 and $0.4 million in 2004. There were no gross realized losses in 2003.

The following tables present the length of time available-for-sale securities were in continuous unrealized loss positions but were not deemed to be other-than-temporarily impaired *(thousands)*:

Consecutive monthly unrealized losses

October 2, 2005	Less Than 12 Months		Greater Than or Equal to 12 Months	
	Gross Unrealized Holding Losses	Fair Value	Gross Unrealized Holding Losses	Fair Value
State and local government obligations	$ (371)	$ 49,527	$ (576)	$ 43,699
U.S. government agency obligations	(21)	11,306	—	—
Asset-backed securities	(34)	3,467	(82)	3,790
Total	$ (426)	$ 64,300	$ (658)	$ 47,489

Consecutive monthly unrealized losses

October 3, 2004	Less Than 12 Months		Greater Than or Equal to 12 Months	
	Gross Unrealized Holding Losses	Fair Value	Gross Unrealized Holding Losses	Fair Value
State and local government obligations	$ (931)	$ 376,318	$ —	$ —
U.S. government agency obligations	(4)	6,651	—	—
Asset-backed securities	(38)	7,097	—	—
Total	$ (973)	$ 390,066	$ —	$ —

Gross unrealized holding losses of $0.4 million for less than twelve months and $0.7 million for greater than or equal to twelve months as of October 2, 2005, pertain to 30 and 31 fixed income securities, respectively, and were primarily caused by interest rate increases. Since Starbucks has the ability and intent to hold these securities until a recovery of fair value, which may be at maturity, and because the unrealized losses were primarily due to higher interest rates, the Company does not consider these securities to be other-than-temporarily impaired.

Additional factors considered by management as of October 2, 2005, included the following, by category:

State and local government obligations

The contractual terms of these securities do not permit the issuer to settle at a price less than the par value of the investment, which is the equivalent of the amount due at maturity. These securities had a minimum credit rating of "A" and an average credit rating above "AA."

U.S. government agency obligations

These securities are obligations of an agency of the U.S. government and are rated "AAA." The contractual terms of these securities do not permit the issuer to settle at a price less than the par value of the investment, which is the equivalent of the amount due at maturity.

Asset-backed securities

These securities are guaranteed by an agency of the U.S. government or have a "AAA" credit rating. Additionally, these securities would not be settled at a price less than the par value of the investment, which the equivalent of the amount due at maturity.

There were no realized losses recorded for other than temporary impairments during fiscal 2005, 2004 or 2003.

Trading securities are comprised mainly of marketable equity mutual funds that approximate a portion of the Company's liability under the Management Deferred Compensation Plan, a defined contribution plan. The corresponding deferred compensation liability of $47.3 million in fiscal 2005 and $32.7 million in fiscal 2004 is included in "Accrued compensation and related costs" on the consolidated balance sheets. In fiscal years 2005 and 2004, the changes in net unrealized holding gains in the trading portfolio included in earnings were $2.4 million and $1.1 million, respectively.

Long-term investments generally mature in less than three years.

Note 2: Business Acquisitions

In November 2004, Starbucks increased its equity ownership from 18% to 100% for its licensed operations in Germany. As a result, management determined that a change in accounting method, from the cost method to the consolidation method, was necessary and included adjusting previously reported information for the Company's proportionate share of net losses of 18% as required by APB No. 18, "The Equity Method of Accounting for Investments in Common Stock." The cumulative effect of the accounting change for prior periods resulted in a reduction of retained earnings of $3.6 million as of October 3, 2004. See Note 19 in the Company's 2004 10-K/A for additional information.

In April 2005, Starbucks acquired substantially all of the assets of Ethos Brands, LLC, (such assets, "Ethos"), a privately held bottled water company based in Santa Monica, California, for $8 million. The earnings of Ethos are included in the accompanying consolidated financial statements from the date of acquisition.

In July 2005, Starbucks increased its equity ownership in its licensed operations in Southern China and Chile, to 51% and 100%, respectively, for purchase prices totaling $15 million, of which $10 million was payable as of October 2, 2005. Previously, Starbucks owned less than 20% in each of these operations, which were accounted for under the cost method. These increases in equity ownership resulted in a change of accounting method, from the cost method to the consolidation method, on the respective dates of acquisition. This accounting change also included adjusting previously reported information for the Company's proportionate share of net losses in Southern China and Chile. As shown in the tables below, the cumulative effect of the accounting change for financial results previously reported under the cost method and as restated in this Report under the equity method resulted in reductions of net earnings of $0.1 million for the 39 weeks ended July 3, 2005, and $0.3 million and $0.1 million for the fiscal years ended October 3, 2004, and September 28, 2003, respectively *(in thousands, except earnings per share)*:

Fiscal Period Ended	Jan 2, 2005 (13 Weeks)	April 3, 2005 (13 Weeks)	July 3, 2005 (13 Weeks)	July 3, 2005 (39 Weeks)
Net earnings, as previously reported	$ 144,753	$ 100,536	$ 125,575	$ 370,864
Effect of change to equity method	(43)	(54)	(47)	(144)
Net earnings, as restated for Southern China and Chile acquisitions	$ 144,710	$ 100,482	$ 125,528	$ 370,720
Net earnings per common share — basic:				
As previously reported	$ 0.18	$ 0.13	$ 0.16	$ 0.47
As restated for Southern China and Chile acquisitions	$ 0.18	$ 0.13	$ 0.16	$ 0.47
Net earnings per common share — diluted:				
As previously reported	$ 0.17	$ 0.12	$ 0.16	$ 0.45
As restated for Southern China and Chile acquisitions	$ 0.17	$ 0.12	$ 0.16	$ 0.45

As shown in the tables below, the cumulative effect of the accounting change for financial results previously reported under the cost method and as restated in this Report under the equity method resulted in reductions of net earnings of $0.1 million for the 39 weeks ended July 3, 2005, and $0.3 million and $0.1 million for the fiscal years ended October 3, 2004, and September 28, 2003, respectively *(in thousands, except earnings per share)*:

Fiscal Period Ended	Jan 2, 2005 (13 Weeks)	April 3, 2005 (13 Weeks)	July 3, 2005 (13 Weeks)	July 3, 2005 (39 Weeks)
Net earnings, as previously reported	$ 144,753	$ 100,536	$ 125,575	$ 370,864
Effect of change to equity method	(43)	(54)	(47)	(144)
Net earnings, as restated for Southern China and Chile acquisitions	$ 144,710	$ 100,482	$ 125,528	$ 370,720
Net earnings per common share — basic:				
As previously reported	$ 0.18	$ 0.13	$ 0.16	$ 0.47
As restated for Southern China and Chile acquisitions	$ 0.18	$ 0.13	$ 0.16	$ 0.47
Net earnings per common share — diluted:				
As previously reported	$ 0.17	$ 0.12	$ 0.16	$ 0.45
As restated for Southern China and Chile acquisitions	$ 0.17	$ 0.12	$ 0.16	$ 0.45

The following table summarizes the effects of the investment accounting change on net earnings and earnings per share for the periods indicated *(in thousands, except earnings per share)*:

Fiscal Year Ended	Oct 3, 2004 (53 Weeks)	Sept 28, 2003 (52 Weeks)
Net earnings, as previously reported	$ 389,272	$ 265,493
Effect of change to equity method	(299)	(138)
Net earnings, as restated for Southern China and Chile acquisitions	$ 388,973	$ 265,355
Net earnings per common share — basic:		
As previously reported	$ 0.49	$ 0.34
As restated for Southern China and Chile acquisitions	$ 0.49	$ 0.34
Net earnings per common share — diluted:		
As previously reported	$ 0.47	$ 0.33
As restated for Southern China and Chile acquisitions	$ 0.47	$ 0.33

Note 3:   **Cash and Cash Equivalents**

Cash and cash equivalents consist of the following *(in thousands)*:

Fiscal Year Ended	Oct 2, 2005	Oct 3, 2004
Operating funds and interest bearing deposits	$ 62,221	$ 65,734
Money market funds	111,588	79,319
Total	$ 173,809	$ 145,053

Note 5: Derivative Financial Instruments

Cash Flow Hedges

Starbucks, which include subsidiaries that use their local currency as their functional currency, enters into cash flow derivative instruments to hedge portions of anticipated revenue streams and inventory purchases. Current forward contracts hedge monthly forecasted revenue transactions denominated in Japanese yen and Canadian dollars, as well as forecasted inventory purchases denominated in U.S. dollars, euros and Swiss francs, for foreign operations. Additionally, the Company has swap contracts to hedge a portion of its forecasted U.S. fluid milk purchases. The effect of these swaps will fix the price paid by Starbucks for the monthly volume of milk purchases covered under the contracts on less than 5% of its forecasted U.S. fluid milk purchases in fiscal 2006.

The Company had accumulated net derivative losses of $4.5 million, net of taxes, in other comprehensive income as of October 2, 2005, related to cash flow hedges. Of this amount, $4.1 million of net derivative losses will be reclassified into earnings within 12 months. No cash flow hedges were discontinued during the fiscal years 2005, 2004 and 2003. Current contracts will expire within 12 months.

Net Investment Hedges

Net investment derivative instruments hedge the Company's equity method investment in Starbucks Coffee Japan, Ltd. to minimize foreign currency exposure to fluctuations in the Japanese yen. The Company had accumulated net derivative gains of $3.3 million, net of taxes, in other comprehensive income as of October 2, 2005, related to net investment derivative hedges. Current contracts expire within 31 months.

The following table presents the net gains and losses reclassified from other comprehensive income into the consolidated statements of earnings during the periods indicated for cash flow and net investment hedges *(in thousands)*:

	Oct 2, 2005	Oct 3, 2004	Sept 28, 2003
Cash flow hedges:			
Reclassified losses into total net revenues	$ (843)	$ (1,488)	$ (1,719)
Reclassified losses into cost of sales	(4,535)	(761)	—
Net reclassified losses — cash flow hedges	(5,378)	(2,249)	(1,719)
Net reclassified gains — net investment hedges	1,058	673	1,446
Total	$ (4,320)	$ (1,576)	$ (273)

Note 6:   Inventories

Inventories consist of the following *(in thousands)*:

Fiscal Year Ended	Oct 2, 2005	Oct 3, 2004
Coffee:		
Unroasted	$ 319,745	$ 233,903
Roasted	56,231	46,070
Other merchandise held for sale	109,094	81,565
Packaging and other supplies	61,229	61,125
Total	$ 546,299	$ 422,663

[There is no page 57.]

As of October 2, 2005, the Company had committed to fixed-price purchase contracts for green coffee totaling $375 million. The Company believes, based on relationships established with its suppliers in the past, the risk of nondelivery on such purchase commitments is remote.

Note 7: Equity and Other Investments

The Company's equity and other investments consist of the following *(in thousands)*:

Fiscal Year Ended	Oct 2, 2005	Oct 3, 2004
Equity method investments	$ 189,735	$ 158,726
Cost method investments	8,920	6,208
Other investments	2,806	2,806
Total	$ 201,461	$ 167,740

Equity Method

The Company's equity investees and ownership interests are as follows:

Fiscal Year Ended	Oct 2, 2005	Oct 3, 2004
The North American Coffee Partnership	50.0%	50.0%
Starbucks Ice Cream Partnership	50.0%	50.0%
Starbucks Coffee Korea Co., Ltd.	50.0%	50.0%
Starbucks Coffee Austria GmbH	50.0%	50.0%
Starbucks Coffee Switzerland AG	50.0%	50.0%
Starbucks Coffee España, S.L	50.0%	50.0%
President Starbucks Coffee Taiwan Ltd.	50.0%	50.0%
Shanghai President Coffee Co.	50.0%	50.0%
Starbucks Coffee France SAS	50.0%	50.0%
Berjaya Starbucks Coffee Company Sdn. Bhd	49.9%	49.9%
Starbucks Coffee Japan, Ltd.	40.1%	40.1%
Coffee Partners Hawaii	5.0%	5.0%
Karstadt Coffee GmbH[1]	—	18.0%
Sur-Andino Café S.A.[1]	—	15.0%
Coffee Concepts (Southern China) Limited[1]	—	5.0%

[1] During fiscal 2005, Starbucks acquired all or a majority of the equity interests in these entities, which were previously accounted for under the cost method. From the respective dates of acquisition, the consolidation method of accounting was applied, and for previously reported information, the equity method of accounting was applied to record the Company's proportionate share of net losses. See Note 2 for additional information.

The Company has licensed the rights to produce and distribute Starbucks branded products to two partnerships in which the Company holds 50% equity interests. The North American Coffee Partnership with the Pepsi-Cola Company develops and distributes bottled Frappuccino® coffee drinks and Starbucks DoubleShot® coffee drink. The Starbucks Ice Cream Partnership with Dreyer's Grand Ice Cream, Inc., develops and distributes superpremium ice creams. The remaining entities, including Coffee Partners Hawaii, which is a general partnership, operate licensed Starbucks retail stores.

During fiscal 2004, Starbucks acquired an equity interest in its licensed operations of Malaysia. During fiscal 2003, Starbucks increased its ownership of its licensed operations in Austria, Shanghai, Spain, Switzerland and Taiwan. The carrying amount of these investments was $24.3 million more than the underlying equity in net assets due to acquired goodwill, which is not subject to amortization in accordance with SFAS No. 142 "Goodwill and Other Intangible Assets." The goodwill is evaluated for impairment in accordance with APB No. 18. No impairment was recorded during fiscal years 2005, 2004 or 2003.

The Company's share of income and losses is included in "Income from equity investees" on the consolidated statements of earnings. Also included is the Company's proportionate share of gross margin resulting from coffee and other product sales to, and royalty and license fee revenues generated from, equity investees. Revenues generated from these related parties, net of eliminations, were $86.1 million, $80.7 million and $71.9 million in fiscal years 2005, 2004 and 2003, respectively. Related costs of sales, net of eliminations, were $43.3 million, $41.2 million and $37.5 million in fiscal years 2005, 2004 and 2003, respectively. As of October 2, 2005 and October 3, 2004, there were $16.7 million and $15.5 million of accounts receivable, respectively, on the consolidated balance sheets from equity investees related to product sales and store license fees.

As of October 2, 2005, the aggregate market value of the Company's investment in Starbucks Coffee Japan, Ltd., was approximately $174.8 million based on its available quoted market price.

Cost Method

The Company has equity interests in entities to develop Starbucks licensed retail stores in Hong Kong, Puerto Rico, Mexico, Cyprus and Greece. As of October 2, 2005, and October 3, 2004, management determined that the estimated fair values of each cost method investment exceeded the related carrying values (no unrealized fair value losses). There were no realized losses recorded for other than temporary impairments during 2005 or 2004. During fiscal 2003, $2.0 million in other than temporary impairment was recorded for the Company's equity interest in its licensed retail stores in Israel, which were fully closed by the end of fiscal 2003.

Starbucks has the ability to acquire additional interests in some of its cost method investees at certain intervals. Depending on the Company's total percentage of ownership interest and its ability to exercise significant influence over financial and operating policies, additional investments may require the retroactive application of the equity method of accounting.

Other Investments

Starbucks has investments in privately held equity securities that are recorded at their estimated fair values. As of October 2, 2005, and October 3, 2004, management determined that the estimated fair values of each investment exceeded the related carrying values (no unrealized fair value losses). There were no realized losses generated from other than temporary impairment during 2005, 2004 or 2003.

60

Note 8: Property, Plant and Equipment

Property, plant and equipment are recorded at cost and consist of the following *(in thousands)*:

Fiscal Year Ended	Oct 2, 2005	Oct 3, 2004
Land	$ 13,833	$ 13,118
Buildings	68,180	66,468
Leasehold improvements	1,947,963	1,605,907
Store equipment	646,792	530,798
Roasting equipment	168,934	152,949
Furniture, fixtures and other	476,372	415,307
	3,322,074	2,784,547
Less accumulated depreciation and amortization	(1,625,564)	(1,326,266)
	1,696,510	1,458,281
Work in progress	145,509	93,135
Property, plant and equipment, net	$ 1,842,019	$ 1,551,416

Note 9: Other Intangible Assets and Goodwill

As of October 2, 2005, indefinite-lived intangibles were $31.6 million and definite-lived intangibles, which collectively had a remaining weighted average useful life of approximately six years, were $3.8 million, net of accumulated amortization of $2.1 million. As of October 3, 2004, indefinite-lived intangibles were $24.3 million and definite-lived intangibles, which collectively had a remaining weighted average useful life of approximately eight years, were $2.5 million, net of accumulated amortization of $1.3 million. The increase in indefinite-lived intangibles was primarily due to trademarks acquired from Ethos. Amortization expense for definite-lived intangibles was $0.8 million, $0.5 million and $0.4 million during fiscal 2005, 2004 and 2003, respectively.

The following table summarizes the estimated amortization expense for each of the next five fiscal years *(in thousands)*:

Fiscal Year Ending	
2006	$ 962
2007	861
2008	400
2009	343
2010	317
Total	$ 2,883

61

The following table summarizes goodwill by operating segment *(in thousands)*:

Fiscal Year Ended	Oct 2, 2005	Oct 3, 2004
United States	$ 61,502	$ 60,540
International	30,972	8,410
Total	$ 92,474	$ 68,950

During fiscal 2005, the United States operating segment acquired substantially all of the assets of Ethos, and the International operating segment increased its equity ownership in its licensed operations in Germany, Southern China and Chile.

Note 10:Long-term Debt and Short-term Borrowings

In August 2005, the Company entered into a $500 million unsecured five-year revolving credit facility (the "Facility") with various banks, of which $100 million may be used for issuances of letters of credit. The Facility is scheduled to expire in August 2010 and is available for working capital, capital expenditures and other corporate purposes, which may include acquisitions and share repurchases. The Company may request an increase up to an additional $500 million under the credit facility, provided there is no default, which would increase total availability to $1 billion.

The interest rate for borrowings under the Facility ranges from 0.150% to 0.275% over LIBOR or an alternate base rate, which is the greater of the bank prime rate or the Federal Funds Rate plus 0.50%. The specific spread over LIBOR will depend upon the Company's performance under specified financial criteria. The Facility contains provisions that require the Company to maintain compliance with certain covenants, including the maintenance of certain financial ratios. As of October 2, 2005, the Company was in compliance with each of these covenants. There were borrowings of $277 million outstanding under the Facility as of October 2, 2005, with no outstanding letters of credit, and the weighted average contractual interest rate was 4.0%.

In September 1999, Starbucks purchased the land and building comprising its York County, Pennsylvania, roasting plant and distribution facility. The total purchase price was $12.9 million. In connection with this purchase, the Company assumed loans totaling $7.7 million from the York County Industrial Development Corporation. The remaining maturities of these loans range from five to six years, with interest rates from 0.0% to 2.0%.

Interest expense was $1.3 million, $0.4 million and $0.3 million in fiscal 2005, 2004 and 2003, respectively.

Scheduled principal payments on long-term debt are as follows *(in thousands)*:

Fiscal Year Ending	
2006	$ 748
2007	762
2008	775
2009	790
2010	337
Thereafter	206
Total principal payments	$ 3,618

Note 11:Other Long-term Liabilities

The Company's other long-term liabilities consist of the following *(in thousands)*:

Fiscal Year Ended	Oct 2, 2005	Oct 3, 2004
Deferred rent liabilities	$ 166,182	$ 136,552
Minority interest liabilities	11,153	1,802
Other	16,230	6,329
Total	$ 193,565	$ 144,683

The deferred rent liabilities as of October 2, 2005 and October 3, 2004, represent amounts for tenant improvement allowances, rent escalation clauses and rent holidays related to certain operating leases. The Company amortizes deferred rent over the terms of the leases as reductions to rent expense on the consolidated statements of earnings.

For operations accounted for under the consolidation method, but in which Starbucks owns less than 100% of the equity interests, long-term liabilities are maintained for the collective ownership interests of minority shareholders. As of October 2, 2005, Starbucks had less than 100% ownership in Coffee Concepts (Southern China) Ltd. (referred to as the Southern China operations in Note 2) as well as in Chengdu Starbucks Coffee Company Limited and Urban Coffee Opportunities, LLC. As of October 3, 2004 the minority interest liability was only for Urban Coffee Opportunities, LLC.

The other remaining long-term liabilities generally include obligations to be settled or paid for one year beyond each respective fiscal year end, for items such as guarantees (see Note 18), donation commitments, hedging instruments and the long-term portion of capital lease obligations.

Note 12:Leases

Rental expense under operating lease agreements was as follows *(in thousands)*:

Fiscal Year Ended	Oct 2, 2005	Oct 3, 2004	Sept 28, 2003
Minimum rentals — retail stores	$ 340,474	$ 285,250	$ 240,016
Minimum rentals — other	43,532	28,108	22,983
Contingent rentals	32,910	24,638	12,274
Total	$ 416,916	$ 337,996	$ 275,273

Minimum future rental payments under noncancelable operating lease obligations as of October 2, 2005, are as follows *(in thousands)*:

Fiscal Year Ending	
2006	$ 423,564
2007	412,146
2008	391,909
2009	363,347
2010	327,491
Thereafter	1,179,036
Total minimum lease payments	$ 3,097,493

The Company has subleases related to certain of its operating lease agreements. During fiscal 2005, 2004 and 2003, the Company recognized sublease income of $4.3 million, $4.0 million and $3.2 million, respectively.

The Company had capital lease obligations of $2.6 million and $0.3 million as of October 2, 2005 and October 3, 3004, respectively. At October 2, 2005, the current portion of the total obligation was $0.8 million and was included in "Other accrued expenses" and the remaining long-term portion of $1.8 million was included in "Other long-term liabilities" on the consolidated balance sheet. Capital lease obligations expire at various dates, with the latest maturity in 2020.

Note 13:Shareholders' Equity

In addition to 1.2 billion shares of authorized common stock with $0.001 par value per share, the Company has authorized 15 million shares of preferred stock, none of which was outstanding at October 2, 2005.

Under the Company's authorized share repurchase program, Starbucks acquired 45.1 million shares at an average price of $25.26 for a total cost of $1.1 billion in fiscal 2005. Starbucks acquired 10.0 million shares at an average price of $20.43 for a total cost of $203.4 million during fiscal 2004. During fiscal 2005, the Starbucks Board of Directors authorized additional repurchases of 30 million shares of the Company's common stock, and as of October 2, 2005, there were 22.1 million remaining shares authorized for repurchase. Share repurchases were funded through cash, cash equivalents, available-for-sale securities and borrowings under the revolving credit facility and were part of the Company's active capital management program.

Comprehensive Income

Comprehensive income includes all changes in equity during the period, except those resulting from transactions with shareholders and subsidiaries of the Company. It has two components: net earnings and other comprehensive income. Accumulated other comprehensive income reported on the Company's consolidated balance sheets consists of foreign currency translation adjustments and the unrealized gains and losses, net of applicable taxes, on available-for-sale securities and on derivative instruments designated and qualifying as cash flow and net investment hedges.

64

Comprehensive income, net of related tax effects, is as follows *(in thousands)*:

Fiscal Year Ended	Oct 2, 2005	Oct 3, 2004	Sept 28, 2003
Net earnings	$ 494,467	$ 388,973	$ 265,355
Unrealized holding gains/(losses) on available-for-sale securities, net of tax benefit/(provision) of $889, $618 and ($53) in 2005, 2004 and 2003, respectively	(1,482)	(1,005)	142
Unrealized holding losses on cash flow hedges, net of tax benefit of $2,268, $2,801 and $804 in 2005, 2004 and 2003, respectively	(3,861)	(4,769)	(1,369)
Unrealized holding gains/(losses) on net investment hedges, net of tax benefit/(provision) of ($609), $328 and $1,903 in 2005, 2004 and 2003, respectively	1,037	(558)	(3,241)
Reclassification adjustment for losses realized in net income, net of tax benefit of $2,751, $832 and $41 in 2005, 2004 and 2003, respectively	4,656	1,407	42
Net unrealized gain/(loss)	350	(4,925)	(4,426)
Translation adjustment	(8,677)	19,892	27,241
Total comprehensive income	$ 486,140	$ 403,940	$ 288,170

The unfavorable translation adjustment change during fiscal year 2005 of $8.7 million was primarily due to the strengthening of the U.S. dollar against the euro, British pound sterling and Japanese yen. The favorable translation adjustment changes during fiscal years 2004 and 2003 of $19.9 million and $27.2 million, respectively, were primarily due to the weakening of the U.S. dollar against several currencies, such as the British pound sterling, Euro, Canadian dollar and Japanese yen.

The components of accumulated other comprehensive income, net of tax, were as follows *(in thousands)*:

Fiscal Year Ended	Oct 2, 2005	Oct 3, 2004
Net unrealized holding losses on available-for-sale securities	$ (651)	$ (523)
Net unrealized holding losses on hedging instruments	(7,786)	(8,264)
Translation adjustment	29,351	38,028
Accumulated other comprehensive income	$ 20,914	$ 29,241

As of October 2, 2005, the translation adjustment of $29.4 million was net of tax provisions of $5.5 million.

Note 14: Employee Stock and Benefit Plans

Stock Option Plans

The Company maintains several equity incentive plans under which it may grant nonqualified stock options, incentive stock options, restricted stock, restricted stock units or stock appreciation rights to employees, consultants and nonemployee directors. Stock options have been granted at prices at or above the fair market value on the date of grant. Options vest and expire according to terms established at the grant date.

The following summarizes all stock option transactions from September 29, 2002, through October 2, 2005 (no restricted stock, restricted stock units or stock appreciation rights were outstanding for any of these periods):

	Shares Subject to Options	Weighted Average Exercise Price per Share	Shares Subject to Exercisable Options	Weighted Average Exercise Price per Share
Outstanding, September 29, 2002	80,919,606	$ 6.78	41,951,196	$ 5.54
Granted	19,075,460	10.55		
Exercised	(16,039,208)	5.85		
Cancelled	(5,824,966)	8.95		
Outstanding, September 28, 2003	78,130,892	7.74	41,777,388	6.28
Granted	18,435,240	15.62		
Exercised	(15,416,982)	7.11		
Cancelled	(4,315,930)	11.88		
Outstanding, October 3, 2004	76,833,220	9.52	53,378,230	7.93
Granted	15,627,550	27.17		
Exercised	(16,169,992)	8.08		
Cancelled	(3,831,872)	17.86		
Outstanding, October 2, 2005	72,458,906	$ 13.22	51,311,418	$ 10.07

As of October 2, 2005, there were 78.4 million shares of common stock available for issuance pursuant to future stock option grants. Additional information regarding options outstanding as of October 2, 2005, is as follows:

	Options Outstanding			Options Exercisable	
Range of Exercise Prices	Shares	Weighted Average Remaining Contractual Life (Years)	Weighted Average Exercise Price	Shares	Weighted Average Exercise Price
$ 2.42 - $ 6.56	17,717,470	2.51	$ 5.01	17,717,470	$ 5.01
6.64 - 10.30	12,918,498	5.69	8.78	12,520,126	8.75
10.32 - 15.20	13,242,074	6.84	10.79	10,145,556	10.71
15.23 - 27.00	15,660,776	8.30	16.53	7,461,918	15.42
27.32 - 30.57	12,920,088	9.14	27.39	3,466,348	27.32
$ 2.42 - $30.57	72,458,906	6.30	$ 13.22	51,311,418	$ 10.07

Employee Stock Purchase Plans

The Company has an employee stock purchase plan which provides that eligible employees may contribute up to 10% of their base earnings toward the quarterly purchase of the Company's common stock. The employee's purchase price is 85% of the lesser of the fair market value of the stock on the first business day or the last business day of the quarterly offering period. Employees may purchase shares having a fair market value of up to $25,000 (measured as of the first day of each quarterly offering period for each calendar year). No

66

compensation expense is recorded in connection with the plan. The total number of shares issuable under the plan is 32.0 million. There were 1,527,880 shares issued under the plan during fiscal 2005 at prices ranging from $20.07 to $21.96. There were 1,959,184 shares issued under the plan during fiscal 2004 at prices ranging from $10.77 to $18.96. There were 1,424,092 shares issued under the plan during fiscal 2003 at prices ranging from $8.66 to $10.43. Since inception of the plan, 14.8 million shares have been purchased, leaving 17.2 million shares available for future issuance. Of the approximately 55,100 employees eligible to participate, approximately 18,800 were participants in the plan as of October 2, 2005.

Starbucks also has a Save-As-You-Earn ("SAYE") plan in the United Kingdom that allows eligible U.K. employees to save toward the purchase of the Company's common stock. The employee's purchase price is 85% of the fair value of the stock on the first business day of a three-year offering period. No compensation expense was recorded in connection with the plan during fiscal years 2005, 2004 or 2003. The total number of shares issuable under the plan is 1.2 million. There were 25,382 shares issued under the plan during fiscal 2005 at $7.93. There were 8,960 shares issued under the plan during fiscal 2004 at prices ranging from $7.07 to $9.48. There were 62,588 shares issued under the plan during fiscal 2003 at prices ranging from $5.66 to $6.01. No shares had been issued prior to fiscal 2003 and 1.1 million shares remain available for future issuance. During fiscal 2004, the Company suspended future offerings under this employee stock purchase plan, with the last offering made in December 2002 and maturing in February 2006.

During fiscal 2004, the Company introduced a U.K. Share Incentive Plan to replace the U.K. SAYE plan. This employee stock purchase plan allows eligible U.K. employees to purchase shares of common stock through payroll deductions during six-month offering periods at the lesser of the fair market value of the stock at the beginning or at the end of the offering period. The Company will award one matching share for each six shares purchased by the employee under the plan. No compensation expense was recorded in connection with the plan. The total number of shares issuable under the plan is 1.4 million, of which 10,732 shares were issued during fiscal 2005 at prices ranging from $19.46 to $24.76. There were no shares issued prior to fiscal 2005, leaving 1,389,268 available for future issuance.

Deferred Stock Plan

Starbucks has a deferred stock plan for certain key employees that enables participants in the plan to defer receipt of ownership of common shares from the exercise of nonqualified stock options. The minimum deferral period is five years. As of October 2, 2005, receipt of 3,394,200 shares was deferred under the terms of this plan. The rights to receive these shares, represented by common stock units, are included in the calculation of basic and diluted earnings per share as common stock equivalents.

Defined Contribution Plans

Starbucks maintains voluntary defined contribution plans covering eligible employees as defined in the plan documents. Participating employees may elect to defer and contribute a portion of their compensation to the plans up to limits stated in the plan documents, not to exceed the dollar amounts set by applicable laws. For employees in the United States and Canada, the Company matched 25% to 150% of each employee's eligible contribution based on years of service, up to a maximum of the first 4% of each employee's compensation. The Company's matching contributions to all plans were approximately $12.4 million, $9.8 million and $6.8 million in fiscal years 2005, 2004 and 2003, respectively.

Note 15:Income Taxes

A reconciliation of the statutory federal income tax rate with the Company's effective income tax rate is as follows:

Fiscal Year Ended	Oct 2, 2005	Oct 3, 2004	Sept 28, 2003
Statutory rate	35.0%	35.0%	35.0%
State income taxes, net of federal income tax benefit	3.9	3.5	3.6
Other, net	(1.0)	(1.2)	—
Effective tax rate	37.9%	37.3%	38.6%

The provision for income taxes consists of the following (in thousands):

Fiscal Year Ended	Oct 2, 2005	Oct 3, 2004	Sept 28, 2003
Current taxes:			
Federal	$ 273,178	$ 188,647	$ 140,138
State	51,949	36,383	25,448
Foreign	14,106	10,193	8,489
Deferred taxes, net	(37,256)	(3,469)	(6,958)
Total	$ 301,977	$ 231,754	$ 167,117

U.S. income and foreign withholding taxes have not been provided on approximately $86.4 million of cumulative undistributed earnings of foreign subsidiaries and equity investees. The Company intends to reinvest these earnings for the foreseeable future. If these amounts were distributed to the United States, in the form of dividends or otherwise, the Company would be subject to additional U.S. income taxes. Because of the availability of U.S. foreign tax credits, the determination of the amount of unrecognized deferred income tax liabilities on these earnings is not practicable.

In December 2004, the FASB issued Staff Position No. FAS 109-1, "Application of SFAS No. 109, Accounting for Income Taxes, to the Tax Deduction on Qualified Production Activities provided by the American Jobs Creation Act of 2004" ("FSP 109-1"). FSP 109-1 states that qualified domestic production activities should be accounted for as a special deduction under SFAS No. 109, "Accounting for Income Taxes," and not be treated as a rate reduction. The provisions of FSP 109-1 are effective immediately. The Company will qualify for a benefit beginning in fiscal 2006, which is not expected to be material to the Company's financial statements.

In December 2004, the FASB issued Staff Position No. FAS 109-2, "Accounting and Disclosure Guidance for the Foreign Earnings Repatriation Provision within the American Jobs Creation Act of 2004" ("FSP 109-2"). The American Jobs Creation Act allows a special one-time dividends received deduction on the repatriation of certain foreign earnings to a U.S. taxpayer (repatriation provision), provided certain criteria are met. The law allows the Company to make an election to repatriate earnings through 2006. FSP 109-2 provides accounting and disclosure guidance for the repatriation provision. Although FSP 109-2 was effective upon its issuance, it allows companies additional time beyond the enactment date to evaluate the effects of the provision on its plan for investment or repatriation of unremitted foreign earnings. The Company continues to evaluate the impact of the new Act to determine whether it will repatriate foreign earnings and the impact, if any, this pronouncement will have on its consolidated financial statements. As of October 2, 2005, the Company has not made an election to repatriate earnings under this provision. The Company may or may not elect to repatriate earnings in fiscal 2006. Earnings under consideration for repatriation range from $0 to $75 million and the related income tax effects range from $0 to $5 million. As provided in FSP 109-2, Starbucks has not adjusted its tax expense or deferred tax liability to reflect the repatriation provision.

The tax effect of temporary differences and carryforwards that comprise significant portions of deferred tax assets and liabilities is as follows *(in thousands)*:

Fiscal Year Ended	Oct 2, 2005	Oct 3, 2004
Deferred tax assets:		
Accrued occupancy costs	$ 31,247	$ 27,006
Accrued compensation and related costs	43,890	37,333
Other accrued expenses	20,199	14,918
Foreign tax credits	15,708	17,514
Other	13,990	16,769
Total	125,034	113,540
Valuation allowance	(8,078)	(929)
Total deferred tax asset, net of valuation allowance	116,956	112,611
Deferred tax liabilities:		
Property, plant and equipment	(32,314)	(58,512)
Other	(11,600)	(12,219)
Total	(43,914)	(70,731)
Net deferred tax asset	$ 73,042	$ 41,880

The Company will establish a valuation allowance if it is more likely than not that these items will either expire before the Company is able to realize their benefits, or that future deductibility is uncertain. Periodically, the valuation allowance is reviewed and adjusted based on management's assessments of realizable deferred tax assets. The valuation allowance as of October 2, 2005 was related to capital loss carryforwards and net operating losses of consolidated foreign subsidiaries. The valuation allowance as of October 2, 2004 related solely to net operating losses of consolidated foreign subsidiaries. The net change in the total valuation allowance for the years ended October 2, 2005, and October 3, 2004, was an increase of $7.1 million and a decrease of $8.4 million, respectively.

As of October 2, 2005, the Company has foreign tax credit carryforwards of $15.7 million with expiration dates between fiscal years 2011 and 2014. As of the end of fiscal 2005, the Company also has capital loss carryforwards of $12.3 million, with $11.1 million and $1.2 million expiring in fiscal years 2006 and 2011, respectively.

Taxes currently payable of $41.5 million and $29.2 million are included in "Accrued taxes" on the consolidated balance sheets as of October 2, 2005, and October 3, 2004, respectively.

The Company has established, and periodically reviews and re-evaluates, an estimated contingent tax liability to provide for the possibility of unfavorable outcomes in tax matters. Contingent tax liabilities totaled $33.1 million as of October 2, 2005, and are included in "Accrued income taxes." These liabilities are provided for in accordance with the requirements of SFAS No. 5, "Accounting for Contingencies." The Company believes its contingent tax liabilities are adequate in the event the tax positions are not ultimately upheld.

Note 16: Earnings per Share

The following table represents the calculation of net earnings per common share — basic and diluted *(in thousands, except earnings per share)*:

Fiscal Year Ended	Oct 2, 2005	Oct 3, 2004	Sept 28, 2003
Net earnings	$ 494,467	$ 388,973	$ 265,355
Weighted average common shares and common stock units outstanding (for basic calculation)	789,570	794,347	781,505
Dilutive effect of outstanding common stock options	25,847	28,583	21,791
Weighted average common and common equivalent shares outstanding (for diluted calculation)	815,417	822,930	803,296
Net earnings per common share — basic	$ 0.63	$ 0.49	$ 0.34
Net earnings per common and common equivalent share — diluted	$ 0.61	$ 0.47	$ 0.33

Options with exercise prices greater than the average market price were not included in the computation of diluted earnings per share. These options totaled 13.7 million, 0.3 million and 1.3 million in fiscal years 2005, 2004 and 2003, respectively.

Note 17: Related Party Transactions

In April 2001, certain members of the Board of Directors and other investors, organized as The Basketball Club of Seattle, LLC ("The Basketball Club"), purchased the franchises for The Seattle Supersonics and The Seattle Storm basketball teams. An executive officer of the Company and member of the Board of Directors, Howard Schultz, owns a controlling interest in The Basketball Club. Starbucks paid approximately $0.8 million, $0.8 million and $0.7 million during fiscal years 2005, 2004 and 2003, respectively, for team sponsorships and ticket purchases. Terms of the team sponsorship agreements did not change as a result of the related party relationship.

Prior to January 2003, a former member of the Company's Board of Directors served as a board member of, and owned an indirect interest in, a privately held company that provides Starbucks with in-store music services. Starbucks paid $0.7 million to the privately held company for music services during fiscal year 2003 while the related party relationship existed.

In June 2005, a member of the Company's Board of Directors was appointed president and chief financial officer of Oracle Corporation. Starbucks had a pre-existing business relationship with Oracle related to financial systems and systems consulting at the time of the appointment and Starbucks continued to make payments for supplies and services subsequent to June 2005 in the ordinary course of business. These payments totaled approximately $2.6 million since the inception of the related party relationship through October 2, 2005. The Board member's employment relationship with Oracle ended on November 15, 2005.

Note 18: Commitments and Contingencies

The Company has unconditionally guaranteed the repayment of certain Japanese yen-denominated bank loans and related interest and fees of an unconsolidated equity investee, Starbucks Coffee Japan, Ltd. The guarantees continue until the loans, including accrued interest and fees, have been paid in full, with the final loan amount due in 2014. The maximum amount is limited to the sum of unpaid principal and interest amounts, as well as other related expenses. These amounts will vary based on fluctuations in the yen foreign exchange rate. As of October 2, 2005, the maximum amount of the guarantees was approximately $9.0 million. Since there has been no modification of these loan guarantees subsequent to the Company's adoption of FASB Interpretation No. 45, "Guarantor's Accounting and Disclosure Requirements for Guarantees, Including Indebtedness of Others," Starbucks has applied the disclosure provisions only and has not recorded the guarantee on its consolidated balance sheet.

During fiscal 2005, Starbucks entered into commitments under which it unconditionally guaranteed its proportionate share, or 50%, of bank line of credit borrowings of certain unconsolidated equity investees. The Company's maximum exposure under these commitments is approximately $4.8 million, excluding interest and other related costs, and the majority of these commitments expire in 2007. As of October 2, 2005, the Company recorded $2.7 million to "Equity and other investments" and "Other long-term liabilities" on the consolidated balance sheet for the fair value of the guarantee arrangements.

Coffee brewing and espresso equipment sold to customers through Company-operated and licensed retail stores, as well as equipment sold to the Company's licensees for use in retail licensing operations, are under warranty for defects in materials and workmanship for a period ranging from 12 to 24 months. The Company establishes an accrual for estimated warranty costs at the time of sale, based on historical experience.

The following table summarizes the activity related to product warranty reserves during fiscal years 2005 and 2004 (in thousands):

Fiscal Year Ended	Oct 2, 2005	Oct 3, 2004
Balance at beginning of fiscal year	$ 3,091	$ 2,227
Provision for warranties issued	7,494	5,093
Warranty claims	(8,827)	(4,229)
Balance at end of fiscal year	$ 1,758	$ 3,091

Legal Proceedings

On June 3, 2004, two current employees of the Company filed a lawsuit, entitled *Sean Pendlebury and Laurel Overton v. Starbucks Coffee Company*, in the U.S. District Court for the Southern District of Florida claiming the Company violated requirements of the Fair Labor Standards Act (FLSA). The suit alleges that the Company misclassified its retail store managers as exempt from the overtime provisions of the FLSA and that the managers are therefore entitled to overtime compensation for any week in which they worked more than 40 hours during the past three years. Plaintiffs seek to represent themselves and all similarly situated U.S. current and former store managers of the Company. Plaintiffs seek reimbursement for an unspecified amount of unpaid overtime compensation, liquidated damages, attorney's fees and costs. Plaintiffs also filed on June 3, 2004 a motion for conditional collective action treatment and court-supervised notice to additional putative class members under the opt-in procedures in section 16(b) of the FLSA. On January 3, 2005, the district court entered an order authorizing nationwide notice of the lawsuit to all current and former store managers employed by the Company during the past three years. The Company filed a motion for summary judgment as to the claims of the named plaintiffs on September 24, 2004. The court denied that motion because this case is in the early stages of discovery, but the court noted that the Company may resubmit this motion at a later date. Starbucks believes that the plaintiffs are properly classified as exempt under the federal wage laws and that a loss in this case is unlikely. Due to the early status of this case, the Company cannot estimate the possible loss to the Company, if any. No trial date currently is set. The Company intends to vigorously defend the lawsuit.

* * *

AUDITORS' REPORT ON CONSOLIDATED FINANCIAL STATEMENTS

REPORT OF INDEPENDENT REGISTERED PUBLIC ACCOUNTING FIRM

To the Board of Directors and Shareholders of Starbucks Corporation

Seattle, Washington

We have audited the accompanying consolidated balance sheets of Starbucks Corporation and subsidiaries (the "Company") as of October 2, 2005, and October 3, 2004, and the related consolidated statements of earnings, shareholders' equity and cash flows for each of the three fiscal years in the period ended October 2, 2005. These financial statements are the responsibility of the Company's management. Our responsibility is to express an opinion on these financial statements based on our audits.

We conducted our audits in accordance with the standards of the Public Company Accounting Oversight Board (United States). Those standards require that we plan and perform the audit to obtain reasonable assurance about whether the financial statements are free of material misstatement. An audit includes examining, on a test basis, evidence supporting the amounts and disclosures in the financial statements. An audit also includes assessing the accounting principles used and significant estimates made by management, as well as evaluating the overall financial statement presentation. We believe that our audits provide a reasonable basis for our opinion.

In our opinion, such consolidated financial statements present fairly, in all material respects, the financial position of Starbucks Corporation and subsidiaries as of October 2, 2005, and October 3, 2004, and the results of their operations and their cash flows for each of the three fiscal years in the period ended October 2, 2005, in conformity with accounting principles generally accepted in the United States of America.

We have also audited, in accordance with the standards of the Public Company Accounting Oversight Board (United States), the effectiveness of the Company's internal control over financial reporting as of October 2, 2005, based on criteria established in *Internal Control — Integrated Framework* issued by the Committee of Sponsoring Organizations of the Treadway Commission and our report dated December 16, 2005 expressed an unqualified opinion on management's assessment of the effectiveness of the Company's internal control over financial reporting and an unqualified opinion of the effectiveness of the Company's internal control over financial reporting.

/s/ DELOITTE & TOUCHE LLP

Seattle, Washington

December 16, 2005

AUDITORS' REPORT ON INTERNAL CONTROL OVER FINANCIAL REPORTING

REPORT OF INDEPENDENT REGISTERED PUBLIC ACCOUNTING FIRM

To the Board of Directors and Shareholders of Starbucks Corporation

Seattle, Washington

We have audited management's assessment, included in the accompanying Report of Management on Internal Control over Financial Reporting, that Starbucks Corporation and subsidiaries (the "Company") maintained effective internal control over financial reporting as of October 2, 2005, based on criteria established in *Internal Control — Integrated Framework* issued by the Committee of Sponsoring Organizations of the Treadway Commission. The Company's management is responsible for maintaining effective internal control over financial reporting and for its assessment of the effectiveness of internal control over financial reporting. Our responsibility is to express an opinion on management's assessment and an opinion on the effectiveness of the Company's internal control over financial reporting based on our audit.

We conducted our audit in accordance with the standards of the Public Company Accounting Oversight Board (United States). Those standards require that we plan and perform the audit to obtain reasonable assurance about whether effective internal control over financial reporting was maintained in all material respects. Our audit included obtaining an understanding of internal control over financial reporting, evaluating management's assessment, testing and evaluating the design and operating effectiveness of internal control, and performing such other procedures as we considered necessary in the circumstances. We believe that our audit provides a reasonable basis for our opinions.

A company's internal control over financial reporting is a process designed by, or under the supervision of, the company's principal executive and principal financial officers, or persons performing similar functions, and effected by the company's board of directors, management, and other personnel to provide reasonable assurance regarding the reliability of financial reporting and the preparation of financial statements for external purposes in accordance with generally accepted accounting principles. A company's internal control over financial reporting includes those policies and procedures that (1) pertain to the maintenance of records that, in reasonable detail, accurately and fairly reflect the transactions and dispositions of the assets of the company; (2) provide reasonable assurance that transactions are recorded as necessary to permit preparation of financial statements in accordance with generally accepted accounting principles, and that receipts and expenditures of the company are being made only in accordance with authorizations of management and directors of the company; and (3) provide reasonable assurance regarding prevention or timely detection of unauthorized acquisition, use, or disposition of the company's assets that could have a material effect on the financial statements.

Because of the inherent limitations of internal control over financial reporting, including the possibility of collusion or improper management override of controls, material misstatements due to error or fraud may not be prevented or detected on a timely basis. Also, projections of any evaluation of the effectiveness of the internal control over financial reporting to future periods are subject to the risk that the controls may become inadequate because of changes in conditions, or that the degree of compliance with the policies or procedures may deteriorate.

In our opinion, management's assessment that the Company maintained effective internal control over financial reporting as of October 2, 2005, is fairly stated, in all material respects, based on criteria established in *Internal Control — Integrated Framework* issued by the Committee of Sponsoring Organizations of the Treadway Commission. Also in our opinion, the Company maintained, in all material respects, effective internal control over financial reporting as of October 2, 2005, based on criteria established in *Internal*

Control — Integrated Framework issued by the Committee of Sponsoring Organizations of the Treadway Commission.

We have also audited, in accordance with the standards of the Public Company Accounting Oversight Board (United States), the consolidated financial statements as of and for the fiscal year ended October 2, 2005 of the Company and our report dated December 16, 2005 expressed an unqualified opinion on those financial statements.

/s/ DELOITTE & TOUCHE LLP

Seattle, Washington

December 16, 2005

Item 9. *Changes in and Disagreements with Independent Registered Public Accounting Firm on Accounting and Financial Disclosure*

Not applicable.

Item 9A. *Controls and Procedures*

Disclosure Controls and Procedures

The Company carried out an evaluation, under the supervision and with the participation of the Company's management, including the chief executive officer and the chief financial officer, of the effectiveness of the design and operation of the disclosure controls and procedures, as defined in Rules 13a-15(e) and 15d-15(e) under the Securities Exchange Act of 1934, as amended (the "Exchange Act"). Based upon that evaluation, the Company's chief executive officer and chief financial officer concluded that the Company's disclosure controls and procedures are effective, as of the end of the period covered by this Report (October 2, 2005), in ensuring that material information relating to Starbucks Corporation, including its consolidated subsidiaries, required to be disclosed by the Company in reports that it files or submits under the Exchange Act is recorded, processed, summarized and reported within the time periods specified in the SEC rules and forms. There were no changes in the Company's internal control over financial reporting during the quarter ended October 2, 2005, that have materially affected, or are reasonably likely to materially affect, the Company's internal control over financial reporting.

Report of Management on Internal Control over Financial Reporting

The management of Starbucks is responsible for establishing and maintaining adequate internal control over financial reporting. Internal control over financial reporting is a process to provide reasonable assurance regarding the reliability of our financial reporting for external purposes in accordance with accounting principles generally accepted in the United States of America. Internal control over financial reporting includes maintaining records that in reasonable detail accurately and fairly reflect our transactions; providing reasonable assurance that transactions are recorded as necessary for preparation of our financial statements; providing reasonable assurance that receipts and expenditures of company assets are made in accordance with management authorization; and providing reasonable assurance that unauthorized acquisition, use or disposition of company assets that could have a material effect on our financial statements would be prevented or detected on a timely basis. Because of its inherent limitations, internal control over financial reporting is not intended to provide absolute assurance that a misstatement of our financial statements would be prevented or detected.

Management conducted an evaluation of the effectiveness of our internal control over financial reporting based on the framework and criteria established in *Internal Control — Integrated Framework*, issued by the Committee of Sponsoring Organizations of the Treadway Commission. This evaluation included review of the documentation of controls, evaluation of the design effectiveness of controls, testing of the operating effectiveness of controls and a conclusion on this evaluation. Based on this evaluation, management concluded that the Company's internal control over financial reporting was effective as of October 2, 2005. Management's assessment of the effectiveness of our internal control over financial reporting as of October 2, 2005 has been audited by Deloitte & Touche LLP, an independent registered public accounting firm, as stated in their report which is included in Item 8 of this Report.

Item 9B. *Other Information*

None.

* * *

TABLE OF CONTENTS

* * *

Audit and Compliance Committee Report

During fiscal 2005, Craig J. Foley, Ms. Hobson, and Messrs. Maffei, Shennan, Teruel and Weatherup served on the Audit Committee. Mr. Foley retired from the Board of Directors and the Audit Committee on February 8, 2005. Ms. Hobson and Mr. Teruel were elected to the Board and appointed to the Audit Committee on February 9, 2005 and September 20, 2005, respectively. Each of Ms. Hobson and Messrs. Maffei, Shennan, Teruel and Weatherup (i) meets the independence criteria prescribed by applicable law and the rules of the SEC for audit committee membership and is an "independent director" as defined in Nasdaq rules; (ii) meets Nasdaq's financial knowledge and sophistication requirements; and (iii) has been determined by the Board of Directors to be an "audit committee financial expert" under SEC rules. The Audit Committee operates pursuant to a written charter, which complies with the applicable provisions of the Sarbanes-Oxley Act of 2002 and related rules of the SEC and Nasdaq. The charter is available on the Company's web site at www.starbucks.com/aboutus/corporate_governance.asp. As more fully described in its charter, the Audit Committee is responsible for overseeing the Company's accounting and financial reporting processes, including the quarterly review and the annual audit of the Company's consolidated financial statements by Deloitte & Touche LLP ("Deloitte"), the Company's independent registered public accounting firm. As part of fulfilling its responsibilities, the Audit Committee reviewed and discussed the audited consolidated financial statements for fiscal 2005 with management and the Company's independent registered public accounting firm and discussed those matters required by Statement on Auditing Standards No. 61 (Communication with Audit Committees), as amended, with the Company's independent registered public accounting firm. The Audit Committee received the written disclosures and the letter required by Independent Standards Board Statement No. 1 (Independence Discussions with Audit Committee) from Deloitte, and discussed that firm's independence with representatives of the firm.

Based upon the Audit Committee's review of the audited consolidated financial statements and its discussions with management, the internal audit function and the Company's independent registered public accounting firm, the Audit Committee recommended to the Board of Directors that the audited consolidated financial statements for the fiscal year ended October 2, 2005 be included in the Company's Annual Report on Form 10-K filed with the SEC.

Respectfully submitted,

Gregory B. Maffei (Chair)
Mellody Hobson
James G. Shennan, Jr.
Javier G. Teruel
Craig E. Weatherup

* * *

EXECUTIVE COMPENSATION

Compensation and Management Development Committee Report on Executive Compensation

The Compensation Committee is comprised entirely of Independent Directors who are also non-employee directors as defined in Rule 16b-3 under the Securities Exchange Act of 1934 and outside directors as defined in Section 162(m) of the Internal Revenue Code.

Role of the Committee: The Committee regularly reviews and approves the Company's executive compensation strategy and principles to ensure that they are aligned with the Company's business strategy and objectives, shareholder interests, desired behaviors and corporate culture.

* * *

Overview of Compensation Philosophy and Program: The Committee believes that compensation paid to executive officers should be closely aligned with the performance of the Company on both a short-term and long-term basis, and that such compensation should assist the Company in attracting and retaining key executives critical to its long-term success. To that end, it is the view of the Committee that the compensation packages for executive officers should consist of three principal components:

- annual base salary;

- annual incentive bonus, the amount of which is dependent on both Company and individual performance during the prior fiscal year; and

- long-term incentive compensation, currently delivered in the form of stock options that are awarded each year based on the prior year's performance and other factors described below, and that are designed to align executive officers' interests with those of shareholders by rewarding outstanding performance and providing long-term incentives.

The Company also provides certain personal benefits to executive officers. Under a program to enhance the safety and effectiveness of management in support of Company business and operations, corporate-owned aircraft are made available to management partners for essential business trips and other Company activities. The chairman and the president and chief executive officer, and other members of management with the approval of the chairman, are permitted limited personal use of the corporate-owned aircraft. Aggregate non-business use of the corporate-owned aircraft may not exceed 20% of total flight hours in any fiscal year. Also under the Company's executive security program, the chairman, the president and chief executive officer and the president, Starbucks Coffee International, are provided security services, including home security systems and monitoring and, in the case of the chairman, personal security services. These security services are provided for the Company's benefit, and the Committee considers the related expenses to be appropriate business expenses rather than personal benefits. The Company also provides executive life insurance and annual physicals to all executive officers. The Company has terminated its obligations to pay premiums with respect to existing split-dollar life insurance arrangements with the chairman, as described on page 28 of this proxy statement, in exchange for an annual cash payment to be used by him to acquire a like benefit. There are no additional perquisites available to the executive officers.

The Company has no severance arrangements with its executive officers. Its only change in control arrangements, which apply to all partners, are accelerated vesting of stock options, which generally will occur under the Company's 2005 Long-Term Equity Incentive Plan and its sub-plans only if a partner's employment is terminated within a year after a change in control or the acquiring company does not assume outstanding awards or substitute equivalent awards, and generally will occur under the Company's other stock option plans (under which options are no longer being granted) upon a change in control. Management partners are eligible to participate in a management deferred compensation plan, described below, which closely mirrors the Company's tax-qualified 401(k) plan that is available to all U.S. partners.

Total Compensation and Peer Comparisons: In establishing total annual compensation for the chairman, the president and chief executive officer and the other executive officers, the Committee reviews each component of the executive's compensation against executive compensation surveys prepared by the Committee's outside compensation consultant.

The surveys used for comparison reflect compensation levels and practices for persons holding comparable positions at targeted peer group companies. The compensation comparator group was determined by the Committee with assistance from its outside consultant, and includes an array of companies in specialty retail and other industries with high growth and strong brand image characteristics. Application of these criteria resulted in a comparator group representing a cross section of 17 leading companies, spanning two Standard & Poor's 500 industry sectors, Consumer Staples and Consumer Discretionary, with annual sales and market capitalizations comparable to that of the Company. A majority of the companies in the comparator group are also in the Standard & Poor's 500 Consumer Discretionary Sector used in the performance comparison graph on page 20 of this proxy statement.

In addition to reviewing executive officers' compensation against the comparator group companies, the Committee also solicits appropriate input from the Company's president and chief executive officer regarding total compensation for those executives reporting directly to him.

Based on the Company's fiscal 2005 performance, the Committee recommended that total direct compensation for executive officers for fiscal 2005 (the sum of base salary, incentive bonus opportunity and long-term compensation delivered through stock option awards) should be positioned at approximately the 75th percentile of the comparator group companies. Actual total direct compensation, however, may range between the 25th and 90th percentiles depending on the Company's financial and market performance, each executive's individual performance, and internal equity considerations among all senior executives. Based on the most recent data available, Starbucks ranked in the top quartile among comparator group companies in one- and three-year revenue growth, one- and three-year earnings per share growth and one-year compounded annual net income growth, and Starbucks ranked in the top 30% among comparator group companies in three-year compounded annual net income growth. The Company ranked at the median in one-year total shareholder return and in the top quartile in three-year total shareholder return.

Base Salary: Base salaries for executive officers are reviewed on an annual basis and at the time of promotion or other increase in responsibilities. Increases in salary are based on subjective evaluation of such factors as the level of responsibility, individual performance, level of pay both of the executive in question and other similarly situated executives, and the comparator group companies' pay levels.

Annual Incentive Bonus: Incentive bonuses are generally granted based on a percentage of each executive officer's base salary. During fiscal 2005, each person who served as president and chief executive officer, the chairman, the segment presidents and all but one of the executive vice presidents of the Company, a total of nine officers, participated in the Company's Executive Management Bonus Plan (the "EMB Plan"). The Committee recommends to the Independent Directors the objective performance measure or measures, bonus target percentages and other terms and conditions of awards under the EMB Plan. During fiscal 2005, target bonus amounts under the EMB Plan were expressed as a percentage of base salary and were established according to the overall intended competitive position and competitive survey data for comparable positions in comparator group companies. For fiscal 2005, the bonus targets for participating officers ranged from 50% to 100% of base salary depending on position. After the end of the fiscal year, the Committee determined the extent to which the performance goals were achieved and recommended to the Independent Directors the amount of the award to be paid to each participant.

Under the EMB Plan as in effect during fiscal 2005, 80% of the target bonus was based on the achievement of the specified objective performance goal recommended by the Committee (and approved by the Independent Directors) for the fiscal year (other than for the chairman and the president and chief executive officer, for whom 100% of the target bonus was based on the objective performance goal). In fiscal 2005, an earnings per share target was the objective performance measure upon which the objective performance goal was based. The terms of the objective performance goal permit bonus payouts of up to 200% of the target bonus in the event (as was the case in fiscal 2005) that the Company's actual financial performance is better than the earnings per share target based on a scale approved by the Independent Directors upon recommendation from the Committee. Twenty percent of the target bonus for each executive officer other than the chairman and the president and chief executive officer was based on specific individual performance goals, which change somewhat each year according to strategic plan initiatives and the responsibilities of the positions. Relative weights assigned to each individual performance goal typically range from 5% to 35% of the 20% target bonus based on specific individual performance. All performance goals were established and approved by the Independent Directors within the first 90 days of fiscal 2005.

The total bonus award is determined according to the level of achievement of both the objective performance and individual performance goals. Below a threshold level of performance, no awards may be granted pursuant to the objective performance goal, and the Independent Directors, acting on the recommendation of the Committee may, in their discretion, reduce the awards pursuant to either objective or individual performance goals.

Long-Term Incentive Compensation: In fiscal 2005, long-term performance-based compensation of executive officers took the form of stock option awards. The Company's equity compensation plan is broad-based, with over 47,000 partners at all levels, including certain part-time retail partners, receiving stock option awards in fiscal 2005. The Committee continues to believe in the importance of equity ownership for all executive officers and the broad-based partner population, for purposes of incentive, retention and alignment with shareholders. In 2005 the Company proposed and shareholders approved a new equity incentive plan that permits a variety of equity award vehicles. The Committee believes the new plan provides the Company with flexibility in the future to achieve a balance between continuing its successful practice of providing equity-based compensation for partners at all levels, and creating and maintaining long-term shareholder value.

In determining the size of stock option grants to executive officers, the Committee bases its recommendations to the Independent Directors on such considerations as the value of total direct compensation for comparable positions in comparator group companies, Company and individual performance against the strategic plan for the prior fiscal year, the number and value of stock options previously granted to the executive officer, the allocation of overall share usage attributed to executive officers and the relative proportion of long-term incentives within the total compensation mix. All stock options granted by the Company during fiscal 2005 were granted as nonqualified stock options with an exercise price equal to the closing price of the Common Stock on the date of grant and, accordingly, will have value only if the market price of the Common Stock increases after that date. The stock options granted to the executive officers vest in three equal annual installments beginning October 1, 2005. The stock options granted to non-management partners generally vest in four equal annual installments.

Compensation of the Chief Executive Officer and the Chairman: Effective March 31, 2005, Orin C. Smith retired as president and chief executive officer of the Company and, effective April 1, 2005, Mr. Donald was appointed president and chief executive officer of the Company. Accordingly, each was compensated as president and chief executive officer for approximately half of the fiscal year.

Base Salary. In fiscal 2005, Mr. Smith's annualized base salary, which was determined in accordance with the factors described above for all executive officers, was $1,190,000. The amount actually paid and reflected in the Summary Compensation Table reflects a lesser amount because the salary was effective for only six months of the fiscal year. His salary was set at the competitive target of the 50th percentile of salaries paid by the comparator group companies. In fiscal 2005, Mr. Donald's annualized base salary, which was also determined in accordance with the factors used for all executive officers, was increased to $900,000 when he became president and chief executive officer. His salary was set somewhat below the median of salaries paid to chief executive officers by the comparator group companies.

Annual Incentive Bonus. For Messrs. Smith and Donald, the EMB Plan provided bonus targets of approximately $1,190,000 and $900,000, respectively, or 100% of base salary in each case, for achievement of the objective performance goal. Under the terms of the EMB Plan and his letter agreement with the Company dated December 8, 2004, Mr. Smith earned a bonus of $1,190,000 for fiscal 2005 based on the achievement of the objective earnings per share performance goal, which was a prorated bonus for the portion of the fiscal year during which Mr. Smith served as president and chief executive officer. Under the terms of the EMB Plan, and confirmed in his letter agreement with the Company dated March 30, 2005, Mr. Donald earned a bonus of $1,800,000 for fiscal 2005. Because the Company achieved earnings per share at a level permitting payout of 200% of the target bonus, as approved by the Independent Directors upon the recommendation of the Committee, the pro rated bonus paid to Mr. Smith and the bonus paid to Mr. Donald were above their annual base salaries (pro rated in Mr. Smith's case) and above the competitive target of the 50th percentile of bonuses paid to chief executive officers by target peer group companies.

Long-Term Incentive Compensation. On November 16, 2004, Messrs. Smith and Donald were granted stock options to purchase 1,000,000 and 600,000 shares of Common Stock, respectively (as adjusted for the two-for-one stock split on October 21, 2005). These grants, like the stock options granted to the other executive officers on the same date, reflect the Company's and such officers' performance for fiscal 2004, and so Mr. Smith's grant was not prorated for the portion of fiscal 2005 during which he served as president and chief executive officer. On April 1, 2005, Mr. Donald was granted an additional stock option to purchase 200,000 shares of Common Stock (as adjusted for the two-for-one stock split on October 21, 2005) in connection with his promotion to president and chief executive officer.

Mr. Smith will continue to provide advisory services to the Company as an employee through June 30, 2007, for which he will be paid $25,000 per year. He will also be provided an office, computer, cell phone and administrative and secretarial assistance as reasonably required and reimbursement for reasonable and customary expenses, including travel expenses.

Compensation of the Chairman. The Committee also annually approves the compensation of Mr. Schultz, the founder of the Company and its chairman. In approving Mr. Schultz's compensation, the Committee considers the factors described above for all executive officers as well as Mr. Schultz's significant role in the Company's leadership and his contribution to the Company's global expansion and international brand development. Mr. Schultz did not receive a salary increase for fiscal 2005. Mr. Schultz's EMB Plan bonus target was approximately $1,190,000, or 100% of base salary, for achievement of the objective earnings per share performance goal. Under the terms of the EMB Plan, Mr. Schultz earned a bonus of $2,380,000 for fiscal 2005, because the Company achieved earnings per share at a level permitting payout of 200% of the target bonus, as approved by the Independent Directors upon the recommendation of the Committee. On November 16, 2004, Mr. Schultz was granted a stock option to purchase 1,000,000 shares of Common Stock (as adjusted for the two-for-one stock split on October 21, 2005). This grant, like the stock options granted to the other executive officers on the same date, reflects the Company's and the chairman's performance for fiscal 2004.

Deferred Compensation Plan: Management partners, including executive officers, are eligible to participate in the Starbucks Management Deferred Compensation Plan (the "MDCP"), which provides an opportunity for eligible partners to defer up to 70% of annual base salary and 100% of bonus compensation into an account that will be credited with earnings at the same rate as one or more investment indices chosen by the partner, which mirror the investment funds available under the Company's 401(k) plan. The Company makes a matching contribution on up to 4% of matchable compensation (maximum $210,000 for 2005). In general, such compensation is matched at rates of 25% to 150%, depending on the length of the partner's service with the Company, with an offset for matching contributions made on the partner's behalf to the 401(k) plan. Annual matching contributions to the 401(k) plan on behalf of partners considered highly compensated are limited to $300.

Review of All Components of Executive Compensation: The Committee and the Independent Directors have reviewed information about all components of the compensation provided to the Company's executive officers, including base salary, annual bonus, equity compensation, including realized gains and accumulated unrealized values on stock options, perquisites and other personal benefits, the accumulated balance under the Company's non-qualified deferred compensation program, and the effect of retirement and change in control of the Company on stock option vesting. A summary of the Company's compensation programs, practices and internal controls, and tables quantifying the estimated values of these components for each executive were presented to and reviewed by the Committee.

Compliance With Section 162(m) of the Internal Revenue Code: Section 162(m) of the Internal Revenue Code disallows a federal income tax deduction to publicly held companies for certain compensation paid to the company's chief executive officer and four other most highly compensated executive officers to the extent that compensation exceeds $1 million per executive officer covered by Section 162(m) in any fiscal year. The limitation applies only to compensation that is not considered "performance-based" as defined in the Section 162(m) rules.

In designing the Company's compensation programs, the Committee carefully considers the effect of Section 162(m) together with other factors relevant to the Company's business needs. The Company has historically taken, and intends to continue taking, appropriate actions, to the extent it believes desirable, to preserve the deductibility of annual incentive and long-term performance awards. However, the Committee has not adopted a policy that all compensation paid must be tax-deductible and qualified under Section 162(m).

* * *

Performance Comparison Graph

The following graph depicts the Company's total return to shareholders from October 1, 2000 through October 2, 2005, relative to the performance of (i) the Standard & Poor's 500 Index, (ii) the Nasdaq Stock Market (U.S. Companies) Index, (iii) the Nasdaq Eating and Drinking Establishments Index, a peer group that includes Starbucks, and (iv) the Standard & Poor's 500 Consumer Discretionary Sector, a peer group that also includes Starbucks. The Company is including the Standard & Poor's 500 Consumer Discretionary Sector in the performance comparison graph for the first time, and after this year will no longer include the Nasdaq Eating and Drinking Establishments Index. Under SEC rules, both the Standard & Poor's 500 Consumer Discretionary Sector and the Nasdaq Eating and Drinking Establishments Index must be shown in this transition year. Management believes it is appropriate to change its peer group index in the performance comparison graph to the Standard & Poor's 500 Consumer Discretionary Sector because that index is more reflective of the companies which the Company considers its peers and includes a majority (10 out of 17) of the companies in the executive compensation comparator group used by the Compensation Committee in connection with recommending compensation for the Company's executive officers. All indices shown in the graph have been reset to a base of 100 as of October 1, 2000, assume an investment of $100 on that date and the reinvestment of dividends paid since that date. The Company has never paid cash dividends on its Common Stock. The points represent index levels based on the last trading day of the Company's fiscal year. The chart set forth below was prepared by Research Data Group, Inc., which holds a license to provide the indices used herein. The stock price performance shown in the graph is not necessarily indicative of future price performance.

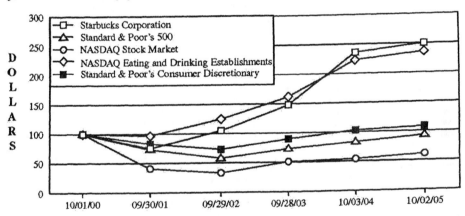

	10/01/00	09/30/01	09/29/02	09/28/03	10/03/04	10/02/05
Starbucks Corporation	$100	$75	$105	$148	$236	$250
Standard & Poor's 500	$100	$73	$ 58	$ 73	$ 83	$ 93
Nasdaq Stock Market	$100	$41	$ 33	$ 51	$ 54	$ 61
Nasdaq Eating and Drinking Establishments	$100	$97	$125	$162	$223	$236
Standard & Poor's Consumer Discretionary	$100	$83	$ 73	$ 90	$103	$108

Summary Compensation Table

The following table sets forth the compensation paid to or earned by (including deferred amounts) (i) the Company's president and chief executive officer, (ii) the Company's four other most highly compensated executive officers in fiscal 2005, and (iii) the Company's former president and chief executive officer (collectively, the "Named Executive Officers"), during each of the Company's last three fiscal years.

		Annual Compensation		Other Annual Compensation ($)[1]	Long-Term Compensation	All Other Compensation ($)
Name and Principal Position	Fiscal Year	Salary ($)	Bonus ($)		Number of Securities Underlying Options[2]	
James L. Donald .... president and chief executive officer	2005	887,308	1,800,000	4,092[3]	800,000	5,982[4]
	2004	832,308	1,404,000[5]	80,308[3]	600,000	3,303[4]
	2003	744,615	1,200,000[5]	156,468[3]	1,000,000	969[4]
Howard Schultz .... chairman	2005	1,176,269	2,380,000	679,542[6]	1,000,000	247,749[7]
	2004	1,179,154	2,490,000[8]	722,300[6]	1,100,000	7,238[7]
	2003	1,132,762	1,417,000	782,651[6]	1,024,000	3,038[7]
James C. Alling .... president, Starbucks Coffee U.S.	2005	476,923	643,500	621[9]	170,000	7,968[10]
	2004	392,006	381,333	1,324[9]	200,000	7,794[10]
	2003	330,475	178,328	—	45,000	4,336[10]
Martin Coles .... president, Starbucks Coffee International	2005	607,885	786,656	3,618[11]	100,000	3,573[12]
	2004	265,385	530,000[13]	501,600[11]	400,000	694[12]
	2003	—	—	—	—	—
Michael Casey .... executive vice president, chief financial officer and chief administrative officer	2005	571,827	574,138	10,244[14]	—	15,670[15]
	2004	555,192	585,000[16]	1,082[14]	1,050,000[17]	13,107[15]
	2003	534,584	334,375	—	350,000	8,432[15]
Orin C. Smith .... Former president and chief executive officer	2005	643,346	1,190,000	77,855[18]	1,000,000	8,968[19]
	2004	1,179,154	2,490,000[20]	152,458[18]	1,100,000	22,169[19]
	2003	1,132,762	1,417,000	246,281[18]	1,024,000	9,920[19]

[1] As shown in footnotes below, "Other Annual Compensation" for some of the Named Executive Officers includes personal use by executives, their families and invited guests of Company aircraft. Amounts reported for such personal use represent the aggregate incremental cost to the Company of such use. The Company calculates the aggregate incremental cost of the personal use of Company aircraft based on a methodology that includes the average weighted cost of fuel, crew hotels and meals, on-board catering, trip-related maintenance, landing fees, trip-related hangar/parking costs and smaller variable costs. Because Company aircraft are used primarily for business travel, the methodology excludes the fixed costs that do not change based on usage, such as pilots' salaries, the purchase or lease costs of the aircraft and the cost of maintenance not related to personal travel. Executives and their families and invited guests occasionally fly on Company aircraft as additional passengers on business flights or personal flights requested by a different executive. In those cases, the aggregate incremental cost to the Company is a *de minimis* amount and so no amount is reflected in the table, except for the Named Executive Officer, if any, who requested a personal flight. The Company formerly reported compensation amounts for personal use of Company aircraft based on the IRS Standard Industry Fare Level (SIFL) tables used for calculating imputed income for such use. Amounts reported for prior years based on the SIFL rate have been restated in this proxy statement to reflect aggregate incremental cost to the Company. "Other Annual Compensation" for some of the Named Executive Officers also includes security services. Under the Company's executive security program, Messrs. Donald, Schultz, Coles and Smith have been provided security services, including home security systems and monitoring and, in the case of Mr. Schultz, personal security services. The Company provides these security services for the Company's benefit and considers the related expenses to be appropriate business expenses. However, in the interest of greater

transparency, the Company is reporting these expenses as "Other Annual Compensation", including for prior years.

(2) Amounts shown for number of securities underlying options have been adjusted to give effect to the Company's two-for-one stock split on October 21, 2005.

(3) The amounts shown represent (i) the aggregate incremental cost to the Company of $4,092 and $62,441, for security services provided to Mr. Donald in fiscal 2005 and 2004, respectively, (ii) relocation and temporary housing expenses paid to Mr. Donald of $16,879 and $156,468 in fiscal 2004 and 2003, respectively, and (iii) the aggregate incremental cost to the Company of $988 for a physical examination provided to Mr. Donald in fiscal 2004.

* * *

Stock Option Grants in Fiscal 2005

The following table sets forth information regarding options to purchase shares of Common Stock granted to the Named Executive Officers during fiscal 2005. The Company has no outstanding stock appreciation rights. The amounts shown for each Named Executive Officer below as potential realizable values are based entirely on hypothetical annualized rates of stock appreciation of five percent and ten percent compounded over the full ten-year terms of the options. These assumed rates of growth were selected by the SEC for illustration purposes only and are not intended to predict future stock prices, which will depend upon overall stock market conditions and the Company's future performance and prospects. Consequently, there can be no assurance that the Named Executive Officers will receive the potential realizable values shown in this table.

Option Grants in Fiscal 2005[1]

Name	Number of Securities Underlying Options Granted	Percent of Total Options Granted to Employees	Exercise Price per Share	Expiration Date	Potential Realizable Value at Assumed Annual Rates of Stock Price Appreciation for Option Term	
					Five Percent ($)	Ten Percent ($)
James L. Donald	600,000[2]	3.9	$27.32	11/16/14	10,308,841	26,124,626
	200,000[3]	1.3	$25.63	04/01/15	3,223,651	8,169,364
Howard Schultz	1,000,000[4]	6.5	$27.32	11/16/14	17,181,401	43,541,044
James C. Alling	170,000[5]	1.1	$27.32	11/16/14	2,920,838	7,401,977
Martin Coles	100,000[6]	0.7	$27.32	11/16/14	1,718,140	4,354,104
Michael Casey	—[7]	—	—	—	—	—
Orin C. Smith	1,000,000[8]	6.5	$27.32	11/16/14	17,181,401	43,541,044

(1) Stock options granted to the executive officers are typically granted in the first fiscal quarter of each year and reflect the Company's and such officers' performance for the prior fiscal year. Other than the options described in note 3 below, all options in this table were granted under the Company's Amended and Restated Key Employee Stock Option Plan — 1994 (the "1994 Key Employee Plan") and vest in three equal annual installments beginning October 1, 2005. The options described in note 3 below were granted under the 2005 Key Employee Sub-Plan to the Starbucks Corporation 2005 Long-Term Equity Incentive Plan (the "2005 Key Employee Plan") and vest in three equal annual installments beginning April 1, 2006. All options in this table have an exercise price equal to the fair market value of the underlying Common Stock on the date of grant. The options will become fully vested and exercisable (i) if the executive terminates his employment after the age of 55 and at least 10 years of credited service with the Company and (ii) upon a change in control of the Company, under the circumstances described for the 1994 Key Employee Plan and 2005 Key Employee Plan, respectively, on pages 27-28 of this proxy statement. Amounts shown for number of securities underlying options and exercise price per share have been adjusted to give effect to the Company's two-for-one stock split on October 21, 2005.

* * *

Exercises of Stock Options in Fiscal 2005

The following table sets forth information regarding stock option exercises during fiscal 2005 by the Named Executive Officers and the value of each Named Executive Officer's exercised and unexercised stock options on October 2, 2005.

Aggregated Option Exercises in Fiscal 2005 and Fiscal Year-End Option Values

Name	Shares Acquired on Exercise[1] (#)	Value Realized[2] ($)	Number of Securities Underlying Unexercised Options at Fiscal Year End[1]		Value of Unexercised In-the-Money Options at Fiscal Year End[3] ($)	
			Exercisable	Unexercisable	Exercisable	Unexercisable
James L. Donald	0	N/A	1,100,000	1,300,000	11,023,000	9,059,000
Howard Schultz	1,482,860	37,941,442	16,603,168	1,033,332	304,180,708	3,600,660
James C. Alling	76,092	1,662,688	685,309	179,999	9,619,980	654,660
Martin Coles	0	N/A	133,334	366,666	545,000	1,635,000
Michael Casey	156,960	3,582,173	1,755,832	350,000	23,636,719	3,437,000
Orin C. Smith	3,508,868	59,485,240	1,489,800	1,033,332	13,878,296	3,600,660

[1] Amounts shown for number of securities underlying unexercised options at fiscal year end and shares acquired on exercise have been adjusted to give effect to the Company's two-for-one stock split on October 21, 2005.

[2] Value realized is calculated by subtracting the aggregate exercise price of the options exercised from the aggregate market value of the shares of Common Stock acquired on the date of exercise.

[3] The value of unexercised options is calculated by subtracting the aggregate exercise price of the options from the aggregate market value of the shares of Common Stock subject thereto as of September 30, 2005 (the last trading day prior to the Company's fiscal year end on October 2, 2005). These values are provided pursuant to SEC rules, but there can be no guarantee that, if and when these stock options are exercised, they will have this value.

Equity Compensation Plan Information

The following table provides information as of October 2, 2005 regarding shares outstanding and available for issuance under the Company's existing equity incentive and employee stock purchase plans *(in millions, except per share amounts)*. All amounts shown have been adjusted to give effect to the Company's two-for-one stock split on October 21, 2005.

Plan Category	(a) Number of Securities to be Issued Upon Exercise of Outstanding Options, Warrants and Rights	(b) Weighted-Average Exercise Price of Outstanding Options, Warrants and Rights	(c) Number of Securities Remaining Available for Future Issuance Under Equity Compensation Plans (Excluding Securities Reflected in Column (a))
Equity compensation plans approved by security holders................................	12,308,976	$ 15.05	95,619,314
Equity compensation plans not approved by security holders	4,882,568	$ 14.45	2,492,338
Total	17,191,544	$ 14.88	98,111,652[1]

[1] Includes 19,699,116 shares remaining available for issuance under employee stock purchase plans and 78,412,536 shares under equity incentive plans.

The shares to be issued under plans not approved by shareholders relate to the Company's 1991 Company-Wide Stock Option Plan (the "Bean Stock Plan"), the Company's UK Share Save Plan and the

Company's UK Share Incentive Plan, the successor to the UK Share Save Plan. The Bean Stock Plan is the Company's former broad-based stock option plan and provided for the annual issuance of stock options to eligible employees. The Bean Stock Plan was approved and adopted by the Board in 1991 and did not require shareholder approval. Generally, options were granted annually under the Bean Stock Plan. These grants required Board approval, were linked to performance goals of the Company and were granted to employees as a percentage of base salary. In fiscal 2005, over 47,000 employees were granted options under the Bean Stock Plan. The Bean Stock Plan was effectively replaced by the 2005 Company-Wide Sub-Plan to the Starbucks Corporation 2005 Long-Term Equity Incentive Plan. The Starbucks Corporation 2005 Long-Term Equity Incentive Plan was approved by the Company's shareholders on February 9, 2005.

The Company's UK Share Save Plan, which is a UK Inland Revenue approved Save-As-You-Earn plan, allows eligible employees in the United Kingdom to save for a three-year period through payroll deductions toward the purchase of the Common Stock at a discount from the fair market value on the first day of business of a three-year offering period. The total number of shares issuable under the plan is 1,200,000, of which 96,930 were issued as of October 2, 2005 (in each case as adjusted to give effect to the two-for-one stock split on October 21, 2005). During fiscal 2003, the Compensation Committee accepted the recommendation of management to suspend future offerings under the UK Share Save Plan, and effectively replace the UK Share Save Plan with the UK Share Incentive Plan in fiscal 2004. The last offering under the UK Share Save Plan was in December 2002 and will mature in February 2006.

The Company's UK Share Incentive Plan, which is a UK Inland Revenue approved plan, allows eligible employees in the United Kingdom to purchase shares of the Common Stock through payroll deductions during six-month offering periods at the lower of the market price at the beginning and the market price at the end of the offering period. The Company awards one matching share for each six shares purchased under the plan. The total number of shares issuable under the plan is 1,400,000, of which 10,732 shares were issued as of October 2, 2005 (in each case as adjusted to give effect to the two-for-one stock split on October 21, 2005).

* * *

PROPOSAL 2 — RATIFICATION OF SELECTION OF INDEPENDENT REGISTERED PUBLIC ACCOUNTING FIRM

Independent Registered Public Accounting Firm Fees

The following table sets forth the aggregate fees billed to the Company for fiscal 2005 and fiscal 2004 by Deloitte:

	Fiscal 2005	Fiscal 2004
Audit Fees	$4,025,000	$1,578,000
Audit-Related Fees	138,000	28,000
Tax Fees	96,000	95,000
All Other Fees	—	—
Total	$4,259,000	$1,701,000

Audit Fees for fiscal 2005 consist of fees paid to Deloitte for (i) the audit of the Company's annual financial statements included in the Annual Report on Form 10-K and review of financial statements included in the Quarterly Reports on Form 10-Q; (ii) the audit of the Company's internal control over financial reporting with the objective of obtaining reasonable assurance about whether effective internal control over financial reporting was maintained in all material respects; (iii) the attestation of management's report on the effectiveness of internal control over financial reporting; and (iv) services that are normally provided by the independent registered public accounting firm in connection with statutory and regulatory filings or engagements. *Audit Fees* for fiscal 2004 consisted of items (i) and (iv) only.

Audit-Related Fees consist of fees for assurance and related services that are reasonably related to the performance of the audit or review of the Company's financial statements and are not reported under *Audit Fees*. This category includes fees related to audit and attest services not required by statute or regulations, due diligence related to mergers, acquisitions and investments and consultations concerning financial accounting and reporting standards.

Tax Fees consist of fees for professional services for tax compliance, tax advice and tax planning. These services include assistance regarding federal, state and international tax compliance, return preparation, tax audits and customs and duties.

The Audit Committee has considered whether the provision of non-audit services is compatible with maintaining the independence of Deloitte and has concluded that it is.

Policy on Audit Committee Pre-Approval of Audit and Permissible Non-Audit Services of the Independent Registered Public Accounting Firm

The Audit Committee is responsible for appointing, setting compensation for and overseeing the work of the independent registered public accounting firm. The Audit Committee has established a policy requiring its pre-approval of all audit and permissible non-audit services provided by the independent registered public accounting firm. The policy is available at www.starbucks.com/aboutus/corporate_governance.asp. The policy provides for the general pre-approval of specific types of services and gives detailed guidance to management as to the specific services that are eligible for general pre-approval, and provides specific cost limits for each such service on an annual basis. The policy requires specific pre-approval of all other permitted services. For both types of pre-approval, the Audit Committee considers whether such services are consistent with the rules of the SEC on auditor independence. The Audit Committee's charter delegates to its Chair the authority to address any requests for pre-approval of services between Audit Committee meetings, and the Chair must report any pre-approval decisions to the Audit Committee at its next scheduled meeting. The policy prohibits the Audit Committee from delegating to management the Audit Committee's responsibility to pre-approve permitted services of the independent registered public accounting firm.

Requests for pre-approval for services that are eligible for general pre-approval must be detailed as to the services to be provided and the estimated total cost and are submitted to the Company's controller. The controller then determines whether the services requested fall within the detailed guidance of the Audit Committee in the policy as to the services eligible for general pre-approval. The independent registered public accounting firm and management must report to the Audit Committee on a timely basis regarding the services provided by the independent registered public accounting firm in accordance with general pre-approval.

None of the services related to the *Audit-Related Fees* or *Tax Fees* described above was approved by the Audit Committee pursuant to the waiver of pre-approval provisions set forth in applicable rules of the SEC.

The Audit Committee requests that shareholders ratify its selection of Deloitte to serve as the Company's independent registered public accounting firm for fiscal 2006. Deloitte audited the consolidated financial statements of the Company and management's report on internal control over financial reporting for fiscal 2005. Representatives of Deloitte will be present at the Annual Meeting and will have an opportunity to make a statement if they so desire and to respond to questions by shareholders.

THE BOARD OF DIRECTORS RECOMMENDS A VOTE FOR THE RATIFICATION OF THE SELECTION OF DELOITTE & TOUCHE LLP AS THE INDEPENDENT REGISTERED PUBLIC ACCOUNTING FIRM OF THE COMPANY FOR FISCAL 2006.

APPENDIX B

PRESENT AND FUTURE VALUE TABLES

Table I

Future Value of $1.00

$f = p\,(1+r)^n$, where $r =$ interest rate; $n =$ number of compounding periods; $p = \$1.00$.

Periods = n	1%	2%	3%	4%	5%	6%	7%	8%	9%	10%	12%	15%
1	1.01000	1.02000	1.03000	1.04000	1.05000	1.06000	1.07000	1.08000	1.09000	1.10000	1.12000	1.15000
2	1.02010	1.04040	1.06090	1.08160	1.10250	1.12360	1.14490	1.16640	1.18810	1.21000	1.25440	1.32250
3	1.03030	1.06121	1.09273	1.12486	1.15763	1.19102	1.22504	1.25971	1.29503	1.33100	1.40493	1.52087
4	1.04060	1.08243	1.12551	1.16986	1.21551	1.26248	1.31080	1.36049	1.41158	1.46410	1.57352	1.74901
5	1.05101	1.10408	1.15927	1.21665	1.27628	1.33823	1.40255	1.46933	1.53862	1.61051	1.76234	2.01136
6	1.06152	1.12616	1.19405	1.26532	1.34010	1.41852	1.50073	1.58687	1.67710	1.77156	1.97382	2.31306
7	1.07214	1.14869	1.22987	1.31593	1.40710	1.50363	1.60578	1.71382	1.82804	1.94872	2.21068	2.66002
8	1.08286	1.17166	1.26677	1.36857	1.47746	1.59385	1.71819	1.85093	1.99256	2.14359	2.47596	3.05902
9	1.09369	1.19509	1.30477	1.42331	1.55133	1.68948	1.83846	1.99900	2.17189	2.35795	2.77308	3.51788
10	1.10462	1.21899	1.34392	1.48024	1.62889	1.79085	1.96715	2.15892	2.36736	2.59374	3.10585	4.04556
11	1.11567	1.24337	1.38423	1.53945	1.71034	1.89830	2.10485	2.33164	2.58043	2.85312	3.47855	4.65239
12	1.12683	1.26824	1.42576	1.60103	1.79586	2.01220	2.25219	2.51817	2.81266	3.13843	3.89598	5.35025
13	1.13809	1.29361	1.46853	1.66507	1.88565	2.13293	2.40985	2.71962	3.06580	3.45227	4.36349	6.15279
14	1.14947	1.31948	1.51259	1.73168	1.97993	2.26090	2.57853	2.93719	3.34173	3.79750	4.88711	7.07571
15	1.16097	1.34587	1.55797	1.80094	2.07893	2.39656	2.75903	3.17217	3.64248	4.17725	5.47357	8.13706
16	1.17258	1.37279	1.60471	1.87298	2.18287	2.54035	2.95216	3.42594	3.97031	4.59497	6.13039	9.35762
17	1.18430	1.40024	1.65285	1.94790	2.29202	2.69277	3.15882	3.70002	4.32763	5.05447	6.86604	10.76126
18	1.19615	1.42825	1.70243	2.02582	2.40662	2.85434	3.37993	3.99602	4.71712	5.55992	7.68997	12.37545
19	1.20811	1.45681	1.75351	2.10685	2.52695	3.02560	3.61653	4.31570	5.14166	6.11591	8.61276	14.23177
20	1.22019	1.48595	1.80611	2.19112	2.65330	3.20714	3.86968	4.66096	5.60441	6.72750	9.64629	16.36654
22	1.24472	1.54598	1.91610	2.36992	2.92526	3.60354	4.43040	5.43654	6.65860	8.14027	12.10031	21.64475
24	1.26973	1.60844	2.03279	2.56330	3.22510	4.04893	5.07237	6.34118	7.91108	9.84973	15.17863	28.62518
26	1.29526	1.67342	2.15659	2.77247	3.55567	4.54938	5.80735	7.39635	9.39916	11.91818	19.04007	37.85680
28	1.32129	1.74102	2.28793	2.99870	3.92013	5.11169	6.64884	8.62711	11.16714	14.42099	23.88387	50.06561
30	1.34785	1.81136	2.42726	3.24340	4.32194	5.74349	7.61226	10.06266	13.26768	17.44940	29.95992	66.21177
32	1.37494	1.88454	2.57508	3.50806	4.76494	6.45339	8.71527	11.73708	15.76333	21.11378	37.58173	87.56507
34	1.40258	1.96068	2.73191	3.79432	5.25335	7.25103	9.97811	13.69013	18.72841	25.54767	47.14252	115.8048
36	1.43077	2.03989	2.89828	4.10393	5.79182	8.14725	11.42394	15.96817	22.25123	30.91268	59.13557	153.1519
38	1.45953	2.12230	3.07478	4.43881	6.38548	9.15425	13.07927	18.62528	26.43668	37.40434	74.17966	202.5433
40	1.48886	2.20804	3.26204	4.80102	7.03999	10.28572	14.97446	21.72452	31.40942	45.25926	93.05097	267.8635
50	1.64463	2.69159	4.38391	7.10668	11.46740	18.42015	29.45703	46.90161	74.35752	117.3909	289.0022	1,083.66
100	2.70481	7.24465	19.21863	50.50495	131.5013	339.3021	867.7163	2,199.76	5,529.04	13,780.6	83,522.3	117 × 10⁴

Table II

Future Value of Annuity of $1.00 in Arrears

$F = [(1 + r)^n - 1]/r$, where $r =$ interest rate; $n =$ number of payments.

No of Payments = n	1%	2%	3%	4%	5%	6%	7%	8%	9%	10%	12%	15%
1	1.00000	1.00000	1.00000	1.00000	1.00000	1.00000	1.00000	1.00000	1.00000	1.00000	1.00000	1.00000
2	2.01000	2.02000	2.03000	2.04000	2.05000	2.06000	2.07000	2.08000	2.09000	2.10000	2.12000	2.15000
3	3.03010	3.06040	3.09090	3.12160	3.15250	3.18360	3.21490	3.24640	3.27810	3.31000	3.37440	3.47250
4	4.06040	4.12161	4.18363	4.24646	4.31013	4.37462	4.43994	4.50611	4.57313	4.64100	4.77933	4.99338
5	5.10101	5.20404	5.30914	5.41632	5.52563	5.63709	5.75074	5.86660	5.98471	6.10510	6.35285	6.74238
6	6.15202	6.30812	6.46841	6.63298	6.80191	6.97532	7.15329	7.33593	7.52333	7.71561	8.11519	8.75374
7	7.21354	7.43428	7.66246	7.89829	8.14201	8.39384	8.65402	8.92280	9.20043	9.48717	10.08901	11.06680
8	8.28567	8.58297	8.89234	9.21423	9.54911	9.89747	10.25980	10.63663	11.02847	11.43589	12.29969	13.72682
9	9.36853	9.75463	10.15911	10.58280	11.02656	11.49132	11.97799	12.48756	13.02104	13.57948	14.77566	16.78584
10	10.46221	10.94972	11.46388	12.00611	12.57789	13.18079	13.81645	14.48656	15.19293	15.93742	17.54874	20.30372
11	11.56683	12.16872	12.80780	13.48635	14.20679	14.97164	15.78360	16.64549	17.56029	18.53117	20.65458	24.34928
12	12.68250	13.41209	14.19203	15.02581	15.91713	16.86994	17.88845	18.97713	20.14072	21.38428	24.13313	29.00167
13	13.80933	14.68033	15.61779	16.62684	17.71298	18.88214	20.14064	21.49530	22.95338	24.52271	28.02911	34.35192
14	14.94742	15.97394	17.08632	18.29191	19.59863	21.01507	22.55049	24.21492	26.01919	27.97498	32.39260	40.50471
15	16.09690	17.29342	18.59891	20.02359	21.57856	23.27597	25.12902	27.15211	29.36092	31.77248	37.27971	47.58041
16	17.25786	18.63929	20.15688	21.82453	23.65749	25.67253	27.88805	30.32428	33.00340	35.94973	42.75328	55.71747
17	18.43044	20.01207	21.76159	23.69751	25.84037	28.21288	30.84022	33.75023	36.97370	40.54470	48.88367	65.07509
18	19.61475	21.41231	23.41444	25.64541	28.13238	30.90565	33.99903	37.45024	41.30134	45.59917	55.74971	75.83636
19	20.81090	22.84056	25.11687	27.67123	30.53900	33.75999	37.37896	41.44626	46.01846	51.15909	63.43968	88.21181
20	22.01900	24.29737	26.87037	29.77808	33.06595	36.78559	40.99549	45.76196	51.16012	57.27500	72.05244	102.4436
22	24.47159	27.29898	30.53678	34.24797	38.50521	43.39229	49.00574	55.45676	62.87334	71.40275	92.50258	137.6316
24	26.97346	30.42186	34.42647	39.08260	44.50200	50.81558	58.17667	66.76476	76.78961	88.49733	118.1552	184.1678
26	29.52563	33.6~091	38.55304	44.31174	51.11345	59.15638	68.67647	79.95442	93.32398	109.1818	150.3339	245.7120
28	32.12910	37.05121	42.93092	49.96758	58.40258	68.52811	80.69769	95.33883	112.9682	134.2099	190.6989	327.1041
30	34.78489	40.56808	47.57542	56.08494	66.43885	79.05819	94.46079	113.2832	136.3075	164.4940	241.3327	434.7451
32	37.49407	44.22703	52.50276	62.70147	75.29883	90.88978	110.2182	134.2135	164.0370	201.1378	304.8477	577.1005
34	40.25770	48.03380	57.73018	69.85791	85.06696	104.1838	128.2588	158.6267	196.9823	245.4767	384.5210	765.3654
36	43.07688	51.99437	63.27594	77.59831	95.83632	119.1209	148.9135	187.1021	236.1247	299.1268	484.4631	1,014.35
38	45.95272	56.11494	69.15945	85.97034	107.7095	135.9042	172.5610	220.3159	282.6298	364.0434	609.8305	1,343.62
40	48.88637	60.40198	75.40126	95.02552	120.7998	154.7620	199.6351	259.0565	337.8824	442.5926	767.0914	1,779.09
50	64.46318	84.57940	112.7969	152.6671	209.3480	290.3359	406.5289	573.7702	815.0836	1,163.91	2,400.02	7,217.72
100	170.4814	312.2323	607.2877	1,237.62	2,610.03	5,638.37	12,381.7	27,484.5	61,422.7	137,796	696,011	783 $\times$ 10⁴

Table III

Present Value of $1.00

$p = f/(1 + r)^n$, where r = discount (interest) rate; n = number of periods until payment; $f = \$1.00$.

Periods = n	1%	2%	3%	4%	5%	6%	7%	8%	9%	10%	12%	15%
1	.99010	.98039	.97087	96154	.95238	.94340	.93458	.92593	.91743	.90909	.89286	.86957
2	.98030	.96117	.94260	92456	.90703	.89000	.87344	.85734	.84168	.82645	.79719	.75614
3	.97059	.94232	.91514	.88900	.86384	.83962	.81630	.79383	.77218	.75131	.71178	.65752
4	96098	.92385	.88849	.85480	.82270	79209	.76290	.73503	.70843	.68301	.63552	.57175
5	.95147	.90573	.86261	82193	.78353	.74726	.71299	.68058	.64993	.62092	.56743	49718
6	.94205	.88797	.83748	.79031	.74622	.70496	.66634	.63017	.59627	.56447	.50663	.43233
7	.93272	.87056	.81309	.75992	.71068	.66506	.62275	.58349	.54703	.51316	.45235	.37594
8	.92348	.85349	.78941	.73069	.67684	.62741	.58201	.54027	.50187	.46651	.40388	.32690
9	.91434	.83676	.76642	.70259	.64461	.59190	.54393	.50025	.46043	.42410	.36061	.28426
10	.90529	.82035	.74409	.67556	.61391	.55839	.50835	.46319	.42241	.38554	.32197	.24718
11	.89632	.80426	.72242	.64958	.58466	.52679	.47509	.42888	.38753	.35049	.28748	.21494
12	.88745	.78849	.70138	.62460	.55684	.49697	.44401	.39711	.35553	.31863	.25668	18691
13	.87866	.77303	.68095	.60057	.53032	.46884	.41496	.36770	.32618	.28966	.22917	16253
14	.86996	.75788	.66112	.57748	.50507	.44230	.38782	.34045	.29925	.26333	.20462	.14133
15	.86135	.74301	.64186	.55526	48102	.41727	.36245	.31524	.27454	.23939	.18270	12289
16	.85282	.72845	.62317	.53391	.45811	.39365	.33873	.29189	.25187	.21763	.16312	.10686
17	.84438	.71416	.60502	.51337	.43630	.37136	.31657	.27027	.23107	.19784	.14564	.09293
18	.83602	.70016	.58739	.49363	.41552	.35034	.29586	.25025	.21199	.17986	.13004	.08081
19	.82774	.68643	.57029	.47464	.39573	.33051	.27651	.23171	.19449	.16351	.11611	.07027
20	81954	.67297	.55368	.45639	.37689	.31180	.25842	.21455	.17843	.14864	.10367	.06110
22	.80340	.64684	.52189	.42196	.34185	.27751	22571	.18394	.15018	.12285	.08264	.04620
24	.78757	.62172	.49193	.39012	.31007	.24698	.19715	.15770	.12640	.10153	.06588	.03493
26	.77205	.59758	.46369	.36069	.28124	.21981	.17220	.13520	.10639	.08391	.05252	.02642
28	75684	.57437	.43706	.33348	.25509	.19563	.15040	.11591	.08955	.06934	.04187	01997
30	.74192	.55207	.41199	.30832	.23138	.17411	.13137	.09938	.07537	.05731	.03338	.01510
32	.72730	.53063	38834	.28506	.20967	.15496	.11474	.08520	.06344	.04736	.02661	.01142
34	.71297	.51003	36604	.26355	.19035	.13791	.10022	.07305	.05339	.03914	.02121	.00864
36	.69892	.49022	34503	.24367	.17266	.12274	.08754	.06262	.04494	.03235	.01691	.00653
38	.68515	.47119	.32523	.22529	.15661	.10924	.07646	.05369	.03783	02673	.01348	.00494
40	.67165	.45289	30656	.20829	14205	.09722	.06678	.04603	.03184	.02209	.01075	.00373
50	.60804	37153	22811	.14071	.08720	.05429	.03395	.02132	.01345	00852	.00346	00092
100	36971	.13803	.05203	.01980	.00760	.00295	.00115	.00045	.00018	.00007	.00001	.00000

Table IV

Present Value of Annuity of $1.00 in Arrears

$P = (1 - 1/[1 + r]^n)/r$, where r = discount (interest) rate; n = number of payments.

No of Payments = n	1%	2%	3%	4%	5%	6%	7%	8%	9%	10%	12%	15%
1	.99010	.98039	.97087	.96154	.95238	.94340	.93458	.92593	.91743	.90909	.89286	.86957
2	1.97040	1.94156	1.91347	1.88609	1.85941	1.83339	1.80802	1.78326	1.75911	1.73554	1.69005	1.62571
3	2.94099	2.88388	2.82861	2.77509	2.72325	2.67301	2.62432	2.57710	2.53129	2.48685	2.40183	2.28323
4	3.90197	3.80773	3.71710	3.62990	3.54595	3.46511	3.38721	3.31213	3.23972	3.16987	3.03735	2.95498
5	4.85343	4.71346	4.57971	4.45182	4.32948	4.21236	4.10020	3.99271	3.88965	3.79079	3.60478	3.35216
6	5.79548	5.60143	5.41719	5.24214	5.07569	4.91732	4.76654	4.62288	4.48592	4.35526	4.11141	3.78448
7	6.72819	6.47199	6.23028	6.00205	5.78637	5.58238	5.38929	5.20637	5.03295	4.86842	4.56376	4.16042
8	7.65168	7.32548	7.01969	6.73274	6.46321	6.20979	5.97130	5.74664	5.53482	5.33493	4.96764	4.48732
9	8.56602	8.16224	7.78611	7.43533	7.10782	6.80169	6.51523	6.24689	5.99525	5.75902	5.32825	4.77158
10	9.47130	8.98259	8.53020	8.11090	7.72173	7.36009	7.02358	6.71008	6.41766	6.14457	5.65022	5.01877
11	10.36763	9.78685	9.25262	8.76048	8.30641	7.88687	7.49867	7.13896	6.80519	6.49506	5.93770	5.23371
12	11.25508	10.57534	9.95400	9.38507	8.86325	8.38384	7.94269	7.53608	7.16073	6.81369	6.19437	5.42062
13	12.13374	11.34837	10.63496	9.98565	9.39357	8.85268	8.35765	7.90378	7.48690	7.10336	6.42355	5.58315
14	13.00370	12.10625	11.29607	10.56312	9.89864	9.29498	8.74547	8.24424	7.78615	7.36669	6.62817	5.72448
15	13.86505	12.84926	11.93794	11.11839	10.37966	9.71225	9.10791	8.55948	8.06069	7.60608	6.81086	5.84737
16	14.71787	13.57771	12.56110	11.65230	10.83777	10.10590	9.44665	8.85137	8.31256	7.82371	6.97399	5.95423
17	15.56225	14.29187	13.16612	12.16567	11.27407	10.47726	9.76322	9.12164	8.54363	8.02155	7.11963	6.04716
18	16.39827	14.99203	13.75351	12.65930	11.68959	10.82760	10.05909	9.37189	8.75563	8.20141	7.24967	6.12797
19	17.22601	15.67846	14.32380	13.13394	12.08532	11.15812	10.33560	9.60360	8.95011	8.36492	7.36578	6.19823
20	18.04555	16.35143	14.87747	13.59033	12.46221	11.46992	10.59401	9.81815	9.12855	8.51356	7.46944	6.25933
22	19.66038	17.65805	15.93692	14.45112	13.16300	12.04158	11.06124	10.20074	9.44243	8.77154	7.64465	6.35866
24	21.24339	18.91393	16.93554	15.24696	13.79864	12.55036	11.46933	10.52876	9.70661	8.98474	7.78432	6.43377
26	22.79520	20.12104	17.87684	15.98277	14.37519	13.00317	11.82578	10.80998	9.92897	9.16095	7.89566	6.49056
28	24.31644	21.28127	18.76411	16.66306	14.89813	13.40616	12.13711	11.05108	10.11613	9.30657	7.98442	6.53351
30	25.80771	22.39646	19.60044	17.29203	15.37245	13.76483	12.40904	11.25778	10.27365	9.42691	8.05518	6.56598
32	27.26959	23.46833	20.38877	17.87355	15.80268	14.08404	12.64656	11.43500	10.40624	9.52638	8.11159	6.59053
34	28.70267	24.49859	21.13184	18.41120	16.19290	14.36814	12.85401	11.58693	10.51784	9.60857	8.15656	6.60910
36	30.10751	25.48884	21.83225	18.90828	16.54685	14.62099	13.03521	11.71719	10.61176	9.67651	8.19241	6.62314
38	31.48466	26.44064	22.49246	19.36786	16.86789	14.84602	13.19347	11.82887	10.69082	9.73265	8.22099	6.63375
40	32.83469	27.35548	23.11477	19.79277	17.15909	15.04630	13.33171	11.92461	10.75736	9.77905	8.24378	6.64178
50	39.19612	31.42361	25.72976	21.48218	18.25593	15.76186	13.80075	12.23348	10.96168	9.91481	8.30450	6.66051
100	63.02888	43.09835	31.59891	24.50500	19.84791	16.61755	14.26925	12.49432	11.10910	9.99927	8.33323	6.66666

YOU'VE GOT A LETTER FROM A FRIEND & THE BUDGET IS DUE.

LET'S TAKE A LOOK AT THE BALANCE SHEET & THE STATEMENT OF INCOME. THERE ARE OTHER FINANCIAL STATEMENTS, BUT WE'LL JUST TAKE THOSE TWO FOR NOW.

AAH, SMART DECISIONS ABOUT BEN & JERRY'S FINANCES - A REALLY IMPORTANT PART OF BEING SOCIALLY RESPONSIBLE - IMPORTANT FOR OUR EMPLOYEES AND OUR STOCKHOLDERS. REMEMBER, WE WOULDN'T BE AROUND TO BE SOCIALLY RESPONSIBLE IF WE DIDN'T MANAGE OUR MONEY RESPONSIBLY.

FRAN SMILED

THE PICTURE ON THE LEFT WE'LL CALL THE BALANCE SHEET. IT'S A SNAPSHOT OF WHAT WE HAVE AT ONE MOMENT. THIS IS A PICTURE OF YOUR FRIENDS. YOU CAN SEE THEY HAVE A DOG, A BIKE FOR THEIR DAUGHTER, A NEW CAR, &... OH YES, A PAYMENT BOOK, PLUS A BUNCH OF OTHER STUFF. SO IN ACCOUNTING LANGUAGE, THIS IS A PICTURE OF THEIR ASSETS & LIABILITIES (AS IN... THEY'RE LIABLE TO COME GET OUR CAR IF WE DON'T MAKE THE NEXT PAYMENT).

THE LETTER ON THE RIGHT IS FROM YOUR FRIENDS IN THE PICTURE. OH JEEZ, IT'S ONE OF THOSE REALLY BORING HOLIDAY LETTERS. IN BUSINESS LANGUAGE, THIS WOULD BE LIKE THE STATEMENT OF INCOME. IT'S A DESCRIPTION OF ALL THE THINGS THAT THEY HAVE DONE IN THE PAST YEAR, LIKE WHAT THEY EARNED, & WHAT THEY BOUGHT & SOLD FOR HOW MUCH. (OR IF YOUR FRIENDS ARE A LITTLE LESS CRASS, WHAT THE KIDS DID IN SCHOOL & WHERE THEY ALL WENT ON VACATION).

NOW IMAGINE THAT YOUR FRIENDS CLOSED THE LETTER BY SAYING, "WE TOOK WHAT WE HAD LEFT AT THE END OF THE YEAR & BOUGHT THE SAILBOAT YOU CAN SEE IN THE ENCLOSED PICTURE." THAT'S HOW THE STATEMENT OF INCOME CONNECTS TO THE BALANCE SHEET. EVERY YEAR THE NET INCOME (THE END OF THE LETTER) GETS ADDED TO THE RETAINED EARNINGS (OVER IN THE CORNER OF THE PICTURE). IT'S NOT QUITE THAT SIMPLE IN A COMPANY, BUT IT'S THE SAME IDEA.

ASSETS — THINGS THE COMPANY OWNS.
- CASH
- ACCOUNTS RECEIVABLE. MONEY OWED TO THE COMPANY.
- INVENTORY. MANUFACTURED PRODUCTS WAITING TO BE SOLD, ALSO INGREDIENTS, PACKAGING & SUPPLIES
- PROPERTY, PLANT & EQUIPMENT. BUILDINGS, MACHINERY, TRUCKS ETC. DEPRECIATION IS THE PART OF THE VALUE OF THESE ASSETS THAT HAS BEEN USED UP, BASED ON HOW LONG IT IS EXPECTED TO LAST.
- PREPAID EXPENSES, DEFERRED INCOME TAXES, OTHER ASSETS. THESE ARE MISCELLANEOUS OTHER PURCHASED ASSETS THE COMPANY HAS THAT HAVE VALUE.

LIABILITIES — WHAT THE COMPANY OWES.
- CURRENT LIABILITIES — BILLS, PAYROLL DUE, TAXES & OTHER OBLIGATIONS THAT HAVE TO BE PAID WITHIN A YEAR.
- LONG TERM DEBT & OBLIGATIONS — LOANS OR UNDER CAPITAL LEASES — AGREEMENTS TO PAY FOR USE OF EQUIPMENT A YEAR OR MORE FROM NOW.
- OTHER LIABILITIES — MISCELLANEOUS OTHER FINANCIAL COMMITMENTS.

STOCKHOLDERS' EQUITY
THIS IS CALLED THE "BOOK VALUE" OF THE OWNERS' STAKE IN THE COMPANY. IT INCLUDES PROCEEDS THE COMPANY RECEIVED FROM THE INITIAL AND SUBSEQUENT SALES OF STOCK TO THE PUBLIC, PLUS ACCUMULATED PROFITS, CALLED RETAINED EARNINGS.

THIS BOOK VALUE IS NOT THE SAME AS THE VALUE OF STOCK ON THE PUBLIC STOCK MARKET WHICH IS CALLED THE "MARKET VALUE". THE STOCK MARKET DETERMINES IN ITS OWN WAYS WHETHER THE COMPANY IS WORTH MORE THAN THE BOOK VALUE OF WHAT IT OWNS MINUS WHAT IT OWES. FOR EXAMPLE, A COMPANY'S STOCK PRICE CHANGES REGULARLY WITHOUT REGARD TO THE VALUE OF THE ASSETS & LIABILITIES IT USES TO RUN ITS BUSINESS.

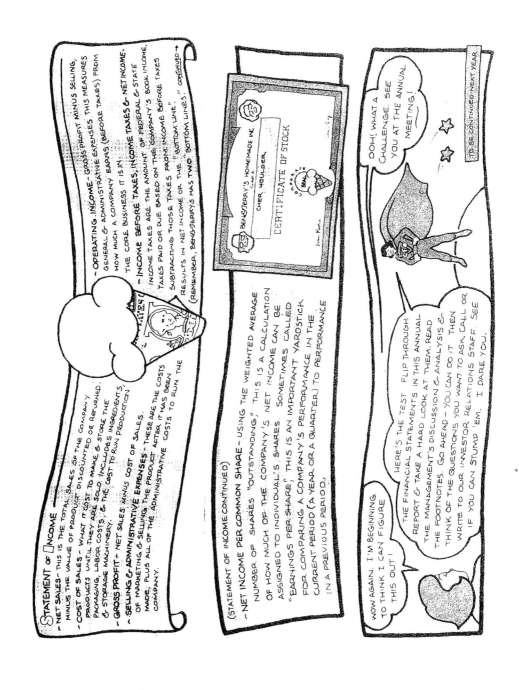

INDEX